Webster's Unabridged Dictionary

Noah Webster

<— p. 100 —>

At·tracĭtivĭlty (?), n. The quality or degree of attractive power.

Atĭtractor (?), n. One who, or that which, attracts.

Sir T. Browne.

Attraĭhent (?), a. [L. attrahens, p. pr. of attrahere. See Attract, v. t.] Attracting; drawing; attractive.

Attraĭhent, n. 1. That which attracts, as a magnet.

The motion of the steel to its attrahent.

Glanvill.

(Med.) A substance which, by irritating the surface, excites action in the part to which it is applied, as a blister, an epispastic, a sinapism.

Atĭtrap (?), v. t. [F. attraper to catch; ... (L. ad + trappe trap. See Trap (for taking game).] To entrap; to insnare. [Obs.]

Grafton.

Atĭtrap , v. t. [Pref. ad + trap to adorn.] To adorn with trapping; to array. [Obs.]

Shall your horse be attrapped ... more richly?

Holland.

At·trecĭtation (?), n. [L. attrectatio; ad + tractare to handle.] Frequent handling or touching. [Obs.]

Jer. Taylor.

Atĭtribuĭtaĭble (?), a. Capable of being attributed; ascribable; imputable.

Errors ... attributable to carelessness.

J.D. Hooker.

Atĭtribute (?), v. t. [imp. & p. p. Attributed; p. pr. & vb. n. Attributing.] [L. attributus, p. p. of attribuere; ad + tribuere to bestow. See Tribute.] To ascribe; to consider (something) as due or appropriate (to); to refer, as an effect to a cause; to impute; to assign; to consider as belonging (to).

We attribute nothing to God that hath any repugnancy or contradiction in it.

Abp. Tillotson.

The merit of service is seldom attributed to the true and exact performer.

Shak.

Syn. Ð See Ascribe.

Attriĭbute (?), n. [L. attributum.] 1. That which is attributed; a quality which is considered as belonging to, or inherent in, a person or thing; an essential or necessary property or characteristic.

But mercy is above this sceptered away; ...

It is an attribute to God himself.

Shak.

Reputation. [Poetic]

Shak.

(Paint. & Sculp.) A conventional symbol of office, character, or identity, added to any particular figure; as, a club is the attribute of Hercules.

(Gram.) Quality, etc., denoted by an attributive; an attributive adjunct or adjective.

At·tri**bu**tion (?), n. [L. attributio: cf. F. attribution.] 1. The act of attributing or ascribing, as a quality, character, or function, to a thing or person, an effect to a cause.

That which is ascribed or attributed.

At**I**tribu**I**tive (?), a. [Cf. F. attributif.] Attributing; pertaining to, expressing, or assigning an attribute; of the nature of an attribute.

At**I**tribu**I**tive, n, (Gram.) A word that denotes an attribute; esp. a modifying word joined to a noun; an adjective or adjective phrase.

At**I**tribu**I**tive**I**ly, adv. In an attributive manner.

At**I**trite (?), a. [L. attritus, p. p. of atterere; ad + terere to rub. See Trite.] 1. Rubbed; worn by friction.

Milton.

(Theol.) Repentant from fear of punishment; having attrition of grief for sin; Đ opposed to contrite.

At**I**trition (?), n. [L. attritio: cf. F. attrition.] 1. The act of rubbing together; friction; the act of wearing by friction, or by rubbing substances together; abrasion.

Effected by attrition of the inward stomach.

Arbuthnot.

The state of being worn.

Johnson.

(Theol.) Grief for sin arising only from fear of punishment or feelings of shame. See Contrition.

Wallis.

Attry (?), a. [See Atter.] Poisonous; malignant; malicious. [Obs.]

Chaucer.

At**I**tune (?), v. t. [imp. & p. p. Attuned (?); p. pr. & vb. n. Attuning.] [Pref. adĐ + tune.]

To tune or put in tune; to make melodious; to adjust, as one sound or musical instrument to another; as, to attune the voice to a harp.

To arrange fitly; to make accordant.

Wake to energy each social aim,
Attuned spontaneous to the will of Jove.
Beattie.

Aïtwain (?), adv. [OE. atwaine, atwinne; pref. aÐ + twain.] In twain; asunder. [Obs. or Poetic] ½Cuts atwain the knots.͵
Tennyson.

Aïtween (?), adv. or prep. [See Atwain, and cf. Between.] Between. [Archaic]
Spenser. Tennyson.

Aïtwirl (?), a. & adv. [Pref. aÐ + twist.] Twisted; distorted; awry. [R.]
Halliwell.

Aïtwite (?), v. t. [OE. attwyten, AS. 'twÆtan. See Twit.] To speak reproachfully of; to twit; to upbraid. [Obs.]

Aïtwixt (?), adv. Betwixt. [Obs.] Spenser.

Aïtwo (?), adv. [Pref. aÐ + two.] In two; in twain; asunder. [Obs.]
Chaucer.

Aïtypic (?), Aïtypicïal,} a. [Pref. aÐ not + typic, typical.] That has no type; devoid of typical character; irregular; unlike the type.

Ø Au · bade (?), n. [F., fr. aube the dawn, fr. L. albus white.] An open air concert in the morning, as distinguished from an evening serenade; also, a pianoforte composition suggestive of morning.
Grove.

The crowing cock ...
Sang his aubade with lusty voice and clear.
Longfellow.

Ø Au · baine (?), n. [F., fr. aubain an alien, fr. L. alibi elsewhere.] Succession to the goods of a stranger not naturalized.
Littr,.

Droit d'aubaine (?), the right, formerly possessed by the king of France, to all the personal property of which an alien died possessed. It was abolished in 1819.
Bouvier.

Aube (?), n. [See Ale.] An alb. [Obs.]
Fuller.

Ø Au · berge (?), n. [F.] An inn.
Beau. & Fl.

Ø Aubin (?), n. [F.] A broken gait of a horse, between an amble and a gallop; Ð commonly called a Canterbury gallop.

Auburn (?), a. [OE. auburne blonde, OF. alborne, auborne, fr. LL. alburnus whitish, fr. L. albus white. Cf. Alburn.] 1. FlaxenÐcolored. [Obs.]
Florio.

Reddish brown.

His auburn locks on either shoulder flowed.

Dryden.

Ø Auĭchenĭĭum (?), n. [NL., fr. Gr. ?, fr. ? the neck.] (Zo"l.) The part of the neck nearest the back.

Auctaĭry (?), n. [L. auctarium.] That which is superadded; augmentation. [Obs.]

Baxter.

Auction (?), n. [L. auctio an increasing, a public sale, where the price was called out, and the article to be sold was adjudged to the last increaser of the price, or the highest bidder, fr. L. augere, auctum, to increase. See Augment.] 1. A public sale of property to the highest bidder, esp. by a person licensed and authorized for the purpose; a vendue.

The things sold by auction or put up to auction.

Ask you why Phryne the whole auction buys ?

Pope.

μ In the United States, the more prevalent expression has been ½sales at auction, that is, by an increase of bids (Lat. auctione). This latter form is preferable.

Dutch auction, the public offer of property at a price beyond its value, then gradually lowering the price, till some one accepts it as purchaser.

P. Cyc.

Auction, v. t. To sell by auction.

Auctionĭaĭry (?), a. [L. auctionarius.] Of or pertaining to an auction or an auctioneer. [R.]

With auctionary hammer in thy hand.

Dryden.

Auc · tionĭeer (?), n. A person who sells by auction; a person whose business it is to dispose of goods or lands by public sale to the highest or best bidder.

Auc · tionĭeer, v. t. To sell by auction; to auction.

Estates ... advertised and auctioneered away.

Cowper.

Au · culpation (?), n. [L. aucupatio, fr. auceps, contr. for aviceps; avis bird + capere to take.] Birdcatching; fowling. [Obs.]

Blount.

Auĭdacious (?), a. [F. audacieux, as if fr. LL. audaciosus (not found), fr. L. audacia audacity, fr. audax, Đacis, bold, fr. audere to dare.] 1. Daring; spirited; adventurous.

As in a cloudy chair, ascending rides

Audacious.

Milton.

Contemning the restraints of law, religion, or decorum; bold in wickedness; presumptuous; impudent; insolent. ½ Audacious traitor. Shak.

½ Such audacious neighborhood.
Milton.

Committed with, or proceedings from, daring effrontery or contempt of law, morality, or decorum. ½Audacious cruelty. ½Audacious prate.

Shak.

Au|da′cious|ly, adv. In an audacious manner; with excess of boldness; impudently.

Au|da′cious|ness, n. The quality of being audacious; impudence; audacity.

Au|dac′i|ty (?), n. 1. Daring spirit, resolution, or confidence; venturesomeness.

The freedom and audacity necessary in the commerce of men.
Tatler.

Reckless daring; presumptuous impudence; Ð implying a contempt of law or moral restraints.

With the most arrogant audacity.
Joye.

Au · di|bil′i|ty (?), n. The quality of being audible; power of being heard; audible capacity.

Au′di|ble (?), a. [LL. audibilis, fr. L. audire, auditum, to hear: cf. Gr. ? ear, L. auris, and E. ear.] Capable of being heard; loud enough to be heard; actually heard; as, an audible voice or whisper.

Au′di|ble, n. That which may be heard. [Obs.]
Visibles are swiftlier carried to the sense than audibles.
Bacon.

Au′di|ble|ness, n. The quality of being audible.

Au′di|bly, adv. So as to be heard.

Au′di|ence (?), n. [F. audience, L. audientia, fr. audire to hear. See Audible, a.] 1. The act of hearing; attention to sounds.

Thou, therefore, give due audience, and attend.
Milton.

Admittance to a hearing; a formal interview, esp. with a sovereign or the head of a government, for conference or the transaction of business.

According to the fair play of the world,
Let me have audience: I am sent to speak.
Shak.

An auditory; an assembly of hearers. Also applied by authors to their readers.

Fit audience find, though few.
Milton.
He drew his audience upward to the sky.

Dryden.

Court of audience, or Audience court (Eng.), a court long since disused, belonging to the Archbishop of Canterbury; also, one belonging to the Archbishop of York. Mozley & W. Ð In general (or open) audience, publicly. Ð To give audience, to listen; to admit to an interview.

Audiĭent (?), a. [L. audiens, p. pr. of audire. See Audible, a.] Listening; paying attention; as, audient souls.

Mrs. Browning.

Audiĭent, n. A hearer; especially a catechumen in the early church. [Obs.] Shelton.

Au·diĭomeĭter (?), n. [L. audire to hear + Ðmeter.] (Acous.) An instrument by which the power of hearing can be gauged and recorded on a scale.

Audiĭphone (?), n. [L. audire to hear + Gr. ? sound.] An instrument which, placed against the teeth, conveys sound to the auditory nerve and enables the deaf to hear more or less distinctly; a dentiphone.

Audit (?), n. [L. auditus a hearing, fr. audire. See Audible, a.] 1. An audience; a hearing. [Obs.]

He appeals to a high audit.

Milton.

An examination in general; a judicial examination.

Specifically: An examination of an account or of accounts, with the hearing of the parties concerned, by proper officers, or persons appointed for that purpose, who compare the charges with the vouchers, examine witnesses, and state the result.

The result of such an examination, or an account as adjusted by auditors; final account.

Yet I can make my audit up.
Shak.

A general receptacle or receiver. [Obs.]

It [a little brook] paid to its common audit no more than the revenues of a little cloud.

Jer. Taylor.

Audit ale, a kind of ale, brewed at the English universities, orig. for the day of audit. Ð Audit house, Audit room, an appendage to a cathedral, for the transaction of its business.

Audit (?), v. t. [imp. & p. p. Audited; p. pr. & vb. n. Auditing.] To examine and adjust, as an account or accounts; as, to audit the accounts of a treasure, or of parties who have a suit depending in court.

Audit, v. i. To settle or adjust an account.

Let Hocus audit; he knows how the money was disbursed.

Arbuthnot.

Ø Auĭdita queĭrela (?). [L., the complaint having been heard.] (Law) A writ which lies for a party against whom judgment is recovered, but to whom good matter of discharge has subsequently accrued which could not have been availed of to prevent such judgment.

Wharton.

Auĭdition (?), n. [L. auditio.] The act of hearing or listening; hearing.

Audition may be active or passive; hence the difference between listening and simple hearing.

Dunglison.

Audiĭtive (?), a. [Cf. F. auditif.] Of or pertaining to hearing; auditory. [R.]

Cotgrave.

Audiĭtor (?), n. [L. auditor, fr. audire. See Audible, a.] 1. A hearer or listener.

Macaulay.

A person appointed and authorized to audit or examine an account or accounts, compare the charges with the vouchers, examine the parties and witnesses, allow or reject charges, and state the balance.

One who hears judicially, as in an audience court.

µ In the United States government, and in the State governments, there are auditors of the treasury and of the public accounts. The name is also applied to persons employed to check the accounts of courts, corporations, companies, societies, and partnerships.

Au · diĭtoriĭal (?), a. Auditory. [R.]

Au · diĭtoriĭum (?), n. [L. See Auditory, n.] The part of a church, theater, or other public building, assigned to the audience.

µ In ancient churches the auditorium was the nave, where hearers stood to be instructed; in monasteries it was an apartment for the reception of strangers.

Audiĭtorĭship (?), n. The office or function of auditor.

Audiĭtoĭry (?), a. [L. auditorius.] Of or pertaining to hearing, or to the sense or organs of hearing; as, the auditory nerve. See Ear.

Auditory canal (Anat.), the tube from the auditory meatus or opening of the ear to the tympanic membrane.

Audiĭtoĭry, n. [L. auditorium.] 1. An assembly of hearers; an audience.

An auditorium.

Udall.

Audiĭtress (?), n. A female hearer.

Milton.

Auĭdituĭal (?), a. Auditory. [R.]

Coleridge.

Auf (?), n. [OE. auph, aulf, fr. Icel. ¾lfr elf. See Elf.] [Also spelt oaf, ouphe.] A changeling or elf child, Ð that is, one left by fairies; a deformed or foolish child; a simpleton; an oaf. [Obs.]

Drayton.

Ø Au · fait (?). [F. Lit., to the deed, act, or point. Fait is fr. L. factum. See Fact.] Expert; skillful; well instructed.

Aulgean (?), a. 1. (Class. Myth.) Of or pertaining to Augeus, king of Elis, whose stable contained 3000 oxen, and had not been cleaned for 30 years. Hercules cleansed it in a single day.

<small>Hence: Exceedingly filthy or corrupt.</small>

Augean stable (Fig.), an accumulation of corruption or filth almost beyond the power of man to remedy.

Auger (?), n. [OE. augoure, nauger, AS. nafeg¾r, fr. nafu, nafa, nave of a wheel + g¾r spear, and therefore meaning properly and originally a naveÐbore. See Nave (of a wheel) and 2d Gore, n.] 1. A carpenter's tool for boring holes larger than those bored by a gimlet. It has a handle placed crosswise by which it is turned with both hands. A pod auger is one with a straight channel or groove, like the half of a bean pod. A screw auger has a twisted blade, by the spiral groove of which the chips are discharge.

<small>An instrument for boring or perforating soils or rocks, for determining the quality of soils, or the nature of the rocks or strata upon which they lie, and for obtaining water.</small>

Auger bit, a bit with a cutting edge or blade like that of an anger.

Ø Aulget (?), n. [F., dim. of auge trough, fr. L. alveus hollow, fr. alvus belly.] (Mining) A priming tube connecting the charge chamber with the gallery, or place where the slow match is applied.

Knight.

Aught (?), Aucht (?), n. [AS. ?ht, fr. ¾gan to own, p. p. ¾hte.] Property; possession. [Scot.]

Sir W. Scott.

Aught (?), n. [OE. aught, ought, awiht, AS. ¾wiht, ¾ ever + wiht. ?136. See Aye ever, and Whit, Wight.] Anything; any part. [Also written ought.]

There failed not aught of any good thing which the Lord has spoken.

Josh. xxi. 45

But go, my son, and see if aught be wanting.

Addison.

<— p. 101 —>

Aught (?), adv. At all; in any degree.

Chaucer.

Augite (?), n. [L. augites, Gr. ?, fr. ? brightness: cf. F. augite.] A variety of pyroxene, usually of a black or dark green color, occurring in igneous rocks, such as basalt; Ð also used instead of the general term pyroxene.

Auïgitic (?), a. Pertaining to, or like, augite; containing augite as a principal constituent; as, augitic rocks.

Augïment (?), v. t. [imp. & p. p. Augmented; p. pr. & vb. n. Augmenting.] [L. augmentare, fr. augmentum an increase, fr. augere to increase; perh. akin to Gr. ?, ?, E. wax, v., and eke, v.: cf. F. augmenter.] 1. To enlarge or increase in size, amount, or degree; to swell; to make bigger; as, to augment an army by re‰forcements; rain augments a stream; impatience augments an evil.

But their spite still serves
His glory to augment.
Milton.

(Gram.) To add an ~ to.

Augïment, v. i. To increase; to grow larger, stronger, or more intense; as, a stream augments by rain.

Augment (?), n. [L. augmentum: cf. F. augment.] 1. Enlargement by addition; increase.

(Gram.) A vowel prefixed, or a lengthening of the initial vowel, to mark past time, as in Greek and Sanskrit verbs.

µ In Greek, the syllabic augment is a prefixed ?, forming an intial syllable; the temporal augment is an increase of the quantity (time) of an initial vowel, as by changing ? to ?.

Augïmentaïble (?), a. Capable of augmentation.
Walsh.

Aug · menïtation (?), n. [LL. augmentatio: cf. F. augmentation.] 1. The act or process of augmenting, or making larger, by addition, expansion, or dilation; increase.

The state of being augmented; enlargement.

The thing added by way of enlargement.

(Her.) A additional charge to a coat of arms, given as a mark of honor.

Cussans.

(Med.) The stage of a disease in which the symptoms go on increasing.

Dunglison.

(Mus.) In counterpoint and fugue, a repetition of the subject in tones of twice the original length.

Augmentation court (Eng. Hist.), a court erected by Stat. 27 Hen. VIII., to augment to revenues of the crown by the suppression of monasteries. It was long ago dissolved.

Encyc. Brit.

Syn. - Increase; enlargement; growth; extension; accession; addition.

Augĭmentaĭtive (?), a. [Cf. F. augmentatif.] Having the quality or power of augmenting; expressing augmentation. Ð Augĭmentaĭtiveĭly, adv.

Augĭmentaĭtive, n. (Gram.) A word which expresses with augmented force the idea or the properties of the term from which it is derived; as, dullard, one very dull. Opposed to diminutive.

Gibbs.

Augĭmenter (?), n. One who, or that which, augments or increases anything.

Augrim (?), n. See Algorism. [Obs.]

Chaucer.

÷ stones, pebbles formerly used in numeration. Ð Noumbres of ~, Arabic numerals.

Chaucer.

Augur (?), n. [L. Of uncertain origin: the first part of the word is perh. fr. L. avis bird, and the last syllable, gur, equiv. to the Skr. gar to call, akin to L. garrulus garrulous.] 1. (Rom. Antiq.) An official diviner who foretold events by the singing, chattering, flight, and feeding of birds, or by signs or omens derived from celestial phenomena, certain appearances of quadrupeds, or unusual occurrences.

One who foretells events by omens; a soothsayer; a diviner; a prophet.

Augur of ill, whose tongue was never found
Without a priestly curse or boding sound.
Dryden.

Augur, v. i. [imp. & p. p. Augured (?); p. pr. & vb. n. Auguring.] 1. To conjecture from signs or omens; to prognosticate; to foreshow.

My auguring mind assures the same success.

Dryden.

To anticipate, to foretell, or to indicate a favorable or an unfavorable issue; as, to augur well or ill.

Augur, v. t. To predict or foretell, as from signs or omens; to betoken; to presage; to infer.

It seems to augur genius.

Sir W. Scott.

I augur everything from the approbation the proposal has met with.

J. F. W. Herschel.

Syn. - To predict; forebode; betoken; portend; presage; prognosticate; prophesy; forewarn.

Augŭral (?), a. [L. auguralis.] Of or pertaining to augurs or to augury; betokening; ominous; significant; as, an augural staff; augural books. ½Portents augural.

Cowper.

Au′gurate (?), v. t. & i. [L. auguratus, p. p. of augurari to augur.] To make or take auguries; to augur; to predict. [Obs.]

C. Middleton.

Au′gurate (?), n. The office of an augur.

Merivale.

Au·gura′tion (?), n. [L. auguratio.] The practice of augury.

Aug′urer (?), n. An augur. [Obs.]

Shak.

Augu′rial (?), a. [L. augurialis.] Relating to augurs or to augury.

Sir T. Browne.

Aug′urist (?), n. An augur. [R.]

Ang′urize (?), v. t. To augur. [Obs.]

Blount.

Au′gurous (?), a. Full of augury; foreboding. [Obs.] ½Augurous hearts.͵ Chapman.

Aug′urship (?), n. The office, or period of office, of an augur.

Bacon.

Au′gury (?), n.; pl. Auguries (?). [L. aucurium.] 1. The art or practice of foretelling events by observing the actions of birds, etc.; divination.

<small>An omen; prediction; prognostication; indication of the future; presage.</small>

From their flight strange auguries she drew.

Drayton.

He resigned himself... with a docility that gave little augury of his future greatness.

Prescott.

<small>A rite, ceremony, or observation of an augur.</small>

Au′gust (?), a. [L. augustus; cf. augere to increase; in the language of religion, to honor by offerings: cf. F. auguste. See Augment.] Of a quality inspiring mingled admiration and reverence; having an aspect of solemn dignity or grandeur; sublime; majestic; having exalted birth, character, state, or authority. ½Forms august.͵ Pope. ½August in visage.͵ Dryden. ½To shed that august blood.͵ Macaulay.

So beautiful and so august a spectacle.

Burke.

To mingle with a body so august.

Byron.

Syn. - Grand; magnificent; majestic; solemn; awful; noble; stately; dignified; imposing.

August (?), n. [L. Augustus. See note below, and August, a.] The eighth month of the year, containing thirtyÐone days.

µ The old Roman name was Sextilis, the sixth month from March, the month in which the primitive Romans, as well as Jews, began the year. The name was changed to August in honor of Augustus C'sar, the first emperor of Rome, on account of his victories, and his entering on his first consulate in that month.

Auĭgustan (?), a. [L. Augustanus, fr. Augustus. See August, n.] 1. Of or pertaining to Augustus C'sar or to his times.

Of or pertaining to the town of Augsburg.

Augustan age of any national literature, the period of its highest state of purity and refinement; Đ so called because the reign of Augustus C'sar was the golden age of Roman literature. Thus the reign of Louis XIV. (b. 1638) has been called the Augustan age of French literature, and that of Queen Anne (b. 1664) the Augustan age of English literature. Đ Augustan confession (Eccl. Hist.), or confession of Augsburg, drawn up at Augusta Vindelicorum, or Augsburg, by Luther and Melanchthon, in 1530, contains the principles of the Protestants, and their reasons for separating from the Roman Catholic church.

Auĭgustine (?), Au · gusĭtiniĭan (?), } n. (Eccl.) A member of one of the religious orders called after St. Augustine; an Austin friar.

Au · gusĭtiniĭan, a. Of or pertaining to St. Augustine, bishop of Hippo in Northern Africa (b. 354 Đ d. 430), or to his doctrines.

÷ canons, an order of monks once popular in England and Ireland; Đ called also regular canons of. Austin, and black canons. Đ ÷ hermits or Austin friars, an order of friars established in 1265 by Pope Alexander IV. It was introduced into the United States from Ireland in 1790. Đ ÷ nuns, an order of nuns following the rule of St. Augustine. Đ ÷ rule, a rule for religious communities based upon the 109th letter of St. Augustine, and adopted by the ÷ orders.

Au · gusĭtiniĭan, n. One of a class of divines, who, following St. Augustine, maintain that grace by its nature is effectual absolutely and creatively, not relatively and conditionally.

Au · gusĭtiniĭanĭism (?), Auĭgustinĭism, n. The doctrines held by Augustine or by the Augustinians.

Auĭgustly , adv. In an august manner.

Auĭgustness, n. The quality of being august; dignity of mien; grandeur; magnificence.

Auk (?), n. [Prov. E. alk; akin to Dan. alke, Icel. & Sw. alka.] (Zo"l.) A name given to various species of arctic sea birds of the family Alcid'. The great ~, now extinct, is Alca (or Plautus) impennis. The razorĐbilled auk is A. torda. See Puffin, Guillemot, and Murre.

Aukward (?), a. See Awkward. [Obs.]

Auïlariïan (?), a. [L. aula hall. Cf. LL. aularis of a court.] Relating to a hall.

Aulariïan, n. At Oxford, England, a member of a hall, distinguished from a collegian.
Chalmers.

Auld (?), a. [See Old.] Old; as, Auld Reekie (old smoky), i. e., Edinburgh. [Scot. & Prov. Eng.]

Auld · lang syne (?). A Scottish phrase used in recalling recollections of times long since past. ½The days of auld lang syne.‚

Auïletic (?), a. [L. auleticus, Gr. ?, fr. ? flute.] Of or pertaining to a pipe (flute) or piper. [R.]
Ash.

Aulic , a. [L. aulicus, Gr. ?, fr. ? hall, court, royal court.] Pertaining to a royal court.

Ecclesiastical wealth and aulic dignities.
Landor.

Aulic council (Hist.), a supreme court of the old German empire; properly the supreme court of the emperor. It ceased at the death of each emperor, and was renewed by his successor. It became extinct when the German empire was dissolved, in 1806. The term is now applied to a council of the war department of the Austrian empire, and the members of different provincial chanceries of that empire are called aulic councilors.
P. Cyc.

Aulic, n. The ceremony observed in conferring the degree of doctor of divinity in some European universities. It begins by a harangue of the chancellor addressed to the young doctor, who then receives the cap, and presides at the disputation (also called the aulic).

Auln (?), n. An ell. [Obs.] See Aune.

Aulnage (?), Aulnaïger (?), } n. See Alnage and Alnager.

Aum (?), n. Same as Aam.

Aulmail (?), v. t. [OE. for amel, enamel.] To figure or variegate. [Obs.]
Spenser.

Aumbry (?), n. Same as Ambry.

Aumelry (?), n. A form of Ambry, a closet; but confused with Almonry, as if a place for alms.

Auncel (?), n. A rude balance for weighing, and a kind of weight, formerly used in England.
Halliwell.

Auncetïry (?), n. Ancestry. [Obs.]
Chaucer.

Ø Aune (?), n. [F. See Alnage.] A French cloth measure, of different parts of the country (at Paris, 0.95 of an English ell); Ð now superseded by the meter.

Aunt (?), n. [OF. ante, F. tante, L. amita father's sister. Cf. Amma.] 1. The sister of one's father or mother; Ð correlative to nephew or niece. Also applied to an uncle's wife.

µ Aunt is sometimes applied as a title or term of endearment to a kind elderly woman not thus related.

An old woman; and old gossip. [Obs.]

Shak.

A bawd, or a prostitute. [Obs.]

Shak.

Aunt Sally, a puppet head placed on a pole and having a pipe in its mouth; also a game, which consists in trying to hit the pipe by throwing short bludgeons at it.

Auntter (?), n. Adventure; hap. [Obs.]

In aunters, perchance.

Aunter, Auntre } (?), v. t. [See Adventure.] To venture; to dare. [Obs.] Chaucer.

Auntie, Aunty } (?), n. A familiar name for an aunt. In the southern United States a familiar term applied to aged negro women.

Auntrous (?), a. Adventurous. [Obs.]

Chaucer.

Ø Aura (?), n.; pl. Aur' (?). [L. aura air, akin to Gr. ?.] 1. Any subtile, invisible emanation, effluvium, or exhalation from a substance, as the aroma of flowers, the odor of the blood, a supposed fertilizing emanation from the pollen of flowers, etc.

(Med.) The peculiar sensation, as of a light vapor, or cold air, rising from the trunk or limbs towards the head, a premonitory symptom of epilepsy or hysterics.

Electric ~, a supposed electric fluid, emanating from an electrified body, and forming a mass surrounding it, called the electric atmosphere. See Atmosphere, 2.

Aural (?), a. [L. aura air.] Of or pertaining to the air, or to an aura.

Aural, a. [L. auris ear.] Of or pertaining to the ear; as, aural medicine and surgery.

Auïran·tiïaceous (?), a. Pertaining to, or resembling, the Aurantiace', an order of plants (formerly considered natural), of which the orange is the type.

Aurate (?), n. [L. auratus, p. p. of aurare to gild, fr. aurum gold: cf. F. aurate.] (Chem.) A combination of auric acid with a base; as, aurate or potassium.

Auraïted (?), a. [See Aurate.] 1. Resembling or containing gold; goldÐcolored; gilded.

2.ÿ(Chem.) Combined with auric acid.

Auraïted (?), a. Having ears. See Aurited.

Aureïate (?), a. [L. aureatus, fr. aureus golden, fr. aurum gold.] Golden; gilded.

Skelton.

Ø Au′reli′a (?; 106), n. [NL., fr. L. aurum gold: cf. F. aur,lie. Cf. Chrysalis.] (Zo"l.) (a) The chrysalis, or pupa of an insect, esp. when reflecting a brilliant golden color, as that of some of the butterflies. (b) A genus of jellyfishes. See Discophora.

Au′reli′an (?), a. Of or pertaining to the aurelia.

Au′reli′an, n. An amateur collector and breeder of insects, esp. of butterflies and moths; a lepidopterist.

Ø Au′reo′la (?), Aure′ole (?), } n. [F. aur,ole, fr. L. aureola, (fem adj.) of gold (sc. corona crown), dim. of aureus. See Aureate, Oriole.] 1. (R. C. Theol.) A celestial crown or accidental glory added to the bliss of heaven, as a reward to those (as virgins, martyrs, preachers, etc.) who have overcome the world, the flesh, and the devil.

> The circle of rays, or halo of light, with which painters surround the figure and represent the glory of Christ, saints, and others held in special reverence.

μ Limited to the head, it is strictly termed a nimbus; when it envelops the whole body, an aureola.
Fairholt.

> A halo, actual or figurative.

The glorious aureole of light seen around the sun during total eclipses.
Proctor.

The aureole of young womanhood.
O. W. Holmes.

4.ÿ(Anat.) See Areola, 2.

Auric (?), a. [L. aurum gold.] 1. Of or pertaining to gold.

> (Chem.) Pertaining to, or derived from, gold; Ð said of those compounds of gold in which this element has its higher valence; as, auric oxide; auric chloride.

Au · ri′chalce′ous (?), a. [L. aurichalcum, for orichalcum brass.] (Zo"l.) BrassÐcolored.

Au · ri′chalcite (?), n. [See Aurichalceous.] (Min.) A hydrous carbonate of copper and zinc, found in pale green or blue crystalline aggregations. It yields a kind of brass on reduction.

Auri′cle (?), n. [L. auricula, dim. of auris ear. See Ear.] 1.ÿ(Anat.) (a) The external ear, or that part of the ear which is prominent from the head. (b) The chamber, or one of the two chambers, of the heart, by which the blood is received and transmitted to the ventricle or ventricles; Ð so called from its resemblance to the auricle or external ear of some quadrupeds. See Heart.

2.ÿ(Zo"l.) An angular or earÐshaped lobe.

> An instrument applied to the ears to give aid in hearing; a kind of ear trumpet.

Mansfield.

Auricled (?), a. ÿHaving ear‐shaped appendages or lobes; auriculate; as, auricled leaves.

Ø Auricula (?), n.; pl. L. Auricul' (?), E. Auriculas (?). [L. auricula. See Auricle.] 1. (Bot.) (a) A species of Primula, or primrose, called also, from the shape of its leaves, bear's‐ear. (b) (b) A species of Hirneola (H. auricula), a membranaceous fungus, called also auricula Jud', or Jew's‐ear.

P. Cyc.

2. ÿ(Zo"l.) (a) A genus of air‐breathing mollusks mostly found near the sea, where the water is brackish

<— p. 102 —>

Auricular (?), a. [LL. auricularis: cf. F. auriculaire. See Auricle.] 1. Of or pertaining to the ear, or to the sense of hearing; as, auricular nerves. 2. Told in the ear, i. e., told privately; as, auricular confession to the priest. This next chapter is a penitent confession of the king, and the strangest... that ever was auricular. Milton. 3. Recognized by the ear; known by the sense of hearing; as, auricular evidence. ½Auricular assurance., Shak. 4. Received by the ear; known by report. ½Auricular traditions., Bacon. 5. (Anat.) Pertaining to the auricles of the heart. Auricular finger, the little finger; so called because it can be readily introduced into the ear passage. Ø Auric · ularia (?), n. pl. [Neut. pl., fr. LL. auricularis.] (Zo"l.) A kind of holothurian larva, with soft, blunt appendages. See Illustration in Appendix. Auricularly, adv. In an auricular manner. Auriculars (?), n. pl. (Zo"l.) A circle of feathers surrounding the opening of the ear of birds. Auriculate (?), Auricula · ted (?), } a. [See Auricle.] (Biol.) Having ears or appendages like ears; eared. Esp.: (a) (Bot.) Having lobes or appendages like the ear; shaped like the ear; auricled. (b) (Zo"l.) Having an angular projection on one or both sides, as in certain bivalve shells, the foot of some gastropods, etc. Auriculate leaf, one having small appended leaves or lobes on each side of its petiole or base. Auriferous (?), a. [L. aurifer; aurum gold + ferre to bear: cf. F. aurifŠre.] Gold‐bearing; containing or producing gold. Whence many a bursting stream auriferous plays. Thomson. ÷ pyrites, iron pyrites (iron disulphide), containing some gold disseminated through it. Auriflamme (?), n. See Oriflamme. Auriform (?), a. [L. auris ear + iform.] Having the form of the human ear; ear‐shaped. Ø Auriga (?), n. [L., charioteer.] (Anat.) The Charioteer, or Wagoner, a constellation in the northern hemisphere, situated between Perseus and Gemini. It contains the bright star Capella. Aurigal (?), a. [L. aurigalis.] Of or pertaining to a chariot. [R.] Au · rigation (?), n. [L. aurigatio, fr. aurigare to be a charioteer, fr. auriga.] The act of driving a chariot or a carriage. [R.] De Quincey. Aurigraphy (?), n. [L. aurum gold + igraphy.] The art of writing with or in gold. Aurin (?), n. [L. aurum gold.] (Chem.) A red coloring matter derived from phenol; ‐ called also, in commerce, yellow coralin. Au · riphrygiate (?), a. [LL. auriphrigiatus; L. aurum gold + LL. phrygiare to adorn with Phrygian needlework, or with embroidery; perhaps corrupted from some other word. Cf. Orfrays.] Embroidered or decorated with gold. [R.] Southey. Au · ri͞pigment (?), n. See Orpiment. [Obs.] Aurĭscalp (?), n. [L. auris ear + scalpere to scrape.] An earpick. Aurĭscope (?), n. [L. auris + ĭscope.] (Med.) An instrument for examining the condition of the ear. Aurĭscŏpy (?), n. Examination of the ear by the aid of the auriscope. Aurist (?), n. [L. auris ear.] One skilled in treating and curing disorders of the ear. Aurĭted (?), a. [L. auritus, fr. auris ear.] (Zo"l.) Having lobes like the ear; auriculate. Aurĭvo͞rous (?), a. [L. aurum gold + vorare to devour.] GoldÐdevouring. [R.] H. Walpole. Au · ro͞cephaĬlous (?), a. [Aurum + cephalous.] (Zo"l.) Having a goldÐcolored head. Au · ro͞chloride (?), n. [Aurum + chloride.] (Chem.) The trichloride of gold combination with the chloride of another metal, forming a double chloride; Ð called also chloraurate. Aurochs (?), n. [G. auerochs, OHG. ?rohso; ?r (cf. AS. ?r) + ohso ox, G. ochs. Cf. Owre, Ox.] (Zo"l.) The European bison (Bison bonasus, or Europ'us), once widely distributed, but now nearly extinct, except where protected in the Lithuanian forests, and perhaps in the Caucasus. It is distinct from the Urus of C'sar, with which it has often been confused. Au · ro͞cya͞nide (?), n. [Aurum + cyanide.] (Chem.) A double cyanide of gold and some other metal or radical; Ð called also cyanaurate. Au͞rora (?), n.; pl. E. Auroras (?), L. (rarely used) Auror' (?). [L. aurora, for ausosa, akin to Gr. ?, ?, dawn, Skr. ushas, and E. east.] 1. The rising light of the morning; the dawn of day; the redness of the sky just before the sun rises. 2. The rise, dawn, or beginning. Hawthorne. 3. (Class. Myth.) The Roman personification of the dawn of day; the goddess of the morning. The poets represented her a rising out of the ocean, in a chariot, with rosy fingers dropping gentle dew. 4. (Bot.) A species of crowfoot. Johnson. 5. The aurora borealis or ~ australis (northern or southern lights). Aurora borealis (?), i. e., northern daybreak; popularly called northern lights. A luminous meteoric phenomenon, visible only at night, and supposed to be of electrical origin. This species of light usually appears in streams, ascending toward the zenith from a dusky line or bank, a few degrees above the northern horizon; when reaching south beyond the zenith, it forms what is called the corona, about a spot in the heavens toward which the dipping needle points. Occasionally the ~ appears as an arch of light across the heavens from east to west. Sometimes it assumes a wavy appearance, and the streams of light are then called merry dancers. They assume a variety of colors, from a pale red or yellow to a deep red or blood color. The Aurora australis (?) is a corresponding phenomenon in the southern hemisphere, the streams of light ascending in the same manner from near the southern horizon. Au͞roral (?). a. Belonging to, or resembling, the aurora (the drawn or the northern lights); rosy. Her cheeks suffused with an auroral blush. Longfellow. Aurous (?), a. 1. Containing gold. 2. (Chem.) Pertaining to, or derived from, gold; Ð said of those compounds of gold in which this element has its lower valence; as, aurous oxide. Ø Aurum (?), n. [L.] Gold. ÷ fulminans (?). See

Fulminate. Ð ÷ mosaicum (?). See Mosaic. Aus̆cult (?), v. i. & t. To auscultate. Auscul̆tate (?), v. i. & t. To practice auscultation; to examine by auscultation. Aus · cul̆tation (?), n. [L. ausculcatio, fr. auscultare to listen, fr. a dim. of auris, orig. ausis, ear. See Auricle, and cf. Scout, n.] 1. The act of listening or hearkening to. Hickes. 2. (Med.) An examination by listening either directly with the ear (immediate auscultation) applied to parts of the body, as the abdomen; or with the stethoscope (mediate ~), in order to distinguish sounds recognized as a sign of health or of disease. Auscul̆ta · tor (?), n. One who practices auscultation. Aus̆cultal̆tor̆y (?), a. Of or pertaining to auscultation. Dunglison. Aul̆sonil̆an (?), a. [L. Ausonia, poetic name for Italy.] Italian. Milton. Auspil̆cate (?), a. [L. auspicatus, p. p. of auspicari to take auspices, fr. auspex a bird seer, an augur, a contr. of avispex; avis bird + specere, spicere, to view. See Aviary, Spy.] Auspicious. [Obs.] Holland. Auspil̆cate (?), v. t. 1. To foreshow; to foretoken. [Obs.] B. Jonson. 2. To give a favorable turn to in commencing; to inaugurate; Ð a sense derived from the Roman practice of taking the auspicium, or inspection of birds, before undertaking any important business. They auspicate all their proceedings. Burke. Auspice (?), n.; pl. Auspices (?). [L. auspicium, fr. auspex: cf. F. auspice. See Auspicate, a.] 1. A divining or taking of omens by observing birds; an omen as to an undertaking, drawn from birds; an augury; an omen or sign in general; an indication as to the future. 2. Protection; patronage and care; guidance. Which by his auspice they will nobler make. Dryden. μ In this sense the word is generally plural, auspices; as, under the auspices of the king. Aus̆picial (?), a. Of or pertaining to auspices; auspicious. [R.] Aus̆picious (?), a. [See Auspice.] 1. Having omens or tokens of a favorable issue; giving promise of success, prosperity, or happiness; predicting good; as, an auspicious beginning. Auspicious union of order and freedom. Macaulay. 2. Prosperous; fortunate; as, auspicious years. ½Auspicious chief., Dryden. 3. Favoring; favorable; propitious; Ð applied to persons or things. ½Thy auspicious mistress., Shak. ½Auspicious gales., Pope. Syn. - See Propitious. Ð Aus̆piciousl̆y, adv. Ð Aus̆piciousl̆ness, n. Ø Auster (?), n. [L. auster a dry, hot, south wind; the south.] The south wind. Pope. Aus̆tere (?), [F. austŠre, L. austerus, fr. Gr. ?, fr. ? to parch, dry. Cf. Sear.] 1. Sour and astringent; rough to the state; having acerbity; as, an austere crab apple; austere wine. 2. Severe in modes of judging, or living, or acting; rigid; rigorous; stern; as, an austere man, look, life. From whom the austere Etrurian virtue rose. Dryden. 3. Unadorned; unembellished; severely simple. Syn. - Harsh; sour; rough; rigid; stern; severe; rigorous; strict. Aus̆terely, adv. Severely; rigidly; sternly. A doctrine austerely logical. Macaulay. Aus̆tereness, n. 1. Harshness or astringent sourness to the taste; acerbity. Johnson. 2. Severity; strictness; austerity. Shak. Aus̆teril̆ty (?), n.; pl. Austeries (?). [F. aust,rit,, L. austerias, fr. austerus. See Austere.] 1. Sourness and harshness to the taste. [Obs.] Horsley. 2. Severity of manners or life; extreme rigor or strictness; harsh discipline. The austerity of John the

Baptist. Milton. 3. Plainness; freedom from adornment; severe simplicity. Partly owing to the studied austerity of her dress, and partly to the lack of demonstration in her manners. Hawthorne. Austin (?), a. Augustinian; as, Austin friars. Austral (?), a. [L. australis, fr. auster: cf. F. austral.] Southern; lying or being in the south; as, austral land; austral ocean. Austral signs (Astron.), the last six signs of the zodiac, or those south of the equator. Aus · tralĪasian (?), a. Of or pertaining to Australasia; as, Australasian regions. Đ n. A native or an inhabitant of Australasia. AusĪtraliĪan (?), a. [From L. Terra Australis southern land.] Of or pertaining to Australia. Đ n. A native or an inhabitant of Australia. Australīize (?), v. i. [See Austral.] To tend toward the south pole, as a magnet. [Obs.] They [magnets] do septentrionate at one extreme, and australize at another. Sir T. Browne. AustriĪan (?), a. Of or pertaining to Austria, or to its inhabitants. Đ n. A native or an inhabitant of Austria. Austrine (?), n. [L. austrinus, from auster south.] Southern; southerly; austral. [Obs.] Bailey. AustroĐHunĪgariĪan (?), a. Of or pertaining to the monarchy composed of Austria and Hungary. AustroĪman · cy (?), n. [L. auster south wind + Īmancy.] Soothsaying, or prediction of events, from observation of the winds. AutarĪchy (?), n. [Gr. ? independence; ? self + ? to sufficient.] SelfĐsufficiency. [Obs.] Milton. AuĪthentic (?), a. [OE. autentik, OF. autentique, F. authentique, L. authenticus coming from the real another, of original or firsthand authority, from Gr. ?, fr. ? suicide, a perpetrator or real author of any act, an absolute master; ? self + a form ? (not found), akin to L. sons and perh. orig. from the p. pr. of ? to be, root as, and meaning the one it really is. See Am, Sin, n., and cf. Effendi.] 1. Having a genuine original or authority, in opposition to that which is false, fictitious, counterfeit, or apocryphal; being what it purports to be; genuine; not of doubtful origin; real; as, an authentic paper or register. To be avenged On him who had stole Jove's authentic fire. Milton. 2. Authoritative. [Obs.] Milton. 3. Of approved authority; true; trustworthy; credible; as, an authentic writer; an authentic portrait; authentic information. 4. (Law) Vested with all due formalities, and legally attested. 5. (Mus.) Having as immediate relation to the tonic, in distinction from plagal, which has a correspondent relation to the dominant in the octave below the tonic. Syn. - Authentic, Genuine,. These words, as here compared, have reference to historical documents. We call a document genuine when it can be traced back ultimately to the author or authors from whom it professes to emanate. Hence, the word has the meaning, ½not changed from the original, uncorrupted, unadulterated:₄ as, a genuine text. We call a document authentic when, on the ground of its being thus traced back, it may be relied on as true and authoritative (from the primary sense of ½having an author, vouched for₄); hence its extended signification, in general literature, of trustworthy, as resting on unquestionable authority or evidence; as, an authentic history; an authentic report of facts. A genuine book is that which was written by the person whose name it bears, as the author of it. An authentic book is that which relates matters of fact as they ?eally happened. A book may be genuine without being, authentic, and a book may be authentic without being genuine. Bp. Watson. It may be said, however, that some writers use authentic (as, an authentic document) in the sense of ½produced by its professed author, not counterfeit.¸ AuĬthentic, n. An original (book or document). [Obs.] ½Authentics and transcripts.¸ Fuller. AuĬthenticĬal (?), a. Authentic. [Archaic] AuĬthenticĬalĬly, adv. In an authentic manner; with the requisite or genuine authority. AuĬthenĬticĬalĬness, n. The quality of being authentic; authenticity. [R.] Barrow. AuĬthentiĬcate (?), v. t. [imp. & p. p. Authenticated (?); p. pr. & vb. n. Authenticating (?).] [Cf. LL. authenticare.] 1. To render authentic; to give authority to, by the proof, attestation, or formalities required by law, or sufficient to entitle to credit. The king serves only as a notary to authenticate the choice of judges. Burke. 2. To prove authentic; to determine as real and true; as, to authenticate a portrait. Walpole. Au · thenĬticiĬty (?), n. [Cf. F. authenticit,.] 1. The quality of being authentic or of established authority for truth and correctness. 2. Genuineness; the quality of being genuine or not corrupted from the original. µ In later writers, especially those on the evidences of Christianity, authenticity is often restricted in its use to the first of the above meanings, and distinguished from qenuineness. AuĬthenticĬly (?), adv. Authentically. AuĬthenticĬness, n The quality of being authentic; authenticity. [R.] Hammond. AuĬthentics (?), n. (Ciwil Law) A collection of the Novels or New Constitutions of Justinian, by an anonymous author; Ð so called on account of its authencity. Bouvier. Author (?), n. [OE. authour, autour, OF. autor, F. auteur, fr. L. auctor, sometimes, but erroneously, written autor or author, fr. augere to increase, to produce. See Auction, n.] 1. The beginner, former, or first ???er of anything; hence, the efficient cause of a thing; a creator; an originator.

<— p. 103 —>

Eternal King; thee, Author of all being. Milton. 2. One who composes or writers a book; a composer, as distinguished from an editor, translator, or compiler. The chief glory every people arises from its authors. Johnson. 3. The editor of a periodical. [Obs.] 4. An informant. [Archaic] Chaucer. Author (?), v. t. 1. To occasion; to originate. [Obs.] Such an overthrow... I have authored. Chapman. 2. To tell; to say; to declare. [Obs.] More of him I dare not author. Massinger. AuthorĬess, n. A female author. Glover. µ The word is not very much used, author being commonly applied to a female writer as well as to a male. AuĬthoriĬal (?), a. Of or pertaining to an author. ½The authorial ?we.'¸ Hare. AuthorĬism (?), n. Authoriship. [R.] AuĬthoriĬtaĬtive (?), a. 1. Having, or proceeding from, due authority; entitled to obedience, credit, or acceptance; determinate; commanding. The sacred functions of authoritative teaching. Barrow. 2. Having an air of authority; positive; dictatorial; peremptory; as, an authoritative tone. The mock authoritative manner of the one, and the insipid mirth of the other.

Swift. Ð Auˈthoriˌtaˈtiveˌly, adv. Ð Auˈthoriˌtaˈtiveˌness, n. Auˈthoriˌty (?), n.; pl. Authorities (?). [OE. autorite, auctorite, F. autorit,, fr. L. auctoritas, fr. auctor. See Author, n.] 1. Legal or rightful power; a right to command or to act; power exercised buy a person in virtue of his office or trust; dominion; jurisdiction; authorization; as, the authority of a prince over subjects, and of parents over children; the authority of a court. Thus can the demigod, Authority, Make us pay down for our offense. Shak. By what authority doest thou these things ? Matt. xxi. 23. 2. Government; the persons or the body exercising power or command; as, the local authorities of the States; the military authorities. [Chiefly in the plural.] 3. The power derived from opinion, respect, or esteem; influence of character, office, or station, or mental or moral superiority, and the like; claim to be believed or obeyed; as, an historian of no authority; a magistrate of great authority. 4. That which, or one who, is claimed or appealed to in support of opinions, actions, measures, etc. Hence: (a) Testimony; witness. ½And on that high authority had believed.ˌ Milton. (b) A precedent; a decision of a court, an official declaration, or an opinion, saying, or statement worthy to be taken as a precedent. (c) A book containing such a statement or opinion, or the author of the book. (d) Justification; warrant. Wilt thou be glass wherein it shall discern Authority for sin, warrant for blame. Shak. Authorˈli·zaˈble (?), a. [LL. authorisabilis.] Capable of being authorized. Hammond. Au·thorˈliˌzation (?), n. [Cf. F. autorisation.] The act of giving authority or legal power; establishment by authority; sanction or warrant. The authorization of laws. Motley. A special authorization from the chief. Merivale. Authorˈize (?), v. t. [imp. & p. p. Authorized (?); p. pr. & vb. n. Authorizing.] [OE. autorize, F. autoriser, fr. LL. auctorizare, authorisare. See Author.] 1. To clothe with authority, warrant, or legal power; to give a right to act; to empower; as, to authorize commissioners to settle a boundary. 2. To make legal; to give legal sanction to; to legalize; as, to authorize a marriage. 3. To establish by authority, as by usage or public opinion; to sanction; as, idioms authorized by usage. 4. To sanction or confirm by the authority of some one; to warrant; as, to authorize a report. A woman's story at a winter's fire, Authorized by her grandam. Shak. 5. To justify; to furnish a ground for. Locke. To ~ one's self, to rely for authority. [Obs.] Authorizing himself, for the most part, upon other histories. Sir P. Sidney. Authorˈlized (?), a. 1. Possessed of or endowed with authority; as, an authorized agent. 2. Sanctioned by authority. The Authorized Version of the Bible is the English translation of the Bible published in 1611 under sanction of King James I. It was ½appointed to be read in churches,ˌ and has been the accepted English Bible. The Revised Version was published in a complete form in 1855. Authorˈli·zer (?), n. One who authorizes. Authorˈless, a. Without an author; without authority; anonymous. Authorˈly, a. Authorial. [R.] Cowper. Authorˈship, n. 1. The quality or state of being an author; function or dignity of an author. 2. Source;

origin; origination; as, the authorship of a book or review, or of an act, or state of affairs. Autho͞type (?), n. A type or block containing a facsimile of an autograph. Knight. Auto- (?). [Gr. ? self.] A combining form, with the meaning of self, one's self, one's own, itself, its own. Au·to͞bi͞ogra͞pher (?), n. [Auto͞ + biographer.] One who writers his own life or biography. Au·to͞bi·o͞graphic (?), Au·to͞bi·o͞graphic͞al (?), } a. Pertaining to, or containing, autobiography; as, an autobiographical sketch. ½Such traits of the autobiographic sort. Carlyle. — Au·to͞bi·o͞graphic͞al͞ly, adv. Au·to͞bi͞ogra͞phist (?), n. One who writes his own life; an autobiographer. [R.] Au·to͞bi͞ogra͞phy (?), n. pl. Autobiographies (?). [Auto͞ + biography.] A biography written by the subject of it; memoirs of one's life written by one's self. Au·to͞carpous (?), Au·to͞carpi͞an (?), } a. [Auto͞ + Gr. ? fruit.] (Bot.) Consisting of the pericarp of the ripened pericarp with no other parts adnate to it, as a peach, a poppy capsule, or a grape. Au·to͞cepha͞lous (?), a. [Gr. ? independent; ? self + ? head.] (Eccl. Hist.) Having its own head; independent of episcopal or patriarchal jurisdiction, as certain Greek churches. Au·to͞chrono͞graph (?), n. [Auto͞ + chronograph.] An instrument for the instantaneous self-recording or printing of time. Knight. Au͞tochthon (?), n.; pl. E. Authochthons (?), L. Autochthones (?). [L., fr. Gr. ?, pl. ?, from the land itself; ? self + ? earth, land.] 1. One who is supposed to rise or spring from the ground or the soil he inhabits; one of the original inhabitants or aborigines; a native; — commonly in the plural. This title was assumed by the ancient Greeks, particularly the Athenians. 2. That which is original to a particular country, or which had there its origin. Au͞tochtho͞nal (?), Au·thochi͞thonic (?), Au͞tochtho͞nous (?), } a. Aboriginal; indigenous; native. Au͞tochtho͞nism (?), n. The state of being autochthonal. Au͞tochtho͞ny, n. An aboriginal or autochthonous condition. Auto͞clave (?), n. [F., fr. Gr. ? self + L. clavis key.] A kind of French stewpan with a steamtight lid. Knight. Au͞tocra͞cy (?), n.; pl. Autocracies. [Gr. ?: cf. F. autocratie. See Autocrat.] 1. Independent or self-derived power; absolute or controlling authority; supremacy. The divine will moves, not by the external impulse or inclination of objects, but determines itself by an absolute autocracy. South. 2. Supreme, uncontrolled, unlimited authority, or right of governing in a single person, as of an autocrat. 3. Political independence or absolute sovereignty (of a state); autonomy. Barlow. 4. (Med.) The action of the vital principle, or of the instinctive powers, toward the preservation of the individual; also, the vital principle. [In this sense, written also autocrasy.] Dunglison. Auto͞crat (?), n. [Gr. ?; ? self + ? strength, ? strong: cf. F. autocrate. See Hard, a.] 1. An absolute sovereign; a monarch who holds and exercises the powers of government by claim of absolute right, not subject to restriction; as, Autocrat of all the Russias (a title of the Czar). 2. One who rules with undisputed sway in any company or relation; a despot. The autocrat of the breakfast table. Holmes. Au·to͞cratic (?), Au·to͞cratic͞al (?), } a. Of or pertaining to autocracy or to an autocrat; absolute; holding independent and arbitrary powers of government. Đ Au · toÏcraticlalĭly, adv. AuÏtocraÏtor (?), n. [Gr. ?.] An autocrat. [Archaic] Au · toÏcraÏtoricÏal (?), a. Pertaining to an autocrator; absolute. [Obs.] Bp. Pearson. Ø AuÏtocraÏtrix (?), n. [NL.] A female sovereign who is independent and absolute; Đ a title given to the empresses of Russia. AutoÏcratĭship (?), n. The office or dignity of an autocrat. Ø AutoĐdaĐf, (?), n.; pl. AutosĐdaĐf? (?). [Pg., act of the faith; auto act, fr. L. actus + da of the + f, faith, fr. L. fides.] 1. A judgment of the Inquisition in Spain and Portugal condemning or acquitting persons accused of religious offenses. 2. An execution of such sentence, by the civil power, esp. the burning of a heretic. It was usually held on Sunday, and was made a great public solemnity by impressive forms and ceremonies. 3. A session of the court of Inquisition. Ø AutoĐdeĐfe (?), n.; pl. AutosĐdeĐfe. [Sp., act of faith.] Same as AutoĐdaĐf?. AutoÏdiÏdact · (?), n. [Gr. ? selfĐtaught.] One who is selfĐtaught; an automath. Au · toÏdyÏnamic (?), a. [AutoÏ + dynamic.] Supplying its own power; Đ applied to an instrument of the nature of a waterĐram. Au · toÏfec · unÏdation (?), n. [AutoÏ + fecundation.] (Biol.) SelfĐimpregnation. Darwin. AuÏtogaÏmous (?), a. (Bot.) Characterized by autogamy; selfĐfertilized. AuÏtogaÏmy (?), n. [AutoÏ + Gr. ? marriage.] (Bot.) SelfĐfertilization, the fertilizing pollen being derived from the same blossom as the pistil acted upon. Au · toÏgeneÏal (?), a. SelfĐproduced; autogenous. Ø Au · toÏgeneÏsis (?), n. [AutoÏ + genesis.] (Biol.) Spontaneous generation. Au · toÏgeÏnetic (?), a. (Biol.) Relating to autogenesis; selfĐgenerated. AuÏtogeÏnous (?), a. [Gr. ?; ? self + root of ? to be born.] 1. (Biol.) SelfĐgenerated; produced independently. 2. (Anat.) Developed from an independent center of ossification. Owen. Autogenous soldering, the junction by fusion of the joining edges of metals without the intervention of solder. AuÏtogeÏnousÏly (?), adv. In an autogenous manner; spontaneously. AutoÏgraph (?), n. [F. autographe, fr. Gr. ? autographic; ? self + ? to write.] That which is written with one's own hand; an original manuscript; a person's own signature or handwriting. AutoÏgraph (?), a. In one's own handwriting; as, an autograph letter; an autograph will. AuÏtograÏphal (?), a. Autographic. [Obs.] Au · toÏgraphic (?), Au · toÏgraphicÏal (?), } a. 1. Pertaining to an autograph, or one's own handwriting; of the nature of an autograph. 2. Pertaining to, or used in, the process of autography; as, autographic ink, paper, or press. AuÏtograÏphy (?), n. [Cf. F. autographie.] 1. The science of autographs; a person's own handwriting; an autograph. 2. A process in lithography by which a writing or drawing is transferred from paper to stone. Ure. AuÏtolaÏtry (?), n. [AutoÏ + Gr. ? worship.] SelfĐworship. Farrar. AutoÏmath (?), n. [Gr. ?; ? self + ?, ?, to learn.] One who is selfĐtaught. [R.] Young. Au · toÏmatic (?), Au · toÏmaticÏal (?), } a. [Cf. F. automatique. See Automaton.] 1.ÿHaving an inherent power of action or motion. Nothing can be said to be automatic. Sir H. Davy. 2. Pertaining to, or produced by, an automaton; of the nature of an automaton; selfĐacting or selfĐregulating under fixed conditions; Đ esp.

applied to machinery or devices in which certain things formerly or usually done by hand are done by the machine or device itself; as, the automatic feed of a lathe; automatic gas lighting; an automatic engine or switch; an automatic mouse. 3. Not voluntary; not depending on the will; mechanical; as, automatic movements or functions. Unconscious or automatic reasoning. H. Spenser. Automatic arts, such economic arts or manufacture as are carried on by selfÐacting machinery. Ure. Au · toÏmaticÏalÏly, adv. In an automatic manner. AuÏtomaÏtism (?), n. The state or quality of being automatic; the power of selfÐmoving; automatic, mechanical, or involuntary action. (Metaph.) A theory as to the activity of matter. AuÏtomaÏton (?), n.; pl. L. Automata (?), E. Automatons (?). [L. fr. Gr. ?, neut. of ? selfÐmoving; ? self + a root ma, man, to strive, think, cf. ? to strive. See Mean, v. i.] 1. Any thing or being regarded as having the power of spontaneous motion or action. Huxley. So great and admirable an automaton as the world. Boyle. These living automata, human bodies. Boyle. 2. A selfÐmoving machine, or one which has its motive power within itself; Ð applied chiefly to machines which appear to imitate spontaneously the motions of living beings, such as men, birds, etc. AuÏtomaÏtous (?), a. {l. automatus, Gr. ?. See Automaton.] Automatic. [Obs.] ½Automatous organs.„ Sir T. Browne. Au · toÏmorphic (?), a. [AutoÏ + Gr. ? for, shape.] Patterned after one's self. The conception which any one frames of another's mind is more or less after the pattern of his own mind, Ð is automorphic. H. Spenser. Au · toÏmorphism (?), n. Automorphic characterization. H. Spenser. Au · toÏnomaÏsy (?), n. [AutoÏ + Gr. ? a name, fr. ? a name; or for E. antonomasia.] (Rhet.) The use of a word of common or general signification for the name of a particular thing; as, ½He has gone to town,„ for, ½He has gone to London.„ Au · toÏnomic (?), a.ÿHaving the power of selfÐgovernment; autonomous. Hickok. AutooÏmist (?), n. [Cf. F. automiste. See Autonomy.] One who advocates autonomy. AuÏtonoÏmous (?), a. [Gr. ?; ? self + ? to assign, hold, sway.] 1. Independent in government; having the right or power of selfÐgovernment. 2. (Biol.) Having independent existence or laws. AuÏtonoÏmy (?), n. [Gr. ?: cf. F. autonomie. See Autonomous.] 1. The power or right of selfÐgovernment; selfÐgovernment, or political independence, of a city or a state. 2. (Metaph.) The sovereignty of reason in the sphere of morals; or man's power, as possessed of reason, to give law to himself. In this, according to Kant, consist the true nature and only possible proof of liberty. Fleming. Ø AuÏtophaÏgi (?), n. pl. [NL., fr. Gr. ? self + ? to eat.] (Zo"l.) Birds which are able to run about and obtain their own food as soon as hatched. AuÏtophoÏby (?), n. [AutoÏ + Gr. ? fear.] Fear of one's self; fear of being egotistical. [R.] Hare. AuÏtophoÏny (?), n. [AutoÏ + Gr. ? a sound.] (Med.) An auscultatory process, which consists in noting the tone of the observer's own voice, while he speaks, holding his head close to the patient's chest. Dunglison. Au · toÏplastic (?), a. Of or pertaining to autoplasty. AutoÏplas · ty (?), n. [AutoÏ + Ïplasty.] (Surg.) The process of artificially repairing lesions by taking a piece of healthy tissue, as from a neighboring part, to supply the deficiency caused by disease or wounds. Auῐtopsic (?), Auῐtopsicῐal (?), } a.ÿPertaining to autopsy; autoptical. [Obs.] Auῐtopsoῐrin (?), n. [Autoï + Gr. ? the itch.] (Med.) That which is given under the doctrine of administering a patient's own virus. Autopῐsy (?), n. [Gr. ?, fr. ? seen by one's self; ? self + ? seen: cf. F. autopsie. See Optic, a.] 1. Personal observation or examination; seeing with one's own eyes; ocular view. By autopsy and experiment. Cudworth. 2. (Med.) Dissection of a dead body, for the purpose of ascertaining the cause, seat, or nature of a disease; a postÐmortem examination. Auῐtoptic (?), Auῐtopticῐal (?), } a. [Gr. ?: cf. F. autoptique.] Seen with one's own eyes; belonging to, or connected with, personal observation; as, autoptic testimony or experience.

<— p. 104 —>

Auῐtopticῐalῐly (?), adv.   By means of ocular view, or one's own observation.

Sir T. Browne.

Au · toῐsche · diῐastic (?), Au · toῐsche · diῐasticῐal (?), } a. [Autoï + Gr. ? to do hastily. See Schediasm.] Extemporary; offhand. [R.]

Dean Martin.

Au · toῐstylic (?), a. [Autoï + Gr. ? pillar.] (Anat.) Having the mandibular arch articulated directly to the cranium, as in the skulls of the Amphibia.

Autoῐthe · ism (?), n. [Autoï + theism.] 1. The doctrine of God's selfÐexistence. [R.]

Deification of one's self; selfÐworship. [R.]

Autoῐthe · ist, n. One given to selfÐworship. [R.]
Autoῐtype (?), n. [Autoï + ῐtype: cf. F. autotype.] 1. A facsimile.

A photographic picture produced in sensitized pigmented gelatin by exposure to light under a negative; and subsequent washing out of the soluble parts; a kind of picture in ink from a gelatin plate.

Au · toῐtyῐpograῐphy (?), n. [Autoï + typography.] A process resembling ½nature printing,„ by which drawings executed on gelatin are impressed into a soft metal plate, from which the printing is done as from copperplate.

Auῐtotyῐpy (?), n. The art or process of making autotypes.
Autumn (?), n. [L. auctumnus, autumnus, perh. fr. a root av to satisfy one's self: cf. F. automne. See Avarice.] 1. The third season of the year, or the season between summer and winter, often called ½the fall.„ Astronomically, it begins in the northern temperate zone at the autumnal equinox, about September 23, and ends at the winter solstice, about December 23; but in popular language, autumn, in America, comprises September, October, and November.

μ In England, according to Johnson, autumn popularly comprises August, September, and October. In the southern hemisphere, the autumn corresponds to our spring.

The harvest or fruits of autumn.

Milton.

The time of maturity or decline; latter portion; third stage.

Dr. Preston was now entering into the autumn of the duke's favor.
Fuller.
Life's autumn past, I stand on winter's verge.
Wordsworth.
Auĭtumnal (?), a. [L. auctumnalis, autumnalis: cf. F. automnal.] 1. Of, belonging to, or peculiar to, autumn; as, an autumnal tint; produced or gathered in autumn; as, autumnal fruits; flowering in autumn; as, an autumnal plant.
Thick as autumnal leaves that strow the brooks
In Vallombrosa.
Milton.

Past the middle of life; in the third stage.

An autumnal matron.
Hawthorne.
Autumnal equinox, the time when the sun crosses the equator, as it proceeds southward, or when it passes the ~ point. Đ ÷ point, the point of the equator intersected by the ecliptic, as the sun proceeds southward; the first point of Libra. Đ ÷ signs, the signs Libra, Scorpio, and Sagittarius, through which the sun passes between the ~ equinox and winter solstice.

Aux·aĭnomeĭter (?), n. [Gr. ? to cause to increase + Ĭmeter.] An instrument to measure the growth of plants.
Goodale.
Ø Auxĭesis (?), n. [NL., Gr. ? increase, fr. ?, ?, to increase.] (Rhet.) A figure by which a grave and magnificent word is put for the proper word; amplification; hyperbole.

Auxĭetic (?), a. [Gr. ?.] Pertaining to, or containing, auxesis; amplifying.
Auxĭiliar (?; 106), a. [L. auxiliaris: cf. F. auxiliaire. See Auxiliary.] Auxiliary. [Archaic]
The auxiliar troops and Trojan hosts appear.
Pope.
Auxĭiliar, n. An auxiliary. [Archaic]
Milton.
Auxĭiliarĭly, adv. By way of help.
Harris.

Auxĭlialry (?; 106), a. [L. auxiliarius, fr. auxilium help, aid, fr. augere to increase.] Conferring aid or help; helping; aiding; assisting; subsidiary; as auxiliary troops.

÷ scales (Mus.), the scales of relative or attendant keys. See under Attendant, a. Ð ÷ verbs (Gram.). See Auxiliary, n., 3.

Auxĭlialry, n.; pl. Auxiliaries (?). 1. A helper; an assistant; a confederate in some action or enterprise.

(Mil.) pl. Foreign troops in the service of a nation at war; (rarely in sing.), a member of the allied or subsidiary force.

(Gram.) A verb which helps to form the voices, modes, and tenses of other verbs; Ð called, also, an auxiliary verb; as, have, be, may, can, do, must, shall, and will, in English; ˆtre and avoir, in French; avere and essere, in Italian; estar and haber, in Spanish.

(Math.) A quantity introduced for the purpose of simplifying or facilitating some operation, as in equations or trigonometrical formulˊ.

Math. Dict.
Auxĭlialtolry (?), a. Auxiliary; helping. [Obs.]
Ø Ava (?), n. Same as Kava.
Johnston.
Av · aĭdalvat (?), n. Same as Amadavat.
Aĭvail (?), v. t. [imp. & p. p. Availed (?); p. pr. & vb. n. Availing.] [OE. availen, fr. F. ? (L. ad) + valoir to be worth, fr. L. valere to be strong, to be worth. See Valiant.] 1. To turn to the advantage of; to be of service to; to profit; to benefit; to help; as, artifices will not avail the sinner in the day of judgment.

O, what avails me now that honor high !
Milton.

To promote; to assist. [Obs.]

Pope.
To avail one's self of, to make use of; take advantage of.
Then shall they seek to avail themselves of names.
Milton.
I have availed myself of the very first opportunity.
Dickens.
Aĭvail, v. i. To be of use or advantage; to answer the purpose; to have strength, force, or efficacy sufficient to accomplish the object; as, the plea in bar must avail, that is, be sufficient to defeat the suit; this scheme will not avail; medicines will not avail to check the disease. ½What signs avail ?ˌ
Milton.
Words avail very little with me, young man.
Sir W. Scott.

A·vail (?), n. 1. Profit; advantage toward success; benefit; value; as, labor, without economy, is of little avail.

The avail of a deathbed repentance.
Jer. Taylor.

pl. Proceeds; as, the avails of a sale by auction.

The avails of their own industry.
Stoddard.

Syn. - Use; benefit; utility; profit; service.

A·vail, v. t. & i. See Avale, v. [Obs.]
Spenser.

A·vail·a·bil·i·ty (?), n.; pl. Availabilities (?). 1. The quality of being available; availableness.

µ The word is sometimes used derogatively in the sense of ½mere availableness,‚ or capability of success without regard to worthiness.

He was... nominated for his availability.
Lowell.

That which is available.

A·vail·a·ble (?), a. 1. Having sufficient power, force, or efficacy, for the object; effectual; valid; as, an available plea. [Obs.]

Laws human are available by consent.
Hooker.

Such as one may avail one's self of; capable of being used for the accomplishment of a purpose; usable; profitable; advantageous; convertible into a resource; as, an available measure; an available candidate.

Struggling to redeem, as he did, the available months and days out of so many that were unavailable.
Carlyle.

Having no available funds with which to pay the calls on new shares.
H. Spenser.

A·vail·a·ble·ness, n. 1. Competent power; validity; efficacy; as, the availableness of a title. [Obs.]

Quality of being available; capability of being used for the purpose intended.

Sir M. Hale.

A·vai·a·bly, adv. In an available manner; profitably; advantageously; efficaciously.

A·vail·ment (?), n. Profit; advantage. [Obs.]

Av·a·lanche· (?; 277), n. [F. avalanche, fr. avaler to descend, to let down, from aval down, downward; ? (L. ad) + val, L. vallis, valley. See Valley.] 1.

A large mass or body of snow and ice sliding swiftly down a mountain side, or falling down a precipice.

A fall of earth, rocks, etc., similar to that of an avalanche of snow or ice.

A sudden, great, or irresistible descent or influx of anything.

Aïvale (?), v. t. & i. [F. avaler to descend, to let down. See Avalanche.] 1. To cause to descend; to lower; to let fall; to doff. [Obs.]
Chaucer.

To bring low; to abase. [Obs.]

Sir H. Wotton.

(v. i.) To descend; to fall; to dismount. [Obs.]

And from their sweaty courses did avale.
Spenser.

Aïvant (?), n. [For avantÐguard. Cf. Avaunt, Van.] The front of an army. [Obs.] See Van.

AïvantÐcou·riÏer (?), n. [F., fr. avant before + courrier. See Avaunt, and Courier.] A person dispatched before another person or company, to give notice of his or their approach.

AïvantÐguard· (?; 277), n. [F. avant before + E. guard, F. avantÐgarde. See Avaunt.] The van or advanced body of an army. See Vanguard.

Avaïrice (?), n. [F. avaritia, fr. avarus avaricious, prob. fr. av?re to covert, fr. a root av to satiate one's self: cf. Gr. ?, ?, to satiate, Skr. av to satiate one's self, rejoice, protect.] 1. An excessive or inordinate desire of gain; greediness after wealth; covetousness; cupidity.

To desire money for its own sake, and in order to hoard it up, is avarice.
Beattie.

An inordinate desire for some supposed good.

All are taught an avarice of praise.
Goldsmith.

Av·aïricious (?), a. [Cf. F. avaricieux.] Actuated by avarice; greedy of gain; immoderately desirous of accumulating property.

Syn. - Greedy; stingy; rapacious; griping; sordid; close. Ð Avaricious, Covetous, Parsimonious, Penurious, Miserly, Niggardly. The avaricious eagerly grasp after it at the expense of others, though not of necessity with a design to save, since a man may be covetous and yet a spendthrift. The penurious, parsimonious, and miserly save money by disgraceful selfÐdenial, and the niggardly by meanness in their dealing with others. We speak of persons as covetous in getting, avaricious in retaining, parsimonious in expending, penurious or miserly in modes of living, niggardly in dispensing.

Ð Av · aĭriciousĭly, adv. Ð Av · aĭriciousĭness, n.

Avaĭrous (?), a. [L. avarus.] Avaricious. [Obs.]

Aĭvast (?), interj. [Corrupted from D. houd vast hold fast. See Hold, v. t., and Fast, a.] (Naut.) Cease; stop; stay. ½Avast heaving.„

Totten.

Av · aĭtar (?), n. [Skr. avatfra descent; ava from + root t? to cross, pass over.] 1. (Hindoo Myth.) The descent of a deity to earth, and his incarnation as a man or an animal; Ð chiefly associated with the incarnations of Vishnu.

Incarnation; manifestation as an object of worship or admiration.

Aĭvaunce (?), v. t. & i. [See Advance.] To advance; to profit.
Chaucer.

Aĭvaunt (?), interj. [F. avant forward, fr. L. ab + ante before. Cf. Avant, Advance.] Begone; depart; Ð a word of contempt or abhorrence, equivalent to the phrase ½Get thee gone.„

Aĭvaunt, v. t. & i. 1. To advance; to move forward; to elevate. [Obs.]
Spenser.

To depart; to move away. [Obs.]

Coverdale.

Aĭvaunt, v. t. & i. [OF. avanter; ? (L. ad) + vanter. See Vaunt.] To vaunt; to boast. [Obs.]
Chaucer.

Aĭvaunt, n. A vaunt; to boast. [Obs.]
Chaucer.

Aĭvauntour (?), n. [OF. avanteur.] A boaster. [Obs.]
Chaucer.

Ø Ave (?), n. [L., hail.] 1. An ave Maria.
He repeated Aves and Credos.
Macaulay.

A reverential salutation.

Their loud applause and aves vehement.
Shak.

Aĭvel (?), v. t. [L. avellere.] To pull away. [Obs.]
Yet are not these parts avelled.
Sir T. Browne.

Aĭvellane (?), a. [Cf. It. avellana a filbert, fr. L. Avella or Abella a city of Campania.] (Her.) In the form of four unhusked filberts; as, an avellane cross.

Ø Ave Maĭria (?), Ave Mary (?). } [From the first words of the Roman Catholic prayer to the Virgin Mary; L. ave hail, Maria Mary.] 1. A salutation and prayer to the Virgin Mary, as mother of God; Ð used in the Roman Catholic church.

To number Ave Maries on his beads.

Shak.

A particular time (as in Italy, at the ringing of the bells about half an hour after sunset, and also at early dawn), when the people repeat the Ave Maria.

Ave Maria ! blessed be the hour !

Byron.

Ø Aïvena (?), n. [L.] (Bot.) A genus of grasses, including the common oat (Avena sativa); the oat grasses.

Av · eïnaceous (?), a. [L. avenaceus, fr. avena oats.] Belonging to, or resembling, oats or the oat grasses.

Aveïnage (?), n. [F. avenage, fr. L. avena oats.] (Old Law) A quantity of oats paid by a tenant to a landlord in lieu of rent.

Jacob.

Aveïner (?), n. [OF. avenier, fr. aveine, avaine, avoine, oats, F. avoine, L. avena.] (Feud. Law) An officer of the king's stables whose duty it was to provide oats for the horses. [Obs.]

Aïvenge (?), v. t. [imp. & p. p. Avenged (?); p. pr. & vb. n. Avenging (?).] [OF. avengier; L. ad + vindicare to lay claim to, to avenge, revenge. See Vengeance.] 1. To take vengeance for; to exact satisfaction for by punishing the injuring party; to vindicate by inflicting pain or evil on a wrongdoer.

He will avenge the blood of his servants.

Deut. xxxii. 43.

Avenge, O Lord, thy slaughtered saints, whose bones
Lie scattered on the Alpine mountains cold.

Milton.

He had avenged himself on them by havoc such as England had never before seen.

Macaulay.

To treat revengefully; to wreak vengeance on. [Obs.]

Thy judgment in avenging thine enemies.

Bp. Hall.

Syn. - To Avenge, Revenge. To avenge is to inflict punishment upon evil doers in behalf of ourselves, or others for whom we act; as, to avenge one's wrongs; to avenge the injuries of the suffering and innocent. It is to inflict pain for the sake of vindication, or retributive justice. To revenge is to inflict pain or injury for the indulgence of resentful and malicious feelings. The former may at times be a duty; the latter is one of the worst exhibitions of human character.

I avenge myself upon another, or I avenge another, or I avenge a wrong. I revenge only myself, and that upon another.

C. J. Smith.

Aïvenge, v. i. To take vengeance.

Levit. xix. 18.

Aïvenge, n. Vengeance; revenge. [Obs.]

Spenser.

Aïvengeance (?), n. Vengeance. [Obs.]

Aïvengeful (?), a. Vengeful. [Obs.]

Spenser.

Aïvengement (?), n. The inflicting of retributive punishment; satisfaction taken. [R.]

Milton.

Aïvenger (?), n. 1. One who avenges or vindicates; as, an avenger of blood.

One who takes vengeance. [Obs.]

Milton.

Aïvengeress, n. A female avenger. [Obs.]

Spenser.

Aïvenilous (?), a. [Pref. aï + L. vena a vein.] (Bot.) Being without veins or nerves, as the leaves of certain plants.

Avelnor (?), n. See Avener. [Obs.]

Avens (?), n. [OF. avence.] (Bot.) A plant of the genus Geum, esp. Geum urbanum, or herb bennet.

Avenitail (?), n. [OF. esventail. Cf. Ventail.] The movable front to a helmet; the ventail.

Avenitine (?), a. Pertaining to Mons Aventinus, one of the seven hills on which Rome stood.

Bryant.

Avenitine, n. A post of security or defense. [Poetic]

Into the castle's tower,

The only Aventine that now is left him.

Beau. & Fl.

Aïventre (?), v. t. To thrust forward (at a venture), as a spear. [Obs.]

Spenser.

Aïventure (?; 135), n. [See Adventure, n.] 1. Accident; chance; adventure. [Obs.]

Chaucer.

(Old Law) A mischance causing a person's death without felony, as by drowning, or falling into the fire.

Aĭventuĭrine (?), n. [F. aventurine: cf. It. avventurino.] 1. A kind of glass, containing goldÐcolored spangles. It was produced in the first place by the accidental (par aventure) dropping of some brass filings into a pot of melted glass.

(Min.) A variety of translucent quartz, spangled throughout with scales of yellow mica.

÷ feldspar, a variety of oligoclase with internal firelike reflections due to the presence of minute crystals, probably of hematite; sunstone.

Aveĭnue (?), n. [F. avenue, fr. avenir to come to, L. advenire. See Advene.] 1. A way or opening for entrance into a place; a passage by which a place may by reached; a way of approach or of exit. ½The avenues leading to the city by land.‚

Macaulay.

On every side were expanding new avenues of inquiry.

Milman.

The principal walk or approach to a house which is withdrawn from the road, especially, such approach bordered on each side by trees; any broad passageway thus bordered.

An avenue of tall elms and branching chestnuts.

W. Black.

A broad street; as, the Fifth Avenue in New York.

Aver (?), n. [OF. aver domestic animal, whence LL. averia, pl. cattle. See Habit, and cf. Average.] A work horse, or working ox. [Obs. or Dial. Eng.]

<— p. 105 —>

Aĭver (?), v. t. [imp. & p. p. Averred (?); p. pr. & vb. n. Averring.] [F. av‚rer, LL. adverare, averare; L. ad + versus true. See Verity.] 1. To assert, or prove, the truth of. [Obs.]

(Law) To avouch or verify; to offer to verify; to prove or justify. See Averment.

To affirm with confidence; to declare in a positive manner, as in confidence of asserting the truth.

It is sufficient that the very fact hath its foundation in truth, as I do seriously aver is the case.

Fielding.

Then all averred I had killed the bird.

Coleridge.

Syn. - To assert; affirm; asseverate. See Affirm.

Averĭage (?), n. [OF. average, LL. averagium, prob. fr. OF. aver, F. avoir, property, horses, cattle, etc.; prop. infin., to have, from L. habere to have. Cf. F. av‚rage small cattle, and avarie (perh. of different origin) damage to ship or cargo, port dues. The first meaning was pe??? the service of carting a feudal lord's wheat, then charge for carriage, the contribution towards loss of things carried, in proportion to the amount of each person's property. Cf. Aver, n., Avercorn, Averpenny.] 1. (OLd Eng. Law) That service which a tenant owed his lord, to be done by the work beasts of the tenant, as the carriage of wheat, turf, etc.

[Cf. F. avarie damage to ship or cargo.] (Com.) (a) A tariff or duty on goods, etc. [Obs.] (b) Any charge in addition to the regular charge for freight of goods shipped. (c) A contribution to a loss or charge which has been imposed upon one of several for the general benefit; damage done by sea perils. (d) The equitable and proportionate distribution of loss or expense among all interested.

General ~, a contribution made, by all parties concerned in a sea adventure, toward a loss occasioned by the voluntary sacrifice of the property of some of the parties in interest for the benefit of all. It is called general average, because it falls upon the gross amount of ship, cargo, and freight at risk and saved by the sacrifice. Kent. Ð Particular ~ signifies the damage or partial loss happening to the ship, or cargo, or freight, in consequence of some fortuitous or unavoidable accident; and it is borne by the individual owners of the articles damaged, or by their insurers. Ð Petty averages are sundry small charges, which occur regularly, and are necessarily defrayed by the master in the usual course of a voyage; such as port charges, common pilotage, and the like, which formerly were, and in some cases still are, borne partly by the ship and partly by the cargo. In the clause commonly found in bills of lading, ½primage and average accustomed,ₓ average means a kind of composition established by usage for such charges, which were formerly assessed by way of average. Arnould. Abbott. Phillips.

A mean proportion, medial sum or quantity, made out of unequal sums or quantities; an arithmetical mean. Thus, if A loses 5 dollars, B 9, and C 16, the sum is 30, and the average 10.

Any medial estimate or general statement derived from a comparison of diverse specific cases; a medium or usual size, quantity, quality, rate, etc. ½The average of sensations.ₓ

Paley.

pl. In the English corn trade, the medial price of the several kinds of grain in the principal corn markets.

On an average, taking the mean of unequal numbers or quantities.

Avérage (?), a. 1. Pertaining to an ~ or mean; medial; containing a mean proportion; of a mean size, quality, ability, etc.; ordinary; usual; as, an average rate of profit; an average amount of rain; the average Englishman; beings of the average stamp.

According to the laws of ~; as, the loss must be made good by average contribution.

Avérage, v. t. [imp. & p. p. Averaged (?); p. pr. & vb. n. Averaging.] 1. To find the mean of, when sums or quantities are unequal; to reduce to a mean.

To divide among a number, according to a given proportion; as, to average a loss.

To do, accomplish, get, etc., on an ~.

Averĭage, v. i. To form, or exist in, a mean or medial sum or quantity; to amount to, or to be, on an ~; as, the losses of the owners will average twenty five dollars each; these spars average ten feet in length.

Averĭcorn · (?), n. [Aver, n. + corn.] (Old Eng. Law) A reserved rent in corn, formerly paid to religious houses by their tenants or farmers.

Kennet.

Aĭverment (?), n. [Cf. OF. averement, LL. averamentum. See Aver, v. t.] 1. The act of averring, or that which is averred; affirmation; positive assertion.

Signally has this averment received illustration in the course of recent events.

I. Taylor.

Verification; establishment by evidence.

Bacon.

(Law) A positive statement of facts; an allegation; an offer to justify or prove what is alleged.

µ In any stage of pleadings, when either party advances new matter, he avers it to be true, by using this form of words: ½and this he is ready to verify.ˬ This was formerly called an averment. It modern pleading, it is termed a verification.

Blackstone.

Aĭvernal (?), Aĭvernĭan (?), } a. Of or pertaining to Avernus, a lake of Campania, in Italy, famous for its poisonous vapors, which ancient writers fancied were so malignant as to kill birds flying over it. It was represented by the poets to be connected with the infernal regions.

Averĭpen · ny (?), n. [Aver, n. + penny.] (Old Eng. Law) Money paid by a tenant in lieu of the service of average.

Aĭverroĭism (?), n. The tenets of the Averroists.

Aĭverroĭist, n. One of a sect of peripatetic philosophers, who appeared in Italy before the restoration of learning; so denominated from Averroes, or Averrhoes, a celebrated Arabian philosopher. He held the doctrine of monopsychism.

Av · erĭruncate (?), v. t. [L. averruncare to avert; a, ab, off + verruncare to turn; formerly derived from ab and eruncare to root out. Cf. Aberuncate.] 1. To avert; to ward off. [Obs.]

Hudibras.

To root up. [Obs.]

Johnson.

Av · er̆run̆ication (?), n. [Cf. OF. averroncation.] 1. The act of averting. [Obs.]

Eradication. [R.]

De Quincey.

Av · er̆run̆icator (?), n. [Cf. Aberuncator.] An instrument for pruning trees, consisting of two blades, or a blade and a hook, fixed on the end of a long rod.

Av · er̆sation (?), n. [L. aversatio, fr. aversari to turn away, v. intens. of avertere. See Avert.] A turning from with dislike; aversion. [Obs.or Archaic]

Some men have a natural aversation to some vices or virtues, and a natural affection to others.

Jer. Taylor.

Āverse (?), a. [L. aversus, p. p. of avertere. See Avert.] 1. Turned away or backward. [Obs.]

The tracks averse a lying notice gave,
And led the searcher backward from the cave.

Dryden.

Having a repugnance or opposition of mind; disliking; disinclined; unwilling; reluctant.

Averse alike to flatter, or offend.

Pope.

Men who were averse to the life of camps.

Macaulay.

Pass by securely as men averse from war.

Micah ii. 8.

μ The prevailing usage now is to employ to after averse and its derivatives rather than from, as was formerly the usage. In this the word is in agreement with its kindred terms, hatred, dislike, dissimilar, contrary, repugnant, etc., expressing a relation or an affection of the mind to an object.

Syn. - Averse, Reluctant, Adverse. Averse expresses an habitual, though not of necessity a very strong, dislike; as, averse to active pursuits; averse to study. Reluctant, a term of the of the will, implies an internal struggle as to making some sacrifice of interest or feeling; as, reluctant to yield; reluctant to make the necessary arrangements; a reluctant will or consent. Adverse denotes active opposition or hostility; as, adverse interests; adverse feelings, plans, or movements; the adverse party.

Āverse, v. t. & i. To turn away. [Obs.]

B. Jonson.

Āversely, adv. 1. Backward; in a backward direction; as, emitted aversely.

With repugnance or aversion; unwillingly.

Aïverseness, n. The quality of being averse; opposition of mind; unwillingness.

Aïversion (?), n. [L. aversio: cf. F. aversion. See Avert.] 1. A turning away. [Obs.]

Adhesion to vice and aversion from goodness.
Bp. Atterbury.

Opposition or repugnance of mind; fixed dislike; antipathy; disinclination; reluctance.

Mutual aversion of races.
Prescott.

His rapacity had made him an object of general aversion.
Macaulay.

µ It is now generally followed by to before the object. [See Averse.] Sometimes towards and for are found; from is obsolete.

A freeholder is bred with an aversion to subjection.
Addison.

His aversion towards the house of York.
Bacon.

It is not difficult for a man to see that a person has conceived an aversion for him.
Spectator.

The Khasias... have an aversion to milk.
J. D. Hooker.

The object of dislike or repugnance.

Pain their aversion, pleasure their desire.
Pope.

Syn. - Antipathy; dislike; repugnance; disgust. See Dislike.

Aïvert (?), v. t. [imp. & p. p. Averted; p. pr. & vb. n. Averting.] [L. avertere; a, ab + vertere to turn: cf. OF. avertir. See Verse, n.] To turn aside, or away; as, to a???t the eyes from an object; to ward off, or prevent, the occurrence or effects of; as, how can the danger be averted? ½To avert his ire.͵
Milton.

When atheists and profane persons do hear of so many discordant and contrary opinions in religion, it doth avert them from the church.
Bacon.

Till ardent prayer averts the public woe.
Prior.

Aïvert, v. i. To turn away. [Archaic]
Co?? and averting from our neighbor's good.
Thomson.

A̤verted, a. Turned away, esp. as an expression of feeling; also, offended; unpropitious.

Who scornful pass it with averted eye.
Keble.

A̤verter (?), n. One who, or that which, averts.

A̤vertḯble (?), a.ÿCapable of being averted; preventable.

A̤vertḯment (?), n. Advertisement. [Obs.]

Ø Aves (?), n. pl. [L., pl. of avis bird.] (Zo"l.) The class of Vertebrata that includes the birds.

μ Aves, or birds, have a complete double circulation, oviparous, reproduction, front limbs peculiarly modified as wings; and they bear feathers. All existing birds have a horny beak, without teeth; but some Mesozoic fossil birds (Odontornithes) had conical teeth inserted in both jaws. The principal groups are: Carinat', including all existing flying birds; Ratit', including the ostrich and allies, the apteryx, and the extinct moas; Odontornithes, or fossil birds with teeth.

The ordinary birds are classified largely by the structure of the beak and feet, which are in direct relating to their habits. See Beak, Bird, Odontonithes.

Ø A̤vesta (?), n. The Zoroastrian scriptures. See ZendÐAvesta.

Avḯan (?), a. Of or instrument to birds.

Avḯa̤ry (?), n.; pl. Aviaries (?). [L. aviarium, fr. aviarius pertaining to birds, fr. avis bird, akin to Gr, ?, Skr. vi.] A house, inclosure, large cage, or other place, for keeping birds confined; a bird house.

Lincolnshire may be termed the aviary of England.
Fuller.

A · vḯation (?), n. The art or science of flying.

Avḯa · tor (?), n. (a) An experimenter in aviation. (b) A flying machine.

Ø A̤vicṳla (?), n. [L., small bird.] (Zo"l.) A genus of marine bivalves, having a pearly interior, allied to the pearl oyster; Ð so called from a supposed resemblance of the typical species to a bird.

A̤vicṳlar (?), a. [L. avicula a small bird, dim. of avis bird.] Of or pertaining to a bird or to birds.

Ø A̤vic · ṳlari̤a (?), n. pl. [NL. See Avicular.] (Zo"l.) See prehensile processes on the cells of some Bryozoa, often having the shape of a bird's bill.

Avḯcul · ture (?; 135), n. [L. avis bird + cultura culture.] (Zo"l.) Rearing and care of birds.

Avid (?), a. [L. avidus, fr. av?re to long: cf. F. avide. See Avarice.] Longing eagerly for; eager; greedy. ½Avid of gold, yet greedier of renown.,
Southey.

A̤vidḯous (?), a. Avid.

A̤vidḯousḯly, adv. Eagerly; greedily.

A̤vidḯty (?), n. [L. aviditas, fr. avidus: cf. F. avidit,. See Avid.] Greediness; strong appetite; eagerness; intenseness of desire; as, to eat with avidity.

His books were received and read with avidity.
Milward.

Aï̆vie (?), adv. [Pref. aï̆ + vie.] Emulously. [Obs.]

Ø A · vi͡fauna (?), n. [NL., fr. L. avis bird + E. fauna.] (Zo"l.) The birds, or all the kinds of birds, inhabiting a region.

Av · iĭgato (?), n. See Avocado.

A · vignon berry (?). (Bot.) The fruit of the Rhamnus infectorius, eand of other species of the same genus; Ð so called from the city of Avignon, in France. It is used by dyers and painters for coloring yellow. Called also French berry.

Aï̆vile (?), v. t. [OF. aviler, F. avilir; a (L. ad) + vil vile. See Vile.] To abase or debase; to vilify; to depreciate. [Obs.]

Want makes us know the price of what we avile.
B. Jonson.

Aï̆vis (?), n. [F. avis. See Advice.] Advice; opinion; deliberation. [Obs.]
Chaucer.

Aï̆vise (?), v. t. [F. aviser. See Advise, v. t.] 1. To look at; to view; to think of. [Obs.]
Chaucer.

To advise; to counsel. [Obs.]

Shak.
To ~ one's self, to consider with one's self, to reflect, to deliberate. [Obs.]
Chaucer.
Now therefore, if thou wilt enriched be,
Avise thee well, and change thy willful mood.
Spenser.

Aï̆vise, v. i. To consider; to reflect. [Obs.]
Aï̆viseful (?), a. Watchful; circumspect. [Obs.]
With sharp, aviseful eye.
Spenser.

Aï̆visely, adv. Advisedly. [Obs.]
Chaucer.

Aï̆visement (?), n. Advisement; observation; deliberation. [Obs.]

Aï̆vision (?), n. Vision. [Obs.]
Chaucer.

Aï̆viso (?), n. [Sp.] 1. Information; advice.

An advice boat, or dispatch boat.

Ø Av · oĭcado (?), n. [Corrupted from the Mexican ahuacatl: cf. Sp. aguacate, F. aguacat,, avocat, G. avogadobaum.] The pulpy fruit of Persea gratissima, a tree of tropical America. It is about the size and shape of a large pear; Ð called also avocado pear, alligator pear, midshipman's butter.

Ø Av · oĭcat (?), n. [F.] An advocate.

Avoĭcate (?), v. t. [L. avocatus, p. p. of avocare; a, ab + vocare to call. Cf. Avoke, and see Vocal, a.] To call off or away; to withdraw; to transfer to another tribunal. [Obs. or Archaic]

One who avocateth his mind from other occupations.
Barrow.
He, at last,... avocated the cause to Rome.
Robertson.

Av · oĭcation (?), n. [L. avocatio.] 1. A calling away; a diversion. [Obs. or Archaic]

Impulses to duty, and powerful avocations from sin.
South.

That which calls one away from one's regular employment or vocation.

Heaven is his vocation, and therefore he counts earthly employments avocations.
Fuller.
By the secular cares and avocations which accompany marriage the clergy have been furnished with skill in common life.

Atterbury. μ In this sense the word is applied to the smaller affairs of life, or occasional calls which summon a person to leave his ordinary or principal business. Avocation (in the singular) for vocation is usually avoided by good writers. 3. pl. Pursuits; duties; affairs which occupy one's time; usual employment; vocation. There are professions, among the men, no more favorable to these studies than the common avocations of women. Richardson. In a few hours, above thirty thousand men left his standard, and returned to their ordinary avocations. Macaulay.

<— p. 106 —>

An irregularity and instability of purpose, which makes them choose the wandering avocations of a shepherd, rather than the more fixed pursuits of agriculture.
Buckle.

Aĭvocaĭtive (?), a. Calling off. [Obs.]
Aĭvocaĭtive, n. That which calls aside; a dissuasive.

Avoĭcet, Avoĭset (?), n. [F. avocette: cf. It. avosetta, Sp. avoceta.] (Zo"l.) A grallatorial bird, of the genus Recurvirostra; the scooper. The bill is long and bend upward toward the tip. The American species is R. Americana. [Written also avocette.] Aĭvoid (?), v. t. [imp. & p. p. Avoided; p. pr. & vb. n. Avoiding.] [OF. esvuidier, es (L. ex) + vuidier, voidier, to empty. See Void, a.] 1. To empty. [Obs.]
Wyclif.

To emit or throw out; to void; as, to avoid excretions. [Obs.]

Sir T. Browne.

To quit or evacuate; to withdraw from. [Obs.]

Six of us only stayed, and the rest avoided
the room.
Bacon.

To make void; to annul or vacate; to refute.

How can these grants of the king's be avoided?
Spenser.

To keep away from; to keep clear of; to endeavor no to meet; to shun; to abstain from; as, to avoid the company of gamesters.

What need a man forestall his date of grief.
And run to meet what he would most avoid ?
Milton.
He carefully avoided every act which could goad them into open hostility.
Macaulay.

To get rid of. [Obs.]

Shak.

(Pleading) To defeat or evade; to invalidate. Thus, in a replication, the plaintiff may deny the defendant's plea, or confess it, and avoid it by stating new matter.

Blackstone.
Syn. - To escape; elude; evade; eschew. Đ To Avoid, Shun. Avoid in its commonest sense means, to keep clear of, an extension of the meaning, to withdraw one's self from. It denotes care taken not to come near or in contact; as, to avoid certain persons or places. Shun is a stronger term, implying more prominently the idea of intention. The words may, however, in many cases be interchanged.

No man can pray from his heart to be kept from temptation, if the take no care of himself to avoid it.
Mason.
So Chanticleer, who never saw a fox,
Yet shunned him as a sailor shuns the rocks.
Dryden.
Aïvoid, v. i. 1. To retire; to withdraw. [Obs.]
David avoided out of his presence.
1 Sam. xviii. 11.

(Law) To become void or vacant. [Obs.]

Ayliffe.

A̤voida̤ble (?), a. 1. Capable of being vacated; liable to be annulled or made invalid; voidable.

The charters were not avoidable for the king's nonage.

Hale.

Capable of being avoided, shunned, or escaped.

A̤voidance (?), n. 1. The act of annulling; annulment.

The act of becoming vacant, or the state of being vacant; Ð specifically used for the state of a benefice becoming void by the death, deprivation, or resignation of the incumbent.

Wolsey,... on every avoidance of St. Peter's chair, was sitting down therein, when suddenly some one or other clapped in before him.

Fuller.

A dismissing or a quitting; removal; withdrawal.

The act of avoiding or shunning; keeping clear of. ½The avoidance of pain.

Beattie.

The courts by which anything is carried off.

Avoidances and drainings of water.

Bacon.

A̤voider (?), n. 1. The person who carries anything away, or the vessel in which things are carried away.

Johnson.

One who avoids, shuns, or escapes.

A̤voidless, a. Unavoidable; inevitable.

Av · oir̤dṳlpois (?), n. & a. [OE. aver de peis, goods of weight, where peis is fr. OF. peis weight, F. poids, L. pensum. See Aver, n., and Poise, n.] 1. Goods sold by weight. [Obs.]

Avoirdupois weight.

Weight; heaviness; as, a woman of much avoirdupois.ÿ[Colloq.]

÷ weight, a system of weights by which coarser commodities are weighed, such as hay, grain, butter, sugar, tea.

µ The standard ~ pound of the United States is equivalent to the weight of 27.7015 cubic inches of distilled water at 620 Fahrenheit, the barometer being at 30 inches, and the water weighed in the air with brass weights. In this system of weights 16 drams make 1 ounce, 16 ounces 1 pound, 25 pounds 1 quarter, 4 quarters 1 hundred weight, and 20 hundred weight 1 ton. The above pound contains 7,000 grains, or 453.54 grams, so that 1 pound avoirdupois is equivalent to 1 31Ð144 pounds troy. (See Troy weight.) Formerly, a hundred weight was reckoned at 112 pounds, the ton being 2,240 pounds (sometimes called a long ton).

A̅voke (?), v. t. [Cf. Avocate.] To call from or back again. [Obs.] Bp. Burnet.

Avo̅ilate (?), v. i. [L. avolare; a (ab) + volare to fly.] To fly away; to escape; to exhale. [Obs.]

Av·o̅ilation (?), n. [LL. avolatio.] The act of flying; flight; evaporation. [Obs.]

Avo̅iset (?), n. Same as Avocet.

A̅vouch (?), v. t. [imp. & p. p. Avouched (?); p. pr. & vb. n. Avouching.] [OF. avochier, LL. advocare to recognize the existence of a thing, to advocate, fr. L. advocare to call to; ad + vocare to call. Cf. Avow to declare, Advocate, and see Vouch, v. t.] 1. To appeal to; to cite or claim as authority. [Obs.]

They avouch many successions of authorities.
Coke.

<small>To maintain a just or true; to vouch for.</small>

We might be disposed to question its authencity, it if were not avouched by the full evidence.
Milman.

<small>To declare or assert positively and as matter of fact; to affirm openly.</small>

If this which he avouches does appear.
Shak.
Such antiquities could have been avouched for the Irish.
Spenser.

<small>To acknowledge deliberately; to admit; to confess; to sanction.</small>

Thou hast avouched the Lord this day to be thy God.
Deut. xxvi. 17.

A̅vouch (?), n. Evidence; declaration. [Obs.]
The sensible and true avouch
Of mine own eyes.
Shak.

A̅voucha̅ible (?), a. Capable of being avouched.

A̅voucher (?), n. One who avouches.

A̅vouchment (?), n. The act of avouching; positive declaration. [Obs.] Milton.

A̅voutrer (?), n. See Advoutrer. [Obs.]

A̅voutrie (?), n. [OF.] Adultery. [Obs.]

Chaucer.

Aïvow (?), v. t. [imp. & p. p. Avowed (?); p. pr. & vb. n. Avowing.] [F. avouver, fr. L. advocare to call to (whence the meanings, to call upon as superior; recognize as lord, own, confess); ad + vocare to call. See Advocate, Avouch.] 1. To declare openly, as something believed to be right; to own or acknowledge frankly; as, a man avows his principles or his crimes.

Which I to be the of Israel's God
Avow, and challenge Dagon to the test.
Milton.

(Law) To acknowledge and justify, as an act done. See Avowry.

Blackstone.

Syn. - To acknowledge; own; confess. See Confess.

Aïvow, n, [Cf. F. aveu.] Avowal. [Obs.]

Dryden.

Aïvow, v. t. & i. [OF. avouer, fr. LL. votare to vow, fr. L. votun. See Vote, n.] To bind, or to devote, by a vow. [Obs.]

Wyclif.

Aïvow, n. A vow or determination. [Archaic]

Aïvowaïble (?), a. Capable of being avowed, or openly acknowledged, with confidence.

Donne.

Aïvowal (?), n. An open declaration; frank acknowledgment; as, an avowal of such principles.

Hume.

Aïvowance (?), n. 1. Act of avowing; avowal.

Upholding; defense; vindication. [Obs.]

Can my avowance of kingÐmurdering be collected from anything here written by me?
Fuller.

Aïvowant (?), n. (Law) The defendant in replevin, who avows the distress of the goods, and justifies the taking.

Cowell.

Aïvowed (?), a. Openly acknowledged or declared; admitted. Ð Aïvowedïly (?), adv.

Aïvow · ee (?), n. [F. avou,. Cf. Advowee, Advocate, n.] The person who has a right to present to a benefice; the patron; an advowee. See Advowson.

Aïvower (?), n. One who avows or asserts.

Aïvowry (?), n. [OE. avouerie protection, authority, OF. avouerie. See Avow to declare.] 1. An advocate; a patron; a patron saint. [Obs.]

Let God alone be our avowry.
Latimer.

The act of the distrainer of goods, who, in an action of replevin, avows and justifies the taking in his own right.

Blackstone.

µ When an action of replevin is brought, the distrainer either makes avowry, that is, avours taking the distress in his own right, or the right of his wife, and states the reason if it, as for arrears of rent, damage done, or the like; or makes cognizance, that is, acknowledges the taking, but justifies in an another's right, as his bailiff or servant.

Aïvowtry, v. t. Adultery. See Advoutry.

Aïvoyer (?), n. [F.] A chief magistrate of a free imperial city or canton of Switzerland. [Obs.]

Aïvulse (?), v. t. [L. avulsus, p. p. of avellere to tear off; a (ab) + vellere to pluck.] To pluck or pull off.

Shenstone.

Aïvulsion (?), n. [L. avulsio.] 1. A tearing asunder; a forcible separation. The avulsion of two polished superficies.

Locke.

A fragment torn off.

J. Barlow.

(Law) The sudden removal of lands or soil from the estate of one man to that of another by an inundation or a current, or by a sudden change in the course of a river by which a part of the estate of one man is cut off and joined to the estate of another. The property in the part thus separated, or cut off, continues in the original owner.

Wharton. Burrill.

Aïvuncuïlar (?), a. [L. avunculus uncle.] Of or pertaining to an uncle.

In these rare instances, the law of pedigree, whether direct or avuncular, gives way.

I. Taylor.

Aïwait (?), v. t. [imp. & p. p. Awaited; p. pr. & vb. n. Awaiting.] [OF. awaitier, agaitier; ? (L. ad) + waitier, gaitier to watch, F. guetter. See Wait.] 1. To watch for; to look out for. [Obs.]

To wait on, serve, or attend. [Obs.]

To wait for; to stay for; to expect. See Expect.

Betwixt these rocky pillars Gabriel sat,
Chief of the angelic guards, awaiting night.
Milton.

To be in store for; to be ready or in waiting for; as, a glorious reward awaits the good.

O Eve, some farther change awaits us night.
Milton.
Aïwait, v. i. 1. To watch. [Obs.]
Chaucer.

To wait (on or upon). [Obs.]

To wait; to stay in waiting.

Darwin.
Aïwait, n. A waiting for; ambush; watch; watching; heed. [Obs.]
Chaucer.
Aïwake (?), v. t. [imp. Awoke (?), Awaked (?); p. p. Awaked; Obs. Awaken, Awoken; p. pr. & vb. n. Awaking. The form Awoke is sometimes used as a p. p.] [AS. ¾w'cnan, v. i. (imp. aw?c), and ¾wacian, v. i. (imp. awacode). See Awaken, Wake.] 1. To rouse from sleep.; to wake; to awaken.
Where morning's earliest ray... awake her.
Tennyson.
And his disciples came to him, and awoke him, saying, Lord, save us; we perish.
Matt. viii. 25.

To rouse from a state resembling sleep, as from death, stupidity., or inaction; to put into action; to give new life to; to stir up; as, to awake the dead; to awake the dormant faculties.

I was soon awaked from this disagreeable reverie.
Goldsmith.
It way awake my bounty further.
Shak.
No sunny gleam awakes the trees.
Keble.
Aïwake (?), v. i. To cease to sleep; to come out of a state of natural sleep; and, figuratively, out of a state resembling sleep, as inaction or death.
The national spirit again awoke.
Freeman.
Awake to righteousness, and sin not.
1 Cor. xv. 34.
Aïwake, a. [From awaken, old p. p. of awake.] Not sleeping or lethargic; roused from sleep; in a state of vigilance or action.
Before whom awake I stood.
Milton.
She still beheld,
Now wide awake, the vision of her sleep.
Keats.
He was awake to the danger.

Froude.

Aïwaken (?), v. t. & i. [imp. & p. p. Awakened (?); p. pr. & vb. n. Awakening.] [OE. awakenen, awaknen, AS. ¾w'cnan, ¾w'cnian, v. i.; pref. onï + w'cnan to wake. Cf. Awake, v. t.] To rouse from sleep or torpor; to awake; to wake.

[He] is dispatched
Already to awaken whom thou nam'st.

Cowper.

Their consciences are thoroughly awakened.

Tillotson.

Syn. - To arouse; excite; stir up; call forth.

Aïwakenïer (?), n. One who, or that which, awakens.

Aïwakenïing, a. Rousing from sleep, in a natural or a figurative sense; rousing into activity; exciting; as, the awakening city; an awakening discourse; the awakening dawn. Ð Aïwakenïingïly, adv.

Aïwakenïing, n. The act of awaking, or ceasing to sleep. Specifically: A revival of religion, or more general attention to religious matters than usual.

Aïwakenïment (?), n. An awakening. [R.]

Aïwanting (?), a. [Pref. aï + wanting.] Missing; wanting. [Prov. Scot. & Eng.]

Sir W. Hamilton.

Aïward (?), v. t. [imp. & p. p. Awarded; p. pr. & vb. n. Awarding.] [OF. eswarder to look at, consider, decide, judge; es (L. ex) + warder, garder, to observe, take heed, keep, fr. OHG. wart?n to watch, guard. See Ward.] To give by sentence or judicial determination; to assign or apportion, after careful regard to the nature of the case; to adjudge; as, the arbitrators awarded damages to the complainant.

To review
The wrongful sentence, and award a new.

Dryden.

Aïward, v. i. To determine; to make an ~.

Aïward, n. [Cf. OF. award, awart, esgart. See Award, v. t.] 1. A judgment, sentence, or final decision. Specifically: The decision of arbitrators in a case submitted.½Impatient for the award.ͺ

Cowper.

An award had been given against.

Gilpin.

The paper containing the decision of arbitrators; that which is warded.

Bouvier.

Aïwarder (?), n. One who awards, or assigns by sentence or judicial determination; a judge.

Aïware (?), a. [OE. iwar, AS. gew'r, fr. w'r wary. The pref. geÏ orig. meant together, completely. ?. See Wary.] 1. Watchful; vigilant or on one's guard against danger or difficulty.

Apprised; informed; cognizant; conscious; as, he was aware of the enemy's designs.

Aware of nothing arduous in a task
They never undertook.
Cowper.

Aïwarn (?), v. t. [Pref. aï + warn, AS. gewarnian. See Warn, v. t.] To warn. [Obs.]
Spenser.

Aïwash (?), a. [Pref. aï + wash.] Washed by the waves or tide; Ð said of a rock or strip of shore, or (Naut.) of an anchor, etc., when flush with the surface of the water, so that the waves break over it.

Aïway (?), adv. [AS. aweg, anweg, onweg; on on + weg way.] 1. From a place; hence.

The sound is going away.
Shak.

Have me away, for I am sore wounded.
2 Chron. xxxv. 23.

Absent; gone; at a distance; as, the master is away from home.

Aside; off; in another direction.

The axis of rotation is inclined away from the sun.
Lockyer.

From a state or condition of being; out of existence.

Be near me when I fade away.
Tennyson.

By ellipsis of the verb, equivalent to an imperative: Go or come ~; begone; take ~.

And the Lord said... Away, get thee down.
Exod. xix. 24.

On; in continuance; without intermission or delay; as, sing away. [Colloq.]

µ It is much used in phrases signifying moving or going from; as, go away, run away, etc.; all signifying departure, or separation to a distance. Sometimes without the verb; as, whither away so fast ? ½Love hath wings, and will away., Waller. It serves to modify the sense of certain verbs by adding that of removal, loss, parting with, etc.; as, to throw away; to trifle away; to squander away, etc. Sometimes it has merely an intensive force; as, to blaze away.

Away with, bear, abide. [Obs. or Archaic] ½The calling of assemblies, I can not away with., (Isa. i. 13), i. e., ½I can not bear or endure [it]., Ð Away with one, signifies, take him away. ½Away with, crucify him., John xix. 15. Ð To make away with. (a) To kill or destroy. (b) To carry off.

<— p. 107 —>

AïwayÐgoing (?), a. (Law) Sown during the last years of a tenancy, but not ripe until after its expiration; Ð said of crops.

Wharton.

Aïwayward (?), adv. Turned away; away. [Obs.]

Chaucer.

Awe (?), n. [OE. a?e, aghe, fr. Icel. agi; akin to AS. ege, ?ga, Goth. agis, Dan. ave chastisement, fear, Gr. ? pain, distress, from the same root as E. ail. ?3. Cf. Ugly.] 1. Dread; great fear mingled with respect. [Obs. or Obsolescent]

His frown was full of terror, and his voice
Shook the delinquent with such fits of awe.

Cowper.

The emotion inspired by something dreadful and sublime; an undefined sense of the dreadful and the sublime; reverential fear, or solemn wonder; profound reverence.

There is an awe in mortals' joy,
A deep mysterious fear.

Keble.

To tame the pride of that power which held the Continent in awe.

Macaulay.

The solitude of the desert, or the loftiness of the mountain, may fill the mind with awe Ð the sense of our own littleness in some greater presence or power.

C. J. Smith.

To stand in awe of, to fear greatly; to reverence profoundly.

Syn. Ð See Reverence.

Awe (?), v. t. [imp. & p. p. Awed (?); p. pr. & vb. n. Awing.] To strike with fear and reverence; to inspire with awe; to control by inspiring dread.

That same eye whose bend doth awe the world.

Shak.

His solemn and pathetic exhortation awed and melted the bystanders.

Macaulay.

Aïwearied (?), p. p. Wearied. [Poetic]

Aïweary (?), a. [Pref. aï + weary.] Weary. [Poetic] ½I begin to be aweary of thee.,

Shak.

Aïweather (?), adv. [Pref. aï + weather.] (Naut.) On the weather side, or toward the wind; in the direction from which the wind blows; Ð opposed to alee; as, helm aweather !

Totten.

Aꞏweigh (?), adv. [Pref. aꞏ + weigh.] (Naut.) Just drawn out of the ground, and hanging perpendicularly; atrip; Ð said of the anchor.

Totten.

Aweless (?), a. See Awless.

Awesome (?), a. 1. Causing awe; appalling; awful; as, an awesome sight. Wright.

<small>Expressive of awe or terror.</small>

An awesome glance up at the auld castle.
Sir W. Scott.

Awesomeꞏness, n. The quality of being awesome.

AweÐstrickꞏen (?), a. AweÐstruck.

AweÐstruckꞏ (?), a. Struck with awe.
Milton.

Awful (?), a. 1. Oppressing with fear or horror; appalling; terrible; as, an awful scene. ½The hour of Nature's awful throes.¸
Hemans.

<small>Inspiring awe; filling with profound reverence, or with fear and admiration; fitted to inspire reverential fear; profoundly impressive.</small>

Heaven's awful Monarch.
Milton.

<small>Struck or filled with awe; terrorÐstricken. [Obs.]</small>

A weak and awful reverence for antiquity.
I. Watts.

<small>Worshipful; reverential; lawÐabiding. [Obs.]</small>

Thrust from the company of awful men.
Shak.

<small>Frightful; exceedingly bad; great; Ð applied intensively; as, an awful bonnet; an awful boaster. [Slang]</small>

Syn. Ð See Frightful.

Awfulꞏly, adv. 1. In an awful manner; in a manner to fill with terror or awe; fearfully; reverently.

<small>Very; excessively. [Slang]</small>

Awfulꞏness, n. 1. The quality of striking with awe, or with reverence; dreadfulness; solemnity; as, the awfulness of this sacred place.

The awfulness of grandeur.
Johnson.

The state of being struck with awe; a spirit of solemnity; profound reverence. [Obs.]

Producing in us reverence and awfulness.
Jer. Taylor.

Aïwhape (?), v. t. [Cf. whap blow.] To confound; to terrify; to amaze. [Obs.]

Spenser.

Aïwhile (?), adv. [Adj. a + while time, interval.] For a while; for some time; for a short time.

Aïwing (?), adv. [Pref. aÐ + wing.] On the wing; flying; fluttering.
Wallace.

Awk (?), a. [OE. auk, awk (properly) turned away; (hence) contrary, wrong, from Icel. "figr, "fugr, afigr, turning the wrong way, fr. af off, away; cf. OHG. abuh, Skr. ap¾c turned away, fr. apa off, away + a root ak, a?k, to bend, from which come also E. angle, anchor.]

Odd; out of order; perverse. [Obs.]

Wrong, or not commonly used; clumsy; sinister; as, the awk end of a rod (the but end). [Obs.]

Golding.

Clumsy in performance or manners; unhandy; not dexterous; awkward. [Obs. or Prov. Eng.]

Awk, adv. Perversely; in the wrong way.
L'Estrange.

Awkly, adv. 1. In an unlucky (leftÐhanded) or perverse manner. [Obs.]
Holland.

Awkwardly. [Obs.]

Fuller.

Awkward (?), a. [Awk + Ïward.] 1. Wanting dexterity in the use of the hands, or of instruments; not dexterous; without skill; clumsy; wanting ease, grace, or effectiveness in movement; ungraceful; as, he was awkward at a trick; an awkward boy.

And dropped an awkward courtesy.
Dryden.

Not easily managed or effected; embarrassing.

A long and awkward process.
Macaulay.

An awkward affair is one that has gone wrong, and is difficult to adjust.
C. J. Smith.

Perverse; adverse; untoward. [Obs.] ½Awkward casualties. ½Awkward wind.

Shak.

O blind guides, which being of an awkward religion, do strain out a gnat, and swallow up a cancel.

Udall.

Syn. Ð Ungainly; unhandy; clownish; lubberly; gawky; maladroit; bungling; ?nelegant; ungraceful; unbecoming. Ð Awkward, Clumsy, Uncouth. Awkward has a special reference to outward deportment. A man is clumsy in his whole person, he is awkward in his gait and the movement of his limbs. Clumsiness is seen at the first view. Awkwardness is discovered only when a person begins to move. Hence the expressions, a clumsy appearance, and an awkward manner. When we speak figuratively of an awkward excuse, we think of a want of ease and grace in making it; when we speak of a clumsy excuse, we think of the whole thing as coarse and stupid. We apply the term uncouth most frequently to that which results from the want of instruction or training; as, uncouth manners; uncouth language.

Ð Awkwardĭly (?), adv. Ð Awkwardĭness, n.

Awl (?), n. [OE. aul, awel, al, AS. ?l, awel; akin to Icel. alr, OHG. ¾la, G. ahle, Lith. yla, Skr. ¾r¾.] A pointed instrument for piercing small holes, as in leather or wood; used by shoemakers, saddlers, cabinetmakers, etc. The blade is differently shaped and pointed for different uses, as in the brad awl, saddler's awl, shoemaker's awl, etc.

Awless (?), a. 1. Wanting reverence; void of respectful fear. ½Awless insolence.

Dryden.

Inspiring no awe. [Obs.] ½The awless throne.

Shak. [Written also aweless.]

Awlessĭness, n. The quality of being awless.

AwlÐshaped · (?), a. 1. Shaped like an awl.

(Nat. Hist.) Subulate. See Subulate.

Gray.

Awlwort · (?), n. [Awl + wort.] (Bot.) A plant (Subularia aquatica), with awlÐshaped leaves.

Awm (?m), n. See Aam.

Awn (?), n. [OE. awn, agune, from Icel. "gn, pl. agnir; akin to Sw. agn, Dan. avne, Goth. ahana, OHG. agana, G. agen, ahne, chaff, Gr. ?, AS. egla; prob. from same root as E. acute. See 3d Ear. ?1.] (Bot.) The bristle or beard of barley, oats, grasses, etc., or any similar bristlelike appendage; arista.

Gray.

Awned (?), a. (Bot.) Furnished with an awn, or long bristleÐshaped tip; bearded.

Gray.

Awning (?), n. [Origin uncertain: cf. F. auvent awing, or Pers. ¾wan, ¾wang, anything suspended, or LG. havening a place sheltered from wind and weather, E. haven.] 1. A rooflike cover, usually of canvas, extended over or before any place as a shelter from the sun, rain, or wind.

(Naut.) That part of the poop deck which is continued forward beyond the bulkhead of the cabin.

Awninged (?), a. Furnished with an awning.

Awnless, a. Without awns or beard.

Awny (?), a. Having awns; bearded.

AÏwork (?), adv. [Pref. aÏ + work.] At work; in action. ½Set awork.„

Shak.

AÏworking, adv. [Pref. aÏ + working.] At work; in action. [Archaic or Colloq.]

Spenser.

AÏwreak, AÏwreke,} (?), v. t. & i. To avenge. [Obs.] See Wreak.

AÏwrong (?), adv. [Pref. aÏ + wrong.] Wrongly.

Ford.

AÏwry (?), adv. & a. [Pref. aÏ + wry.] 1. Turned or twisted toward one side; not in a straight or true direction, or position; out of the right course; distorted; obliquely; asquint; with oblique vision; as, to glance awry. ½Your crown's awry.„

Shak.

Blows them transverse, ten thousand leagues awry.

Into the devious air.

Milton.

Aside from the line of truth, or right reason; unreasonable or unreasonably; perverse or perversely.

Or by her charms

Draws him awry, enslaved.

Milton.

Nothing more awry from the law of God and nature than that a woman should give laws to men.

Milton.

Awsome (?), a. Same as Awesome.

Ax, Axe,} (?), n. [OE. ax, axe, AS. eax, ′x, acas; akin to D. akse, OS. accus, OHG. acchus, G. axt, Icel. ″x, ″xi, Sw. yxe, Dan. ″kse, Goth. aqizi, Gr. ?, L. ascia; not akin to E. acute.] A tool or instrument of steel, or of iron with a steel edge or blade, for felling trees, chopping and splitting wood, hewing timber, etc. It is wielded by a wooden helve or handle, so fixed in a socket or eye as to be in the same plane with the blade. The broadax, or carpenter's ax, is an ax for hewing timber, made heavier than the chopping ax, and with a broader and thinner blade and a shorter handle.

The ancient battle-ax had sometimes a double edge.

¶ The word is used adjectively or in combination; as, axhead or ax head; ax helve; ax handle; ax shaft; ax-shaped; axlike.

This word was originally spelt with e, axe; and so also was nearly every corresponding word of one syllable: as, flaxe, taxe, waxe, sixe, mixe, pixe, oxe, fluxe, etc. This superfluous e is not dropped; so that, in more than a hundred words ending in x, no one thinks of retaining the e except in axe. Analogy requires its exclusion here.

½The spelling ax is better on every ground, of etymology, phonology, and analogy, than axe, which has of late become prevalent.

New English Dict. (Murray).

Ax (?), v. t. & i. [OE. axien and asken. See Ask.] To ask; to inquire or inquire of.

¶ This word is from Saxon, and is as old as the English language. Formerly it was in good use, but now is regarded as a vulgarism. It is still dialectic in England, and is sometimes heard among the uneducated in the United States. ½And Pilat axide him, Art thou kyng of Jewis? ½Or if he axea fish.

Wyclif.

½The king axed after your Grace's welfare.

Pegge.

Axal (?), a. [See Axial.] [R.]

Axe (?), Axeman (?), etc. See Ax, Axman.

Axïal (?), a. 1. Of or pertaining to an axis; of the nature of, or resembling, an axis; around an axis.

To take on an axial, and not an equatorial, direction.

Nichol.

(Anat.) Belonging to the axis of the body; as, the axial skeleton; or to the axis of any appendage or organ; as, the axial bones.

Axial line (Magnetism), the line taken by the magnetic force in passing from one pole of a horseshoe magnet to the other.

Faraday.

Axïallly (?), adv. In relation to, or in a line with, an axis; in the axial (magnetic) line.

Axil (?), n. [L. axilla. Cf. Axle.] (Bot.) The angle or point of divergence between the upper side of a branch, leaf, or petiole, and the stem or branch from which it springs.

Gray.

Axile (?), a. Situated in the axis of anything; as an embryo which lies in the axis of a seed.

Gray.

Ø Axĭlla (?), n.; pl. Axillae (?). [L.] (Anat.) The armpit, or the cavity beneath the junction of the arm and shoulder.

(Bot.) An axil.

Axĭlˈlar (?), a. Axillary.

Axilˈlaĭries (?), Axilˈlars (?),} n. pl. (Zo"l.) Feathers connecting the under surface of the wing and the body, and concealed by the closed wing.

Axilˈlaĭry (?), a. [See Axil.] 1. (Anat.) Of or pertaining to the axilla or armpit; as, axillary gland, artery, nerve.

(Bot.) Situated in, or rising from, an axil; of or pertaining to an axil. ½Axillary buds.„

Gray.

Axĭnite (?), n. [Named in allusion to the form of the crystals, fr. Gr. ? an ax.] (Min.) A borosilicate of alumina, iron, and lime, commonly found in glassy, brown crystals with acute edges.

Axĭinoĭman · cy (?), n. [L. axinomantia, Gr. ? ax + ĭmancy.] A species of divination, by means of an ax or hatchet.

Axĭom (?), n. [L. axioma, Gr. ? that which is thought worthy, that which is assumed, a basis of demonstration, a principle, fr. ? to think worthy, fr. ? worthy, weighing as much as; cf. ? to lead, drive, also to weigh so much: cf F. axiome. See Agent, a.] 1. (Logic & Math.) A selfÐevident and necessary truth, or a proposition whose truth is so evident as first sight that no reasoning or demonstration can make it plainer; a proposition which it is necessary to take for granted; as, ½The whole is greater than a part;„ ½A thing can not, at the same time, be and not be.„

An established principle in some art or science, which, though not a necessary truth, is universally received; as, the axioms of political economy.

Syn. Ð Axiom, Maxim, Aphorism, Adage. An axiom is a selfÐevident truth which is taken for granted as the basis of reasoning. A maxim is a guiding principle sanctioned by experience, and relating especially to the practical concerns of life. An aphorism is a short sentence pithily expressing some valuable and general truth or sentiment. An adage is a saying of longÐestablished authority and of universal application.

Ax · iĭoĭmatic (?), Ax · iĭoĭmaticĭal,} a. [Gr. ?.] Of or pertaining to an axiom; having the nature of an axiom; selfÐevident; characterized by axioms. ½Axiomatical truth.„

Johnson.

The stores of axiomatic wisdom.

I. Taylor.

Ax · iĭoĭmaticĭalĭly, adv. By the use of axioms; in the form of an axiom.

Ø Axis (?), n. [L.] (Zo"l.) The spotted deer (Cervus axis or Axis maculata) of India, where it is called hog deer and parrah (Moorish name).

Axis (?), n.; pl. Axes (?). [L. axis axis, axle. See Axle.] 1. A straight line, real or imaginary, passing through a body, on which it revolves, or may be supposed to revolve; a line passing through a body or system around which the parts are symmetrically arranged.

> (Math.) A straight line with respect to which the different parts of a magnitude are symmetrically arranged; as, the axis of a cylinder, i. e., the axis of a cone, that is, the straight line joining the vertex and the center of the base; the axis of a circle, any straight line passing through the center.

> (Bot.) The stem; the central part, or longitudinal support, on which organs or parts are arranged; the central line of any body.

Gray.

> (Anat.) (a) The second vertebra of the neck, or vertebra dentata. (b) Also used of the body only of the vertebra, which is prolonged anteriorly within the foramen of the first vertebra or atlas, so as to form the odontoid process or peg which serves as a pivot for the atlas and head to turn upon.

> (Crystallog.) One of several imaginary lines, assumed in describing the position of the planes by which a crystal is bounded.

> (Fine Arts) The primary of secondary central line of any design.

Anticlinal axis (Geol.), a line or ridge from which the strata slope downward on the two opposite sides. Ð Synclinal axis, a line from which the strata slope upward in opposite directions, so as to form a valley. Ð Axis cylinder (Anat.), the neuraxis or essential, central substance of a nerve fiber; Ð called also axis band, axial fiber, and cylinder axis. Ð Axis in peritrochio, the wheel and axle, one of the mechanical powers. Ð Axis of a curve (Geom.), a straight line which bisects a system of parallel chords of a curve; called a principal axis, when cutting them at right angles, in which case it divides the curve into two symmetrical
<— p. 108 —>
portions, as in the parabola, which has one such axis, the ellipse, which has two, or the circle, which has an infinite number. The two axes of the ellipse are the major axis and the minor axis, and the two axes of the hyperbola are the transverse axis and the conjugate axis. Ð Axis of a lens, the straight line passing through its center and perpendicular to its surfaces. Ð Axis of a telescope or microscope, the straight line with which coincide the axes of the several lenses which compose it. Ð Axes of co"rdinates in a plane, to straight lines intersecting each other, to which points are referred for the purpose of determining their relative position: they are either rectangular or oblique. Ð Axes of co"rdinates in space, the three straight lines in which the co"rdinate planes intersect each other. Ð Axis of a balance, that line about which it turns. Ð Axis of oscillation, of a pendulum, a right line passing through the center

about which it vibrates, and perpendicular to the plane of vibration. Ð Axis of polarization, the central line around which the prismatic rings or curves are arranged. Brewster. Ð Axis of revolution (Descriptive Geom.), a straight line about which some line or plane is revolved, so that the several points of the line or plane shall describe circles with their centers in the fixed line, and their planes perpendicular to it, the line describing a surface of revolution, and the plane a solid of revolution. Ð Axis of symmetry (Geom.), any line in a plane figure which divides the figure into two such parts that one part, when folded over along the axis, shall coincide with the other part. Ð Axis of the equator, ecliptic, horizon (or other circle considered with reference to the sphere on which it lies), the diameter of the sphere which is perpendicular to the plane of the circle. Hutton. Ð Axis of the Ionic capital (Arch.), a line passing perpendicularly through the middle of the eye of the volute. Ð Neutral axis (Mech.), the line of demarcation between the horizontal elastic forces of tension and compression, exerted by the fibers in any cross section of a girder. Ð Optic ~ of a crystal, the direction in which a ray of transmitted light suffers no double refraction. All crystals, not of the isometric system, are either uniaxial or biaxial. Ð Optic ~, Visual ~ (Opt.), the straight line passing through the center of the pupil, and perpendicular to the surface of the eye. Ð Radical ~ of two circles (Geom.), the straight line perpendicular to the line joining their centers and such that the tangents from any point of it to the two circles shall be equal to each other. Ð Spiral ~ (Arch.), the ~ of a twisted column drawn spirally in order to trace the circumvolutions without. Ð Axis of abscissas and Axis of ordinates. See Abscissa. Axle (?), n. [OE. axel, exel, shoulder, AS. ?axl; akin to AS. eax axle, Sw. & Dan. axel shoulder, ~, G. achse axle, achsel shoulder, L. axis axle, Gr. ?, Skr. aksha, L. axillaÿshoulder joint: cf. F. essieu, axle, OF. aissel, fr. dim. of L. axis. ?. Cf. 2d Axis.] 1. The pin or spindle on which a wheel revolves, or which revolves with a wheel. 2. A transverse bar or shaft connecting the opposite wheels of a car or carriage; an axletree. 3. An axis; as, the sun's axle. Had from her axle torn The steadfast earth. Milton. µ Railway axles are called leading and trailing from their position in the front or in the rear of a car or truck respectively. Axle box · (?). 1. A bushing in the hub of a wheel, through which the axle passes. 2. The journal box of a rotating axle, especially a railway axle. µ In railway construction, the axle guard, or pedestal, with the superincumbent weight, rests on the top of the box (usually with a spring intervening), and holds it in place by flanges. The box rests upon the journal bearing and key, which intervene between the inner top of the box and the axle. Axled (?), a. Having an axle; Ð used in composition. Merlin's agateÐaxled car. T. Warton. Axle guard · (?). The part of the framing of a railway car or truck, by which an axle box is held laterally, and in which it may move vertically; Ð also called a jaw in the United States, and a housing in England. AxleÏtree · (?), n. [Cf. Icel. "xultr?.] 1. A bar or beam of wood or iron, connecting the opposite wheels of a carriage, on the ends of which the wheels revolve. 2. A spindle or axle of a wheel. [Obs.] Axman (?), n.; pl. Axmen (?). One who wields an ax. Axmin·ster (?), n. An ÷ carpet, ?n imitation Turkey carpet, noted for its thick and soft pile; Ð so called from Axminster, Eng. Ø Axoïlotl (?), n. [The native name.] (Zo"l.) An amphibian of the salamander tribe found in the elevated lakes of Mexico; the siredon. µ When it breeds in captivity the young develop into true salamanders of the genus Amblystoma. This also occurs naturally under favorable conditions, in its native localities; although it commonly lives and breeds in a larval state, with persistent external gills. See Siredon. Axstone· (?), n. (Min.) A variety of jade. It is used by some savages, particularly the natives of the South Sea Islands, for making axes or hatchets. Axtree (?), n. Axle or axletree. [Obs.] Drayton. Axunge (?), n. [F. axonge, L. axungia; axis wheel + ungere to grease.] Fat; grease; esp. the fat of pigs or geese; usually (Pharm.), lard prepared for medical use. Ay (?), interj. Ah! alas! ½Ay me! I fondly dream ? Had ye been there.'ͺ Milton. Ay (?), adv. Same as Aye. Ø Ayah (?), n. [Pg. aia, akin to Sp. aya a governess, ayo a tutor.] A native nurse for children; also, a lady's maid. [India] Aye, Ay } (?), adv. [Perh. a modification of yea, or from the interjection of admiration or astonishment, OE. ei, ey, why, hey, ay, well, ah, ha. Cf. MHG. & G. ei, Dan. ej. Or perh. akin to aye ever.] Yes; yea; Ð a word expressing assent, or an affirmative answer to a question. It is much used in viva voce voting in legislative bodies, etc. µ This word is written I in the early editions of Shakespeare and other old writers. Aye (?), n. An affirmative vote; one who votes in the affirmative; as, ½To call for the ayes and noes;ͺ ½The ayes have it.ͺ Aye, Ay } (?), adv. [Icel. ei, ey; akin to AS. ¾, ¾wa, always, Goth. aiws an age, Icel. 'fi, OHG, ?wa, L. aevum, Gr. ? an age, ?, ?, ever, always, G. je, Skr. ?va course. ?,?. Cf. Age, v., Either, a., Or, conj.] Always; ever; continually; for an indefinite time. For his mercies aye endure. Milton. For aye, always; forever; eternally. AyeÐaye· (?), n. [From the native name, prob. from its cry.] (Zo"l.) A singular nocturnal quadruped, allied to the lemurs, found in Madagascar (Cheiromys Madagascariensis), remarkable for its long fingers, sharp nails, and rodentÐlike incisor teeth. Ayegreen· (?), n. [Aye ever + green.] (Bot.) The houseleek (Sempervivum tectorum). Halliwell. Aïyen, Aïyein (?), Aïyeins (?), adv. & prep. [OE. ?, ?. See Again.] Again; back against. [Obs.] Chaucer. Aïyenward (?), adv. Backward. [Obs.] Chaucer. Ayle (?), n. [OE. ayel, aiel, OF. aiol, aiel, F. a‹eul, a dim. of L. avus grandfather.] A grandfather. [Obs.] Writ of Ayle, an ancient English writ which lay against a stranger who had dispossessed the demandant of land of which his grandfather died seized. Ayme· (?), n. [Cf. F. ahi interj.] The utterance of the ejaculation ½Ay me !ͺ [Obs.] See Ay, interj. ½Aymees and hearty heighÐhoes.ͺ J. Fletcher. Aïyond (?), prep. & adv. Beyond. [North of Eng.] Aïyont (?), prep. & adv. Beyond. [Scot.] Ayïrie, Ayïry (?), n. See Aerie. Drayton. Ayrshire (?), n. (Agric.) One of a superior breed of cattle from Ayrshire, Scotland. Ayrshires are notable for the quantity and quality of their milk. Ø Aïyun·taïmiïento (?), n. [Sp., fr. OSp. ayuntar to join.] In Spain and Spanish America, a corporation or body of magistrates in cities and towns, corresponding to mayor and aldermen. Aïzaleïa (?; 97), h.; pl. Azaleas (?). [NL., fr. Gr. ? dry, Ð so called because supposed to grow best in dry ground.] (Bot.) A genus of showy flowering shrubs, mostly natives of China or of North America; false honeysuckle. The genus is scarcely distinct from Rhododendron. Azaïrole (?), n. [F. azerole, the name of the fruit, fr. Ar. azïzo'r?r: cf. It. azzeruolo, Sp. acerolo.] (Bot.) The Neapolitan medlar (Crat'gus azarolus), a shrub of southern Europe; also, its fruit. Aïzedaïrach (?), n. [F. az,darac, Sp. acederaque, Pers. ¾z¾ddirakht noble tree.] 1. (Bot.) A handsome Asiatic tree (Melia azedarach), common in the southern United States; Ð called also, Pride of India, Pride of China, and Bead tree. 2. (Med.) The bark of the roots of the azedarach, used as a cathartic and emetic. Aziïmuth (?), n. [OE. azimut, F. azimut, fr. Ar. asÐsum?t, pl. of asÐsamt a way, or perh., a point of the horizon and a circle extending to it from the zenith, as being the Arabic article: cf. It. azzimutto, Pg. azimuth, and Ar. samtÐalÐr¾'s the vertex of the heaven. Cf. Zenith.] (Astron. & Geodesy) (a) The quadrant of an ~ circle. (b) An arc of the horizon intercepted between the meridian of the place and a vertical circle passing through the center of any object; as, the azimuth of a star; the azimuth or bearing of a line surveying. µ In trigonometrical surveying, it is customary to reckon the azimuth of a line from the south point of the horizon around by the west from 00 to 3600. Azimuth circle, or Vertical circle, one of the great circles of the sphere intersecting each other in the zenith and nadir, and cutting the horizon at right angles. Hutton. Ð Azimuth compass, a compass resembling the mariner's compass, but having the card divided into degrees instead of rhumbs, and having vertical sights; used for taking the magnetic ~ of a heavenly body, in order to find, by comparison with the true ~, the variation of the needle. Ð Azimuth dial, a dial whose stile or gnomon is at right angles to the plane of the horizon. Hutton. Ð Magnetic ~, an arc of the horizon, intercepted between the vertical circle passing through any object and the magnetic meridian. This is found by observing the object with an ~ compass. Aziïmuth · al (?), a. Of or pertaining to the azimuth; in a horizontal circle. ÷ error of a transit instrument, its deviation in azimuth from the plane of the meridian. Azoï (?). [See Azote.] (Chem.) A combining form of azote; (a) Applied loosely to compounds having nitrogen variously combined, as in cyanides, nitrates, etc. (b) Now especially applied to compounds containing a two atom nitrogen group uniting two hydrocarbon radicals, as in azobenzene, azobenzoic, etc. These compounds furnish many artificial dyes. See Diazoï. Az · oïbenzene (?), n. [Azoï + benzene.] (Chem.) A substance (C6H5.H2.C6H5) derived from nitrobenzene, forming orange red crystals which are easily fusible. Aïzoic (?), a. [Gr. ? priv. + ? life, from ? to live.] Destitute of any vestige of organic life, or at least of animal life; anterior to the existence of animal life; formed when there was no animal life on the globe; as, the azoic. rocks. ÷ age (Geol.), the age preceding the existence of animal life, or anterior to the paleozoic tome. Azoic is also used as a noun, age being understood. See Arch'an, and Eozoic. Az · oïleic (?), a. [Azoï + oleic.] (Chem.) Pertaining to an acid produced by treating oleic with nitric acid. [R.] Aïzonic (?), a. [Gr. ?; ? priv. + ? zone, region.] Confined to no zone or region; not local. Aïzoriïan (?), a. Of or pertaining to the Azores. Đ n. A native of the Azores. Azote (?; 277), n. [F. azote, fr. Gr. ? priv. + ? life; Đ so named by Lavoisier because it is incapable of supporting life.] Same as Nitrogen. [R.] Azoth (?), n. [LL. azoch, azoth, fr. Ar. azĐzauq mercury.] (Alchemy) (a) The first principle of metals, i. e., mercury, which was formerly supposed to exist in all metals, and to be extractable from them. (b) The universal remedy of Paracelsus. Aïzotic (?), a.ÿ(Chem.) Pertaining to azote, or nitrogen; formed or consisting of azote; nitric; as, azotic gas; azotic acid. [R.] Carpenter. Azoïtite (?), n.ÿ(Chem.) A salt formed by the combination of azotous, or nitrous, acid with a base; a nitrite. [R.] Azoïtize (?), v. t. [imp. & p. p. Azotized (?); p. pr. & vb. n. Azotizing (?).] To impregnate with azote, or nitrogen; to nitrogenize. Az · oïtomeïter (?), n. [Azote + Ïmeter.] (Chem.) An apparatus for measuring or determining the proportion of nitrogen; a nitrometer. Aïzotous (?), a: Nitrous; as, azotous acid. [R.] Aztec (?), a. Of or relating to one of the early races in Mexico that inhabited the great plateau of that country at the time of the Spanish conquest in 1519. Đ n. One of the Aztec race or people. Azure (?; 277), a. [F. & OSp. azur, Sp. azul, through Ar. from Per. 1¾jaward, or 1¾juward, lapis lazuli, a blue color, 1¾jawardÆ, 1¾juwardÆ, azure, cerulean, the initial l having been dropped, perhaps by the influence of the Ar. azrĐaq azure, blue. Cf. G. lasur, lasurstein, azure color, azure stone, and NL. lapis lazuli.] SkyĐblue; resembling the clear blue color of the unclouded sky; cerulean; also, cloudless. ÷ stone (Min.), the lapis lazuli; also, the lazulite. Azure, n. 1. The lapis lazuli. [Obs.] 2. The clear blue color of the sky; also, a pigment or dye of this color. ½In robes of azure., Wordsworth. 3. The blue vault above; the unclouded sky. Not like those steps On heaven's azure. Milton. 4. (Her.) A blue color, represented in engraving by horizontal parallel lines. Azure, v. t. To color blue. Azured (?), a. Of an azure color; skyĐblue. ½The azured harebell., Shak. Aïzureïous (?), a. (Zo"l.) Of a fine blue color; azure. Azuïrine (?), a. [Cf. Azurn.] Azure. Azuïrine, n. (Zo"l.) The blue roach of Europe (Leuciscus c'ruleus); Đ so called from its color. Azuïrite (?), n. (Min.) Blue carbonate of copper; blue malachite. Azurn (?), a. [Cf. OF. azurin, asurin, LL. azurinus. See Azure, a.] Azure. [Obs.] Thick set with agate, and the azurn sheen Of turkis blue, and emerald green. Milton. Azyïgous (?), a. [Gr. ?; ? priv. + ? yoke.] Odd; having no fellow; not one of a pair; single; as, the azygous muscle of the uvula. Azym, Azyme (?), n. [F. azyme unleavened, L. azymus, fr. Gr. ?; ? priv. + ? leaven.] Unleavened bread. Aïzymic (?), a. Azymous. Azyïmite (?), n. [Cf. F. azymite.] (Eccl. Hist.) One who administered the Eucharist with unleavened bread; Đ a name of reproach given by those of the Greek church to the Latins. Azyïmous (?),

a. [See Azym.] Unleavened; unfermented. ½Azymous bread., Dunglison.

<— p. 109 —>

<— p. 109 —>

B (?) is the second letter of the English alphabet. (See Guide to Pronunciation, 196,220.) It is etymologically related to ÿpÿ,ÿvÿ,ÿfÿ,ÿwÿ and ÿmÿ, letters representing sounds having a close organic affinity to its own sound; as in Eng. bursar andÿpurser;ÿEng. ÿbear and Lat. ÿpear; Eng. silver and Ger. ÿsilber; Lat. cubitum and It. gomito; Eng. seven, Anglo-Saxon seofon, Ger. sieben, Lat. septem, Gr.?, Sanskrit saptan. The form of letter B is Roman, from Greek B (Beta), of Semitic origin. The small ÿbÿ was formed by gradual change from the capital B.

In ÿMusic, B is the nominal of the sevens tone in the model major scale ÿ(the scale of C majorÿ), or of the second tone in it's relative minor scale (that of A minorÿ)ÿ. B? stands for B flat, the tone a half step , or semitone, lower than B. In German, B stands for our B?, while our B natural is called H (pronounced h„).

Ba (?), v.i. [Cf. OF. ÿbaer to open mouth, F. baer.] To kiss. [Obs.] Chaucer.

Baa (?), v.i. [Cf. G. b„en; an imitative word.] To cry baa, or bleat as a sheep.

  He treble baas for help, but none can get.

Sir P.Sidney.

Baa (?), n.; pl.ÿBaas. [Cf. G. ÿb„.] The cry or bleating of a sheep; a bleat.

Baaing, n. The bleating of a sheep.

Marryat.

  Baal (?), n.; Heb.pl. ÿBaalim (?). [Heb. ba'al lord.] 1. (Myth.) The supreme male divinity of the Ph?nitian and Canaanitish nations.

μ The name of this god occurs in the Old Testament and elsewhere with qualifying epithets subjoined, answering to the different ideas of his character; as, ÿBaal-berith (the Covenant Baal), Baal-zebub (Baal of the fly).

2. pl. The whole class of divinities to whom the name Baal was applied. Judges x. 6.

Baal̈ism (?), n. Worship of Baal; idolatry.

  Baal̈ist (?), Baal̈ite (?), } n. A worshiper of Baal; a devotee of any false religion; an idolater.

ØBaba (?), n. [F.] A kind of plum cake.

Babbitt (?), v.t. To line with Babbitt metal.

Babbitt met·al (?). [From the inventor, Isaac Babbittÿ of Massachusetts.] A soft white alloy of variable composition (as a none parts of tin to one of copper, or of fifty parts of tin to five of antimony and one of copper) used in bearings to diminish friction.

Babble, v.i. [imp. & p.p. Babbled (?);p. pr. & vb. n. Babbling.] [Cf.LG. babbeln, D. babbelen, G. bappeln, bappern, F. babiller, It. babbolare; prob.

orig., to keep saying baÿ0, imitative of a child learning to talk.]

To utter words indistinctly or unintelligibly; to utter inarticulate sounds; as a child babbles.

To talk incoherently; to utter unmeaning words.

To talk much; to chatter; to prate.

To make a continuous murmuring noise, as shallow water running over stones.

In every babbling he finds a friend.
Wordsworth.

µ Hounds are said to babble, or to be babbling, when they are too noisy after having found a good scent.

Syn. - To prate; prattle; chatter; gossip.

Babble, v.i. 1. To utter in an indistinct or incoherent way; to repeat, as words, in a childish way without understanding.

These [words] he used to babble in all companies.
Arbuthnot.

To disclose by too free talk, as a secret.

Babble, n. 1. Idle talk; senseless prattle; gabble; twaddle. ½This is mere moral babble.
Milton.

Inarticulate speech; constant or confused murmur.

The babble of our young children.
Darwin.
The babble of the stream.
Tennyson.
BabbleIment (?), n. Babble.
Hawthorne.
Babbler (?), n. 1. An idle talker; an irrational prater; a teller of secrets.
Great babblers, or talkers, are not fit for trust.
L'Estrange.

A hound too noisy on finding a good scent.

(Zo"l.) A name given to any one of family (Timalin') of thrushlike birds, having a chattering note.

BabbleIry (?), n. Babble. [Obs.]
Sir T. More
Babe (?), n. [Cf. Ir. bab, baban, W. baban, maban.]

An infant; a young child of either sex; a baby.

A doll for children.

Spenser.

Babehood (?), n. Babyhood. [R.]

Udall.

Babel (?), n. [Heb. B¾bel, the name of the capital of Babylonia; in Genesis associated with the idea of ½confusion‚] 1. The city and tower in the land of Shinar, where the confusion of languages took place.

Therefore is the name of it called Babel.

Gen.xi.9.

> Hence: A place or scene of noise and confusion; a confused mixture of sounds, as of voices or languages.

That babel of strange heathen languages.

Hammond.

The grinding babel of the street.

R.L.Stevenson.

Baberly (?), n. [Perh. orig. for baboonery. Cf. Baboon, and also Babe.] Finery of a kind to please a child. [Obs.] ½Painted ÿbabery.‚

Sir P.Sidney.

Babilan (?), Babilon (?), n. [See Baboon] A baboon. [Obs.]

B.Jonson.

ØBabillard (?), n. [F., a babbler.] (Zo"l.) The lesser whitethroat of Europe; - called also ÿbabbling warbler.

Babingtonlite (?), n. [From Dr. Babbington.] (Min.) A mineral occurring in triclinic crystals approaching pyroxene in angle, and of a greenish black color.It is a silicate of iron, manganese, and lime.

ØBab · ilroussa, ØBab · ilrussa (?), n. [F. babiroussa, fr.Malay ÿb¾bÆ hog + r?sa deer.] (Zo"l.) A large hoglike quadruped (Sus, or Porcus, babirussa) of the East Indies, sometimes domesticated; the Indian hog. Its upper canine

teeth or tusks are large and recurved.

Babish (?), a. Like a babe; a childish; babyish. [R.] ½Babish imbecility.‚ Drayton. - Babishly, adv. - Babishiness, n. [R.]

Babism (?), n. [From Bab (Pers.ÿbab a gate), the title assumed by the founder, Mirza Ali Mohammed.] The doctrine of a modern religious sect, which originated in Persia in 1843, being a mixture of Mohammedan, Christian,Jewish and Parsee elements.

Babist, n. A believer in Babism.

ØBablah (?), n. [Cf. Per. bab?l a species of mimosa yielding gum arabic.] The ring of the fruit of several East Indian species of acacia; neb-neb. It contains gallic acid and tannin, and is used for dyeing drab.

ØBaboo, ØBabu (?), n. [Hind. b¾b?ÿ] A Hindoo gentleman; native clerk who writes English; also, a Hindoo title answering to Mr.ÿ or Esquire.

Whitworth.

Baboon (?), n. [OE. babewin, baboin, fr.F. babouin, or LL.ÿbabewynus. Of unknown origin; cf. D. baviaan, G. pavian, baboon, F. babin lip of ape, dogs, etc., dial. G. b„ppe mouth.] (Zo"l.) One of the Old World Quadrumana, of the genera Cynocephalus and Papio; the dog-faced ape. Baboons have dog-like muzzles and large canine teeth, cheek pouches, a short tail, and naked callosities on the buttocks. They are mostly African. See Mandrill, and Chacma, and Drill an ape.

Baboonery (?), n. Baboonish behavior.

Marryat.

Baboonish, a. Like a baboon.

Baby (?), n.; pl. Babies. [Dim. of babe] 1. An infant or young child of either sex; a babe.

A small image of an infant; a doll.

Babies in the eyes, the minute reflection which one sees of one's self in the eyes of another.

She clung about his neck, gave him ten kisses,

Toyed with his locks, looked babies in his eyes.

Heywood.

Baby, a. Pertaining to, or resembling, an infant; young or little; as, ÿbaby swans. ½Baby figure.

Shak.

Baby, v.i. [imp. & p.p. Babied (?); p. pr. & vb. n.Babying.] To treat like a young child; to keep dependent; to humor; to fondle.

Young.

Baby farm · (?). A place where the nourishment and care of babies are offered for hire.

Baby farm · er (?). One who keeps a baby farm.

Baby farm · ing. The business of keeping a baby farm.

Babyhood (?), n. The state or period of infancy.

Babyhouse · (?), a. A place for children's dolls and dolls' furniture.

Swift.

Babyish, a. Like a baby; childish; puerile; simple. - Babyishly, adv. - Babyishness, n.

Babyism (?), n. 1. The state of being a baby.

A babyish manner of acting or speaking.

Baby jump · er (?). A hoop suspended by an elastic strap, in which a young child may be held secure while amusing itself by jumping on the floor.

Bab · ylonïan (?), a. Of or pertaining to the real or to the mystical Babylon, or to the ancient kingdom of Babylonia; Chaldean.

Bab · ylonïan, n. 1. An inhabitant of Babylonia (which included Chaldea); a Chaldean.

An astrologer; - so called because the Chaldeans were remarkable for the study of astrology.

Bab·ylonic (?), Bab·ylonicIal (?), } a. 1. Pertaining to Babylon, or made there; as Babylonic garments,carpets, or hangings.

Tumultuous; disorderly. [Obs.]

Sir J.Harrington.
Babylo·nish (?), n. 1. Of or pertaining to, or made in, Babylon or Babylonia. ½A Babylonishÿgarment.

Josh. vii.21.

Pertaining to the Babylon of Revelation xiv.8.

Pertaining to Rome and papal power. [Obs.]

The... injurious nickname of Babylonish.
Gape.
4.Confused; Babel-like.
ØBab·yIroussa, ØBab·yIrussa (?), n. (Zo"l.) See Babyroussa.
BabyIship (?), n. The quality of being a baby; the personality of an infant.
Bac (?), n. [F. See Back a vat]

A broad, flatbottomed ferryboat, usually worked by a rope.

A vat or cistern. See 1st Back.

BaccaIlaureIate (?), n. [NL. baccalaureatus, fr.LL. baccalaureus a bachelor of arts, fr. baccalarius, but as if fr L. bacca lauri bayberry, from the practice of the bachelor's wearing a garland of bayberries. See Bachelor.]

The degree of bachelor of arts. (B.A. or A.B.), the

first or lowest academical degree conferred by universities and colleges.

A baccalaureate sermon. [U.S.]

Bac·caIlaureIate, a. Pertaining to a bachelor of arts.
Baccalaureate sermon, in some American colleges, a sermon delivered as a farewell discourse graduating class.
ØBac·caIra, Bac·caIrat (?), n. [F.] A French game of cards, played by a banker and punters.
BacIcare, BacIkare } (?), interj. Stand back! give place! - a cant word of the Elizabethan writers, probably in ridicule of some person who pretended to a knowledge of Latin which he did not possess.
Baccare! you are marvelous forward.
Shak.

Baccate (?), a. [L. baccatus, fr. L. bacca berry.]
(Bot.) Pulpy throughout, like a berry; - said of fruits.
Gray.

Baccated (?), a. 1. Having many berries.

Set or adorned with pearls. [Obs.]

Bacchanal (?), a.ÿ[L. Bacchanalis. See Bacchanalia.]

Relating to Bacchus or his festival.

Engaged in drunken revels; drunken and riotous or noisy.

Bacchanal (?), n. 1. A devotee of Bacchus; one who indulges in drunken revels; one who is noisy and riotous when intoxicated; a carouser. ½Tipsy bacchanals.‚
Shak.

pl. The festival of Bacchus; the bacchanalia.

Drunken revelry; an orgy.

A song or dance in honor of Bacchus.

ØBac · chaïnalila (?), n. pl. [L. Bacchanalÿa place devoted to Bacchus; in the pl. Bacchanalia a feast of Bacchus, fr. Bacchusÿthe god of wine, Gr. ?]

(Myth.) A feast or an orgy in honor of Bacchus.

Hence: A drunken feast; drunken reveler.

Bac · chaïnalilan (?), a. Of or pertaining to the festival of Bacchus; relating to or given to reveling and drunkenness.
Even bacchanalian madness has its charms.
Cowper.
Bac · ahaïnalilan, n. A bacchanal; a drunken reveler.
Bac · chaïnalilanïism (?), n. The practice of bacchanalians; bacchanals; drunken revelry.
Bacchant (?), n.; pl. E. Bacchants, L. Bacchantes. [L. bacchans, -antis, p. pr. of bacchariÿ to celebrate the festival of Bacchus.]

A priest of Bacchus.

A bacchanal; a reveler.

Croly.
Bacchant, a. Bacchanalian; fond of drunken revelry; wine-loving; reveling; carousing.
Byron.
Bacchante (?), n.; L. pl. Bacchantes 1. A priestess of Bacchus.

A female bacchanal.

Bacchantic (?), a. Bacchanalian.

Bacchic (?), Bacchical (?) }, a. [L. Bacchicus, Gr. ?] Of or relating to Bacchus; hence, jovial, or riotous,with intoxication.

ØBacchius (?), n.; pl. Bacchii. [L. Bacchiusӱpes, Gr. ? (sc. ? foot).] (Pros.) A metrical foot composed of a short syllable and two long ones; according to some, two long and a short.

Bacchus (?), n. [L., fr. Gr. ?] (Myth.) The god of wine, son of Jupiter and Semele.

Bacciferious (?), a. [L.ӱbaccifer;ӱbaccaӱberry + ferre to bear] Producing berries. ½ӱBacciferousӱtrees.

Ray.

Bacciform (?), a. [L. bacca berry + -form.] Having the form of a berry.

Baccivolrous (?), a. [L. bacca berry + varare to devour.] (Zo"l.) Eating, or subsisting on, berries; as,ӱbaccivorous birds.

Bace (?), n., a., &v. See Base. [Obs.]

Spenser.

Bachairach, Backairack } (?), n. A kind of wine made at Bacharach on the Rhine.

Bacheellor (?), n. [OF. bacheler young man, F. bacheliery (cf.Pr. bacalar, Sp.bachiller, Pg. bacharel, It. baccalare), LL. baccalarius the tenant of a kind of farm called baccalaria, a soldier not old or rich enough to lead his retainers into battle with a banner, person of an inferior academical degree aspiring to a doctorate. In the latter sense, it was afterward changed to baccalaureus. See Baccalaureate, n.]

A man of any age who has not been married.

As merry and mellow an old bachelor as ever followed a hound.
W.Irving.

An unmarried woman. [Obs.]

B.Jonson.

<— p. 110 —>

A person who has taken the first or lowest degree in the liberal arts, or in some branch of science, at a college or university; as, a bacheloryof arts.

A knight who had no standard of his own, but fought under the standard of another in the field; often, a young knight.

In the companies of London tradesmen, one not yet admitted to wear the livery; a junior member. [Obs.]

(Zo"l.) A kind of bass, an edible fresh-water fish (Pomoxys annularis) of the southern United States.

Bachelloridom (?), n. The state of bachelorhood; the whole body of bachelors.

Bachĕlorĭhood (?), n. The state or condition of being a bachelor; bachelorship.

Bachĕlorĭism (?), n. Bachelorhood; also, a manner or peculiarity belonging to bachelors.

W.Irving.

Bachĕlor's button (?), (Bot.) A plant with flowers shaped like buttons; especially, several species of Ranunculus, and the cornflower (ÿCentaures cyanus) and globe amaranth (Gomphrena).

µ Bachelor's buttons, a name given to several flowers ½from their similitude to the jagged cloathe buttons, anciently worne in this kingdom„, according to Johnson's Gerarde, p.472(1633); but by other writers ascribed to " a habit of country fellows to carry them in their pockets to divine their success with their sweethearts.„

Dr.Prior.

Bachĕlorĭship , n. The state of being a bachelor.

Bachelĭry (?), n. [OF. bachelerie.] The body of young aspirants for knighthood. [Obs.]

Chaucer.

Băcillar (?), a. [L. bacillum little staff.] (Biol.) Shaped like a rod or staff.

ØBacillĭla·rĭĭ' (?), n. pl. [NL., fr.L. bacillum, dim. of baculum stick.] (Biol.) See ÿDiatom.

Bacillĭlaĭry (?), a. Of or pertaining to little rods; rod-shaped.

Băcillĭiform (?), a. [L. bacillum little staff + ĭform.] Rod-shaped.

Băcillus (?), n.; pl. Bacilli (?). [NL., for L. bacillum. See Bacillarle.] (Biol.) A variety of bacterium; a microscopic, rod-shaped vegetable organism.

Back (?), n. [F. bac: cf. Arm. bak tray, bowl.] 1. A large shallow vat; a cistern, tub, or trough, used by brewers, distillers, dyers, picklers, gluemakers, and others, for mixing or cooling wort, holding water, hot glue, etc.

Hop back, Jack back, the cistern which receives the infusion of malt and hops from the copper.- Wash back, a vat in which distillers ferment the wort to form wash. - Water back, a cistern to hold a supply of water; esp. a small cistern at the back of a stove, or a group of pipes set in the fire box of a stove or furnace, through which water circulates and is heated.

A ferryboat. See Bac, 1

Back (?), n. [As b'c, bac; akin to Icel., Sw., & LG. bak, Dan. bag; cf. OHG. bahho ham, Skr. bhaj to turn, OSlav. b?g? flight. Cf. Bacon.] 1. In human beings, the hinder part of the body, extending from the neck to the end o the spine; in other animals, that part of the body which corresponds most nearly to such part of a human being; as, the ÿback of a horse, fish, or lobster.

An extended upper part, as of a mountain or ridge.

[The mountains] their broad bare backs upheave
Into the clouds.
Milton.

<small>The outward or upper part of a thing, as opposed to the inner or lower part; as, the back of the hand, the back of the foot, the back of a hand rail.</small>

Methought Love pitying me, when he saw this,
Gave me your hands, the ÿbacksÿand palms to kiss.
Donne.

<small>The part opposed to the front; the hinder or rear part of a thing; as, the back of a book; the back of an army; the ÿback of a chimney.</small>

<small>The part opposite to, or most remote from, that which fronts the speaker or actor; or the part out of sight, or not generally seen; as, the back of an island, of a hill, or of a village.</small>

<small>The part of a cutting tool on the opposite side from its edge; as, the back of a knife, or of a saw.</small>

<small>A support or resource in reserve.</small>

This project
Should have a back or second, that might hold,
If this should blast in proof.
Shak.

<small>(Naut.) The keel and keelson of a ship.</small>

<small>(Mining) The upper part of a lode, or the roof of a horizontal underground passage.</small>

<small>A garment for the back; hence, clothing.</small>

A bak to walken inne by daylight.
Chaucer.

Behind one's back, when one is absent; without one's knowledge;as, to ridicule a person behind his back. - Full back, Half back, Quarter back (Football), players stationed behind those in the front line. - To be or lie on one's back, to be helpless. - To put, or get, one's back up, to assume an attitude of obstinate resistance (from the action of a cat when attacked.). [Colloq.] - To see the back of, to get rid of. - To turn the back, to go away; to flee. - To turn the back on one, to forsake or neglect him.

Back, a. 1. Being at the back or in the rear; distant; remote; as, the back door; back settlements.

<small>Being in arrear; overdue; as, back rent.</small>

<small>Moving or operating backward; as, back action.</small>

Back charges, charges brought forward after an account has been made up. - Back filling (Arch.), the mass of materials used in filling up the space between two walls, or between the inner and outer faces of a wall, or upon the haunches of an arch or vault. - Back pressure. (Steam Engine) See under Pressure.ÿ- Back rest, a guide attached to the slide rest of a lathe, and placed in contact with the work, to steady it in turning.- Back slang, a kind of slang in which every word is written or pronounced backwards; as, nam for ÿman. - Back stairs, stairs in the back part of a house; private stairs. Also used adjectively. See ÿBack stairs, Backstairs, and Backstair, in the Vocabulary. - Back step (Mil.), the retrograde movement of a man or body of men, without changing front. - Back stream, a current running against the main current of a stream; an eddy. - To take the back track, to retrace one's steps; to retreat. [Colloq.]

Back (?), v.i.ÿ[imp. & p.p. Backed (?); p. pr. & vb. n. Backing.]

To get upon the back of; to mount.

I will back him [a horse] straight.
Shak.

To place or seat upon the back. [R.]

Great Jupiter, upon his eagle backed,
Appeared to me.
Shak.

To drive or force backward; to cause to retreat or recede; as, to back oxen.

To make a back for; to furnish with a back; as, to back books.

To adjoin behind; to be at the back of.

A garden ... with a vineyard backed.
Shak.
The chalk cliffs which back the beach.
Huxley.

To write upon the back of; as, to back a letter; to indorse; as, to back a note or legal document.

To support; to maintain; to second or strengthen by aid or influence; as, to backÿ a friend. ½Parliament would be backed by the people.⸲

Macaulay.
Have still found it necessary to back and fortify their laws with rewards and punishments.
South.
The mate backed the captain manfully.
Blackw. Mag.

To bet on the success of; - as, to back a race horse.

To back an anchor (Naut.), to lay down a small anchor ahead of a large one, the cable of the small one being fastened to the crown of the large one. - To back the field, in horse racing, to bet against a particular horse or horses, that some one of all the other horses, collectively designated ½the field, will win. - To back the oars, to row backward with the oars. - To back a rope, to put on a preventer. - To back the sails, to arrange them so as to cause the ship to move astern. - To back up, to support; to sustain; as, to back up one's friends. - To back a warrant (Law), is for a justice of the peace, in the county where the warrant is to be executed, to sign or indorse a warrant, issued in another county, to apprehend an offender. - To back water (Naut.), to reverse the action of the oars, paddles, or propeller, so as to force the boat or ship backward.}

Back, v.i. 1. To move or go backward; as, the horse refuses to back.

(Naut.) To change from one quarter to another by a course opposite to that of the sun; - used of the wind.

(Sporting) To stand still behind another dog which

has pomted; - said of a dog. [Eng.]

To back and fill, to manage the sails of a ship so that the wind strikes them alternately in front and behind, in order to keep the ship in the middle of a river or channel while the current or tide carries the vessel against the wind. Hence: (Fig.) To take opposite positions alternately; to assert and deny. [Colloq.] - To back out, To back down, to retreat or withdraw from a promise, engagement, or contest; to recede. [Colloq.]

Cleon at first ... was willing to go; but, finding that he [Nicias] was in earnest, he tried to ÿback out.

Jowett (Thucyd.)

Back, adv. [Shortened from aback.] 1. In, to, or toward, the rear; as, to stand back; to step ÿback.

To the place from which one came; to the place or person from which something is taken or derived; as, to go back for something left behind; to go ÿback to one's native place; to put a book back after reading it.

To a former state, condition, or station; as, to go back to private life; to go back to barbarism.

(Of time) In times past; ago. ½Sixty or seventy years back.

Gladstone.

Away from contact; by reverse movement.

The angel of the Lord ... came, and rolled back the stone from the door.
Matt. xxvii.2.

In concealment or reserve; in one's own possession; as, to keep ÿback the truth; to keep back part of the money due to another.

In a state of restraint or hindrance.

The Lord hath kept thee back from honor.
Numb. xxiv.11.

In return, repayment, or requital.

What have I to give you ÿback!
Shak.

In withdrawal from a statement, promise, or undertaking; as, he took back0 the offensive words.

In arrear; as, to be back in one's rent. [Colloq.]

Back and forth, backwards and forwards; to and fro. - To go back on, to turn back from; to abandon; to betray;as, to go back on a friend; to go back on one's professions. [Colloq.]

Bacaĭrack (?), n. See Bacharach.

Bacĭkare (?), interj. Same as Baccare.

Backband · (?),n. [2nd backÿ, n. + band.] (Saddlery) The band which passes over the back of a horse and holds up the shafts of a carriage.

Backbite · , v.i. [2nd back, n., + bite] To wound by clandestine detraction; to censure meanly or spitefully (as absent person); to slander or speak evil of (one absent).

Spenser.

Backbite · , v.i. To censure or revile the absent.

They are arrant knaves, and will ÿbackbite.

Shak.

Backbit · er (?), n. One who backbites; a secret calumniator or detractor.

Backbit · ing (?), n. Secret slander; detraction.

Backbiting, and bearing of false witness.

Piers Plowman.

Backboard · (?), n. [2nd ÿbackÿ,n. + board.]

A board which supports the back wen one is sitting;

specifically, the board athwart the after part of a boat.

A board serving as the back part of anything, as of a wagon.

A thin stuff used for the backs of framed pictures, mirrors, etc.

A board attached to the rim of a water wheel to prevent the water from running off the floats or paddies into the interior of the wheel.

W.Nicholson.

A board worn across the back to give erectness to the figure.

Thackeray.

Backbond · (?), n. [Back, adv. + ÿbond.] (Scots Law) An instrument which, in conjunction with another making an absolute disposition, constitutes a trust.

Backbone, n. [2d back, n. + bone.ÿ]

> The column of bones in the back which sustains and gives firmness to the frame; the spine; the vertebral or spinal column.

> Anything like, or serving the purpose of, a backbone.

The lofty mountains on the north side compose the granitic axis, or backbone of the country.

Darwin.

We have now come to the backbone of our subject.

Earle.

> Firmness; moral principle; steadfastness.

Shelley's thought never had any ÿbackbone.

Shairp.

To the backbone, through and through; thoroughly; entirely. ½Staunch to ÿthe backbone.ˏ

Lord Lytton.

Backboned (?), a. Vertebrate.

Backcast · (?), n. [Back, adv.+ ÿcast.] Anything which brings misfortune upon one, or causes failure in an effort or enterprise; a reverse. [Scot.]

Back door (?). A door in the back part of a building; hence, an indirect way.

Atterbury.

Backdoor, a. Acting from behind and in concealment; as backdoor intrigues.

Backdown · (?), n. A receding or giving up; a complete surrender. [Colloq.]

Backed (?), a. Having a back; fitted with a back; as, a backed electrotype or stereotype plate. Used in composition; as, broad-ÿbacked; hump-backed.

Backer (?), n. One who, or that which, backs; especially one who backs a person or thing in a contest.

Backfall · (?), n. [2nd back ,n. + fall] A fall or throw on the back in wrestling.

Backfriend · (?), n. [Back, n. or adv. + friend] A secret enemy. [Obs.]

South.

Backgam · mon (?), n. [Origin unknown; perhaps fr.Dan. bakke tray + E.ÿgame; or very likely the first part is from E.back, adv., and the game is so called because the men are often set back.] A game of chance and skill, played by two persons on a ½boardˏ marked off into twenty-four spaces called

½points͵. Each player has fifteen pieces, or ½men͵, the movements of which from point to point are determined by throwing dice. Formerly called ÿtables.

Backgammon board , a board for playing backgammon, often made in the form of two rectangular trays hinged together, each tray containing two ½tables͵.

Backgam · mon, v.i. In the game of backgammon, to beat by ending the game before the loser is clear of his first ½table͵.

Background · (?), n. [ÿBack, a. + ground.]
Ground in the rear or behind, or in the distance,

as opposed to the foreground, or the ground in front.
(Paint.) The space which is behind and subordinate to a portrait or group of figures.

μ The distance in a picture is usually divided into foreground, middle distance, and background.
Fairholt.
Anything behind, serving as a foil; as, the statue had a background of red hangings.
A place in obscurity or retirement, or out of sight.

I fancy there was a background of grinding and waiting before Miss Torry could produce this highly finished ... performance.
Mrs.Alexander.
A husband somewhere in the background.
Thackeray.
Backhand · (?), n. [Back, adv. + ÿhand.] A kind of handwriting in which the downward slope of the letters is from left to right.

Backhand · , a. 1. Sloping from left to right; - said of handwriting.
Backhanded; indirect; oblique. [R.]

Backhand · ed, a. 1. With the hand turned backward; as, a ÿbackhanded blow.
Indirect; awkward; insincere; sarcastic; as, a ÿbackhandedÿ compliment.

3.Turned back, or inclining to the left; as, a backhanded letters.

Backhand · edĭness, n.   State of being backhanded; the using of backhanded or indirect methods.

Backhand · er (?), n. A backhanded blow.

Backhouse · (?), n. [ÿBack, a. + house.] A building behind the main building. Specifically: A privy; a necessary.

Backing, n. 1. The act of moving backward, or of putting or moving anything backward.

That which is behind, and forms the back of, anything, usually giving strength or stability.

Support or aid given to a person or cause.

(Bookbinding) The preparation of the back of a book with glue, etc., before putting on the cover.

Backjoint · (?), n. [Backÿ, a. or adv. + joint.] (a) A rebate or chase in masonry left to receive a permanent slab or other filling.

Backlash · (?), n. [ÿBackÿ, adv. + lash.] (Mech.) The distance through which one part of connected machinery, as a wheel, piston, or screw, can be moved without moving the connected parts, resulting from looseness in fitting or from wear; also, the jarring or reflex motion caused in badly fitting machinery by irregularities in velocity or a reverse of motion.

Backless, a. Without a back.

Backlog · (?), n. [ÿBack, a. + log.] A large stick of wood, forming the of a fire on the hearth. [U.S.]

There was first a backlog, from fifteen to four and twenty inches in diameter and five feet long, imbedded in the ashes.

S.G. Goodrich.

Backpiece · (?), Backplate · (?),} n. [ÿBack, n. or a. + ÿpiece, plate.ÿ] A piece, or plate which forms the back of anything, or which covers the back; armor for the back.

<— p. 111 —>

Backrack (?), Backrag (?),} n. See Bacharach.

Backs (?), n. pl. Among leather dealers, the thickest and stoutest tanned hides.

Backsaw · (?), n. [2d back,n.+ saw.] A saw (as a tenon saw) whose blade is stiffened by an added metallic back.

Backset · (?), n. [ÿBack, adv. + ÿset.] 1. A check; a relapse; a discouragement; a setback.

Whatever is thrown back in its course, as water.

Slackwater, or the ÿbackset caused by the overflow.

Harper's Mag.

Backset · , v.i. To plow again, in the fall; - said of prairie land broken up in the spring. [Western U.S.]

Backsettler (?), n. [Back, a. + settler.] One living in the back or outlying districts of a community.

The English backsettlers of Leinster and Munster.

Macaulay.

ØBacksheesh · , ØBackshish · } (?), n. [Pers.ÿbakhshÆsh, fr. ÿbakhshÆdan to give.] In Egypt and the Turkish empire, a gratuity; a ½tip‚.

Backside · (?), n. [ÿBack, a. + side.ÿ] The hinder part, posteriors, or rump of a person or animal.

µBackside (one word) was formerly used of the rear part or side of any thing or place, but in such senses is now two words.

Backsight · (?), n. [Back, adv. + sight.ÿ] (Surv.) The reading of the leveling staff in its unchanged position when the leveling instrument has been taken to a new position; a sight directed backwards to a station previously occupied. Cf. Foresight,ÿn., 3.

Back · slide (?), v.i. [imp. Backslidÿ(?); p.p. Backslidden (?), Backslid; p.pr.&vb.n. ÿBacksliding.ÿ] [Backÿ, adv.+ slide.] To slide back; to fall away; esp. to abandon gradually the faith and practice of a religion that has been professed.

Backslider (?), n. One who backslides.

Backsliding, a. Slipping back; falling back into sin or error; sinning.

Turn, O backsliding children, saith the Lord.

Jer. iii. 14.

Backsliding, n. The act of one who backslides; abandonment of faith or duty.

Our backslidings are many.

Jer. xiv.7.

Backstaff · (?), n. An instrument formerly used for taking the altitude of the heavenly bodies, but now superseded by the quadrant and sextant; - so called because the observer turned his back to the body observed.

Back stairs · . Stairs in the back part of a house, as distinguished from the front stairs; hence, a private or indirect way.

Backstairs · , Backstair · , a. Private; indirect; secret; intriguing; as if finding access by the back stairs.

A backstairs influence.

Burke.

Female caprice and ÿbackstairs influence.

Trevelyan.

Backstay · (?), n. [ÿBack, a. or n. + stay.] 1.(Naut.) A rope or stay extending from the masthead to the side of a ship, slanting a little aft, to assist the shrouds in supporting the mast. [Often used in the plural.]

A rope or strap used to prevent excessive forward motion.

Backster (?), n. [See Baxter.] A backer. [Obs.]

Backstitch · (?), n. [ÿBack, adv. + ÿstitch.] A stitch made by setting the needle back of the end of the last stitch, and bringing it out in front of the end.

Backstitch · , v.i. To sew with backstitches; as, to backstitch a seam.

Backstress (?), n. A female baker. [Obs.]

Backsword · (?), n. [2d back, n. + sword.] 1. A sword with one sharp edge.

In England, a stick with a basket handle, used in rustic amusements; also, the game in which the stick is used. Also called ÿsinglestick.

Halliwell.

Backward (?), Backwards (?),} adv. [ÿBack, ÿadv. + Ïward.] 1. With the back in advance or foremost; as, to ride backward.

Toward the back; toward the rear; as, to throw the arms ÿbackward.

On the back, or with the back downward.

Thou wilt fall ÿbackward.ÿ
Shak.

Toward, or in, past time or events; ago.

Some reigns ÿbackward. ÿ
Locke.

By way of reflection; reflexively.

Sir J.Davies.

From a better to a worse state, as from honor to shame, from religion to sin.

The work went ÿbackward.ÿ
Dryden.

In a contrary or reverse manner, way, or direction; contrarily; as, to read ÿbackwards.

We might have ... beat them ÿbackward home.
Shak.

Backward, a. 1. Directed to the back or rear; as, backward glances.

Unwilling; averse; reluctant; hesitating; loath.

For wiser brutes were ÿbackwardÿ to be slaves.
Pope.

Not well advanced in learning; not quick of apprehension; dull; inapt; as, a ÿbackward ÿchild. ½The backward learner.

South.

Late or behindhand; as, a ÿbackward season.

Not advanced in civilization; undeveloped; as, the country or region is in a backward ÿstate.

Already past or gone; bygone. [R.]

And flies unconscious o'er each ÿbackwardÿ year.
Byron.

Backward, n. The state behind or past. [Obs.]
In the dark ÿbackwardÿ and abysm of time.

Shak.

Backward, v.i. To keep back; to hinder. [Obs.]

Back · warĭdation (?), n. [Backward, v.i.+ ĭation.] (Stock Exchange) The seller's postponement of delivery of stock or shares, with the consent of the buyer, upon payment of a premium to the latter; - also, the premium so paid. See ÿContango.

Biddle.

Backwardĭly (?), adv. 1. Reluctantly; slowly; aversely. [Obs.]

Sir P.Sidney.

Perversely; ill.[Obs.]

And does he think so ÿbackwardlyÿ of me?

Shak.

Backwardĭness, n. The state of being backward.

Backwash · (?), v.i. To clean the oil from (wood) after combing.

Backwa · ter (?), n. [ÿBack, a. or adv. + ÿĭward.ÿ] 1. Water turned back in its course by an obstruction, an opposing current , or the flow of the tide, as in a sewer or river channel, or across a river bar.

An accumulation of water overflowing the low lands, caused by an obstruction.

Water thrown back by the turning of a waterwheel, or by the paddle wheels of a steamer.

Backwoods (?), n. pl. [Back,ÿ a. + ÿwoods.] The forests or partly cleared grounds on the frontiers.

Backwoodsman (?), n.; pl. Backwoodsmen (?). A men living in the forest in or beyond the new settlements, especially on the western frontiers of the older portions of the United States.

Fisher Ames.

Backworm · (?), n. [2d ÿback, n. + worm.ÿ] A disease of hawks. See Filanders.

Wright.

Bacon (?), n. [OF. bacon, fr. OHG. bacho, bahho, flitch of bacon, ham; akin to E. back. ÿCf. ÿBack the back side.] The back and sides of a pig salted and smoked; formerly, the flesh of a pig salted or fresh.

Bacon beetle (Zo"l.), a beetle (Dermestes lardarius) which, especially in the larval state, feeds upon bacon, woolens, furs, etc. See Dermestes. - To save one's bacon, to save one's self or property from harm or less. [Colloq.]

Baĭconiĭan (?), a. Of or pertaining to Lord Bacon, or to his system of philosophy.

Baconian method, the inductive method. See Induction.

Bacĭteriĭa (?), n.p. See ÿBacterium.

Bacĭteriĭal (?), a. (Biol.) Of or pertaining to bacteria.

Bacĭteriĭci · dal (?), a. Destructive of bacteria.

Bacĭterĭcide (?), n. [ÿBacterium ÿ+ L. ÿcaedere to kill] (Biol.) Same as Germicide.

Bacĭterĭoĭlog · icĭal (?), a.   Of or pertaining to bacteriology; as, ÿbacteriological ÿstudies.

Bacĭterĭol · oĭgist, n. One skilled in bacteriology.

Bacĭterĭol · oĭgy (?), n. [ÿBacterium + Ĭlogy.ÿ] (Biol.)   The science relating to bacteria.

Bacĭte · riĭoĭscopic (?), a.   (Biol.)   Relating to bacterioscopy; as, a ÿbacterioscopic examination.

Bacĭte · riĭoscoĭpist (?), n.   (Biol.)   One skilled in bacterioscopic examinations.

Bacĭte · riĭoscoĭpy (?), n. [ÿBacterium + Ĭscopyÿ] (Biol.) The application of a knowledge of bacteria for their detection and identification, as in the examination of polluted water.

Bacĭterĭum (?), n.; pl. ÿBacteria (?). [NL., fr. Gr.?, ?, a staff: cf. F. bact,rie.ÿ] (Biol.) A microscopic vegetable organism, belonging to the class Alg', usually in the form of a jointed rodlike filament, and found in putrefying organic infusions. Bacteria are destitute of chlorophyll, and are the smallest of microscopic organisms. They are very widely diffused in nature, and multiply with marvelous rapidity, both by fission and by spores. Certain species are active agents in fermentation, while others appear to be the cause of certain infectious diseases. See ÿBacillus.

Bacteĭroid (?), Bac · teĭroidal (?),} a.   [ÿBacterium + Ĭoid.]   (Biol.) Resembling bacteria; as, bacteroid particles.

Bactriĭan (?), a. Of or pertaining to Bacteria in Asia. - n. A native of Bacteria.

Bactrian camel, the two-humped camel.

Bacule (?), n. [F.] (Fort.) See ÿBascule.

Bacuĭline (?), a. [L. baculum staff.] Of or pertaining to the rod or punishment with the rod.

Bacuĭlite (?), n. [L. baculune stick, staff; cf. F. baculite.] (Paleon.) A cephalopod of the extinct genus Baculites, found fossil in the Cretaceous rocks. It is like an uncoiled ammonite.

Bac · uĭlomeĭtry (?), n. [L. baculum staff + Ĭmetry] Measurement of distance or altitude by a staff or staffs.

Bad (?), imp. of Bid.ÿ Bade. [Obs.]

Dryden.

Bad (?), a. [Compar. Worse (?); ÿsuperl. ÿWorst (?).ÿ] [Probably fr. AS. ÿb'ddel hermaphrodite; cf. b'dling effeminate fellow.] Wanting good qualities, whether physical or moral; injurious, hurtful, inconvenient, offensive, painful, unfavorable, or defective, either physically or morally; evil; vicious; wicked; - the opposite of good; as a ÿbad man; ÿbad conduct; bad habits; bad soil; ÿbad health; bad crop; bad news.

Sometimes used substantively.

The strong antipathy of good to ÿbad.ÿ
Pope.

Syn. - Pernicious; deleterious; noxious; baneful; injurious; hurtful; evil; vile; wretched; corrupt; wicked; vicious; imperfect.

Badder (?), compar. of ÿBad, a.[Obs.]
Chaucer.

Badderïlocks (?), n. [Perh. for Balderlocks, ÿfr. Balder the Scandinavian deity.] (Bot.) A large black seaweed (Alaria esculenta) sometimes eaten in Europe; - also called ÿmurlins, honeyware, ÿand henware.

Baddish, a. Somewhat bad; inferior.
Jeffrey.

Bade (?). A form of the pat tense of ÿBid.

Badge (?), n. [LL. bagea, bagia, ÿsign, prob. of German origin; cf. AS. be g, be h, bracelet, collar, crown, OS ÿb?g- in comp., AS. b?gan ÿto bow, bend, G. ÿbiegen. See Bow to bend.] 1. A distinctive mark, token, sign, or cognizance, worn on the person; as, the ÿbadge of a society; the ÿbadge of a policeman. ½Tax gatherers, recognized by their official ÿbadges.ÿ͵
Prescott.

Something characteristic; a mark; a token.

Sweet mercy is nobility's true ÿbadge.ÿ
Shak.

(Naut.) A carved ornament on the stern of a vessel, containing a window or the representation of one.

Badge (?), v.t. To mark or distinguish with a badge.

Badgeless, a. Having no badge.
Bp. Hall.

Badger (?), n. [Of uncertain origin; perh. fr. an old verb ÿbadge to lay up provisions to sell again.] An itinerant licensed dealer in commodities used for food; a hawker; a huckster; - formerly applied especially to one who bought grain in one place and sold it in another. [Now dialectic, Eng.]

Badger, n. [OE. bageard, prob. fr. badge + ɩ̈ard, in reference to the white mark on its forehead. See Badge,n.] 1. A carnivorous quadruped of the genus ÿMeles or of an allied genus. It is a burrowing animal, with short, thick legs, and long claws on the fore feet. One species (M. vulgaris), called also brock, inhabits the north of Europe and Asia; another species (Taxidea Americana or Labradorica) inhabits the northern parts of North America. See ÿTeledu.

A brush made of badgers' hair, used by artists.

Badger dog. (Zo"l.) See ÿDachshund.

Badger, v.t. [imp. & p.p. Badgered (?);p. pr. & vb. n. Badgering.] [For sense 1, see 2d ÿBadger; for 2, see 1st Badger.] 1. To tease or annoy, as a badger when baited; to worry or irritate persistently.

To beat down; to cheapen; to barter; to bargain.

BadgerÏer (?), n. 1. One who badgers.

A kind of dog used in badger baiting.

BadgerÏing, n. 1. The act of one who badgers.

The practice of buying wheat and other kinds of food in one place and selling them in another for a profit. [Prov. Eng.]

BadgerÏlegged · (?), a. Having legs of unequal length, as the badger was thought to have.
Shak.
ØBad · iÏaga (?), n. [Russ. badiaga.] (Zo"l.) A freshÐwater sponge (Spongilla), common in the north of Europe, the powder of which is used to take away the livid marks of bruises.
ØBadiÏan (?), n. [F.badiane, fr. Per. b¾di¾n anise.] [Bot.] An evergreen Chinese shrub of the Magnolia family (Illicium anisatum), and its aromatic seeds; Chinese anise; star anise.
BaÏdigeon (?), n. [F.] A cement or paste (as of plaster and freestone, or of sawdust and glue or lime) used by sculptors, builders, and workers in wood or stone, to fill holes, cover defects, or finish a surface.
ØBa · di · nage (?),n. [F., fr. badiner to joke, OF. to trifle, be silly, fr. badin silly.] Playful raillery; banter. ½He ...indulged himself only in an elegant badinage.¸
Warbur?on.
Bad lands (?). Barren regions, especially in the western United States, where horizontal strata (Tertiary deposits) have been often eroded into fantastic forms, and much intersected by canons, and where lack of wood, water, and forage increases the difficulty of traversing the country, whence the name, first given by the Canadian French, Mauvaises Terres (bad lands).
Badly, adv. In a bad manner; poorly; not well; unskillfully; imperfectly; unfortunately; grievously; so as to cause harm; disagreeably; seriously.

µ Badly is often used colloquially for very much or very greatly, with words signifying to want or need.

BadminÏton (?), n. [From the name of the seat of the Duke of Beaufort in England.] 1. A game, similar to lawn tennis, played with shuttlecocks.

A preparation of claret, spiced and sweetened.

Badness, n. The state of being bad.

ØB'noïmere (?), n. [Gr. ? to walk + Ðmere.] (Zo"l.) One of the somites (arthromeres) that make up the thorax of Arthropods.
Packard.
B'noïpod (?), n. [Gr. ? to walk + Ðpod.] (Zo"l.) One of the thoracic legs of Arthropods.
ØB'noïsome (?), n. [Gr. ? to walk + Ðsome body.] (Zo"l.) The thorax of Arthropods.
Packard.
Baff (?), n. A blow; a stroke. [Scot.]
H.Miller.
Baffle (?), v.i. [imp. & p.p. Baffled (?); p.pr. & vb.n. Baffling (?).] [Cf. Lowland Scotch bauchle to treat contemptuously, bauch tasteless, abashed, jaded, Icel. b¾gr uneasy, poor, or b¾gr, n., struggle, b'gja to push, treat harshly, OF. beffler, beffer, to mock, deceive, dial. G. b„ppe mouth, beffen to bark, chide.]

To cause to undergo a disgraceful punishment, as a recreant knight. [Obs.]

He by the heels him hung upon a tree,
And baffled so, that all which passed by
The picture of his punishment might see.
Spenser.

To check by shifts and turns; to elude; to foil.

The art that baffles time's tyrannic claim.
Cowper.

To check by perplexing; to disconcert, frustrate, or defeat; to thwart. ½A baffled purpose.

De Quincey.
A suitable scripture ready to repel and baffle them all.
South.
Calculations so difficult as to have baffled, until within a ... recent period, the most enlightened nations.
Prescott.
The mere intricacy of a question should not baffle us.
Locke.
Baffling wind (Naut.), one that frequently shifts from one point to another.
Syn. Ð To balk; thwart; foil; frustrate; defeat.
Baffle, v.i. 1. To practice deceit. [Obs.]
Barrow.

To struggle against in vain; as, a ship baffles with the winds. [R.]

Baffle, n. A defeat by artifice, shifts, and turns; discomfiture. [R.] ½A baffle to philosophy.

South.

Bafflement (?), n. The process or act of baffling, or of being baffled; frustration; check.

Baffler (?), n. One who, or that which, baffles.

<— p. 112 —>

Baffling (?), a. Frustrating; discomfiting; disconcerting; as, baffling currents, winds, tasks, Đ ? Baft (?). n. Same as Bafta. Bafta (?), n. [Cf. Per. baft. woven, wrought.] A coarse stuff, usually of cotton, originally made in India. Also, an imitation of this fabric made for export. Bag (?), n. [OE. bagge; cf. Icel. baggi, and also OF. bague, bundle, LL. baga.] 1. A sack or pouch, used for holding anything; as, a bag of meal or of money. 2. A sac, or dependent gland, in animal bodies, containing some fluid or other substance; as, the bag of poison in the mouth of some serpents; the bag of a cow. 3. A sort of silken purse formerly tied about men's hair behind, by way of ornament. [Obs.] 4. The quantity of game bagged. 5. (Com.) A certain quantity of a commodity, such as it is customary to carry to market in a sack; as, a bag of pepper or hops; a bag of coffee. Bag and baggage, all that belongs to one. Đ To give one the bag, to disappoint him. [Obs.] Bunyan.

Bag, v.t. [imp. & p.p. Bagged(?); p.pr. & vb.n. Bagging] 1. To put into a bag; as, to bag hops.

To seize, capture, or entrap; as, to bag an army; to bag game.

To furnish or load with a bag or with a well filled bag.

A bee bagged with his honeyed venom.

Dryden.

Bag, v.i. 1. To swell or hang down like a full bag; as, the skin bags from containing morbid matter.

To swell with arrogance. [Obs.]

Chaucer.

To become pregnant. [Obs.]

Warner.(Alb.Eng.).

ØBaĭgasse (?), n. [F.] Sugar cane, as it ?omes crushed from the mill. It is then dried and used as fuel. Also extended to the refuse of beetroot sugar.

ØBag · aĭtelle (?), n. [F., fr. It. bagatella; cf. Prov. It. bagata trifle, OF. bague, Pr. bagua, bundle. See Bag, n.] 1. A trifle; a thing of no importance.

Rich trifles, serious bagatelles.

Prior.

A game played on an oblong board, having, at one end, cups or arches into or through which balls are to be driven by a rod held in the hand of the player.

Baggage (?), n. [F. bagage, from OF. bague bungle. In senses 6 and 7 cf. F. bagasse a prostitute. See Bag, n.] 1. The clothes, tents, utensils, and provisions of an army.

µ ½The term itself is made to apply chiefly to articles of clothing and to small personal effects.

Farrow.

<blockquote>The trunks, valises, satchels, etc., which a traveler carries with him on a journey; luggage.</blockquote>

The baronet's baggage on the roof of the coach.
Thackeray.
We saw our baggage following below.
Johnson.
µ The English usually call this luggage.
<blockquote>Purulent matter. [Obs.]</blockquote>

Barrough.
<blockquote>Trashy talk. [Obs.]</blockquote>

Ascham.
<blockquote>A man of bad character. [Obs.]</blockquote>

Holland.
<blockquote>A woman of loose morals; a prostitute.</blockquote>

A disreputable, daring, laughing, painted French baggage.
Thackeray.
<blockquote>A romping, saucy girl. [Playful]</blockquote>

Goldsmith.
Baggage mas·ter (?). One who has charge of the baggage at a railway station or upon a line of public travel. [U.S.]
Baggager (?), n. One who takes care of baggage; a camp follower. [Obs.]
Sir W.Raleigh.
ØBaggaïla (?), n. [Ar. ½fem. of baghl a mule. Balfour.] (Naut.) A twoÐmasted Arab or Indian trading vessel, used in Indian Ocean.
Baggily (?), adv. In a loose, baggy way.
Bagging, n. 1. Cloth or other material for bags.
<blockquote>The act of putting anything into, or as into, a bag.

The act of swelling; swelling.</blockquote>

Bagging, n. [Etymol. uncertain.] Reaping peas, beans, wheat, etc., with a chopping stroke. [Eng.]

Baggy (?), a. Resembling a bag; loose or puffed out, or pendent, like a bag; flabby; as, baggy trousers; baggy cheeks.

Bagman (?), n.; pl. Bagmen (?). A commercial traveler; one employed to solicit orders for manufacturers and tradesmen.

Thackeray.

Bag net · (?). A bagÐshaped net for catching fish.

Bagnio (?), n. [It. bagno, fr. L. balneum. Cf. Bain.] 1. A house for bathing, sweating, etc.; Ð also, in Turkey, a prison for slaves. [Obs.]

A brothel; a stew; a house of prostitution.

Bagpipe (?), n. A musical wind instrument, now used chiefly in the Highlands of Scotland.

µ It consists of a leather bag, which receives the air by a tube that is stopped by a valve; and three sounding pipes, into which the air is pressed by the performer. Two of these pipes produce fixed tones, namely, the bass, or key tone, and its fifth, and form together what is called the drone; the third, or chanter, gives the melody.

Bagpipe, v.t. To make to look like a bagpipe.

To bagpipe the mizzen (Naut.), to lay it aback by bringing the sheet to the mizzen rigging.

Totten.

Bagpip · er (?), n. One who plays on a bagpipe; a piper.

Shak.

Bagreef · (?), n. [Bag + reef.] (Naut.) The lower reef of fore and aft sails; also, the upper reef of topsails.

Ham. Nav. Encyc.

ØBague (?), n. [F., a ring] (Arch.) The annular molding or group of moldings dividing a long shaft or clustered column into two or more parts.

Baïguet, Baïguette } (?), n. [F. baguette, prop. a rod? It. bacchetta, fr. L. baculum, baculi? stick, staff.] 1. (Arch.) A small molding, like the astragal, but smaller; a bead.

(Zo"l) One of the minute bodies seen in the divided nucleoli of some Infusoria after conjugation.

Bagwig (?), n. A wig, in use in the 18th century, with the hair at the back of the head in a bag.

Bagworm · (?), n. (Zo"l.) One of several lepidopterous insects which construct, in the larval state, a baglike case which they carry about for protection. One species (Plat?ceticus Gloveri) feeds on the orange tree. See Basket worm.

Bahÿ(?), interj. An exclamation expressive of extreme contempt.

TwentyÐfive years ago the vile ejaculation, Bah! was utterly unknown to the English public.

De Quincey.

ØBaĭhar (?), n. [Ar. bah¾r, from bahara to charge with a load.] A weight used in certain parts of the East Indies, varying considerably in different localities, the range being from 223 to 625 pounds.

Baigne (?), v.i. [F. baigner to bathe, fr. L. balneum bath.] To soak or drench. [Obs.]

Bail (?), n. [F. baille a bucket, pail; cf. LL. bacula, dim. of bacca a sort of vessel. Cf. Bac.] A bucket or scoop used in bailing water out of a boat. [Obs.]

The bail of a canoe ... made of a human skull.

Capt. Cook.

Bail, v.t. [imp. & p.p. Bailed (?); p. pr. & vb.n. Bailing.] 1. To lade; to dip and throw; Ð usually with out; as, to bail water out of a boat.

Buckets ... to bail out the water.

Capt. J. Smith.

To dip or lade water from; Ð often with out to express completeness; as, to bail a boat.

By the help of a small bucket and our hats we bailed her out.

R.H.Dana, Jr.

Bail, v.?t. [OF. bailler to give, to deliver, fr. L. bajulare to bear a burden, keep in custody, fr. bajulus ? who bears burdens.] 1. To deliver; to release. [Obs.]

Ne none there was to rescue her, ne none to bail.

Spenser.

(Law) (a) To set free, or deliver from arrest, or out of custody, on the undertaking of some other person or persons that he or they will be responsible for the appearance, at a certain day and place, of the person bailed.

µ The word is applied to the magistrate or the surety. The magistrate bails (but admits to bail is commoner) a man when he liberates him from arrest or imprisonment upon bond given with sureties. The surety bails a person when he procures his release from arrest by giving bond for his appearance.

Blackstone.

(b) To deliver, as goods in trust, for some special object or purpose, upon a contract, expressed or implied, that the trust shall be faithfully executed on the part of the bailee, or person intrusted; as, to bail cloth to a tailor to be made into a garment; to bail goods to a carrier.

Blackstone. Kent.

Bail, n. [OF. bail guardian, administrator, fr. L. bajulus. See Bail to deliver.] 1. Custody; keeping. [Obs.]

Silly Faunus now within their bail.

Spenser.

(Law) (a) The person or persons who procure the release of a prisoner from the custody of the officer, or from imprisonment, by becoming surely for his appearance in court.

The bail must be real, substantial bondsmen.
Blackstone.
A. and B. were bail to the arrest in a suit at law.
Kent.
(b) The security given for the appearance of a prisoner in order to obtain his release from custody of the officer; as, the man is out on bail; to go bail for any one.
Excessive bail ought not to be required.
Blackstone.
Bail, n. [OE. beyl; cf. Dan. b"ile an bending, ring, hoop, Sw. b"gel, bygel, and Icel. beyla hump, swelling, akin to E. bow to bend.] 1. The arched handle of a kettle, pail, or similar vessel, usually movable.
Forby.
A half hoop for supporting the cover of a carrier's wagon, awning of a boat, etc.

Bail, n. [OF. bail, baille. See Bailey.] 1. (Usually pl.) A line of palisades serving as an exterior defense. [Written also bayle.] [Obs.]
The outer wall of a feudal castle. Hence: The space inclosed by it; the outer court.

Holinshed.
A certain limit within a forest. [Eng.]
A division for the stalls of an open stable.
(Cricket) The top or cross piece (or either of the two cross pieces) of the wicket.

Bailaïble (?), a. 1. Having the right or privilege of being admitted to bail, upon bond with sureties; Ð used of persons. ½He's bailable, I'm sure.¸
Ford.
Admitting of bail; as, a bailable offense.
That can be delivered in trust; as, bailable goods.

Bail bond · (?). (Law) (a) A bond or obligation given by a prisoner and his surety, to insure the prisoner's appearance in court, at the return of the writ. (b) Special bail in court to abide the judgment.
Bouvier.
Bail · ee (?), n. [OF. baill,, p.p. of bailler. See Bail to deliver.] (Law) The person to whom goods are committed in trust, and who has a temporary possession and a qualified property in them, for the purposes of the trust.
Blackstone.

µ In penal statutes the word includes those who receive goods for another in good faith.

Wharton.

Bailerÿ(?), n. (Law) See Bailor.

Bailer, n. 1. One who bails or lades.

<small>A utensil, as a bucket or cup, used in bailing; a machine for bailing water out of a pit.</small>

Bailey (?), n. [The same word as bail line of palisades; cf. LL. ballium bailey, OF. bail, baille, a palisade, baillier to inclose, shut.] 1. The outer wall of a feudal castle. [Obs.]

<small>The space immediately within the outer wall of a castle or fortress. [Obs.]</small>

<small>A prison or court of justice; Ð used in certain proper names; as, the Old Bailey in London; the New Bailey in Manchester. [Eng.]</small>

Oxf. Gloss.

Bailie (?), n. [See Bailiff.] An officer in Scotland, whose office formerly corresponded to that of sheriff, but now corresponds to that of an English alderman.

Bailiff (?), n. [OF. baillif, F. bailli, custodia? magistrate, fr. L. bajulus porter. See Bail to deliver.]

<small>Originally, a person put in charge of something especially, a chief officer, magistrate, or keeper, as of a county, town, hundred, or castle; one to whom power? of custody or care are intrusted.</small>

Abbott.

Lausanne is under the canton of Berne, governed by a bailiff sent every three years from the senate.

Addison.

<small>(Eng. Law) A sheriff's deputy, appointed to make arrests, collect fines, summon juries, etc.</small>

µ In American law the term bailiff is seldom used except sometimes to signify a sheriff's officer or constable, or a party liable to account to another for the rent and profits of real estate.

Burrill.

<small>An overseer or under steward of an estate, who directs husbandry operations, collects rents, etc. [Eng.]</small>

Bailiffïwick (?), n. See Bailiwick. [Obs.]

Bailïwick (?), n. [Bailie, bailiff + wick a village.] (Law) The precincts within which a bailiff has jurisdiction; the limits of a bailiff's authority.

Baillie (?), n. 1. Bailiff. [Obs.]

<small>Same as Bailie. [Scot.]</small>

Bailment (?), n. 1. (Law) The action of bailing a person accused.

Bailment ...is the saving or delivery of a man out of prison before he hath satisfied the law.

Dalton.

(Law) A delivery of goods or money by one person to another in trust, for some special purpose, upon a contract, expressed or implied, that the trust shall be faithfully executed.

Blackstone.

µ In a general sense it is sometimes used as comprehending all duties in respect to property.

Story.

Bail · or (?), n. (Law) One who delivers goods or money to another in trust.

Bailpiece · (?), n. (Law) A piece of parchment, or paper, containing a recognizance or bail bond.

Bain (?), n. [F. bain, fr. L. balneum. Cf. Bagnio.] A bath; a bagnio. [Obs.]

Holland.

ØBain · Ïma · rie (?), n. [F.] A vessel for holding hot water in which another vessel may be heated without scorching its contents; Đ used for warming or preparing food or pharmaceutical preparations.

ØBairam (?), n. [Turk. ba‹r¾m.] The name of two Mohammedan festivals, of which one is held at the close of the fast called Ramadan, and the other seventy days after the fast.

Bairn (?), n. [Scot. bairn, AS. bearn, fr. beran to bear; akin to Icel., OS., &Goth. barn. See Bear to support.] A child. [Scot. & Prov. Eng.]

Has he not well provided for the bairn !

Beau. & Fl.

Baisemains · (?), n. pl. [F., fr. baiser to kiss + mains hands.] Respects; compliments. [Obs.]

Bait (?), n. [Icel. beita food, beit pasture, akin to AS. b¾t food, Sw. bete. See Bait, v.i.] 1. Any substance, esp. food, used in catching fish, or other animals, by alluring them to a hook, snare, inclosure, or net.

Anything which allures; a lure; enticement; temptation.

Fairfax.

A portion of food or drink, as a refreshment taken on a journey; also, a stop for rest and refreshment.

A light or hasty luncheon.

Bait bug (Zo"l), a crustacea? of the genus Hippa found burrowing in sandy beaches. See Anomura.

Bait, v.t. [imp. & p.p. Baited; p. pr. & vb. n. Baiting.] [OE. baiten, beit?n, to feed, harass, fr. Icel. beita, orig. to cause to bite, fr. bÆta. ?87. See Bite.]

> To provoke and harass; esp., to harass or torment for sport; as, to bait a bear with dogs; to bait a bull.

> To give a portion of food and drink to, upon the road; as, to bait horses.

Holland.

> To furnish or cover with bait, as a trap or hook.

A crooked pin ... bailed with a vile earthworm.
W.Irving.

Bait, v.i. To stop to take a portion of food and drink for refreshment of one's self or one's beasts, on a journey.

Evil news rides post, while good news baits.
Milton.

My lord's coach conveyed me to Bury, and thence baiting a? Newmarket.
Evelyn.

Bait, v.i. [F. battre de l'aile (or des ailes), to flap o? flutter. See Batter, v.i.] To flap the wings; to flutter as if to fly; or to hover, as a hawk when she stoops to her prey. ½Kites that bait and beat.‚

Shak.

Baiter (?), n. One who baits; a tormentor.

Baize (?), n. [For bayes, pl. fr. OF. baie; cf. F. bai bayÐcolored. See Bay a color.] A coarse woolen stuff with a long nap; Ð usually dyed in plain colors.

A new black baize waistcoat lined with silk.
Pepys.

ØBaĭjocco (?), n. [It., fr. bajo brown, bay, from its color.] A small cooper coin formerly current in the Roman States, worth about a cent and a half.

Bake (?), v. t. [imp.& p.p. Baked (?); p. pr. & vb. n. Baking.] [AS. bacan; akin to D. bakken, OHG. bacchan, G. backen, Icel. & Sw. baca, Dan. bage, Gr. ? to roast.] 1. To prepare, as food, by cooking in a dry heat, either in an oven or under coals, or on heated stone or metal; as, to bake bread, meat, apples.

µ Baking is the term usually applied to that method of cooking which exhausts the moisture in food more than roasting or broiling; but the distinction of meaning between roasting and baking is not always observed.

> To dry or harden (anything) by subjecting to heat, as, to bake bricks; the sun bakes the ground.

> To harden by cold.

The earth ... is baked with frost.
Shak.
They bake their sides upon the cold, hard stone.
Spenser.
Bake, v.i. 1. To do the work of baking something; as, she brews, washes, and bakes.
Shak.

To be baked; to become dry and hard in heat; as, the bread bakes; the ground bakes in the hot sun.

Bake, n. The process, or result, of baking.
Bakehouse · ÿ(?), n. [AS. b'ch?s. See Bak?, v.i., and House.] A house for baking; a bakery.
<— p. 113 —>
Bakemeat · (?), BakedImeat · (?), } n. A pie; baked food. [Obs.]
Gen. xl.17. Shak.
Baken (?), p.p. of Bake. [Obs. or. Archaic]
Baker (?), n. [AS. b'cere. See Bake, v.i.] 1. One whose business it is to bake bread, biscuit, etc.

A portable oven in which baking is done. [U.S.]

A baker's dozen, thirteen. Đ Baker foot, a distorted foot. [Obs.] Jer.Taylor. Đ Baker's itch, a rash on the back of the hand, caused by the irritating properties of yeast. Đ Baker's salt, the subcarbonate of ammonia, sometimes used instead of soda, in making bread.
BakerĐlegged · (?), a. Having legs that bend inward at the knees.
BakerIy (?), n. 1. The trade of a baker. [R.]

The place for baking bread; a bakehouse.

Baking, n. 1. The act or process of cooking in an oven, or of drying and hardening by heat or cold.

The quantity baked at once; a batch; as, a baking of bread.

Baking powder, a substitute for yeast, usually consisting of an acid, a carbonate, and a little farinaceous matter.
BakingIly, adv. In a hot or baking manner.
BakisItre (?), n. [See Baxter.] A baker. [Obs.]
Chaucer.
ØBaksheesh · , Bakshish · (?), n. Same as Backsheesh.
Balaam (?), n. A paragraph describing something wonderful, used to fill out a newspaper column; Đ an allusion to the miracle of Balaam's ass speaking. Numb. xxii.30. [Cant]

Balaam basket or box (Print.), the receptacle for rejected articles.

Black?. Mag.

ØBalaïchong (?), n. [Malay b¾lach¾n.] A condiment formed of small fishes or shrimps, pounded up with salt and spices, and then dried. It is much esteemed in China.

ØBal · 'Ïnoideïa (?), n. [NL., from L. balaena whale + Đoid.] (Zo"l) A division of the Cetacea, including the right whale and all other whales having the mouth fringed with baleen. See Baleen.

Balance (?), n. [OE. balaunce, F. balance, fr. L. bilan?, bilancis, having two scales; bis twice (akin to E. two) + lanx plate, scale.] 1. An apparatus for weighing.

μ In its simplest form, a balance consists of a beam or lever supported exactly in the middle, having two scales or basins of equal weight suspended from its extremities. Another form is that of the Roman balance, our steelyard, consisting of a lever or beam, suspended near one of its extremities, on the longer arm of which a counterpoise slides. The name is also given to other forms of apparatus for weighing bodies, as to the combinations of levers making up platform scales; and even to devices for weighing by the elasticity of a spring.

Act of weighing mentally; comparison; estimate.

A fair balance of the advantages on either side.
Atterbury.

Equipoise between the weights in opposite scales.

The state of being in equipoise; equilibrium; even adjustment; steadiness.

And hung a bottle on each side
To make his balance true.
Cowper.

The order and balance of the country were destroyed.
Buckle.

English workmen completely lose their balance.
J. S. Mill.

An equality between the sums total of the two sides of an account; as, to bring one's accounts to a balance; Đ also, the excess on either side; as, the balance of an account. ½ A balance at the banker's.

Thackeray.

I still think the balance of probabilities leans towards the account given in the text.
J. Peile.

(Horol.) A balance wheel, as of a watch, or clock. See Balance wheel (in the Vocabulary).

(Astron.) (a) The constellation Libra. (b) The seventh sign in the Zodiac, called Libra, which the sun enters at the equinox in September.

A movement in dancing. See Balance, v. i., S.

Balance electrometer, a kind of balance, with a poised beam, which indicates, by weights suspended from one arm, the mutual attraction of oppositely electrified surfaces. Knight. Ð Balance fish. (Zo"l) See Hammerhead. Ð Balance knife, a carving or table knife the handle of which overbalances the blade, and so keeps it from contact with the table. Ð Balance of power. (Politics), such an adjustment of power among sovereign states that no one state is in a position to interfere with the independence of the others; international equilibrium; also, the ability (of a state or a third party within a state) to control the relations between sovereign states or between dominant parties in a state. Ð Balance sheet (Bookkeeping), a paper showing the balances of the open accounts of a business, the debit and credit balances footing up equally, if the system of accounts be complete and the balances correctly taken. Ð Balance termometer, a termometer mounted as a balance so that the movement of the mercurial column changes the indication of the tube. With the aid of electrical or mechanical devices adapted to it, it is used for the automatic regulation of the temperature of rooms warmed artificially, and as a fire alarm. Ð Balance of torsion. See Torsion Balance. Ð Balance of trade (Pol. Econ.), an equilibrium between the money values of the exports and imports of a country; or more commonly, the amount required on one side or the other to make such an equilibrium. Ð Balance valve, a valve whose surfaces are so arranged that the fluid pressure tending to seat, and that tending to unseat the valve, are nearly in equilibrium; esp., a puppet valve which is made to operate easily by the admission of steam to both sides. See Puppet valve. Ð Hydrostatic balance. See under Hydrostatic. Ð To lay in balance, to put up as a pledge or security. [Obs.] Chaucer. Ð To strike a balance, to find out the difference between the debit and credit sides of an account.

Balance (?), v. t. [imp. & p.p. Balanced (?); p. pr. & vb. n. Balancing (?).] [From Balance, n.: cf. F. balancer.] 1. To bring to an equipoise, as the scales of a balance by adjusting the weights; to weigh in a balance.

> To support on a narrow base, so as to keep from falling; as, to balance a plate on the end of a cane; to balance one's self on a tight rope.

> To equal in number, weight, force, or proportion; to counterpoise, counterbalance, counteract, or neutralize.

One expression ... must check and balance another.
Kent.

> To compare in relative force, importance, value, etc.; to'estimate.

Balance the good and evil of things.

L'Estrange.

To settle and adjust, as an account; to make two accounts equal by paying the difference between them.

I am very well satisfied that it is not in my power to balance accounts with my Maker.
Addison.

To make the sums of the debits and credits of an account equal; Ð said of an item; as, this payment, or credit, balances the account.

To arrange accounts in such a way that the sum total of the debits is equal to the sum total of the credits; as, to balance a set of books.

(Dancing) To move toward, and then back from, reciprocally; as, to balance partners.

(Naut.) To contract, as a sail, into a narrower compass; as, to balance the boom mainsail.

Balanced valve. See Balance valve, under Balance, n.
Syn. Ð To poise; weigh; adjust; counteract; neutralize; equalize.
Balance, v.i. 1. To have equal weight on each side; to be in equipoise; as, the scales balance.

To fluctuate between motives which appear of equal force; to waver; to hesitate.

He would not balance or err in the determination of his choice.
Locke.

(Dancing) To move toward a person or couple, and then back.

BalanceÏaÏble (?), a. Such as can be balanced.
BalanceÏment (?), n. The act or result of balancing or adjusting; equipoise; even adjustment of forces. [R.]
Darwin.
BalanÏcerÿ(?), n. 1. One who balances, or uses a balance.

(Zo"l.) In Diptera, the rudimentary posterior wing.

BalanceÏreef · (?), n. (Naut.) The last reef in a foreÐandÐaft sail, taken to steady the ship.
Balance wheel · (?). 1. (Horology) (a) A wheel which regulates the beats or pulses of a watch or chronometer, answering to the pendulum of a clock; Ð often called simply a balance. (b) A ratchetÐshaped scape wheel, which in some watches is acted upon by the axis of the balance wheel proper (in those watches called a balance).

(Mach.) A wheel which imparts regularity to the movements of any engine or machine; a fly wheel.

Bal·a̤niferĭous (?), a. [L. balanus acorn + Ðferous.] Bearing or producing acorns.

Bala̤nite (?), n. [L. balanus acorn: cf. F. balanite.] (Paleon.) A fossil balanoid shell.

ØBal·a̤noĭglossusӱ(?), n. [NL., fr. Gr. ? acorn + ? tongue.] (Zo"l) A peculiar marine worm. See Enteropneusta, and Tornaria.

Bala̤noid (?), a. [Gr. ? acorn + Ðoid.] (Zo"l.) Resembling an acorn; Ð applied to a group of barnacles having shells shaped like acorns. See Acornshell, and Barnacle.

Balas ru·by (?). [OE. bales, balais, F. balais, LL. balascus, fr. Ar. balakhsh, so called from Badakhshan, Balashan, or Balaxiam, a place in the neighborhood of Samarcand, where this ruby is found.] (Min.) A variety of spinel ruby, of a pale rose red, or inclining to orange. See Spinel.

Ba̤llaustineӱ(?), n. [L. balaustium, Gr. ?.] (Bot.) The pomegranate tree (Punica granatum). The bark of the root, the rind of the fruit, and the flowers are used medicinally.

Bal̤butĭ̤late (?), Bal̤ĭbucĭ̤lnateӱ(?),} v.i. [L. balbutire, fr. balbus stammering: cf. F. balbutier.] To stammer. [Obs.]

ØBal̤ĭbutĭ̤lesӱ(?), n. (Med.) The defect of stammering; also, a kind of incomplete pronunciation.

Balconӱ(?), n. A balcony. [Obs.]

Pepys.

Balco̤lniedӱ(?), a. Having balconies.

Balco̤lny (?), n.; pl. Balconies (?). [It. balcone; cf. It. balco, palco, scaffold, fr. OHG. balcho, pa?cho, beam, G. balken. See Balk beam.] 1. (Arch.) A platform projecting from the wall of a building, usually resting on brackets or consoles, and inclosed by a parapet; as, a balcony in front of a window. Also, a projecting gallery in places of amusement; as, the balcony in a theater.

<small>A projecting gallery once common at the stern of large ships.</small>

μ ½The accent has shifted from the second to the first syllable within these twenty years.͵

Smart (1836).

Bald (?), a. [OE. balled, ballid, perh. the p.p. of ball to reduce to the roundness or smoothness of a ball, by removing hair. ?85. But cf. W. bali whiteness in a horse's forehead.] 1. Destitute of the natural or common covering on the head or top, as of hair, feathers, foliage, trees, etc.; as, a bald head; a bald oak.

On the bald top of an eminence.

Wordsworth.

<small>Destitute of ornament; unadorned; bare; literal.</small>

In the preface to his own bald translation.
Dryden.

Undisguised. ½ Bald egotism.

Lowell.

Destitute of dignity or value; paltry; mean. [Obs.]

(Bot.) Destitute of a beard or awn; as, bald wheat.

(Zo"l.) (a) Destitute of the natural covering. (b) Marked with a white spot on the head; baldÐfaced.

Bald buzzard (Zo"l.), the fishhawk or osprey. Ð Bald coot (Zo"l.), a name of the European coot (Fulica atra), alluding to the bare patch on the front of the head.

Baldaĭchin (?), n. [LL. baldachinus, baldechinus, a canopy of rich silk carried over the host; fr. Bagdad, It. Baldacco, a city in Turkish Asia from whence these rich silks came: cf. It. baldacchino. Cf. Baudekin.] 1. A rich brocade; baudekin. [Obs.]

(Arch.) A structure in form of a canopy, sometimes supported by columns, and sometimes suspended from the roof or projecting from the wall; generally placed over an altar; as, the baldachin in St. Peter's.

A portable canopy borne over shrines, etc., in procession.

[Written also baldachino, baldaquin, etc.]

Bald eagle (?). (Zo"l.) The whiteÐheaded eagle (Hali'etus ?eucocephalus) of America. The young, until several years old, lack the white feathers on the head.

µ The bald eagle is represented in the coat of arms, and on the coins, of the United States.

Balder (?), n. [Icel. Baldr, akin to E. bold.] (Scan. Myth.) The most beautiful and beloved of the gods; the god of peace; the son of Odin and Freya. [Written also Baldur.]

BalderĬdash (?), n. [Of uncertain origin: cf. Dan. balder noise, clatter, and E. dash; hence, perhaps, unmeaning noise, then hodgepodge, mixture; or W. baldorduss a prattling, baldordd, baldorddi, to prattle.] 1. A worthless mixture, especially of liquors.

Indeed beer, by a mixture of wine, hath lost both name and nature, and is called balderdash.

Taylor (Drink and Welcome).

Senseless jargon; ribaldry; nonsense; trash.

BalderĬdash (?), v.t. To mix or adulterate, as liquors.
The wine merchants of Nice brew and balderdash, and even
mix it with pigeon's dung and quicklime.

Smollett.

Baldḯfaced· (?), a. Having a white face or a white mark on the face, as a stag.

Baldhead· ÿ(?), n. 1. A person whose head is bald.

2 Kings ii. 23.

(Zo"l.) A whiteÐheaded variety of pigeon.

Baldhead· ed, a. Having a bald head.

Baldly, adv. Nakedly; without reserve; inelegantly.

Baldness, n. The state or condition of being bald; as, baldness of the head; baldness of style.

This gives to their syntax a peculiar character of simplicity and baldness. W.D. Whitney.

Baldpate· (?), n. 1. A baldheaded person.

Shak.

(Zo"l.) The American widgeon (Anas Americana).

Baldpate· (?), Baldpat· ed (?), } a. Destitute of hair on the head; baldheaded.

Shak.

Baldrib· (?),n. A piece of pork cut lower down than the sparerib, and destitute of fat. [Eng.]

Southey.

Baldric (?), n. [OE. baudric, bawdrik, through OF. (cf. F. baudrier and LL. baldringus, baldrellus), from OHG. balderich, cf. balz, palz, akin to E. belt. See Belt, n.] A broad belt, sometimes richly ornamented, worn over one shoulder, across the breast, and under the opposite arm; less properly, any belt. [Also spelt bawdrick.]

A radiant baldric o'er his shoulder tied

Sustained the sword that glittered at his side.

Pope.

Baldwin (?), n. (Bot.) A kind of reddish, moderately acid, winter apple. [U.S.]

Bale (?), n. [OE. bale, OF. bale, F. balle, LL. bala, fr. OHG. balla, palla, pallo, G. ball, balle, ballen, ball round pack; cf. D. baal. Cf. Ball a round body.] A bundle or package of goods in a cloth cover, and corded for storage or transportation; also, a bundle of straw ? hay, etc., put up compactly for transportation.

Bale of dice, a pair of dice. [Obs.]

B. Jonson.

Bale, v.t. [imp. & p.p. Baled (?); p.pr. & vb.n. Baling.] To make up in a bale.

Goldsmith.

Bale, v.t. See Bail, v.t., to lade.

<— p. 114 —>

Bale (?), n. [AS. bealo, bealu, balu; akin to OS. ?alu, OHG. balo, Icel. b"l, Goth. balweins.] 1. Misery; ?alamity; misfortune; sorrow.

Let now your bliss be turned into bale.

Spenser.

Evil; an evil, pernicious influence; something causing great injury. [Now chiefly poetic]

Bal·eǐaric (?), a. [L. Balearicus, fr. Gr. ? the Balearic Islands.] Of or pertaining to the isles of Majorca, Minorca, Ivica, etc., in the Mediterranean Sea, off the coast of Valencia.

Balearic crane. (Zo"l.) See Crane.

Baǐleen (?), n. [F. baleine whale and whalibone, L. balaena a whale; cf. Gr. ?.] (Zo"l. & Com.) Plates or blades of ½whalebone,ͺ from two to twelve feet long, and sometimes a foot wide, which in certain whales (Bal'noidea) are attached side by side along the upper jaw, and form a fringelike sieve by which the food is retained in the mouth.

Balefire· (?), n. [AS. b?lj?r the fire of the ?uneral pile; b?l fire, flame (akin to Icel. b¾l, OSlav. b?l?, white, Gr. ? bright, white, Skr. bh¾la brightness) + f?r, E. fire.] A signal fire; an alarm fire.

Sweet Teviot! on thy silver tide
The glaring balefires blaze no more.

Sir W. Scott.

Baleful (?), a. [AS. bealoful. See Bale misery.] 1. Full of deadly or pernicious influence; destructive. ½Baleful enemies.ͺ

Shak.

Four infernal rivers that disgorge
Into the burning lake their baleful streams.

Milton.

Full of grief or sorrow; woeful; sad. [Archaic]

Balefulǐly, adv. In a baleful manner; perniciously.

Balefulǐness, n. The quality or state of being baleful.

ØBaliǐsa·ur (?), n. [Hind.] (Zo"l.) A badgerlike animal of India (Arcionyx collaris).

Balisǐter (?), n. [OF. balestre. See Ballista.] A crossbow. [Obs.]

Blount.

Balisǐtoid (?), a. (Zo"l.) Like a fish of the genus Balistes; of the family Balistid'. See Filefish.

ØBal·isǐtrariǐa (?), n. [LL.] (Anc. Fort.) A narrow opening, often cruciform, through which arrows might be discharged.

ØBaǐlize (?), n. [F. balise; cf. Sp. balisa.] A pole or a frame raised as a sea beacon or a landmark.

Balk (?), n. [AS. balca beam, ridge; akin to Icel. b¾lkr partition, bj¾lki beam, OS. balko, G. balken; cf. Gael. balc ridge of earth between two furrows. Cf. Balcony, Balk, v.i., 3d Bulk.] 1. A ridge of land left unplowed between furrows, or at the end of a field; a piece missed by the plow slipping aside.

Bad plowmen made balks of such ground.
Fuller.

A great beam, rafter, or timber; esp., the tieDbeam ?f a house. The loft above was called ½the balks.

Tubs hanging in the balks.
Chaucer.

(Mil.) One of the beams connecting the successive supports of a trestle bridge or bateau bridge.

A hindrance or disappointment; a check.

A balk to the confidence of the bold undertaker.
South.

A sudden and obstinate stop; a failure.

(Baseball) A deceptive gesture of the pitcher, as if to deliver the ball.

Balk line (Billiards), a line across a billiard table near one end, marking a limit within which the cue balls are placed in beginning a game; also, a line around the table, parallel to the sides, used in playing a particular game, called the balk line game.

Balk, v.t. [imp. & p.p. Balked (?); p.pr. & vb.n. Balking.] [From Balk a beam; orig. to put a balk or beam in one's way, in order to stop or hinder. Cf., for sense 2, AS. on balcan legan to lay in heaps.]

To leave or make balks in. [Obs.]

Gower.

To leave heaped up; to heap up in piles. [Obs.]

Ten thousand bold Scots, two and twenty knights,
Balk'd in their own blood did Sir Walter see.
Shak.

To omit, miss, or overlook by chance. [Obs.]

To miss intentionally; to avoid; to shun; to refuse; to let go by; to shirk. [Obs. or Obsolescent]

By reason of the contagion then in London, we balked the ?nns.
Evelyn.

Sick he is, and keeps his bed, and balks his meat.

Bp. Hall.
Nor doth he any creature balk,
But lays on all he meeteth.
Drayton.

To disappoint; to frustrate; to foil; to baffle; to ?hwart; as, to balk expectation.

They shall not balk my entrance.
Byron.
Balk, v.i. 1. To engage in contradiction; to be in opposition. [Obs.]
In strifeful terms with him to balk.
Spenser.

To stop abruptly and stand still obstinately; to jib; to stop short; to swerve; as, the horse balks.

µ This has been regarded as an Americanism, but it occurs in Spenser's ½Fa‰orie Queene, Book IV., 10, xxv.
Ne ever ought but of their true loves talkt,
Ne ever for rebuke or blame of any balkt.

Balk, v.i. [Prob. from D. balken to bray, bawl.] To indicate to fishermen, by shouts or signals from shore, the direction taken by the shoals of herring.

Balker (?), n. [See 2d Balk.] One who, or that which balks.

Balker (?), n. [See last Balk.] A person who stands on a rock or eminence to espy the shoals of herring, etc., and to give notice to the men in boats which way they pass; a conder; a huer.

Baleingïly, adv. In manner to balk or frustrate.

Balkish, a. Uneven; ridgy. [R.]
Holinshed.

Balky (?), a. Apt to balk; as, a balky horse.

Ball (?), n. [OE. bal, balle; akin to OHG. balla, palla, G. ball, Icel. b"llr, ball; cf. F. balle. Cf. 1st Bale, n., Pallmall.] 1. Any round or roundish body or mass; a sphere or globe; as, a ball of twine; a ball of snow.

A spherical body of any substance or size used to play with, as by throwing, knocking, kicking, etc.

A general name for games in which a ball is thrown, kicked, or knocked. See Baseball, and Football.

Any solid spherical, cylindrical, or conical projectile of lead or iron, to be discharged from a firearm; as, a cannon ball; a rif?e ball; Ð often used collectively; as, powder and ball. Spherical balls for the smaller firearms are commonly called bullets.

(Pirotechnics & Mil.) A flaming, roundish body shot into the air; a case filled with combustibles intended to burst and give light or set fire, or to produce smoke or stench; as, a fire ball; a stink ball.

(Print.) A leatherÐcovered cushion, fastened to a handle called a ballstock; Ð formerly used by printers for inking the form, but now superseded by the roller.

A roundish protuberant portion of some part of the body; as, the ball of the thumb; the ball of the foot.

(Far.) A large pill, a form in which medicine is commonly given to horses; a bolus.

White.

The globe or earth.

Pope.

Move round the dark terrestrial ball.

Addison.

Ball and socket joint, a joint in which a ball moves within a socket, so as to admit of motion in every direction within certain limits. Ð Ball bearings, a mechanical device for lessening the friction of axle bearings by means of small loose metal balls. Ð Ball cartridge, a cartridge containing a ball, as distinguished from a blank cartridge, containing only powder. Ð Ball cock, a faucet or valve which is opened or closed by the fall or rise of a ball floating in water at the end of a lever. Ð Ball gudgeon, a pivot of a spherical form, which permits lateral deflection of the arbor or shaft, while retaining the pivot in its socket. Knight. Ð Ball lever, the lever used in a ball cock. Ð Ball of the eye, the eye itself, as distinguished from its lids and socket; Ð formerly, the pupil of the eye. Ð Ball valve (Mach.), a contrivance by which a ball, placed in a circular cup with a hole in its bottom, operates as a valve. Ð Ball vein (Mining), a sort of iron ore, found in loose masses of a globular form, containing sparkling particles. Ð Three balls, or Three golden balls, a pawnbroker's sign or shop.

Syn.Ð See Globe.

Ball, v.i. [imp. & p.p. Balled (?); p.pr. & vb.n. Balling.] To gather balls which cling to the feet, as of damp snow or clay; to gather into balls; as, the horse balls; the snow balls.

Ball, v.t. 1. (Metal.) To heat in a furnace and form into balls for rolling.

To form or wind into a ball; as, to ball cotton.

Ball, n. [F. bal, fr. OF. baler to dance, fr. LL. ballare. Of uncertain origin; cf. Gr. ? to toss or throw, or ?, ?, to leap, bound, ? to dance, jump about; or cf. 1st Ball, n.] A social assembly for the purpose of dancing.

Ballad (?), n. [OE. balade, OF. balade, F. ballade, fr. Pr. ballada a dancing song, fr. ballare to dance; cf. It. ballata. See 2d Ball, n., and Ballet.] A popular kind of narrative poem, adapted for recitation or singing; as, the ballad of Chevy Chase; esp., a sentimental or romantic poem in short stanzas.

Ballad, v.i. To make or sing ballads. [Obs.]

Ballad, v.t. To make mention of in ballads. [Obs.]

Balïlade (?), n. [See Ballad, n.] A form of French versification, sometimes imitated in English, in which three or four rhymes recur through three stanzas of eight or ten lines each, the stanzas concluding with a refrain, and the whole poem with an envoy.

Balladǐer (?), n. A writer of ballads.

Ballad mon · ger (?). [See Monger.] A seller or maker of ballads; a poetaster.

Shak.

Balladǐry (?), n. [From Ballad, n.] Ballad poems; the subject or style of ballads. ½Base balladry is so beloved.„

Drayton.

Ballaǐhoo, Ballaǐhou } (?), n. A fastÐsailing schooner, used in the Bermudas and West Indies.

Ballaǐrag (?), v.i. [Corrupted fr. bullirag.] To bully; to threaten. [Low]

T. Warton.

Ballast (?), n. [D. ballast; akin to Dan. baglast, ballast, OSw. barlast, Sw. ballast. The first part is perh. the same word as E. bare, adj.; the second is last a burden, and hence the meaning a bare, or mere, load. See Bare, a., and Last load.] 1. (Naut.) Any heavy substance, as stone, iron, etc., put into the hold to sink a vessel in the water to such a depth as to prevent capsizing.

Any heavy matter put into the car of a balloon to give it steadiness.

Gravel, broken stone, etc., laid in the bed of a railroad to make it firm and solid.

The larger solids, as broken stone or gravel, used in making concrete.

Fig.: That which gives, or helps to maintain, uprightness, steadiness, and security.

It [piety] is the right ballast of prosperity.

Barrow.

Ballast engine, a steam engine used in excavating and for digging and raising stones and gravel for ballast. Ð Ship in ballast, a ship carring only ballast.

Ballast, v.t. [imp. & p.p. Ballasted; p.pr. & vb.n. Ballasting.] 1. To steady, as a vessel, by putting heavy substances in the hold.

To fill in, as the bed of a railroad, with gravel, stone, etc., in order to make it firm and solid.

To keep steady; to steady, morally.

'T is charity must ballast the heart.

Hammond.

Ballastǐage (?), n. (Law) A toll paid for the privilege of taking up ballast in a port or harbor.

Ballastǐing, n. That which is used for steadying anything; ballast.

Ballaǐtry (?), n. See Balladry. [Obs.]

Milton.

ØBallet · (?), n. [F., a dim. of bal dance. See 2d Ball, n.] 1. An artistic dance performed as a theatrical entertainment, or an interlude, by a number of persons, usually women. Sometimes, a scene accompanied by pantomime and dancing.

> The company of persons who perform the ballet.

> (Mus.) A light part song, or madrigal, with a fa la burden or chorus, Ð most common with the Elizabethan madrigal composers.

> (Her.) A bearing in coats of arms, representing one or more balls, which are denominated bezants, plates, etc., according to color.

Ball′flow · er (?), n. (Arch.) An ornament resembling a ball placed in a circular flower, the petals of which form a cup round it, Ð usually inserted in a hollow molding.

ØBal′listaÿ(?), n.; pl. Ballist?e (?). [L. ballista, balista, fr. Gr. ? to throw.] An ancient military engine, in the form of a crossbow, used for hurling large missiles.

Ballis′ter (?), n. [L. ballista. Cf. Balister.] A crossbow. [Obs.]

Bal′listic (?), a. 1. Of or pertaining to the ballista, or to the art of hurling stones or missile weapons by means of an engine.

> Pertaining to projection, or to a projectile.

Ballistic pendulum, an instrument consisting of a mass of wood or other material suspended as a pendulum, for measuring the force and velocity of projectiles by means of the arc through which their impact impels it.

Bal′listics (?), n. [Cf. F. balistique. See Ballista.] The science or art of hurling missile weapons by the use of an engine.

Whewell.

ØBalli′umÿ(?),n. [LL.] See Bailey.

Bal′loonÿ(?), n. [F. ballon, aug. of balle ball: cf. It. ballone. See 1st Ball, n., and cf. Pallone.] 1. A bag made of silk or other light material, and filled with hydrogen gas or heated air, so as to rise and float in the atmosphere; especially, one with a car attached for a‰rial navigation.

> (Arch.) A ball or globe on the top of a pillar, church, etc., as at St. Paul's, in London. [R.]

> (Chem.) A round vessel, usually with a short neck, to hold or receive whatever is distilled; a glass vessel of a spherical form.

> (Pyrotechnics) A bomb or shell. [Obs.]

> A game played with a large inf?ated ball. [Obs.]

> (Engraving) The outline inclosing words represented as coming from the mouth of a pictured figure.

Air balloon, a balloon for a‰rial navigation. Ð Balloon frame (Carp.), a house frame constructed altogether of small timber. Ð Balloon net, a variety of woven lace in which the weft threads are twisted in a peculiar manner around the warp.

Bal'loon, v.t. To take up in, or as if in, a balloon.

Bal'loon, v.i. 1. To go up or voyage in a balloon.

To expand, or puff out, like a balloon.

Bal'looned (?),a. Swelled out like a balloon.

Bal'looner (?), n. One who goes up in a balloon; an a%oronaut.

Bal'loon fish · (?). (Zo"l.) A fish of the genus Diodon or the genus Tetraodon, having the power of distending its body by taking air or water into its dilatable esophagus. See Globefish, and Bur fish.

Bal'looning, n. 1. The art or practice of managing balloons or voyaging in them.

(Stock Exchange) The process of temporarily raising the value of a stock, as by fictitious sales. [U.S.]

Bal'looning spider (?). (Zo"l.) A spider which has the habit of rising into the air. Many kinds (esp. species of Lycosa) do this while young by ejecting threads of silk until the force of the wind upon them carries the spider aloft.

Bal'loonist, n. An a%oronaut.

Bal'loonryÿ(?), n. The art or practice of ascending in a balloon; a%oronautics.

Ballot (?), n. [F. ballotte, fr. It. ballotta. See Ball round body.]

Originally, a ball used for secret voting. Hence: Any printed or written ticket used in voting.

The act of voting by balls or written or printed ballots or tickets; the system of voting secretly by balls or by tickets.

The insufficiency of the ballot.
Dickens.

<— p. 115 —>

The whole number of votes cast at an election, or in a given territory or electoral district.

Ballot box, a box for receiving ballots.

Ballot (?), v.i. [imp. & p.p. Balloted; p.pr. & vb. n. Balloting.] [F. ballotter to toss, to ballot, or It. ballottare. See Ballot, n.] To vote or decide by ballot; as, to ballot for a candidate.

Ballot, v.t. To vote for or in opposition to.

None of the competitors arriving to a sufficient number of balls, they fell to ballot some others.

Sir H. Wotton.

Balloïtade · (?), n. [F. ballottade, fr. ballotter to toss. See Ballot, v.i.] (Man.) A leap of a horse, as between two pillars, or upon a straight line, so that when his four feet are in the air, he shows only the shoes of his hind feet, without jerking out.

Bal·loïtation (?), n. Voting by ballot. [Obs.]
Sir H. Wotton.
Ballotïer (?), n. One who votes by ballot.
Balloïtin (?),n. [F.] An officer who has charge of a ballot box. [Obs.]
Harrington.
Ballow (?),n. A cudgel. [Obs.]
Shak.
Ballproof· (?), a. Incapable of being penetrated by balls from firearms.
Ballroom· (?), n. A room for balls or dancing.
Balm (?), n. [OE. baume, OF. bausme, basme, F. baume, L. balsamum balsam, from Gr. ?; perhaps of Semitic origin; cf. Heb. b¾s¾m. Cf. Balsam.]

(Bot.) An aromatic plant of the genus Melissa.

The resinous and aromatic exudation of certain trees or shrubs.

Dryden.

Any fragrant ointment.

Shak.

Anything that heals or that mitigates pain. ½Balm for each ill.‚

Mrs. Hemans.
Balm cricket (Zo"l.), the European cicada. Tennyson. Ð Balm of Gilead (Bot.), a small evergreen African and Asiatic tree of the terebinthine family (Balsamodendron Gileadense). Its leaves yield, when bruised, a strong aromatic scent; and from this tree is obtained the balm of Gilead of the shops, or balsam of Mecca. This has a yellowish or greenish color, a warm, bitterish, aromatic taste, and a fragrant smell. It is valued as an unguent and cosmetic by the Turks. The fragrant herb Dracocephalum Canariense is familiarly called balm of Gilead, and so are the American trees, Populus balsamifera, variety candicans (balsam poplar), and Abies balsamea (balsam fir).

Balm, v.i. To anoint with balm, or with anything medicinal. Hence: To soothe; to mitigate. [Archaic]
Shak.
Balmiïfy (?), v. t. [Balm + Ðfy.] To render balmy. [Obs.]
Cheyne.
Balmiïly, adv. In a balmy manner.
Coleridge.
Balïmoral (?), n. [From Balmoral Castle, in Aberdeenshire, Scotland.] 1. A long woolen petticoat, worn immediately under the dress.

A kind of stout walking shoe, laced in front.

A man who uses his balmorals to tread on your toes.
George Eliot.

Balmy (?), a. 1. Having the qualities of balm; odoriferous; aromatic; assuaging; soothing; refreshing; mild. ½The balmy breeze.

Tickell.

Tired nature's sweet restorer, balmy sleep !
Young.

Producing balm. ½The balmy tree.

Pope.

Syn. Ð Fragrant; sweetÐscented; odorous; spicy.

Balneïalÿ(?), a. [L. balneum bath.] Of or pertaining to a bath.
Howell.

Balneïaïry (?), n. [L. balnearium, fr. balneum bath.] A bathing room.
Sir T. Browne.

Bal·neïation (?), n. [LL. balneare to bathe, fr. L. balneum bath.] The act of bathing. [R.]

Balneïaïtoïry (?), a. [L. balneatorius.] Belonging to a bath. [Obs.]

Bal·neïograïphy (?), n. [L. balneum bath + Ðgraphy.] A description of baths.

Bal·neïoloïgy (?), n. [L. balneum bath + Ðlogy.] A treatise on baths; the science of bathing.

Bal·neïoïtheraïpy (?), n. [L. balneum bath + Gr. ? to heal.] The treatment of disease by baths.

Baloïtade· (?), n. See Ballotade.

ØBalsa (?), n. [Sp. or Pg. balsa.] (Naut.) A raft or float, used principally on the Pacific coast of South America.

Balsam (?), n. [L. balsamum the balsam tree or its resin, Gr. ?. See Balm, n.] 1. A resin containing more or less of an essential o? volatile oil.

µ The balsams are aromatic resinous substances, flowing spontaneously r by incision from certain plants. A great variety of substances pass under this name, but the term is now usually restricted to resins which, in addition to a volatile oil, contain benzoic and cinnamic acid. Among the true balsams are the balm of Gilead, and the balsams of copaiba, Peru, and Tolu. There are also many pharmaceutical preparations and resinous substances, possessed of a balsamic smell, to which the name balsam has been given.

(Bot.) (a) A species of tree (Abies balsamea). (b) An annual garden plant (Impatiens balsamina) with beautiful flowers; balsamine.

Anything that heals, soothes, or restores.

Was not the people's blessing a balsam to thy blood?
Tennyson.

Balsam apple (Bot.), an East Indian plant (Momordica balsamina), of the gourd family, with red or orangeÐyellow cucumberÐshaped fruit of the size of a walnut, used as a vulnerary, and in liniments and poultices. ÐBalsam fir (Bot.), the American coniferous tree, Abies balsamea, from which the useful Canada balsam is derived. Ð Balsam of copaiba. See Copaiba. Ð Balsam of Mecca, balm of Gilead. Ð Balsam of Peru, a reddish brown, syrupy balsam, obtained from a Central American tree (Myroxylon Pereir' and used as a stomachic and expectorant, and in the treatment of ulcers, etc. It was long supposed to be a product of Peru. Ð Balsam of Tolu, a reddish or yellowish brown semisolid or solid balsam, obtained from a South American tree (Myxoxylon toluiferum.). It is highly fragrant, and is used as a stomachic and expectorant. Ð Balsam tree, any tree from which balsam is obtained, esp. the Abies balsamea. Ð Canada balsam, Balsam of fir, Canada turpentine, a yellowish, viscid liquid, which, by time and exposure, becomes a transparent solid mass. It is obtained from the balm of Gilead (or balsam) fir (Abies balsamea) by breaking the vesicles upon the trunk and branches. See Balm.

Balsam (?), v.t. To treat or anoint with balsam; to relieve, as with balsam; to render balsamic.

Bal · samÏationÿ(?), n. 1. The act of imparting balsamic properties.

The art or process of embalming.

BalÏsamicÿ(?), BalÏsamicÏalÿ(?), } a. [Cf. F. balsamique.] Having the qualities of balsam; containing, or resembling, balsam; soft; mitigative; soothing; restorative.

Bal · samÏiferÏous (?), a. [Balsam + Ðferous.] Producing balsam.

BalsamÏineÿ(?), n. [Cf. F. balsamine, fr. Gr. ? balsam plant.] (Bot.) The Impatiens balsamina, or garden balsam.

BalsamÏous (?), a. Having the quality of balsam; containing balsam. ½A balsamous substance.

Sterne.

Balterÿ(?), v. t. [Etymol. uncertain. Cf. Bloodboltered.] To stick together.[Obs.]

Holland.

Baltic (?), a. [NL. mare Balticum, fr. L. balteus belt, from certain straits or channels surrounding its isles, called belts. See Belt.] Of or pertaining to the sea which separates Norway and Sweden from Jutland, Denmark, and Germany; situated on the Baltic Sea.

BaltiÏmore bird · (?). BaltiÏmore oriÏoleÿ(?). } (Zo"l.) A common American bird (Icterus galbula), named after Lord Baltimore, because its colors (black and orange red) are like those of his coat of arms; Ð called also golden robin.

BalusÏter (?), n. [F. balustre, It. balaustro, fr. L. balaustium the flower of the wild pomegranate, fr. Gr. ?; Ð so named from the similarity of form.]

(Arch.) A row of balusters topped by a rail, serving as an open parapet, as along the edge of a balcony, terrace, bridge, staircase, or the eaves of a building.

Bam (?), n. [Prob. a contr. of bamboozle.] An imposition; a cheat; a hoax.

Garrick.

To relieve the tedium? he kept plying them with all manner of bams.

Prof. Wilson.

Bam, v.t. To cheat; to wheedle. [Slang]

Foote.

ØBamĭbinoÿ(?), n. [It., a little boy, fr. bambo silly; cf. Gr. ?, ?, to chatter.] A child or baby; esp., a representation in art of the infant Christ wrapped in swaddling clothes.

Bamĭboc · ciĭadeÿ(?), n. [It. bambocciata, fr. Bamboccio a nickname of Peter Van Laer, a Dutch genre painter; properly, a child, simpleton, puppet, fr. bambo silly.] (Paint.) A representation of a grotesque scene from common or rustic life.

Bamĭboo (?), n. [Malay bambu, mambu.] (Bot.) A plant of the family of grasses, and genus Bambusa, growing in tropical countries.

μ The most useful species is Bambusa arundinacea, which has a woody, hollow, round, straight, jointed stem, and grows to the height of forty feet and upward. The flowers grow in large panicles, from the joints of the stalk, placed three in a parcel, close to their receptacles. Old stalks grow to five or six inches in diameter, and are so hard and durable as to be used for building, and for all sorts of furniture, for water pipes, and for poles to support palanquins. The smaller stalks are used for walking sticks, flutes, etc.

Bamĭboo, v.t. To flog with the bamboo.

Bamĭboozle (?), v.t. [Imp. & p.p. Bamboozled (?); p.pr. & vb.n. Bamboozlingÿ(?).] [Said to be of Gipsy origin.] To deceive by trickery; to cajole by confusing the senses; to hoax; to mystify; to humbug. [Colloq.]

Addison.

What oriental tomfoolery is bamboozling you?

J.H.Newman.

Bamĭboozler (?), n. A swindler; one who deceives by trickery. [Colloq.]

Arbuthnot.

ØBan (?), n. [AS. bann command, edict; akin to D. ban, Icel. bann, Dan. band, OHG. ban, G. bann, a public proclamation, as of interdiction or excommunication, Gr. ? to say, L. fari to speak, Skr. bhan to speak; cf. F. ban, LL. bannum, of G. origin. ?. Cf. Abandon, Fame.] 1. A public proclamation or edict; a public order or notice, mandatory or prohibitory; a summons by public proclamation.

(Feudal & Mil.) A calling together of the king's (esp. the French king's) vassals for military service; also, the body of vassals thus assembled or summoned. In present usage, in France and Prussia, the most effective part of the population liable to military duty and not in the standing army.

pl. Notice of a proposed marriage, proclaimed in church. See Banns (the common spelling in this sense).

An interdiction, prohibition, or proscription. ½Under ban to touch.

Milton.

A curse or anathema. ½Hecate's ban.

Shak.

A pecuniary mulct or penalty laid upon a delinquent for offending against a ban; as, a mulct paid to a bishop by one guilty of sacrilege or other crimes.

Ban of the empire (German Hist.), an imperial interdict by which political rights and privileges, as those of a prince, city, or district, were taken away.

Ban, v.t. [imp. & p.p. Banned (?); p. pr. & vb. n. Banning.] [OE. bannen, bannien, to summon, curse, AS. bannan to summon; akin to Dan. bande, forbande, to curse, Sw. banna to revile, bannas to curse. See Ban an edict, and cf. Banish.] 1. To curse; to invoke evil upon.

Sir W. Scott.

To forbid; to interdict.

Byron.

Ban, v.i. To curse; to swear. [Obs.]

Spenser.

Ban, n. [Serv. ban; cf. Russ. & Pol. pan a master? lord, Per. ban.] An ancient title of the warden of the eastern marches of Hungary; now, a title of the viceroy of Croatia and Slavonia.

Banalÿ(?), a. [F., fr. ban an ordinance.] Commonplace; trivial; hackneyed; trite.

Ba͏̈nalii̇ty (?), n.; pl. Banalities (?). [F. banalit,. See Banal.] Something commonplace, hackneyed, or trivial; the commonplace, in speech.

The highest things were thus brought down to the banalities of discourse. J. Morley.

Ba͏̈nana (?), n. [Sp. banana, name of the fruit.] (Bot.) A perennial herbaceous plant of almost treelike size (Musa sapientum); also, its edible fruit. See Musa.

µ The banana has a soft, herbaceous stalk, with leaves of great length and breadth. The flowers grow in bunches, covered with a sheath of a green or purple color; the fruit is five or six inches long, and over an inch in diameter; the pulp is soft, and of a luscious taste, and is eaten either raw or cooked. This plant is a native of tropical countries, and furnishes an important article of food.

Banana bird (Zo"l.), a small American bird (Icterus leucopteryx), which feeds on the banana. Ð Banana quit (Zo"l.), a small bird of tropical America, of the genus Certhiola, allied to the creepers.

Banat (?), n. [Cf. F. & G. banat. See Ban a warden.] The territory governed by a ban.

Banc (?), ØBancus (?), Bank (?), } n. [OF. banc, LL. bancus. See Bank, n.] A bench; a high seat, or seat of distinction or judgment; a tribunal or court.

In banc, In banco (the ablative of bancus), In bank, in full court, or with full judicial authority; as, sittings in banc (distinguished from sittings at nini prius).

ØBanco (?), n. [It. See Bank.] A bank, especially that of Venice.

μ This term is used in some parts of Europe to indicate bank money, as distinguished from the current money, when this last has become depreciated.

Bandÿ(?), n. [OE. band, bond, Icel. band; akin to G., Sw., & D. band, OHG. bant, Goth. banti, Skr. bandha a binding, bandh to bind, for bhanda, bhandh, also to E. bend, bind. In sense 7, at least, it is fr. F. bande, from OHG. bant. ? See Bind, v.t., and cf. Bend, Bond, 1st Bandy.] 1. A fillet, strap, or any narrow ligament with which a thing is encircled, or fastened, or by which a number of things are tied, bound together, or confined; a fetter.

Every one's bands were loosed.
Acis xvi 26.

(Arch.) (a) A continuous tablet, stripe, or series of ornaments, as of carved foliage, of color, or of brickwork, etc. (b) In Gothic architecture, the molding, or suite of moldings, which encircles the pillars and small shafts.

That which serves as the means of union or connection between persons; a tie. ½To join in Hymen's bands.

Shak.

A linen collar or ruff worn in the 16th and 17th centuries.

pl. Two strips of linen hanging from the neck in front as part of a clerical, legal, or academic dress.

A narrow strip of cloth or other material on any article of dress, to bind, strengthen, ornament, or complete it. ½Band and gusset and seam.

Hood.
<— p. 116 —>

A company of persons united in any common design, especially a body of armed men. Troops of horsemen with his bands of foot. Shak.

A number of musicians who play together upon portable musical instruments, especially those making a loud sound, as certain wind instruments (trumpets, clarinets, etc.), and drums, or cymbals.

(Bot.) A space between elevated lines or ribs, as of the fruits of umbelliferous plants.

(Zo"l.) A stripe, streak, or other mark transverse to the axis of the body.

(Mech.) A belt or strap.

A bond [Obs.] ½Thy oath and band., Shak.

Pledge; security. [Obs.] Spenser. Band saw, a saw in the form of an endless steel belt, with teeth on one edge, running over wheels. Band (?), v.t. [imp. & p.p. Banded; p.pr. & vb.n. Banding.] 1. To bind or tie with a band.

To mark with a band.

To unite in a troop, company, or confederacy. ½Banded against his throne., Milton. Banded architrave, pier, shaft, etc. (Arch.), an architrave, pier, etc., of which the regular profile is interrupted by blocks or projections crossing it at right angles. Band, v.i. To confederate for some common purpose; to unite; to conspire together. Certain of the Jews banded together. Acts xxiii. 12. Band, v.t. To bandy; to drive away. [Obs.] Band, imp. of Bind. [Obs.] Bandage (?), n. [F. bandage, fr. bande. See Band.] 1. A fillet or strip of woven material, used in dressing and binding up wounds, etc.

Something resembling a bandage; that which is bound over or round something to cover, strengthen, or compress it; a ligature. Zeal too had a place among the rest, with a bandage over her eyes. Addison. Bandage, v.t. [imp. & p.p. Bandaged (?); p.pr. & vb.n. Bandaging (?).] To bind, dress, or cover, with a bandage; as, to bandage the eyes. ØBanÏdala (?), n. A fabric made in Manilla from the older leaf sheaths of the abaca (Musa textilis). BanÏdanna, BanÏdana } (?), n. [Hind. b¾ndhn? a mode of dyeing in which the cloth is tied in different places so as to prevent the parts tied from receiving the dye. Cf. Band, n.] 1. A species of silk or cotton handkerchief, having a uniformly dyed ground, usually of red or blue, with white or yellow figures of a circular, lozenge, or other simple form.

A style of calico printing, in which white or bright spots are produced upon cloth previously dyed of a uniform red or dark color, by discharging portions of the color by chemical means, while the rest of the cloth is under pressure. Ure. Bandbox · ÿ(?), n. A light box of pasteboard or thin wood, usually cylindrical, for holding ruffs (the bands of the 17th century), collars, caps, bonnets, etc. ØBandeauÿ(?), n.; pl. Bandeauxÿ(?). [F.] A narrow band or fillet; a part of a headÐdress. Around the edge of this cap was a stiff bandeau of leather. Sir W.Scott. BandeÏlet (?), Bandletÿ(?), n. [F. bandelette, dim. of bande. See Band, n., and ch. Bendlet.] (Arch.) A small band or fillet; any little band or flat molding, compassing a column, like a ring. Gwilt. Bander (?), n. One banded with others. [R.] BandeÎrole (?), Bandrolÿ(?), n. [F. banderole, dim. of bandiŠre, banniŠre, banner; cf. It. banderuola a little banner. See Banner.] A little banner, flag, or streamer. [Written also bannerol.] From the extremity of which fluttered a small banderole or streamer bearing a cross. Sir W. Scott. Band fish · (?). (Zo"l.) A small red fish of the genus Cepola; the ribbon fish. BandÏcoot (?), n. [A corruption of the native name.] (Zo"l.) (a) A species of very large rat (Mus giganteus), found in India and Ceylon. It does much injury to rice fields and gardens. (b) A ratlike marsupial animal (genus Perameles) of several species, found in Australia and Tasmania. Banding plane · (?). A plane used for cutting out grooves and inlaying strings and bands in straight and circular work. Bandit (?), n.; pl.Bandits (?), or Banditti (?). [It. bandito outlaw, p.p. of bandire to proclaim, to banish, to proscribe, LL. bandire, bannire. See Ban an edict, and cf. Banish.] An outlaw; a brigand. No savage fierce, bandit, or mountaineer. Milton. µ The plural banditti was formerly used as a collective noun. Deerstealers are ever a desperate banditti. Sir W. Scott. Bandle (?),n. [Ir. bannlamh cubit, fr. bann a measure + lamh hand, arm.] An Irish measure of two feet in length. Bandlet (?),n. Same as Bandelet. Bandmas · ter (?), n. The conductor of a musical band. Bandog · (?),n. [Band + dog, i.e., bound dog.] A mastiff or other large and fierce dog, usually kept chained or tied up. The keeper entered leading his bandog, a large bloodhound, tied in a leam, or band, from which he takes his name. Sir W. Scott. Ban · doÏleer, Ban · doÏlier (?), n. [F. bandouliŠre (cf.It. bandoliera, Sp.bandolera), fr.F. bande band, Sp.&It. banda. See Band, n.] 1. A broad leather belt formerly worn by soldiers over the right shoulder and across the breast under the left arm. Originally it was used for supporting the musket and twelve cases for charges, but later only as a cartridge belt.

One of the leather or wooden cases in which the charges of powder were carried. [Obs.] Bandoĺline (?), n. [Perh. allied to band.] A glutinous pomatum for the fair. Bandon (?), n. [OF. bandon. See Abandon.] Disposal; control; license. [Obs.] Rom. of R. Bandore (?), n. [Sp. bandurria, fr. L. pandura, pandurium, a musical instrument of three strings, fr. Gr. ?. Cf. Pandore, Banjo, Mandolin.] A musical stringed instrument, similar in form to a guitar; a pandore. Bandrol (?), n. Same as Banderole. Bandy (?), n. [Telugu bandi.] A carriage or cart used in India, esp. one drawn by bullocks. Bandy, n. pl. Bandies (?). [Cf. F. band,, p.p. of bander to bind, to bend (a bow), to bandy, fr. bande. See Band, n.] 1. A club bent at the lower part for striking a ball at play; a hockey stick. Johnson.

The game played with such a club; hockey; shinney; bandy ball. Bandy, v.t. [imp. & p.p. Bandied (?); p.pr. & vb.n. Bandying.] 1. To beat to and fro, as a ball in playing at bandy. Like tennis balls bandied and struck upon us ... by rackets from without. Cudworth.

To give and receive reciprocally; to exchange. ½To bandy hasty words., Shak.

To toss about, as from man to man; to agitate. Let not obvious and known truth be bandied about in a disputation. I. Watts. Bandy, v.i. To content, as at some game in which each strives to drive the ball his own way. Fit to bandy with thy lawless sons. Shak. Bandy, a. Bent; crooked; curved laterally, esp. with the convex side outward; as, a bandy leg. BandyÐlegged · (?), a. Having crooked legs. Bane (?), n. [OE. bane destruction, AS. bana murderer; akin to Icel. bani death, murderer, OHG. bana murder, bano murderer, ? murder, OIr. bath death, benim I strike. ?.] 1. That which destroys life, esp. poison of a deadly quality. [Obs. except in combination, as in ratsbane, henbane, etc.]

Destruction; death. [Obs.] The cup of deception spiced and tempered to their bane. Milton.

Any cause of ruin, or lasting injury; harm; woe. Money, thou bane of bliss, and source of woe. Herbert.

A disease in sheep, commonly termed the rot. Syn. Ð Poison; ruin; destruction; injury; pest. Bane, v.t. To be the bane of; to ruin. [Obs.] Fuller. Baneber · ry (?), n.(Bot.) A genus (Act'a) of plants, of the order Ranunculace', native in the north temperate zone. The red or white berries are poisonous. Baneful (?), a. Having poisonous qualities; deadly; destructive; injurious; noxious; pernicious. ½Baneful hemlock., Garth. ½Baneful wrath., ? Chapman. ?ÐBanefullly, adv.ÐBanefullness, n. Banewort (?), n. (Bot.) Deadly nightshade. Bang (?), v.t. [imp. & p.p. Banged; p.pr. & vb.n. Banging.] [Icel. banga to hammer; akin to Dan. banke to beat, Sw.b†ngas to be impetuous, G. bengel club, clapper of a bell.] 1. To beat, as with a club or cudgel; to treat with violence; to handle roughly. The desperate tempest hath so banged the Turks. Shak.

To beat or thump, or to cause (something) to hit or strike against another object, in such a way as to make a loud noise; as, to bang a drum or a piano; to bang a door (against the doorpost or casing) in shutting it. Bang, v.i. To make a loud noise, as if with a blow or succession of blows; as, the window blind banged and waked me; he was banging on the piano. Bang, n. 1. A blow as with a club; a heavy blow. Many a stiff thwack, many a bang. Hudibras.

The sound produced by a sudden concussion. Bang, v.t. To cut squarely across, as the tail of a hors, or the forelock of human beings; to cut (the hair). His hair banged even with his eyebrows. The Century Mag. Bang, n. The short, front hair combed down over the forehead, esp. when cut squarely across; a false front of hair similarly worn. His hair cut in front like a young lady's bang. W. D. Howells. Bang, Bangue (?), n. See Bhang. Banging, a. Huge; great in size. [Colloq.] Forby. Bangle (?), v.t. [From 1st

Bang.] To waste by little and little; to fritter away. [Obs.] Bangle, n. [Hind. bangrÆ bracelet, bangle.] An ornamental circlet, of glass, gold, silver, or other material, worn by women in India and Africa, and in some other countries, upon the wrist or ankle; a ring bracelet. Bangle ear, a loose hanging ear of a horse, like that of a spaniel. Banian (?),n. [Skr. banij merchant. The tree was so named by the English, because used as a market place by the merchants.] 1. A Hindoo trader, merchant, cashier, or money changer. [Written also banyan.]

A man's loose gown, like that worn by the Banians.

(Bot.) The Indian fig. See Banyan. Banian days (Naut.), days in which the sailors have no flesh meat served out to them. This use seems to be borrowed from the Banians or Banya race, who eat no flesh. Banish (?), v.t. [imp. & p.p. Banished(?); p.pr. & vb.n. Banishing.] [OF. banir, F. bannir, LL. bannire, fr. OHG. bannan to summon, fr. ban ban. See Ban an edict, and Finish, v.t.] 1. To condemn to exile, or compel to leave one's country, by authority of the ruling power. ½We banish you our territories.„ Shak.

To drive out, as from a home or familiar place; Đ used with from and out of. How the ancient Celtic tongue came to be banished from the Low Countries in Scotland. Blair.

To drive away; to compel to depart; to dispel. ½Banish all offense.„ Shak. Syn. Đ To Banish, Exile, Expel. The idea of a coercive removal from a place is common to these terms. A man is banished when he is forced by the government of a country (be he a foreigner or a native) to leave its borders. A man is exiled when he is driven into banishment from his native country and home. Thus to exile is to banish, but to banish is not always to exile. To expel is to eject or banish, summarily or authoritatively, and usually under circumstances of disgrace; as, to expel from a college; expelled from decent society. Banishĭer (?), n. One who banishes. Banishĭment (?), n. [Cf. F. bannissement.] The act of banishing, or the state of being banished. He secured himself by the banishment of his enemies. Johnson. Round the wide world in banishment we roam. Dryden. Syn. Đ Expatriation; ostracism; expulsion; proscription; exile; outlawry. Banisĭter (?),n. [Formerly also banjore and banjer; corrupted from bandore, through negro slave pronunciation.] A stringed musical instrument having a head and neck like the guitar, and its body like a tambourine. It has five strings, and is played with the fingers and hands. Bank (?), n. [OE. banke; akin to E. bench, and prob. of Scand. origin.; cf. Icel. bakki. See Bench.] 1. A mound, pile, or ridge of earth, raised above the surrounding level; hence, anything shaped like a mound or ridge of earth; as, a bank of clouds; a bank of snow. They cast up a bank against the city. 2 Sam. xx. 15.

A steep acclivity, as the slope of a hill, or the side of a ravine.

The margin of a watercourse; the rising ground bordering a lake, river, or sea, or forming the edge of a cutting, or other hollow. Tiber trembled underneath her banks. Shak.

An elevation, or rising ground, under the sea; a shoal, shelf, or shallow; as, the banks of Newfoundland.

(Mining) (a) The face of the coal at which miner? are working. (b) A deposit of ore or coal, worked by excavations above water level. (c) The ground at the top of a shaft; as, ores are brought to bank. Bank beaver (Zo"l.), the otter. [Local, U.S.] Đ Bank swallow, a small American and European swallow (Clivicola riparia) that nests in a hole which it excavates in a bank. Bank, v.t. [imp. & p.p. Banked(?); p.pr. & vb.n. Banking.] 1. To raise a mound or dike about; to inclose, defend, or fortify with a bank; to embank. ½Banked well with earth.„ Holland.

To heap or pile up; as, to bank sand.

To pass by the banks of. [Obs.] Shak. To bank a fire, To bank up a fire, to cover the coals or embers with ashes or cinders, thus keeping the fire low but alive. Bank, n. [Prob. fr. F. banc. Of German origin, and akin to E. bench. See Bench.] 1. A bench, as for rowers in a galley; also, a tier of oars. Placed on their banks, the lusty Trojan sweep Neptune's smooth face, and cleave the yielding deep. Waller.

(Law) (a) The bench or seat upon which the judges sit. (b) The regular term of a court of law, or the full court sitting to hear arguments upon questions of law, as distinguished from a sitting at Nisi Prius, or a court held for jury trials. See Banc. Burrill.

(Printing) A sort of table used by printers.

(Music) A bench, or row of keys belonging to a keyboard, as in an organ. Knight. Bank, n. [F. banque, It. banca, orig. bench, table, counter, of German origin, and akin to E. bench; cf. G. bank bench, OHG. banch. See Bench, and cf. Banco, Beach.] 1. An establishment for the custody, loan, exchange, or issue, of money, and for facilitating the transmission of funds by drafts or bills of exchange; an institution incorporated for performing one or more of such functions, or the stockholders (or their representatives, the directors), acting in their corporate capacity.

The building or office used for banking purposes.

A fund from deposits or contributions, to be used in transacting business; a joint stock or capital. [Obs.] Let it be no bank or common stock, but every man be master of his own money. Bacon.

(Gaming) The sum of money or the checks which the dealer or banker has as a fund, from which to draw his stakes and pay his losses.

In certain games, as dominos, a fund of pieces from which the players are allowed to draw. Bank credit, a credit by which a person who has give? the required security to a bank has liberty to draw to ? certain extent agreed upon. Ð Bank of deposit, a bank which receives money for safe keeping. Ð Bank of issue, a bank which issues its own notes payable to bearer. Bank, v.t. To deposit in a bank. Bank, v.i. 1. To keep a bank; to carry on the business of a banker.

<— p. 117 —>

To deposit money in a bank; to have an account with a banker. Bankaïble (?), a. Receivable at a bank. Bank bill · (?). 1. In America (and formerly in England), a promissory note of a bank payable to the bearer on demand, and used as currency; a bank note.

In England, a note, or a bill of exchange, of a bank, payable to order, and usually at some future specified time. Such bills are negotiable, but form, in the strict sense of the term, no part of the currency. Bank book · (?). A book kept by a depositor, in which an officer of a bank enters the debits and credits of the depositor's account with the bank. Banker (?), n.[See the nouns Bank and the verbs derived from them.] 1. One who conducts the business of banking; one who, individually, or as a member of a company, keeps an establishment for the deposit or loan of money, or for traffic in money, bills of exchange, etc.

A money changer. [Obs.]

The dealer, or one who keeps the bank in a gambling house.

A vessel employed in the cod fishery on the banks of Newfoundland. Grabb. J.Q. Adams.

A ditcher; a drain digger. [Prov. Eng.]

The stone bench on which masons cut or square their work. Weale. Bankerĭess (?), n. A female banker. Thackeray. Banking, n. The business of a bank or of a banker. Banking house, an establishment or office in which, or a firm by whom, banking is done. Bank note · (?). 1. A promissory note issued by a bank or banking company, payable to bearer on demand. μ In the United States popularly called a bank bill.

Formerly, a promissory note made by a banker, or banking company, payable to a specified person at a fixed date; a bank bill. See Bank bill, 2. [Obs.]

A promissory note payable at a bank. Bankruptÿ(?), n. [F. banqueroute, fr. It. bancarotta bankruptcy; banca bank (fr. OHG. banch, G. bank, bench) + rotta broken, fr. L. ruptus, p.p. of rumpere to break. At Florence, it is said, the bankrupt had his bench (i.e., money table) broken. See 1st Bank, and Rupture, n.] 1. (Old Eng. Low) A trader who secretes himself, or does certain other acts tending to defraud his creditors. Blackstone.

A trader who becomes unable to pay his debts; an insolvent trader; popularly, any person who is unable to pay his debts; an insolvent person. M?Culloch.

(Law) A person who, in accordance with the terms of a law relating to bankruptcy, has been judicially declared to be unable to meet his liabilities. µ In England, until the year 1861 none but a ½trader‚ could be made a bankrupt; a nonÐtrader failing to meet his liabilities being an ½insolvent‚. But this distinction was abolished by the Bankruptcy Act of 1861. The laws of 1841 and 1867 of the United States relating to bankruptcy applied this designation bankrupt to others besides those engaged in trade. Bankrupt, a. 1. Being a bankrupt or in a condition of bankruptcy; unable to pay, or legally discharged from paying, one's debts; as, a bankrupt merchant.

Depleted of money; not having the means of meeting pecuniary liabilities; as, a bankrupt treasury.

Relating to bankrupts and bankruptcy.

Destitute of, or wholly wanting (something once possessed, or something one should possess). ½Bankrupt in gratitude.‚ Sheridan. Bankrupt law, a law by which the property of a person who is unable or unwilling to pay his debts may be taken and distributed to his creditors, and by which a person who has made a full surrender of his property, and is free from fraud, may be discharged from the legal obligation of his debts. See Insolvent, a. Bankrupt, v.t. [imp. & p. p. Bankrupted; p. pr. & vb.n. Bankrupting.] To make bankrupt; to bring financial ruin upon; to impoverish. BankruptĬcy (?), n.; pl. Bankruptcies(?).

The state of being actually or legally bankrupt.

The act or process of becoming a bankrupt.

Complete loss; Ð followed by of. Bankside · (?), n. The slope of a bank, especially of the bank of a steam. BankĬsid · ed(?), a. (Naut.) Having sides inclining inwards, as a ship; Ð opposed to wallÐsided. Bank swallow (?). See under 1st Bank, n. ØBanliĭeue · (?), n. [F., fr. LL. bannum leucae, banleuca; bannum jurisdiction + leuca league.] The territory without the walls, but within the legal limits, of a town or city. Brande & C. Banner (?), n. [OE. banere, OF. baniere, F. banniŠre, bandiŠre, fr. LL. baniera, banderia, fr. bandum banner, fr. OHG. bant band, strip of cloth; cf. bindan to bind, Goth. bandwa, bandwo, a sign. See Band, n.] 1. A kind of flag attached to a spear or pike by a crosspiece, and used by a chief as his standard in battle. Hang out our banners on the outward walls. Shak.

A large piece of silk or other cloth, with a device or motto, extended on a crosspiece, and borne in a procession, or suspended in some conspicuous place.

Any flag or standard; as, the starÐspangled banner. Banner fish (Zo"l.), a large fish of the genus Histiophorus, of the Swordfish family, having a broad bannerlike dorsal fin; the sailfish. One species (H. Americanus) inhabits the North Atlantic. Bannered (?), a. Furnished with, or bearing, banners. ½A bannered host.‚ Milton. BannerĬet (?), n.[OE. baneret, OF. baneret, F. banneret; properly a dim. of OF. baniere. See Banner.]

Originally, a knight who led his vassals into the field under his own banner; Ð commonly used as a title of rank.

A title of rank, conferred for heroic deeds, and hence, an order of knighthood; also, the person bearing such title or rank. µ The usual mode of conferring the rank on the field of battle was by cutting or tearing off the point of the pennon or pointed flag on the spear of the candidate, thereby making it a banner.

A civil officer in some Swiss cantons.

A small banner. Shak. Bannerïol (?), n. A banderole; esp. a banner displayed at a funeral procession and set over the tomb. See Banderole. Banïnition (?), n. [LL. bannitio. See Banish.] The act of expulsion.[Obs.] Abp. Laud. Bannock (?), n. [Gael. bonnach.] A kind of cake or bread, in shape flat and roundish, commonly made of oatmeal or barley meal and baked on an iron plate, or griddle; Ð used in Scotland and the northern counties of England. Jamieson. Bannock fluke, the turbot. [Scot.] Banns (?), n. pl. [See Ban.] Notice of a proposed marriage, proclaimed in a church, or other place prescribed by law, in order that any person may object, if he knows of just cause why the marriage should not take place. Banquet (?), n. [F., a feast, prop. a dim. of banc bench; cf. It. banchetto, dim. of banco a bench, counter. See Bank a bench, and cf. Banquette.] 1. A feast; a sumptuous entertainment of eating and drinking; often, a complimentary or ceremonious feast, followed by speeches.

A dessert; a course of sweetmeats; a sweetmeat or sweetmeats. [Obs.] We'll dine in the great room, but let the music And banquet be prepared here. Massinger. Banquet,v.t. [imp. & p.p. Banqueted; p. pr. & vb.n. Banqueting.] To treat with a banquet or sumptuous entertainment of food; to feast. Just in time to banquet The illustrious company assembled there. Coleridge.

Banquet, v.i. 1. To regale one's self with good eating and drinking; to feast.
Were it a draught for Juno when she banquets,
I would not taste thy treasonous offer.
Milton.

To partake of a dessert after a feast. [Obs.]

Where they did both sup and banquet.
Cavendish.
Banquetïter (?), n. One who banquets; one who feasts or makes feasts.
Banïquette (?), n. [F. See Banquet, n.] 1. (Fort.) A raised way or foot bank, running along the inside of a parapet, on which musketeers stand to fire upon the enemy.

(Arch.) A narrow window seat; a raised shelf at the back or the top of a buffet or dresser.

Banshee, Banshie (?), n. [Gael. beanÐshith fairy; Gael. & Ir. bean woman + Gael. sith fairy.] A supernatural being supposed by the Irish and Scotch peasantry to warn a family of the speedy death of one of its members, by wailing or singing in a mournful voice under the windows of the house.

Banstic · kle (?), n. [OE. ban, bon, bone + stickle prickle, sting. See Bone, n., Stickleback.] (Zo"l.) A small fish, the threeÐspined stickleback.

Bantam (?), n. A variety of small barnyard fowl, with feathered legs, probably brought from Bantam, a district of Java.

Bantam work · . Carved and painted work in imitation of Japan ware.

ØBanteng (?), n. (Zo"l.) The wild ox of Java (Bibos Banteng).

Banter (?), v.t. [imp. & p.p. Bantered(?); p. pr. & vb.n. Bantering.] [Prob. corrupted fr. F. badiner to joke, or perh. fr. E. bandy to beat to and fro. See Badinage, and cf. Barter fr. OF. barater.]

1. To address playful goodÐnatured ridicule to, Ð the person addressed, or something pertaining to him, being the subject of the jesting; to rally; as, he bantered me about my credulity.

HagÐridden by my own fancy all night, and then bantered on
my haggard looks the next day.
W. Irving.

To jest about; to ridicule in speaking of, as some trait, habit, characteristic, and the like. [Archaic]

If they banter your regularity, order, and love of study, banter in return their neglect of them.
Chatham.

To delude or trick, Ð esp. by way of jest. [Obs.]

We diverted ourselves with bantering several poor scholars
with hopes of being at least his lordship's chaplain.
De Foe.

To challenge or defy to a match. [Colloq. Southern and Western U.S.]

Banter, n. The act of bantering; joking or jesting; humorous or goodÐhumored raillery; pleasantry.

Part banter, part affection.
Tennyson.

Banterïer (?), n. One who banters or rallies.

Bantinglism (?), n. A method of reducing corpulence by avoiding food containing much farinaceous, saccharine, or oily matter; Ð so called from William Banting of London.

Bantling (?), n. [Prob. for bandling, from band, and meaning a child wrapped in swaddling bands; or cf. G. b„ntling a bastard, fr. bank bench. Cf. Bastard, n.] A young or small child; an infant. [Slightly contemptuous or depreciatory.]

In what out of the way corners genius produces her bantlings.
W. Irving.

Banxring (?), n.(Zo"l.) An East Indian insectivorous mammal of the genus Tupaia.

Banyan (?), n. [See Banian.] (Bot.) A tree of the same genus as the common fig, and called the Indian fig (Ficus Indica), whose branches send shoots to the ground, which take root and become additional trunks, until it may be the tree covers some acres of ground and is able to shelter thousands of men.

Baobab (?), n. [The native name.] (Bot.) A gigantic African tree (Adansonia digitata), also naturalized in India. See Adansonia.

Baphomet (?), n.[A corruption of Mahomet or Mohammed, the Arabian prophet: cf. Pr. Bafomet, OSp. Mafomat, OPg. Mafameda.] An idol or symbolical figure which the Templars were accused of using in their mysterious rites.

Baptism (?), n. [OE. baptim, baptem, OE. baptesme, batisme, F. bapt^me, L. baptisma, fr. Gr. ?, fr. ? to baptize, fr. ? to dip in water, akin to ? deep, Skr. g¾h to dip, bathe, v.i.] The act of baptizing; the application of water to a person, as a sacrament or religious ceremony, by which he is initiated into the visible church of Christ. This is performed by immersion, sprinkling, or pouring.

Baptismal (?), a. [Cf. F. baptismal.] Pertaining to baptism; as, baptismal vows.

Baptismal name, the Christian name, which is given at baptism.

Baptismally, adv. In a baptismal manner.

Baptist (?), n. [L. baptista, G. ?]

One who administers baptism; Ð specifically applied to John, the forerunner of Christ.

Milton.

One of a denomination of Christians who deny the validity of infant baptism and of sprinkling, and maintain that baptism should be administered to believers alone, and should be by immersion. See Anabaptist.

? In doctrine the Baptists of this country [the United States] are Calvinistic, but with much freedom and moderation.

Amer. Cyc.

Freewill Baptists, a sect of Baptists who are Arminian in doctrine, and practice open communion. Ð SeventhÐday Baptists, a sect of Baptists who keep the seventh day of the week, or Saturday, as the Sabbath. See Sabbatarian. The Dunkers and Campbellites are also Baptists.

Baptisterly (?),Baptistry(?), n.; pl. Baptisteries (?), Ïtries (?). [L. baptisterium, Gr. ?: cf. F. baptistŠre.] (Arch.) (a) In early times, a separate building, usually polygonal, used for baptismal services. Small churches were often changed into baptisteries when larger churches were built near. (b) A part of a church containing a font and used for baptismal services.

Baptistic (?), a. [Gr. ?] Of or for baptism; baptismal.

Baptistical(?), a. Baptistic. [R.]

Baptizable(?), a. Capable of being baptized; fit to be baptized.

Baxter.

Bap · tization(?), n. Baptism. [Obs.]

Their baptizations were null.

Jer. Taylor.

BapĬtize (?), v. t. [imp. & p.p. Baptized (?); p. pr. & vb.n. Baptizing.] [F. baptiser, L. baptizare, fr.Gr. ?. See Baptism.] 1.To administer the sacrament of baptism to.

To christen (because a name is given to infants at their baptism); to give a name to; to name.

I'll be new baptized;
Henceforth I never will be Romeo.
Shak.

To sanctify; to consecrate.

BapĬtizement (?),n. The act of baptizing.[R.]
BapĬtizer(?), n. One who baptizes.
Bar (?), n. [OE. barre, F. barre, fr. LL. barra, W. bar the branch of a tree, bar, baren branch, Gael. & Ir. barra bar. ? 91.] 1. A piece of wood, metal, or other material, long in proportion to its breadth or thickness, used as a lever and for various other purposes, but especially for a hindrance, obstruction, or fastening; as, the bars of a fence or gate; the bar of a door.

Thou shalt make bars of shittim wood.
Ex. xxvi. 26.

An indefinite quantity of some substance, so shaped as to be long in proportion to its breadth and thickness; as, a bar of gold or of lead; a bar of soap.

Anything which obstructs, hinders, or prevents; an obstruction; a barrier.

Must I new bars to my own joy create?
Dryden.
<— p. 118 —>

A bank of sand, gravel, or other matter, esp. at the mouth of a river or harbor, obstructing navigation.

Any railing that divides a room, or office, or hall of assembly, in order to reserve a space for those having special privileges; as, the bar of the House of Commons.

(Law) (a) The railing that incloses the place which counsel occupy in courts of justice. Hence, the phrase at the bar of the court signifies in open court. (b) The place in court where prisoners are stationed for arraignment, trial, or sentence. (c) The whole body of lawyers licensed in a court or district; the legal profession. (d) A special plea constituting a sufficient answer to plaintiff's action.

Any tribunal; as, the bar of public opinion; the bar of God.

A barrier or counter, over which liquors and food are passed to customers; hence, the portion of the room behind the counter where liquors for sale are kept.

(Her.) An ordinary, like a fess but narrower, occupying only one fifth part of the field.

A broad shaft, or band, or stripe; as, a bar of light; a bar of color.

(Mus.) A vertical line across the staff. Bars divide the staff into spaces which represent measures, and are themselves called measures. µ A double bar marks the end of a strain or main division of a movement, or of a whole piece of music; in psalmody, it marks the end of a line of poetry. The term bar is very often loosely used for measure, i.e., for such length of music, or of silence, as is included between one bar and the next; as, a passage of eight bars; two bars' rest.

(Far.) pl. (a) The space between the tusks and grinders in the upper jaw of a horse, in which the bit is placed. (b) The part of the crust of a horse's hoof which is bent inwards towards the frog at the heel on each side, and extends into the center of the sole.

(Mining) (a) A drilling or tamping rod. (b) A vein or dike crossing a lode.

(Arch.) (a) A gatehouse of a castle or fortified town. (b) A slender strip of wood which divides and supports the glass of a window; a sash bar. Bar shoe (Far.), a kind of horseshoe having a bar across the usual opening at the heel, to protect a tender frog from injury. Ð Bar shot, a double headed shot, consisting of a bar, with a ball or half ball at each end; Ðformerly used for destroying the masts or rigging in naval combat. Ð Bar sinister (Her.), a term popularly but erroneously used for baton, a mark of illegitimacy. See Baton. Ð Bar tracery (Arch.), ornamental stonework resembling bars of iron twisted into the forms required. Ð Blank bar (Law). See Blank. Ð Case at bar (Law), a case presently before the court; a case under argument. Ð In bar of, as a sufficient reason against; to prevent. Ð Matter in bar, or Defence in bar, a plea which is a final defense in an action. Ð Plea in bar, a plea which goes to bar or defeat the plaintiff's action absolutely and entirely. Ð Trial at bar (Eng. Law), a trial before all the judges of one the superior courts of Westminster, or before a quorum representing the full court. Bar (?), v.t. [imp. & p.p. Barred (?); p. pr. & vb. n. Barring.] [F. barrer. See Bar, n.] 1. To fasten with a bar; as, to bar a door or gate.

To restrict or confine, as if by a bar; to hinder; to obstruct; to prevent; to prohibit; as, to bar the entrance of evil; distance bars our intercourse; the statute bars my right; the right is barred by time; a release bars the plaintiff's recovery; Ð sometimes with up. He barely looked the idea in the face, and hastened to bar it in its dungeon. Hawthorne.

To except; to exclude by exception. Nay, but I bar toÐnight: you shall not gauge me By what we do toÐnight. Shak.

To cross with one or more stripes or lines. For the sake of distinguishing the feet more clearly, I have barred them singly. Burney. Barb(?), n. [F. barbe, fr. L. barba beard. See Beard, n.] 1. Beard, or that which resembles it, or grows in the place of it. The barbel, so called by reason of his barbs, or wattles in his mouth. Walton.

A muff?er, worn by nuns and mourners. [Obs.]

pl. Paps, or little projections, of the mucous membrane, which mark the opening of the submaxillary glands under the tongue in horses and cattle. The name is mostly applied when the barbs are inflamed and swollen. [Written also barbel and barble.]

The point that stands backward in an arrow, fishhook, etc., to prevent it from being easily extracted. Hence: Anything which stands out with a sharp point obliquely or crosswise to something else. ½Having two barbs or points.¸ Ascham.

A bit for a horse. [Obs.] Spenser.

(Zo"l.) One of the side branches of a feather, which collectively constitute the vane. See Feather.

(Zo"l.) A southern name for the kingfishes of the eastern and southeastern coasts of the United States; Ð also improperly called whiting.

(Bot.) A hair or bristle ending in a double hook. Barb, v.t. [imp. & p.p. Barbed (?); p. pr. & vb. n. Barbing.] 1. To shave or dress the beard of. [Obs.]

To clip; to mow. [Obs.] Marston.

To furnish with barbs, or with that which will hold or hurt like barbs, as an arrow, fishhook, spear, etc. But rattling storm of arrows barbed with fire. Milton. Barb, n. [F. barbe, fr. Barbarie.] 1. The Barbary horse, a superior breed introduces from Barbary into Spain by the Moors.

(Zo"l.) A blackish or dun variety of the pigeon, originally brought from Barbary. Barb, n. [Corrupted fr. bard.] Armor for a horse. Same as 2d Bard, n., 1. Barbaĭcan (?), n. See Barbican. Barbaĭcanĭage (?), n. See Barbicanage. Barĭbadiĭanÿ(?), a. Of or pertaining to Barbados. Ð n. A native of Barbados. Barĭbados or Barĭbadoes (?), n. A West Indian island, giving its name to a disease, to a cherry, etc. Barbados cherry (Bot.), a genus of trees of the West Indies (Malpighia) with an agreeably acid fruit resembling a cherry. Ð Barbados leg (Med.), a species of elephantiasis incident to hot climates. Ð Barbados nuts, the seeds of the Jatropha curcas, a plant growing in South America and elsewhere. The seeds and their acrid oil are used in medicine as a purgative. See Physic nut. ØBarbaĭra (?), n. [Coined by logicians.] (Logic) The first word in certain mnemonic lines which represent the various forms of the syllogism. It indicates a syllogism whose three propositions are universal affirmatives. Whately. Bar · baĭresque (?), a. Barbaric in form or style; as, barbaresque architecture. De Quincey. Barĭbariĭan (?), n. [See Barbarous.]

A foreigner. [Historical] Therefore if I know not the meaning of the voice, I shall be unto him that speaketh a barbarian, and he that speaketh shall be a barbarian unto me. ? Cor. xiv. 11.

A man in a rule, savage, or uncivilized state.

A person destitute of culture. M. Arnold.

A cruel, savage, brutal man; one destitute of pity or humanity. ½Thou fell barbarian. Philips. Barĭbariĭan, a. Of, or pertaining to, or resembling, barbarians; rude; uncivilized; barbarous; as, barbarian governments or nations. Barĭbaic (?), a. [L. barbaricus foreign, barbaric, Gr. ?.] 1. Of, or from, barbarian nations; foreign; Ð often with reference to barbarous nations of east. ¸Barbaric pearl and gold.¸ Milton.

Of or pertaining to, or resembling, an uncivilized person or people; barbarous; barbarian; destitute of refinement. ½Wild, barbaric music.¸ Sir W. Scott. Barbaĭrism (?), n. [L. barbarismus, Gr.?; cf. F. barbarisme.] 1. An uncivilized state or condition; rudeness of manners; ignorance of arts, learning, and literature; barbarousness. Prescott.

A barbarous, cruel, or brutal action; an outrage. A heinous barbarism ... against the honor of marriage. Milton.

An offense against purity of style or language; any form of speech contrary to the pure idioms of a particular language. See Solecism. The Greeks were the first that branded a foreign term in any of their writers with the odious name of barbarism. G. Campbell. Barĭbariĭty (?), n.; pl. Barbarities (?). [From Barbarous.] 1. The state or manner of a barbarian; lack of civilization.

Cruelty; ferociousness; inhumanity. Treating Christians with a barbarity which would have shocked the very Moslem. Macaulay.

A barbarous or cruel act.

Barbarism; impurity of speech. [Obs.] Swift. Barbaĭrize (?), v.i. [imp. & p.p. Barbarized (?); p. pr. & vb. n. Barbarizing (?).]

To become barbarous. The Roman empire was barbarizing rapidly from the time of Trajan. De Quincey.

To adopt a foreign or barbarous mode of speech. The ill habit ... of wretched barbarizing against the Latin and Greek idiom, with their untutored Anglicisms. Milton. Barbaĭrize (?),v.t. [Cf. F. barbariser, LL. barbarizare.] To make barbarous. The hideous changes which have barbarized France. Burke. Barbaĭrous (?), a. [L. barbarus, Gr. ?, strange, foreign; later, slavish, rude, ignorant; akin to L. balbus stammering, Skr. barbara stammering, outlandish. Cf. Brave, a.] 1. Being in the state of a barbarian; uncivilized; rude; peopled with barbarians; as, a barbarous people; a barbarous country.

Foreign; adapted to a barbaric taste.[Obs.] Barbarous gold. Dryden.

Cruel; ferocious; inhuman; merciless. By their barbarous usage he died within a few days, to the grief of all that knew him. Clarendon.

Contrary to the pure idioms of a language. A barbarous expression G. Campbell.

Syn. Ð Uncivilized; unlettered; uncultivated; untutored; ignorant; merciless; brutal. See Ferocious.

Barbaïrousïly, adv. In a barbarous manner.

Barbaïrousïness, n. The quality or state of being barbarous; barbarity; barbarism.

Barbaïry(?), n. [Fr. Ar. Barbar the people of Barbary.] The countries on the north coast of Africa from Egypt to the Atlantic. Hence: A Barbary horse; a barb. [Obs.] Also, a kind of pigeon.

Barbary ape (Zo"l.), an ape (Macacus innus) of north Africa and Gibraltar Rock, being the only monkey inhabiting Europe. It is very commonly trained by showmen.

Barbaïstel · (?),n. [F. barbastelle.] (Zo"l.) A European bat (Barbastellus communis), with hairy lips.

Barbate (?), a. [L. barbatus, fr. barba beard. See Barb beard.] (Bot.) Bearded; beset with long and weak hairs.

Barbaïted (?), a. Having barbed points.

A dart uncommonly barbated.

T. Warton.

Barbeïcue (?), n. [In the language of Indians of Guiana, a frame on which all kinds of flesh and fish are roasted or smokeÐdried.] 1. A hog, ox, or other large animal roasted or broiled whole for a feast.

A social entertainment, where many people assemble, usually in the open air, at which one or more large animals are roasted or broiled whole.

A floor, on which coffee beans are sunÐdried.

Barbeïcue (?), v.t. [imp. & p.p. Barbecued(?); p. pr. & vb. n. Barbecuing.] 1. To dry or cure by exposure on a frame or gridiron.

They use little or no salt, but barbecue their game and fish in the smoke. Stedman.

To roast or broil whole, as an ox or hog.

Send me, gods, a whole hog barbecued.
Pope.

Barbed (?), a. [See 4th Bare.] Accoutered with defensive armor; Ð said of a horse. See Barded (which is the proper form.)

Sir W. Raleigh.

Barbed, a. Furnished with a barb or barbs; as, a barbed arrow; barbed wire.

Barbed wire, a wire, or a strand of twisted wires, armed with barbs or sharp points. It is used for fences.

Barbel (?), n.[OE. barbel, F. barbeau, dim. of L. barbus barbel, fr. barba beard. See 1st Barb.]

(Zo"l.) A slender tactile organ on the lips of certain fished.

(Zo"l.) A large freshÐwater fish (Barbus vulgaris) found in many European rivers. Its upper jaw is furnished with four barbels.

pl. Barbs or paps under the tongued of horses and cattle. See 1st Barb,3.

Barbelĭlate (?),a. [See 1st Barb.] (Bot.) Having short, stiff hairs, often barbed at the point.

Gray.

Barĭbelluĭlate (?), a. (Bot.) Barbellate with diminutive hairs or barbs.

Barber (?), n. [OE. barbour, OF. barbeor, F. barbier, as if fr. an assumed L. barbator, fr. barba beard. See 1st Barb.] One whose occupation it is to shave or trim the beard, and to cut and dress the hair of his patrons.

Barber's itch. See under Itch.

μ Formerly the barber practiced some offices of surgery, such as letting blood and pulling teeth. Hence such terms as barber surgeon (old form barber chirurgeon), barber surgery, etc.

Barber, v.t. [imp. & p.p. Barbered (?); p. pr. & vb. n. Barbering.] To shave and dress the beard or hair of.

Shak.

Barber fish. (Zo"l.) See Surgeon fish.

Barberĭmon · ger (?), n. A fop. [Obs.]

Barberĭry (?),n. [OE. barbarin, barbere, OF. berbere.] (Bot.) A shrub of the genus Berberis, common along roadsides and in neglected fields. B. vulgaris is the species best known; its oblong red berries are made into a preserve or sauce, and have been deemed efficacious in fluxes and fevers. The bark dyes a fine yellow, esp. the bark of the root. [Also spelt berberry.]

Barbet (?),n. [F. barbet, fr.barbe beard, long hair of certain animals. See Barb beard.] (Zo"l.) (a) A variety of small dog, having long curly hair. (b) A bird of the family Bucconid', allied to the Cuckoos, having a large, conical beak swollen at the base, and bearded with five bunches of stiff bristles; the puff bird. It inhabits tropical America and Africa. (c) A larva that feeds on aphides.

Barĭbette (?), n. [F. Cf. Barbet.] (Fort.) A mound of earth or a platform in a fortification, on which guns are mounted to fire over the parapet.

En barbette, In barbette, said of guns when they are elevated so as to fire over the top of a parapet, and not through embrasures. Ð Barbette gun, or

Barbette battery, a single gun, or a number of guns, mounted in barbette, or partially protected by a parapet or turret. Ð Barbette carriage, a gun carriage which elevates guns sufficiently to be in barbette. [See Illust. of Casemate.]

Barbĭcan (?), Barbāĭcan(?), n. [OE. barbican, barbecan, F. barbacane, LL. barbacana, barbicana, of uncertain origin: cf. Ar. barbakh aqueduct, sewer. F. barbacane also means, an opening to let out water, loophole.] 1. (Fort.) A tower or advanced work defending the entrance to a castle or city, as at a gate or bridge. It was often large and strong, having a ditch and drawbridge of its own.

An opening in the wall of a fortress, through which missiles were discharged upon an enemy.

Barbĭcanĭage (?), Barbāĭcanĭage (?), n. [LL. barbicanagium. See Barbican.] Money paid for the support of a barbican. [Obs.]

Barbĭcel (?), n. [NL. barbicella, dim. of L. barba. See 1st Barb.] (Zo"l.) One of the small hooklike processes on the barbules of feathers.

ØBarbiers (?), n. (Med.) A variety of paralysis, peculiar to India and the Malabar coast; Ð considered by many to be the same as beriberi in chronic form.

Barĭbigerĭous (?), a. [L. barba a beard + gerous.] Having a beard; bearded; hairy.

ØBarbĭton (?), n. [L., fr. Gr. ?.] (Mus.) An ancient Greek instrument resembling a lyre.

Bar · bĭturic acid (?). (Chem.) A white, crystalline substance, ?, derived
<— p. 119 —>
from alloxantin, also from malonic acid and urea, and regarded as a substituted urea.

Barble (?), n. See Barbel.

Barboĭtine (?), n. [F.] A paste of clay used in decorating coarse pottery in relief.

Barbre (?), a. Barbarian. [Obs.]
Chaucer.

Barbule (?), n. [L. barbula, fr. barba beard.]

A very minute barb or beard.

Booth.

(Zo"l.) One of the processes along the edges of the barbs of a feather, by which adjacent barbs interlock. See Feather.

Barcaĭrolle (?), n. [F. barcarolle, fr. It. barcaruola, fr. barca bark, barge.] (Mus.) (a) A popular song or melody sung by Venetian gondoliers. (b) A piece of music composed in imitation of such a song.

Barcon (?), n. [It. barcone, fr. barca a bark.] A vessel for freight; Đ used in Mediterranean.

Bard (?), n. [Of Celtic origin; cf. W. bardd, Arm. barz, Ir. & Gael. bard, and F. barde.] 1. A professional poet and singer, as among the ancient Celts, whose occupation was to compose and sing verses in honor of the heroic achievements of princes and brave men.

Hence: A poet; as, the bard of Avon.

Bard, Barde (?), n. [F. barde, of doubtful origin.]

A piece of defensive (or, sometimes, ornamental) armor for a horse's neck, breast, and flanks; a barb. [Often in the pl.]

pl. Defensive armor formerly worn by a man at arms.

(Cookery) A thin slice of fat bacon used to cover any meat or game.

Bard, v.t. (Cookery) To cover (meat or game) with a thin slice of fat bacon.

Barded, p.a. [See Bard horse armor.] 1. Accoutered with defensive armor; Đ said of a horse.

(Her.) Wearing rich caparisons.

Fifteen hundred men ... barded and richly trapped.
Stow.

Bardic, a. Of or pertaining to bards, or their poetry.

½The bardic lays of ancient Greece.‚

G.P. Marsh.

Bardish, a. Pertaining to, or written by, a bard or bards. ½Bardish impostures.‚

Selden.

Bardism (?), n. The system of bards; the learning and maxims of bards.

Bardling (?), n. An inferior bard.

J. Cunningham.

Bardship, n. The state of being a bard.

Bare (?), a. [OE. bar, bare, AS. b'r; akin to D. & G. baar, OHG. par, Icel. berr, Sw. & Dan. bar, OSlav. bos? barefoot, Lith. basas; cf. Skr. bh¾s to shine ?.]

Without clothes or covering; stripped of the usual covering; naked; as, his body is bare; the trees are bare.

With head uncovered; bareheaded.

When once thy foot enters the church, be bare.
Herbert.

Without anything to cover up or conceal one's thoughts or actions; open to view; exposed.

Bare in thy guilt, how foul must thou appear !
Milton.

Plain; simple; unadorned; without polish; bald; meager. ½Uttering bare truth.

Shak.

Destitute; indigent; empty; unfurnished or scantily furnished; Ð used with of (rarely with in) before the thing wanting or taken away; as, a room bare of furniture. ½A bare treasury.

Dryden.

Threadbare; much worn.

It appears by their bare liveries that they live by your bare words.
Shak.

Mere; alone; unaccompanied by anything else; as, a bare majority. ½The bare necessaries of life.

Addison.
Nor are men prevailed upon by bare of naked truth.
South.
Under bare poles (Naut.), having no sail set.
Bare, n. 1. Surface; body; substance. [R.]
You have touched the very bare of naked truth.
Marston.

(Arch.) That part of a roofing slate, shingle, tile, or metal plate, which is exposed to the weather.

Bare, v.t. [imp. & p.p. Bared(?); p. pr. & vb. n. Baring.] [AS. barian. See Bare, a.] To strip off the covering of; to make bare; as, to bare the breast.
Bare. Bore; the old preterit of Bear, v.
Bareback · (?), adv. On the bare back of a horse, without using a saddle; as, to ride bareback.
Barebacked · (?), a. Having the back uncovered; as, a barebacked horse.
Barebone · (?), n. A very lean person; one whose bones show through the skin.
Shak.
Barefaced · (?), a. 1. With the face uncovered; not masked. ½You will play barefaced.
Shak.

Without concealment; undisguised. Hence: Shameless; audacious. ½Barefaced treason.

J. Baillie.

Barefaced · ly, adv. Openly; shamelessly.

Locke.

Barefaced · ness, n. The quality of being barefaced; shamelessness; assurance; audaciousness.

Barefoot (?), a. & adv. With the feet bare; without shoes or stockings.

Barefoot · ed, a. Having the feet bare.

ØBaïr,ge (?), n. [F. bar,ge, so called from Bar,ges, a town in the Pyrenees.] A gauzelike fabric for ladies' dresses, veils, etc. of worsted, silk and worsted, or cotton and worsted.

Barehand · ed (?), n. Having bare hands.

Barehead · ed (?), Barehead, a. & adv. Having the head uncovered; as, a bareheaded girl.

Barelegged · (?), a. Having the legs bare.

Barely, adv. 1. Without covering; nakedly.

Without concealment or disguise.

Merely; only.

R. For now his son is duke.
W. Barely in title, not in revenue.
Shak.

But just; without any excess; with nothing to spare (of quantity, time, etc.); hence, scarcely; hardly; as, there was barely enough for all; he barely escaped.

Barenecked · (?), a. Having the neck bare.

Bareness, n. The state of being bare.

Baresark (?), n. [Literally, bare sark or shirt.] A Berserker, or Norse warrior who fought without armor, or shirt of mail. Hence, adverbially: Without shirt of mail or armor.

Barfish · (?), n. (Zo"l.) Same as Calico bass.

Barful (?), a. Full of obstructions. [Obs.]
Shak.

Bargain (?), n. [OE. bargayn, bargany, OF. bargaigne, bargagne, prob. from a supposed LL. barcaneum, fr. barca a boat which carries merchandise to the shore; hence, to traffic to and fro, to carry on commerce in general. See Bark a vessel.] 1. An agreement between parties concerning the sale of property; or a contract by which one party binds himself to transfer the right to some property for a consideration, and the other party binds himself to receive the property and pay the consideration.

A contract is a bargain that is legally binding.

Wharton.

An agreement or stipulation; mutual pledge.

And whon your honors mean to solemnize
The bargain of your faith.
Shak.

A purchase; also (when not qualified), a gainful transaction; an advantageous purchase; as, to buy a thing at a bargain.

The thing stipulated or purchased; also, anything bought cheap.

She was too fond of her most filthy bargain.
Shak.

Bargain and sale (Law), a species of conveyance, by which the bargainor contracts to convey the lands to the bargainee, and becomes by such contract a trustee for and seized to the use of the bargainee. The statute then completes the purchase; i.e., the bargain vests the use, and the statute vests the possession. Blackstone. Ð Into the bargain, over and above what is stipulated; besides. Ð To sell bargains, to make saucy (usually indelicate) repartees. [Obs.] Swift. Ð To strike a bargain, to reach or ratify an agreement. ½A bargain was struck. Macaulay.

Syn. Ð Contract; stipulation; purchase; engagement.

Bargain, v.i. [OE. barganien, OF. bargaigner, F. barguigner, to hesitate, fr. LL. barcaniare. See Bargain, n.] To make a bargain; to make a contract for the exchange of property or services; Ð followed by with and for; as, to bargain with a farmer for a cow.

So worthless peasants bargain for their wives.
Shak.

Bargain, v.t. [imp. & p.p. Bargained (?); p. pr. & vb. n. Bargaining.] To transfer for a consideration; to barter; to trade; as, to bargain one horse for another.

To bargain away, to dispose of in a bargain; Ð usually with a sense of loss or disadvantage; as, to bargain away one's birthright. ½The heir ... had somehow bargained away the estate.
G.Eliot.

Bar · fainĭee (?), n. [OF. bargaign,, p.p. See Bargain, v.i.] (Law) The party to a contract who receives, or agrees to receive, the property sold.
Blackstone.

Bargainĭer (?), n. One who makes a bargain; Ð sometimes in the sense of bargainor.

Bar · gainĭor (?), n. (Law) One who makes a bargain, or contracts with another; esp., one who sells, or contracts to sell, property to another.
Blackstone.

Barge (?), n. [OF. barge, F. berge, fr. LL. barca, for barica (not found), prob. fr. L. baris an Egyptian rowboat, fr. Gr. ?, prob. fr. Egyptian: cf. Coptic bari a boat. Cf. Bark a vessel.] 1. A pleasure boat; a vessel or boat of state, elegantly furnished and decorated.

A large, roomy boat for the conveyance of passengers or goods; as, a ship's barge; a charcoal barge.

A large boat used by flag officers.

A double-decked passenger or freight vessel, towed by a steamboat. [U.S.]

A large omnibus used for excursions. [Local, U.S.]

Barge'board· (?), n. [Perh. corrup. of vergeboard; or cf. LL. bargus a kind of gallows.] A vergeboard.

Barge'course· (?), n. [See Bargeboard.] (Arch.) A part of the tiling which projects beyond the principal rafters, in buildings where there is a gable.

Gwilt.

Bar'gee (?), n. A bargeman. [Eng.]

Barge'man (?), n. The man who manages a barge, or one of the crew of a barge.

Barge'mas·ter (?), n. The proprietor or manager of a barge, or one of the crew of a barge.

Bar'ger (?), n. The manager of a barge. [Obs.]

Barg'hest· (?), n. [Perh. G. berg mountain + geist demon, or b„r a bear + geist.] A goblin, in the shape of a large dog, portending misfortune. [Also written barguest.]

Ba·ri'la (?), n. [Cf. Barium.] (Chem.) Baryta.

Bar'ic (?), a. (Chem.) Of or pertaining to barium; as, baric oxide.

Bar'ic, a. [Gr. ? weight.] (Physics) Of or pertaining to weight, esp. to the weight or pressure of the atmosphere as measured by the barometer.

Ba·ril'la (?), n. [Sp. barrilla.] 1. (Bot.) A name given to several species of Salsola from which soda is made, by burning the barilla in heaps and lixiviating the ashes.

(Com.) (a) The alkali produced from the plant, being an impure carbonate of soda, used for making soap, glass, etc., and for bleaching purposes. (b) Impure soda obtained from the ashes of any seashore plant, or kelp.

Ure.

Copper barilla (Min.), native copper in granular form mixed with sand, an ore brought from Bolivia; — called also Barilla de cobre.

∅Ba·ril'let (?), n. [F., dim. of baril barrel.] A little cask, or something resembling one.

Smart.

Bar i·ron (?). See under Iron.

Bar'ite (?), n. (Min.) Native sulphate of barium, a mineral occurring in transparent, colorless, white to yellow crystals (generally tabular), also in granular form, and in compact massive forms resembling marble. It has a high specific gravity, and hence is often called heavy spar. It is a common mineral in metallic veins.

Bar'i·tone (?), a. & n. See Barytone.

Barium (?), n. [NL., fr. Gr. ? heavy.] (Chem.) One of the elements, belonging to the alkaline earth group; a metal having a silver‐white color, and melting at a very high temperature. It is difficult to obtain the pure metal, from the facility with which it becomes oxidized in the air. Atomic weight, ?137. Symbol, Ba. Its oxide called baryta. [Rarely written barytum.]

¶ Some of the compounds of this element are remarkable for their high specific gravity, as the sulphate, called heavy spar, and the like. The oxide was called barote, by Guyton de Morveau, which name was changed by Lavoisier to baryta, whence the name of the metal.

Bard (?), n. [Akin to Dan. & Sw. bark, Icel. b"rkr, LG. & HG. borke.] 1. The exterior covering of the trunk and branches of a tree; the rind.

Specifically, Peruvian bark.

Bark bed. See Bark stove (below). Ð Bark pit, a pit filled with bark and water, in which hides are steeped in tanning. Ð Bark stove (Hort.), a glazed structure for keeping tropical plants, having a bed of tanner's bark (called a bark bed) or other fermentable matter which produces a moist heat.

Bark, v.t. [imp. & p.p. Barked (?); p. pr. & vb. n. Barking.] 1. To strip the bark from; to peel.

To abrade or rub off any outer covering from; as to bark one's heel.

To girdle. See Girdle, v.t., 3.

To cover or inclose with bark, or as with bark; as, to bark the roof of a hut.

Bark, v.i. [OE. berken, AS. beorcan; akin to Icel. berkja, and prob. to E. break.] 1. To make a short, loud, explosive noise with the vocal organs; Ð said of some animals, but especially of dogs.

To make a clamor; to make importunate outcries.

They bark, and say the Scripture maketh heretics.
Tyndale.
Where there is the barking of the belly, there no other commands will be heard, much less obeyed.
Fuller.
Bark, n. The short, loud, explosive sound uttered by a dog; a similar sound made by some other animals.

Bark, Barque (?), n. [F. barque, fr. Sp. or It. barca, fr. LL. barca for barica. See Barge.]

Formerly, any small sailing vessel, as a pinnace, fishing smack, etc.; also, a rowing boat; a barge. Now applied poetically to a sailing vessel or boat of any kind.

Byron.

(Naut.) A three‐masted vessel, having her foremast and mainmast square‐rigged, and her mizzenmast schooner‐rigged.

Barkanĭtine (?), n. Same as Barkentine.

Bark bee·tle (?). (Zo"l.) A small beetle of many species (family Scolytid'), which in the larval state bores under or in the bark of trees, often doing great damage.

Barkbound· (?), a. Prevented from growing, by having the bark too firm or close.

Barkeep·er (?), n. One who keeps or tends a bar for the sale of liquors.

Barken (?), a. Made of bark. [Poetic]

Whittier.

Barkenĭtine (?), n. [See Bark, n., a vessel.] (Naut.) A threemasted vessel, having the foremast squareÐrigged, and the others schoonerÐrigged. [Spel? also barquentine, barkantine, etc.] See Illust. in Append.

Barker (?), n. 1. An animal that barks; hence, any one who clamors unreasonably.

> One who stands at the doors of shops to urg? passers by to make purchases. [Cant, Eng.]
>
> A pistol. [Slang]

Dickens.

(Zo"l.) The spotted redshank.

Barker, n. One who strips trees of their bark.

Barker's mill· (?). [From Dr. Barker, the inventor.] A machine, invented in the 17th century, worked by a form of reaction wheel. The water flows into a vertical tube and gushes from apertures in hollow horizontal arms, causing the machine to revolve on its axis.

Barkerĭy (?), n. A tanhouse.

Barking i·rons (?). 1. Instruments used in taking off the bark of trees.

Gardner.

> A pair of pistols. [Slang]

Barkless, a. Destitute of bark.

Bark louse· (?). (Zo"l.) An insect of the family Coccid', which infests the bark of trees and vines.

µ The wingless females assume the shape of scales. The bark louse of vine is Pulvinaria innumerabilis; that of the pear is Lecanium pyri. See Orange scale.

Barky (?), a. Covered with, or containing, bark. ½The barky fingers of the elm.„

Shak.

Barley (?), n. [OE. barli, barlich, AS. b'rlic; bere barley + lÆc (which is prob. the same as E. like, adj., or perh. a form of AS. le¾c leek). AS. bere is akin to Icel, barr barley, Goth. barizeins made of barley, L. far spelt; cf.

W. barlys barley, bara bread. ?92. Cf. Farina, 6th Bear.] (Bot.) A valuable grain, of the family of grasses, genus Hordeum, used for food, and for making malt, from which are prepared beer, ale, and whisky.

<— p. 120 —>
<— p. 120 —>

Barley bird (Zo"l.), the siskin. Ð Barley sugar, sugar boiled till it is brittle (formerly with a decoction of barley) and candied. Ð Barley water, a decoction of barley, used in medicine, as a nutritive and demulcent.

BarleyÏbrake · BarleyÏbreak · } (?), n. An ancient rural game, commonly played round stacks of barley, or other grain, in which some of the party attempt to catch others who run from a goal.

BarleyÐbree · (?), n. [Lit. barley broth. See Brew.] Liquor made from barley; strong ale. [Humorous] [Scot.]

Burns.

BarleyÏcorn · (?), n. [See Corn.] 1. A grain or ½corn ͕ of barley.

Formerly , a measure of length, equal to the average length of a grain of barley; the third part of an inch.

John Barleycorn, a humorous personification of barley as the source of malt liquor or whisky.

Barm (?), n. [OE. berme, AS. beorma; akin to Sw. b„rma, G. b„rme, and prob. L. fermenium. û93. Foam rising upon beer, or other malt liquors, when fermenting, and used as leaven in making bread and in brewing; yeast.

Shak.

Barm , n. [OE. bearm, berm, barm, AS. beorma; akin to E. bear to support.] The lap or bosom. [Obs.]

Chaucer.

Barmaid · (?), n. A girl or woman who attends the customers of a bar, as in a tavern or beershop.

A bouncing barmaid.

W. Irving.

Barmas · ter (?), n. [Berg + master: cf. G. Bergmeister.] Formerly, a local judge among miners; now, an officer of the barmote. [Eng.]

Barmcloth · (?), n. Apron. [Obs.]

Chaucer.

BarmeÏci · dal (?), a. [See Barmecide.] Unreal; illusory. ½A sort of Barmecidal feast. ͕

Hood.

BarmeÏcide (?), n. [A prince of the Barmecide family, who, as related in the ½Arabian Nights' Tales ͕, pretended to set before the hungry Shacabac food, on which the latter pretended to feast.] One who proffers some illusory advantage or benefit. Also used as an adj.: Barmecidal. ½A Barmecide feast. ͕

Dickens.

Barmote · (?), n. [Barg + mote meeting.] A court held in Derbyshire, in England, for deciding controversies between miners.
Blount.
Balmy (?), a. Full of barm or froth; in a ferment. ½Barmy beer.
Dryden.
Barn (?), n. [OE. bern, AS. berern, bern; bere barley + ern, 'rn, a close place. ?92. See Barley.] A covered building used chiefly for storing grain, hay, and other productions of a farm. In the United States a part of the barn is often used for stables.
Barn owl (Zo"l.), an owl of Europe and America (Aluco flammeus, or Strix flammea), which frequents barns and other buildings. Ð Barn swallow (Zo"l.), the common American swallow (Hirundo horreorum), which attaches its nest of mud to the beams and rafters of barns.
Barn, v.t. To lay up in a barn. [Obs.]
Shak.
Men ... often barn up the chaff, and burn up the grain.
Fuller.
Barn, n. A child. [Obs.] See Bairn.
Barnaïbite (?), n. (Eccl. Hist.) A member of a religious order, named from St. Barnabas.
Barnaïcle (?), n. [Prob. from E. barnacle a kind of goose, which was popularly supposed to grow from this shellfish; but perh. from LL. bernacula for pernacula, dim. of perna ham, sea mussel; cf. Gr. ? ham Cf. F. bernacle, barnacle, E. barnacle a goose; and Ir. bairneach, barneach, limpet.] (Zo"l.) Any cirriped crustacean adhering to rocks, floating timber, ships, etc., esp. (a) the sessile species (genus Balanus and allies), and (b) the stalked or goose barnacles (genus Lepas and allies). See Cirripedia, and Goose barnacle.
Barnacle eater (Zo"l.), the orange filefish. Ð Barnacle scale (Zo"l.), a bark louse (Ceroplastes cirripediformis) of the orange and quince trees in Florida. The female scale curiously resembles a sessile barnacle in form.
Barnaïcle, n. [See Bernicle.] A bernicle goose.
Barnaïcle, n. [OE. bernak, bernacle; cf. OF. bernac, and Prov. F. (Berri) berniques, spectacles.] 1. pl. (Far.) An instrument for pinching a horse's nose, and thus restraining him. [Formerly used in the sing.]
The barnacles ... give pain almost equal to that of the
switch.
Youatt.
pl. Spectacles; Ð so called from their resemblance to the barnacles used by farriers. [Cant, Eng.]

Dickens.
Barnyard · (?), n. A yard belonging to a barn.
ØBaïrocco (?), a. [It.] (Arch.) See Baroque.

Baro̅graph (?), n. [Gr. ? weight + Ðgraph.] (Meteor.) An instrument for recording automatically the variations of atmospheric pressure.

Ba̅roko (?), n. [A mnemonic word.] (Logic) A form or mode of syllogism of which the first proposition is a universal affirmative, and the other two are particular negative.

Ba̅rolo̅gy (?), n. [Gr. ? weight + Ðlogy.] The science of weight or gravity.

Bar · o̅ma̅crome̅ter (?), n. [Gr. ? weight + ? long + Ðmeter.] (Med.) An instrument for ascertaining the weight and length of a newborn infant.

Ba̅rome̅ter (?), n. [Gr. ? weight + Ðmeter: cf. F. baromŠtre.] An instrument for determining the weight or pressure of the atmosphere, and hence for judging of the probable changes of weather, or for ascertaining the height of any ascent.

µ The barometer was invented by Torricelli at Florence about 1643. It is made in its simplest form by filling a graduated glass tube about 34 inches long with mercury and inverting it in a cup containing mercury. The column of mercury in the tube descends until balanced by the weight of the atmosphere, and its rise or fall under varying conditions is a measure of the change in the atmospheric pressure. At the sea level its ordinary height is about 30 inches (760 millimeters). See Sympiesometer.

Nichol.

Aneroid barometer. See Aneroid barometer, under Aneroid. Ð Marine barometer, a barometer with tube contracted at bottom to prevent rapid oscillations of the mercury, and suspended in gimbals from an arm or support on shipboard. Ð Mountain barometer, a portable mercurial barometer with tripod support, and long scale, for measuring heights. Ð Siphon barometer, a barometer having a tube bent like a hook with the longer leg closed at the top. The height of the mercury in the longer leg shows the pressure of the atmosphere. Ð Wheel barometer, a barometer with recurved tube, and a float, from which a cord passes over a pulley and moves an index.

Bar · o̅metric (?), Bar · o̅metric̅al (?), } a. Pertaining to the barometer; made or indicated by a barometer; as, barometric changes; barometrical observations.

Bar · o̅metric̅al̅ly, adv. By means of a barometer, or according to barometric observations.

Bar · o̅metro̅graph (?), n. [Gr. ? weight + ? measure + Ðgraph.] A form of barometer so constructed as to inscribe of itself upon paper a record of the variations of atmospheric pressure.

Ba̅rome̅try (?), n. The art or process of making barometrical measurements.

Baro̅metz (?), n. [Cf. Russ. baranets' clubmoss.] (Bot.) The woollyÐskinned rhizoma or rootstock of a fern (Dicksonia barometz), which, when specially prepared and inverted, somewhat resembles a lamb; Ð called also Scythian lamb.

Baron (?), n. [OE. baron, barun, OF. baron, accus. of ber, F. baron, prob. fr. OHG. baro (not found) bearer, akin to E. bear to support; cf. O. Frisian bere, LL. baro, It. barone, Sp. varon. From the meaning bearer (of burdens) seem to have come the senses strong man, man (in distinction from woman), which is the oldest meaning in French, and lastly, nobleman. Cf. L. baro, simpleton. See Bear to support.]

> A title or degree of nobility; originally, the possessor of a fief, who had feudal tenants under him; in modern times, in France and Germany, a nobleman next in rank below a count; in England, a nobleman of the lowest grade in the House of Lords, being next below a viscount.

µ ½The tenants in chief from the Crown, who held lands of the annual value of four hundred pounds, were styled Barons; and it is to them, and not to the members of the lowest grade of the nobility (to whom the title at the present time belongs), that reference is made when we read of the Barons of the early days of England's history.... Barons are addressed as 'My Lord,' and are styled 'Right Honorable.' All their sons and daughters 'Honorable.',
Cussans.

> (Old Law) A husband; as, baron and feme, husband and wife. [R.]

Cowell.
Baron of beef, two sirloins not cut asunder at the backbone. Ð Barons of the Cinque Ports, formerly members of the House of Commons, elected by the seven Cinque Ports, two for each port. Ð Baron of the exchequer, the judges of the Court of Exchequer, one of the three ancient courts of England, now abolished.

Baronïage (?), n. [OE. barnage, baronage, OF.barnage, F. baronnage; cf. LL. baronagium.]

> The whole body of barons or peers.

The baronage of the kingdom.
Bp. Burnet.

> The dignity or rank of a baron.

> The land which gives title to a baron. [Obs.]

Baronïess (?), n. A baron's wife; also, a lady who holds the baronial title in her own right; as, the Baroness BurdettÐCoutts.

Baronïet (?), n. [Baron + Ðet.] A dignity or degree of honor next below a baron and above a knight, having precedency of all orders of knights except those of the Garter. It is the lowest degree of honor that is hereditary. The baronets are commoners.

µ The order was founded by James I. in 1611, and is given by patent. The word, however, in the sense of a lesser baron, was in use long before.

½Baronets have the title of 'Sir' prefixed to their Christian names; their surnames being followed by their dignity, usually abbreviated Bart. Their wives are addressed as 'Lady' or 'Madam'. Their sons are possessed of no title beyond 'Esquire.'

Cussans.

Baronĕtḁge (?), n. 1. State or rank of a baronet.

The collective body of baronets.

Baronĕtĭcy (?), n. The rank or patent of a baronet.

Baronial (?), a. Pertaining to a baron or a barony. ½Baronial tenure.

Hallam.

Barŏny (?), n.; pl. Baronies (?). [OF. baronie, F. baronnie, LL. baronia. See Baron.] 1. The fee or domain of a baron; the lordship, dignity, or rank of a baron.

In Ireland, a territorial division, corresponding nearly to the English hundred, and supposed to have been originally the district of a native chief. There are 252 of these baronies. In Scotland, an extensive freehold. It may be held by a commoner.

Brande & C.

Baroque (?), a. [F.; cf. It. barocco.] (Arch.) In bad taste; grotesque; odd.

Barŏscope (?), n. [Gr. ? weight + Ðscope: cf. F. baroscope.] Any instrument showing the changes in the weight of the atmosphere; also, less appropriately, any instrument that indicates Ðor foreshadows changes of the weather, as a deep vial of liquid holding in suspension some substance which rises and falls with atmospheric changes.

Bar · oĭscopic (?), Bar · oĭscopicĭal (?), } a. Pertaining to, or determined by, the baroscope.

Barouche (?), n. [G. barutsche, It. baroccio, biroccio, LL. barrotium, fr. L. birotus twoÐwheeled; bi=bis twice + rota wheel.] A fourÐwheeled carriage, with a falling top, a seat on the outside for the driver, and two double seats on the inside arranged so that the sitters on the front seat face those on the back seat.

Ba · rouĭchet(?), n. A kind of light barouche.

Barpost · (?), n. A post sunk in the ground to receive the bars closing a passage into a field.

Barque (?), n. Same as 3d Bark, n.

Barraĭcan (?), n. [F. baracan, bouracan (cf. Pr. barracan, It. baracane, Sp. barragan, Pg. barregana, LL. barracanus), fr. Ar. barrak¾n a kind of black gown, perh. fr. Per. barak a garment made of camel's hair.] A thick, strong stuff, somewhat like camlet; Ð still used for outer garments in the Levant.

Barrack (?), n. [F. baraque, fr. It. baracca (cf. Sp. barraca), from LL. barra bar. See Bar, n.]

(Mil.) A building for soldiers, especially when in garrison. Commonly in the pl., originally meaning temporary huts, but now usually applied to a permanent structure or set of buildings.

He lodged in a miserable hut or barrack, composed of dry branches and thatched with straw.
Gibbon.

A movable roof sliding on four posts, to cover hay, straw, etc. [Local, U.S.]

Barrack, v.t. To supply with barracks; to establish in barracks; as, to barrack troops.

Barrack, v.i. To live or lodge in barracks.

Barraclade (?), n. [D. baar, OD. baer, naked, bare + kleed garment, i.e., cloth undressed or without nap.] A home‐made woolen blanket without nap. [Local, New York]
Bartlett.

Barracoon · (?), n. [Sp. or Pg. barraca. See Barrack.] A slave warehouse, or an inclosure where slaves are quartered temporarily.
Du Chaillu.

Bar · racuda (?), Bar · racouata (?), } n. 1. (Zo"l.) A voracious pikelike, marine fish, o? the genus Sphyr'na, sometimes used as food.

μ That of Europe and our Atlantic coast is Sphyr'na spet (or S. vulgaris); a southern species is S. picuda; the Californian is S. argentea.

(Zo"l.) A large edible fresh‐water fish of Australia and New Zealand (Thyrsites atun).

Barrage (?), n. [F., fr. barrer to bar, from barre bar.] (Engin.) An artificial bar or obstruction placed in a river or water course to increase the depth of water; as, the barrages of the Nile.

ØBarïranca (?), n. [Sp.] A ravine caused by heavy rains or a watercourse. [Texas & N. Mex.]

ØBarras (?), n. [F.] A resin, called also galipot.

Barrator (?), n. [OE. baratour, OF. barateor deceiver, fr. OF. barater, bareter, to deceive, cheat, barter. See Barter, v.i.] One guilty of barratry.

Barratrous (?), ? (Law) Tainter with, or constituting, barratry. Ð Barratrously, adv.
Kent.

Barratry (?), n. [Cf. F. baraterie, LL. barataria. See Barrator, and cf. Bartery.] 1. (Law) The practice of exciting and encouraging lawsuits and quarrels. [Also spelt barretry.]
Coke. Blackstone.

(Mar. Law) A fraudulent breach of duty or willful act of known illegality on the part of a master of a ship, in his character of master, or of the mariners, to the injury of the owner of the ship or cargo, and without his consent. It includes every breach of trust committed with dishonest purpose, as by running away with the ship, sinking or deserting her, etc., or by embezzling the cargo.

Kent. Part.

(Scots Law) The crime of a judge who is influenced by bribery in pronouncing judgment.

Wharton.

Barred owl (?). (Zo"l.) A large American owl (Syrnium nebulosum); Ð so called from the transverse bars of a dark brown color on the breast.

Barrel (?), n.[OE. barel, F. baril, prob. fr. barre bar. Cf. Barricade.] 1.A round vessel or cask, of greater length than breadth, and bulging in the middle, made of staves bound with hoops, and having flat ends or heads.

The quantity which constitutes a full barrel. This varies for different articles and also in different places for the same article, being regulated by custom or by law. A barrel of wine is 31 1/2 gallons; a barrel of flour is 196 pounds.

A solid drum, or a hollow cylinder or case; as, the barrel of a windlass; the barrel of a watch, within which the spring is coiled.

<— p. 121 —>

A metallic tube, as of a gun, from which a projectile is discharged.

Knight.

A jar. [Obs.]

1 Kings xvii. 12.

(Zo"l.) The hollow basal part of a feather.

Barrel bulk (Com.), a measure equal to five cubic feet, used in estimating capacity, as of a vessel for freight. Ð Barrel drain (Arch.), a drain in the form of a cylindrical tube. Ð Barrel of a boiler, the cylindrical part of a boiler, containing the flues. Ð Barrel of the ear (?), the tympanum, or tympanic cavity. Ð Barrel organ, an instrument for producing music by the action of a revolving cylinder. Ð Barrel vault. See under Vault.

Barrel (?), v.t. [imp. & p.p. Barreled (?), or Barrelled; p. pr. & vb. n. Barreling, or Barrelling.] To put or to pack in a barrel or barrels.

Barreled, Barrelled (?), a. Having a barrel; Ð used in composition; as, a doubleÐbarreled gun.

Barren (?), a. [OE. barein, OF. brehaing, ?em. brehaigne, baraigne, F. br,haigne; of uncertain origin; cf. Arm. br,kha?, markha?, sterile; LL. brana a sterile mare, principally in Aquitanian and Spanish documents; Bisc. barau, baru, fasting.] 1. Incapable of producing offspring; producing no young; sterile; Ð ?aid of women and female animals.

She was barren of children.
Bp. Hall.

Not producing vegetation, or useful vegetation; ?rile. ½Barren mountain tracts.

Macaulay.

Unproductive; fruitless; unprofitable; empty.

Brilliant but barren reveries.
Prescott.
Some schemes will appear barren of hints and matter.
Swift.

Mentally dull; stupid.

Shak.
Barren flower, a flower which has only stamens without a pistil, or which as neither stamens nor pistils. Ð Barren Grounds (Geog.), a vast tract in British America northward of the forest regions. Ð Barren Ground bear (Zo"l.), a peculiar bear, inhabiting the Barren Grounds, now believed to be a variety of the brown bear of Europe. Ð Barren Ground caribou (Zo"l.), a small reindeer (Rangifer Gr?nlandicus) peculiar to the Barren Grounds and Greenland.

Barren, n. 1. A tract of barren land.

pl. Elevated lands or plains on which grow small trees, but not timber; as, pine barrens; oak barrens. They are not necessarily sterile, and are often fertile. [Amer.]

J. Pickering.
Barrenİly, adv. Unfruitfully; unproductively.
Barrenİness, n. The condition of being barren; sterility; unproductiveness.
A total barrenness of invention.
Dryden.
Barrenİwort · (?), n. (Bot.) An herbaceous plant of the Barberry family (Epimedium alpinum), having leaves that are bitter and said to be sudorific.

Barret (?), n. [F. barrette, LL. barretum a cap. See Berretta, and cf. Biretta.] A kind of cap formerly worn by soldiers; Ð called also barret cap. Also, the flat cap worn by Roman Catholic ecclesiastics.

Bar · riİcade (?), n. [F. barricade, fr. Sp. barricada, orig. a barring up with casks; fr. barrica cask, perh. fr. LL. barra bar. See Bar, n., and cf. Barrel, n.]

(Mil.) A fortification, made in haste, of trees, earth, palisades, wagons, or anything that will obstruct the progress or attack of an enemy. It is usually an obstruction formed in streets to block an enemy's access.

Any bar, obstruction, or means of defense.

Such a barricade as would greatly annoy, or absolutely stop, the currents of the atmosphere.

Derham.

Bar·ri‖cade, v. t. [imp. & p.p. Barricaded; p. pr. & vb. n. Barricading.] [Cf. F. barricader. See Barricade, n.] To fortify or close with a barricade or with barricades; to stop up, as a passage; to obstruct; as, the workmen barricaded the streets of Paris.

The further end whereof [a bridge] was barricaded with barrels.

Hakluyt.

Bar·ri‖cader (?), n. One who constructs barricades.

Bar·ri‖cado (?), n. & v.t. See Barricade.

Shak.

Barri‖er (?), n. [OE. barrere, barere, F. barriŠre, fr. barre bar. See Bar, n.] 1. (Fort.) A carpentry obstruction, stockade, or other obstacle made in a passage in order to stop an enemy.

A fortress or fortified town, on the frontier of a country, commanding an avenue of approach.

pl. A fence or railing to mark the limits of a place, or to keep back a crowd.

No sooner were the barriers opened, than he paced into the lists.

Sir W. Scott.

An any obstruction; anything which hinders approach or attack. ½Constitutional barriers.

Hopkinson.

Any limit or boundary; a line of separation.

'Twixt that [instinct] and reason, what a nice barrier !

Pope.

Barrier gate, a heavy gate to close the opening through a barrier. Ð Barrier reef, a form of coral reef which runs in the general direction of the shore, and incloses a lagoon channel more or less extensive. Ð To fight at barriers, to fight with a barrier between, as a martial exercise. [Obs.]

ØBar·ri‖gudo (?),n. [Native name, fr. Sp. barrigudo bigÐbellied.] (Zo"l.) A large, darkÐcolored, South American monkey, of the genus Lagothrix, having a long prehensile tail.

Bar·ring‖out (?), n. The act of closing the doors of a schoolroom against a schoolmaster; Ð a boyish mode of rebellion in schools.

Swift.

Barris‖ter (?), n. [From Bar, n.] Counselor at law; a counsel admitted to plead at the bar, and undertake the public trial of causes, as distinguished from an attorney or solicitor. See Attorney. [Eng.]

Barroom · (?), n. A room containing a bar or counter at which liquors are sold.

Barrow (?), n. [OE. barow, fr. AS. beran to bear. See Bear to support, and cf. Bier.] 1. A support having handles, and with or without a wheel, on which heavy or bulky things can be transported by hand. See Handbarrow, and Wheelbarrow.

(Salt Works) A wicker case, in which salt is put to drain.

Barrow (?), n. [OE. barow, bargh, AS. bearg, bearh; akin to Icel. b"rgr, OHG. barh, barug, G. barch. ?95.] A hog, esp. a male hog castrated.
Holland.

Barrow, n. [OE. bergh, AS. beorg, beorh, hill, sepulchral mound; akin to G. berg mountain, Goth. bairgahei hill, hilly country, and perh. to Skr. b?hant high, OIr. brigh mountain. Cf. Berg, Berry a mound, and Borough an incorporated town.] 1. A large mound of earth or stones over the remains of the dead; a tumulus.

(Mining) A heap of rubbish, attle, etc.

Barrowïst, n. (Eccl. Hist.) A follower of Henry Barrowe, one of the founders of Independency or Congregationalism in England. Barrowe was executed for nonconformity in 1953.

Barruïlet (?), n. [Dim. of bar, n.] (Her.) A diminutive of the bar, having one fourth its width.

Barruïly (?), a. (Her.) Traversed by barrulets or small bars; Ð said of the field.

Barry (?), a. (Her.), Divided into bars; Ð said of the field.

Barse (?), n. [AS. bears, b'rs, akin to D. baars, G. bars, barsch. Cf. 1st Bass, n.] The common perch. See 1st Bass. [Prov. Eng.]
Halliwell.

Bartend · er (?), n. A barkeeper.

Barter (?), v.i. [imp. & p.p. Bartered (?); p. pr. & vb. n. Bartering.] [OE. bartren, OF. barater, bareter, to cheat, exchange, perh. fr. Gr. ? to do, deal (well or ill), use practices or tricks, or perh. fr. Celtic; cf. Ir. brath treachery, W. brad. Cf. Barrator.] To traffic or trade, by exchanging one commodity for another, in distinction from a sale and purchase, in which money is paid for the commodities transferred; to truck.

Barter, v.t. To trade or exchange in the way of barter; to exchange (frequently for an unworthy consideration); to traffic; to truck; Ð sometimes followed by away; as, to barter away goods or honor.

Barter, n. 1. The act or practice of trafficking by exchange of commodities; an exchange of goods.

The spirit of huckstering and barter.
Burke.

The thing given in exchange.

Syn. Ð Exchange; dealing; traffic; trade; truck.

Barterïer (?), n. One who barters.

Barterïy (?), n. Barter. [Obs.]

Camden.

Barth (?), n. [Etymol. unknown.] A place of shelter for cattle. [Prov. Eng.]

Halliwell.

Barïtholoïmew tide · (?). Time of the festival of St. Bartholomew, August 24th.

Shak.

Bartiïzan · (?), n. [Cf. Brettice.] (Arch.) A small, overhanging structure for lookout or defense, usually projecting at an angle of a building or near an entrance gateway.

Bartlett (?), n. (Bot.) A Bartlett pear, a favorite kind of pear, which originated in England about 1770, and was called Williams' Bonchr‚tien. It was brought to America, and distributed by Mr. Enoch Bartlett, of Dorchester, Massachusetts.

Barton (?), n. [AS. beret?n courtyard, grange; bere barley + t?n an inclosure.] 1. The demesne lands of a manor; also, the manor itself. [Eng.]

Burton.

A farmyard. [Eng.]

Southey.

Bartram (?), n. (Bot.) See Bertram.

Johnson.

Barway · (?), n. A passage into a field or yard, closed by bars made to take out of the posts.

Barwise · (?), adv. (Her.) Horizontally.

Barwood · (?), n. A red wood of a leguminous tree (Baphia nitida), from Angola and the Gaboon in Africa. It is used as a dyewood, and also for ramrods, violin bows and turner's work.

Bar · yïcentric (?), a. [Gr. ? heavy + ? center.] Of or pertaining to the center of gravity. See Barycentric calculus, under Calculus.

Baïryphoïny (?), n. [Gr. ? heavy + ? a sound voice.] (Med.) Difficulty of speech.

Baïryta (?), n. [Gr. ? heavy. Cf. Baria.] (Chem.) An oxide of barium (or barytum); a heavy earth with a specific gravity above 4.

Baïrytes (?), n. [Gr. ? heavy: cf. Gr. ? heaviness, F. baryte.] (Min.) Barium sulphate, generally called heavy spar or barite. See Barite.

Baïrytic (?), a. Of or pertaining to baryta.

Ba′ryto‐calcite (?), n. [Baryta + calcite.] (Min.) A mineral of a white or gray color, occurring massive or crystallized. It is a compound of the carbonates of barium and calcium.

Bar′ytone, Bar′itone (?), a. [Gr. ?; ? heavy + ? tone.] 1. (Mus.) Grave and deep, as a kind of male voice.

<small>(Greek Gram.) Not marked with an accent on the last syllable, the grave accent being understood.</small>

Bar′ytone, Bar′itone, n. [F. baryton: cf. It. baritono.] 1. (Mus.) (a) A male voice, the compass of which partakes of the common bass and the tenor, but which does not descend as low as the one, nor rise as high as the other. (b) A person having a voice of such range. (c) The viola di gamba, now entirely disused.

<small>(Greek Gram.) A word which has no accent marked on the last syllable, the grave accent being understood.</small>

Ba′rytum (?), n. [NL.] (Chem.) The metal barium. See Barium. [R.]

Basal (?), a. Relating to, or forming, the base.

Basal cleavage. See under Cleavage. — Basal plane (Crystallog.), one parallel to the lateral or horizontal axis.

Basal‐nerved · (?), a. (Bot.) Having the nerves radiating from the base; — said of leaves.

Ba′salt (?), n. [N. basaltes (an African word), a dark and hard species of marble found in Ethiopia: cf. F. basalte.] 1. (Geol.) A rock of igneous origin, consisting of augite and triclinic feldspar, with grains of magnetic or titanic iron, and also bottle‐green particles of olivine frequently disseminated.

μ It is usually of a greenish black color, or of some dull brown shade, or black. It constitutes immense beds in some regions, and also occurs in veins or dikes cutting through other rocks. It has often a prismatic structure as at the Giant's Causeway, in Ireland, where the columns are as regular as if the work of art. It is a very tough and heavy rock, and is one of the best materials for macadamizing roads.

<small>An imitation, in pottery, of natural basalt; a kind of black porcelain.</small>

Ba‐sal′tic (?), a. [Cf. F. basaltique.] Pertaining to basalt; formed of, or containing, basalt; as basaltic lava.

Ba‐sal′ti‐form (?), a. [Basalt + ‐form.] In the form of basalt; columnar.

Ba‐sal′toid (?), a. [Basalt + ‐oid.] Formed like basalt; basaltiform.

Basan (?), n. Same as Basil, a sheepskin.

Bas′a‐nite (?), n. [L. basanites lapis, Gr. ? the touchstone: cf. F. basanite.] (Min.) Lydian stone, or black jasper, a variety of siliceous or flinty slate, of a grayish or bluish black color. It is employed to test the purity of gold, the amount of alloy being indicated by the color left on the stone when rubbed by the metal.

ØBas · bleu (?), n. [F., fr. bas stocking + bleu blue.] A bluestocking; a literary woman. [Somewhat derisive]

Bascïnet (?), n. [OE. bacinet, basnet, OF. bassinet, bacinet, F. bassinet, dim. of OF. bacin, F. bassin, a helmet in the form of a basin.] A light helmet, at first open, but later made with a visor. [Written also basinet, bassinet, basnet.]

Bascule (?), n. [F., a seesaw.] In mechanics an apparatus on the principle of the seesaw, in which one end rises as the other falls.

Bascule bridge, a counterpoise or balanced drawbridge, which is opened by sinking the counterpoise and thus lifting the footway into the air.

Base (?), a. [OE. bass, F. bas, low, fr. LL. bassus thick, fat, short, humble; cf. L. Bassus, a proper name, and W. bas shallow. Cf. Bass a part in music.] 1. Of little, or less than the usual, height; of low growth; as, base shrubs. [Archaic]
Shak.

Low in place or position. [Obs.]

Shak.

Of humble birth; or low degree; lowly; mean. [Archaic] ½A pleasant and base swain.⹂

Bacon.

Illegitimate by birth; bastard. [Archaic]

Why bastard? wherefore base?
Shak.

Of little comparative value, as metal inferior to gold and silver, the precious metals.

Alloyed with inferior metal; debased; as, base coin; base bullion.

Morally low. Hence: LowÐminded; unworthy; without dignity of sentiment; ignoble; mean; illiberal; menial; as, a base fellow; base motives; base occupations. ½A cruel act of a base and a cowardish mind.⹂ Robynson (More's Utopia). ½Base ingratitude.⹂

Milton.

Not classical or correct. ½Base Latin.⹂

Fuller.

Deep or grave in sound; as, the base tone of a violin. [In this sense, commonly written bass.]

(Law) Not held by honorable service; as, a base estate, one held by services not honorable; held by villenage. Such a tenure is called base, or low, and the tenant, a base tenant.

Base fee, formerly, an estate held at the will of the lord; now, a qualified fee. See note under Fee, n., 4. Ð Base metal. See under Metal.

Syn. Ð Dishonorable; worthless; ignoble; lowÐminded; infamous; sordid; degraded. Ð Base, Vile, Mean. These words, as expressing moral qualities, are here arranged in the order of their strength, the strongest being placed first. Base marks a high degree of moral turpitude; vile and mean denote, in different degrees, the want of what is valuable or worthy of esteem. What is base excites our abhorrence; what is vile provokes our disgust or indignation; what is mean awakens contempt. Base is opposed to highÐminded; vile, to noble; mean, to liberal or generous. Ingratitude is base; sycophancy is vile; undue compliances are mean.

Base, n.[F. base, L. basis, fr. Gr. ? a stepping step, a base, pedestal, fr. ? to go, step, akin to E. come. Cf. Basis, and see Come.] 1. The bottom of anything, considered as its support, or that on which something rests for support; the foundation; as, the base of a statue. ½The base of mighty mountains.¸ Prescott.

Fig.: The fundamental or essential part of a thing; the essential principle; a groundwork.

(Arch.) (a) The lower part of a wall, pier, or column, when treated as a separate feature, usually in projection, or especially ornamented. (b) The lower part of a complete architectural design, as of a monument; also, the lower part of any elaborate piece of furniture or decoration.

(Bot.) That extremity of a leaf, fruit, etc., at which it is attached to its support.

<— p. 122 —>

(Chem.) The positive, or nonÐacid component of a salt; a substance which, combined with an acid, neutralizes the latter and forms a salt; Ð applied also to the hydroxides of the positive elements or radicals, and to certain organic bodies resembling them in their property of forming salts with acids.

(Pharmacy) The chief ingredient in a compound.

(Dyeing) A substance used as a mordant. Ure.

(Fort.) The exterior side of the polygon, or that imaginary line which connects the salient angles of two adjacent bastions.

(Geom.) The line or surface constituting that part of a figure on which it is supposed to stand.

(Math.) The number from which a mathematical table is constructed; as, the base of a system of logarithms.

[See Base low.] A low, or deep, sound. (Mus.) (a) The lowest part; the deepest male voice. (b) One who sings, or the instrument which plays, base. [Now commonly written bass.] The trebles squeak for fear, the bases roar. Dryden.

(Mil.) A place or tract of country, protected by fortifications, or by natural advantages, from which the operations of an army proceed, forward movements are made, supplies are furnished, etc.

(Mil.) The smallest kind of cannon. [Obs.]

(Zo"l.) That part of an organ by which it is attached to another more central organ.

(Crystallog.) The basal plane of a crystal.

(Geol.) The ground mass of a rock, especially if not distinctly crystalline.

(Her.) The lower part of the field. See Escutcheon.

The housing of a horse. [Obs.]

pl. A kind of skirt (often of velvet or brocade, but sometimes of mailed armor) which hung from the middle to about the knees, or lower. [Obs.]

The lower part of a robe or petticoat. [Obs.]

An apron. [Obs.] ½Bakers in their linen bases., Marston.

The point or line from which a start is made; a starting place or a goal in various games. To their appointed base they went. Dryden.

(Surv.) A line in a survey which, being accurately determined in length and position, serves as the origin from which to compute the distances and positions of any points or objects connected with it by a system of triangles. Lyman.

A rustic play; Ð called also prisoner's base, prison base, or bars. ½To run the country base., Shak.

(Baseball) Any one of the four bounds which mark the circuit of the infield. Altern base. See under Altern. Ð Attic base. (Arch.) See under Attic. Ð Base course. (Arch.) (a) The first or lower course of a foundation wall, made of large stones of a mass of concrete; Ð called also foundation course. (b) The architectural member forming the transition between the basement and the wall above. Ð Base hit (Baseball), a hit, by which the batsman, without any error on the part of his opponents, is able to reach the first base without being put out. Ð Base line. (a) A main line taken as a base, as in surveying or in military operations. (b) A line traced round a cannon at the rear of the vent. Ð Base plate, the foundation plate of heavy machinery, as of the steam engine; the bed plate. Ð Base ring (Ordnance), a projecting band of metal around the breech, connected with the body of the gun by a concave molding. H.L. Scott. Base (?), v. t. [imp. & p.p. Based (?); p. pr. & vb. n. Basing.] [From Base, n.] To put on a base or basis; to lay the foundation of; to found, as an argument or conclusion; Ð used with on or upon. Bacon. Base, v. t. [See Base, a., and cf. Abase.] 1. To abase; to let, or cast, down; to lower. [Obs.] If any ... based his pike. Sir T. North.

To reduce the value of; to debase. [Obs.] Metals which we can not base. Bacon. Baseball (?), n. 1. A game of ball, so called from the bases or bounds (four in number) which designate the circuit which each player must endeavor to make after striking the ball.

The ball used in this game. Baseboard (?), n. (Arch.) A board, or other woodwork, carried round the walls of a room and touching the floor, to form a base and protect the plastering; Ð also called washboard (in England), mopboard, and scrubboard. Baseborn · (?), a. 1. Born out of wedlock. Gay.

Born of low parentage.

Vile; mean. ½Thy baseborn heart., Shak. BaseÐburn · er (?), n. A furnace or stove in which the fuel is contained in a hopper or chamber, and is fed to the fire as the lower stratum is consumed. BaseÐcourt · (?), n. [F. basseÐcour. See Base, a., and Court, n.] 1. The secondary, inferior, or rear courtyard of a large house; the outer court of a castle.

(Law) An inferior court of law, not of record. Based (?), p.p. & a. 1. Having a base, or having as a base; supported; as, broadÐbased.

[See Base, n., 18Ð21.] Wearing, or protected by, bases. [Obs.] ½Based in lawny velvet., E.Hall. Baseĭdow's disĭease (?). [Named for Dr. Basedow, a German physician.] (Med.) A disease characterized by enlargement of the thyroid gland, prominence of the eyeballs, and inordinate action of the heart; Ð called also exophthalmic goiter. Flint. Baseĭlard

(?), n. [OF. baselarde, LL. basillardus.] A short sword or dagger, worn in the fifteenth century. [Written also baslard.] Fairholt. Baseless, a. Without a base; having no foundation or support. ½The baseless fabric of this vision., Shak. Basely, adv. 1. In a base manner; with despicable meanness; dishonorably; shamefully.

Illegitimately; in bastardy. [Archaic] Knolles. Basement (?), n. [F. soubassement. Of uncertain origin. Cf. Base, a., Bastion.] (Arch.) The outer wall of the ground story of a building, or of a part of that story, when treated as a distinct substructure. (See Base, n., 3 (a).) Hence: The rooms of a ground floor, collectively. Basement membrane (Anat.), a delicate membrane composed of a single layer of flat cells, forming the substratum upon which, in many organs, the epithelioid cells are disposed. Baseness (?), n. The quality or condition of being base; degradation; vileness. I once did hold it a baseness to write fair. Shak. Baseĭnet (?), n. See Bascinet. [Obs.] Base vi · ol (?). See Bass viol. Bash (?), v. t. & i. [OE. baschen, baissen. See Abash.] To abash; to disconcert or be disconcerted or put out of countenance. [Obs.] His countenance was bold and bashed not. Spenser. Baĭshaw (?), n. [See Pasha.] 1. A Turkish title of honor, now written pasha. See Pasha.

Fig.: A magnate or grandee.

(Zo"l.) A very large siluroid fish (Leptops olivaris) of the Mississippi valley; Ð also called goujon, mud cat, and yellow cat. Bashful (?), a. [See Bash.] 1. Abashed; daunted; dismayed. [Obs.]

Very modest, or modest excess; constitutionally disposed to shrink from public notice; indicating extreme or excessive modesty; shy; as, a bashful person, action, expression. Syn. Ð Diffident; retiring; reserved; shamefaced; sheepish. Bashfulĭly, adv. In a bashful manner. Bashfulĭness, n. The quality of being bashful. Syn. Ð Bashfulness, Modesty, Diffidence, Shyness. Modesty arises from a low estimate of ourselves; bashfulness is an abashment or agitation of the spirits at coming into contact with others; diffidence is produced by an undue degree of selfÐdistrust; shyness usually arises from an excessive selfÐconsciousness, and a painful impression that every one is looking at us. Modesty of deportment is becoming at all; bashfulness often gives rise to mistakes and blundering; diffidence is society frequently makes a man a burden to himself; shyness usually produces a reserve or distance which is often mistaken for haughtiness. ØBashiĭbaĭzouk (?), n. [Turkish, lightÐheaded, a foolish fellow.] A soldier belonging to the irregular troops of the Turkish army. Bashless, a. Shameless; unblushing. [Obs.] Spenser. Bashyle (?), n. (Chem.) See Basyle. Basiĭ (?). A combining form, especially in anatomical and botanical words, to indicate the base or position at or near a base; forming a base; as, basibranchials, the most ventral of the cartilages or bones of the branchial arches; basicranial, situated at the base of the cranium; basifacial, basitemporal, etc. Basic (?), a. 1. (Chem.) (a) Relating to a base; performing the office of a base in a salt. (b) Having the base in excess, or the amount of the base atomically greater than that of the acid, or exceeding in proportion that of the related neutral salt. (c) Apparently alkaline, as certain normal salts which exhibit alkaline reactions with test paper.

(Min.) Said of crystalline rocks which contain a relatively low percentage of silica, as basalt. Basic salt (Chem.), a salt formed from a base or hydroxide by the partial replacement of its hydrogen by a negative or acid element or radical. Baĭsicerĭlite (?), n. [BasiÐ + Gr. ? horn, antenna.] (Zo"l.) The second joint of the antenn' of crustaceans. Baĭsiciĭty, n. (Chem.) (a) The quality or state of being a base. (b) The power of an acid to unite with one or more atoms or equivalents of a base, as indicated by the number of replaceable hydrogen atoms contained in the acid. Baĭsidiĭloĭspore (?), n. [Basidium + spore.] (Bot.) A spore borne by a basidium. Ð Baĭsid · iĭloĭsporous (?), a. ØBaĭsidiĭum (?), n. [NL., dim. of Gr. ? base.] (Bot.) A special oblong or pyriform cell, with slender branches, which bears the spores in that division of fungi called Basidiomycetes, of which the common mushroom is an example. Basiĭfi · er (?), n. (Chem.) That which converts into a salifiable base. Ba̱sifu̱gal (?), a. [Base, n. + L. fugere to flee.] (Bot.) Tending or proceeding away from the base; as, a basifugal growth. Basi̱fy (?), v.t. [Base + Ðfy.] (Chem.) To convert into a salifiable base. ØBa · si̱gyni̱um (?), n. [NL., fr. Gr. ? base + ? woman.] (Bot.) The pedicel on which the ovary of certain flowers, as the passion flower, is seated; a carpophore or thecaphore. Ba · si̱hyal (?), a. [BasiÐ + Gr. ? (the letter ½upsilon‸); from the shape.] (Anat.) Noting two small bones, forming the body of the inverted hyoid arch. Ba · si̱hyoid (?), n. [BasiÐ + hyoid.] (Anat.) The central tongue bone. Basil (?), n. [Cf. F. basile and E. Bezel.] The slope or angle to which the cutting edge of a tool, as a plane, is ground. Grier. Basil, v.t. [imp. & p.p. Basiled (?); p. pr. & vb. n. Basiling.] To grind or form the edge of to an angle. Moxon. Basil, n. [F. basilic, fr. L. badilicus royal, Gr. ?, fr. ? king.] (Bot.) The name given to several aromatic herbs of the Mint family, but chiefly to the common or sweet basil (Ocymum basilicum), and the bush basil, or lesser basil (O. minimum), the leaves of which are used in cookery. The name is also given to several kinds of mountain mint (Pycnanthemum). Basil thyme, a name given to the fragrant herbs Calamintha Acinos and C. Nepeta. Ð Wild basil, a plant (Calamintha clinopodium) of the Mint family. Basil (?), n. [Corrupt. from E. basan, F. basane, LL. basanium, bazana, fr. Ar. bith¾na, prop., lining.] The skin of a sheep tanned with bark. Basi̱lar (?), Basi̱la̱ry (?), } a. [F. basilaire, fr. L. basis. See Base, n.] 1. Relating to, or situated at, the base.

Lower; inferior; applied to impulses or springs of action. [R.] ½Basilar instincts.‸ H. W. Beecher. Ba̱silic (?), n. [F. basilique.] Basilica. Ba̱silic (?), Ba̱silici̱al (?), } a. [See Basilica.] 1. Royal; kingly; also, basilican.

(Anat.) Pertaining to certain parts, anciently supposed to have a specially important function in the animal economy, as the middle vein of the right arm. Ba̱sili̱ca (?), n.; pl. Basilicas (?); sometimes Basilic?e (?). [L. basilica, Gr. ? (sc. ?, or ?) fr. ? royal, fr. ? king.] 1. Originally, the place of a king; but afterward, an apartment provided in the houses of persons of importance, where assemblies were held for dispensing justice; and hence, any large hall used for this purpose.

(Arch.) (a) A building used by the Romans as a place of public meeting, with court rooms, etc., attached. (b) A church building of the earlier centuries of Christianity, the plan of which was taken from the basilica of the Romans. The name is still applied to some churches by way of honorary distinction. Ba̱sili̱ca, n. A digest of the laws of Justinian, translated from the original Latin into Greek, by order of Basil I., in the ninth century. P. Cyc. Ba̱sili̱can (?), a. Of, relating to, or resembling, a basilica; basilical. There can be no doubt that the first churches in Constantinople were in the basilican form. Milman. Ba̱sili̱cok (?), n. [OF. basilicoc.] The basilisk. [Obs.] Chaucer ØBa̱sili̱con (?), n. [L. basilicon, Gr. ?, neut. of ?: cf. F. basilicon. See Basilica.] (Med.) An ointment composed of wax, pitch, resin, and olive oil, lard, or other fatty substance. Basi̱lisk (?), n. [L. basiliscus, Gr. ? little king, kind of serpent, dim. of ? king; Ð so named from some prominences on the head resembling a crown.] 1. A fabulous serpent, or dragon. The ancients alleged that its hissing would drive away all other serpents, and that its breath, and even its look, was fatal. See Cockatrice. Make me not sighted like the basilisk. Shak.

(Zo"l.) A lizard of the genus Basiliscus, belonging to the family Iguanid‘. µ This genus is remarkable for a membranous bag rising above the occiput, which can be filled with air at pleasure; also for an elevated crest along the back, that can be raised or depressed at will.

(Mil.) A large piece of ordnance, so called from its supposed resemblance to the serpent of that name, or from its size. [Obs.] Basin (?), n. [OF. bacin, F. bassin, LL. bacchinus, fr. bacca a water vessel, fr. L. bacca berry, in allusion to the round shape; or perh. fr. Celtic. Cf. Bac.]

A hollow vessel or dish, to hold water for washing, and for various other uses.

The quantity contained in a basin.

A hollow vessel, of various forms and materials, used in the arts or manufactures, as that used by glass grinders for forming concave glasses, by hatters for molding a hat into shape, etc.

A hollow place containing water, as a pond, a dock for ships, a little bay.

(Physical Geog.) (a) A circular or oval valley, or depression of the surface of the ground, the lowest part of which is generally occupied by a lake, or traversed by a river. (b) The entire tract of country drained by a river, or sloping towards a sea or lake.

(Geol.) An isolated or circumscribed formation, particularly where the strata dip inward, on all sides, toward a center; Ð especially applied to the coal formations, called coal basins or coal fields. Basined (?), a. Inclosed in a basin. ½Basined rivers., Young. Basilnet (?), n. Same as Bascinet. Ba · silocÏcipiÏtal (?), a. [BasiÐ + occipital.] (Anat.) Of or pertaining to the bone in the base of the cranium, frequently forming a part of the occipital in the adult, but usually distinct in the young. Ð n. The basioccipital bone. ØBasiÏon (?), n. [Gr. ? a base.] (Anat.) The middle of the anterior margin of the great foramen of the skull. BaÏsipoÏdite (?), n. [BasiÐ + ?, ?, foot.] (Anat.) The basal joint of the legs of Crustacea. ØBaÏsip · teÏrygiÏum (?), n. [NL., fr. Gr. ? a base + ? a fin.] (Anat.) A bar of cartilage at the base of the embryonic fins of some fishes. It develops into the metapterygium. Ð BaÏsip · terÏygiÏal (?), a. Ba · sipÏteryÏgoid (?), a. & n. [BasiÐ + pierygoid.] (Anat.) Applied to a protuberance of the base of the sphenoid bone. Basis (?),n.; pl. Bases (?). [L. basis, Gr. ?. See Base, n.] 1. The foundation of anything; that on which a thing rests. Dryden.

The pedestal of a column, pillar, or statue. [Obs.] If no basis bear my rising name. Pope.

<— p. 123 —>

The ground work the first or fundamental principle; that which supports.

The basis of public credit is good faith.
A. Hamilton.

The principal component part of a thing.

BaÏsisoÏlute (?), a. [BasiÏ + solute, a.] (Bot.) Prolonged at the base, as certain leaves.

Ba · siÏsphenoid (?), Ba · siÏspheÏnoidal (?), } a. [BasiÏ + spheroid.] (Anat.) Of or pertaining to that part of the base of the cranium between the basioccipital and the presphenoid, which usually ossifies separately in the embryo or in the young, and becomes a part of the sphenoid in the adult.

Ba · siÏsphenoid, n. (Anat.) The basisphenoid bone.

Bask, v. i. [imp. & p.p. Basked (?); p. pr. & vb. n. Basking.] [OScand. ba?ask to bathe one's self, or perh. bakask to bake one's self, sk being reflexive. See Bath, n., Bake, v. t.] To lie in warmth; to be exposed to genial heat.

Basks in the glare, and stems the tepid wave.
Goldsmith.

Bask, v. t. To warm by continued exposure to heat; to warm with genial heat.

Basks at the fire his hairy strength.
Milton.

Basket (?), n. [Of unknown origin. The modern Celtic words seem to be from the English.] 1. A vessel made of osiers or other twigs, cane, rushes, splints, or other flexible material, interwoven. ½Rude baskets ... woven of the flexile willow.˳

Dyer.

<small>The contents of a basket; as much as a basket contains; as, a basket of peaches.</small>

<small>(Arch.) The bell or vase of the Corinthian capital. [Improperly so used.]</small>

Gwilt.

<small>The two back seats facing one another on the outside of a stagecoach. [Eng.]</small>

Goldsmith.

Basket fish (Zo"l.), an ophiuran of the genus Astrophyton, having the arms much branched. See Astrophyton. Ð Basket hilt, a hilt with a covering wrought like basketwork to protect the hand. Hudibras. Hence, Baskethilted, a. Ð Basket work, work consisting of plaited osiers or twigs. Ð Basket worm (Zo"l.), a lepidopterous insect of the genus Thyridopteryx and allied genera, esp. T. ephemer'formis. The larva makes and carries about a bag or basketÐlike case of silk and twigs, which it afterwards hangs up to shelter the pupa and wingless adult females.

Basket, v. t. To put into a basket. [R.]

BasketÏful (?), n.; pl. Basketfuls (?). As much as a basket will contain.

BasketÏry (?), n. The art of making baskets; also, baskets, taken collectively.

Basking shark · (?). (Zo"l.) One of the largest species of sharks (Cetorhinus maximus), so called from its habit of basking in the sun; the liver shark, or bone shark. It inhabits the northern seas of Europe and America, and grows to a length of more than forty feet. It is a harmless species.

Basnet (?), n. Same as Bascinet.

ØBaÏsom · maÏtophoÏra (?), n. pl. [NL., fr. Gr. ? base + ? eye + ? to bear.] (Zo"l.) A group of Pulmonifera having the eyes at the base of the tentacles, including the common pond snails.

Bason (?), n. A basin. [Obs. or Special form]

Basque (?), a. [F.] Pertaining to Biscay, its people, or their language.

Basque (?), n. [F.] 1. One of a race, of unknown origin, inhabiting a region on the Bay of Biscay in Spain and France.

<small>The language spoken by the Basque people.</small>

<small>A part of a lady's dress, resembling a jacket with a short skirt; Ð probably so called because this fashion of dress came from the Basques.</small>

Basquish (?), a. [F. Basque Biscayan: cf. G. Baskisch.] Pertaining to the country, people, or language of Biscay; Basque [Obs.]

Sir T. Browne.

Bas·Đrellief (?), n. [F. basĭrelief; bas law + relief raised work, relever to raise: cf. It. bassorilievo.] Low relief; sculpture, the figures of which project less than half of their true proportions; Đ called also bassrelief and bassolrilievo. See Altolrilievo.

Bass (?), n.; pl. Bass, and sometimes Basses (?). [A corruption of barse.] (Zo"l.) 1. An edible, spinyĐfinned fish, esp. of the genera Roccus, Labrax, and related genera. There are many species.

μ The common European bass is Labrax lupus. American species are: the striped bass (Roccus lineatus); white or silver bass of the lakes. (R. chrysops); brass or yellow bass (R. interruptus).

The two American freshĐwater species of black bass (genus Micropterus). See Black bass.

Species of Serranus, the sea bass and rock bass. See Sea bass.

The southern, red, or channel bass (Sci'na ocellata). See Redfish.

μ The name is also applied to many other fishes. See Calico bass, under Calico.

Bass, n. [A corruption of bast.] 1. (Bot.) The linden or lime tree, sometimes wrongly called whitewood; also, its bark, which is used for making mats. See Bast.

(Pron. ?) A hassock or thick mat.

Bass (?), n. [F. basse, fr. bas low. See Base, a.]

A bass, or deep, sound or tone.

(Mus.) (a) The lowest part in a musical composition. (b) One who sings, or the instrument which plays, bass. [Written also base.]

Thorough bass. See Thorough bass.

Bass, a. Deep or grave in tone.

Bass clef (Mus.), the character placed at the beginning of the staff containing the bass part of a musical composition. [See Illust. under Clef.] Đ Bass voice, a deepsounding voice; a voice fitted for singing bass.

Bass, v. t. To sound in a deep tone. [R.]

Shak.

Bassa (?), Baslsaw (?), n. See Bashaw.

Bass· drum (?). (Mus.) The largest of the different kinds of drums, having two heads, and emitting a deep, grave sound. See Bass, a.

Basset (?),n. [F. bassette, fr.It. bassetta. Cf. Basso.] A game at cards, resembling the modern faro, said to have been invented at Venice.

Some dress, some dance, some play, not to forget

Your piquet parties, and your dear basset.

Rowe.

Basset (?), a. [Cf. OF. basset somewhat low, dim. of bas low.] (Geol.) Inclined upward; as, the basset edge of strata.

Lyell.

Basset, n. (Geol.) The edge of a geological stratum at the surface of the ground; the outcrop.

Basset, v. i. [imp. & p.p. Basseted; p. pr. & vb. n. Basseting.] (Geol.) To inclined upward so as to appear at the surface; to crop out; as, a vein of coal bassets.

Basset horn · (?). [See Basset, a.] (Mus.) An instrument blown with a reed, and resembling a clarinet, but of much greater compass, embracing nearly four octaves.

Basset hound · (?). [F. basset.] (Zo"l.) A small kind of hound with a long body and short legs, used as an earth dog.

Bassetïing, n. The upward direction of a vein in a mine; the emergence of a stratum at the surface.

ØBasïsetto (?),n. [It., adj., somewhat low; n., counter tenor. See Basso.] (Mus.) A tenor or small bass viol.

Bass horn (?). (Mus.) A modification of the bassoon, much deeper in tone.

Bassiïnet (?), n. [Cf. F. bassinet, dim. of bassin. See Basin, and cf. Bascinet.] 1. A wicker basket, with a covering or hood over one end, in which young children are placed as in a cradle.

See Bascinet.

Lord Lytton.

ØBasso (?), n. [It., fr. LL. bassus. See Base, a.] (Mus.) (a) The bass or lowest part; as, to sing basso. (b) One who sings the lowest part. (c) The double bass, or contrabasso.

ØBasso continuo (?). [It., bass continued.] (Mus.) A bass part written out continuously, while the other parts of the harmony are indicated by figures attached to the bass; continued bass.

Bassock (?), n. A hassock. See 2d Bass, 2.

Basïsoon (?), n. [F. basson, fr. basse bass; or perh. fr. bas son low sound. See Bass a part in music.] (Mus.) A wind instrument of the double reed kind, furnished with holes, which are stopped by the fingers, and by keys, as in flutes. It forms the natural bass to the oboe, clarinet, etc.

μ Its compass comprehends three octaves. For convenience of carriage it is divided into two parts; whence it is also called a fagot.

Basïsoonist, n. A performer on the bassoon.

Busby.

ØBassoÐriïlievo (?), BassoÐreïlievo (?), n. [It. bassoÐrilievo.] Same as BasÐrelief.

Bassoĭrin (?), n. [Cf. F. bassorine.] (Chem.) A constituent part of a species of gum from Bassora, as also of gum tragacanth and some gum resins. It is one of the amyloses.

Ure.

BassÐreĭlief· (?), n. Some as BasÐrelief.

Bass vi · ol (?). (Mus.) A stringed instrument of the viol family, used for playing bass. See 3d Bass, n., and Violoncello.

Basswood· (?), n. (Bot.) The bass (Tilia) or its wood; especially, T. Americana. See Bass, the lime tree.

All the bowls were made of basswood,
White and polished very smoothly.

Longfellow.

Bast (?), n. [AS. b'st; akin to Icel., Sw., Dan., D., & G. bast, of unknown origin. Cf. Bass the tree.] 1. The inner fibrous bark of various plants; esp. of the lime tree; hence, matting, cordage, etc., made therefrom.

A thick mat or hassock. See 2d Bass, 2.

ØBasta (?), interj. [It.] Enough; stop.

Shak.

Bastard (?),n. [OF. bastard, bastart, F. b?tard, prob. fr. OF. bast, F. b?t, a packsaddle used as a bed by the muleteers (fr. LL. bastum) + ĭard. OF. fils de bast son of the packsaddle; as the muleteers were accustomed to use their saddles for beds in the inns. See Cervantes, ½Don Quixote,͵ chap. 16; and cf.G. bankert, fr. bank bench.] 1. A ½natural͵ child; a child begotten and born out of wedlock; an illegitimate child; one born of an illicit union.

µ By the civil and canon laws, and by the laws of many of the United States, a bastard becomes a legitimate child by the intermarriage of the parents at any subsequent time. But by those of England, and of some states of the United States, a child, to be legitimate, must at least be born after the lawful marriage.

Kent. Blackstone.

(Sugar Refining) (a) An inferior quality of soft brown sugar, obtained from the sirups that ? already had several boilings. (b) A large size of mold, in which sugar is drained.

A sweet Spanish wine like muscadel in flavor.

Brown bastard is your only drink.

Shak.

A writing paper of a particular size. See Paper.

Bastard (?), a. 1. Begotten and born out of lawful matrimony; illegitimate. See Bastard, n., note.

Lacking in genuineness; spurious; false; adulterate; Ð applied to things which resemble those which are genuine, but are really not so.

That bastard self=love which is so vicious in itself, and productive of so many vices.
Barrow.

Of an unusual make or proportion; as, a bastard musket; a bastard culverin. [Obs.]

(Print.) Abbreviated, as the half title in a page preceding the full title page of a book.

Bastard ashlar (Arch.), stones for ashlar work, roughly squared at the quarry. — Bastard file, a file intermediate between the coarsest and the second cut. — Bastard type (Print.), type having the face of a larger or a smaller size than the body; e. g., a nonpareil face on a brevier body. — Bastard wing (Zo"l.), three to five quill feathers on a small joint corresponding to the thumb in some mammalia; the alula.

Bastard, v. t. To bastardize. [Obs.]
Bacon.
Bastardism (?),n. The state of being a bastard; bastardy.
Bastardize (?), v. t. [imp. & p.p. Bastardized (?); p. pr. & vb. n. Bastardizing.] 1. To make or prove to be a bastard; to stigmatize as a bastard; to declare or decide legally to be illegitimate.

The law is so indulgent as not to bastardize the child, if born, though not begotten, in lawful wedlock.
Blackstone.

To beget out of wedlock. [R.]

Shak.
Bastardly, a. Bastardlike; baseborn; spurious; corrupt. [Obs.] — adv. In the manner of a bastard; spuriously. [Obs.]
Shak. Donne.
Bastardy (?), n. 1. The state of being a bastard; illegitimacy.

The procreation of a bastard child.

Wharton.
Baste (?), v. t. [imp. & p.p. Basted; p. pr. & vb. n. Basting.] [Cf. Icel. beysta to strike, powder; Sw. basa to beat with a rod: perh. akin to E. beat.]

To beat with a stick; to cudgel.

One man was basted by the keeper for carrying some people
over on his back through the waters.
Pepys.

(Cookery) To sprinkle flour and salt and drip butter or fat on, as on meat in roasting.

To mark with tar, as sheep. [Prov. Eng.]

Baste, v. t. [OE. basten, OF. bastir, F. b?tir, prob. fr. OHG. bestan to sew, MHG. besten to bind, fr. OHG. bast bast. See Bast.] To sew loosely, or with long stitches; Ð usually, that the work may be held in position until sewed more firmly.

Shak.

Basĭtile Basĭtille } (?), n. [F. bastille fortress, OF. bastir to build, F. b?tir.]

(Feud. Fort.) A tower or an elevated work, used for the defense, or in the siege, of a fortified place.

The high bastiles ... which overtopped the walls.
Holland.

½The Bastille„, formerly a castle or fortress in Paris, used as a prison, especially for political offenders; hence, a rhetorical name for a prison.

Bas · tiĭnade (?), n. See Bastinado, n.
Bas · tiĭnade, v. t. To bastinado. [Archaic]
Bas · tiĭnado (?), n.; pl. Bastinadoes (?). [Sp. bastonada (cf. F. bastonnade), fr. baston (cf. F. b?ton) a stick or staff. See Baston.]

A blow with a stick or cudgel.

A sound beating with a stick or cudgel. Specifically: A form of punishment among the Turks, Chinese, and others, consisting in beating an offender on the soles of his feet.

Bas · tiĭnado, v. t. [imp. & p.p. Bastinadoes (?); p. pr. & vb. n. Bastinadoing.] To beat with a stick or cudgel, especially on the soles of the feet.

Bastion (?), n. [F. bastion (cf. It. bastione), fr. LL. bastire to build (cf. F. b?tir, It. bastire), perh. from the idea of support for a weight, and akin to Gr. ? to lift, carry, and to E. baston, baton.] (Fort.) A work projecting outward from the main inclosure of a fortification, consisting of two faces and two flanks, and so constructed that it is able to defend by a flanking fire the adjacent curtain, or wall which extends from one bastion to another. Two adjacent bastions are connected by the curtain, which joins the flank of one with the adjacent flank of the other. The distance between the flanks of a bastion is called the gorge. A lunette is a detached bastion. See Ravelin.

Bastioned (?),a. Furnished with a bastion; having bastions.

<— p. 124 —>

Basto (?), n. [Sp.] The ace of clubs in qua?rille and omber. Pope. Baston (?), n. [OF. baston, F. b?ton, LL. basto. See Bastion, and cf. Baton, and 3d Batten.]

A staff or cudgel. [Obs.] ½To fight with blunt bastons.„ Holland.

(Her.) See Baton.

An officer bearing a painted staff, who formerly was in attendance upon the king's court to take into custody persons committed by the court. Mozley & W. Basyle (?), n. [Gr. ? base + ? wood. See Ïyl.] (Chem.) A positive or nonacid constituent of compound, either elementary, or, if compound, performing the functions of an element. Basyïlous (?), a. Pertaining to, or having the nature of, a basyle; electroÐpositive; basic; Ð opposed to chlorous. Graham. Bat (?), n. [OE. batte, botte, AS. batt; perhaps fr. the Celtic; cf. Ir. bat, bata, stick, staff; but cf. also F. batte a beater (thing), wooden sword, battre to beat.]

A large stick; a club; specifically, a piece of wood with one end thicker or broader than the other, used in playing baseball, cricket, etc.

(Mining) Shale or bituminous shale. Kirwan.

A sheet of cotton used for filling quilts or comfortables; batting.

A part of a brick with one whole end. Bat bolt (Machinery), a bolt barbed or jagged at its butt or tang to make it hold the more firmly. Knight. Bat, v. t. [imp. & p.p. Batted (?); p. pr. & vb. n. Batting.] To strike or hit with a bat or a pole; to cudgel; to beat. Holland. Bat, v. i. To use a bat, as in a game of baseball. Bat, n. [Corrupt. from OE. back, backe, balke; cf. Dan. aftenÐbakke (aften evening), Sw. nattÐbacka (natt night), Icel. le?rÐblaka (le?r leather), Icel. blaka to flutter.] (Zo"l.) One of the Cheiroptera, an order of flying mammals, in which the wings are formed by a membrane stretched between the elongated fingers, legs, and tail. The common bats are small and insectivorous. See Cheiroptera and Vampire. Bat tick (Zo"l.), a wingless, dipterous insect of the genus Nycteribia, parasitic on bats. Bataïble (?), a. [Abbrev. from debatable.] Disputable. [Obs.] µ The border land between England and Scotland, being formerly a subject of contention, was called batable or debatable ground. Batailled (?), a. Embattled. [Obs.] Chaucer. ØBa · tarïdeau (?),n. [F.] 1. A cofferdam. Brande & C.

(Mil.) A wall built across the ditch of a fortification, with a sluice gate to regulate the height of water in the ditch on both sides of the wall. ØBaïtatas (?), ØBaïtata (?), } n. An aboriginal American name for the sweet potato (Ipom'a batatas). Baïtaviïan (?), a. Of or pertaining to (a) the Batavi, an ancient Germanic tribe; or to (b) ?atavia or Holland; as, a Batavian legion. Batavian Republic, the name given to Holland by the French after its conquest in 1795. Baïtaviïan, n. A native or inhabitant of Batavia or Holland. [R.] Bancroft. Batch (?), n. [OE. bache, bacche, fr. AS. bacan to bake; cf. G. geb„ck and D. baksel. See Bake, v. t.]

The quantity of bread baked at one time.

A quantity of anything produced at one operation; a group or collection of persons or things of the same kind; as, a batch of letters; the next batch of business. ½A new batch of Lords.¸ Lady M. W. Montagu. Bate (?), n. [Prob. abbrev. from debate.] Strife; contention. [Obs.] Shak. Bate, v. t. [imp. & p.p. Bated; p. pr. & vb. n. Bating.] [From abate.] 1. To lessen by retrenching, deducting, or reducing; to abate; to beat down; to lower. He must either bate the laborer's wages, or not employ or not pay him. Locke.

To allow by way of abatement or deduction. To whom he bates nothing or what he stood upon with the parliament. South.

To leave out; to except. [Obs.] Bate me the king, and, be he flesh and blood. He lies that says it. Beau. & Fl.

To remove. [Obs.] About autumn bate the earth from about the roots of olives, and lay them bare. Holland.

To deprive of. [Obs.] When baseness is exalted, do not bate The place its honor for the person's sake. Herbert. Bate, v. i. 1. To remit or retrench a part; Ð with of. Abate thy speed, and I will bate of mine. Dryden.

To waste away. [Obs.] Shak. Bate (?), v. t. To attack; to bait. [Obs.] Spenser. Bate, imp. of Bite. [Obs.] Spenser. Bate, v. i. [F. battre des ailes to flutter. Cf. Bait to flutter.] To flutter as a hawk; to bait. [Obs.] Bacon. Bate, n. (Jewish Antiq.) See 2d Bath. Bate, n. [Cf. Sw. beta maceration, soaking, G. beize, and E. bite.] An alkaline solution consisting of the dung of certain animals; Ð employed in the preparation of hides; grainer. Knight. Bate, v. t. To steep in bate, as hides, in the manufacture of leather. ØBaĭteau (?), n.; pl. Bateaux (?). [F. bateau, LL. batellus, fr. battus, batus, boa, which agrees with AS. b¾t boat: cf. W. bad boat. See Boat, n.] A boat; esp. a flatÐbottomed, clumsy boat used on the Canadian lakes and rivers. [Written also, but less properly, batteau.] Bateau bridge, a floating bridge supported by bateaux. Bated (?), a. Reduced; lowered; restrained; as, to speak with bated breath. Macaulay. Bateful (?), a. Exciting contention; contentious. [Obs.] ½It did bateful question frame. ˳ Sidney. Bateless, a. Not to be abated. [Obs.] Shak. Batement (?), n. [For Abatement. See 2d Bate.] Abatement; diminution. Moxon. Batement light (Arch.), a window or one division of a window having vertical sides, but with the sill not horizontal, as where it follows the rake of a staircase. Batfish · (?), n. (Zo"l.) A name given to several species of fishes: (a) The Malthe vespertilio of the Atlantic coast. (b) The flying gurnard of the Atlantic (Cephalacanthus spinarella). (c) The California batfish or sting ray (Myliobatis Californicus.) Batfowl · er (?), n. One who practices or finds sport in batfowling. Batfowl · ing (?), n. [From Bat a stick.] A mode of catching birds at night, by holding a torch or other light, and beating the bush or perch where they roost. The birds, flying to the light, are caught with nets or otherwise. Batful (?), a. [Icel. bati amelioration, batna to grow better; akin to AS. bet better. Goth. gaĭbatnan to profit. ?255. Cf. Batten, v. i., Better.] Rich; fertile. [Obs.] ½Batful valleys.˳ Drayton. Bath (?), n.; pl. Baths (?). [AS. b'?; akin to OS. & Icel. ba?, Sw., Dan., D., & G. bad, and perh. to G. b„hen to foment.] 1. The act of exposing the body, or part of the body, for purposes of cleanliness, comfort, health, etc., to water, vapor, hot air, or the like; as, a cold or a hot bath; a medicated bath; a steam bath; a hip bath.

Water or other liquid for bathing.

A receptacle or place where persons may immerse or wash their bodies in water.

A building containing an apartment or a series of apartments arranged for bathing. Among the ancients, the public baths were of amazing extent and magnificence. Gwilt.

(Chem.) A medium, as heated sand, ashes, steam, hot air, through which heat is applied to a body.

(Photog.) A solution in which plates or prints are immersed; also, the receptacle holding the solution. µ Bath is used adjectively or in combination, in an obvious sense of or for baths or bathing; as, bathroom, bath tub, bath keeper. Douche bath. See Douche. Ð Order of the Bath, a high order of British knighthood, composed of three classes, viz., knights grand cross, knights commanders, and knights companions, abbreviated thus: G. C. B., K. C. B., K. B. Ð Russian bath, a kind of vapor bath which consists in a prolonged exposure of the body to the influence of the steam of water, followed by washings and shampooings. Ð Turkish bath, a kind of bath in which a profuse perspiration is produced by hot air, after which the body is washed and shampooed. Ð Bath house, a house used for the purpose of bathing; Ð also a small house, near a bathing place, where a bather undresses and dresses. Bath (?), n. [Heb.] A Hebrew measure containing the tenth of a homer, or five gallons and three pints, as a measure for liquids; and two pecks and five quarts, as a dry measure. Bath (?), n. A city in the west of England, resorted to for its hot springs, which has given its name to various objects. Bath brick, a preparation of calcareous earth, in the form of a brick, used for cleaning knives, polished metal, etc. Ð Bath chair, a kind of chair on wheels, as used by invalids at Bath. ½People walked out, or drove out, or were pushed out in their Bath chairs.˳ Dickens. Ð Bath metal, an alloy consisting of four and a half ounces of zinc and one pound of copper. Ð Bath note, a folded writing paper, 8 1/2 by 14 inches. Ð Bath stone, a species of limestone (o"lite) found near Bath, used for building. Bathe (?), v. t. [imp. & p.p. Bathed (?); p. pr. & vb. n. Bathing.] [OE. ba?ien, AS. ba?ian, fr. b‘? bath. See 1st Bath, and cf. Bay to bathe.] 1. To wash by immersion, as in a bath; to subject to a bath. Chancing to bathe himself in the River Cydnus. South.

To lave; to wet. ½The lake which bathed the foot of the Alban mountain., T. Arnold.

To moisten or suffuse with a liquid. And let us bathe our hands in C‘sar's blood. Shak.

To apply water or some liquid medicament to; as, to bathe the eye with warm water or with sea water; to bathe one's forehead with camphor.

To surround, or envelop, as water surrounds a person immersed. ½The rosy shadows bathe me. , Tennyson. ½The bright sunshine bathing all the world., Longfellow. Bathe (?), v. i. 1. To bathe one's self; to take a bath or baths. ½They bathe in summer., Waller.

To immerse or cover one's self, as in a bath. ½To bathe in fiery floods., Shak. ½Bathe in the dimples of her cheek., Lloyd.

To bask in the sun. [Obs.] Chaucer. Bathe, n. The immersion of the body in water; as to take one's usual bathe. Edin. Rev. Bather (?), n. One who bathes. Bathetic (?), a. Having the character of bathos. [R.] Bathing (?), n. Act of taking a bath or baths. Bathing machine, a small room on wheels, to be driven into the water, for the convenience of bathers, who undress and dress therein. Bathmism (?), n. See Vital force. Bathometer (?), n. [Gr. ? depth + ?meter.] An instrument for measuring depths, esp. one for taking soundings without a sounding line. Bathorse · (?), n. [F. b?t packsaddle (cheval de b?t packhorse) + E. horse. See Bastard.] A horse which carries an officer's baggage during a campaign. Bathos (?), n. [Gr. ? depth, fr. ? deep.] (Rhet.) A ludicrous descent from the elevated to the low, in writing or speech; anticlimax. ØBathybilus (?), n. [NL., fr. Gr. ? deep + ? life] (Zo"l.) A name given by Prof. Huxley to a gelatinous substance found in mud dredged from the Atlantic and preserved in alcohol. He supposed that it was free living protoplasm, covering a large part of the ocean bed. It is now known that the substance is of chemical, not of organic, origin. Bath · ymetric (?), Bath · ymetrical (?), } a. Pertaining to bathymetry; relating to the measurement of depths, especially of depths in the sea. Bathymetry (?), n. [Gr. ? depth + ?metry.] The art or science of sounding, or measuring depths in the sea. Bating (?), prep. [Strictly p. pr. of Bat? to abate.] With the exception of; excepting. We have little reason to think that they bring many ideas with them, bating some faint ideas of hunger and thirst. Locke. Batiste (?), n. [F. batiste, from the name of the alleged first maker, Baptiste of Cambrai. Littr,.] Originally, cambric or lawn of fine linen; now applied also to cloth of similar texture made of cotton. Batlet (?), n. [Bat stick + Ilet.] A short bat for beating clothes in washing them; Ð called also batler, batling staff, batting staff. Shak. ØBatman (?), n. [Turk. batman.] A weight used in the East, varying according to the locality; in Turkey, the greater batman is about 157 pounds, the lesser only a fourth of this; at Aleppo and Smyrna, the batman is 17 pounds. Simmonds. Batman (?), n.; pl. Batmen (?). [F. b?t packsaddle + E. man. Cf. Bathorse.] A man who has charge of a bathorse and his load. Macaulay. ØBatoideli (?), n. pl. [NL., fr. Gr. ? a kind of ray + Ioid.] (Zo"l.) The division of fishes which includes the rays and skates. Baton (?), n. [F. b?ton. See Baston.] 1. A staff or truncheon, used for various purposes; as, the baton of a field marshal; the baton of a conductor in musical performances. He held the baton of command. Prescott.

(Her.) An ordinary with its ends cut off, borne sinister as a mark of bastardy, and containing one fourth in breadth of the bend sinister; Ð called also bastard bar. See Bend sinister. Batoon (?), n. See Baton, and Baston. Bat print · ing (?). (Ceramics) A mode of printing on glazed ware. ØBatrachila (?), n. pl. [NL., fr. Gr. ? belonging to a frog, fr. ? frog.] (Zo"l.) The order of amphibians which includes the frogs and toads; the Anura. Sometimes the word is used in a wider sense as equivalent to Amphibia. Batrachilan (?), a. (Zo"l.) Pertaining to the Batrachia. Ð n. One of the Batrachia.

Batraïchoid (?), a. [Batrachia + ïoid.] (Zo"l.) Froglike. Specifically: Of or pertaining to the Batrachid‘, a family of marine fishes, including the toadfish. Some have poisonous dorsal spines. Bat·raïcholmyïomaïchy (?), n. [Gr. ?; ? frog + ? mouse + ? battle.] The battle between the frogs and mice; Ð a Greek parody on the Iliad, of uncertain authorship. Bat·raïchophaïgous (?), a. [Gr. ? frog + ? to eat.] Feeding on frogs. Quart. Rev. Batsman (?), n.; pl. Batsmen (?). The one who wields the bat in cricket, baseball, etc. Bat'sÐwing (?) or Batwing, a. Shaped like a bat's wing; as, a bat'sÐwing burner. ØBatta (?), n. [Prob. through Pg. for Canarese bhatta rice in the husk.] Extra pay; esp. an extra allowance to an English officer serving in India. Whitworth.

<— p. 125 —>

ØBatta (?), n. [Hind. ba??a.] Rate of exchange; also, the discount on uncurrent coins. [India] Battaïble (?), a. [See Batful.] Capable of culti?ation; fertile; productive; fattening. [Obs.] Burton. Battaillant (?), a. [F. bataillant, p. pr. See Battle, v. i.] [Obs.] Prepared for battle; combatant; warlike. Spenser. Ð n. A combatant. Shelton. Battaillous (?), a. [OF. bataillos, fr. bataille. See Battle, n.] Arrayed for battle; fit or eager for battle; warlike. [Obs.] ½In battailous aspect.¸ Milton. Batïtalia (?), n. [LL. battalia battle, a body of troops. See Battle, n.] 1. Order of battle; disposition or arrangement of troops (brigades, regiments, battalions, etc.), or of a naval force, for action. A drawing up the armies in battalia. Jer. Taylor. 2. An army in battle array; also, the main battalia or body. [Obs.] Shak. Batïtalion (?), n. [F. bataillon, fr. It. battaglione. See Battalia.] 1. A body of troops; esp. a body of troops or an army in battle array. ½The whole battalion views.¸ Milton. 2. (Mil.) A regiment, or two or more companies of a regiment, esp. when assembled for drill or battle. Batïtalion (?), v. t. To form into battalions. [R.] Battel (?), n. [Obs. form. of Battle.] (Old Eng. Law) A single combat; as, trial by battel. See Wager of battel, under Wager. Battel, n. [Of uncertain etymology.] Provisions ordered from the buttery; also, the charges for them; Ð only in the pl., except when used adjectively. [Univ. of Oxford, Eng.] Battel, v. i. To be supplied with provisions from the buttery. [Univ. of Oxford, Eng.] Battel, v. t. [Cf. Batful, Batten, v. i.] To make fertile. [Obs.] ½To battel barren land.¸ Ray. Battel, a. Fertile; fruitful; productive. [Obs.] A battel soil for grain, for pasture good. Fairfax. Batteller (?), Battler (?), n. [See 2d Battel, n.] A student at Oxford who is supplied with provisions from the buttery; formerly, one who paid for nothing but what he called for, answering nearly to a sizar at Cambridge. Wright. Batten (?), v. t. [imp. & p.p. Battened (?); p. pr. & vb. n. Battening.] [See Batful.] 1. To make fat by plenteous feeding; to fatten. ½Battening our flocks.¸ Milton. 2. To fertilize or enrich, as land. Batten, v. i. To grow fat; to grow fat in ease and luxury; to glut one's self. Dryden. The pampered monarch lay battening in ease. Garth. Skeptics, with a taste for carrion, who batten on the hideous facts in history, Ð persecutions, inquisitions. Emerson. Batten, n . [F. b?ton stick, staff. See Baton.] A strip of sawed stuff, or a scantling; as, (a) pl. (Com. & Arch.) Sawed timbers about 7 by 2 1/2 inches and not less than

6 feet long. Brande & C. (b) (Naut.) A strip of wood used in fastening the edges of a tarpaulin to the deck, also around masts to prevent chafing. (c) A long, thin strip used to strengthen a part, to cover a crack, etc. Batten door (Arch.), a door made of boards of the whole length of the door, secured by battens nailed crosswise. Batten, v. t. To furnish or fasten with battens. To batten down, to fasten down with battens, as the tarpaulin over the hatches of a ship during a storm. Batten, n. [F. battant. See Batter, v. t.] The movable bar of a loom, which strikes home or closes the threads of a woof. Battenĭing (?), n. (Arch.) Furring done with small pieces nailed directly upon the wall. Batter (?), v. t. [imp. & p.p. Battered (?); p. pr. & vb. n. Battering.] [OE. bateren, OF. batre, F. battre, fr. LL. battere, for L. batuere to strike, beat; of unknown origin. Cf. Abate, Bate to abate.]

> To beat with successive blows; to beat repeatedly and with violence, so as to bruise, shatter, or demolish; as, to batter a wall or rampart.
>
> To wear or impair as if by beating or by hard usage. ½Each battered jade., Pope.
>
> (Metallurgy) To flatten (metal) by hammering, so as to compress it inwardly and spread it outwardly. Batter, n. [OE. batere, batire; cf. OF. bateure, bature, a beating. See Batter, v. t.] 1. A semiÐliquid mixture of several ingredients, as, flour, eggs, milk, etc., beaten together and used in cookery. King.
>
> Paste of clay or loam. Holland.
>
> (Printing) A bruise on the face of a plate or of type in the form. Batter, n. A backward slope in the face of a wall or of a bank; receding slope. Batter rule, an instrument consisting of a rule or frame, and a plumb line, by which the batter or slope of a wall is regulated in building. Batter, v. i. (Arch.) To slope gently backward. Batter, n. One who wields a bat; a batsman. Batterĭer (?), n. One who, or that which, batters. BatterĭingÐram · (?), n. 1. (Mil.) An engine used in ancient times to beat down the walls of besieged places. µ It was a large beam, with a head of iron, which was sometimes made to resemble the head of a ram. It was suspended by ropes t a beam supported by posts, and so balanced as to swing backward and forward, and was impelled by men against the wall. Grose.
>
> A blacksmith's hammer, suspended, and worked horizontally. Batterĭing train · (?). (Mil.) A train of artillery for siege operations. Batterĭy (?), n.; pl. Batteries (?). [F. batterie, fr. battre. See Batter, v. t.] 1. The act of battering or beating.
>
> (Law) The unlawful beating of another. It includes every willful, angry and violent, or negligent touching of another's person or clothes, or anything attached to his person or held by him.
>
> (Mil.) (a) Any place where cannon or mortars are mounted, for attack or defense. (b) Two or more pieces of artillery in the field. (c) A company or division of artillery, including the gunners, guns, horses, and all equipments. In the United States, a battery of flying artillery consists usually of six guns. Barbette battery. See Barbette. Ð Battery d'enfilade, or Enfilading battery, one that sweeps the whole length of a line of troops or part of a work. Ð Battery en ,charpe, one that plays obliquely. Ð Battery gun, a gun capable of firing a number, of shots simultaneously or successively without stopping to load. Ð Battery wagon, a wagon employed to transport the tools and materials for repair of the carriages, etc., of the battery. Ð In battery, projecting, as a gun, into an embrasure or over a parapet in readiness for firing. Ð Masked battery, a battery artificially concealed until required to open upon the enemy. Ð Out of battery, or From battery, withdrawn, as a gun, to a position for loading.

(Elec.) (a) A number of coated jars (Leyden jars) so connected that they may be charged and discharged simultaneously. (b) An apparatus for generating voltaic electricity. µ In the trough battery, copper and zinc plates, connected in pairs, divide the trough into cells, which are filled with an acid or oxidizing liquid; the effect is exhibited when wires connected with the two endÐplates are brought together. In Daniell's battery, the metals are zinc and copper, the former in dilute sulphuric acid, or a solution of sulphate of zinc, the latter in a saturated solution of sulphate of copper. A modification of this is the common gravity battery, so called from the automatic action of the two fluids, which are separated by their specific gravities. In Grove's battery, platinum is the metal used with zinc; two fluids are used, one of them in a porous cell surrounded by the other. In Bunsen's or the carbon battery, the carbon of gas coke is substituted for the platinum of Grove's. In Leclanch,'s battery, the elements are zinc in a solution of ammonium chloride, and gas carbon surrounded with manganese dioxide in a porous cell. A secondary battery is a battery which usually has the two plates of the same kind, generally of lead, in dilute sulphuric acid, and which, when traversed by an electric current, becomes charged, and is then capable of giving a current of itself for a time, owing to chemical changes produced by the charging current. A storage battery is a kind of secondary battery used for accumulating and storing the energy of electrical charges or currents, usually by means of chemical work done by them; an accumulator.

A number of similar machines or devices in position; an apparatus consisting of a set of similar parts; as, a battery of boilers, of retorts, condensers, etc.

(Metallurgy) A series of stamps operated by one motive power, for crushing ores containing the precious metals. Knight.

The box in which the stamps for crushing ore play up and down.

(Baseball) The pitcher and catcher together. Batting (?), n. 1. The act of one who bats; the management of a bat in playing games of ball. Mason.

Cotton in sheets, prepared for use in making quilts, etc.; as, cotton batting. Battle (?), a. Fertile. See Battel, a. [Obs.] Battle, n. [OE. bataille, bataile, F. bataille battle, OF., battle, battalion, fr. L. battalia, battualia, the fighting and fencing exercises of soldiers and gladiators, fr. batuere to strike, beat. Cf. Battalia, 1st Battel, and see Batter, v. t.] 1. A general action, fight, or encounter, in which all the divisions of an army are or may be engaged; an engagement; a combat.

A struggle; a contest; as, the battle of life. The whole intellectual battle that had at its center the best poem of the best poet of that day. H. Morley.

A division of an army; a battalion. [Obs.] The king divided his army into three battles. Bacon. The cavalry, by way of distinction, was called the battle, and on it alone depended the fate of every action. Robertson.

The main body, as distinct from the van and rear; battalia. [Obs.] Hayward. µ Battle is used adjectively or as the first part of a selfÐexplaining compound; as, battle brand, a ½brand, or sword used in battle; battle cry; battlefield; battle ground; battlearray; battle song. Battle piece, a painting, or a musical composition, representing a battle. Ð Battle royal. (a) A fight between several gamecocks, where the one that stands longest is the victor. Grose. (b) A contest with fists or cudgels in which more than two are engaged; a mˆl,e. Thackeray. Ð Drawn battle, one in which neither party gains the victory. Ð To give battle, to attack an enemy. Ð To join battle, to meet the attack; to engage in battle. Ð Pitched battle, one in which the armies are previously drawn up in form, with a regular disposition of the forces. Ð Wager of battle. See under Wager, n. Syn. Ð Conflict; encounter; contest; action. Battle, Combat, Fight, Engagement. These words agree in denoting a close encounter between contending parties. Fight is a word of less dignity than the others. Except in poetry, it is more naturally applied to the encounter of a few individuals, and more commonly an accidental one; as, a street fight. A combat is a close encounter, whether between few or many, and is usually premeditated. A battle is commonly more general and prolonged. An engagement supposes large numbers on each side, engaged or intermingled in the conflict. Battle (?), v. i. [imp. & p.p. Battled (?); p. pr. & vb. n. Battling.] [F. batailler, fr. bataille. See Battle, n.] To join in battle; to contend in fight; as, to battle over theories. To meet in arms, and battle in the plain. Prior. Battle, v. t. To assail in battle; to fight. BattleĐax · BattleĐaxe · } (?), n. (Mil.) A kind of broadax formerly used as an offensive weapon. Battled (?), p. p. Embattled. [Poetic] Tennyson. Battleĭdoor · (?), n. [OE. batyldour. A corrupted form of uncertain origin; cf. Sp. batallador a great combatant, he who has fought many battles, Pg. batalhador, Pr. batalhador, warrior, soldier, fr. L. battalia; or cf. Pr. batedor batlet, fr. batre to beat, fr. L. batuere. See Battle, n.] 1. An instrument, with a handle and a flat part covered with parchment or crossed with catgut, used to strike a shuttlecock in play; also, the play of battledoor and shuttlecock.

[OE. battleder.] A child's hornbook. [Obs.] Halliwell. Battleĭment (?), n. [OE. batelment; cf. OF. bataillement combat, fr. batailler, also OF. bastillier, bateillier, to fortify. Cf. Battle, n., Bastile, Bastion.] (Arch.) (a) One of the solid upright parts of a parapet in ancient fortifications. (b) pl. The whole parapet, consisting of alternate solids and open spaces. At first purely a military feature, afterwards copied on a smaller scale with decorative features, as for churches. Battleĭmentĭed (?), a. Having battlements. A battlemented portal. Sir W. Scott. Batĭtoloĭgist (?), n. One who battologizes. Batĭtoloĭgize (?), v. t. To keep repeating needlessly; to iterate. Sir T. Herbert. Batĭtoloĭgy (?), n. [F. battologie, fr. Gr. ?; ? a stammerer + ? speech.] A needless repetition of words in speaking or writing. Milton. Batton (?), n. See Batten, and Baton. ØBattue · (?), n. [F. battue, fr. battre to beat. See Batter, v. t., and cf. Battuta.] (Hunting) (a) The act of beating the woods, bushes, etc., for game. (b) The game itself. (c) The wanton slaughter of game. Howitt. ØBat · ture (?), n. [F., fr. battre to beat.] An elevated river bed or sea bed. ØBatĭtuta (?), n. [It. battuta, fr. battere to beat.] (Mus.) The measuring of time by beating. Batty (?), a. Belonging to, or resembling, a bat. ½Batty wings., Shak. Batule (?), n. A springboard in a circus or gymnasium; Đ called also batule board. ØBatz (?), n.; pl. Batzen (?). [Ger. batz, batze, batzen, a coin bearing the image of a bear, Ger. b„tz, betz, bear,] A small copper coin, with a mixture of silver, formerly current in some parts of Germany and Switzerland. It was worth about four cents. Bauĭbee (?), n. Same as Bawbee. Bauble (?), n. [Cf. OF. baubel a child's plaything, F. babiole, It. babbola, LL. baubellum gem, jewel, L. babulus,a baburrus, foolish.] 1. A trifling piece of finery; a gewgaw; that which is gay and showy without real value; a cheap, showy plaything. The ineffective bauble of an Indian pagod. Sheridan.

The fool's club. [Obs.] ½A fool's bauble was a short stick with a head ornamented with an ass's ears fantastically carved upon it., Nares. Baubling (?), a. See Bawbling. [Obs.] Baudeĭkin (?), n. [OE. bawdekin rich silk stuff, OF. baudequin. See Baldachin.] The richest kind of stuff used in garments in the Middle Ages, the web being gold, and the woof silk, with embroidery : Đ made originally at Bagdad. [Spelt also baudkin, baudkyn, bawdekin, and baldakin.] Nares. Baudrick (?), n. A belt. See Baldric. Bauk, Baulk (?), n. & v. See Balk. BaunscheidtĬism (?), n. [From the introducer, a German named Baunscheidt.] (Med.) A form of acupuncture, followed by the rubbing of the part with a stimulating fluid. Bauxite, Beauxite (?), n. [F., fr. Baux or Beaux, near Arles.] (Min.) A ferruginous hydrate of alumina. It is largely used in the preparation of aluminium and alumina, and for the lining of furnaces which are exposed to intense heat. Baĭvariĭan (?), a. Of or pertaining to Bavaria. Đ n. A native or an inhabitant of Bavaria. Bavarian cream. See under Cream. Bavaĭroy (?), n. [F. Bavarois Bavarian.] A kind of cloak or surtout. [Obs.] Johnson. Let the looped bavaroy the fop embrace. Gay.

<— p. 126 —>

Bavian (?), n. [See Baboon.] A baboon.

Bavin (?), n. [Cf. Gael. & Ir. baban tuft, tassel.] 1. A fagot of brushwood, or other light combustible matter, for kindling fires; refuse of brushwood. [Obs. or Dial. Eng.]

Impure limestone. [Prov. Eng.]

Wright.

Bawbee (?), n. [Perh. corrupt. fr. halfpenny.] A halfpenny. [Spelt also baubee.] [Scot. & Prov. Eng.]

Bawble (?), n. A trinket. See Bauble.

Bawbling, a. Insignificant; contemptible. [Obs.]

Bawcock (?), n. [From F. beau fine + E. cock (the bird); or more prob. fr. OF. baud bold, gay + E. cock. Cf. Bawd.] A fine fellow; Ð a term of endearment. [Obs.] ½How now, my bawcock ?ˏ

Shak.

Bawd (?), n. [OE. baude, OF. balt, baut, baude, bold, merry, perh. fr. OHG. bald bold; or fr. Celtic, cf. W. baw dirt. Cf. Bold, Bawdry.] A person who keeps a house of prostitution, or procures women for a lewd purpose; a procurer or procuress; a lewd person; Ð usually applied to a woman.

Bawd, v. i. To procure women for lewd purposes.

Bawdily (?), adv. Obscenely; lewdly.

Bawdiness, n. Obscenity; lewdness.

Bawdrick (?), n. A belt. See Baldric.

Bawdry (?), n. [OE. baudery, OF. bauderie, balderie, boldness, joy. See Bawd.] 1. The practice of procuring women for the gratification of lust.

Illicit intercourse; fornication.

Shak.

Obscenity; filthy, unchaste language. ½The pert style of the pit bawdry.ˏ

Steele.

Bawdy, a. /1. Dirty; foul; Ð said of clothes. [Obs.]

It [a garment] is al bawdy and toÐtore also.

Chaucer.

Obscene; filthy; unchaste. ½A bawdy story.ˏ

Burke.

BawdyÏhouse· (?), n. A house of prostitution; a house of ill fame; a brothel.

Bawhorse· (?), n. Same as Bathorse.

Bawl (?), v. i. [imp. & p.p. Bawled (?); p. pr. & vb. n. Bawling.] [Icel. baula to low, bellow, as a cow; akin to Sw. b"la; cf. AS bellan, G. bellen to bark, E. bellow, bull.] 1. To cry out with a loud, full sound; to cry with vehemence, as in calling or exultation; to shout; to vociferate.

To cry loudly, as a child from pain or vexation.

Bawl, v. t. To proclaim with a loud voice, or by outcry, as a hawker or townƉcrier does.
Swift.
Bawl, n. A loud, prolonged cry; an outcry.
Bawler (?), n. One who bawls.
Bawn (?), n. [Ir. & Gael. babhun inclosure, bulwark.] 1. An inclosure with mud or stone walls, for keeping cattle; a fortified inclosure. [Obs.]
Spenser.

A large house. [Obs.]

Swift.
Bawrel (?), n. [Cf. It. barletta a tree falcon, or hobby.] A kind of hawk. [Obs.]
Halliwell.
Bawsin (?), Bawson (?), } n. [OE. bawson, baucyne, badger (named from its color), OF. bauzan, baucant, bauchant, spotted with white, pied; cf. It. balzano, F. balzan, a whiteƉfooted horse, It. balza border, trimming, fr. L. balteus belt, border, edge. Cf. Belt.] 1. A badger. [Obs.]
B. Jonson.

A large, unwieldy person. [Obs.]

Nares.
Baxter (?), n. [OE. bakestre, bakistre, AS. b'cestre, prop. fem. of b'cere baker. See Baker.] A baker; originally, a female baker. [Old Eng. & Scotch]
Bay (?), a. [F. bai, fr. L. badius brown, chestnutcolored; Ɖ used only of horses.] Reddish brown; of the color of a chestnut; Ɖ applied to the color of horses.

Bay cat (Zo"l.), a wild cat of Africa and the East Indies (Felis aurata). Ɖ Bay lynx (Zo"l.), the common American lynx (Felis, or Lynx, rufa).

Bay, n. [F. baie, fr. LL. baia. Of uncertain origin: cf. Ir. & Gael. badh or bagh bay harbor, creek; Bisc. baia, baiya, harbor, and F. bayer to gape, open the mouth.] 1. (Geol.) An inlet of the sea, usually smaller than a gulf, but of the same general character.

µ The name is not used with much precision, and is often applied to large tracts of water, around which the land forms a curve; as, Hudson's Bay. The name is not restricted to tracts of water with a narrow entrance, but is used foe any recess or inlet between capes or headlands; as, the Bay of Biscay.

A small body of water set off from the main body; as a compartment containing water for a wheel; the portion of a canal just outside of the gates of a lock, etc.

A recess or indentation shaped like a bay.

A principal compartment of the walls, roof, or other part of a building, or of the whole building, as marked off by the buttresses, vaulting, mullions of a window, etc.; one of the main divisions of any structure, as the part of a bridge between two piers.

A compartment in a barn, for depositing hay, or grain in the stalks.

A kind of mahogany obtained from Campeachy Bay.

Sick bay, in vessels of war, that part of a deck appropriated to the use of the sick.
Totten.
Bay, n. [F. baie a berry, the fruit of the laurel and other trees, fr. L. baca, bacca, a small round fruit, a berry, akin to Lith. bapka laurel berry.] 1. A berry, particularly of the laurel. [Obs.]

The laurel tree (Laurus nobilis). Hence, in the plural, an honorary garland or crown bestowed as a prize for victory or excellence, anciently made or consisting of branches of the laurel.

The patriot's honors and the poet's bays.
Trumbull.

A tract covered with bay trees. [Local, U. S.]

Bay leaf, the leaf of the bay tree (Laurus nobilis). It has a fragrant odor and an aromatic taste.

Bay, v. i. [imp. & p.p. Bayed (?); p. pr. & vb. n. Baying.] [OE. bayen, abayen, OF. abaier, F. aboyer, to bark; of uncertain origin.] To bark, as a dog with a deep voice does, at his game.

The hounds at nearer distance hoarsely bayed.
Dryden.

Bay (?), v. t. To bark at; hence, to follow with barking; to bring or drive to bay; as, to bay the bear.
Shak.

Bay (?), n. [See Bay, v. i.] 1. DeepÐtoned, prolonged barking. ½The bay of curs.„
Cowper.

[OE. bay, abay, OF. abai, F. aboi barking, pl. abois, prop. the extremity to which the stag is reduced when surrounded by the dogs, barking (aboyant); aux abois at or a difficulty, when escape has become impossible.

Embolden'd by despair, he stood at bay.
Dryden.

The most terrible evils are just kept at bay by incessant efforts.
I. Taylor

Bay, v. t. [Cf. OE. b'wen to bathe, and G. b„hen to foment.] To bathe. [Obs.]

Spenser.

Bay, n. A bank or dam to keep back water.

Bay, v. t. To dam, as water; Ð with up or back.

ØBaya (?), n. [Native name.] (Zo"l.) The East Indian weaver bird (Ploceus Philippinus).

ØBaïyad (?), Baïyatte (?), n. [Ar. bayad.] (Zo"l.) A large, edible, siluroid fish of the Nile, of two species (Bagrina bayad and B. docmac).

Ba · yaïdere (?), n. [F., from Pg. bailadeira a female dancer, bailar to dance.] A female dancer in the East Indies. [Written also bajadere.]

BayÐant · ler (?), n. [See BezÐAntler.] (Zo"l.) The second tine of a stag's horn. See under Antler.

Bayard (?), n. 1. [OF. bayard, baiart, bay horse; bai bay + ïard. See Bay, a., and ïard.] Properly, a bay horse, but often any horse. Commonly in the phrase blind bayard, an old blind horse.

Blind bayard moves the mill.

Philips.

[Cf. F. bayeur, fr. bayer to gape.] A stupid, clownish fellow. [Obs.]

B. Jonson.

Bayardïly, a. Blind; stupid. [Obs.] ½A formal and bayardly round of duties.„

Goodman.

Bayberïry (?), n. (Bot.) (a) The fruit of the bay tree or Laurus nobilis. (b) A tree of the West Indies related to the myrtle (Pimenta acris). (c) The fruit of Myrica cerifera (wax myrtle); the shrub itself; Ð called also candleberry tree.

Bayberry tallow, a fragrant green wax obtained from the bayberry or wax myrtle; Ð called also myrtle wax.

Baybolt · (?), n. A bolt with a barbed shank.

Bayed (?), a. Having a bay or bays. ½The large bayed barn.„

Drayton.

Bay ice · (?). See under Ice.

Bay leaf · (?). See under 3d Bay.

Bayoïnet (?), n. [F. bayonnette, ba‹onnette; Ð so called, it is said, because the first bayonets were made at Bayonne.]

(Mil.) A pointed instrument of the dagger kind fitted on the muzzle of a musket or rifle, so as to give the soldier increased means of offense and defense.

µ Originally, the bayonet was made with a handle, which required to be fitted into the bore of the musket after the soldier had fired.

(Mach.) A pin which plays in and out of holes made to receive it, and which thus serves to engage or disengage parts of the machinery.

Bayonet clutch. See Clutch. Ð Bayonet joint, a form of coupling similar to that by which a bayonet is fixed on the barrel of a musket.

Knight.

Bayonet, v. t. [imp. & p.p. Bayoneted; p. pr. & vb. n. Bayoneting.] 1. To stab with a bayonet.

To compel or drive by the bayonet.

To bayonet us into submission.

Burke.

Bayou (?), n.; pl. Bayous (?). [North Am. Indian bayuk, in F. spelling bayouc, bayouque.] An inlet from the Gulf of Mexico, from a lake, or from a large river, sometimes sluggish, sometimes without perceptible movement except from tide and wind. [Southern U. S.]

A dark slender thread of a bayou moves loiteringly northeastward into a swamp of huge cypresses.

G. W. Cable.

Bay rum (?). A fragrant liquid, used for cosmetic and medicinal purposes.

µ The original bay rum, from the West Indies, is prepared, it is believed, by distillation from the leaves of the bayberry (Myrcia acris). The bay rum of the Pharmacop?ia (spirit of myrcia) is prepared from oil of myrcia (bayberry), oil of orange peel, oil of pimento, alcohol, and water.

Bays, Bayze (?), n. See Baize. [Obs.]

Bay salt · (?). Salt which has been obtained from sea water, by evaporation in shallow pits or basins, by the heat of the sun; the large crystalline salt of commerce.

Bacon. Ure.

Bay tree · . A species of laurel. (Laurus nobilis).

Bay window (?). (Arch.) A window forming a bay or recess in a room, and projecting outward from the wall, either in a rectangular, polygonal, or semicircular form; Ð often corruptly called a bow window.

Bay yarn · (?). Woolen yarn. [Prov. Eng.]

Wright.

Balzaar Balzar } (?), n. [Per. b¾zar market.] 1. In the East, an exchange, marketplace, or assemblage of shops where goods are exposed for sale.

A spacious hall or suite of rooms for the sale of goods, as at a fair.

A fair for the sale of fancy wares, toys, etc., commonly for a charitable objects.

Macaulay.

Bdellium (?), n. [L., fr. Gr. ?; cf. Heb. b'dolakh bdellium (in sense 1).] 1. An unidentified substance mentioned in the Bible (Gen. ii. 12, and Num. xi. 7), variously taken to be a gum, a precious stone, or pearls, or perhaps a kind of amber found in Arabia.

A gum resin of reddish brown color, brought from India, Persia, and Africa.

¶ Indian bdellium or false myrrh is an exudation from Balsamodendron Roxb?rghii. Other kinds are known as African, Sicilian, etc.

ØBdelÏloideÏa (?), n. pl. [NL., fr. Gr. ? leech + ïoid.] (Zo"l.) The order of Annulata which includes the leeches. See Hirudinea.

BdelÏlomeÏter (?), n. [Gr. ? leech + ïmeter.] (Med.) A cupping glass to which are attached a scarificator and an exhausting syringe.

Dunglison.

ØBdel·loïmorpha (?), n. [NL., fr. Gr. ? leech + ? form.] (Zo"l.) An order of Nemertina, including the large leechlike worms (Malacobdella) often parasitic in clams.

Be (?), v. i. [imp. Was (?); p. p. Been (?); p. pr. & vb. n. Being.] [OE. been, beon, AS. beçn to be, beçm I am; akin to OHG. bim, pim, G. bin, I am, Gael. & Ir. bu was, W. bod to be, Lith. buÐti, O. Slav. byÐti, to be, L. fuÐi I have been, fuÐturus about to be, foÐre to be about to be, and perh to fieri to become, Gr. ? to be born, to be, Skr. bh? to be. This verb is defective, and the parts lacking are supplied by verbs from other roots, is, was, which have no radical connection with be. The various forms, am, are, is, was, were, etc., are considered grammatically as parts of the verb ½to be„, which, with its conjugational forms, is often called the substantive verb. ?97. Cf. Future, Physic.] 1. To exist actually, or in the world of fact; to have ex?stence.

To be contents his natural desire.

Pope.

To be, or not to be: that is the question.

Shak.

To exist in a certain manner or relation, Ð whether as a reality or as a product of thought; to exist as the subject of a certain predicate, that is, as having a certain attribute, or as belonging to a certain sort, or as identical with what is specified, Ð a word or words for the predicate being annexed; as, to be happy; to be here; to be large, or strong; to be an animal; to be a hero; to be a nonentity; three and two are five; annihilation is the cessation of existence; that is the man.

To take place; to happen; as, the meeting was on Thursday.

To signify; to represent or symbolize; to answer to.

The field is the world.

Matt. xiii. 38.

The seven candlesticks which thou sawest are the seven churches.

Rev.i. 20.

¶ The verb to be (including the forms is, was, etc.) is used in forming the passive voice of other verbs; as, John has been struck by James. It is also used with the past participle of many intransitive verbs to express a state of the subject. But have is now more commonly used as the auxiliary, though expressing a different sense; as, ½Ye have come too late Ð but ye are come. „ ½The minstrel boy to the war is gone.„ The present and imperfect tenses form, with the infinitive, a particular future tense, which expresses necessity, duty, or purpose; as, government is to be supported; we are to pay our just debts; the deed is to be signed toÐmorrow.

Have or had been, followed by to, implies movement. ½I have been to Paris.͵ Sydney Smith. ½Have you been to Franchard ?͵ R. L. Slevenson.

µ Been, or ben, was anciently the plural of the indicative present. ½Ye ben light of the world.͵ Wyclif, Matt. v. 14. Afterwards be was used, as in our Bible: ½They that be with us are more than they that be with them.͵ 2 Kings vi. 16. Ben was also the old infinitive: ½To ben of such power.͵ R. of Gloucester. Be is used as a form of the present subjunctive: ½But if it be a question of words and names.͵ Acis xviii. 15. But the indicative forms, is and are, with if, are more commonly used.

Be it so, a phrase of supposition, equivalent to suppose it to be so; or of permission, signifying let it be so. Shak. Ð If so be, in case. Ð To be from, to have come from; as, from what place are you ? I am from Chicago. Ð To let be, to omit, or leave untouched; to let alone. ½Let be, therefore, my vengeance to dissuade.͵

Spenser.

Syn. Ð To be, Exist. The verb to be, except in a few rare case, like that of Shakespeare's ½To be, or not to be͵, is used simply as a copula, to connect a subject with its predicate; as, man is mortal; the soul is immortal. The verb to exist is never properly used as a mere copula, but points to things that stand forth, or have a substantive being; as, when the soul is freed from all corporeal alliance, then it truly exists. It is not, therefore, properly synonymous with to be when used as a copula, though occasionally made so by some writers for the sake of variety; as in the phrase ½there exists [is] no reason for laying new taxes.͵ We may, indeed, say, ½a friendship has long existed between them,͵ instead of saying, ½there has long been a friendship between them;͵ but in this case, exist is not a mere copula. It is used in its appropriate sense to mark the friendship as having been long in existence.

BeÏ. [AS. be, and in accented form bÆ, akin to OS. be and bÆ, OHG. bi, pi, and pÆ, MHG. be and bÆ, G. be and bei, Goth. bi, and perh. Gr. ? about (cf. AS. beseen to look about). ?203. Gr. By, AmbÏ.] A prefix, originally the same word as by; joined with verbs, it serves: (a) To intensify the meaning; as, bespatter, bestir. (b) To render an intransitive verb transitive; as, befall (to fall upon); bespeak (to speak for). (c) To make the action of a verb particular or definite; as, beget (to get as offspring); beset (to set around).

It is joined with certain substantives, and a few adjectives, to form verbs; as, bedew, befriend, benight, besot; belate (to make late); belittle (to make little). It also occurs in certain nouns, adverbs, and prepositions,

<— p. 127 —>

often with something of the force of the preposition by, or about; as, belief (believe), behalf, bequest (bequeath); because, before, beneath, beside, between. In some words the original force of be is obscured or lost; as, in become, begin, behave, behoove, belong. Beach (?), n.; pl. Beaches (?). [Cf.

Sw. backe hill, Dan. bakke, Icel. bakki hill, bank. Cf. Bank.] 1. Pebbles, collectively; shingle. 2. The shore of the sea, or of a lake, which is washed by the waves; especially, a sandy or pebbly shore; the strand.

Beach flea (Zo"l.), the common name of many species of amphipod Crustacea, of the family Orchestid', living on the sea beaches, and leaping like fleas. Ð Beach grass (Bot.), a coarse grass (Ammophila arundinacea), growing on the sandy shores of lakes and seas, which, by its interlaced running rootstocks, binds the sand together, and resists the encroachment of the waves. Ð Beach wagon, a light open wagon with two or more seats. Ð Raised beach, an accumulation of waterÐworn stones, gravel, sand, and other shore deposits, above the present level of wave action, whether actually raised by elevation of the coast, as in Norway, or left by the receding waters, as in many lake and river regions.

Beach, v. t. [imp. & p.p. Beached (?); p. pr. & vb. n. Beaching.] To run or drive (as a vessel or a boat) upon a beach; to strand; as, to beach a ship.

Beach comb · er (?). A long, curling wave rolling in from the ocean. See Comber. [Amer.]

Beached (?), p. p. & a. 1. Bordered by a beach.
The beached verge of the salt flood.
Shak.

Driven on a beach; stranded; drawn up on a beach; as, the ship is beached.

Beachy (?), a. Having a beach or beaches; formed by a beach or beaches; shingly.
The beachy girdle of the ocean.
Shak.

Beacon (?), n. [OE. bekene, AS. be cen, b?cen; akin to OS. b?kan, Fries. baken, beken, sign, signal, D. baak, OHG. bouhhan, G. bake; of unknown origin. Cf. Beckon.] 1. A signal fire to notify of the approach of an enemy, or to give any notice, commonly of warning.
No flaming beacons cast their blaze afar.
Gay.

A signal or conspicuous mark erected on an eminence near the shore, or moored in shoal water, as a guide to mariners.

A high hill near the shore. [Prov. Eng.]

That which gives notice of danger.

Modest doubt is called
The beacon of the wise.
Shak.

Beacon fire, a signal fire.

Beacon, v. t. [imp. & p.p. Beaconed (?); p. pr. & vb. n. Beaconing.] 1. To give light to, as a beacon; to light up; to illumine.

That beacons the darkness of heaven.
Campbell.

To furnish with a beacon or beacons.

Beaconǐage (?), n. Money paid for the maintenance of a beacon; also, beacons, collectively.

Beaconǐless, a. Having no beacon.

Bead (?), n. [OE. bede prayer, prayer bead, AS. bed, gebed, prayer; akin to D. bede, G. bitte, AS. biddan, to ask, bid, G. bitten to ask, and perh. to Gr. ? to persuade, L. fidere to trust. Beads are used by the Roman Catholics to count their prayers, one bead being dropped down a string every time a prayer is said. Cf. Sp. cuenta bead, fr. contar to count. See Bid, in to bid beads, and Bide.] 1. A prayer. [Obs.]

A little perforated ball, to be strung on a thread, and worn for ornament; or used in a rosary for counting prayers, as by Roman Catholics and Mohammedans, whence the phrases to tell beads, to at one's beads, to bid beads, etc., meaning, to be at prayer.

Any small globular body; as, (a) A bubble in spirits. (b) A drop of sweat or other liquid. ½Cold beads of midnight dew., Wordsworth. (c) A small knob of metal on a firearm, used for taking aim (whence the expression to draw a bead, for, to take aim). (d) (Arch.) A small molding of rounded surface, the section being usually an arc of a circle. It may be continuous, or broken into short embossments. (e) (Chem.) A glassy drop of molten flux, as borax or microcosmic salt, used as a solvent and color test for several mineral earths and oxides, as of iron, manganese, etc., before the blowpipe; as, the borax bead; the iron bead, etc.

Bead and butt (Carp.), framing in which the panels are flush, having beads stuck or run upon the two edges. Knight. Ð Beat mold, a species of fungus or mold, the stems of which consist of single cells loosely jointed together so as to resemble a string of beads. [Written also bead mould.] Ð Bead tool, a cutting tool, having an edge curved so as to make beads or beading. Ð Bead tree (Bot.), a tree of the genus Melia, the best known species of which (M. azedarach), has blue flowers which are very fragrant, and berries which are poisonous.

Bead, v. t. [imp. & p.p. Beaded; p. pr. & vb. n. Beading.] To ornament with beads or beading.

Bead, v. i. To form beadlike bubbles.

Beadhouse · , Bedehouse · (?), n. [OE. bede prayer + E. house. See Bead, n.] An almshouse for poor people who pray daily for their benefactors.

Beading, n. 1. (Arch.) Molding in imitation of beads.

The beads or beadÐforming quality of certain liquors; as, the beading of a brand of whisky.

Beadle (?), n. [OE. bedel, bidel, budel, OF. bedel, F. bedeau, fr. OHG. butil, putil, G. bttel, fr. OHG. biotan, G. bieten, to bid, confused with AS. bydel, the same word as OHG. butil. See. Bid, v.] 1. A messenger or crier of a court; a servitor; one who cites or bids persons to appear and answer; Ð called also an apparitor or summoner.

<small>An officer in a university, who precedes public processions of officers and students. [Eng.]</small>

μ In this sense the archaic spellings bedel (Oxford) and bedell (Cambridge) are preserved.

<small>An inferior parish officer in England having a variety of duties, as the preservation of order in church service, the chastisement of petty offenders, etc.</small>

Beadleĭry (?), n. Office or jurisdiction of a beadle.]
Beadleĭship, n. The state of being, or the personality of, a beadle.
A. Wood.

Bead proof· (?). 1. Among distillers, a certain degree of strength in alcoholic liquor, as formerly ascertained by the floating or sinking of glass globules of different specific gravities thrown into it; now ascertained by more accurate meters.

<small>A degree of strength in alcoholic liquor as shown by beads or small bubbles remaining on its surface, or at the side of the glass, when shaken.</small>

Beadroll· (?), n. (R. C. Ch.) A catalogue of persons, for the rest of whose souls a certain number of prayers are to be said or counted off on the beads of a chaplet; hence, a catalogue in general.

On Fame's eternal beadroll worthy to be field.
Spenser.

It is quite startling, on going over the beadroll of English worthies, to find how few are directly represented in the male line.
Quart. Rev.

Beadsman, Bedesman (?), n.; pl. Ĭmen (?). A poor man, supported in a beadhouse, and required to pray for the soul of its founder; an almsman.

Whereby ye shall bind me to be your poor beadsman for ever unto Almighty God.
Fuller.

Beadsnake· (?), n. (Zo"l.) A small poisonous snake of North America (Elaps fulvius), banded with yellow, red, and black.

Beadswom·an, Bedeswom·an (?), n.; pl. Ĭwomen (?). Fem. of Beadsman.

Beadwork· (?), n. Ornamental work in beads.

Beady (?), a. 1. Resembling beads; small, round, and glistening. ½Beady eyes.
Thackeray.

<small>Covered or ornamented with, or as with, beads.</small>

<small>Characterized by beads; as, beady liquor.</small>

Beagle (?), n. [OE. begele; perh. of Celtic origin; cf. Ir. & Gael. beag small, little, W. bach. F. bigle is from English.] 1. A small hound, or hunting dog, twelve to fifteen inches high, used in hunting hares and other small game. See Illustration in Appendix.

Fig.: A spy or detective; a constable.

Beak (?), n. [OE. bek, F. bec, fr. Celtic; cf. Gael. & Ir. bac, bacc, hook, W. bach.] 1. (Zo"l.) (a) The bill or nib of a bird, consisting of a horny sheath, covering the jaws. The form varied much according to the food and habits of the bird, and is largely used in the classification of birds. (b) A similar bill in other animals, as the turtles. (c) The long projecting sucking mouth of some insects, and other invertebrates, as in the Hemiptera. (d) The upper or projecting part of the shell, near the hinge of a bivalve. (e) The prolongation of certain univalve shells containing the canal.

Anything projecting or ending in a point, like a beak, as a promontory of land.

Carew.

(Antiq.) A beam, shod or armed at the end with a metal head or point, and projecting from the prow of an ancient galley, in order to pierce the vessel of an enemy; a beakhead.

(Naut.) That part of a ship, before the forecastle, which is fastened to the stem, and supported by the main knee.

(Arch.) A continuous slight projection ending in an arris or narrow fillet; that part of a drip from which the water is thrown off.

(Bot.) Any process somewhat like the beak of a bird, terminating the fruit or other parts of a plant.

(Far.) A toe clip. See Clip, n. (Far.)

A magistrate or policeman. [Slang, Eng.]

Beaked (?), a. 1. Having a beak or a beaklike point; beakÐshaped. ½Each beaked promontory.¸

Milton.

(Biol.) Furnished with a process or a mouth like a beak; rostrate.

Beaked whale (Zo"l.), a cetacean of the genus Hyperoodon; the bottlehead whale.

Beaker (?), n. [OE. biker; akin to Icel. bikarr, Sw. b„gare, Dan. baeger, G. becher, It. bicchiere; Ð all fr. LL. bicarium, prob. fr. Gr. ? wine jar, or perh. L. bacar wine vessel. Cf. Pitcher a jug.] 1. A large drinking cup, with a wide mouth, supported on a foot or standard.

An openÐmouthed, thin glass vessel, having a projecting lip for pouring; Ð used for holding solutions requiring heat.

Knight.

Beakhead· (?), n. 1. (Arch.) An ornament used in rich Norman doorways, resembling a head with a beak.

Parker.

(Naut.) (a) A small platform at the fore part of the upper deck of a vessel, which contains the water closets of the crew. (b) (Antiq.) Same as Beak, 3.

Beakiron (?), n. [From Bickern.] A bickern; a bench anvil with a long beak, adapted to reach the interior surface of sheet metal ware; the horn of an anvil.

Beal (?), n. [See Boil a tumor.] (Med.) A small inflammatory tumor; a pustule. [Prov. Eng.]

Beal, v. i. [imp. & p.p. Bealed (?); p. pr. & vb. n. Bealing.] To gather matter; to swell and come to a head, as a pimple. [Prov. Eng.]

BeÐall· (?), n. The whole; all that is to be. [Poetic]

Shak.

Beam (?), n. [AS. be m beam, post, tree, ray of light; akin to OFries. b¾m tree, OS. b?m, D. boom, OHG. boum, poum, G. baum, Icel. ba?mr, Goth. bahms and Gr. ? a growth, ? to become, to be. Cf. L. radius staff, rod, spoke of a wheel, beam or ray, and G. strahl arrow, spoke of a wheel, ray or beam, flash of lightning. ?97. See Be; cf. Boom a spar.] 1. Any large piece of timber or iron long in proportion to its thickness, and prepared for use.

One of the principal horizontal timbers of a building or ship.

The beams of a vessel are strong pieces of timber stretching across from side to side to support the decks.

Totten.

The width of a vessel; as, one vessel is said to have more beam than another.

The bar of a balance, from the ends of which the scales are suspended.

The doubtful beam long nods from side to side.

Pope.

The principal stem or horn of a stag or other deer, which bears the antlers, or branches.

The pole of a carriage. [Poetic]

Dryden.

A cylinder of wood, making part of a loom, on which weavers wind the warp before weaving; also, the cylinder on which the cloth is rolled, as it is woven; one being called the fore beam, the other the back beam.

The straight part or shank of an anchor.

The main part of a plow, to which the handles and colter are secured, and to the end of which are attached the oxen or horses that draw it.

(Steam Engine) A heavy iron lever having an oscillating motion on a central axis, one end of which is connected with the piston rod from which it receives motion, and the other with the crank of the wheel shaft? Ð called also working beam or walking beam.

A ray or collection of parallel rays emitted from the sun or other luminous body; as, a beam of light, or of heat.

How far that little candle throws his beams !
Shak.

Fig.: A ray; a gleam; as, a beam of comfort.

Mercy with her genial beam.
Keble.

One of the long feathers in the wing of a hawk; Ð called also beam feather.

Abaft the beam (Naut.), in an are of the horizon between a line that crosses the ship at right angles, or in the direction of her beams, and that point of the compass toward which her stern is directed. Ð Beam center (Mach.), the fulcrum or pin on which the working beam of an engine vibrates. Ð Beam compass, an instrument consisting of a rod or beam, having sliding sockets that carry steel or pencil points; Ð used for drawing or describing large circles. Ð Beam engine, a steam engine having a working beam to transmit power, in distinction from one which has its piston rod attached directly to the crank of the wheel shaft. Ð Before the beam (Naut.), in an arc of the horizon included between a line that crosse the ship at right angles and that point of the compass toward which the ship steers. Ð On the beam , in a line with the beams, or at right angled with the keel. Ð On the weather beam, on the side of a ship which faces the wind. Ð To be on her beam ends, to incline, as a vessel, so much on one side that her beams approach a vertical position.

Beam, v. t. [imp. & p.p. Beamed (?); p. pr. & vb. n. Beaming.] To send forth; to emit; Ð followed ordinarily by forth; as, to beam forth light.

Beam, v. i. To emit beams of light.

He beamed, the daystar of the rising age.
Trumbull.

Beambird· (?), n. (Zo"l.) A small European flycatcher (Muscicapa gricola), so called because it often nests on a beam in a building.

Beamed (?), a. Furnished with beams, as the head of a stag.

Tost his beamed frontlet to the sky.
Sir W. Scott.

Beamful (?), a. Beamy; radiant.

Beamil̇ly (?), adv. In a beaming manner.

Beamil̇ness, n. The state of being beamy.

Beaming, a. Emitting beams; radiant.

Beamingĭly, adv. In a beaming manner; radiantly.

Beamless, a. 1. Not having a beam.

Not emitting light.

Beamlet (?), n. A small beam of light.

Beam tree · (?). [AS. be m a tree. See Beam.] (Bot.) A tree (Pyrus aria) related to the apple.

Beamy (?), a. 1. Emitting beams of light; radiant; shining. ½Beamy gold.,
Tickell.

<— p. 128 —>

Resembling a beam in size and weight; massy. His doubleÐbiting ax, and beamy spear. Dryden.

Having horns, or antlers. Beamy stags in toils engage. Dryden. Bean (?), n. [OE. bene, AS.be n; akin to D. boon, G. bohne, OHG. p?na, Icel. baun, Dan. b"nne, Sw. b"na, and perh. to Russ. bob, L. faba.] 1. (Bot.) A name given to the seed of certain leguminous herbs, chiefly of the genera Faba, Phaseolus, and Dolichos; also, to the herbs. µ The origin and classification of many kinds are still doubtful. Among true beans are: the blackÐeyed bean and China bean, included in Dolichos Sinensis; black Egyptian bean or hyacinth bean, D. Lablab; the common haricot beans, kidney beans, string beans, and pole beans, all included in Phaseolus vulgaris; the lower bush bean, Ph. vulgaris, variety nanus; Lima bean, Ph. lunatus; Spanish bean and scarlet runner, Ph. maltiflorus; Windsor bean, the common bean of England, Faba vulgaris. As an article of food beans are classed with vegetables.

The popular name of other vegetable seeds or fruits, more or less resembling true beans. Bean aphis (Zo"l.), a plant louse (Aphis fab') which infests the bean plant. Ð Bean fly (Zo"l.), a fly found on bean flowers. Ð Bean goose (Zo"l.), a species of goose (Anser se?etum). Ð Bean weevil (Zo"l.), a small weevil that in the larval state destroys beans. The American species in Bruchus fab'. Ð Florida bean (Bot.), the seed of Mucuna urens, a West Indian plant. The seeds are washed up on the Florida shore, and are often polished and made into ornaments. Ð Ignatius bean, or St. Ignatius's bean (Bot.), a species of Strychnos. Ð Navy bean, the common dried white bean of commerce; probably so called because an important article of food in the navy. Ð Pea bean, a very small and highly esteemed variety of the edible white bean; Ð so called from its size. Ð Sacred bean. See under Sacred. Ð Screw bean. See under Screw. Ð Sea bean. (a) Same as Florida bean. (b) A red bean of unknown species used for ornament. Ð Tonquin bean, or Tonka bean, the fragrant seed of Dipteryx odorata, a leguminous tree. Ð Vanilla bean. See under Vanilla. Bean ca · per. (Bot.) A deciduous plant of warm climates, generally with fleshy leaves and flowers of a yellow or whitish yellow color, of the genus Zygophyllum. Bean trefoil. (Bot.) A leguminous shrub of southern Europe, with trifoliate leaves (Anagyris f?tida). Bear (?), v. t. [imp. Bore (?) (formerly Bare (?)); p. p. Born (?), Borne (?); p. pr. & vb. n. Bearing.] [OE. beren, AS. beran, beoran, to bear, carry, produce; akin to D. baren to bring forth, G. geb„ren, Goth. baįran to bear or carry, Icel. bera, Sw. b„ra, Dan. b're, OHG. beran, peran, L. ferre to bear, carry, produce, Gr. ?, OSlav brati to take, carry, OIr. berim I bear, Skr. bh? to bear. ?92. Cf. Fertile.]

To support or sustain; to hold up.

To support and remove or carry; to convey. I 'll bear your logs the while. Shak.

To conduct; to bring; Ð said of persons. [Obs.] Bear them to my house. Shak.

To possess and use, as power; to exercise. Every man should bear rule in his own house. Esther i. 22.

To sustain; to have on (written or inscribed, or as a mark), as, the tablet bears this inscription.

To possess or carry, as a mark of authority or distinction; to wear; as, to bear a sword, badge, or name.

To possess mentally; to carry or hold in the mind; to entertain; to harbor Dryden. The ancient grudge I bear him. Shak.

To endure; to tolerate; to undergo; to suffer. Should such a man, too fond to rule alone, Bear, like the Turk, no brother near the throne. Pope. I cannot bear The murmur of this lake to hear. Shelley. My punishment is greater than I can bear. Gen. iv. 13.

To gain or win. [Obs.] Some think to bear it by speaking a great word. Bacon. She was ... found not guilty, through bearing of friends and bribing of the judge. Latimer.

To sustain, or be answerable for, as blame, expense, responsibility, etc. He shall bear their iniquities. Is. liii. 11. Somewhat that will bear your charges. Dryden.

To render or give; to bring forward. ½Your testimony bear‚ Dryden.

To carry on, or maintain; to have. ½The credit of bearing a part in the conversation.‚ Locke.

To admit or be capable of; that is, to suffer or sustain without violence, injury, or change. In all criminal cases the most favorable interpretation should be put on words that they can possibly bear. Swift.

To manage, wield, or direct. ½Thus must thou thy body bear.‚ Shak. Hence: To behave; to conduct. Hath he borne himself penitently in prison ? Shak.

To afford; to be to ; to supply with. ?is faithful dog shall bear him company. Pope.

To bring forth or produce; to yield; as, to bear apples; to bear children; to bear interest. Here dwelt the man divine whom Samos bore. Dryden. µ In the passive form of this verb, the best modern usage restricts the past participle born to the sense of brought forth, while borne is used in the other senses of the word. In the active form, borne alone is used as the past participle. To bear down. (a) To force into a lower place; to carry down; to depress or sink. ½His nose, ... large as were the others, bore them down into insignificance.‚ Marryat. (b) To overthrow or crush by force; as, to bear down an enemy. Ð To bear a hand. (a) To help; to give assistance. (b) (Naut.) To make haste; to be quick. Ð To bear in hand, to keep (one) up in expectation, usually by promises never to be realized; to amuse by false pretenses; to delude. [Obs.] ½How you were borne in hand, how crossed.‚ Shak. Ð To bear in mind, to remember. Ð To bear off. (a) To restrain; to keep from approach. (b) (Naut.) To remove to a distance; to keep clear from rubbing against anything; as, to bear off a blow; to bear off a boat. (c) To gain; to carry off, as a prize. Ð To bear one hard, to owe one a grudge. [Obs.] ½C‘sar doth bear me hard.‚ Shak. Ð To bear out. (a) To maintain and support to the end; to defend to the last. ½Company only can bear a man out in an ill thing.‚ South. (b) To corroborate; to confirm. Ð To bear up, to support; to keep from falling or sinking. ½Religious hope bears up the mind under sufferings.‚ Addison. Syn. Ð To uphold; sustain; maintain; support; undergo; suffer; endure; tolerate; carry; convey; transport; waft. Bear (?), v. i. 1. To produce, as fruit; to be fruitful, in opposition to barrenness. This age to blossom, and the next to bear. Dryden.

To suffer, as in carrying a burden. But man is born to bear. Pope.

To endure with patience; to be patient. I can not, can not bear. Dryden.

To press; Ð with on or upon, or against. These men bear hard on the suspected party. Addison.

To take effect; to have influence or force; as, to bring matters to bear.

To relate or refer; Ð with on or upon; as, how does this bear on the question?

To have a certain meaning, intent, or effect. Her sentence bore that she should stand a certain time upon the platform. Hawthorne.

To be situated, as to the point of compass, with respect to something else; as, the land bears N. by E. To bear against, to approach for attack or seizure; as, a lion bears against his prey. [Obs.] Ð To bear away (Naut.), to change the course of a ship, and make her run before the wind. Ð To bear back, to retreat. ½Bearing back from the blows of their sable antagonist., Sir W. Scott. Ð To bear down upon (Naut.), to approach from the windward side; as, the fleet bore down upon the enemy. Ð To bear in with (Naut.), to run or tend toward; as, a ship bears in with the land. Ð To bear off (Naut.), to steer away, as from land. Ð To bear up. (a) To be supported; to have fortitude; to be firm; not to sink; as, to bear up under afflictions. (b) (Naut.) To put the helm up (or to windward) and so put the ship before the wind; to bear away. Ha?ersly. Ð To bear upon (Mil.), to be pointed or situated so as to affect; to be pointed directly against, or so as to hit (the object); as, to bring or plant guns so as to bear upon a fort or a ship; the artillery bore upon the center. Ð To bear up to, to tend or move toward; as, to bear up to one another. Ð To bear with, to endure; to be indulgent to; to forbear to resent, oppose, or punish. Bear (?), n. A bier. [Obs.] Spenser. Bear (?), n. [OE. bere, AS. bera; akin to D. beer, OHG. bero, pero, G. b„r, Icel. & Sw. bj"rn, and possibly to L. fera wild beast, Gr. ? beast, Skr. bhalla bear.]

(Zo"l.) Any species of the genus Ursus, and of the closely allied genera. Bears are plantigrade Carnivora, but they live largely on fruit and insects. The European brown bear (U. arctos), the white polar bear (U. maritimus), the grizzly bear (U. horribilis), the American black bear, and its variety the cinnamon bear (U. Americanus), the Syrian bear (Ursus Syriacus), and the sloth bear, are among the notable species.

(Zo"l.) An animal which has some resemblance to a bear in form or habits, but no real affinity; as, the woolly bear; ant bear; water bear; sea bear.

(Astron.) One of two constellations in the northern hemisphere, called respectively the Great Bear and the Lesser Bear, or Ursa Major and Ursa Minor.

Metaphorically: A brutal, coarse, or morose person.

(Stock Exchange) A person who sells stocks or securities for future delivery in expectation of a fall in the market. µ The bears and bulls of the Stock Exchange, whose interest it is, the one to depress, and the other to raise, stocks, are said to be so called in allusion to the bear's habit of pulling down, and the bull's of tossing up.

(Mach.) A portable punching machine.

(Naut.) A block covered with coarse matting; Ð used to scour the deck. Australian bear. (Zo"l.) See Koala. Ð Bear baiting, the sport of baiting bears with dogs. Ð Bear caterpillar (Zo"l.), the hairy larva of a moth, esp. of the genus Euprepia. Ð Bear garden. (a) A place where bears are kept for diversion or fighting. (b) Any place where riotous conduct is common or permitted. M. Arnold. Ð Bear leader, one who leads about a performing bear for money; hence, a facetious term for one who takes charge of a young man on his travels. Bear, v. t. (Stock Exchange) To endeavor to depress the price of, or prices in; as, to bear a railroad stock; to bear the market. Bear, Bere (?), n. [AS. bere. See Barley.] (Bot.) Barley; the sixÐrowed barley or the fourÐrowed barley, commonly the former (Hord?um hexastichon or H. vulgare). [Obs. except in North of Eng. and Scot.] BearaÏble (?), a. Capable of being borne or endured; tolerable. Ð BearaÏbly, adv. BearberÏry (?), n. (Bot.) A trailing plant of the heath family (Arctostaphylos uvaÐursi), having leaves which are tonic and astringent, and glossy red berries of which bears are said to be fond. Bearbind· (?), n. (Bot.) The bindweed (Convolvulus arvensis). Beard (?), n. [OE. berd, AS. beard; akin to Fries. berd, D. baard, G. bart, Lith. barzda, OSlav. brada, Pol. broda, Russ. boroda, L. barba, W. barf. Cf. 1st Barb.]

The hair that grows on the chin, lips, and adjacent parts of the human face, chiefly of male adults.

(Zo"l.) (a) The long hairs about the face in animals, as in the goat. (b) The cluster of small feathers at the base of the beak in some birds (c) The appendages to the jaw in some Cetacea, and to the mouth or jaws of some fishes. (d) The byssus of certain shellfish, as the muscle. (e) The gills of some bivalves, as the oyster. (f) In insects, the hairs of the labial palpi of moths and butterflies.

(Bot.) Long or stiff hairs on a plant; the awn; as, the beard of grain.

A barb or sharp point of an arrow or other instrument, projecting backward to prevent the head from being easily drawn out.

That part of the under side of a horse's lower jaw which is above the chin, and bears the curb of a bridle.

(Print.) That part of a type which is between the shoulder of the shank and the face.

An imposition; a trick. [Obs.] Chaucer. Beard grass (Bot.), a coarse, perennial grass of different species of the genus Andropogon. Ð To one's beard, to one's face; in open defiance. Beard (?), v. t. [imp. & p.p. Bearded; p. pr. & vb. n. Bearding.] 1. To take by the beard; to seize, pluck, or pull the beard of (a man), in anger or contempt.

To oppose to the gills; to set at defiance. No admiral, bearded by three corrupt and dissolute minions of the palace, dared to do more than mutter something about a court martial. Macaulay.

To deprive of the gills; Ð used only of oysters and similar shellfish. Bearded, a. Having a beard. ½Bearded fellow.¸ Shak. ½Bearded grain.¸ Dryden. Bearded vulture, Bearded eagle. (Zo"l.) See Lammergeir. Ð Bearded tortoise. (Zo"l.) See Matamata. Beardie (?), n. [From Beard, n.] (Zo"l.) The bearded loach (Nemachilus barbatus) of Europe. [Scot.] Beardless, a. 1. Without a beard. Hence: Not having arrived at puberty or manhood; youthful.

Destitute of an awn; as, beardless wheat. Beardless̈ness, n. The state or quality of being destitute of beard. Bearer (?), n. 1. One who, or that which, bears, sustains, or carries. ½Bearers of burdens.¸ 2 Chron. ii. 18. ½The bearer of unhappy news.¸ Dryden.

Specifically: One who assists in carrying a body to the grave; a pallbearer. Milton.

A palanquin carrier; also, a house servant. [India]

A tree or plant yielding fruit; as, a good bearer.

(Com.) One who holds a check, note, draft, or other order for the payment of money; as, pay to bearer.

(Print.) A strip of reglet or other furniture to bear off the impression from a blank page; also, a type or typeÐhigh piece of metal interspersed in blank parts to support the plate when it is shaved. Bearherd· (?), n. A man who tends a bear. Bearhound· (?), n. A hound for baiting or hunting bears. Car??le. Bearing (?), n. 1. The manner in which one bears or conducts one's self; mien; behavior; carriage. I know him by his bearing. Shak.

Patient endurance; suffering without complaint.

The situation of one object, with respect to another, such situation being supposed to have a connection with the object, or influence upon it, or to be influenced by it; hence, relation; connection. But of this frame, the bearings and the ties, The strong connections, nice dependencies. Pope.

Purport; meaning; intended significance; aspect.

The act, power, or time of producing or giving birth; as, a tree in full bearing; a tree past bearing. [His mother] in travail of his bearing. R. of Gloucester.

(Arch.) (a) That part of any member of a building which rests upon its supports; as, a lintel or beam may have four inches of bearing upon the wall. (b) The portion of a support on which anything rests. (c) Improperly, the unsupported span; as, the beam has twenty feet of bearing between its supports.

(Mach.) (a) The part of an axle or shaft in contact with its support, collar, or boxing; the journal. (b) The part of the support on which a journal rests and rotates.

(Her.) Any single emblem or charge in an escutcheon or coat of arms Ð commonly in the pl. A carriage covered with armorial bearings. Thackeray.

(Naut.) (a) The situation of a distant object, with regard to a ship's position, as on the bow, on the lee quarter, etc.; the direction or point of the compass in which an object is seen; as, the bearing of the cape was M. N. W. (b) pl. The widest part of a vessel below the plankÐsheer. (c) pl. The line of flotation of a vessel when properly trimmed with cargo or ballast. Ball bearings. See under Ball. Ð To bring one to his bearings, to bring one to his senses. Ð To lose one's bearings, to become bewildered. Ð To take bearings, to ascertain by the compass the position of an object; to ascertain the relation of one object or place to another; to ascertain one's position by reference to landmarks or to the compass; hence (Fig.), to ascertain the condition of things when one is in trouble or perplexity. Syn. Ð Deportment; gesture; mien; behavior; manner; carriage; demeanor; port; conduct; direction; relation; tendency; influence. Bearing cloth · (?). A cloth with which a child is covered when carried to be baptized. Shak. Bearing rein · (?). A short rein looped over the check hook or the hames to keep the horse's head up; Ð called in the United States a checkrein. Bearish, a. Partaking of the qualities of a bear; resembling a bear in temper or manners. Harris. Bearishĭness, n. Behavior like that of a bear. Bearn (?), n. See Bairn. [Obs.] Bear'sÐbreech · (?), n. (Bot.) (a) See Acanthus, n., 1. (b) The English cow parsnip (Heracleum sphondylium) Dr. Prior.

<— p. 129 —>

Bear'sÐear · (?), n. (Bot.) A kind of primrose (Primula auricula), so called from the shape of the leaf. Bear'sÐroot · (?), n. (Bot.) A species of hellebore (Helleborus f?tidus), with digitate leaves. It has an offensive smell and acrid taste, and is a powerful emetic, cathartic, and anthelmintic. Bearskin · (?), n. 1. The skin of a bear. 2. A coarse, shaggy, woolen cloth for overcoats. 3. A cap made of bearskin, esp. one worn by soldiers. Bear'sÐpaw · (?), n. (Zo"l.) A large bivalve shell of the East Indies (Hippopus maculatus), often used as an ornament. Bearward · (?), n. [Bear + ward a keeper.] A keeper of bears. See Bearherd. [R.] Shak. Beast (?), n. [OE. best, beste, OF. beste, F. bˆte, fr. L. bestia.] 1. Any living creature; an animal; Ð including man, insects, etc. [Obs.] Chaucer. 2. Any fourÐfooted animal, that may be used for labor, food, or sport; as, a beast of burden. A righteous man regardeth the life of his beast. Prov. xii. 10. 3. As opposed to man: Any irrational animal. 4. Fig.: A coarse, brutal, filthy, or degraded fellow. 5. A game at cards similar to loo. [Obs.] Wright. 6. A penalty at beast, omber, etc. Hence: To be beasted, to be beaten at beast, omber, etc. Beast royal, the lion. [Obs.] Chaucer. Syn. Ð Beast, Brute. When we use these words in a figurative sense, as applicable to human beings, we think of beasts as mere animals governed by animal appetite; and of brutes as being destitute of reason or moral feeling, and governed by unrest?ained passion. Hence we speak of beastly appetites; beastly indulgences, etc.; and of brutal manners; brutal inhumanity; brutal ferocity. So, also, we say of a drunkard, that he first made himself a beast, and then treated his family like a brute. Beasthood (?), n. State or nature of a beast. Beastings (?), n. pl. See Biestings. Beastlihead (?), n. [Beastly + Ihead state.] Beastliness. [Obs.] Spenser. Beastlike (?), a. Like a beast. Beastliness, n. The state or quality of being beastly. Beastly (?), a. 1. Pertaining to, or having the form, nature, or habits of, a beast. Beastly divinities and droves of gods. Prior. 2. Characterizing the nature of a beast; contrary to the nature and dignity of man; brutal; filthy. The beastly vice of drinking to excess. Swift. 3. Abominable; as, beastly weather. [Colloq. Eng.] Syn. Ð Bestial; brutish; irrational; sensual; degrading. Beat (?), v. t. [imp. Beat; p.p. Beat, Beaten (?); p. pr. & vb. n. Beating.] [OE. beaten, beten, AS. be tan; akin to Icel. bauta, OHG. b?zan. Cf. 1st Butt, Button.] 1. To strike repeatedly; to lay repeated blows upon; as, to beat one's breast; to beat iron so as to shape it; to beat grain, in order to force out the ?eeds; to beat eggs and sugar; to beat a drum. Thou shalt beat some of it [spices] very small. Ex. xxx. 36. They did beat the gold into thin plates. Ex. xxxix. 3. 2. To punish by blows; to thrash. 3. To scour or range over in hunting, accompanied with the noise made by striking bushes, etc., for the purpose of rousing game. To beat the woods, and rouse the bounding prey. Prior. 4. To dash against, or strike, as with water or wind. A frozen continent ... beat with perpetual storms. Milton. 5. To tread, as a path. Pass awful gulfs, and beat my painful way. Blackmore. 6. To overcome in a battle, contest, strife, race, game, etc.; to vanquish or conquer; to surpass. He beat them in a bloody battle. Prescott. For loveliness, it would be hard to beat that. M. Arnold. 7. To cheat; to chouse; to swindle; to defraud; Ð often with out. [Colloq.] 8. To exercise severely; to perplex; to trouble. Why should any one ... beat his head about the Latin grammar who does not intend to be a critic? Locke. 9. (Mil.) To give the signal for, by beat of drum; to sound by beat of drum; as, to beat an alarm, a charge, a parley, a retreat; to beat the general, the reveille, the tattoo. See Alarm, Charge, Parley, etc. To beat down, to haggle with (any one) to secure a lower price; to force down. [Colloq.] Ð To beat into, to teach or instill, by repetition. Ð To beat off, to repel or drive back. Ð To beat out, to extend by hammering. Ð To beat out of a thing, to cause to relinquish it, or give it up. ½Nor can anything beat their posterity out of it to this day., South. Ð To beat the dust. (Man.) (a) To take in too little ground with the fore legs, as a horse. (b) To perform curvets too precipitately or too low. Ð To beat the hoof, to walk; to go on foot. Ð To beat the wing, to flutter; to move with fluttering agitation. Ð To beat time, to measure or regulate time in music by the motion of the hand or foot. Ð To beat up, to attack suddenly; to alarm or disturb; as, to beat up an enemy's quarters. Syn. Ð To strike; pound; bang; buffet; maul; drub; th?ap; baste; thwack; thrash; pommel; cudgel; belabor; conquer; defeat; vanquish; overcome. Beat, v. i. 1. To strike repeatedly; to inflict repeated bla?s; to knock vigorously or loudly.

The men of the city ... beat at the door. Judges. xix. 22. 2. To move with pulsation or throbbing. A thousand hearts beat happily. Byron. 3. To come or act with violence; to dash or fall with force; to strike anything, as, rain, wind, and waves do. Sees rolling tempests vainly beat below. Dryden. They [winds] beat at the crazy casement. Longfellow. The sun beat upon the head of Jonah, that he fainted, and wisbed in himself to die. Jonah iv. 8. Public envy seemeth to beat chiefly upon ministers. Bacon. 4. To be in agitation or doubt. [Poetic] To still my beating mind. Shak. 5. (Naut.) To make progress against the wind, by sailing in a zigzag line or traverse. 6. To make a sound when struck; as, the drums beat. 7. (Mil.) To make a succession of strokes on a drum; as, the drummers beat to call soldiers to their quarters. 8. (Acoustics & Mus.) To sound with more or less rapid alternations of greater and less intensity, so as to produce a pulsating effect; Ð said of instruments, tones, or vibrations, not perfectly in unison. A beating wind (Naut.), a wind which necessitates tacking in order to make progress. Ð To beat about, to try to find; to search by various means or ways. Addison. Ð To beat about the bush, to approach a subject circuitously. Ð To beat up and down (Hunting), to run first one way and then another; Ð said of a stag. Ð To beat up for recruits, to go diligently about in order to get helpers or participators in an enterprise. Beat (?), n. 1. A stroke; a blow. He, with a careless beat, Struck out the mute creation at a heat. Dryden. 2. A recurring stroke; a throb; a pulsation; as, a beat of the heart; the beat of the pulse. 3. (Mus.) (a) The rise or fall of the hand or foot, marking the divisions of time; a division of the measure so marked. In the rhythm of music the beat is the unit. (b) A transient grace note, struck immediately before the one it is intended to ornament. 4. (Acoustics & Mus.) A sudden swelling or re‰onforcement of a sound, recurring at regular intervals, and produced by the interference of sound waves of slightly different periods of vibrations; applied also, by analogy, to other kinds of wave motions; the pulsation or throbbing produced by the vibrating together of two tones not quite in unison. See Beat, v. i., 8. 5. A round or course which is frequently gone over; as, a watchman's beat. 6. A place of habitual or frequent resort. 7. A cheat or swindler of the lowest grade; Ð often emphasized by dead; as, a dead beat. [Low] Beat of drum (Mil.), a succession of strokes varied, in different ways, for particular purposes, as to regulate a march, to call soldiers to their arms or quarters, to direct an attack, or retreat, etc. Ð Beat of a watch, or clock, the stroke or sound made by the action of the escapement. A clock is in beat or out of beat, according as the strokes is at equal or unequal intervals. Beat, a. Weary; tired; fatigued; exhausted. [Colloq.] Quite beat, and very much vexed and disappointed. Dickens. Beaten (?), a. 1. Made smooth by beating or treading; worn by use. ½A broad and beaten way.¸ Milton. ½Beaten gold.¸ Shak. 2. Vanquished; conquered; baffled. 3. Exhausted; tired out. 4. Become common or trite; as, a beaten phrase. [Obs.] 5. Tried; practiced. [Obs.] Beau. & Fl. Beater (?), n. 1. One who, or that which, beats. 2. A person who beats up game for the hunters. Black. Beath (?), v. t. [AS. be?ian to foment.] To bathe; also, to dry or heat, as unseasoned wood. [Obs.] Spenser. Be·aĭtific (?), Be·aĭtificĭal (?), } a. [Cf. F. b,atifique, L. beatificus. See Beatify.] Having the power to impart or complete blissful enjoyment; blissful. ½The beatific vision.͵ South. Ð Be·aĭtificĭalĭly, adv. Be·aĭtifĭĭcate (?), v. t. To beatify. [Obs.] Fuller. Beĭat·iĭfiĭcation (?), n. [Cf. F. b,atification.] The act of beatifying, or the state of being beatified; esp., in the R. C. Church, the act or process of ascertaining and declaring that a deceased person is one of ½the blessed,͵ or has attained the second degree of sanctity, Ð usually a stage in the process of canonization. ½The beatification of his spirit.͵ Jer. Taylor. Beĭatiĭfy (?), v. t. [imp. & p.p. Beatified (?); p. pr. & vb. n. Beatifying.] [L. beatificare; beatus happy (fr. beare to bless, akin to bonus good) + facere to make: cf. F. b,atifier. See Bounty.] 1. To pronounce or regard as happy, or supremely blessed, or as conferring happiness. The common conceits and phrases that beatify wealth. Barrow. 2. To make happy; to bless with the completion of celestial enjoyment. ½Beatified spirits.͵ Dryden. 3. (R. C. Ch.) To ascertain and declare, by a public process and decree, that a deceased person is one of ½the blessed͵ and is to be reverenced as such, though not canonized. Beating (?), n. 1. The act of striking or giving blows; punishment or chastisement by blows. 2. Pulsation; throbbing; as, the beating of the heart. 3. (Acoustics & Mus.) Pulsative sounds. See Beat, n. 4. (Naut.) The process of sailing against the wind by tacks in zigzag direction. Beĭatiĭtude (?), n. [L. beatitudo: cf. F. b,atitude. See Beatify.] 1. Felicity of the highest kind; consummate bliss. 2. Any one of the nine declarations (called the Beatitudes), made in the Sermon on the Mount (Matt. v. 3Ð12), with regard to the blessedness of those who are distinguished by certain specified virtues. 3. (R. C. Ch.) Beatification. Milman. Syn. Ð Blessedness; felicity; happiness. Beau (?), n.; pl. F. Beaux (E. pron. b?z), E. Beaus (?). [F., a fop, fr. beau fine, beautiful, fr. L. bellus pretty, fine, for bonulus, dim. of bonus good. See Bounty, and cf. Belle, Beauty.] 1. A man who takes great care to dress in the latest fashion; a dandy. 2. A man who escorts, or pays attentions to, a lady; an escort; a lover. Beaucatch·er (?), n. A small flat curl worn on the temple by women. [Humorous] Beaufet (?), n. [See Buffet.] A niche, cupboard, or sideboard for plate, china, glass, etc.; a buffet. A beaufet ... filled with gold and silver vessels. Prescott. Beaufin (?), n. See Biffin. Wright. Beau iĭdeal (?). [F. beau beautiful + id,al ideal.] A conception or image of consummate beauty, moral or physical, formed in the mind, free from all the deformities, defects, and blemishes seen in actual existence; an ideal or faultless standard or model. Beauish (?), n. Like a beau; characteristic of a beau; foppish; fine. ½A beauish young spark.͵ Byrom. ØBeau· monde (?). [F. beau fine + monde world.] The fashionable world; people of fashion and gayety. Prior. Beaupere· (?), n. [F. beau p,re; beau fair + p,re father.] 1. A father. [Obs.] Wyclif. 2. A companion. [Obs.] Spenser. ØBeau·se·ant (?), n. [F. beauc,ant.] The black and white standard of the Knights Templars. Beauship

(?), n. The state of being a beau; the personality of a beau. [Jocular] Dryden. Beauteous (?), a. Full of beauty; beautiful; very handsome. [Mostly poetic] Ð Beauteously, adv. Ð Beauteousness, n. Beautied (?), p. a. Beautiful; embellished. [Poetic] Shak. Beautifi·er (?), n. One who, or that which, beautifies or makes beautiful. Beautiful (?), a. Having the qualities which constitute beauty; pleasing to the sight or the mind. A circle is more beautiful than a square; a square is more beautiful than a parallelogram. Lord Kames. Syn. Ð Handsome; elegant; lovely; fair; charming; graceful; pretty; delightful. See Fine. Ð Beautifully, adv. Ð Beautifulness, n. Beautify (?), v. t. [imp. & p.p. Beautified (?); p. pr. & vb. n. Beautifying.] [Beauty + Ify.] To make or render beautiful; to add beauty to; to adorn; to deck; to grace; to embellish. The arts that beautify and polish life. Burke. Syn. Ð To adorn; grace; ornament; deck; decorate. Beautify, v. i. To become beautiful; to advance in beauty. Addison. Beautiless, a. Destitute of beauty. Hammond. Beauty (?), n.; pl. Beauties (?). [OE. beaute, beute, OF. beaut,, biaut,, Pr. beltat, F. beaut,, fr. an assumed LL. bellitas, from L. bellus pretty. See Beau.]

An assemblage or graces or properties pleasing to the eye, the ear, the intellect, the 'sthetic faculty, or the moral sense. Beauty consists of a certain composition of color and figure, causing delight in the beholder. Locke. The production of beauty by a multiplicity of symmetrical parts uniting in a consistent whole. Wordsworth. The old definition of beauty, in the Roman school, was, ½multitude in unity;₎ and there is no doubt that such is the principle of beauty. Coleridge.

A particular grace, feature, ornament, or excellence; anything beautiful; as, the beauties of nature.

A beautiful person, esp. a beautiful woman. All the admired beauties of Verona. Shak.

Prevailing style or taste; rage; fashion. [Obs.] She stained her hair yellow, which was then the beauty. Jer. Taylor. Beauty spot, a patch or spot placed on the face with intent to heighten beauty by contrast. Beaux (?), n., pl. of Beau. Beauxite (?), n. (Min.) See Bauxite. Beaver (?), n. [OE. bever, AS. beofer, befer; akin to D. bever, OHG. bibar, G. biber, Sw. b„fver, Dan. b'ver, Lith. bebru, Russ. bobr', Gael. beabhar, Corn. befer, L. fiber, and Skr. babhrus large ichneumon; also as an adj., brown, the animal being probably named from its color. ?253. See Brown.]

(Zo"l.) An amphibious rodent, of the genus Castor. µ It has palmated hind feet, and a broad, flat tail. It is remarkable for its ingenuity in constructing its valued for its fur, and for the material called castor, obtained from two small bags in the groin of the animal. The European species is Castor fiber, and the American is generally considered a variety of this, although sometimes called Castor Canadensis.

The fur of the beaver.

A hat, formerly made of the fur of the beaver, but now usually of silk. A brown beaver slouched over his eyes. Prescott.

Beaver cloth, a heavy felted woolen cloth, used chiefly for making overcoats. Beaver rat (Zo"l.), an aquatic ratlike quadruped of Tasmania (Hydromys chrysogaster). Ð Beaver skin, the furry skin of the beaver. Ð Bank beaver. See under 1st Bank. Beaver, n. [OE. baviere, bauier, beavoir, bever; fr. F. bavišre, fr. bave slaver, drivel, foam, OF., prattle, drivel, perh. orig. an imitative word. Bavišre, according to Cotgrave, is the bib put before a (slavering) child.] That piece of armor which protected the lower part of the face, whether forming a part of the helmet or fixed to the breastplate. It was so constructed (with joints or otherwise) that the wearer could raise or lower it to eat and drink. Beavered (?), a. Covered with, or wearing, a beaver or hat. ½His beavered brow., Pope. Beaverĭteen (?), n. A kind of fustian made of coarse twilled cotton, shorn after dyeing. Simmonds.

<— p. 130 —>

Beĭbeerine, or Beĭbirine (?), n. (Chem.) An alkaloid got from the bark of the bebeeru, or green heart of Guiana (Nectandra Rodi?i). It is a tonic, antiperiodic, and febrifuge, and is used in medicine as a substitute for quinine. [Written also bibirine.]

Beĭbleed (?), v. t. To make bloody; to stain with blood. [Obs.]
Chaucer.

Beĭblood (?), Beĭbloody (?), v. t. To make bloody; to stain with blood. [Obs.]
Sheldon.

Beĭblot (?), v. t. To blot; to stain.
Chaucer.

Beĭblubber (?), v. t. To make swollen and disfigured or sullied by weeping; as, her eyes or cheeks were beblubbered.

Beĭcalm (?), v. t. [imp. & p.p. Becalmed (?); p. pr. & vb. n. Becalming.]
1. To render calm or quiet; to calm; to still; to appease.

Soft whispering airs ... becalm the mind.
Philips.

To keep from motion, or stop the progress of, by the stilling of the wind; as, the fleet was becalmed.

Beĭcame (?), imp. of Become.

ØBecard (?), n. (Zo"l.) A South American bird of the flycatcher family. (Tityra inquisetor).

Beĭcause (?), conj. [OE. bycause; by + cause.] 1. By or for the cause that; on this account that; for the reason that.
Milton.

In order that; that. [Obs.]

And the multitude rebuked them because they should hold their peace.
Matt. xx. 31.

Because of, by reason of, on account of. [Prep. phrase.]

Because of these things cometh the wrath of God upon the children of disobedience.
Eph. v. 6.

Syn. Ð Because, For, Since, As, Inasmuch As. These particles are used, in certain connections, to assign the reason of a thing, or that ½on account of, which it is or takes place. Because (by cause) is the strongest and most emphatic; as, I hid myself because I was afraid. For is not quite so strong;

as, in Shakespeare, ½I hate him, for he is a Christian., Since is less formal and more incidental than because; as, I will do it since you request me. It more commonly begins a sentence; as, Since your decision is made, I will say no more. As is still more incidental than since, and points to some existing fact by way of assigning a reason. Thus we say, as I knew him to be out of town, I did not call. Inasmuch as seems to carry with it a kind of qualification which does not belong to the rest. Thus, if we say, I am ready to accept your proposal, inasmuch as I believe it is the best you can offer, we mean, it is only with this understanding that we can accept it.

ØBec · caïbunga (?), n. [NL. (cf. It. beccabunga, G. bachbunge), fr. G. bach brook + bunge, OHG. bungo, bulb. See Beck a brook.] See Brooklime.

ØBec · caïfico (?), n.; pl. Beccaficos (?). [It., fr. beccare to peck + fico fig.] (Zo"l.) A small bird. (Silvia hortensis), which is highly prized by the Italians for the delicacy of its flesh in the autumn, when it has fed on figs, grapes, etc.

ØBachaïmel (?), n. [F. b,chamel, named from its inventor, Louis de B,chamel.] (Cookery) A rich, white sauce, prepared with butter and cream.

Beïchance (?), adv. [Pref. beï for by + chance.] By chance; by accident. [Obs.]

Grafton.

Beïchance, v. t. & i. To befall; to chance; to happen to.

God knows what hath bechanced them.

Shak.

Beïcharm (?), v. t. To charm; to captivate.

ØB^che · de mer (?). [F., lit., a sea spade.] (Zo"l.) The trepang.

Bechic (?), a. [L. bechicus, adj., for a cough, Gr. ?, fr. ? cough: cf. F. b,chique.] (Med.) Pertaining to, or relieving, a cough. Thomas. Ð n. A medicine for relieving coughs.

Quincy.

Beck (?), n. See Beak. [Obs.]

Spenser.

Beck, n. [OE. bek, AS. becc; akin to Icel. bekkr brook, OHG. pah, G. bach.] A small brook.

The brooks, the becks, the rills.

Drayton.

Beck, n. A vat. See Back.

Beck, v. i. [imp. & p.p. Becked (?); p. pr. & vb. n. Becking.] [Contr. of beckon.] To nod, or make a sign with the head or hand. [Archaic]

Drayton.

Beck, v. t. To notify or call by a nod, or a motion of the head or hand; to intimate a command to. [Archaic]

When gold and silver becks me to come on.

Shak.

Beck, n. A significant nod, or motion of the head or hand, esp. as a call or command.

They have troops of soldiers at their beck.

Shak.

Becker (?), n. (Zo"l.) A European fish (Pagellus centrodontus); the sea bream or braise.

Becket (?), n. [Cf. D. bek beak, and E. beak.]

(Naut.) A small grommet, or a ring or loop of rope ? metal for holding things in position, as spars, ropes, etc.; also a bracket, a pocket, or a handle made of rope.

A spade for digging turf. [Prov. Eng.]

Wright.

Beckon, v. t. [imp. & p.p. Beckoned (?); p. pr. & vb. n. Beckoning.] To make a significant sign to; hence, to summon, as by a motion of the hand.

His distant friends, he beckons near.

Dryden.

It beckons you to go away with it.

Shak.

Beckon, n. A sign made without words; a beck. ½At the first beckon.

Bolingbroke.

Beïclap (?), v. t. [OE. biclappen.] To catch; to grasp; to insnare. [Obs.]

Chaucer.

Beïclip (?), v. t. [imp. & p.p. Beclipped (?).] [AS. beclyppan; pref. be + clyppan to embrace.] To embrace; to surround. [Obs.]

Wyclif.

Beïcloud (?), v. t. [imp. & p.p. Beclouded; p. pr. & vb. n. Beclouding.] To cause obscurity or dimness to; to dim; to cloud.

If thou becloud the sunshine of thine eye.

Quarles.

Beïcome (?), v. i. [imp. Became (?); p.p. Become; p. pr. & vb. n. Becoming.] [OE. bicumen, becumen, AS. becuman to come to, to happen; akin to D. bekomen, OHG.a piqu‰oman, Goth. biquiman to come upon, G. bekommen to get, suit. See Beï, and Come.] 1. To pass from one state to another; to enter into some state or condition, by a change from another state, or by assuming or receiving new properties or qualities, additional matter, or a new character.

The Lord God ... breathed into his nostrils the breath of life; and man became a living soul.

Gen. ii. 7.

That error now which is become my crime.

Milton.

To come; to get. [Obs.]

But, madam, where is Warwick then become!
Shak.

To become of, to be the present state or place of; to be the fate of; to be the end of; to be the final or subsequent condition of.

What is then become of so huge a multitude?
Sir W. Raleigh.

Beĭcome, v. t. To suit or be suitable to; to be con???ous with; to befit; to accord with, in character or circumstances; to be worthy of, or proper for; to cause to appear well; Ð said of persons and things.

It becomes me so to speak of so excellent a poet.
 Dryden.

I have known persons so anxious to have their dress become them, as to convert it, at length, into their proper self, and thus actually to become the dress.
 Coleridge.

Beĭcomed (?), a. Proper; decorous. [Obs.]
And gave him what becomed love I might.
Shak.

Beĭcoming, a. Appropriate or fit; congruous; suitable; graceful; befitting.
A low and becoming tone.
Thackeray.

Formerly sometimes followed by of.
Such discourses as are becoming of them.
Dryden.

Syn. Ð Seemly; comely; decorous; decent; proper.

Beĭcoming, n. That which is becoming or appropriate. [Obs.]

Beĭcomingĭly, adv. In a becoming manner.

Beĭcomingĭness, n. The quality of being becoming, appropriate, or fit; congruity; fitness.

The becomingness of human nature.
Grew.

Beĭcripple (?), v. t. To make a cripple of; to cripple; to lame. [R.]
Dr. H. More.

ØBeĭcuna (?), n. [Sp.] (Zo"l.) A fish of the Mediterranean (Sphyr'na spet.) See Barracuda.

Beĭcurl (?), v. t. To curl; to adorn with curls.

Bed (?), n. [AS. bed, bedd; akin to OS. bed, D. bed, bedde, Icel. be?r, Dan. bed, Sw. b„dd, Goth. badi, OHG. betti, G. bett, bette, bed, beet a plat of ground; all of uncertain origin.] 1. An article of furniture to sleep or take rest in or on; a couch. Specifically: A sack or mattress, filled with some soft material, in distinction from the bedstead on which it is placed (as, a feather bed), or this with the bedclothes added. In a general sense, any thing or place used for sleeping or reclining on or in, as a quantity of hay, straw, leaves, or twigs.

And made for him [a horse] a leafy bed.
Byron.
I wash, wring, brew, bake, ... make the beds.
Shak.
In bed he slept not for my urging it.
Shak.

(Used as the symbol of matrimony) Marriage.

George, the eldest son of his second bed.
Clarendon.

A plat or level piece of ground in a garden, usually a little raised above the adjoining ground. ½Beds of hyacinth and roses.

Milton.

A mass or heap of anything arranged like a bed; as, a bed of ashes or coals.

The bottom of a watercourse, or of any body of water; as, the bed of a river.

So sinks the daystar in the ocean bed.
Milton.

(Geol.) A layer or seam, or a horizontal stratum between layers; as, a bed of coal, iron, etc.

(Gun.) See Gun carriage, and Mortar bed.

(Masonry) (a) The horizontal surface of a building stone; as, the upper and lower beds. (b) A course of stone or brick in a wall. (c) The place or material in which a block or brick is laid. (d) The lower surface of a brick, slate, or tile.

Knight.

(Mech.) The foundation or the more solid and fixed part or framing of a machine; or a part on which something is laid or supported; as, the bed of an engine.

The superficial earthwork, or ballast, of a railroad.

(Printing) The flat part of the press, on which the form is laid.

μ Bed is much used adjectively or in combination; as, bed key or bedkey; bed wrench or bedwrench; bedchamber; bedmaker, etc.

Bed of justice (French Hist.), the throne (F. lit bed) occupied by the king when sitting in one of his parliaments (judicial courts); hence, a session of a refractory parliament, at which the king was present for the purpose of causing his decrees to be registered. Ð To be brought to bed, to be delivered of a child; Ð often followed by of; as, to be brought to bed of a son. Ð To make a bed, to prepare a bed; to arrange or put in order a bed and its bedding. Ð From bed and board (Law), a phrase applied to a separation by partial divorce of man and wife, without dissolving the bonds of matrimony.

If such a divorce (now commonly called a judicial separation) be granted at the instance of the wife, she may have alimony.

Bed, v. t. [imp. & p.p. Bedded; p. pr. & vb. n. Bedding.] 1. To place in a bed. [Obs.]
Bacon.

To make partaker of one's bed; to cohabit with.

I'll to the Tuscan wars, and never bed her.
Shak.

To furnish with a bed or bedding.

To plant or arrange in beds; to set, or cover, as in a bed of soft earth; as, to bed the roots of a plant in mold.

To lay or put in any hollow place, or place of rest and security, surrounded or inclosed; to embed; to furnish with or place upon a bed or foundation; as, to bed a stone; it was bedded on a rock.

Among all chains or clusters of mountains where large bodies of still water are bedded.
Wordsworth.

(Masonry) To dress or prepare the surface of stone) so as to serve as a bed.

To lay flat; to lay in order; to place in a horizontal or recumbent position. ½Bedded hair.͵

Shak.
Bed (?), v. i. To go to bed; to cohabit.
If he be married, and bed with his wife.
Wiseman.

Bedabĭble (?), v. t. [imp. & p.p. Bedabbled (?); p. pr. & vb. n. Bedabbling (?). To dabble; to sprinkle or wet.
Shak.

Bedaff (?), v. t. To make a daff or fool of. [Obs.]
Chaucer.

ØBedaĭgat (?), n. The sacred books of the Buddhists in Burmah.
Malcom.

Bedaggle (?), v. t. To daggle.

Bedash (?), v. t. [imp. & p.p. Bedashed (?); p. pr. & vb. n. Bedashing.] To wet by dashing or throwing water or other liquid upon; to bespatter. ½Trees bedashed with rain.͵
Shak.

Bedaub (?), v. t. [imp. & p.p. Bedaubed (?); p. pr. & vb. n. Bedaubing.] To daub over; to besmear or soil with anything thick and dirty.

Bedaub foul designs with a fair varnish.
Barrow.

Bedazzle (?), v. t. [imp. & p.p. Bedazzled (?); p. pr. & vb. n. Bedazzling (?).] To dazzle or make dim by a strong light. ½Bedazzled with the sun.

Shak.

Bedbug · (?), n. (Zo"l.) A wingless, bloodsucking, hemipterous insect (Cimex Lectularius), sometimes infesting houses and especially beds. See Illustration in Appendix.

Bedchair · (?), n. A chair with adjustable back, for the sick, to support them while sitting up in bed.

Bedcham · ber (?), n. A chamber for a bed; an apartment form sleeping in.

Shak.

Lords of the bedchamber, eight officers of the royal household, all of noble families, who wait in turn a week each. [Eng.] Ð Ladies of the bedchamber, eight ladies, all titled, holding a similar official position in the royal household, during the reign of a queen. [Eng.]

Bedclothes · (?), n. pl. Blankets, sheets, coverlets, etc., for a bed.

Shak.

Bedcord · (?), n. A cord or rope interwoven in a bedstead so as to support the bed.

Bedded (?), a. Provided with a bed; as, doublebedded room; placed or arranged in a bed or beds.

Bedding (?), n. [AS. bedding, beding. See Bed.] 1. A bed and its furniture; the materials of a bed, whether for man or beast; bedclothes; litter.

(Geol.) The state or position of beds and layers.

Bede (?), v. t. [See Bid, v. t.] To pray; also, to offer; to proffer. [Obs.]
R. of Gloucester. Chaucer.

Bede, n. (Mining) A kind of pickax.

Bedeck (?), v. t. [imp. & p.p. Bedecked (?); p. pr. & vb. n. Bedecking.] To deck, ornament, or adorn; to grace.

Bedecked with boughs, flowers, and garlands.

Pennant.

ØBedelguar, Bedelgar (?), n. [F., fr. Per. b¾dÐ¾ward, or b¾dÐ¾wardag, prop., a kind of white thorn or thistle.] A gall produced on rosebushes, esp. on the sweetbrier or eglantine, by a puncture from the ovipositor of a gallfly (Rhodites ros'). It was once supposed to have medicinal properties.

Bedehouse · (?), n. Same as Beadhouse.

Bedel, Bedell (?), n. Same as Beadle.

Bedelry (?), n. Beadleship. [Obs.]

Blount.

ØBeden (?), n. (Zo"l.) The Abyssinian or Arabian ibex (Capra Nubiana). It is probably the wild goat of the Bible.

Bedesman (?), n. Same as Beadsman. [Obs.]

Beïdevil (?), v. t. [imp. & p.p. Bedevilled (?); p. pr. & vb. n. Bedeviling or Bedevilling.] 1. To throw into utter disorder and confusion, as if by the agency of evil spirits; to bring under diabolical influence; to torment.

Bedeviled and used worse than St. Bartholomew.

Sterne.

To spoil; to corrupt.

Wright.

Beïdevilĭment (?), n. The state of being bedeviled; bewildering confusion; vexatious trouble. [Colloq.]

Beïdew (?), v. t. [imp. & p.p. Bedewed (?); p. pr. & vb. n. Bedewing.] To moisten with dew, or as with dew. ½Falling tears his face bedew.

Dryden.

Beïdewer (?), n. One who, or that which, bedews.

Beïdewy (?), a. Moist with dew; dewy. [Obs.]

Night with her bedewy wings.

A. Brewer.

Bedfel · low (?), n. One who lies with another in the same bed; a person who shares one's couch.

Bedfere · Bedphere · } (?), n. [Bed + AS. fera a companion.] A bedfellow. [Obs.]

Chapman.

Bedgown · (?), n. A nightgown.

Beïdight (?), v. t. [p. p. Bedight, Bedighted.] TO bedeck; to array or equip; to adorn. [Archaic]

Milton.

Beïdim (?), v. t. [imp. & p.p. Bedimmed (?); p. pr. & vb. n. Bedimming.] To make dim; to obscure or darken.

Shak.

Beïdizen (?), v. t. To dress or adorn tawdrily or with false taste.

Remnants of tapestried hangings, ... and shreds of pictures with which he had bedizened his tatters.

Sir W. Scott.

Beïdizenĭment (?), n. That which bedizens; the act of dressing, or the state of being dressed, tawdrily.

Bedkey · (?), n. An instrument for tightening the parts of a bedstead.

Bedlam (?), n. [See Bethlehem.] 1. A place appropriated to the confinement and care of the insane; a madhouse.

Abp. Tillotson.

An insane person; a lunatic; a madman. [Obs.]

Let's get the bedlam to lead him.
Shak.

Any place where uproar and confusion prevail.

Bedlam, a. Belonging to, or fit for, a madhouse. ½The bedlam, brainsick duchess.
Shak.

Bedlamĭte (?), n. An inhabitant of a madhouse; a madman. ½Raving bedlamites.
Beattie.

Bedmak·er (?), n. One who makes beds.

<— p. 131 —>

BedÐmold·ing BedÐmould·ing } (?), n. (Arch.) The molding of a cornice immediately below the corona.
Oxf. Gloss.

Beïdote (?), v. t. To cause to dote; to deceive. [Obs.]
Chaucer.

Bedouĭin (?), n. [F. b,douin, OF. b,duin, fr. Ar. bedawÆ rural, living in the desert, fr. badw desert, fr. bad¾ to live in the desert, to lead a nomadic life.] One of the nomadic Arabs who live in tents, and are scattered over Arabia, Syria, and northern Africa, esp. in the deserts. Ð Bedouĭinĭism (?), n.

Bedouĭin, a. Pertaining to the Bedouins; nomad.

Bedpan· (?), n. 1. A pan for warming beds.
Nares.

A shallow chamber vessel, so constructed that it can be used by a sick person in bed.

Bedphere· (?), n. See Bedfere. [Obs.]
B. Jonson.

Bedpiece· (?), Bedplate· (?), } n. (Mach.) The foundation framing or piece, by which the other parts are supported and held in place; the bed; Ð called also baseplate and soleplate.

Bedpost· (?), n. 1. One of the four standards that support a bedstead or the canopy over a bedstead.

Anciently, a post or pin on each side of the bed to keep the clothes from falling off. See Bedstaff.

Brewer.

Bedquilt· (?), n. A quilt for a bed; a coverlet.

Beïdrabble (?), v. t. To befoul with rain and mud; to drabble.

Beïdraggle (?), v. t. [imp. & p.p. Bedraggled (?); p. pr. & vb. n. Bedraggling (?). To draggle; to soil, as garments which, in walking, are suffered to drag in dust, mud, etc.

Swift.

Be·drench (?), v. t. [imp. & p.p. Bedrenched (?); p. pr. & vb. n. Bedrenching.] To drench; to saturate with moisture; to soak.

Shak.

Be·dribble (?), v. t. To dribble upon.

Bedrid · (?), Bedrid · den (?), } a. [OE. bedrede, AS. bedreda, bedrida; from bed, bedd, a bed or couch + ridda a rider; cf. OHG. pettiriso, G. bettrise. See Bed, n., and Ride, v. i.] Confined to the bed by sickness or infirmity. ½Her decrepit, sick, and bedrid father.¸ Shak. ½The estate of a bedridden old gentleman.¸ Macaulay.

Bedright · Bedrite · } (?), n. [Bed + right, rite.] The duty or privilege of the marriage bed.

Shak.

Be·drizzle (?), v. t. To drizzle upon.

Bed rock (?). (Mining) The solid rock underlying superficial formations. Also Fig.

Bedroom (?), n. 1. A room or apartment intended or used for a bed; a lodging room.

Room in a bed. [In this sense preferably bed room.]

Then by your side no bed room me deny.
 Shak.

Be·drop (?), v. t. To sprinkle, as with drops.

The yellow carp, in scales bedropped with gold.

Pope.

Be·drug (?), v. t. To drug abundantly or excessively.

Bed screw · (?). 1. (Naut.) A form of jack screw for lifting large bodies, and assisting in launching.

A long screw formerly used to fasten a bedpost to one of the adjacent side pieces.

Bedside · (?), n. The side of a bed.

Bedsite · (?), n. A recess in a room for a bed.

Of the three bedrooms, two have fireplaces, and all are of fair size, with windows and bedsite well placed.

Quart. Rev.

Bedsore · (?), n. (Med.) A sore on the back or hips caused by lying for a long time in bed.

Bedspread · (?), n. A bedquilt; a counterpane; a coverlet. [U. S.]

Bedstaff · (?), n.; pl. Bedstaves (?). ½A wooden pin stuck anciently on the sides of the bedstead, to hold the clothes from slipping on either side.¸

Johnson.

Hostess, accommodate us with a bedstaff.

B. Jonson.

Say there is no virtue in cudgels and bedstaves.
Brome.

Bedstead (?), n. [Bed + stead a frame.] A framework for supporting a bed.

Bed steps · (?). Steps for mounting a bed of unusual height.

Bedstock (?), n. The front or the back part of the frame of a bedstead. [Obs. or Dial. Eng.]

Bedstraw · (?), n. 1. Straw put into a bed.
Bacon.

(Bot.) A genus of slender herbs, usually with square stems, whorled leaves, and small white flowers.

Our Lady's bedstraw, which has yellow flowers, is Galium verum. Ð White bedstraw is G. mollugo.

Bedswerv · er (?), n. One who swerves from and is unfaithful to the marriage vow. [Poetic]
Shak.

Bedtick · (?), n. A tick or bag made of cloth, used for inclosing the materials of a bed.

Bedtime · (?), n. The time to go to bed.
Shak.

Beïduck (?), v. t. [imp. & p.p. Beducked (?).] To duck; to put the head under water; to immerse. ½Deep himself beducked.
Spenser.

Beduin (?), n. See Bedouin.

Beïdung (?), v. t. [imp. & p.p. Bedunged (?).] To cover with dung, as for manuring; to bedaub or defile, literally or figuratively.
Bp. Hall.

Beïdust (?), v. t. To sprinkle, soil, or cover with dust.
Sherwood.

Bedward (?), adv. Towards bed.

Beïdwarf (?), v. t. [imp. & p.p. Bedwarfed (?).] To make a dwarf of; to stunt or hinder the growth of; to dwarf.
Donne.

Beïdye (?), v. t. [imp. & p.p. Bedyed (?); p. pr. & vb. n. Bedyeing.] To dye or stain.
Briton fields with Sarazin blood bedyed.
Spenser.

Bee (?), p. p. of Be; Ð used for been. [Obs.]
Spenser.

Bee (?), n. [AS. beç; akin to D. bij and bije, Icel. b?, Sw. & Dan. bi, OHG. pini, G. biene, and perh. Ir. beach, Lith. bitis, Skr. bha. ?97.] 1. (Zo"l.) An insect of the order Hymenoptera, and family Apid' (the honeybees), or family Andrenid' (the solitary bees.) See Honeybee.

µ There are many genera and species. The common honeybee (Apis mellifica) lives in swarms, each of which has its own queen, its males or drones, and its very numerous workers, which are barren females. Besides the A. mellifica there are other species and varieties of honeybees, as the A. ligustica of Spain and Italy; the A. Indica of India; the A. fasciata of Egypt. The bumblebee is a species of Bombus. The tropical honeybees belong mostly to Melipoma and Trigona.

<blockquote>A neighborly gathering of people who engage in united labor for the benefit of an individual or family; as, a quilting bee; a husking bee; a raising bee. [U. S.]</blockquote>

The cellar ... was dug by a bee in a single day.
S. G. Goodrich.

pl. [Prob. fr. AS. be h ring, fr. b?gan to bend. See 1st Bow.] (Naut.) Pieces of hard wood bolted to the sides of the bowsprit, to reeve the foreĭtopmast stays through; Đ called also bee blocks.

Bee beetle (Zo"l.), a beetle (Trichodes apiarius) parasitic in beehives. Đ Bee bird (Zo"l.), a bird that eats the honeybee, as the European flycatcher, and the American kingbird. Đ Bee flower (Bot.), an orchidaceous plant of the genus Ophrys (O. apifera), whose flowers have some resemblance to bees, flies, and other insects. Đ Bee fly (Zo"l.), a two winged fly of the family Bombyliid'. Some species, in the larval state, are parasitic upon bees. Đ Bee garden, a garden or inclosure to set beehives in ; an apiary. Mortimer. Đ Bee glue, a soft, unctuous matter, with which bees cement the combs to the hives, and close up the cells; Đ called also propolis. Đ Bee hawk (Zo"l.), the honey buzzard. Đ Bee killer (Zo"l.), a large twoĐwinged fly of the family Asilid' (esp. Trupanea apivora) which feeds upon the honeybee. See Robber fly. Đ Bee louse (Zo"l.), a minute, wingless, dipterous insect (Braula c'ca) parasitic on hive bees. Đ Bee martin (Zo"l.), the kingbird (Tyrannus Carolinensis) which occasionally feeds on bees. Đ Bee moth (Zo"l.), a moth (Galleria cereana) whose larv' feed on honeycomb, occasioning great damage in beehives. Đ Bee wolf (Zo"l.), the larva of the bee beetle. See Illust. of Bee beetle. Đ To have a bee in the head or in the bonnet. (a) To be choleric. [Obs.] (b) To be restless or uneasy. B. Jonson. (c) To be full of fancies; to be a little crazy. ½She's whiles crackĐbrained, and has a bee in her head., Sir W. Scott.

Beebread · (?), n. A brown, bitter substance found in some of the cells of honeycomb. It is made chiefly from the pollen of flowers, which is collected by bees as food for their young.

Beech (?), n.; pl. Beeches (?). [OE. beche, AS. b?ce; akin to D. beuk, OHG. buocha, G. buche, Icel. beyki, Dan. b"g, Sw. bok, Russ. buk, L. fagus, Gr. ? oak, ? to eat, Skr. bhaksh; the tree being named originally from the esculent fruit. See Book, and cf. 7th Buck, Buckwheat.] (Bot.) A tree of the genus Fagus.

µ It grows to a large size, having a smooth bark and thick foliage, and bears an edible triangular nut, of which swine are fond. The Fagus sylvatica is the European species, and the F. ferruginea that of America.

Beech drops (Bot.), a parasitic plant which grows on the roots of beeches (Epiphegus Americana).Ð Beech marten (Zo"l.), the stone marten of Europe (Mustela foina). Ð Beech mast, the nuts of the beech, esp. as they lie under the trees, in autumn. Ð Beech oil, oil expressed from the mast or nuts of the beech tree. Ð Cooper beech, a variety of the European beech with copperÐcolored, shining leaves.

Beechen (?), a. [AS. b?cen.] Consisting, or made, of the wood or bark of the beech; belonging to the beech. ½Plain beechen vessels.‚

Dryden.

Beechnut · (?), n. The nut of the beech tree.

Beech tree · (?). The beech.

Beechy (?), a. Of or relating to beeches.

BeeÐeat · er (?), n. (Zo"l.) (a) A bird of the genus Merops, that feeds on bees. The European species (M. apiaster) is remarkable for its brilliant colors. (b) An African bird of the genus Rhinopomastes.

Beef (?), n. [OE. boef, befe, beef, OF. boef, buef, F. b?ef, fr. L. bos, bovis, ox; akin to Gr. ?, Skr. g? cow, and E. cow. See 2d Cow.] 1. An animal of the genus Bos, especially the common species, B. taurus, including the bull, cow, and ox, in their full grown state; esp., an ox or cow fattened for food. [In this, which is the original sense, the word has a plural, beeves (?).]

A herd of beeves, fair oxen and fair kine.
Milton.

The flesh of an ox, or cow, or of any adult bovine animal, when slaughtered for food. [In this sense, the word has no plural.] ½Great meals of beef.‚

Shak.

Applied colloquially to human flesh.

Beef (?), a. Of, pertaining to, or resembling, beef.

Beef tea, essence of beef, or strong beef broth.

Beefeat · er (?), n. [Beef + eater; prob. one who eats another's beef, as his servant. Cf. AS. hl¾f?ta servant, properly a loaf eater.] 1. One who eats beef; hence, a large, fleshy person.

One of the yeomen of the guard, in England.

(Zo"l.) An African bird of the genus Buphaga, which feeds on the larv' of botflies hatched under the skin of oxen, antelopes, etc. Two species are known.

Beefsteak · (?), n. A steak of beef; a slice of beef broiled or suitable for broiling.

BeefÐwit · ted (?), n. Stupid; dull.

Shak.

Beefwood · (?), n. An Australian tree (Casuarina), and its red wood, used for cabinetwork; also, the trees Stenocarpus salignus of New South Wales, and Banksia compar of Queensland.

Beefy, a. Having much beef; of the nature of beef; resembling beef; fleshy.

Beehive · (?), n. A hive for a swarm of bees. Also used figuratively.

µ A common and typical form of beehive was a domeshaped inverted basket, whence certain ancient Irish and Scotch architectural remains are called beehive houses.

Beehouse · (?), n. A house for bees; an apiary.

Bee lark · spur (?). (Bot.) See Larkspur.

Beeld (?), n. Same as Beild.

Fairfax.

Bee line · (?). The shortest line from one place to another, like that of a bee to its hive when loaded with honey; an air line. ½A bee line for the brig.‚

Kane.

Beḯelzeḯbub (?), n. The title of a heathen deity to whom the Jews ascribed the sovereignty of the evil spirits; hence, the Devil or a devil. See Baal.

Beem (?), n. [AS. b?me, b?me.] A trumpet. [Obs.]

Beemas · ter (?), n. One who keeps bees.

Been (?). [OE. beon, ben, bin, p. p. of been, beon, to be. See Be.] The past participle of Be. In old authors it is also the pr. tense plural of Be. See 1st Bee.

Assembled been a senate grave and stout.

Fairfax.

Beer (?), n. [OE. beor, ber, AS. beꞓr; akin to Fries. biar, Icel. bj?rr, OHG. bior, D. & G. bier, and possibly E. brew. ?93, See Brew.] 1. A fermented liquor made from any malted grain, but commonly from barley malt, with hops or some other substance to impart a bitter flavor.

µ Beer has different names, as small beer, ale, porter, brown stout, lager beer, according to its strength, or other qualities. See Ale.

A fermented extract of the roots and other parts of various plants, as spruce, ginger, sassafras, etc.

Small beer, weak beer; (fig.) insignificant matters. ½To suckle fools, and chronicle small beer.‚

Shak.

Beereḯgar (?), n. [Beer + eager.] Sour beer. [Obs.]

Beerhouse · (?), n. A house where malt liquors are sold; an alehouse.

Beeriḯness (?), n. Beery condition.

Beery (?), a. Of or resembling beer; affected by beer; maudlin.

Beestings (?), n. Same as Biestings.

Beeswax · (?), n. The wax secreted by bees, and of which their cells are constructed.

Beeswing · (?), n. The second crust formed in port and some other wines after long keeping. It consists of pure, shining scales of tartar, supposed to resemble the wing of a bee.

Beet (?), n. [AS. bete, from L. beta.] 1. (Bot.) A biennial plant of the genus Beta, which produces an edible root the first year and seed the second year.

> The root of plants of the genus Beta, different species and varieties of which are used for the table, for feeding stock, or in making sugar.

µ There are many varieties of the common beet (Beta vulgaris). The Old ½white beet₃, cultivated for its edible leafstalks, is a distinct species (Beta Cicla).

Beete, Bete (?), v. t. [AS. b?tan to mend. See Better.] 1. To mend; to repair. [Obs.]

Chaucer.

> To renew or enkindle (a fire). [Obs.]

Chaucer.

Beetle (?), n. [OE. betel, AS. bÆtl, b?tl, mallet, hammer, fr. be tan to beat. See Beat, v. t.] 1. A heavy mallet, used to drive wedges, beat pavements, etc.

> A machine in which fabrics are subjected to a hammering process while passing over rollers, as in cotton mills; Ð called also beetling machine.

Knight.
<— p. 132 —>
Beetle (?), v. t. [imp. & p.p. Beetled (?); p. pr. & vb. n. Beetling.] 1. To beat with a heavy mallet.

> To finish by subjecting to a hammering process in a beetle or beetling machine; as, to beetle cotton goods.

Beetle, n. [OE. bityl, bittle, AS. b?tel, fr. b?tan to bite. See Bite, v. t.] Any insect of the order Coleoptera, having four wings, the outer pair being stiff cases for covering the others when they are folded up. See Coleoptera.

Beetle mite (Zo"l.), one of many species of mites, of the family Oribatid', parasitic on beetles. Ð Black beetle, the common large black cockroach (Blatta orientalis).

Beetle, v. i. [See Beetlebrowed.] To extend over and beyond the base or support; to overhang; to jut.

To the dreadful summit of the cliff
That beetles o'er his base into the sea.
Shak.
Each beetling rampart, and each tower sublime.

Wordsworth.

Beetle brow · (?). An overhanging brow.

BeetleÐbrowed · (?), a. [OE. bitelbrowed; cf. OE. bitel, adj., sharp, projecting, n., a beetle. See Beetle an insect.] Having prominent, overhanging brows; hence, lowering or sullen.

µ The earlier meaning was, ½Having bushy or overhanging eyebrows.͵

BeetleÏhead · (?), n. [Beetle a mallet + head.]

A stupid fellow; a blockhead.

Sir W. Scott.

(Zo"l.) The blackÏbellied plover, or bullhead (Squatarola helvetica). See Plover.

BeetleÐhead · ed (?), a. Dull; stupid.
Shak.

BeetleÏstock · (?), n. The handle of a beetle.

Beet rad · ish (?). Same as Beetrave.

Beetrave · (?), n. [F. betterave; bette beet + rave radish.] The common beet (Beta vulgaris).

Beeve (?), n. [Formed from beeves, pl. of beef.] A beef; a beef creature.

They would knock down the first beeve they met with.

W. Irving.

Beeves (?), n.; plural of Beef, the animal.

BeÏfall (?), v. t. [imp. Befell (?); p. p. Befallen (?); p. pr. & vb. n. Befalling.] [AS. befeallan; pref. beÏ + feallan to fall.] To happen to.

I beseech your grace that I may know
The worst that may befall me.

Shak.

BeÏfall, v. i. To come to pass; to happen.

I have revealed ... the discord which befell.

Milton.

BeÏfit (?), v. t. [imp. & p.p. Befitted; p. pr. & vb. n. Befitting.] To be suitable to; to suit; to become.

That name best befits thee.

Milton.

BeÏfitting, a. Suitable; proper; becoming; fitting.

BeÏfittingÏly, adv. In a befitting manner; suitably.

BeÏflatter (?), v. t. To flatter excessively.

BeÏflower (?), v. t. To besprinkle or scatter over with, or as with, flowers.
Hobbes.

BeÏfog (?), v. t. [imp. & p.p. Befogged (?); p. pr. & vb. n. Befogging (?).] 1. To involve in a fog; Ð mostly as a participle or part. adj.

Hence: To confuse; to mystify.

Beïfool (?), v. t. [imp. & p.p. Befooled (?); p. pr. & vb. n. Befooling.] [OE. befolen; pref. beï + fol fool.] 1. To fool; to delude or lead into error; to infatuate; to deceive.

This story ... contrived to befool credulous men.
Fuller.

To cause to behave like a fool; to make foolish. ½Some befooling drug.‚

G. Eliot.

Beïfore (?), prep. [OE. beforen, biforen, before, AS. beforan; pref. beï + foran, fore, before. See Beï, and Fore.] 1. In front of; preceding in space; ahead of; as, to stand before the fire; before the house.

His angel, who shall go
Before them in a cloud and pillar of fire.
Milton.

Preceding in time; earlier than; previously to; anterior to the time when; Đ sometimes with the additional idea of purpose; in order that.

Before Abraham was, I am.
John viii. 58.
Before this treatise can become of use, two points are necessary.
Swift.

μ Formerly before, in this sense, was followed by that. ½Before that Philip called thee... I saw thee.‚
John i. 48.

An advance of; farther onward, in place or time.

The golden age ... is before us.
Carlyle.

Prior or preceding in dignity, order, rank, right, or worth; rather than.

He that cometh after me is preferred before me.
John i. 15.
The eldest son is before the younger in succession.
Johnson.

In presence or sight of; face to face with; facing.

Abraham bowed down himself before the people.
Gen. xxiii. 12.
Wherewith shall I come before the Lord?
Micah vi. 6.

Under the cognizance or jurisdiction of.

If a suit be begun before an archdeacon.
Ayliffe.

Open for; free of access to; in the power of.

The world was all before them where to choose.
Milton.

Before the mast (Naut.), as a common sailor, — because the sailors live in the forecastle, forward of the foremast. — Before the wind (Naut.), in the direction of the wind and by its impulse; having the wind aft.

Be‖fore, adv. 1. On the fore part; in front, or in the direction of the front; — opposed to in the rear.

The battle was before and behind.
2 Chron. xiii. 14.

In advance. ½I come before to tell you.

Shak.

In time past; previously; already.

You tell me, mother, what I knew before.
Dryden.

Earlier; sooner than; until then.

When the butt is out, we will drink water; not a drop before.
Shak.

µ Before is often used in self—explaining compounds; as, before—cited, before—mentioned; beforesaid.

Be‖forehand · (?), adv. [Before + hand.]

In a state of anticipation ore preoccupation; in advance; — often followed by with.

Agricola ... resolves to be beforehand with the danger.
Milton.
The last cited author has been beforehand with me.
Addison.

By way of preparation, or preliminary; previously; aforetime.

They may be taught beforehand the skill of speaking.
Hooker.

Be‖forehand · , a. In comfortable circumstances as regards property; forehanded.

Rich and much beforehand.
Bacon.

Be̅foretime · (?), adv. Formerly; aforetime.

[They] dwelt in their tents, as beforetime.
  2 Kings xiii. 5.

Be̅fortune (?), v. t. To befall. [Poetic]

I wish all good befortune you.
  Shak.

Be̅foul (?), v. t. [imp. & p.p. Befouled (?); p. pr. & vb. n. Befouling.] [Cf. AS. bef?lan; pref. be̅ + f?lan to foul. See Foul, a.] 1. To make foul; to soil.

> To entangle or run against so as to impede motion.

Be̅friend (?), v. t. [imp. & p.p. Befriended; p. pr. & vb. n. Befriending.] To act as a friend to; to favor; to aid, benefit, or countenance.

By the darkness befriended.
  Longfellow.

Be̅friendment (?), n. Act of befriending. [R.]

Be̅frill (?), v. t. To furnish or deck with a frill.

Be̅fringe (?), v. t. To furnish with a fringe; to form a fringe upon; to adorn as with fringe.
  Fuller.

Be̅fuddle (?), v. t. [imp. & p.p. Befuddled (?)] To becloud and confuse, as with liquor.

Beg (?), n. [Turk. beg, pronounced bay. Cf. Bey, Begum.] A title of honor in Turkey and in some other parts of the East; a bey.

Beg (?), v. t. [imp. & p.p. Begged (?); p. pr. & vb. n. Begging.] [OE. beggen, perh. fr. AS. bedecian (akin to Goth. bedagwa beggar), biddan to ask. (Cf. Bid, v. t.); or cf. beghard, beguin.] 1. To ask earnestly for; to entreat or supplicate for; to beseech.

I do beg your good will in this case.
  Shak.

[Joseph] begged the body of Jesus.
  Matt. xxvii. 58.

Sometimes implying deferential and respectful, rather than earnest, asking; as, I beg your pardon; I beg leave to disagree with you.

> To ask for as a charity, esp. to ask for habitually or from house to house.

Yet have I not seen the righteous forsaken, nor his seed begging bread.
  Ps. xxxvii. 25.

> To make petition to; to entreat; as, to beg a person to grant a favor.

> To take for granted; to assume without proof.

> (Old Law) To ask to be appointed guardian for, or to ask to have a guardian appointed for.

Else some will beg thee, in the court of wards.
Harrington.

Hence: To beg (one) for a fool, to take him for a fool.

I beg to, is an elliptical expression for I beg leave to; as, I beg to inform you. Ð To bag the question, to assume that which was to be proved in a discussion, instead of adducing the proof or sustaining the point by argument. Ð To go aïbegging, a figurative phrase to express the absence of demand for something which elsewhere brings a price; as, grapes are so plentiful there that they go aïbegging.

Syn. Ð To Beg, Ask, Request. To ask (not in the sense of inquiring) is the generic term which embraces all these words. To request is only a polite mode of asking. To beg, in its original sense, was to ask with earnestness, and implied submission, or at least deference. At present, however, in polite life, beg has dropped its original meaning, and has taken the place of both ask and request, on the ground of its expressing more of deference and respect. Thus, we beg a person's acceptance of a present; we beg him to favor us with his company; a tradesman begs to announce the arrival of new goods, etc. Crabb remarks that, according to present usage, ½we can never talk of asking a person's acceptance of a thing, or of asking him to do us a favor., This can be more truly said of usage in England than in America.

Beg, v. i. To ask alms or charity, especially to ask habitually by the wayside or from house to house; to live by asking alms.

I can not dig; to beg I am ashamed.
 Luke xvi. 3.

ØBega (?), n. See Bigha.

Beïgem (?), v. t. [imp. & p.p. Begemmed (?); p. pr. & vb. n. Begemming.] To adorn with gems, or as with gems.

Begemmed with dewdrops.
Sir W. Scott.

Those lonely realms bright garden isles begem.
Shelley.

Beïget (?), v. t. [imp. Begot (?), (Archaic) Begat (?); p. p. Begot, Begotten (?); p. pr. & vb. n. Begetting.] [OE. bigiten, bigeten, to get, beget, AS. begitan to get; pref. beï + gitan. See Get, v. t.] 1. To procreate, as a father or sire; to generate; Ð commonly said of the father.

Yet they a beauteous offspring shall beget.
 Milton.

To get (with child.) [Obs.]

Shak.

To produce as an effect; to cause to exist.

Love is begot by fancy.

Granville.

Begetter (?), n. One who begets; a father.

Beggable (?), a. Capable of being begged.

Beggar (?), n. [OE. beggere, fr. beg.] 1. One who begs; one who asks or entreats earnestly, or with humility; a petitioner.

> One who makes it his business to ask alms.

> One who is dependent upon others for support; Ð a contemptuous or sarcastic use.

> One who assumes in argument what he does not prove.

Abp. Tillotson.

Beggar, v. t. [imp. & p.p. Beggared (?); p. pr. & vb. n. Beggaring.] 1. To reduce to beggary; to impoverish; as, he had beggared himself.

Milton.

> To cause to seem very poor and inadequate.

It beggared all description.

Shak.

Beggarhood (?), n. The condition of being a beggar; also, the class of beggars.

Beggarism (?), n. Beggary. [R.]

Beggarliness (?), n. The quality or state of being beggarly; meanness.

Beggarly (?), a. 1. In the condition of, or like, a beggar; suitable for a beggar; extremely indigent; poverty‖stricken; mean; poor; contemptible. ½A bankrupt, beggarly fellow.„ South.   ½A beggarly fellowship.„ Swift. ½Beggarly elements.„ Gal. iv. 9.

> Produced or occasioned by beggary. [Obs.]

Beggarly sins, that is, those sins which idleness and beggary usually betray men to; such as lying, flattery, stealing, and dissimulation.

Jer. Taylor.

Beggarly, adv. In an indigent, mean, or despicable manner; in the manner of a beggar.

Beggar's lice · (?). (Bot.) The prickly fruit or seed of certain plants (as some species of Echinospermum and Cynoglossum) which cling to the clothing of those who brush by them.

Beggar's ticks · (?). The bur marigold (Bidens) and its achenes, which are armed with barbed awns, and adhere to clothing and fleeces with unpleasant tenacity.

Beggary (?), n. [OE. beggerie. See Beggar, n.] 1. The act of begging; the state of being a beggar; mendicancy; extreme poverty.

> Beggarly appearance. [R.]

The freedom and the beggary of the old studio.
Thackeray.
Syn. Ð Indigence; want; penury; mendicancy.
Beggarly̆, a. Beggarly. [Obs.]
B. Jonson.
Beggeĭstere (?), n. [Beg + ĭster.] A beggar. [Obs.]
Chaucer.
Beĭghard Beĭguard } (?), n. [F. b,gard, b,guard; cf. G. beghard, LL. Beghardus, Begihardus, Begardus. Prob. from the root of beguine + ĭard or ĭhard. See Beguine.] (Eccl. Hist.) One of an association of religious laymen living in imitation of the Beguines. They arose in the thirteenth century, were afterward subjected to much persecution, and were suppressed by Innocent X. in 1650. Called also Beguins.
Beĭgild (?), v. t. [imp. & p.p. Begilded or Begilt (?).] To gild.
B. Jonson.
Beĭgin (?), v. i. [imp. & p.p. Began (?), Begun (?); p. pr. & vb. n. Beginning (?).] [AS. beginnan (akin to OS. biginnan, D. & G. beginnen, OHG. biginnan, Goth., duĭginnan, Sw. begynna, Dan. begynde); pref. beĭ + an assumed ginnan. ?31. See Gin to begin.] 1. To have or commence an independent or first existence; to take rise; to commence.

Vast chain of being ! which from God began.
Pope.

To do the first act or the first part of an action; to enter upon or commence something new, as a new form or state of being, or course of action; to take the first step; to start.
½Tears began to flow.

Dryden.
When I begin, I will also make an end.
1 Sam. iii. 12.
Beĭgin, v. t. 1. To enter on; to commence.
Ye nymphs of Solyma ! begin the song.
Pope.

To trace or lay the foundation of; to make or place a beginning of.

The apostle begins our knowledge in the creatures, which leads us to the knowledge of God.
Locke.
Syn. Ð To commence; originate; set about; start.
Beĭgin, n. Beginning. [Poetic & Obs.]
Spenser.
Beĭginner (?), n. One who begins or originates anything. Specifically: A young or inexperienced practitioner or student; a tyro.
A sermon of a new beginner.

Swift.

Be̅ginning (?), n. 1. The act of doing that which begins anything; commencement of an action, state, or space of time; entrance into being or upon a course; the first act, effort, or state of a succession of acts or states.

In the beginning God created the heaven and the earth.
Gen. i. 1.

That which begins or originates something; the first cause; origin; source.

I am ... the beginning and the ending.
Rev. i. 8.

That which is begun; a rudiment or element.

Mighty things from small beginnings grow.
Dryden.

Enterprise. ½To hinder our beginnings.

Shak.
Syn. Ð Inception; prelude; opening; threshold; origin; outset; foundation.

Be̅gird (?), v. t. [imp. Begirt (?), Begirded; p. p. Begirt; p. pr. & vb. n. Begirding.] [AS. begyrdan (akin to Goth. bigairdan); pref. be̅ + gyrdan to gird.] 1. To bind with a band or girdle; to gird.

To surround as with a band; to encompass.

Be̅girdle (?), v. t. To surround as with a girdle.
Be̅girt (?), v. t. To encompass; to begird.
Milton.

ØBegler̅beg · (?), n. [Turk. beglerbeg, fr. beg, pl. begler. See Beg, n.] The governor of a province of the Ottoman empire, next in dignity to the grand vizier.

Be̅gnaw (?), v. t. [p. p. Begnawed (?), (R.) Begnawn (?).] [AS. begnagan; pref. be̅ + gnagan to gnaw.] To gnaw; to eat away; to corrode.

The worm of conscience still begnaw thy soul.
Shak.

Be̅god (?), v. t. [imp. & p.p. Begodded.] To exalt to the dignity of a god; to deify. [Obs.] ½Begodded saints.

South.

Be̅gone (?), interj. [Be, v. i. + gone, p. p.] Go away; depart; get you gone.

Be̅gone, p. p. [OE. begon, AS. big¾n; pref. be̅ + g¾n to go.] Surrounded; furnished; beset; environed (as in woe̅begone). [Obs.]

Gower. Chaucer.

Beǐgoniǐa (?), n. [From Michel Begon, a promoter of botany.] (Bot.) A genus of plants, mostly of tropical America, many species of which are grown as ornamental plants. The leaves are curiously oneÐsided, and often exhibit brilliant colors.

<— p. 133 —>

Beǐgore (?), v. t. To besmear with gore.

Beǐgot (?), imp. & p. p. of Beget.

Beǐgotten (?), p. p. of Beget.

Beǐgrave (?), v. t. [Pref. beǐ + grave; akin to G. begraben, Goth. bigraban to dig a ditch around.] To bury; also, to engrave. [Obs.]

Gower.

Beǐgrease (?), v. t. To soil or daub with grease or other oily matter.

Beǐgrime (?), v. t. [imp. & p.p. Begrimed (?); p. pr. & vb. n. Begriming.] To soil with grime or dirt deeply impressed or rubbed in.

Books falling to pieces and begrimed with dust.

Macaulay.

Beǐgrimer (?), n. One who, or that which, begrimes.

Beǐgrudge (?), v. t. [imp. & p.p. Begrudged (?); p. pr. & vb. n. Begrudging.] To grudge; to envy the possession of.

Beǐguile (?), v. t. [imp. & p.p. Beguiled (?); p. pr. & vb. n. Beguiling.] 1. To delude by guile, artifice, or craft; to deceive or impose on, as by a false statement; to lure.

The serpent beguiled me, and I did eat.

Gen. iii. 13.

To elude, or evade by craft; to foil. [Obs.]

When misery could beguile the tyrant's rage.

Shak.

To cause the time of to pass without notice; to relieve the tedium or weariness of; to while away; to divert.

Ballads ... to beguile his incessant wayfaring.

W. Irving.

Syn. Ð To delude; deceive; cheat; insnare; mislead; amuse; divert; entertain.

Beǐguilement (?), n. The act of beguiling, or the state of being beguiled.

Beǐguiler (?), n. One who, or that which, beguiles.

Beǐguiling, a. Alluring by guile; deluding; misleading; diverting. Ð Beǐguilingǐly, adv.

ØBe · guin (?), n. [F.] See Beghard.

ØBe · gui · nage (?), n. [F.] A collection of small houses surrounded by a wall and occupied by a community of Beguines.

ØBe·guine (?), n. [F. b,guine; LL. beguina, beghina; fr. Lambert le BŠgue (the Stammerer) the founder of the order. (Du Cange.)] A woman belonging to one of the religious and charitable associations or communities in the Netherlands, and elsewhere, whose members live in beguinages and are not bound by perpetual vows.

ØBegum (?), n. [Per., fr. Turk., perh. properly queen mother, fr. Turk. beg (see Beg, n.) + Ar. umm mother.] In the East Indies, a princess or lady of high rank.

Malcom.

Beïgun (?), p. p. of Begin.

Beïhalf (?), n. [OE. onïbehalve in the name of, bihalven by the side of, fr. AS. healf half, also side, part: akin to G. halb half, halber on account of. See Beï, and Half, n.] Advantage; favor; stead; benefit; interest; profit; support; defense; vindication.

In behalf of his mistress's beauty.

Sir P. Sidney.

Against whom he had contracted some prejudice in behalf of his nation.

Clarendon.

In behalf of, in the interest of. Đ On behalf of, on account of; on the part of.

Beïhappen (?), v. t. To happen to. [Obs.]

Beïhave (?), v. t. [imp. & p.p. Behaved (?); p. pr. & vb. n. Behaving.] [AS. behabban to surround, restrain, detain (akin to G. gehaben (obs.) to have, sich gehaben to behave or carry one's self); pref. beï + habban to have. See Have, v. t.] 1. To manage or govern in point of behavior; to discipline; to handle; to restrain. [Obs.]

He did behave his anger ere 't was spent.

Shak.

To carry; to conduct; to comport; to manage; to bear; Đ used reflexively.

Those that behaved themselves manfully.

2 Macc. ii. 21.

Beïhave, v. i. To act; to conduct; to bear or carry one's self; as, to behave well or ill.

µ This verb is often used colloquially without an adverb of manner; as, if he does not behave, he will be punished. It is also often applied to inanimate objects; as, the ship behaved splendidly.

Beïhavior (?), n. Manner of behaving, whether good or bad; mode of conducting one's self; conduct; deportment; carriage; Đ used also of inanimate objects; as, the behavior of a ship in a storm; the behavior of the magnetic needle.

A gentleman that is very singular in his behavior.

Steele.

To be upon one's good behavior, To be put upon one's good behavior, to be in a state of trial, in which something important depends on propriety of conduct. Ð During good behavior, while (or so long as) one conducts one's self with integrity and fidelity or with propriety.

Syn. Ð Bearing; demeanor; manner. Ð Behavior, Conduct. Behavior is the mode in which we have or bear ourselves in the presence of others or toward them; conduct is the mode of our carrying ourselves forward in the concerns of life. Behavior respects our manner of acting in particular cases; conduct refers to the general tenor of our actions. We may say of soldiers, that their conduct had been praiseworthy during the whole campaign, and their behavior admirable in every instance when they met the enemy.

Beïhead (?), v. t. [imp. & p.p. Beheaded; p. pr. & vb. n. Beheading.] [OE. bihefden, AS. behe fdian; pref. beï + he fod head. See Head.] To sever the head from; to take off the head of.

Beïheadal (?), n. Beheading. [Modern]

Beïheld (?), imp. & p. p. of Behold.

Beheïmoth (?), n. [Heb. behem?th, fr. Egyptian Pïeheïmaut hippopotamus.] An animal, probably the hippopotamus, described in Job xl. 15Ð24.

Behen (?), Behn (?), n. [Per. & Ar. bahman, behmen, an herb, whose leaves resemble ears of corn, saffron.] (Bot.) (a) The Centaurea behen, or sawÐleaved centaury. (b) The Cucubalus behen, or bladder campion, now called Silene inflata. (c) The Statice limonium, or sea lavender.

Beïhest (?), n. [OE. biheste promise, command, AS. beh?s promise; pref. beï + h?s command. See Hest, Hight.] 1. That which is willed or ordered; a command; a mandate; an injunction.

To do his master's high behest.

Sir W. Scott.

A vow; a promise. [Obs.]

The time is come that I should send it her, if I keep the behest that I have made.

Paston.

Beïhest, v. t. To vow. [Obs.]

Paston.

Beïhete (?), v. t. See Behight. [Obs.]

Chaucer.

Beïhight (?), v. t. [imp. Behight; p. p. Behight, Behoten.] [OE. bihaten, AS. beh¾tan to vow, promise; pref. beï + h¾tan to call, command. See Hight, v.] [Obs. in all its senses.] 1. To promise; to vow.

Behight by vow unto the chaste Minerve.

Surrey.

To give in trust; to commit; to intrust.

The keys are to thy hand behight.
Spenser.

To adjudge; to assign by authority.

The second was to Triamond behight.
Spenser.

To mean, or intend.

More than heart behighteth.
Mir. for Mag.

To consider or esteem to be; to declare to be.

All the lookersÏon him dead behight.
Spenser.

To call; to name; to address.

Whom ... he knew and thus behight.
Spenser.

To command; to order.

He behight those gates to be unbarred.
Spenser.
Beïhight, n. A vow; a promise. [Obs.]
Surrey.
Beïhind (?), prep. [AS. behindan; pref. beÏ + hindan. See Hind, a.] 1. On the side opposite the front or nearest part; on the back side of; at the back of; on the other side of; as, behind a door; behind a hill.
A tall Brabanter, behind whom I stood.
Bp. Hall.

Left after the departure of, whether this be by removing to a distance or by death.

A small part of what he left behind him.
Pope.

Left a distance by, in progress of improvement Hence: Inferior to in dignity, rank, knowledge, or excellence, or in any achievement.

I was not a whit behind the very chiefest apostles.
2 Cor. xi. 5.
Beïhind, adv. 1. At the back part; in the rear. ½I shall not lag behind.,
Milton.

Toward the back part or rear; backward; as, to look behind.

Not yet brought forward, produced, or exhibited to view; out of sight; remaining.

We can not be sure that there is no evidence behind.
Locke.

Backward in time or order of succession; past.

Forgetting those things which are behind.
   Phil. ii. 13.

After the departure of another; as, to stay behind.

Leave not a rack behind.
Shak.
Be͏̈hind, n. The backside; the rump. [Low]
Be͏̈hindhand · (?), adv. & a. [Behind + hand.]

In arrears financially; in a state where expenditures have exceeded the receipt of funds.

In a state of backwardness, in respect to what is seasonable or appropriate, or as to what should have been accomplished; not equally forward with some other person or thing; dilatory; backward; late; tardy; as, behindhand in studies or in work.

In this also [dress] the country are very much behindhand.
Addison.
Be͏̈hither (?), prep. On this side of. [Obs.]
Two miles behither Clifden.
Evelyn.
Be͏̈hold (?), v. t. [imp. & p.p. Beheld (?) (p. p. formerly Beholden (?), now used only as a p. a.); p. pr. & vb. n. Beholding.] [OE. bihalden, biholden, AS. behealdan to hold, have in sight; pref. be͏̈ + healdan to hold, keep; akin to G. behalten to hold, keep. See Hold.] To have in sight; to see clearly; to look at; to regard with the eyes.

When he beheld the serpent of brass, he lived.
   Num. xxi. 9.

Behold the Lamb of God, which taketh away the sin of the world.
   John. i. 29.

Syn. Ð To scan; gaze; regard; descry; view; discern.

Be͏̈hold, v. i. To direct the eyes to, or fix them upon, an object; to look; to see.

And I beheld, and, lo, in the midst of the throne, ... a lamb as it had been slain.
   Rev. v. 6.

Be͏̈holden (?), p. a. [Old p. p. of behold, used in the primitive sense of the simple verb hold.] Obliged; bound in gratitude; indebted.

But being so beholden to the Prince.
Tennyson.

Beïholder (?), n. One who beholds; a spectator.

Beïholding, a. Obliged; beholden. [Obs.]

I was much bound and beholding to the right reverend father.

Robynson (More's Utopia).

So much hath Oxford been beholding to her nephews, or sister's children.

Fuller.

Beïholding, n. The act of seeing; sight; also, that which is beheld.
  Shak.

Beïholdingĭness, n., The state of being obliged or beholden. [Obs.]

Sir P. Sidney.

Beïhoof (?), n. [OE. to bihove for the use of, AS. beh?f advantage, a word implied in beh?flÆc necessary; akin to Sw. behof, Dan. behov, G. behuf, and E. heave, the root meaning to seize, hence the meanings ½to hold, make use of.¸ See Heave, v. t.] Advantage; profit; benefit; interest; use.

  No mean recompense it brings
  To your behoof.

Milton.

Beïhoovaĭble (?), a. Supplying need; profitable; advantageous. [Obs.]

Udall.

Beïhoove (?), v. t. [imp. & p.p. Behooved (?); p. pr. & vb. n. Behooving.] [OE. bihoven, behoven, AS. beh?fian to have need of, fr. beh?f. See Behoof.] To be necessary for; to be fit for; to be meet for, with respect to necessity, duty, or convenience; Ð mostly used impersonally.

  And thus it behooved Christ to suffer.
   Luke xxiv. 46.

[Also written behove.]

Beïhoove (?), v. i. To be necessary, fit, or suitable; to befit; to belong as due.

    Chaucer.

Beïhoove, n. Advantage; behoof. [Obs.]

  It shall not be to his behoove.

Gower.

Beïhooveful (?), a. Advantageous; useful; profitable. [Archaic] Ð Beïhoovefulĭly, adv. Ð Beïhoovefulĭness, n. [Archaic]

Beïhove (?), v., and derivatives. See Behoove, & c.

Beïhovely, a. & adv. Useful, or usefully. [Obs.]

Beïhowl (?), v. t. To howl at. [Obs.]

  The wolf behowls the moon.

Shak.

ØBeige (?), n. [F.] Debeige.

Beild (?), n. [Prob. from the same root as build, v. t.] A place of shelter; protection; refuge. [Scot. & Prov. Eng.] [Also written bield and beeld.]

  The random beild o' clod or stane.

Burns.

Being (?), p. pr. from Be. Existing.

µ Being was formerly used where we now use having. ½Being to go to a ball in a few days. Miss Edgeworth.

µ In modern usage, is, are, was or were being, with a past participle following (as built, made, etc.) indicates the process toward the completed result expressed by the participle. The form is or was building, in this passive signification, is idiomatic, and, if free from ambiguity, is commonly preferable to the modern is or was being built. The last form of speech is, however, sufficiently authorized by approved writers. The older expression was is, or was, aÐbuilding or in building.

A man who is being strangled.
Lamb.
While the article on Burns was being written.
Froude.
Fresh experience is always being gained.
  Jowett (Thucyd.)

Being, n. 1. Existence, as opposed to nonexistence; state or sphere of existence.

In Him we live, and move, and have our being.
Acts xvii. 28.

That which exists in any form, whether it be material or spiritual, actual or ideal; living existence, as distinguished from a thing without life; as, a human being; spiritual beings.

What a sweet being is an honest mind !
Beau. & Fl.
A Being of infinite benevolence and power.
Wordsworth.

Lifetime; mortal existence. [Obs.]

Claudius, thou
Wast follower of his fortunes in his being.
Webster (1654).

An abode; a cottage. [Prov. Eng.]

Wright.
It was a relief to dismiss them [Sir Roger's servants] into little beings within my manor.
  Steele.
Being, adv. Since; inasmuch as. [Obs. or Colloq.]
And being you have
Declined his means, you have increased his malice.
Beau. & Fl.
Be˙jade (?), v. t. To jade or tire. [Obs.]

Milton.

Be′jape (?), v. t. To jape; to laugh at; to deceive. [Obs.]
Chaucer.

Be′jaun′dice (?), v. t. To infect with jaundice.

Be·jew′el (?), v. t. [imp. & p.p. Bejeweled or Bejewelled (?); p. pr. & vb. n. Bejeweling or Bejewelling.] To ornament with a jewel or with jewels; to spangle. ½Bejeweled hands.

Thackeray.

Be·jum′ble (?), v. t. To jumble together.

ØBe′kah (?), n. [Heb.] Half a shekel.

Be·knave′ (?), v. t. To call knave. [Obs.]
Pope.

Be·know′ (?), v. t. To confess; to acknowledge. [Obs.]
Chaucer.

Bel (?), n. The Babylonian name of the god known among the Hebrews as Baal. See Baal.
Baruch vi. 41.

Be·la′bor (?), v. t. [imp. & p.p. Belabored (?); p. pr. & vb. n. Belaboring.] 1. To ply diligently; to work carefully upon. ½If the earth is belabored with culture, it yieldeth corn.

Barrow.

To beat soundly; to cudgel.

Ajax belabors there a harmless ox.
Dryden.

Bel · Đac′coyle (?), n. [F. bel beautiful + accueil reception.] A kind or favorable reception or salutation. [Obs.]

Be·lace′ (?), v. t. [imp. & p.p. Belaced (?).]

To fasten, as with a lace or cord. [Obs.]

To cover or adorn with lace. [Obs.]

Beaumont.

To beat with a strap. See Lace. [Obs.]

Wright.

Be·lam′ (?), v. t. [See Lam.] To beat or bang. [Prov. & Low, Eng.]
Todd.

Bel·a′mour (?), n. [F. bel amour fair love.] 1. A lover. [Obs.]
Spenser.

A flower, but of what kind is unknown. [Obs.]

Her snowy brows, like budded belamours.

Spenser.

Belaïmy (?), n. [F. bel ami fair friend.] Good friend; dear friend. [Obs.]

Chaucer.

Beïlate (?), v. t. [imp. & p.p. Belated; p. pr. & vb. n. Belating.] To retard or make too late.

Davenant.

Beïlated, a. Delayed beyond the usual time; too late; overtaken by night; benighted. ½Some belated peasant., Milton. Ð Beïlatedïness, n. Milton.

Beïlaud (?), v. t. To laud or praise greatly.

Beïlay (?), v. t. [imp. & p.p. Belaid, Belayed (?); p. pr. & vb. n. Belaying.] [For senses 1 & 2, D. beleggen to cover, belay; akin to E. pref. beÏ, and lay to place: for sense 3, OE. beleggen, AS. belecgan. See pref. BeÏ, and Lay to place.] 1. To lay on or cover; to adorn. [Obs.]

Jacket ... belayed with silver lace.

Spenser.

(Naut.) To make fast, as a rope, by taking several turns with it round a pin, cleat, or kevel.

Totten.

To lie in wait for with a view to assault. Hence: to block up or obstruct. [Obs.]

Dryden.

Belay thee! Stop.

<— p. 134 —>

Beïlaying pin · (?). (Naut.) A strong pin in the side of a vessel, or by the mast, round which ropes are wound when they are fastened or belayed.

Belch (?), v. t. [imp. & p.p. Belched (?); p. pr. & vb. n. Belching.] [OE. belken, AS. bealcan, akin to E. bellow. See Bellow, v. i.] 1. To eject or throw up from the stomach with violence; to eruct.

I belched a hurricane of wind.

Swift.

To eject violently from within; to cast forth; to ?mit; to give vent to; to vent.

Within the gates that now
Stood open wide, belching outrageous flame.

Milton.

Belch, v. i. 1. To eject wind from the stomach through the mouth; to eructate.

To issue with spasmodic force or noise.

Dryden.

Belch, n. 1. The act of belching; also, that which is belched; an eructation.

Malt liquor; Đ vulgarly so called as causing eructation. [Obs.]

Dennis.

Belcher (?), n. One who, or that which, belches.

Beldam Beldame } (?), n. [Pref. belï, denoting relationship + dame mother: cf. F. belledame fair lady, It. belladonna. See Belle, and Dame.]

Grandmother; Đ corresponding to belsire.

To show the beldam daughters of her daughter.
Shak.

An old woman in general; especially, an ugly old woman; a hag.

Around the beldam all erect they hang.
Akenside.

Beïleaguer (?), v. t. [imp. & p.p. Beleaguered (?); p. pr. & vb. n. Beleaguering.] [D. belegeren (akin to G. belagern, Sw. bel„gra, Dan. beleire); pref. beï = E. beï + leger bed, camp, army, akin to E. lair. See Lair.] To surround with an army so as to preclude escape; to besiege; to blockade.

The wail of famine in beleaguered towns.
Longfellow.

Syn. Đ To block up; environ; invest; encompass.

Beïleaguerïer (?), n. One who beleaguers.

Beïleave (?), v. t. & i. [imp. & p.p. Beleft (?).] To leave or to be left. [Obs.]

May.

Beïlecture (?), v. t. [imp. & p.p. Belectured (?); p. pr. & vb. n. Belecturing.] To vex with lectures; to lecture frequently.

Beïlee (?), v. t. To place under the lee, or unfavorably to the wind.
Shak.

Beïlemnite (?), n. [Gr. ? dart, fr. ? dart, fr. ? to throw: cf. F. b‚lemnite.] (Paleon.) A conical calcareous fossil, tapering to a point at the lower extremity, with a conical cavity at the other end, where it is ordinarily broken; but when perfect it contains a small chambered cone, called the phragmocone, prolonged, on one side, into a delicate concave blade; the thunderstone. It is the internal shell of a cephalopod related to the sepia, and belonging to an extinct family. The belemnites are found in rocks of the Jurassic and Cretaceous ages. Đ Belïemïnitic, a.

Beïleper (?), v. t. [imp. & p.p. Belepered (?).] To infect with leprosy. [Obs.]

Beau. & Fl.

ØBelĐesïprit (?), n.; pl. Beauxïesprits (?). [F., fine wit.] A fine genius, or man of wit. ½A man of letters and a bel esprit.‚

W. Irving.

Belfry (?), n. [OE. berfray movable tower used in sieges, OF. berfreit, berfroit, F. beffroi, fr. MHG. bervrit, bercvrit, G. bergfriede, fr. MHG. bergen to protect (G. bergen to conceal) + vride peace, protection, G. friede peace; in compounds often taken in the sense of security, or place of security; orig. therefore a place affording security. G. friede is akin to E. free. See Burg, and Free.] 1. (Mil. Antiq.) A movable tower erected by besiegers for purposes of attack and defense.

> A bell tower, usually attached to a church or other building, but sometimes separate; a campanile.
>
> A room in a tower in which a bell is or may be hung; or a cupola or turret for the same purpose.
>
> (Naut.) The framing on which a bell is suspended.

Belïgard (?), n. [It. bel guardo.] A sweet or loving look. [Obs.]
Spenser.

Belgiïan (?), a. Of or pertaining to Belgium. Ð n. A native or inhabitant of Belgium.

Belgic (?), a. [L. Belgicus, fr. Belgae the Belgians.] 1. Of or pertaining to the Belg‘, a German tribe who anciently possessed the country between the Rhine, the Seine, and the ocean.

How unlike their Belgic sires of old.
Goldsmith.

> Of or pertaining to the Netherlands or to Belgium.

Belïgraviïan (?), a. Belonging to Belgravia (a fashionable quarter of London, around Pimlico), or to fashionable life; aristocratic.

Beliïal (?), n. [Heb. beli ya'al; beli without + ya'al profit.] An evil spirit; a wicked and unprincipled person; the personification of evil.

What concord hath Christ with Belia?
2 Cor. vi. 15.

A son (or man) of Belial, a worthless, wicked, or thoroughly depraved person.
1 Sam. ii. 12.

Beïlibel (?), v. t. [See Libel, v. t.] To libel or traduce; to calumniate.
Fuller.

Beïlie (?), v. t. [imp. & p.p. Belied (?); p. pr. & vb. n. Belying (?).] [OE. bilien, bili?en, AS. beleᴄgan; pref. beï + leᴄgan to lie. See Lie, n.] 1. To show to be false; to convict of, or charge with, falsehood.

Their trembling hearts belie their boastful tongues.
Dryden.

> To give a false representation or account of.

Should I do so, I should belie my thoughts.
Shak.

To tell lie about; to calumniate; to slander.

Thou dost belie him, Percy, thou dost belie him.
Shak.

To mimic; to counterfeit. [Obs.]

Dryden.

To fill with lies. [Obs.] ½The breath of slander] doth belie all corners of the world.

Shak.

Be**lief** (?), n. [OE. bileafe, bileve; cf. AS. gele fa. See Believe.] 1. Assent to a proposition or affirmation, or the acceptance of a fact, opinion, or assertion as real or true, without immediate personal knowledge; reliance upon word or testimony; partial or full assurance without positive knowledge or absolute certainty; persuasion; conviction; confidence; as, belief of a witness; the belief of our senses.

Belief admits of all degrees, from the slightest suspicion to the fullest assurance.

Reid.

(Theol.) A persuasion of the truths of religion; faith.

No man can attain [to] belief by the bare contemplation of heaven and earth.

Hooker.

The thing believed; the object of belief.

Superstitious prophecies are not only the belief of fools, but the talk sometimes of wise men.

Bacon.

A tenet, or the body of tenets, held by the advocates of any class of views; doctrine; creed.

In the heat of persecution to which Christian belief was subject upon its first promulgation.

Hooker.

Ultimate belief, a first principle incapable of proof; an intuitive truth; an intuition.

Sir W. Hamilton.

Syn. Ð Credence; trust; reliance; assurance; opinion.

Be**lief**ful (?), a. Having belief or faith.

Be**liev**a**ble** (?), a. Capable of being believed; credible. Ð Be**liev**a**ble**ness, n. Ð Be**liev** · a**bili**ty (?), n.

Bel̈lieve (?), v. t. [imp. & p.p. Believed (?); p. pr. & vb. n. Believing.] [OE. bileven (with pref. bel̈ for AS. gel̈), fr. AS. gel?fan, gel?fan; akin to D. gelooven, OHG. gilouban, G. glauben, OS. gil?bian, Goth. galaubjan, and Goth. liubs dear. See Lief, a., Leave, n.] To exercise belief in; to credit upon the authority or testimony of another; to be persuaded of the truth of, upon evidence furnished by reasons, arguments, and deductions of the mind, or by circumstances other than personal knowledge; to regard or accept as true; to place confidence in; to think; to consider; as, to believe a person, a statement, or a doctrine.

Our conqueror (whom I now
Of force believe almighty).
Milton.
King Agrippa, believest thou the prophets ?
Acts xxvi. ?7.
Often followed by a dependent clause.
I believe that Jesus Christ is the Son of God.
Acts viii. 37.
Syn. Ð See Expect.

Bel̈lieve, v. i. 1. To have a firm persuasion, esp. of the truths of religion; to have a persuasion approaching to certainty; to exercise belief or faith.

Lord, I believe; help thou mine unbelief.
Mark ix. 24.
With the heart man believeth unto righteousness.
Rom. x. 10.

To think; to suppose.

I will not believe so meanly of you.
Fielding.

To believe in. (a) To believe that the subject of the thought (if a person or thing) exists, or (if an event) that it has occurred, or will occur; Ð as, to believe in the resurrection of the dead. ½She does not believe in Jupiter.₎ J. H. Newman. (b) To believe that the character, abilities, and purposes of a person are worthy of entire confidence; Ð especially that his promises are wholly trustworthy. ½Let not your heart be troubled: ye believe in God, believe also in me.₎ John xiv. 1. (c) To believe that the qualities or effects of an action or state are beneficial: as, to believe in sea bathing, or in abstinence from alcoholic beverages. Ð To believe on, to accept implicitly as an object of religious trust or obedience; to have faith in.

Bel̈liever (?), n. 1. One who believes; one who is persuaded of the truth or reality of some doctrine, person, or thing.

(Theol.) One who gives credit to the truth of the Scriptures, as a revelation from God; a Christian; Ð in a more restricted sense, one who receives Christ as his Savior, and accepts the way of salvation unfolded in the gospel.

Thou didst open the Kingdom of Heaven to all believers.
Book of Com. Prayer.

(Eccl. Hist.) One who was admitted to all the rights of divine worship and instructed in all the mysteries of the Christian religion, in distinction from a catechumen, or one yet under instruction.

Belïeving, a. That believes; having belief. Đ Belïevinglÿ, adv.

Belïight (?), v. t. To illuminate. [Obs.]
Cowley.

Belïike (?), adv. [Pref. belï (for by) + like.] It is likely or probably; perhaps. [Obs. or Archaic] Đ Belïikely, adv.

Belike, boy, then you are in love.
Shak.

Belïime (?), v. t. [imp. & p.p. Belimed (?).] To besmear or insnare with birdlime.

Belïittle (?), v. t. [imp. & p.p. Belittled (?); p. pr. & vb. n. Belittling.] To make little or less in a moral sense; to speak of in a depreciatory or contemptuous way.
T. Jefferson.

Belïive (?), adv. [Cf. Live, a.] Forthwith; speedily; quickly. [Obs.]
Chaucer.

Belk (?), v. t. [See Belch.] To vomit. [Obs.]

Bell (?), n. [AS. belle, fr. bellan to bellow. See Bellow.] 1. A hollow metallic vessel, usually shaped somewhat like a cup with a flaring mouth, containing a clapper or tongue, and giving forth a ringing sound on being struck.

μ Bells have been made of various metals, but the best have always been, as now, of an alloy of copper and tin.

The Liberty Bell, the famous bell of the Philadelphia State House, which rang when the Continental Congress declared the Independence of the United States, in 1776. It had been cast in 1753, and upon it were the words ½Proclaim liberty throughout all the land, to all the inhabitants thereof.

A hollow perforated sphere of metal containing a loose ball which causes it to sound when moved.

Anything in the form of a bell, as the cup or corol of a flower. ½In a cowslip's bell I lie.

Shak.

(Arch.) That part of the capital of a column included between the abacus and neck molding; also used for the naked core of nearly cylindrical shape, assumed to exist within the leafage of a capital.

pl. (Naut.) The strikes of the bell which mark the time; or the time so designated.

μ On shipboard, time is marked by a bell, which is struck eight times at 4, 8, and 12 o'clock. Half an hour after it has struck ½eight bells, it is struck once, and at every succeeding half hour the number of strokes is increased by one, till at the end of the four hours, which constitute a watch, it is struck eight times.

To bear away the bell, to win the prize at a race where the prize was a bell; hence, to be superior in something. Fuller. Ð To bear the bell, to be the first or leader; Ð in allusion to the bellwether or a flock, or the leading animal of a team or drove, when wearing a bell. Ð To curse by bell, book, and candle, a solemn form of excommunication used in the Roman Catholic church, the bell being tolled, the book of offices for the purpose being used, and three candles being extinguished with certain ceremonies. Nares. Ð To lose the bell, to be worsted in a contest. ½In single fight he lost the bell.„ Fairfax. Ð To shake the bells, to move, five notice, or alarm.

Shak.

µ Bell is much used adjectively or in combinations; as, bell clapper; bell foundry; bell hanger; bellïmouthed; bell tower, etc., which, for the most part, are selfïexplaining.

Bell arch (Arch.), an arch of unusual form, following the curve of an ogee. Ð Bell cage, or Bell carriage (Arch.), a timber frame constructed to carry one or more large bells. Ð Bell cot (Arch.), a small or subsidiary construction, frequently corbeled out from the walls of a structure, and used to contain and support one or more bells. Ð Bell deck (Arch.), the floor of a belfry made to serve as a roof to the rooms below. Ð Bell founder, one whose occupation it is to found or cast bells. Ð Bell foundry, or Bell foundery, a place where bells are founded or cast. Ð Bell gable (Arch.), a small gableïshaped construction, pierced with one or more openings, and used to contain bells. Ð Bell glass. See Bell jar. Ð Bell hanger, a man who hangs or puts up bells. Ð Bell pull, a cord, handle, or knob, connecting with a bell or bell wire, and which will ring the bell when pulled. Aytoun. Ð Bell punch, a kind of conductor's punch which rings a bell when used. Ð Bell ringer, one who rings a bell or bells, esp. one whose business it is to ring a church bell or chime, or a set of musical bells for public entertainment. Ð Bell roof (Arch.), a roof shaped according to the general lines of a bell. Ð Bell rope, a rope by which a church or other bell is rung. Ð Bell tent, a circular conicalïtopped tent. Ð Bell trap, a kind of bell shaped stench trap.

Bell (?), v. t. [imp. & p.p. Belled (?); p. pr. & vb. n. Belling.] 1. To put a bell upon; as, to bell the cat.

To make bellïmouthed; as, to bell a tube.

Bell, v. i. To develop bells or corollas; to take the form of a bell; to blossom; as, hops bell.

Bell, v. t. [AS. bellan. See Bellow.] To utter by bellowing. [Obs.]

Bell, v.i. To call or bellow, as the deer in rutting time; to make a bellowing sound; to roar.

As loud as belleth wind in hell.
Chaucer.
The wild buck bells from ferny brake.
Sir W. Scott.

Bel·ladonna (?), n. [It., literally fine lady; bella beautiful + donna lady.] (Bot.) (a) An herbaceous European plant (Atropa belladonna) with reddish bell-shaped flowers and shining black berries. The whole plant and its fruit are very poisonous, and the root and leaves are used as powerful medicinal agents. Its properties are largely due to the alkaloid atropine which it contains. Called also deadly nightshade. (b) A species of Amaryllis. (A. belladonna); the belladonna lily.

Bell an·imalcule (?). (Zo"l.) An infusorian of the family Vorticellid‘, common in fresh-water ponds.

Bell bear·er (?). (Zo"l.) A Brazilian leaf hopper (Bocydium tintinnabuliferum), remarkable for the four bell-shaped appendages of its thorax.

Bellbird· (?), n. [So called from their notes.] (Zo"l.) (a) A South American bird of the genus Casmarhincos, and family Cotingid‘, of several species; the campanero. (b) The Myzantha melanophrys of Australia.

Bell crank· (?). A lever whose two arms form a right angle, or nearly a right angle, having its fulcrum at the apex of the angle. It is used in bell pulls and in changing the direction of bell wires at angles of rooms, etc., and also in machinery.

<— p. 135 —>

Belle (?), n. [F. belle, fem. of bel, beau, beautiful, fine. See Beau.] A young lady of superior beauty and attractions; a handsome lady, or one who attracts notice in society; a fair lady.

Belled (?), a. Hung with a bell or bells.

Belle-lettrist (?), n. One versed in belleslettres.

Ø Bellerophon (?), n. (Paleon.) A genus of fossil univalve shells, believed to belong to the Heteropoda, peculiar to the Paleozoic age.

Ø Belles-lettres (?), n. pl. [F.] Polite or elegant literature; the humanities; Đ used somewhat vaguely for literary works in which imagination and taste are predominant.

Bel·letristic (?), Bel·letristical (?), } a. Occupied with, or pertaining to, belles-lettres. ½An unlearned, belletristic trifler.„
M. Arnold.

Bell-faced· (?), a. Having the striking surface convex; Đ said of hammers.

Bellflow·er (?), n. (Bot.) A plant of the genus Campanula; Đ so named from its bell-shaped flowers.

Bellflow·er, n. [F. bellefleur, lit., beautiful flower.] A kind of apple. The yellow bellflower is a large, yellow winter apple. [Written also bellefleur.]

Bellibone (?), n. [F. belle et bonne, beautiful and good.] A woman excelling both in beauty and goodness; a fair maid. [Obs.]

Spenser.

Bellic (?), Bellical (?), } a. [L. bellicus. See Bellicose.] Of or pertaining to war; warlike; martial. [Obs.] ½Bellic C'sar.͵

Feltham.

Bellicose· (?), a. [L. bellicosus, fr. bellicus of war, fr. bellum war. See Duel.] Inclined to war or contention; warlike; pugnacious.

Arnold was, in fact, in a bellicose vein.

W. Irving.

Bellicose·ly, adv. In a bellicose manner.

Bellicous (?), a. Bellicose. [Obs.]

Bellied (?), a. Having (such) a belly; puffed out; Ð used in composition; as, potïbellied; shadïbellied.

Belligerience (?), Belligerienïcy (?), } n. The quality of being belligerent; act or state of making war; warfare.

Belligerïent (?), a. [L. bellum war + gerens, ïentis, waging, p. pr. of gerere to wage: cf. F. bellig͵rant. See Bellicose, Jest.] 1. Waging war; carrying on war. ½Belligerent powers.͵

E. Everett.

Pertaining, or tending, to war; of or relating to belligerents; as, a belligerent tone; belligerent rights.

Belligerïent, n. A nation or state recognized as carrying on war; a person engaged in warfare.

Belligerïentïly, adv. In a belligerent manner; hostilely.

Belling (?), n. [From Bell to bellow.] A bellowing, as of a deer in rutting time.

Johnson.

Bellipoïtent (?), a. [L. bellipotens; bellum war + potens powerful, p. pr. of posse to be able.] Mighty in war; armipotent. [R.]

Blount.

Bell jar· (?). (Phys.) A glass vessel, varying in size, open at the bottom and closed at the top like a bell, and having a knob or handle at the top for lifting it. It is used for a great variety of purposes; as, with the air pump, and for holding gases, also for keeping the dust from articles exposed to view.

Bellman (?), n. A man who rings a bell, especially to give notice of anything in the streets. Formerly, also, a night watchman who called the hours.

Milton.

Bell met·al (?). A hard alloy or bronze, consisting usually of about three parts of copper to one of tin; Ð used for making bells.

Bell metal ore, a sulphide of tin, copper, and iron; the mineral stannite.

BellÐmouthed· (?), a. Expanding at the mouth; as, a bellÐmouthed gun.

Byron.

Bellon (?), n. Lead colic.

ØBellona (?), n. [L., from bellum war.] (Rom. Myth.) The goddess of war.

Bellow (?), v. i. [imp. & p.p. Bellowed ; p. pr. & vb. n. Bellowing.] [OE. belwen, belowen, AS. bylgean, fr. bellan; akin to G. bellen, and perh. to L. flere to weep, OSlav. bleja to bleat, Lith. balsas voice. Cf. Bell, n. & v., Bawl, Bull.] 1. To make a hollow, loud noise, as an enraged bull.

> To bowl; to vociferate; to clamor.

Dryden.

> To roar; as the sea in a tempest, or as the wind when violent; to make a loud, hollow, continued sound.

The bellowing voice of boiling seas.
Dryden.

Bellow, v. t. To emit with a loud voice; to shout; Ð used with out. ½Would bellow out a laugh.͵
Dryden.

Bellow, n. A loud resounding outcry or noise, as of an enraged bull; a roar.

Bellow′er (?), n. One who, or that which, bellows.

Bellows (?), n. sing. & pl. [OE. bely, below, belly, bellows, AS. b‘lg, b‘lig, bag, bellows, belly. Bellows is prop. a pl. and the orig. sense is bag. See Belly.] An instrument, utensil, or machine, which, by alternate expansion and contraction, or by rise and fall of the top, draws in air through a valve and expels it through a tube for various purposes, as blowing fires, ventilating mines, or filling the pipes of an organ with wind.

Bellows camera, in photography, a form of camera, which can be drawn out like an accordion or bellows. Ð Hydrostatic bellows. See Hydrostatic. Ð A pair of bellows, the ordinary household instrument for blowing fires, consisting of two nearly heartÐshaped boards with handles, connected by leather, and having a valve and tube.

Bellows fish · (?). (Zo"l.) A European fish (Centriscus scolopax), distinguished by a long tubular snout, like the pipe of a bellows; Ð called also trumpet fish, and snipe fish.

Bell pep · per (?). (Bot.) A species of Capsicum, or Guinea pepper (C. annuum). It is the red pepper of the gardens.

BellÐshaped · (?), a. Having the shape of a widemouthed bell; campanulate.

Bellu′ine (?), a. [L. belluinus, fr. bellua beast.] Pertaining to, or like, a beast; brutal. [R.]

Animal and belluine life.

Atterbury.

Bellweth·er (?), n. 1. A wether, or sheep, which leads the flock, with a bell on his neck.

Hence: A leader. [Contemptuous]

Swift.

Bellwort (?), n. (Bot.) A genus of plants (Uvularia) with yellowish bellïshaped flowers.

Belly (?), n.; pl. **Bellies** (?). [OE. bali, bely, AS. belg, b‘lg, b‘lig, bag, bellows, belly; akin to Icel. belgr bag, bellows, Sw. b„lg, Dan. b‘lg, D. & G. balg, cf. W. bol the paunch or belly, dim. boly, Ir. bolg. Cf. Bellows, Follicle, Fool, Bilge.] 1. That part of the human body which extends downward from the breast to the thighs, and contains the bowels, or intestines; the abdomen.

µ Formerly all the splanchnic or visceral cavities were called bellies; Ð the lower belly being the abdomen; the middle belly, the thorax; and the upper belly, the head.

Dunglison.

The under part of the body of animals, corresponding to the human belly.

Underneath the belly of their steeds.
Shak.

The womb. [Obs.]

Before I formed thee in the belly I knew thee.
Jer. i. 5.

The part of anything which resembles the human belly in protuberance or in cavity; the innermost part; as, the belly of a flask, muscle, sail, ship.

Out of the belly of hell cried I.
Jonah ii. 2.

(Arch.) The hollow part of a curved or bent timber, the convex part of which is the back.

Belly doublet, a doublet of the 16th century, hanging down so as to cover the belly. Shak. Ð **Belly fretting**, the chafing of a horse's belly with a girth. Johnson. Ð **Belly timber**, food. [Ludicrous] Prior. Ð **Belly worm**, a worm that breeds or lives in the belly (stomach or intestines). Johnson.

Belly, v. t. [imp. & p.p. Bellied (?); p. pr. & vb. n. Bellying.] To cause to swell out; to fill. [R.]

Your breath of full consent bellied his sails.
Shak.

Belly, v. i. To swell and become protuberant, like the belly; to bulge.

The bellying canvas strutted with the gale.
Dryden.

Bellyïache · (?), n. Pain in the bowels; colic.

Bellyïband · (?), n. 1. A band that passes under the belly of a horse and holds the saddle or harness in place; a girth.

<small>A band of flannel or other cloth about the belly.</small>

<small>(Naut.) A band of canvas, to strengthen a sail.</small>

Bellyïbound · (?), a. Costive; constipated.

Bellyïcheat · (?), n. An apron or covering for the front of the person. [Obs.]
Beau. & Fl.

Bellyïcheer · (?), n. [Perh. from F. belle chŠre.] Good cheer; viands. [Obs.] ½Bellycheer and banquets.„ Rowlands. ½Loaves and bellycheer.„ Milton.

Bellyïcheer · , v. i. To revel; to feast. [Obs.]

A pack of clergymen [assembled] by themselves to bellycheer in their presumptuous Sion.
Milton.

Bellyïful (?), n. As much as satisfies the appetite. Hence: A great abundance; more than enough.
Lloyd.

King James told his son that he would have his bellyful of parliamentary impeachments.
Johnson.

BellyÐgod · (?), n. One whose great pleasure it is to gratify his appetite; a glutton; an epicure.

BellyÐpinched · (?), a. Pinched with hunger; starved. ½The bellyÐpinched wolf.„
Shak.

Beïlock (?), v. t. [imp. & p.p. Belocked (?).] [Pref. beï + lock: cf. AS. bel?can.] To lock, or fasten as with a lock. [Obs.]
Shak.

Beloïman · cy (?), n. [Gr. ?; ? arrow + ? a diviner: cf. F. b‚lomancie.] A kind of divination anciently practiced by means of marked arrows drawn at random from a bag or quiver, the marks on the arrows drawn being supposed to foreshow the future.
Encyc. Bri?.

Beïlong (?), v. i. [imp. & p.p. Belonged (?); p. pr. & vb. n. Belonging.] [OE. belongen (akin to D. belangen to concern, G. belangen to attain to, to concern); pref. beï + longen to desire. See Long, v. i.] [Usually construed with to.] 1. To be the property of; as, Jamaica belongs to Great Britain.

<small>To be a part of, or connected with; to be appendant or related; to owe allegiance or service.</small>

A desert place belonging to ... Bethsaids.
Luke ix. 10.
The mighty men which belonged to David.
1 Kings i. 8.

To be the concern or proper business or function of; to appertain to. ½Do not interpretations belong to God ?

Gen. xl. 8.

To be suitable for; to be due to.

Strong meat belongeth to them that are of full age.
Heb. v. 14.
No blame belongs to thee.
Shak.

To be native to, or an inhabitant of; esp. to have a legal residence, settlement, or inhabitancy, whether by birth or operation of law, so as to be entitled to maintenance by the parish or town.

Bastards also are settled in the parishes to which the mothers belong.
Blackstone.
Beïlong (?), v. t. To be deserved by. [Obs.]
More evils belong us than happen to us.
B. Jonson.
Beïlonging, n. [Commonly in the pl.] 1. That which belongs to one; that which pertains to one; hence, goods or effects. ½Thyself and thy belongings.
Shak.

That which is connected with a principal or greater thing; an appendage; an appurtenance.

Family; relations; household. [Colloq.]

Few persons of her ladyship's belongings stopped, before they did her bidding, to ask her reasons.
Thackeray.
Beloïnite (?), n. [Gr. ? a needle.] (Min.) Minute acicular or dendritic crystalline forms sometimes observed in glassy volcanic rocks.
Belïooche Belïoochee } (?), a. Of or pertaining to Beloochistan, or to its inhabitants. Ð n. A native or an inhabitant of Beloochistan.
Beïlord (?), v. t. 1. To act the lord over.

To address by the title of ½lord.

Beïlove (?), v. t. [imp. & p.p. Beloved (?).] [OE. bilufien. See pref. Beï, and Love, v. t.] To love. [Obs.]

Wodroephe.

Beḷoved (?), p. p. & a. Greatly loved; dear to the heart.

Antony, so well beloved of C'sar.

Shak.

This is my beloved Son.

Matt. iii. 17.

Beḷoved (?), n. One greatly loved.

My beloved is mine, and I am his.

Cant. ii. 16.

Beḷow (?), prep. [Pref. beḷ by + low.] 1. Under, or lower in place; beneath not so high; as, below the moon; below the knee.

Shak.

Inferior to in rank, excellence, dignity, value, amount, price, etc.; lower in quality. ½One degree below kings.

Addison.

Unworthy of; unbefitting; beneath.

They beheld, with a just loathing and disdain, ... how below all history the persons and their actions were.

Milton.

Who thinks no fact below his regard.

Hallam.

Syn. Ð Underneath; under; beneath.

Beḷow, adv. 1. In a lower place, with respect to any object; in a lower room; beneath.

Lord Marmion waits below.

Sir W. Scott.

On the earth, as opposed to the heavens.

The fairest child of Jove below.

Prior.

In hell, or the regions of the dead.

What businesss brought him to the realms below.

Dryden.

In court or tribunal of inferior jurisdiction; as, at the trial below.

Wheaton.

In some part or page following.

Bellowt (?), v. t. To treat as a lout; to talk abusively to. [Obs.]
Camden.

Belsire· (?), n. [Pref. bell + sire. Cf. Beldam.] A grandfather, or ancestor. ½His great belsire Brute., [Obs.]
Drayton.

Belswag·ger (?), n. [Contr. from bellyswagger.] A lewd man; also, a bully. [Obs.]
Dryden.

Belt (?), n. [AS. belt; akin to Icel. belti, Sw. b„lte, Dan. b'lte, OHG. balz, L. balteus, Ir. & Gael. balt bo?der, belt.] 1. That which engirdles a person or thing; a band or girdle; as, a lady's belt; a sword belt.

The shining belt with gold inlaid.
Dryden.

That which restrains or confines as a girdle.

He cannot buckle his distempered cause
Within the belt of rule.
Shak.

Anything that resembles a belt, or that encircles or crosses like a belt; a strip or stripe; as, a belt of trees; a belt of sand.

(Arch.) Same as Band, n., 2. A very broad band ? more properly termed a belt.

(Astron.) One of certain girdles or zones on the surface of the planets Jupiter and Saturn, supposed to be of the nature of clouds.

(Geog.) A narrow passage or strait; as, the Great Belt and the Lesser Belt, leading to the Baltic Sea.

(Her.) A token or badge of knightly rank.

(Mech.) A band of leather, or other flexible substance, passing around two wheels, and communicating motion from one to the other. [See Illust. of Pulley.]

(Nat. Hist.) A band or stripe, as of color, round any organ; or any circular ridge or series of ridges.

Belt lacing, thongs used for lacing together the ends of machine belting.

Belt, v. t. [imp. & p.p. Belted; p. pr. & vb. n. Belting.] 1. To encircle with, or as with, a belt; to encompass; to surround.

A coarse black robe belted round the waist.
C. Reade.

They belt him round with hearts undaunted.
Wordsworth.

To shear, as the buttocks and tails of sheep. [Prov. Eng.]

Halliwell.

Beltane (?), n. [Gael. bealltainn, bealltuinn.]
The first day of May (Old Style).

The quarterĐdays anciently in Scotland were Hallowmas, Candlemas, Beltane, and Lammas.

New English Dict.

A festival of the heathen Celts on the first day of May, in the observance of which great bonfires were kindled. It still exists in a modified form in some parts of Scotland and Ireland.

Belted (?), a. 1. Encircled by, or secured with, a belt; as, a belted plaid; girt with a belt, as an honorary distinction; as, a belted knight; a belted earl.

Marked with a band or circle; as, a belted stalk.

Worn in, or suspended from, the belt.

Three men with belted brands.

Sir W. Scott.

Belted cattle, cattle originally from Dutch stock, having a broad band of white round the middle, while the rest of the body is black; Đ called also blanketed cattle.

Beltein (?), Beltin (?), n. See Beltane.

Belting (?), n. The material of which belt? for machinery are made; also, belts, taken collectively.

<— p. 136 —>

Beïluga (?), n. [Russ. bieluga a sort of large sturgeon, prop. white fish, fr. bieluii white.] (Zo"l.) A ??tacean allied to the dolphins.

μ The northern beluga (Delphinapterus catodon) is the white whale and white fish of the whalers. It grows to be from twelve to eighteen feet long.

Beïlute (?), v. t. [imp. & p.p. Beluted; p. pr. & vb. n. Beluting.] [Pref. beï + L. lutum mud.] To bespatter, as with mud. [R.]

Sterne.

Bel · veïdere (?), n. [It., fr. bello, bel, beautiful + vedere to see.] (Arch.) A small building, or a part of a building, more or less open, constructed in a place commanding a fine prospect.

ØBelzeïbuth (?), n. [From Beelzebub.] (Zo"l.) A spider monkey (Ateles belzebuth) of Brazil.

ØBema (?), n. [Gr. ? step, platform.]

(Gr. Antiq.) A platform from which speakers addressed an assembly.

Mitford.

(Arch.) (a) That part of an early Christian church which was reserved for the higher clergy; the inner or eastern part of the chancel. (b) Erroneously: A pulpit.

Beïmad (?), v. t. To make mad. [Obs.]

Fuller.

Beïmangle (?), v. t. To mangle; to tear ?sunder. [R.]

Beaumont.

Bemask (?), v. t. To mask; to conceal.

Bemaster (?), v. t. To master thoroughly.

Bemaul (?), v. t. To maul or beat severely; to bruise. ½In order to bemaul Yorick.‚

Sterne.

Bemaze (?), v. t. [OE. bimasen; pref. beï + masen to maze.] To bewilder. Intellects bemazed in endless doubt.

Cowper.

Bemean (?), v. t. To make mean; to lower.

C. Reade.

Bemeet (?), v. t. [imp. & p.p. Bemet (?); p. pr. & vb. n. Bemeeting.] To meet. [Obs.]

Our very loving sister, well bemet.
    Shak.

Bemete (?), v. t. To mete. [Obs.]
Shak.

Bemingle (?), v. t. To mingle; to mix.

Bemire (?), v. t. [imp. & p.p. Bemired (?); p. pr. & vb. n. Bemiring.] To drag through, encumber with, or fix in, the mire; to soil by passing through mud or dirt.

Bemired and benighted in the dog.
    Burke.

Bemist (?), v. t. To envelop in mist. [Obs.]

Bemoan (?), v. t. [imp. & p.p. Bemoaned (?); p. pr. & vb. n. Bemoaning.] [OE. bimenen, AS. bem?nan; pref. beï + m?nan to moan. See Moan.] To express deep grief for by moaning; to express sorrow for; to lament; to bewail; to pity or sympathize with.

Implores their pity, and his pain bemoans.
    Dryden.

Syn. Đ See Deplore.

Bemoaner (?), n. One who bemoans.

Bemock (?), v. t. To mock; to ridicule.

Bemock the modest moon.
    Shak.

Bemoil (?), v. t. [Pref. beï + moil, fr. F. mouiller to wet; but cf. also OE. bimolen to soil, fr. AS. m¾l spot: cf. E. mole.] To soil or encumber with mire and dirt. [Obs.]

Shak.

Bemol (?), n. [F. b‚mol, fr. b, ? + mol soft.] (Mus.) The sign ?; the same as B flat. [Obs.]

Bemonster (?), v. t. To make monstrous or like a monster. [Obs.]
    Shak.

Bemourn (?), v. t. To mourn over.

Wyclif.

Bemuddle (?), v. t. To muddle; to stupefy or bewilder; to confuse.

Bemuffle (?), v. t. To cover as with a muffler; to wrap up.

Bemuffled with the externals of religion.

Sterne.

Bemuse (?), v. t. To muddle, daze, or partially stupefy, as with liquor.

A parson much bemused in beer.

Pope.

Ben (?), Ben nut · (?). [Ar. b¾n, name of the tree.] (Bot.) The seed of one or more species of moringa; as, oil of ben. See Moringa.

Ben, adv. & prep. [AS. binnan; pref. beï by + innan within, in in.] Within; in; in or into the interior; toward the inner apartment. [Scot.]

Ben, n. [See Ben, adv.] The inner or principal room in a hut or house of two rooms; Đ opposed to but, the outer apartment. [Scot.]

Ben. An old form of the pl. indic. pr. of Be. [Obs.]

Bename (?), v. t. [p. p. Benamed, Benempt.] To promise; to name. [Obs.]

Bench (?), n.; pl. Benches (?). [OE. bench, benk, AS. benc; akin to Sw. b„nk, Dan b'nk, Icel. bekkr, OS., D., & G. bank. Cf. Bank, Beach.] 1. A long seat, differing from a stool in its greater length.

Mossy benches supplie? ?ne place of chairs.

Sir W. Scott.

A long table at which mechanics and other work; as, a carpenter's bench.

The seat where judges sit in court.

To pluck down justice from your awful bench.

Shak.

The persons who sit as judges; the court; as, the opinion of the full bench. See King's Bench.

A collection or group of dogs exhibited to the public; Đ so named because the animals are usually placed on benches or raised platforms.

A conformation like a bench; a long stretch of flat ground, or a kind of natural terrace, near a lake or river.

Bench mark (Leveling), one of a number of marks along a line of survey, affixed to permanent objects, to show where leveling staffs were placed. Đ Bench of bishops, the whole body of English prelates assembled in council. Đ Bench plane, any plane used by carpenters and joiners for working a flat surface, as jack planes, long planes. Đ Bench show, an exhibition of dogs. Đ Bench table (Arch.), a projecting course at the base of a building, or round a pillar, sufficient to form a seat.

Bench (?), v. t. [imp. & p.p. Benched (?); p. pr. & vb. n. Benching.] 1. To furnish with benches.

'T was benched with turf.
Dryden.
Stately theaters benched crescentwise.
Tennyson.

To place on a bench or seat of honor.

Whom I ... have benched and reared to worship.
 Shak.
Bench, v. i. To sit on a seat of justice. [R.]
Shak.
Bencher (??), n. 1. (Eng. Law) One of the senior and governing members of an Inn of Court.

An alderman of a corporation. [Eng.]

Ashmole.

A member of a court or council. [Obs.]

Shak.

One who frequents the benches of a tavern; an idler. [Obs.]

Bench war · rant (?). (Law) A process issued by a presiding judge or by a court against a person guilty of some contempt, or indicted for some crime; Đ so called in distinction from a justice's warrant.

Bend (?), v. t. [imp. & p.p. Bended or Bent (?); p. pr. & vb. n. Bending.] [AS. bendan to bend, fr. bend a band, bond, fr. bindan to bind. See Bind, v. t., and cf. 3d & 4th Bend.] 1. To strain or move out of a straight line; to crook by straining; to make crooked; to curve; to make ready for use by drawing into a curve; as, to bend a bow; to bend the knee.

To turn toward some certain point; to direct; to incline. ½Bend thine ear to supplication.

Milton.
Towards Coventry bend we our course.
Shak.
Bending her eyes ... upon her parent.
Sir W. Scott.

To apply closely or with interest; to direct.

To bend his mind to any public business.
Temple.
But when to mischief mortals bend their will.
Pope.

To cause to yield; to render submissive; to subdue. ½Except she bend her humor.ˏ

Shak.

(Naut.) To fasten, as one rope to another, or as a sail to its yard or stay; or as a cable to the ring of an anchor.

Totten.

To bend the brow, to knit the brow, as in deep thought or in anger; to scowl; to frown.

Camden.

Syn. Ð To lean; stoop; deflect; bow; yield.

Bend, v. i. 1. To be moved or strained out of a straight line; to crook or be curving; to bow.

The green earth's end
Where the bowed welkin slow doth bend.
Milton.

To jut over; to overhang.

There is a cliff, whose high and bending head
Looks fearfully in the confined deep.
Shak.

To be inclined; to be directed.

To whom our vows and wished bend.
Milton.

To bow in prayer, or in token of submission.

While each to his great Father bends.
Coleridge.

Bend, n. [See Bend, v. t., and cf. Bent, n.] 1. A turn or deflection from a straight line or from the proper direction or normal position; a curve; a crook; as, a slight bend of the body; a bend in a road.

Turn; purpose; inclination; ends. [Obs.]

Farewell, poor swain; thou art not for my bend.
Fletcher.

(Naut.) A knot by which one rope is fastened to another or to an anchor, spar, or post.

Totten.

(Leather Trade) The best quality of sole leather; a butt. See Butt.

(Mining) Hard, indurated clay; bind.

Bends of a ship, the thickest and strongest planks in her sides, more generally called wales. They have the beams, knees, and foothooks bolted to them. Also, the frames or ribs that form the ship's body from the keel to the top of the sides; as, the midship bend.

Bend, n. [AS. bend. See Band, and cf. the preceding noun.] 1. A band. [Obs.]

Spenser.

[OF. bende, bande, F. bande. See Band.] (Her.) One of the honorable ordinaries, containing a third or a fifth part of the field. It crosses the field diagonally from the dexter chief to the sinister base.

Bend sinister (Her.), an honorable ordinary drawn from the sinister chief to the dexter base.

Bendaïble (?), a. Capable of being bent.

Bender (?), n. 1. One who, or that which, bends.

An instrument used for bending.

A drunken spree. [Low, U. S.]

Bartlett.

A sixpence. [Slang, Eng.]

Bending, n. The marking of the clothes with stripes or horizontal bands. [Obs.]

Chaucer.

Bendlet (?), n. [Bend + ïlet: cf. E. bandlet.] (Her.) A narrow bend, esp. one half the width of the bend.

Bendwise (?), adv. (Her.) Diagonally.

Bendy (?), a. [From Bend a band.] (Her.) Divided into an even number of bends; Ð said of a shield or its charge.

Cussans.

Bene (?), n. (Bot.) See Benne.

Bene (?), n. [AS. b?n.] A prayer; boon. [Archaic]

What is good for a bootless bene ?

Wordsworth.

ØBene, Ben (?), n. [Native name.] (Zo"l.) A hoglike mammal of New Guinea (Porcula papuensis).

Beïneaped (?), a. (Naut.) See Neaped.

Beïneath (?), prep. [OE. benethe, bineo?en, AS. beneo?an, beny?an; pref. beï + neo?an, ny?an, downward, beneath, akin to E. nether. See Nether.] 1. Lower in place, with something directly over or on; under; underneath; hence, at the foot of. ½Beneath the mount.

Ex. xxxii. 19.

Beneath a rude and nameless stone he lies.

Pope.

Under, in relation to something that is superior, or that oppresses or burdens.

Our country sinks beneath the yoke.
Shak.

Lower in rank, dignity, or excellence than; as, brutes are beneath man; man is beneath angels in the scale of beings. Hence: Unworthy of; unbecoming.

He will do nothing that is beneath his high station.
Atterbury.
Bėneath (?), adv. 1. In a lower place; underneath.
The earth you take from beneath will be barren.
Mortimer.

Below, as opposed to heaven, or to any superior region or position; as, in earth beneath.

ØBen · ėdiciïte (?), n. [L., (imperative pl.,) bless ye, praise ye.] A canticle (the Latin version of which begins with this word) which may be used in the order for morning prayer in the Church of England. It is taken from an apocryphal addition to the third chapter of Daniel.

ØBen · ėdiciïte, interj. [See Benedicite, n.] An exclamation corresponding to Bless you !.

Benėdict (?), Benėdick (?), } n. [From Benedick, one of the characters in Shakespeare's play of ½Much Ado about Nothing.ˌ] A married man, or a man newly married.

Benėdict, a. [L. benedictus, p. p. of benedicere to bless. See Benison, and cf. Bennet.] Having mild and salubrious qualities. [Obs.]
Bacon.

Ben · ėdictine (?), a. Pertaining to the monks of St. Benedict, or St. Benet.

Ben · ėdictine, n. (Eccl. Hist.) One of a famous order of monks, established by St. Benedict of Nursia in the sixth century. This order was introduced into the United States in 1846.

μ The Benedictines wear black clothing, and are sometimes called Black Monks. The name Black Fr????rs which belongs to the Dominicans, is also sometimes applied to the Benedictines.

Ben · ėdiction (?), n. [L. benedictio: cf. F. b,n,diction. See Benison.] 1. The act of blessing.

A blessing; an expression of blessing, prayer, or kind wishes in favor of any person or thing; a solemn or affectionate invocation of happiness.

So saying, he arose; whom Adam thus
Followed with benediction.
Milton.
Homeward serenely she walked with God's benediction upon her.

Longfellow.

Specifically: The short prayer which closes public worship; as, to give the benediction.

(Eccl.) The form of instituting an abbot, answering to the consecration of a bishop.

Ayliffe.

(R. C. Ch.) A solemn rite by which bells, banners, candles, etc., are blessed with holy water, and formally dedicated to God.

Ben · e̅ȋdiction̑ȋal (?), n. A book of benedictions.
Ben · e̅ȋdiction̑ȋa̅ȋry (?), n. A collected series of benedictions.
The benedictionary of Bishop Athelwold.
  G. Gurton's Needle.
Ben · e̅ȋdictive (?), a. Tending to bless.
  Gauden.
Ben · e̅ȋdictȏȋry (?), a. Expressing wishes for good; as, a benedictory prayer.
  Thackeray.
ØBen · e̅ȋdictus (?), n. [L., blessed. See Benedict, a.] The song of Zacharias at the birth of John the Baptist (Luke i. 68); Ð so named from the first word of the Latin version.
Bene̅ȋdight (?), a. Blessed. [R.]
  Longfellow.
Ben · e̅ȋfaction (?), n. [L. benefactio, fr. benefacere to do good to one; bene well + facere to do. See Benefit.] 1. The act of conferring a benefit.
  Johnson.

A benefit conferred; esp. a charitable donation.

Syn. Ð Gift; present; gratuity; boon; alms.
Ben · e̅ȋfactor (?), n. [L.] One who confers a benefit or benefits.
  Bacon.
Ben · e̅ȋfactress, n. A woman who confers a benefit.
His benefactress blushes at the deed.
  Cowper.
Be̅ȋnefic (?), a. [L. beneficus. See Benefice.] Favorable; beneficent.
  Milton.
Bene̅ȋfice (?), n. [F. b,n,fice, L. beneficium, a kindness , in LL. a grant of an estate, fr. L. beneficus beneficent; bene well + facere to do. See Benefit.]

A favor or benefit. [Obs.]

Baxter.

(Feudal Law) An estate in lands; a fief.

μ Such an estate was granted at first for life only, and held on the mere good pleasure of the donor; but afterward, becoming hereditary, it received the appellation of fief, and the term benefice became appropriated to church livings.

An ecclesiastical living and church preferment, as in the Church of England; a church endowed with a revenue for the maintenance of divine service. See Advowson.

μ All church preferments are called benefices, except bishoprics, which are called dignities. But, ordinarily, the term dignity is applied to bishoprics, deaneries, archdeaconries, and prebendaryships; benefice to parsonages, vicarages, and donatives.

Beneïfice, v. t. [imp. & p.p. Beneficed.] To endow with a benefice. [Commonly in the past participle.]

Beneïficed (?), a. Possessed of a benefice o? church preferment. ½Beneficed clergymen.ͺ
Burke.

Beneïficeïless (?), a. Having no benefice. ½Beneficeless precisians.ͺ
Sheldon.

Beïnefiïcence (?), n. [L. beneficentia, fr. beneficus: cf. F. b,n,ficence. See Benefice.] The practice of doing good; active goodness, kindness, or charity; bounty springing from purity and goodness.

And whose beneficence no charge exhausts.
Cowper.

Syn. Ð See Benevolence.

Beïnef · iïcent (?), a. Doing or producing good; performing acts of kindness and charity; characterized by beneficence.

The beneficent fruits of Christianity.
Prescott.

Syn. Ð See Benevolent.

Beïnef · iïcential (?), a. Relating to beneficence.

<— p. 137 —>

Beïnefiïcentïly (?), adv. In a beneficent manner; with beneficence. Ben · eïficial (?), a. [Cf. F. b,n,ficial, LL. beneficialis.] 1. Conferring benefits; useful; profi?table; helpful; advantageous; serviceable; contributing to a valuable end; Ð followed by to. The war which would have been most beneficial to us. Swift. 2. (Law) Receiving, or entitled to have or receive, advantage, use, or benefit; as, the beneficial owner of an estate. Kent. 3. King. [Obs.] ½A beneficial foe.ͺ B. Jonson. Syn. Ð See Advantage. Ben · eïficialïly, adv. In a beneficial or advantageous manner; profitably; helpfully. Ben · eïficialïness, n. The quality of being beneficial; profitableness. Ben · eïficiïaïry (?), a. [Cf. F. b,n,ficiaire, LL. beneficiarius.] 1. Holding some office or valuable possession, in subordination to another; holding under a feudal or other superior; having a dependent and secondary possession. A feudatory or beneficiary king of England. Bacon. 2. Bestowed as a gratuity; as, beneficiary gifts. Ben·eﬁciary, n.; pl. Beneficiaries (?). 1. A feudatory or vassal; hence, one who holds a benefice and uses its proceeds. Ayliffe. 2. One who receives anything as a gift; one who receives a benefit or advantage; esp. one who receives help or income from an educational fund or a trust estate. The rich men will be offering sacrifice to their Deity whose beneficiaries they are. Jer. Taylor. Ben·eﬁciate (?), v. t. [Sp. beneficiar to benefit, to work mines.] (Mining) To reduce (ores). Ð Ben·eﬁ·ciation (?), n. Ben·eﬁcient (?), a. Beneficent. [Obs.] Beneﬁt (?), n. [OE. benefet, benfeet, bienfet, F. bienfait, fr. L. benefactum; bene well (adv. of bonus good) + factum, p. p. of facere to do. See Bounty, and Fact.] 1. An act of kindness; a favor conferred. Bless the Lord, O my soul, and forget not all his benefits. Ps. ciii. 2. 2. Whatever promotes prosperity and personal happiness, or adds value to property; advantage; profit. Men have no right to what is not for their benefit. Burke. 3. A theatrical performance, a concert, or the like, the proceeds of which do not go to the lessee of the theater or to the company, but to some individual actor, or to some charitable use. 4. Beneficence; liberality. [Obs.] Webster (1623). 5. pl. Natural advantaged; endowments; accomplishments. [R.] ½The benefits of your own country.„ Shak. Benefit of clergy. (Law) See under Clergy. Syn. Ð Profit; service; use; avail. See Advantage. Beneﬁt, v. t. [imp. & p.p. Benefited; p. pr. & vb. n. Benefitting.] To be beneficial to; to do good to; to advantage; to advance in health or prosperity; to be useful to; to profit. I will repent of the good, wherewith I said I would benefit them. Jer. xviii. 10. Beneﬁt, v. i. To gain advantage; to make improvement; to profit; as, he will benefit by the change. Beneﬁt·er (?), n. One who confers a benefit; Ð also, one who receives a benefit. Beïneme (?), v. t. [AS. ben?man. Cf. Benim.] To deprive (of), or take away (from). [Obs.] Beïnempt (?), p. p. of Bename. 1. Promised; vowed. [Obs.] Spenser. 2. Named; styled. [Archaic] Sir W. Scott. ØBe·ne placiïto (?). [It. beneplacito pleasure, fr. L. bene well + placitus pleasing.] 1. At or during pleasure. For our English judges there never was ... any bene placito as their tenure. F. Harrison. 2. (Mus.) At pleasure; ad libitum. Beïnet (?), v. t. [imp. & p.p. Benetted.] To catch in a net; to insnare. Shak. Beïnevoïlence (?), n. [OF. benevolence, L. benevolentia. See Benevolent.] 1. The disposition to do good; good will; charitableness; love of mankind, accompanied with a desire to promote their happiness. The wakeful benevolence of the gospel. Chalmers. 2. An act of kindness; good done; charity given. 3. A species of compulsory contribution or tax, which has sometimes been illegally exacted by arbitrary kings of England, and falsely represented as a gratuity. Syn. Ð Benevolence, Beneficence, Munificence. Benevolence marks a disposition made up of a choice and desire for the happiness of others. Beneficence marks the working of this disposition in dispensing good on a somewhat broad scale. Munificence shows the same disposition, but acting on a still broader scale, in conferring gifts and favors. These are not necessarily confined to objects of immediate utility. One may show his munificence in presents of pictures or jewelry, but this would not be beneficence. Benevolence of heart; beneficence of life; munificence in the encouragement of letters. BeÏnevoÏlent (?), a. [L. benevolens, Ïentis; bene well (adv. of bonus good) + volens, p. pr. of volo I will, I wish. See Bounty, and Voluntary.] Having a disposition to do good; possessing or manifesting love to mankind, and a desire to promote their prosperity and happiness; disposed to give to good objects; kind; charitable. Ð BeÏnevoÏlentÏly, adv. Syn. Ð Benevolent, Beneficent. Etymologically considered, benevolent implies wishing well to others, and beneficent, doing well. But by degrees the word benevolent has been widened to include not only feelings, but actions; thus, we speak of benevolent operations, benevolent labors for the public good, benevolent societies. In like manner, beneficent is now often applied to feelings; thus, we speak of the beneficent intentions of a donor. This extension of the terms enables us to mark nicer shades of meaning. Thus, the phrase ½benevolent labors¸ turns attention to the source of these labors, viz., benevolent feeling; while beneficent would simply mark them as productive of good. So, ½beneficent intentions¸ point to the feelings of the donor as bent upon some specific good act; while ½benevolent intentions¸ would only denote a general wish and design to do good. BeÏnevoÏlous (?), a. [L. benevolus.] Kind; benevolent. [Obs.] T. Puller. BenÏgal (?), n. 1. A province in India, giving its name to various stuffs, animals, etc. 2. A thin stuff, made of silk and hair, originally brought from Bengal. 3. Striped gingham, originally brought from Bengal; Bengal stripes. Bengal light, a firework containing niter, sulphur, and antimony, and producing a sustained and vivid colored light, used in making signals and in pyrotechnics; Ð called also blue light. Ð Bengal stripes, a kind of cotton cloth woven with colored stripes. See Bengal, 3. Ð Bengal tiger. (Zo"l.). See Tiger. BenÏgalee, BenÏgali (?), n. The language spoken in Bengal. Ben · gallese (?), a. Of or pertaining to Bengal. Ð n. sing. & pl. A native or natives of Bengal. BenÏgola (?), n. A Bengal light. BeÏnight (?), v. t. [imp. & p.p. Benighted; p. pr. & vb. n. Benighting.] 1. To involve in darkness; to shroud with the shades of night; to obscure. [Archaic] The clouds benight the sky. Garth. 2. To overtake with night or darkness, especially before the end of a day's journey or task. Some virgin, sure, ... benighted in these woods. Milton. 3. To involve in moral darkness, or ignorance; to debar from intellectual light. Shall we to men benighted The lamp of life deny ? Heber. BeÏnightment (?), n. The condition of being benighted. BeÏnign (?), a. [OE. benigne, bening, OF. benigne, F. b‚nin, fem. b‚nigne, fr. L. benignus, contr. from benigenus; bonus good + root of genus kind. See Bounty, and Genus.] 1. Of a kind or gentle disposition; gracious; generous; favorable; benignant. Creator bounteous and benign. Milton. 2. Exhibiting or manifesting kindness, gentleness, favor, etc.; mild; kindly; salutary; wholesome. Kind influences and benign aspects. South. 3. Of a mild type or character; as, a benign disease. Syn. Ð Kind; propitious; bland; genial; salubrious; favorable salutary; gracious; liberal. BeÏnignanÏcy

(?), n. Benignant quality; kindliness. Benignant (?), a. [LL. benignans, p. pr. of benignare, from L. benignus. See Benign.] Kind; gracious; favorable. Ð Benignantly, adv. Benignity (?), n. [OE. benignite, F. b‚nignit‚, OF. b‚nignet‚, fr. L. benignitas. See Benign.] 1. The quality of being benign; goodness; kindness; graciousness. ½Benignity of aspect.„ Sir W. Scott. 2. Mildness; gentleness. The benignity or inclemency of the season. Spectator. 3. Salubrity; wholesome quality. Wiseman. Benignly (?), adv. In a benign manner. Benim (?), v. t. [AS. beniman. See Benumb, and cf. Nim.] To take away. [Obs.] Ire … benimeth the man fro God. Chaucer. Benison (?), n. [OE. beneysun, benesoun, OF. bene‹?›un, bene‹son, fr. L. benedictio, fr. benedicere to bless; bene (adv. of bonus good) + dicere to say. See Bounty, and Diction, and cf. Benediction.] Blessing; beatitude; benediction. Shak. More precious than the benison of friends. Talfourd. ØB‚Œnitier · (?), n. [F., fr. b‚nir to bless.] (R. C. Ch.) A holyÐwater stoup. Shipley. Benjamin (?), n. [Corrupted from benzoin.] See Benzoin. Benjamin, n. A kind of upper coat for men. [Colloq. Eng.] Benjamite (?), n. A descendant of Benjamin; one of the tribe of Benjamin. Judg. iii. 15. Benne (?), n. [Malay bijen.] (Bot.) The name of two plants (Sesamum orientale and S. indicum), originally Asiatic; Ð also called oil plant. From their seeds an oil is expressed, called benne oil, used mostly for making soap. In the southern United States the seeds are used in candy. Bennet (?), n. [F. benoŒte, fr. L. benedicta, fem. of benedictus, p. p., blessed. See Benedict, a.] (Bot.) The common yellow‹flowered avens of Europe (Geum urbanum); herb bennet. The name is sometimes given to other plants, as the hemlock, valerian, etc. Benshee (?), n. See Banshee. Bent (?), imp. & p. p. of Bend. Bent, a. & p. p. 1. Changed by pressure so as to be no longer straight; crooked; as, a bent pin; a bent lever. 2. Strongly inclined toward something, so as to be resolved, determined, set, etc.; Ð said of the mind, character, disposition, desires, etc., and used with on; as, to be bent on going to college; he is bent on mischief. Bent, n. [See Bend, n. & v.] 1. The state of being curved, crooked, or inclined from a straight line; flexure; curvity; as, the bent of a bow. [Obs.] Wilkins. 2. A declivity or slope, as of a hill. [R.] Dryden. 3. A leaning or bias; proclivity; tendency of mind; inclination; disposition; purpose; aim. Shak. With a native bent did good pursue. Dryden. 4. Particular direction or tendency; flexion; course. Bents and turns of the matter. Locke. 5. (Carp.) A transverse frame of a framed structure. 6. Tension; force of acting; energy; impetus. [Archaic] The full bent and stress of the soul. Norris. Syn. Ð Predilection; turn. Bent, Bias, Inclination, Prepossession. These words agree in describing a permanent influence upon the mind which tends to decide its actions. Bent denotes a fixed tendency of the mind in a given direction. It is the widest of these terms, and applies to the will, the intellect, and the affections, taken conjointly; as, the whole bent of his character was toward evil practices. Bias is literally a weight fixed on one side of a ball used in bowling, and causing it to swerve from a straight course. Used figuratively, bias applies particularly to the judgment, and denotes something which acts with a permanent force on the character through that faculty; as, the bias of early education, early habits, etc. Inclination is an excited state of desire or appetency; as, a strong inclination to the study of the law. Prepossession is a mingled state of feeling and opinion in respect to some person or subject, which has laid hold of and occupied the mind previous to inquiry. The word is commonly used in a good sense, an unfavorable impression of this kind being denominated a prejudice. ½Strong minds will be strongly bent, and usually labor under a strong bias; but there is no mind so weak and powerless as not to have its inclinations, and none so guarded as to be without its prepossessions. Crabb. Bent (?), n. [AS. beonet; akin to OHG. pinuz, G. binse, rush, bent grass; of unknown origin.] 1. A reedlike grass; a stalk of stiff, coarse grass. His spear a bent, both stiff and strong. Drayton. 2. (Bot.) A grass of the genus Agrostis, esp. Agrostis vulgaris, or redtop. The name is also used of many other grasses, esp. in America. 3. Any neglected field or broken ground; a common; a moor. [Obs.] Wright. Bowmen bickered upon the bent. Chevy Chase. Bent grass · (?). (Bot.) Same as Bent, a kind of grass. Benthal (?), a. [Gr. ? the depth of the sea.] Relating to the deepest zone or region of the ocean. Benĭthamic (?), a. Of or pertaining to Bentham or Benthamism. Benthamĭism (?), n. That phase of the doctrine of utilitarianism taught by Jeremy Bentham; the doctrine that the morality of actions is estimated and determined by their utility; also, the theory that the sensibility to pleasure and the recoil from pain are the only motives which influence human desires and actions, and that these are the sufficient explanation of ethical and jural conceptions. Benthamĭite (?), n. One who believes in Benthamism. Benting time (?). The season when pigeons are said to feed on bents, before peas are ripe. Bare benting times ... may come. Dryden. Benty (?), a. 1. A bounding in bents, or the stalks of coarse, stiff, withered grass; as, benty fields. 2. Resembling bent. Holland. Beĭnumb (?), v. t. [imp. & p.p. Benumbed (?); p. pr. & vb. n. Benumbing.] [OE. binomen, p. p. of binimen to take away, AS. beniman; pref. be + niman to take. See Numb, a., and cf. Benim.] To make torpid; to deprive of sensation or sensibility; to stupefy; as, a hand or foot benumbed by cold. The creeping death benumbed her senses first. Dryden. Beĭnumbed (?), a. Made torpid; numbed; stupefied; deadened; as, a benumbed body and mind. Đ Beĭnumbedness, n. Beĭnumbment (?), n. Act of benumbing, or state of being benumbed; torpor. Kirby. Benzal (?), n. [Benzoic + aldehyde.] (Chem.) A transparent crystalline substance,? $C_6H_5.CO.NH_2$, obtained by the action of ammonia upon chloride of benzoyl, as also by several other reactions with benzoyl compounds. Benĭzamide (?), n. [Benzoin + amide.] (Chem.) A transparent crystalline substance, $C_6H_5.CO.NH_2$, obtained by the action of ammonia upon chloride of benzoyl, as also by several other reactions with benzoyl compounds. Benzene (?), n. [From Benzoin.] (Chem.) A volatile, very inflammable liquid, C_6H_6, contained in the naphtha produced by the destructive distillation of coal, from which it is separated by fractional distillation. The name is sometimes applied also to the impure commercial product or benzole, and also, but rarely, to a similar mixed product of petroleum. Benzene nucleus, Benzene ring (Chem.), a closed chain or ring, consisting of six carbon atoms, each with one hydrogen atom attached, regarded as the type from which the aromatic compounds are derived. This ring formula is provisionally accepted as representing the probable constitution of the benzene molecule, C6H6, and as the type on which its derivatives are formed. Benzile (?), n. [From Benzoin.] (Chem.) A yellowish crystalline substance, C6H5.CO.CO.C6H5, formed from benzoin by the action of oxidizing agents, and consisting of a doubled benzoyl radical. Benzine (?), n. [From Benzoin.] (Chem.) 1. A liquid consisting mainly of the lighter and more volatile hydrocarbons of petroleum or kerosene oil, used as a solvent and for cleansing soiled fabrics; Ð called also petroleum spirit, petroleum benzine. Varieties or similar products are gasoline, naphtha, rhigolene, ligroin, etc. 2. Same as Benzene. [R.] µ The hydrocarbons of benzine proper are essentially of the marsh gas series, while benzene proper is the typical hydrocarbon of the aromatic series. Benzoïate (?), n. [Cf. F. benzoate.] (Chem.) A salt formed by the union of benzoic acid with any salifiable base.

<— p. 138 —>

BenÏzoic (?), a. [Cf. F. benzo‹que.] Pertaining to, or obtained from, benzoin.

Benzoic acid, or flowers of benzoin, a peculiar vegetable acid, C6H5.CO2H, obtained from benzoin, and some other balsams, by sublimation or decoction. It is also found in the urine of infants and herbivorous animals. It crystallizes in the form of white, satiny flakes; its odor is aromatic; its taste is pungent, and somewhat acidulous. Ð Benzoic aldehyde, oil of bitter almonds; the aldehyde, C6H5.CHO, intermediate in composition between benzoic or benzyl alcohol, and benzoic acid. It is a thin colorless liquid.

BenÏzoin (?), n. [Cf. F. benjoin, Sp. benjui, Pg. beijoin; all fr. Ar. lub¾nÐj¾wÆ incense form Sumatra (named Java in Arabic), the first syllable being lost. Cf. Benjamin.] [Called also benjamin.] 1. A resinous substance, dry and brittle, obtained from the Styrax benzoin, a tree of Sumatra, Java, etc., having a fragrant odor, and slightly aromatic taste. It is used in the preparation of benzoic acid, in medicine, and as a perfume.

A white crystalline substance, C14H12O2, obtained from benzoic aldehyde and some other sources.

(Bot.) The spicebush (Lindera benzoin).

Flowers of benzoin, benzoic acid. See under Benzoic.

BenÏzoinaÏted (?), a. (Med.) Containing or impregnated with benzoin; as, benzoinated lard.

Benzole Benzol } (?), n. [Benzoin + L. oleum oil.] (Chem.) An impure benzene, used in the arts as a solvent, and for various other purposes. See

Benzene.

µ It has great solvent powers, and is used by manufacturers of India rubber and gutta percha; also for cleaning soiled kid gloves, and for other purposes.

Benzoïline (?), n. (Chem.) (a) Same as Benzole. (b) Same as Amarine. [R.]

Watts.

Benzoyl (?), n. [Benzoic + Gr. ? wood. See Ïyl.] (Chem.) A compound radical, C6H5.CO; the base of benzoic acid, of the oil of bitter almonds, and of an extensive series of compounds. [Formerly written also benzule.]

Benzyl (?), n. [Benzoic + Ïyl.] (Chem.) A compound radical, C6H5.CH2, related to toluene and benzoic acid; Ð commonly used adjectively.

Beïpaint (?), v. t. To paint; to cover or color with, or as with, paint.

Else would a maiden blush bepaint my cheek.

Shak.

Beïpelt (?), v. t. To pelt roundly.

Beïpinch (?), v. t. [imp. & p.p. Bepinched (?).] To pinch, or mark with pinches.

Chapman.

Beïplaster (?), v. t. [imp. & p.p. Beplastered (?); p. pr. & vb. n. Beplastering.] To plaster over; to cover or smear thickly; to bedaub.

Beplastered with rouge.

Goldsmith.

Beïplumed (?), a. Decked with feathers.

Beïpommel (?), v. t. [imp. & p.p. Bepommeled (?); p. pr. & vb. n. Bepommeling.] To pommel; to beat, as with a stick; figuratively, to assail or criticise in conversation, or in writing.

Thackeray.

Beïpowder (?), v. t. To sprinkle or cover with powder; to powder.

Beïpraise (?), v. t. To praise greatly or extravagantly.

Goldsmith.

Beïprose (?), v. t. To reduce to prose. [R.] ½To beprose all rhyme.

Mallet.

Beïpuffed (?), a. Puffed; praised.

Carlyle.

Beïpurple (?), v. t. To tinge or dye with a purple color.

Beïqueath (?), v. t. [imp. & p.p. Bequeathed (?); p. pr. & vb. n. Bequeathing.] [OE. biquethen, AS. becwe?an to say, affirm, bequeath; pref. beï + cwe?an to say, speak. See Quoth.] 1. To give or leave by will; to give by testament; Ð said especially of personal property.

My heritage, which my dead father did bequeath to me.

Shak.

To hand down; to transmit.

To bequeath posterity somewhat to remember it.
Glanvill.

To give; to offer; to commit. [Obs.]

To whom, with all submission, on my knee
I do bequeath my faithful services
And true subjection everlastingly.
Shak.

Syn. Ð To Bequeath, Devise. Both these words denote the giving or disposing of property by will. Devise, in legal usage, is property used to denote a gift by will of real property, and he to whom it is given is called the devisee. Bequeath is properly applied to a gift by will or legacy; i. e., of personal property; the gift is called a legacy, and he who receives it is called a legatee. In popular usage the word bequeath is sometimes enlarged so as to embrace devise; and it is sometimes so construed by courts.

BeÏqueathaÏble (?), a. Capable of being bequeathed.

BeÏqueathal (?), n. The act of bequeathing; bequeathment; bequest. Fuller.

BeÏqueathment (?), n. The act of bequeathing, or the state of being bequeathed; a bequest.

BeÏquest (?), n. [OE. biquest, corrupted fr. bequide; pref. beÏ + AS. cwide a saying, becwe?an to bequeath. The ending Ïest is probably due to confusion with quest. See Bequeath, Quest.] 1. The act of bequeathing or leaving by will; as, a bequest of property by A. to B.

That which is left by will, esp. personal property; a legacy; also, a gift.

BeÏquest, v. t. To bequeath, or leave as a legacy. [Obs.] ½All I have to bequest.¸
Gascoigne.

BeÏquethen (?), old p. p. of Bequeath. [Obs.]
Chaucer.

BeÏquote (?), v. t. To quote constantly or with great frequency.

BeÏrain (?), v. t. [imp. & p.p. Berained (?); p. pr. & vb. n. Beraining.] To rain upon; to wet with rain. [Obs.]
Chaucer.

BeÏrate (?), v. t. [imp. & p.p. Berated; p. pr. & vb. n. Berating.] To rate or chide vehemently; to scold. Holland. Motley.

BeÏrattle (?), v. t. To make rattle; to scold vociferously; to cry down. [Obs.] Shak.

BeÏray (?), v. t. [Pref. beÏ + ray to defile.] To make foul; to soil; to defile. [Obs.] Milton.

ØBerbe (?), n. [Cf. Berber, Barb a Barbary horse.] (Zo"l.) An African genet (Genetta pardina). See Genet.

Berber (?), n. [See Barbary.] A member of a race somewhat resembling the Arabs, but often classed as Hamitic, who were formerly the inhabitants of the whole of North Africa from the Mediterranean southward into the Sahara, and who still occupy a large part of that region; Ð called also Kabyles. Also, the language spoken by this people.

Berberïne (?), n. (Chem.) An alkaloid obtained, as a bitter, yellow substance, from the root of the barberry, gold thread, and other plants.

Berberïry (?), n. See Barberry.

Berdash (?), n. A kind of neckcloth. [Obs.]

A treatise against the cravat and berdash. Steele.

Bere (?), v. t. [Cf. OIcel. berja to strike.] To pierce. [Obs.] Chaucer.

Bere, n. See Bear, barley. [Scot.]

Beïreave (?), v. t. [imp. & p.p. Bereaved (?), Bereft (?); p. pr. & vb. n. Bereaving.] [OE. bireven, AS. bere fian. See Beï, and Reave.]

To make destitute; to deprive; to strip; Ð with of before the person or thing taken away.

Madam, you have bereft me of all words. Shak.
Bereft of him who taught me how to sing. Tickell.

To take away from. [Obs.]

All your interest in those territories
Is utterly bereft you; all is lost. Shak.

To take away. [Obs.]

Shall move you to bereave my life. Marlowe.

μ The imp. and past pple. form bereaved is not used in reference to immaterial objects. We say bereaved or bereft by death of a relative, bereft of hope and strength.

Syn. Ð To dispossess; to divest.

Beïreavement (?), n. The state of being bereaved; deprivation; esp., the loss of a relative by death.

Beïreaver (?), n. One who bereaves.

Beïreft (?), imp. & p. p. of Bereave.

Beïretta (?), n. Same as Berretta.

Berg (?), n. [?95. See Barrow hill, and cf. Iceberg.] A large mass or hill, as of ice.

Glittering bergs of ice. Tennyson.

Bergaïmot (?), n. [F. bergamote, fr. It. bergamotta; prob. a corruption of Turk. beg arm?di a lord's pear.] 1. (Bot.) (a) A tree of the Orange family (Citrus bergamia), having a roundish or pearïshaped fruit, from the rind of which an essential oil of delicious odor is extracted, much prized as a perfume. Also, the fruit. (b) A variety of mint (Mentha aquatica, var. glabrata).

The essence or perfume made from the fruit.

A variety of pear. Johnson.

A variety of snuff perfumed with bergamot.

The better hand ... gives the nose its bergamot. Cowper.

A coarse tapestry, manufactured from flock of cotton or hemp, mixed with ox's or goat's hair; Ð said to have been invented at Bergamo, Italy. Encyc. Brit.

Wild bergamot (Bot.), an American herb of the Mint family (Monarda fistulosa).

Berganïder (?), n. [Berg, for burrow + gander a male goose ? Cf. G. bergente, Dan. gravgaas.] (Zo"l.) A European duck (Anas tadorna). See Sheldrake.

Bergerïet (?), n. [OF. bergerete, F. berger a shepherd.] A pastoral song. [Obs.]

Bergh (?), n. [AS. beorg.] A hill. [Obs.]

Bergmas · ter (?), n. See Barmaster.

Bergmeal (?), n. [G. berg mountain + mehl meal.] (Min.) An earthy substance, resembling fine flour. It is composed of the shells of infusoria, and in Lapland and Sweden is sometimes eaten, mixed with flour or ground birch bark, in times of scarcity. This name is also given to a white powdery variety of calcite.

Bergmote (?), n. See Barmote.

Bergoïmask (?), n. A rustic dance, so called in ridicule of the people of Bergamo, in Italy, once noted for their clownishness.

Bergylt (?), n. [Etymol. uncertain.] (Zo"l.) The Norway haddock. See Rosefish.

Beïrhyme (?), v. t. [imp. & p.p. Berhymed (?); p. pr. & vb. n. Berhyming.] To mention in rhyme or verse; to rhyme about. [Sometimes use depreciatively.] Shak.

ØBe · riïberi (?), n. [Singhalese beri weakness.] An acute disease occurring in India, characterized by multiple inflammatory changes in the nerves, producing great muscular debility, a painful rigidity of the limbs, and cachexy.

Beïrime (?), v. t. To berhyme. [The earlier and etymologically preferable spelling.]

Berkeïleian (?), a. Of or relating to Bishop Berkeley or his system of idealism; as, Berkeleian philosophy. Ð Berkeleyïism , n.

Berlin (?), n. [The capital of Prussia] 1. A fourïwheeled carriage, having a sheltered seat behind the body and separate from it, invented in the 17th century, at Berlin.

Fine worsted for fancyïwork; zephyr worsted; Ð called also Berlin wool.

Berlin black, a black varnish, drying with almost a dead surface; Ð used for coating the better kinds of ironware. Ure. Ð Berlin blue, Prussian blue. Ure. Ð Berlin green, a complex cyanide of iron, used as a green dye, and similar to Prussian blue. Ð Berlin iron, a very fusible variety of cast iron, from which figures and other delicate articles are manufactured. These are often stained or lacquered in imitation of bronze. Ð Berlin shop, a shop for the sale of worsted embroidery and the materials for such work. Ð Berlin work, worsted embroidery.

Berm Berme } (?), n. [F. berme, of German origin; cf. G. brame, br„me, border, akin to E. brim.] 1. (Fort.) A narrow shelf or path between the bottom of a parapet and the ditch.

> (Engineering) A ledge at the bottom of a bank or cutting, to catch earth that may roll down the slope, or to strengthen the bank.

Berĭmuda grass · (?). (Bot.) A kind of grass (Cynodon Dactylon) esteemed for pasture in the Southern United States. It is a native of Southern Europe, but is now wideĭspread in warm countries; Ð called also scutch grass, and in Bermuda, devil grass.

Bernaĭcle (?), n. See Barnacle.

Berna fly · (?). (Zo"l.) A Brazilian dipterous insect of the genus Trypeta, which lays its eggs in the nostrils or in wounds of man and beast, where the larv' do great injury.

Bernarĭdine (?), a. Of or pertaining to St. Bernard of Clairvaux, or to the Cistercian monks. Ð n. A Cistercian monk.

Berĭnese (?), a. Pertaining to the city o? canton of Bern, in Switzerland, or to its inhabitants. Ð n. sing. & pl. A native or natives of Bern.

Berniĭcle (?), n. [OE. bernak, bernacle; cf. OF. bernac; prob. fr. LL. bernacula for hibernicula, bernicula, fr. Hibernia; the birds coming from Hibernia o? Ireland. Cf. 1st Barnacle.] A bernicle goose. [Written also barnacle.]

Bernicle goose (Zo"l.), a goose (Branta leucopsis), of Arctic Europe and America. It was formerly believed that it hatched from the cirripeds of the sea (Lepas), which were, therefore, called barnacles, goose barnacles, or Anatifers. The name is also applied to other related species. See Anatifa and Cirripedia.

Berĭnouse (?), n. Some as Burnoose.

Beĭrob (?), v. t. To rob; to plunder. [Obs.]

ØBeroĭe (?), n. [L. Beroe, one of the Oceanid' Gr. ?: cf. F. bero,.] (Zo"l.) A small, oval, transparent jellyfish, belonging to the Ctenophora.

Berĭretta (?), n. [It., fr. LL. birrettum, berretum, a cap, dim. of L. birrus, birrum, a cloak to keep off rain, cf. Gr. ? tawny, red: cf. Sp. birreta, Pg. barrete, and E. Barret.] A square cap worn by ecclesiastics of the Roman Catholic Church. A cardinal's berretta is scarlet; that worn by other clerics is black, except that a bishop's is lined with green. [Also spelt beretta, biretta, etc.]

Berried (?), a. Furnished with berries; consisting of a berry; baccate; as, a berried shrub.

Berry (?), n.; pl. Berries. [OE. berie, AS. berie, berige; akin to D. bes, G. beere, OS. and OHG. beri, Icel. ber, Sw. b„r, Goth. basi, and perh. Skr. bhas to eat.]

> Any small fleshy fruit, as the strawberry, mulberry, huckleberry, etc.

> (Bot.) A small fruit that is pulpy or succulent throughout, having seeds loosely imbedded in the pulp, as the currant, grape, blueberry.

> The coffee bean.

> One of the ova or eggs of a fish.

Travis.

In berry, containing ova or spawn.

Berry, v. i. [imp. & p.p. Berried (?); p. pr. & vb. n. Berrying.] To bear or produce berries.

Berry, n. [AS. beorh. See Barrow a hill.] A mound; a hillock.

W. Browne.

Berrying, n. A seeking for or gathering of berries, esp. of such as grow wild.

Berserk (?), Berserkïer (?), } n. [Icel. berserkr.] 1. (Scand. Myth.) One of a class of legendary heroes, who fought frenzied by intoxicating liquors, and naked, regardless of wounds.

Longfellow.

> One who fights as if frenzied, like a Berserker.

Berstle (?), n. See Bristle. [Obs.]

Chaucer.

Berth (?), n. [From the root of bear to produce, like birth nativity. See Birth.] [Also written birth.]

> (Naut.) (a) Convenient sea room. (b) A room in which a number of the officers or ship's company mess and reside. (c) The place where a ship lies when she is at anchor, or at a wharf.

> An allotted place; an appointment; situation or employment. ½He has a good berth.„

Totten.

> A place in a ship to sleep in; a long box or shelf on the side of a cabin or stateroom, or of a railway car, for sleeping in.

Berth deck, the deck next below the lower gun deck. Ham. Nav. Encyc. Ð To give (the land or any object) a wide berth, to keep at a distance from it.

Berth, v. t. [imp. & p.p. Berthed (?); p. pr. & vb. n. Berthing.] 1. To give an anchorage to, or a place to lie at; to place in a berth; as, she was berthed stem to stern with the Adelaide.

To allot or furnish berths to, on shipboard; as, to berth a ship's company.

Totten.

Bertha (?), n. [F. berthe, fr. Berthe, a woman's name.] A kind of collar or cape worn by ladies.

Berthage (?), n. A place for mooring vessels in a dock or harbor.

Berthierlite (?), n. [From Berthier, a French naturalist.] (Min.) A double sulphide of antimony and iron, of a dark steel‖gray color.

Berthing (?), n. (Naut.) The planking outside of a vessel, above the sheer strake.

Smyth.

Bertram (?), n. [Corrupted fr. L. pyrethrum, Gr. ? a hot spicy plant, fr. ? fire.] (Bot.) Pellitory of Spain (Anacyclus pyrethrum).

<— p. 139 —>

Berylcoid (?), a. [NL. beryx, the name of the typical genus + Ioid.] (Zo"l.) Of or pertaining to the Berycid‘, a family of marine fishes.

Beryl (?), n. [F. b,ryl, OF. beril, L. beryllus, Gr. ?, prob. fr. Skr. vaid?rya. Cf. Brilliant.] (Min.) A mineral of great hardness, and, when transparent, of much beauty. It occurs in hexagonal prisms, commonly of a green or bluish green color, but also yellow, pink, and white. It is a silicate of aluminium and glucinum (beryllium). The aquamarine is a transparent, sea‖green variety used as a gem. The emerald is another variety highly prized in jewelry, and distinguished by its deep color, which is probably due to the presence of a little oxide of chromium.

Berylline (?), a. Like a beryl; of a light or bluish green color.

Beryllilum (?), n. [NL.] (Chem.) A metallic element found in the beryl. See Glucinum.

Berylloid (?), n. [Beryl + Ioid.] (Crystallog.) A solid consisting of a double twelve‖sided pyramid; Ð so called because the planes of this form occur on crystals of beryl.

Be‖saiel, Be‖saile, Be‖sayle (?), n. [OF. beseel, F. bisa‹eul, fr. L. bis twice + LL. avolus, dim. of L. avus grandfather.] 1. A great‖grandfather. [Obs.]

(Law) A kind of writ which formerly lay where a great‖grandfather died seized of lands in fee simple, and on the day of his death a stranger abated or entered and kept the heir out. This is now abolished.

Blackstone.

Be‖saint (?), v. t. To make a saint of.

Be‖sant (?), n. See Bezant.

BesÐantler (?), n. Same as BezÐantler.

Be‖scatter (?), v. t. 1. To scatter over.

To cover sparsely by scattering (something); to strew. ½With flowers bescattered.

Spenser.

Beïscorn (?), v. t. To treat with scorn. ½Then was he bescorned.͵
Chaucer.

Beïscratch (?), v. t. To tear with the nails; to cover with scratches.

Beïscrawl (?), v. t. To cover with scrawls; to scribble over.
Milton.

Beïscreen (?), v. t. To cover with a screen, or as with a screen; to shelter; to conceal.
Shak.

Beïscribble (?), v. t. To scribble over. ½Bescribbled with impertinences.͵
Milton.

Beïscumber (?), Beïscummer (?), } v. t. [Pref. beï + scumber, scummer.] To discharge ordure or dung upon. [Obs.]
B. Jonson.

Beïsee (?), v. t. & i. [AS. beseen; pref. beï + ?ecn to see.] To see; to look; to mind. [Obs.]
Wyclif.

Beïseech (?), v. t. [imp. & p.p. Besought (?); p. pr. & vb. n. Beseeching.] [OE. bisechen, biseken (akin to G. besuchen to visit); pref. beï + sechen, seken, to seek. See Seek.] 1. To ask or entreat with urgency; to supplicate; to implore.

I beseech you, punish me not with your hard thoughts.
Shak.

But Eve ... besought his peace.
Milton.

Syn. Ð To beg; to crave. Ð To Beseech, Entreat, Solicit, Implore, Supplicate. These words agree in marking that sense of want which leads men to beg some favor. To solicit is to make a request, with some degree of earnestness and repetition, of one whom we address as a superior. To entreat implies greater urgency, usually enforced by adducing reasons or arguments. To beseech is still stronger, and belongs rather to the language of poetry and imagination. To implore denotes increased fervor of entreaty, as addressed either to equals or superiors. To supplicate expresses the extreme of entreaty, and usually implies a state of deep humiliation. Thus, a captive supplicates a conqueror to spare his life. Men solicit by virtue of their interest with another; they entreat in the use of reasoning and strong representations; they beseech with importunate earnestness; they implore from a sense of overwhelming distress; they supplicate with a feeling of the most absolute inferiority and dependence.

Beïseech, n. Solicitation; supplication. [Obs. or Poetic]
Shak.

Beïseecher (?), n. One who beseeches.

Beïseeching, a. Entreating urgently; imploring; as, a beseeching look. Ð Beïseechingïly, adv. Ð Beïseechingïness, n.

Beïseechment (?), n. The act of beseeching or entreating earnestly. [R.] Goodwin.

Beïseek (?), v. t. To beseech. [Obs.] Chaucer.

Beïseem (?), v. t. [imp. & p.p. Beseemed (?); p. pr. & vb. n. Beseeming.] [Pref. beï + seem.] Literally: To appear or seem (well, ill, best, etc.) for (one) to do or to have. Hence: To be fit, suitable, or proper for, or worthy of; to become; to befit.

A duty well beseeming the preachers.
Clarendon.

What form of speech or behavior beseemeth us, in our prayers to God ?
Hocker.

Beïseem, v. i. To seem; to appear; to be fitting. [Obs.] ½As beseemed best.
Spenser.

Beïseeming, n. 1. Appearance; look; garb. [Obs.]
I ... did company these three in poor beseeming.
Shak.

Comeliness.

Baret.

Beïseeming, a. Becoming; suitable. [Archaic] Đ Beïseemingĭly, adv. Đ Beïseemingĭness, n.

Beïseemly, a. Fit; suitable; becoming. [Archaic]
In beseemly order sitten there.
Shenstone.

Beïseen (?), a. [Properly the p. p. of besee.]

Seen; appearing. [Obs. or Archaic]

Decked or adorned; clad. [Archaic]

Chaucer.

Accomplished; versed. [Archaic]

Spenser.

Beïset (?), v. t. [imp. & p.p. Beset; p. pr. & vb. n. Besetting.] [AS. besettan (akin to OHG. bisazjan, G. besetzen, D. bezetten); pref. beï + settan to set. See Set.] 1. To set or stud (anything) with ornaments or prominent objects.

A robe of azure beset with drops of gold.
Spectator.

The garden is so beset with all manner of sweet shrubs that it perfumes the air.
Evelyn.

To hem in; to waylay; to surround; to besiege; to blockade. ½Beset with foes.

Milton.
Let thy troops beset our gates.
Addison.

To set upon on all sides; to perplex; to harass; Ð said of dangers, obstacles, etc. ½Adam, sore beset, replied. Milton. ½Beset with ills. Addison. ½Incommodities which beset old age. Burke.

To occupy; to employ; to use up. [Obs.]

Chaucer.
Syn. Ð To surround; inclose; environ; hem in; besiege; encircle; encompass; embarrass; urge; press.

Beïsetment (?), n. The act of besetting, or the state of being beset; also, that which besets one, as a sin. ½Fearing a besetment.
Kane.

Beïsetter (?), n. One who, or that which, besets.

Beïsetting, a. Habitually attacking, harassing, or pressing upon or about; as, a besetting sin.

Beïshine (?), v. t. [imp. & p.p. Beshone; p. pr. & vb. n. Beshining.] To shine upon; to ullumine.

ØBeïshow (?), n. [Native name.] (Zo"l.) A large food fish (Anoplopoma fimbria) of the north Pacific coast; Ð called also candlefish.

Beïshrew (?), v. t. To curse; to execrate.
Beshrew me, but I love her heartily.
Shak.

µ Often a very mild form of imprecation; sometimes so far from implying a curse, as to be uttered coaxingly, nay even with some tenderness.
Schmidt.

Beïshroud (?), v. t. To cover with, or as with, a shroud; to screen.

Beïshut (?), v. t. To shut up or out. [Obs.]

Beïside (?), prep. [OE. biside, bisiden, bisides, prep. and adv., beside, besides; pref. beï by + side. Cf. Besides, and see Side, n.] 1. At the side of; on one side of. ½Beside him hung his bow.
Milton.

Aside from; out of the regular course or order of; in a state of deviation from; out of.

[You] have done enough
To put him quite beside his patience.
Shak.

Over and above; distinct from; in addition to. [In this use besides is now commoner.]

Wise and learned men beside those whose names are in the Christian records.

Addison.

To be beside one's self, to be out ob one's wits or senses.

Paul, thou art beside thyself.

Acts xxvi. 24.

Syn. Ð Beside, Besides. These words, whether used as prepositions or adverbs, have been considered strictly synonymous, from an early period of our literature, and have been freely interchanged by our best writers. There is, however, a tendency, in present usage, to make the following distinction between them: 1. That beside be used only and always as a preposition, with the original meaning ½by the side of; ˳ as, to sit beside a fountain; or with the closely allied meaning ½aside from˳, ½apart from˳, or ½out of˳; as, this is beside our present purpose; to be beside one's self with joy. The adverbial sense to be wholly transferred to the cognate word. 2. That besides, as a preposition, take the remaining sense ½in addition to˳, as, besides all this; besides the considerations here offered. ½There was a famine in the land besides the first famine.˳ Gen. xxvi. 1. And that it also take the adverbial sense of ½moreover˳, ½beyond˳, etc., which had been divided between the words; as, besides, there are other considerations which belong to this case. The following passages may serve to illustrate this use of the words: Ð

Lovely Thais sits beside thee.

Dryden.

Only be patient till we have appeased
The multitude, beside themselves with fear.

Shak.

It is beside my present business to enlarge on this speculation.

Locke.

Besides this, there are persons in certain situations who are expected to be charitable.

Bp. Porteus.

And, besides, the Moor
May unfold me to him; there stand I in much peril.

Shak.

That man that does not know those things which are of necessity for him to know is but an ignorant man, whatever he may know besides.

Tillotson.

See Moreover.

Beïsides (?), Beïside (?), } adv. [OE. Same as beside, prep.; the ending Ïs is an adverbial one, prop. a genitive sign.] 1. On one side. [Obs.]

Chaucer. Shak.

More than that; over and above; not included in the number, or in what has been mentioned; moreover; in addition.

The men said unto Lot, Hast thou here any besides ?
Gen. xix. 12.
To all beside, as much an empty shade,
An Eugene living, as a C'sar dead.
Pope.

µ These sentences may be considered as elliptical.

Be‖sides (?), prep. Over and above; separate or distinct from; in addition to; other than; else than. See Beside, prep., 3, and Syn. under Beside.

Besides your cheer, you shall have sport.
Shak.

Be‖siege (?), v. t. [imp. & p.p. Besieged (?); p. pr. & vb. n. Besieging.] [OE. bisegen; pref. be‖ + segen to siege. See Siege.] To beset or surround with armed forces, for the purpose of compelling to surrender; to lay s?ege to; to beleaguer; to beset.

Till Paris was besieged, famished, and lost.
Shak.

Syn. Ð To environ; hem in; invest; encompass.

Be‖siegement (?), n. The act of besieging, or the state of being besieged.
Golding.

Be‖sieger (?), n. One who besieges; Ð opposed to the besieged.

Be‖sieging (?), a. That besieges; laying siege to. Ð Be‖siegingĭly, adv.

Be‖sit (?), v. t. [Pref. be‖ + sit.] To suit; to fit; to become. [Obs.]

Be‖slabber (?), v. t. To beslobber.

Be‖slave (?), v. t. To enslave. [Obs.]
Bp. Hall.

Be‖slaver (?), v. t. [imp. & p.p. Beslavered (?); p. pr. & vb. n. Beslavering.] To defile with slaver; to beslobber.

Be‖slime (?), v. t. To daub with slime; to soil. [Obs.]
B. Jonson.

Be‖slobber (?), v. t. To slobber on; to smear with spittle running from the mouth. Also Fig.: as, to beslobber with praise.

Be‖slubber (?), v. t. To beslobber.

Be‖smear (?), v. t. [imp. & p.p. Besmeared (?); p. pr. & vb. n. Besmearing.] To smear with any viscous, glutinous matter; to bedaub; to soil.

Besmeared with precious balm.
Spenser.

Be‖smearer (?), n. One that besmears.

Be‖smirch (?), v. t. [imp. & p.p. Besmirched (?); p. pr. & vb. n. Besmirching.] To smirch or soil; to disoolor; to obscure. Hence: To dishonor; to sully.
Shak.

Be‖smoke (?), v. t. 1. To foul with smoke.

To harden or dry in smoke.

Johnson.

Beïsmut (?), v. t. [imp. & p.p. Besmutted; p. pr. & vb. n. Besmutting.] [Pref. beï + smut: cf. AS. besmÆtan, and also OE. besmotren.] To blacken with smut; to foul with soot.

Beïsnow (?), v. t. [imp. & p.p. Besnowed (?).] [OE. bisnewen, AS. besnÆwan; pref. beï + snÆwan to snow.] 1. To scatter ? snow; to cover thick, as with snow flakes. [R.]

Gower.

To cover with snow; to whiten with snow, or as with snow.

Beïsnuff (?), v. t. To befoul with snuff.

Young.

Beïsogne (?), n. [F. bisogne.] A worthless fellow; a bezonian. [Obs.]

Besom (?), n. [OE. besme, besum, AS. besma; akin to D. bezem, OHG pesamo, G. besen; of uncertain origin.] A brush of twigs for sweeping; a broom; anything which sweeps away or destroys. [Archaic or Fig.]

I will sweep it with the besom of destruction.

Isa. xiv. 23.

The housemaid with her besom.

W. Irving.

Besom, v. t. [imp. & p.p. Besomed (?).] To sweep, as with a besom. [Archaic or Poetic]

Cowper.

Rolls back all Greece, and besoms wide the plain.

Barlow.

Besomïer (?), n. One who uses a besom. [Archaic]

Beïsort (?), v. t. To assort or be congruous with; to fit, or become. [Obs.]

Such men as may besort your age.

Shak.

Beïsort, n. Befitting associates or attendants. [Obs.]

With such accommodation and besort

As levels with her breeding.

Shak.

Beïsot (?), v. t. [imp. & p.p. Besotted (?); p. pr. & vb. n. Besotting.] To make sottish; to make dull or stupid; to stupefy; to infatuate.

Fools besotted with their crimes.

Hudibras.

Beïsotted, a. Made sottish, senseless, or infatuated; characterized by drunken stupidity, or by infatuation; stupefied. ½Besotted devotion.„ Sir W. Scott. Ð Beïsottedïly, adv. Ð Beïsottedïness, n.

Milton.

Beïsottingïly, adv. In a besotting manner.

Beïsought (?), p. p. of Beseech.

Beïspangle (?), v. t. [imp. & p.p. Bespangled (?); p. pr. & vb. n. Bespangling (?).] To adorn with spangles; to dot or sprinkle with something brilliant or glittering.

The grass ... is all bespangled with dewdrops.
Cowper.

Beïspatter (?), v. t. [imp. & p.p. Bespattered (?); p. pr. & vb. n. Bespattering.] 1. To soil by spattering; to sprinkle, esp. with dirty water, mud, or anything which will leave foul spots or stains.

To asperse with calumny or reproach.

Whom never faction could bespatter.
Swift.

Beïspawl (?), v. t. To daub, soil, or make foul with spawl or spittle. [Obs.] Milton.

Beïspeak (?), v. t. [imp. Bespoke (?), Bespake (Archaic); p. p. Bespoke, Bespoken (?); p. pr. & vb. n. Bespeaking.] [OE. bispeken, AS. besprecan, to speak to, accuse; pref. beï + sprecan to speak. See Speak.] 1. To speak or arrange for beforehand; to order or engage against a future time; as, to bespeak goods, a right, or a favor.

Concluding, naturally, that to gratify his avarice was to bespeak his favor.
Sir W. Scott.

To show beforehand; to foretell; to indicate.

[They] bespoke dangers ... in order to scare the allies.
Swift.

To betoken; to show; to indicate by external marks or appearances.

When the abbot of St. Martin was born, he had so little the figure of a man that it bespoke him rather a monster.
Locke.

To speak to; to address. [Poetic]

He thus the queen bespoke.
Dryden.

Beïspeak, v. i. To speak. [Obs.]
Milton.

Beïspeak, n. A bespeaking. Among actors, a benefit (when a particular play is bespoken.) ½The night of her bespeak.
Dickens.

Beïspeaker (?), n. One who bespeaks.

Beïspeckle (?), v. t. [imp. & p.p. Bespeckled (?); p. pr. & vb. n. Bespeckling.] To mark with speckles or spots.

Milton.

Bespew (?), v. t. To soil or daub with spew; to vomit on.

Bespice (?), v. t. To season with spice, or with some spicy drug. Shak.

Bespirt (?), v. t. Same as Bespurt.

<— p. 140 —>
<— p. 140 —>

Bespit (?), v. t. [imp. Bespit; p. p. Bespit, Bespitten (?); p. pr. & vb. n. Bespitting.] To daub or soil with spittle.

Johnson.

Bespoke (?), imp. & p.p. of Bespeak.

Bespot (?), v. t. [imp. & p.p. Bespotted (?); p. pr. & vb. n. Bespotting.] To mark with spots, or as with spots.

Bespread (?), v. t. [imp. & p.p. Bespread; p. pr. & vb. n. Bespreading.] To spread or cover over.

The carpet which bespread
His rich pavilion's floor.

 Glover.

Besprent (?), p. p. [OE. bespreynt, p. p. of besprengen, bisprengen, to besprinkle, AS. besprengan, akin to D. & G. besprengen; pref. beï + sprengan to sprinkle. See Sprinkle.] Sprinkled over; strewed.

His face besprent with liquid crystal shines.

Shenstone.

The floor with tassels of fir was besprent.

Longfellow.

Besprinkle (?), v. t. [imp. & p.p. Besprinkled (?); p. pr. & vb. n. Besprinkling (?).] To sprinkle over; to scatter over.

The bed besprinkles, and bedews the ground.

Dryden.

Besprinkler (?), n. One who, or that which, besprinkles.

Besprinkling (?), n. The act of sprinkling anything; a sprinkling over.

Bespurt (?), v. t. To spurt on or over; to asperse. [Obs.]

Milton.

Bessemer steel · (?). Steel made directly from cast iron, by burning out a portion of the carbon and other impurities that the latter contains, through the agency of a blast of air which is forced through the molten metal; Ð so called from Sir Henry Bessemer, an English engineer, the inventor of the process.

Best (?), a.; superl. of Good. [AS. besta, best, contr. from betest, betst, betsta; akin to Goth. batists, OHG. pezzisto, G. best, beste, D. best, Icel. beztr, Dan. best, Sw. b„st. This word has no connection in origin with good. See Better.] 1. Having good qualities in the highest degree; most good, kind, desirable, suitable, etc.; most excellent; as, the best man; the best road; the best cloth; the best abilities.

When he is best, he is a little worse than a man.
Shak.
Heaven's last, best gift, my ever new delight.
Milton.

<small>Most advanced; most correct or complete; as, the best scholar; the best view of a subject.</small>

<small>Most; largest; as, the best part of a week.</small>

Best man, the only or principal groomsman at a wedding ceremony.

Best, n. Utmost; highest endeavor or state; most nearly perfect thing, or being, or action; as, to do one's best; to the best of our ability.

At best, in the utmost degree or extent applicable to the case; under the most favorable circumstances; as, life is at best very short. Ð For best, finally. [Obs.] ½Those constitutions ... are now established for best, and not to be mended.„ Milton. Ð To get the best of, to gain an advantage over, whether fairly or unfairly. Ð To make the best of. (a) To improve to the utmost; to use or dispose of to the greatest advantage. ½Let there be freedom to carry their commodities where they can make the best of them.„ Bacon. (b) To reduce to the least possible inconvenience; as, to make the best of ill fortune or a bad bargain.

Best, adv.; superl. of Well. 1. In the highest degree; beyond all others. ½Thou serpent ! That name best befits thee.„
Milton.
He prayeth best, who loveth best
All things both great and small.
Coleridge.

<small>To the most advantage; with the most success, case, profit, benefit, or propriety.</small>

Had we best retire? I see a storm.
Milton.
Had I not best go to her?
Thackeray.

<small>Most intimately; most thoroughly or correctly; as, what is expedient is best known to himself.</small>

Best, v. t. To get the better of. [Colloq.]
Beïstad (?), imp. & p. p. of Bestead. Beset; put in peril. [Obs.]
Chaucer.
Beïstain (?), v. t. To stain.
Beïstar (?), v. t. [imp. & p.p. Bestarred (?).] To sprinkle with, or as with, stars; to decorate with, or as with, stars; to bestud. ½Bestarred with anemones.„
W. Black.

Bestead (?), v. t. [imp. & p.p. Bestead or Bested, also (Obs.) Bestad. In sense 3 imp. also Besteaded.] [Pref. be- + stead a place.] 1. To put in a certain situation or condition; to circumstance; to place. [Only in p. p.]

They shall pass through it, hardly bestead and hungry: ... and curse their king and their God.

Is. viii. 21.

Many far worse bestead than ourselves.

Barrow.

To put in peril; to beset. [Only in p. p.]

Chaucer.

To serve; to assist; to profit; to avail.

Milton.

Bestial (?), a. [F. bestial, L. bestialis, fr. bestia beast. See Beast.] 1. Belonging to a beast, or to the class of beasts.

Among the bestial herds to range.

Milton.

Having the qualities of a beast; brutal; below the dignity of reason or humanity; irrational; carnal; beastly; sensual.

Shak.

Syn. Ð Brutish; beastly; brutal; carnal; vile; low; depraved; sensual; filthy.

Bestial, n. A domestic animal; also collectively, cattle; as, other kinds of bestial. [Scot.]

Bestiality (?), n. [F. bestialit,.] 1. The state or quality of being bestial.

Unnatural connection with a beast.

Bestialize (?), v. t. [imp. & p.p. Bestialized (?); p. pr. & vb. n. Bestializing.] To make bestial, or like a beast; to degrade; to brutalize.

The process of bestializing humanity.

Hare.

Bestially, adv. In a bestial manner.

Bestick (?), v. t. [imp. & p.p. Bestuck (?); p. pr. & vb. n. Besticking.] To stick over, as with sharp points pressed in; to mark by infixing points or spots here and there; to pierce.

Truth shall retire
Bestuck with slanderous darts.

Milton.

Bestill (?), v. t. To make still.

Bestir (?), v. t. [imp. & p.p. Bestirred (?); p. pr. & vb. n. Bestirring.] To put into brisk or vigorous action; to move with life and vigor; Ð usually with the reciprocal pronoun.

You have so bestirred your valor.
Shak.
Rouse and bestir themselves ere well awake.
Milton.
Bestorm (?), v. i. & t. To storm.
Young.
Bestow (?), v. t. [imp. & p.p. Bestowed (?); p. pr. & vb. n. Bestowing.] [OE. bestowen; pref. be + stow a place. See Stow.] 1. To lay up in store; to deposit for safe keeping; to stow; to place; to put. ½He bestowed it in a pouch.
Sir W. Scott.
See that the women are bestowed in safety.
Byron.

To use; to apply; to devote, as time or strength in some occupation.

To expend, as money. [Obs.]

To give or confer; to impart; Đ with on or upon.

Empire is on us bestowed.
Cowper.
Though I bestow all my goods to feed the poor.
1 Cor. xiii. 3.

To give in marriage.

I could have bestowed her upon a fine gentleman.
Tatler.

To demean; to conduct; to behave; Đ followed by a reflexive pronoun. [Obs.]

How might we see Falstaff bestow himself tonight in his true colors, and not ourselves be seen?
Shak.
Syn. Đ To give; grant; present; confer; accord.
Bestowal (?), n. The act of bestowing; disposal.
Bestower (?), n. One that bestows.
Bestowment (?), n. 1. The act of giving or bestowing; a conferring or bestowal.
If we consider this bestowment of gifts in this view.
Chauncy.

That which is given or bestowed.

They almost refuse to give due praise and credit to God's own bestowments.
I. Taylor.

Beïstraddle (?), v. t. To bestride.

Beïstraught (?), a. [Pref. beï + straught; prob. here used for distraught.] Out of one's senses; distracted; mad. [Obs.]

Shak.

Beïstreak (?), v. t. To streak.

Beïstrew (?), v. t. [imp. Bestrewed (?); p. p. Bestrewed, Bestrown (?); p. pr. & vb. n. Bestrewing.] To strew or scatter over; to besprinkle. [Spelt also bestrow.]

Milton.

Beïstride (?), v. t. [imp. Bestrode (?), (Obs. or R.) Bestrid (?); p. p. Bestridden (?), Bestrid, Bestrode; p. pr. & vb. n. Bestriding.] [AS. bestrÆdan; pref. beï + strÆdan to stride.] 1. To stand or sit with anything between the legs, or with the legs astride; to stand over

That horse that thou so often hast bestrid.

Shak.

Why, man, he doth bestride the narrow world
Like a Colossus.

Shak.

To step over; to stride over or across; as, to bestride a threshold.

Beïstrode (?), imp. & p. p. of Bestride.

Beïstrown (?), p. p. of Bestrew.

Beïstuck (?), imp. & p. p. Bestick.

Beïstud (?), v. t. [imp. & p.p. Bestudded; p. pr. & vb. n. Bestudding.] To set or adorn, as with studs or bosses; to set thickly; to stud; as, to bestud with stars.

Milton.

Beïswike, v. t. [AS. beswÆcan; beï + swÆcan to deceive, entice; akin to OS. swÆkan, OHG. swÆhhan, Icel. svÆkja.] To lure; to cheat. [Obs.]

Gower.

Bet (?), n. [Prob. from OE. abet abetting, OF. abet, fr. abeter to excite, incite. See Abet.] That which is laid, staked, or pledged, as between two parties, upon the event of a contest or any contingent issue; the act of giving such a pledge; a wager. ½Having made his bets.„

Goldsmith.

Bet, v. t. [imp. & p.p. Bet, Betted (?); p. pr. & vb. n. Betting.] To stake or pledge upon the event of a contingent issue; to wager.

John a Gaunt loved him well, and betted much money on his head.

Shak.

I'll bet you two to one I'll make him do it.

O. W. Holmes.

Bet, imp. & p. p. of Beat. [Obs.]

Bet, a. & adv. An early form of Better. [Obs.]

To go bet, to go fast; to hurry. [Obs.]
Chaucer.

Beta̤line (?), n. [From beta, generic name of the beet.] (Chem.) A nitrogenous base, C5H11NO2, produced artificially, and also occurring naturally in beetroot molasses and its residues, from which it is extracted as a white crystalline substance; Ð called also lycine and oxyneurine. It has a sweetish taste.

Be̤Itake (?), v. t. [imp. Betook (?); p. p. Betaken (?); p. pr. & vb. n. Betaking.] [Pref. be̤I + take.] 1. To take or seize. [Obs.]
Spenser.

To have recourse to; to apply; to resort; to go; Ð with a reflexive pronoun.

They betook themselves to treaty and submission.
Burke.
The rest, in imitation, to like arms
Betook them.
Milton.
Whither shall I betake me, where subsist ?
Milton.

To commend or intrust to; to commit to. [Obs.]

Be̤Itaught (?), a. [P. p. of OE. bitechen, AS. bet?can, to assign, deliver. See Teach.] Delivered; committed in trust. [Obs.]

Bete (?), v. t. To better; to mend. See Beete. [Obs.]
Chaucer.

Be̤Iteela (?), n. [Pg. beatilha.] An East India muslin, formerly used for cravats, veils, etc. [Obs.]

Be̤Iteem (?), v. t. [Pref. be̤I + an old verb teem to be fitting; cf. D. betamen to beseem, G. ziemen, Goth. gatiman, and E. tame. See Tame, a.] 1. To give ; to bestow; to grant; to accord; to consent. [Obs.]
   Spenser. Milton.

To allow; to permit; to suffer. [Obs.]

So loving to my mother,
That he might not beteem the winds of heaven
Visit her face too roughly.
Shak.

Betel (?), n. [Pg., fr. Tamil vettilei, prop. meaning, a mere leaf.] (Bot.) A species of pepper (Piper betle), the leaves of which are chewed, with the areca or betel nut and a little shell lime, by the inhabitants of the East Indies. I is a woody climber with ovate manynerved leaves.

Betelĭguese (?), n. [F. B,telgeuse, of Arabic origin.] (Astron.) A bright star of the first magnitude, near one shoulder of Orion. [Written also Betelgeux and Betelgeuse.]

Betel nut · (?). The nutlike seed of the areca palm, chewed in the East with betel leaves (whence its name) and shell lime.

ØB^te noire (?). [Fr., lit. black beast.] Something especially hated or dreaded; a bugbear.

Bethĭabaĭra wood · (?). (Bot.) A highly elastic wood, used for fishing rods, etc. The tree is unknown, but it is thought to be East Indian.

Bethel (?), n. [Heb. b?thĭel house of God.]

A place of worship; a hallowed spot.

S. F. Adams.

A chapel for dissenters. [Eng.]

A house of worship for seamen.

Beĭthink (?), v. t. [imp. & p.p. Bethought (?); p. pr. & vb. n. Bethinking.] [AS. be?encan; pref. beĭ + ?encan to think. See Think.] To call to mind; to recall or bring to recollection, reflection, or consideration; to think; to consider; Ð generally followed by a reflexive pronoun, often with of or that before the subject of thought.

I have bethought me of another fault.

Shak.

The rest ... may ... bethink themselves, and recover.

Milton.

We bethink a means to break it off.

Shak.

Syn. Ð To recollect; remember; reflect.

Beĭthink, v. i. To think; to recollect; to consider. ½Bethink ere thou dismiss us.͵

Byron.

Bethleĭhem (?), n. [Heb. b?thĭlekhem house of food; b?th house + lekhem food, 1¾kham to eat. Formerly the name of a hospital for the insane, in London, which had been the priory of St. Mary of Bethlehem. Cf. Bedlam.] 1. A hospital for lunatics; Ð corrupted into bedlam.

(Arch.) In the Ethiopic church, a small building attached to a church edifice, in which the bread for the eucharist is made.

Audsley.

Bethleĭhemĭite (?), Bethlemĭite (?), } n. 1. An inhabitant of Bethlehem in Judea.

An insane person; a madman; a bedlamite.

One of an extinct English order of monks.

Bethought (?), imp. & p. p. of Bethink.
Bethrall (?), v. t. To reduce to thralldom; to inthrall. [Obs.]
Spenser.
Bethumb (?), v. t. To handle; to wear or soil by handling; as books.
Poe.
Bethump (?), v. t. [imp. & p.p. Bethumped (?), or Bethumpt; p. pr. & vb. n. Bethumping.] To beat or thump soundly.
Shak.
Betide (?), v. t. [imp. & p.p. Betided (?), Obs. Betid (?); p. pr. & vb. n. Betiding.] [OE. bitiden; pref. bi, be + tiden, fr. AS. tÆdan, to happen, fr. tÆd time. See Tide.] To happen to; to befall; to come to ; as, woe betide the wanderer.
What will betide the few ?
Milton.
Betide, v. i. To come to pass; to happen; to occur.
A salve for any sore that may betide.
Shak.
μ Shakespeare has used it with of. ½What would betide of me ?
Betime (?), Betimes (?), } adv. [Pref. be (for by) + time; that is, by the proper time. The Is is an adverbial ending.] 1. In good season or time; before it is late; seasonably; early.
To measure life learn thou betimes.
Milton.
To rise betimes is often harder than to do all the day's work.
Barrow.

In a short time; soon; speedily; forth with.

He tires betimes that spurs too fast betimes.
Shak.
Betitle (?), v. t. To furnish with a title or titles; to entitle. [Obs.]
Carlyle.
Betoken (?), v. t. [imp. & p.p. Betokened (?); p. pr. & vb. n. Betokening.] 1. To signify by some visible object; to show by signs or tokens.
A dewy cloud, and in the cloud a bow ...
Betokening peace from God, and covenant new.
Milton.

To foreshow by present signs; to indicate something future by that which is seen or known; as, a dark cloud often betokens a storm.

Syn. Ð To presage; portend; indicate; mark; note.

ØB, ·ton (?), n. [F. b,ton, fr. L. bitumen bitumen.] (Masonry) The French name for concrete; hence, concrete made after the French fashion.

Be͡tongue (?), v. t. To attack with the tongue; to abuse; to insult.

Betoŏny (?), n.; pl. Betonies (?). [OE. betony, betany, F. betoine, fr. L. betonica, vettonica.] (Bot.) A plant of the genus Betonica (Linn.).

µ The purple or wood betony (B. officinalis, Linn.) is common in Europe, being formerly used in medicine, and (according to Loudon) in dyeing wool a yellow color.

Be͡took (?), imp. of Betake.

Be͡torn (?), a. Torn in pieces; tattered.

Be͡toss (?), v. t. [imp. & p.p. Betossed (?).] To put in violent motion; to agitate; to disturb; to toss. ½My betossed soul.

Shak.

Be͡trap (?), v. t. [imp. & p.p. Betrapped (?).] 1. To draw into, or catch in, a trap; to in? snare; to circumvent.

Gower.

To put trappings on; to clothe; to deck.

After them followed two other chariots covered with red satin, and the horses betrapped with the same.

Stow.

<— p. 141 —>

Be͡tray (?), v. t. [imp. & p.p. Betrayed (?); p. pr. & vb. n. Betraying.] [OE. betraien, bitraien; pref. be͡ + OF. tra‹r to bertray, F. trahir, fr. L. tradere. See Traitor.] 1. To deliver into the hands of an enemy by treachery or fraud, in violation of trust; to give up treacherously or faithlessly; as, an officer betrayed the city.

Jesus said unto them, The Son of man shall be betrayed into the hands of men.

Matt. xvii. 22.

To prove faithless or treacherous to, as to a trust or one who trusts; to be false to; to deceive; as, to betray a person or a cause.

But when I rise, I shall find my legs betraying me.

Johnson.

To violate the confidence of, by disclosing a secret, or that which one is bound in honor not to make known.

Willing to serve or betray any government for hire.

Macaulay.

To disclose or discover, as something which prudence would conceal; to reveal unintentionally.

Be swift to hear, but cautious of your tongue, lest you betray your ignorance.

T. Watts.

To mislead; to expose to inconvenience not foreseen to lead into error or sin.

Genius ... often betrays itself into great errors.

T. Watts.

To lead astray, as a maiden; to seduce (as under promise of marriage) and then abandon.

To show or to indicate; Ð said of what is not obvious at first, or would otherwise be concealed.

All the names in the country betray great antiquity.

Bryant.

Beïtrayal (?) n. The act or the result of betraying.

Beïtrayer (?), n. One who, or that which, betrays.

Beïtrayment (?), n. Betrayal. [R.]

Udall.

Beïtrim (?), v. t. [imp. & p.p. Betrimmed (?); p. pr. & vb. n. Betrimming.] To set in order; to adorn; to deck, to embellish; to trim.

Shak.

Beïtroth (?), v. t. [imp. & p.p. Betrothed (?); p. pr. & vb. n. Betrothing.] [Pref. beï + troth, i. e., truth. See Truth.] 1. To contract to any one for a marriage; to engage or promise in order to marriage; to affiance; Ð used esp. of a woman.

He, in the first flower of my freshest age,
Betrothed me unto the only heir.

Spenser.

Ay, and we are betrothed.

Shak.

To promise to take (as a future spouse); to plight one's troth to.

What man is there that hath betrothed a wife, and hath not taken her?

Deut. xx. 7.

To nominate to a bishopric, in order to consecration.

Ayliffe.

Beïtrothal (?), n. The act of betrothing, or the fact of being betrothed; a mutual promise, engagement, or contract for a future marriage between the persons betrothed; betrothment; affiance. ½The feast of betrothal.„

Longfellow.

Beïtrothment (?), n. The act of betrothing, or the state of being betrothed; betrothal.

Beïtrust (?), v. t. To trust or intrust. [Obs.]

Beïtrustment (?), n. The act of intrusting, or the thing intrusted. [Obs.] Chipman.

ØBetso (?), n. [It. bezzo.] A small brass Venetian coin. [Obs.]

Better (?), a.; compar. of Good. [OE. betere, bettre, and as adv. bet, AS. betera, adj., and bet, adv.; akin to Icel. betri, adj., betr, adv., Goth. batiza, adj., OHG. bezziro, adj., baz, adv., G. besser, adj. and adv., bass, adv., E. boot, and prob. to Skr. bhadra excellent. See Boot advantage, and cf. Best, Batful.] 1. Having good qualities in a greater degree than another; as, a better man; a better physician; a better house; a better air.

Could make the worse appear
The better reason.
Milton.

Preferable in regard to rank, value, use, fitness, acceptableness, safety, or in any other respect.

To obey is better than sacrifice.
1 Sam. xv. 22.
It is better to trust in the Lord than to put confidence in princes.
Ps. cxviii. 9.

Greater in amount; larger; more.

Improved in health; less affected with disease; as, the patient is better.

More advanced; more perfect; as, upon better acquaintance; a better knowledge of the subject.

All the better. See under All, adv. Ð Better half, an expression used to designate one's wife.

My dear, my better half (said he),
I find I must now leave thee.
Sir P. Sidney.

Ð To better off, to be in a better condition. Ð Had better. (See under Had) The phrase had better, followed by an infinitive without to, is idiomatic. The earliest form of construction was ½were better‚ with a dative; as, ½Him were better go beside.‚ (Gower.) i. e., It would be better for him, etc. At length the nominative (I, he, they, etc.) supplanted the dative and had took the place of were. Thus we have the construction now used.

By all that's holy, he had better starve
Than but once think this place becomes thee not.
Shak.

Better, n. 1. Advantage, superiority, or victory; Ð usually with of; as, to get the better of an enemy.

One who has a claim to precedence; a superior, as in merit, social standing, etc.; Ð usually in the plural.

Their betters would hardly be found.
Hooker.

For the better, in the way of improvement; so as to produce improvement.
½If I have altered him anywhere for the better.͵
Dryden.

Better, adv.; compar. of Well. 1. In a superior or more excellent manner; with more skill and wisdom, courage, virtue, advantage, or success; as, Henry writes better than John; veterans fight better than recruits.

I could have better spared a better man.
Shak.

More correctly or thoroughly.

The better to understand the extent of our knowledge.
Locke.

In a higher or greater degree; more; as, to love one better than another.

Never was monarch better feared, and loved.
Shak.

More, in reference to value, distance, time, etc.; as, ten miles and better. [Colloq.]

To think better of (any one), to have a more favorable opinion of any one. Ð To think better of (an opinion, resolution, etc.), to reconsider and alter one's decision.

Better (?), v. t. [imp. & p.p. Bettered (?); p. pr. & vb. n. Bettering.] [AS. beterian, betrian, fr. betera better. See Better, a.] 1. To improve or ameliorate; to increase the good qualities of.

Love betters what is best.
Wordsworth.

He thought to better his circumstances.
Thackeray.

To improve the condition of, morally, physically, financially, socially, or otherwise.

The constant effort of every man to better himself.
Macaulay.

To surpass in excellence; to exceed; to excel.

The works of nature do always aim at that which can not be bettered.
Hooker.

To give advantage to; to support; to advance the interest of. [Obs.]

Weapons more violent, when next we meet,
May serve to better us and worse our foes.
Milton.

Syn. Ð To improve; meliorate; ameliorate; mend; amend; correct; emend; reform; advance; promote.

Better, v. i. To become better; to improve.
Carlyle.

Better, n. One who bets or lays a wager.

Betterment (?), n. 1. A making better; amendment; improvement.
W. Montagu.

(Law) An improvement of an estate which renders it better than mere repairing would do; Ð generally used in the plural. [U. S.]

Bouvier.

Bettermost · (?), a. Best. [R.] ½The bettermost classes.„
Brougham.

Betteriness, n. 1. The quality of being better or superior; superiority. [R.]
Sir P. Sidney.

The difference by which fine gold or silver exceeds in fineness the standard.

ØBettong (?), n. [Native name.] (Zo"l.) A small, leaping Australian marsupial of the genus Bettongia; the jerboa kangaroo.

Bettor (?), n. One who bets; a better.
Addison.

Betty (?), n. 1. [Supposed to be a cant word, from Betty, for Elizabeth, as such an instrument is also called Bess (i. e., Elizabeth) in the Canting Dictionary of 1725, and Jenny (i. e., Jane).] A short bar used by thieves to wrench doors open. [Written also bettee.]

The powerful betty, or the artful picklock.
Arbuthnot.

[Betty, nickname for Elizabeth.] A name of contempt given to a man who interferes with the duties of women in a household, or who occupies himself with womanish matters.

A pearlshaped bottle covered round with straw, in which olive oil is sometimes brought from Italy; Ð called by chemists a Florence flask. [U. S.]

Bartlett.

Betulin (?), n. [L. betula birch tree.] (Chem.) A substance of a resinous nature, obtained from the outer bark of the common European birch (Betula alba), or from the tar prepared therefrom; Ð called also birch camphor.
Watts.

Betumble (?), v. t. [imp. & p.p. Betumbled (?).] To throw into disorder; to tumble. [R.]

From her betumbled couch she starteth.

Shak.

Beïtutor (?), v. t. [imp. & p.p. Betutored (?).] To tutor; to instruct.
Coleridge.

Beïtween (?), prep. [OE. bytwene, bitweonen, AS. betwecnan, betwecnum; prefix beï by + a form fr. AS. tw¾ two, akin to Goth. tweihnai two apiece. See Twain, and cf. Atween, Betwixt.] 1. In the space which separates; betwixt; as, New York is between Boston and Philadelphia.

> Used in expressing motion from one body or place to another; from one to another of two.

If things should go so between them.
Bacon.

> Belonging in common to two; shared by both.

Castor and Pollux with only one soul between them.
Locke.

> Belonging to, or participated in by, two, and involving reciprocal action or affecting their mutual relation; as, opposition between science and religion.

An intestine struggle, open or secret, between authority and liberty.
Hume.

> With relation to two, as involved in an act or attribute of which another is the agent or subject; as, to judge between or to choose between courses; to distinguish between you and me; to mediate between nations.

> In intermediate relation to, in respect to time, quantity, or degree; as, between nine and ten o'clock.

Between decks, the space, or in the space, between the decks of a vessel. Ð Between ourselves, Between you and me, Between themselves, in confidence; with the understanding that the matter is not to be communicated to others.

Syn. Ð Between, Among. Between etymologically indicates only two; as, a quarrel between two men or two nations; to be between two fires, etc. It is however extended to more than two in expressing a certain relation.

I ... hope that between public business, improving studies, and domestic pleasures, neither melancholy nor caprice will find any place for entrance.
Johnson.

Among implies a mass or collection of things or persons, and always supposes more than two; as, the prize money was equally divided among the ship's crew.

Beïtween, n. Intermediate time or space; interval. [Poetic & R.]
Shak.

Beïtwixt (?), prep. [OE. betwix, bitwix, rarely bitwixt, AS. betweox, betweohs, betweoh, betwÆh; pref. beï by + a form fr. AS. tw¾ two. See Between.]

In the space which separates; between.

From betwixt two aged oaks.
Milton.

From one to another of; mutually affecting.

There was some speech of marriage
Betwixt myself and her.
Shak.

Betwixt and between, in a midway position; soÏso; neither one thing nor the other. [Colloq.]

ØBeurÏr, (?), n. [F., fr. beurre butter.] (Bot.) A beurr, (or buttery) pear, one with the me?? soft and melting; Ð used with a distinguishing word; as, Beurr, d'Anjou; Beurr, Clairgeau.

Bevel (?), n. [C. F. biveau, earlier buveau, Sp. baivel; of unknown origin. Cf. Bevile.] 1. Any angle other than a right angle; the angle which one surface makes with another when they are not at right angles; the slant or inclination of such surface; as, to give a bevel to the edge of a table or a stone slab; the bevel of a piece of timber.

An instrument consisting of two rules or arms, jointed together at one end, and opening to any angle, for adjusting the surfaces of work to the same or a given inclination; Ð called also a bevel square.

Gwilt.
Bevel, a. 1. Having the slant of a bevel; slanting.

Hence: Morally distorted; not upright. [Poetic]

I may be straight, though they themselves be bevel.
Shak.

A bevel angle, any angle other than one of 90?. Ð Bevel wheel, a cogwheel whose working face is oblique to the axis.
Knight.

Bevel, v. t. [imp. & p.p. Beveled (?) or Bevelled; p. pr. & vb. n. Beveling or Bevelling.] To cut to a bevel angle; to slope the edge or surface of.

Bevel, v. i. To deviate or incline from an angle of 90?, as a surface; to slant.

Their houses are very ill built, the walls bevel.
Swift.

Beveled, Bevelled (?), a. 1. Formed to a bevel angle; sloping; as, the beveled edge of a table.

(Min.) Replaced by two planes inclining equally upon the adjacent planes, as an edge; having its edges replaces by sloping planes, as a cube or other solid.

Bevel gear · (?). (Mech.) A kind of gear in which the two wheels working together lie in different planes, and have their teeth cut at right angles to the surfaces of two cones whose apices coincide with the point where the axes of the wheels would meet.

Bevelment (?), n. (Min.) The replacement of an edge by two similar planes, equally inclined to the including faces or adjacent planes.

Bever (?), n. [OE. bever a drink, drinking time, OF. beivre, boivre, to drink, fr. L. bibere.] A light repast between meals; a lunch. [Obs.]

Beau. & Fl.

Bever, v. i. [imp. & p.p. Bevered (?).] To take a light repast between meals. [Obs.]

Beverage (?), n. [OF. bevrage, F. breuvage, fr. beivre to drink, fr. L. bibere. Cf. Bib, v. t., Poison, Potable.] 1. Liquid for drinking; drink; Ð usually applied to drink artificially prepared and of an agreeable flavor; as, an intoxicating beverage.

He knew no beverage but the flowing stream.
Thomson.

Specifically, a name applied to various kinds of drink.

A treat, or drink money. [Slang]

Bevile (?), n. [See Bevel.] (Her.) A chief broken or opening like a carpenter's bevel.

Encyc. Brit.

Beviled, Bevilled (?), a. (Her.) Notched with an angle like that inclosed by a carpenter's bevel; Ð said of a partition line of a shield.

Bevy (?), n.; pl. Bevies (?). [Perhaps orig. a drinking company, fr. OF. bev‚e (cf. It. beva) a drink, beverage; then, perh., a company in general, esp. of ladies; and last applied by sportsmen to larks, quails, etc. See Beverage.] 1. A company; an assembly or collection of persons, especially of ladies.

What a bevy of beaten slaves have we here !
Beau. & Fl.

A flock of birds, especially quails or larks; also, a herd of roes.

Bewail (?), v. t. [imp. & p.p. Bewailed (?); p. pr. & vb. n. Bewailing.] To express deep sorrow for, as by wailing; to lament; to wail over.

Hath widowed and unchilded many a one,
Which to this hour bewail the injury.
Shak.

Syn. Ð To bemoan; grieve. Ð See Deplore.

Bewail, v. i. To express grief; to lament.
Shak.

Bewailaïble (?), a. Such as may, or ought to, be bewailed; lamentable.

Bewailer (?), n. One who bewails or laments.

Bewailing, a. Wailing over; lamenting. Ð Bewailingly, adv.
Bewailment (?), n. The act of bewailing.
Bewake (?), v. t. & i. To keep watch over; to keep awake. [Obs.]
Gower.
Beware (?), v. i. [Be, imperative of verb to be + ware. See Ware, Wary.] 1. To be on one's guard; to be cautious; to take care; Ð commonly followed by of or lest before the thing that is to be avoided.

Beware of all, but most beware of man !
  Pope.
Beware the awful avalanche.
Longfellow.

To have a special regard; to heed. [Obs.]

Behold, I send an Angel before thee. ... Beware of him, and obey his voice. Ex. xxiii. 20, 21.

µ This word is a compound from be and the Old English ware, now wary, which is an adjective. ½Be ye? war of false prophetis.¸ Wyclif, Matt. vii. 15. It is used commonly in the imperative and infinitive modes, and with such auxiliaries (shall, should, must, etc.) as go with the infinitive.

<— p. 142 —>

Beware (?), v. t. To avoid; to take care of; to have a care for. [Obs.] ½Priest, beware your beard.¸
Shak.
To wish them beware the son.
Milton.
Bewash (?), v. t. To drench or souse with water. ½Let the maids bewash the men.¸
Herrick.
Beweep (?), v. t. [imp. & p.p. Bewept (?); p. pr. & vb. n. Beweeping.] [AS. bew?pan; pref. be + weep.] To weep over; to deplore; to bedew with tears. ½His timeless death beweeping.¸
Drayton.
Beweep, v. i. To weep. [Obs.]
Chaucer.
Bewet (?), v. t. [imp. & p.p. Bewet, Bewetted.] To wet or moisten.
Gay.
Bewhore (?), v. t. 1. To corrupt with regard to chastity; to make a whore of.
J. Fletcher.

To pronounce or characterize as a whore.

Shak.

Be̤wig (?), v. t. [imp. & p.p. Bewigged (?).] To cover (the head) with a wig.

Hawthorne.

Be̤wilder (?), v. t. [imp. & p.p. Bewildered (?); p. pr. & vb. n. Bewildering.] [Pref. be̤ + wilder.] To lead into perplexity or confusion, as for want of a plain path; to perplex with mazes; or in general, to perplex or confuse greatly.

Lost and bewildered in the fruitless search.

Addison.

Syn. Ð To perplex; puzzle; entangle; confuse; confound; mystify; embarrass; lead astray.

Be̤wildered (?), a. Greatly perplexed; as, a bewildered mind.

Be̤wilderedĭness (?), n. The state of being bewildered; bewilderment. [R.]

Be̤wilderĭing (?), a. Causing bewilderment or great perplexity; as, bewildering difficulties. Ð Be̤wilderĭingĭly, adv.

Be̤wilderĭment (?), n. 1. The state of being bewildered.

A bewildering tangle or confusion.

He ... soon lost all traces of it amid bewilderment of tree trunks and underbrush.

Hawthorne.

Be̤winter (?), v. t. To make wintry. [Obs.]

Bewit (?), n. [Cf. OF. buie bond, chain, fr. L. boja neck collar, fetter. Cf. Buoy.] A double slip of leather by which bells are fastened to a hawk's legs.

Be̤witch (?), v. t. [imp. & p.p. Bewitched (?); p. pr. & vb. n. Bewitching.] 1. To gain an ascendency over by charms or incantations; to affect (esp. to injure) by witchcraft or sorcery.

See how I am bewitched; behold, mine arm
Is like a blasted sapling withered up.

Shak.

To charm; to fascinate; to please to such a degree as to take away the power of resistance; to enchant.

The charms of poetry our souls bewitch.

Dryden.

Syn. Ð To enchant; captivate; charm; entrance.

Be̤witchedĭness (?), n. The state of being bewitched.

Gauden.

Be̤witcher (?), n. One who bewitches.

Be̤witcherĭy (?), n. The power of bewitching or fascinating; bewitchment; charm; fascination.

There is a certain bewitchery or fascination in words.

South.

Bewitching, a. Having power to bewitch or fascinate; enchanting; captivating; charming. Ð Bewitchingly, adv. Ð Bewitchingness, n.

Bewitchment (?), n. 1. The act of bewitching, or the state of being bewitched.

Tylor.

The power of bewitching or charming.

Shak.

Bewonder (?), v. t. [imp. & p.p. Bewondered (?).] 1. To fill with wonder. [Obs.]

To wonder at; to admire. [Obs.]

Bewrap (?), v. t. [imp. & p.p. Bewrapped (?).] To wrap up; to cover.
Fairfax.

Bewray (?), v. t. To soil. See Beray.

Bewray, v. t. [imp. & p.p. Bewrayed (?); p. pr. & vb. n. Bewraying.] [OE. bewraien, biwreyen; pref. be + AS. wr?gan to accuse, betray; akin to OS. wr?gian, OHG. ruog?n, G. rgen, Icel. r'gja, Goth. wr?hjan to accuse.] To expose; to reveal; to disclose; to betray. [Obs. or Archaic]

The murder being once done, he is in less fear, and in more hope that the deed shall not be bewrayed or known.

Robynson (More's Utopia.)

Thy speech bewrayeth thee.

Matt. xxvi. 73.

Bewrayer (?), n. One who, or that which, bewrays; a revealer. [Obs. or Archaic]

Addison.

Bewrayment (?), n. Betrayal. [R.]

Bewreck (?), v. t. To wreck. [Obs.]

Bewreke (?), v. t. [Pref. be + wreak.] To wreak; to avenge. [Obs.]
Ld. Berners.

Bewrought (?), a. [Pref. be + wrought, p. p. of work, v. t.] Embroidered. [Obs.]

B. Jonson.

Bey (?), n. [See Beg a bey.] A governor of a province or district in the Turkish dominions; also, in some places, a prince or nobleman; a beg; as, the bey of Tunis.

Beylic (?), n. [Turk.] The territory ruled by a bey.

Beyond (?), prep. [OE. biyonde, bi?eonde, AS. begeondan, prep. and adv.; pref. be + geond yond, yonder. See Yon, Yonder.] 1. On the further side of; in the same direction as, and further on or away than.

Beyond that flaming hill.

G. Fletcher.

At a place or time not yet reached; before.

A thing beyond us, even before our death.
Pope.

Past, out of the reach or sphere of; further than; greater than; as, the patient was beyond medical aid; beyond one's strength.

In a degree or amount exceeding or surpassing; proceeding to a greater degree than; above, as in dignity, excellence, or quality of any kind. ½Beyond expectation.

Barrow.
Beyond any of the great men of my country.
Sir P.Sidney.

Beyond sea. (Law) See under Sea. Đ To go beyond, to exceed in ingenuity, in research, or in anything else; hence, in a bed sense, to deceive or circumvent.

That no man go beyond and defraud his brother in any matter.
1 Thess. iv. 6.

Beÿond (?), adv. Further away; at a distance; yonder.
Lo, where beyond he lyeth languishing.
Spenser.

Beÿzant (?), n. [See Byzant.] 1. A gold coin of Byzantium or Constantinople, varying in weight and value, usually (those current in England) between a sovereign and a half sovereign. There were also white or silver bezants. [Written also besant, byzant, etc.]

(Her.) A circle in or, i. e., gold, representing the gold coin called bezant.

Burke.

A decoration of a flat surface, as of a band or belt, representing circular disks lapping one upon another.

Bez · Đantler (?), n. [L. bis twice (OF. bes) + E. antler.] The second branch of a stag's horn.

Bezel (?), n. [From an old form of F. biseau sloping edge, prob. fr. L. bis double. See Biÿ.] The rim which encompasses and fastens a jewel or other object, as the crystal of a watch, in the cavity in which it is set.

B,Ïzique (?), n. [F. b,sigue.] A game at cards in which various combinations of cards in the hand, when declared, score points.

Bezoar (?), n. [F. b,zoard, fr. Ar. b¾zahr, b¾dizahr, fr. Per. p¾dÏzahr bezoar; p¾d protecting + zahr poison; cf. Pg. & Sp. bezoar.] A calculous concretion found in the intestines of certain ruminant animals (as the wild goat, the gazelle, and the Peruvian llama) formerly regarded as an unfailing antidote for poison, and a certain remedy for eruptive, pestilential, or putrid diseases. Hence: Any antidote or panacea.

μ Two kinds were particularly esteemed, the Bezoar orientale of India, and the Bezoar occidentale of Peru.

Bezoar antelope. See Antelope. Ð Bezoar goat (Zo"l.), the wild goat (Capra 'gagrus). Ð Bezoar mineral, an old preparation of oxide of antimony. Ure.

Bez·oïardic (?), a. [Cf. F. b,zoardique, b,zoartique.] Pertaining to, or compounded with, bezoar. Ð n. A medicine containing bezoar.

Bez·oïartic (?), Bez·oïarticïal (?), } a. [See Bezoardic.] Having the qualities of an antidote, or of bezoar; healing. [Obs.]

Beïzoniïan (?), n. [Cf. F. besoin need, want, It bisogno.] A low fellow or scoundrel; a beggar.

Great men oft die by vile bezonians.
Shak.

Bezzle (?), v. t. [imp. & p.p. Bezzled (?); p. pr. & vb. n. Bezzling (?).] [OF. besillier, besiler, to maltreat, pillage; or shortened fr. embezzle. Cf. Embezzle.] To plunder; to waste in riot. [Obs.]

Bezzle, v. i. To drink to excess; to revel. [Obs.]

Bhang (?), n. [Per. bang; cf. Skr. bhang¾ hemp.] An astringent and narcotic drug made from the dried leaves and seed capsules of wild hemp (Cannabis Indica), and chewed or smoked in the East as a means of intoxication. See Hasheesh.

ØBhunder (?), n. [Native name.] (Zo"l.) An Indian monkey (Macacus Rhesus), protected by the Hindoos as sacred. See Rhesus.

Biï (?). [L. bis twice, which i composition drops the ïs, akin to E. two. See Bisï, Two, and cf. Diï, Disï.]

> In most branches of science biï in composition denotes two, twice, or doubly; as, bidentate, twoïtoothed; biternate, doubly ternate, etc.

> (Chem.) In the composition of chemical names biï denotes two atoms, parts, or equivalents of that constituent to the name of which it is prefixed, to one of the other component, or that such constituent is present in double the ordinary proportion; as, bichromate, bisulphide. Beï and diï are often used interchangeably.

Biïacid (?), a. [Pref. biï + acid.] (Chem.) Having two hydrogen atoms which can be replaced by negative atoms or radicals to form salts; Ð said of bases. See Diacid.

Bi·aïcumiïnate (?), a. [Pref. biï + acuminate.] (Bot.) Having points in two directions.

Beïanguïlar (?), a. [Pref. biï + angular.] Having two angles or corners.

Biïanguïlate (?), Biïanguïla·ted (?), } a. [Pref. biï + angulate, angulated.] Biangular.

Biïanguïlous (?), a. [Pref. biï + angulous.] Biangular. [R.]

Biïan·therïiferïous (?), a. [Pref. biï + antherigerous.] (Bot.) Having two anthers.

Bi·arĭcuĭlate (?), a. [Pref. biĭ + articulate.] (Zo"l.) Having, or consisting of, tow joints.

Bias (?), n.; pl. Biases (?). [F. biasis, perh. fr. LL. bifax twoĭfaced; L. bis + facies face. See Biĭ, and cf. Face.] 1. A weight on the side of the ball used in the game of bowls, or a tendency imparted to the ball, which turns it from a straight line.

Being ignorant that there is a concealed bias within the spheroid, which will ... swerve away.
Sir W. Scott.

A learning of the mind; propensity or prepossession toward an object or view, not leaving the mind indifferent; bent inclination.

Strong love is a bias upon the thoughts.
South.
Morality influences men's lives, and gives a bias to all their actions.
Locke.

A wedgeĭshaped piece of cloth taken out of a garment (as the waist of a dress) to diminish its circumference.

A slant; a diagonal; as, to cut cloth on the bias.

Syn. Ð Prepossession; prejudice; partiality; inclination. See Bent.
Bias, a. 1. Inclined to one side; swelled on one side. [Obs.]
Shak.

Cut slanting or diagonally, as cloth.

Bias, adv. In a slanting manner; crosswise; obliquely; diagonally; as, to cut cloth bias.

Bias, v. t. [imp. & p.p. Biased (?); p. pr. & vb. n. Biasing.] To incline to one side; to give a particular direction to; to influence; to prejudice; to prepossess.

Me it had not biased in the one direction, nor should it have biased any just critic in the counter direction.
De. Quincey.

Bi·auĭricuĭlate (?), a. [Pref. biĭ + au riculate.] 1. (Anat.) Having two auricles, as the heart of mammals, birds, and reptiles.

(Bot. & Zo"l.) Having two earlike projections at its base, as a leaf.

Biĭaxal (?), Biĭaxiĭal (?), } a. [Pref. biĭ + axal, axial.] (Opt.) Having two axes; as, biaxial polarization. Brewster. Ð Biĭaxiĭalĭly, adv.

Bib (?), n. [From Bib, v., because the bib receives the drink that the child slavers from the mouth.] 1. A small piece of cloth worn by children over the breast, to protect the clothes.

(Zo"l.) An arctic fish (Gadus luscus), allied to the cod; Ð called also pout and whiting pout.

A bibcock.

Bib, Bibbe (?), v. t. [L. bibere. See Beverage, and cf. Imbibe.] To drink; to tipple. [Obs.]

This miller hath ... bibbed ale.

Chaucer.

Bib, v. i. To drink; to sip; to tipple.

He was constantly bibbing.

Locke.

Biĭbacious (?), a. [L. bibax, bibacis, fr. bibere. See Bib.] Addicted to drinking.

Bibaciĭty (?), n. The practice or habit of drinking too much; tippling.

Blount.

Bibasic (?), a. [Pref. biĭ + basic.] (Chem.) Having to hydrogen atoms which can be replaced by positive or basic atoms or radicals to form salts; Ð said of acids. See Dibasic.

Bibb (?), n. A bibcock. See Bib, n., 3.

Bibber (?), n. One given to drinking alcoholic beverages too freely; a tippler; Ð chiefly used in composition; as, winebibber.

BibbleÐbabble (?), n. [A reduplication of babble.] Idle talk; babble.

Shak.

Bibbs (?), n. pl. (Naut.) Pieces of timber bolted to certain parts of a mast tp support the trestletrees.

Bibcock · (?), n. A cock or faucet having a bent down nozzle.

Knight.

Biĭbirine (?), n. (Chem.) See Bebeerine.

Bibiĭtoĭry (?), a. Of or pertaining to drinking or tippling.

Bible (?), n. [F. bible, L. biblia, pl., fr. Gr. ?, pl. of ?, dim. of ?, ?, book, prop. Egyptian papyrus.] 1. A book. [Obs.]

Chaucer.

The Book by way of eminence, Ð that is, the book which is made up of the writings accepted by Christians as of divine origin and authority, whether such writings be in the original language, or translated; the Scriptures of the Old and New Testaments; Ð sometimes in a restricted sense, the Old Testament; as, King James's Bible; Douay Bible; Luther's Bible. Also, the book which is made up of writings similarly accepted by the Jews; as, a rabbinical Bible.

A book containing the sacred writings belonging to any religion; as, the Koran is often called the Mohammedan Bible.

Bible Society, an association for securing the multiplication and wide distribution of the Bible. Ð Douay Bible. See Douay Bible. Ð Geneva Bible. See under Geneva.

Bibler (?), n. [See Bib, v. t.] A great drinker; a tippler. [Written also bibbler and bibbeler.]

Bibliĭcal (?), a. Pertaining to, or derived from, the Bible; as, biblical learning; biblical authority.

Bib‧liĭcaliĭty (?), n. The quality of being biblical; a biblical subject. [R.]

Bibliĭcalĭly (?), adv. According to the Bible.

Bibliĭcism (?), n. [Cf. F. biblicisme.] Learning or literature relating to the Bible. [R.]

Bibliĭcist (?), n. One skilled in the knowledge of the Bible; a demonstrator of religious truth by the Scriptures.

Biblĭĭoĭgraph‧ (?), n. Bibliographer.

Bib‧liĭograĭpher (?), n. [Gr. ?, fr. ? book + ? to write : cf. F. bibliographe.] One who writes, or is versed in, bibliography.

Bib‧liĭoĭgraphic (?), Bib‧liĭoĭgraphicĭal (?), } a. [Cf. F. bibliographique.] Pertaining to bibliography, or the history of books. Ð Bib‧liĭoĭgraphicĭalĭly, adv.

Bib‧liĭograĭphy (?) n.; pl. Bibliographies (?). [Gr. ?: cf. F. bibliographie.] A history or description of books and manuscripts, with notices of the different editions, the times when they were printed, etc.

Bib‧liĭolaĭter (?), Bib‧liĭolaĭtrist (?), } n. [See. Bibliolatry.] A worshiper of books; especially, a worshiper of the Bible; a believer in its verbal inspiration.

De Quincey.

Bib‧liĭolaĭtry (?), n. [Gr. ? book + ? service, worship, ? to serve.] Book worship, esp. of the Bible; Ð applied by Roman Catholic divine? to the exaltation of the authority of the Bible over that of the pope or the church, and by Protestants to an excessive regard to the letter of the Scriptures.

Coleridge. F. W. Newman.

Bib‧liĭoĭlogicĭal (?), a. Relating to bibliology.

Bib‧liĭoloĭgy (?), n. [Gr. ? book + ĭlogy.]

An account of books; book lore; bibliography.

The literature or doctrine of the Bible.

Biblĭĭoĭman‧cy (?), n. [Gr. ? book + ĭmancy: cf. F. bibliomancie.] A kind of divination, performed by selecting passages of Scripture at hazard, and drawing from them indications concerning future events.

Bib‧liĭoĭmaniĭa (?), n. [Gr. ? book + ? madness: cf. F. bibliomanie.] A mania for acquiring books.

Bib‧liĭoĭmaniĭac (?), n. One who has a mania for books. Ð a. Relating to a bibliomaniac.

Bib‧liĭoĭmaĭniacĭal (?), a. Pertaining to a passion for books; relating to a bibliomaniac.

Bib·li̇ȯi̇pegic (?), a. [Gr. ? book + ? to make fast.] Relating to the binding of books. [R.]

<— p. 143 —>

Bib·li̇i̇opei̇gist (?), n. A bookbinder.

Bib·li̇i̇op·ei̇gistic (?), a. Pertaining to the art of binding books. [R.] Dibdin.

Bib·li̇i̇opei̇gy (?), n. [See Bibliopegic.] The art of binding books. [R.]

Bibli̇i̇ȯi̇phile (?), n. [Gr. ? book + ? to love: cf. F. bibliophile.] A lover of books.

Bib·li̇i̇ophi̇i̇lism (?), n. Love of books.

Bib·li̇i̇ophi̇i̇list (?), n. A lover of books.

Bib·li̇i̇ȯi̇phobi̇i̇a (?), n. [Gr. ? book + ? to fear.] A dread of books. [R.]

Bibli̇i̇ȯi̇pole (?), n. [L. bibliopola, Gr. ?; ? book + ? to sell: cf. F. bibliopole.] One who sells books.

Bib·li̇i̇ȯi̇polic (?), Bib·li̇i̇opoi̇lar (?), a. [See Bibliopole.] Of or pertaining to the sale of books. ½Bibliopolic difficulties., Carlyle.

Bib·li̇i̇opoi̇lism (?), n. The trade or business of selling books.

Bib·li̇i̇opoi̇list (?), n. Same as Bibliopole.

Bib·li̇i̇op·oi̇listic (?), a. Of or pertaining to bibliopolism. Dibdin.

Bibli̇i̇ȯi̇taph (?), Bib·li̇i̇otai̇phist (?), } n. [Gr. ? book + ? a burial.] One who hides away books, as in a tomb. [R.] Crabb.

Bibli̇i̇ȯi̇thec (?), n. A librarian.

ØBib·li̇i̇ȯi̇theca (?), n. [L. See Bibliotheke.] A library.

Bib·li̇i̇ȯi̇thecal (?), a. [L. bibliothecalis. See Bibliotheke.] Belonging to a library. Byrom.

Bib·li̇i̇othei̇cai̇ry (?), n. [L. bibliothecarius: cf. F. biblioth,caire.] A librarian. [Obs.] Evelin.

Bibli̇i̇ȯi̇theke (?), n. [L. bibliotheca, Gr. ?; ? book + ? a case, box, fr. ? to place: cf. F. bibliothŠque.] A library. [Obs.] Bale.

Biblist (?), n. [Cf. F. bibliste. See Bible.]

One who makes the Bible the sole rule of faith.

A biblical scholar; a biblicist.

I. Taylor.

Bi̇i̇bracteİate (?), a. [Pref. bii̇ + bracteate.] (Bot.) Furnished with, or having, two bracts.

Bibui̇lous (?), a. [L. bibulus, fr. bibere to drink. See Bib, v. t.] 1. Readily imbibing fluids or moisture; spongy; as, bibulous blotting paper.

283

Inclined to drink; addicted to tippling.

Bibulously, adv. In a bibulous manner; with profuse imbibition or absorption.

De Quincey.

Bicalcarate (?), a. [Pref. bi- + calcarate.] Having two spurs, as the wing or leg of a bird.

Bicallose (?), **Bicallous** (?), } a. [Pref. bi- + callose, callous.] (Bot.) Having two callosities or hard spots.

Gray.

Bicameral (?), a. [Pref. bi- + camera.] Consisting of, or including, two chambers, or legislative branches.

Bentham.

Bicapsular (?), a. [Pref. bi- + capsular: cf. F. bicapsulaire.] (Bot.) Having two capsules; as, a bicapsular pericarp.

Bicarbonate (?), n. [Pref. bi-+ carbonate.] (Chem.) A carbonate in which but half the hydrogen of the acid is replaced by a positive element or radical, thus making the proportion of the acid to the positive or basic portion twice what it is in the normal carbonates; an acid carbonate; -- sometimes called supercarbonate.

Bicarbureted or **-retted** (?), a. [Pref. bi- + carbureted.] (Chem.) Containing two atoms or equivalents of carbon in the molecule. [Obs. or R.]

Bicarinate (?), a. [Pref. bi- + carinate.] (Biol.) Having two keellike projections, as the upper palea of grasses.

Bicaudal (?), a. [Pref. bi- + caudal.] Having, or terminating in, two tails.

Bicaudate (?), a. [Pref. bi- + caudate.] Twotailed; bicaudal.

Bicched (?), a. [Of unknown origin.] Pecked; pitted; notched. [Obs.]

Chaucer.

Bicched bones, pecked, or notched, bones; dice.

Bice, Bise (?), n. [F. bis, akin to It. bigio light gray, tawny.] (Paint.) A pale blue pigment, prepared from the native blue carbonate of copper, or from smalt; -- called also blue bice.

Green bice is prepared from the blue, by adding yellow orpiment, or by grinding down the green carbonate of copper.

Cooley. Brande & C.

Bicentenary (?), a. [Pref. bi- + centenary.] Of or pertaining to two hundred, esp. to two hundred years; as, a bicentenary celebration. -- n. The two hundredth anniversary, or its celebration.

Bi·centennial, a. [Pref. bi- + centennial.] 1. Consisting of two hundred years.

Occurring every two hundred years.

Bi·cen̆ten̆ni̇al, n. The two hundredth year or anniversary, or its celebration.

Bi̇cephaĭlous (?), a. [Pref. bĭ + cephalous: cf. F. bic,phale.] Having two heads.

ØBiceps (?), n. [L., twoĭheaded; bis twice + caput head. See Capital.] (Anat.) A muscle having two heads or origins; Đ applied particularly to a flexor in the arm, and to another in the thigh.

ØBĭĭchir (?), n. [Native name.] (Zo"l.) A remarkable ganoid fish (Polypterus bichir) found in the Nile and other African rivers. See Brachioganoidei.

Bĭchloride (?), n. [Pref. bĭĭ + chloride.] (Chem.) A compound consisting of two atoms of chlorine with one or more atoms of another element; Đ called also dichloride.

Bichloride of mercury, mercuric chloride; Đ sometimes called corrosive sublimate.

ØBicho (?), n. [Sp.] (Zo"l.) See Jigger.

Bĭchromate (?), n. [Pref. bĭĭ + chromate.] (Chem.) A salt containing two parts of chromic acid to one of the other ingredients; as, potassfum bichromate; Đ called also dichromate.

Bĭchromaĭtize (?), v. t. To combine or treat with a bichromate, esp. with bichromate of potassium; as, bichromatized gelatine.

Bĭcipiĭtal (?), a. [L. biceps, bicipitis: cf. F. bicipital. See Biceps.] 1. (Anat.) (a) Having two heads or origins, as a muscle. (b) Pertaining to a biceps muscle; as, bicipital furrows, the depressions on either side of the biceps of the arm.

(Bot.) Dividing into two parts at one extremity; having two heads or two supports; as, a bicipital tree.

Bĭcipiĭtous (?), a. Having two heads; bicipital. ½Bicipitous serpents., Sir T. Browne.

Bicker, n. [See Beaker.] A small wooden vessel made of staves and hoops, like a tub. [Prov. Eng.]

Bicker (?), v. i. [imp. & p.p. Bickered (?); p. pr. & vb. n. Bickering.] [OE. bikeren, perh. fr. Celtic; cf. W. bicra to fight, bicker, bicre conflict, skirmish; perh. akin to E. beak.] 1. To skirmish; to exchange blows; to fight. [Obs.]

Two eagles had a conflict, and bickered together.
Holland.

To contend in petulant altercation; to wrangle.

Petty things about which men cark and bicker.
Barrow.

To move quickly and unsteadily, or with a pattering noise; to quiver; to be tremulous, like flame.

They [streamlets] bickered through the sunny shade.
Thomson.
Bicker, n. 1. A skirmish; an encounter. [Obs.]

A fight with stones between two parties of boys. [Scot.]

Jamieson.

A wrangle; also, a noise, as in angry contention.

Bicker´er (?), n. One who bickers.
Bicker´ing, n. 1. A skirmishing. ½Frays and bickerings.,
Milton.

Altercation; wrangling.

Bicker´iment (?), n. Contention. [Obs.]
Spenser.
Bickern (?), n. [F. bigorne. See Bicorn.] An anvil ending in a beak or point (orig. in two beaks); also, the beak or horn itself.
Bi´colli´gate (?), a. [L. bis twice + colligatus, p. p. See Colligate, v. t.] (Zo"l.) Having the anterior toes connected by a basal web.
Bicol · or (?), Bicol · ored (?), } a. [L. bicolor; bis twice + color color.] Of two colors.
Bi´concave (?), a. [Pref. bi´ + concave.] Concave on both sides; as, biconcave vertebr‘.
Bi´conju´gate (?), a. [Pref. bi´ + conjugate, a.] (Bot.) Twice paired, as when a petiole forks twice.
Gray.
Bi´convex (?), a. [Pref. bi´ + convex.] Convex on both sides; as, a biconvex lens.
Bicorn (?), Bicorned (?), Bi´cornous (?), } a. [L. bicornis; bis twice + cornu horn: cf. F. bicorne. Cf. Bickern.] Having two horns; twoÐhorned; crescentlike.
Bi´corpo´ral (?), a. [Pref. bi´ + corporal.] Having two bodies.
Bi´corpo´rate (?), a. [Pref. bi´ + corporate.] (Her.) DoubleÐbodied, as a lion having one head and two bodies.
Bi´costate (?), a. [Pref. bi´ + costate.] (Bot.) Having two principal ribs running longitudinally, as a leaf.
Bi´crenate (?), a. [Pref. bi´ + crenate.] (Bot.) Twice crenated, as in the case of leaves whose crenatures are themselves crenate.
Bi · cres´centic (?), a. [Pref. bi´ + crescent.] Having the form of a double crescent.
Bi´crural (?), a. [Pref. bi´ + crural.] Having two legs.
Hooker.

Bi̇́cuspid (?), Bi̇́cuspidi̇́ate (?), } a. [See pref. Bi̇́, and Cuspidate.] Having two points or prominences; ending in two points; Ð said of teeth, leaves, fruit, etc.

Bi̇́cuspid, n. (Anat.) One of the two doublei̇́pointed teeth which intervene between the canines (cuspids) and the molars, on each side of each jaw. See Tooth, n.

Bi̇́cyai̇́nide (?), n. See Dicyanide.

Bicy̆cle (?), n. [Pref. bi̇́ + cycle.] A light vehicle having two wheels one behind the other. It has a saddle seat and is propelled by the rider's feet acting on cranks or levers.

Bicy̆cler (?), n. One who rides a bicycle.

Bi̇́cyclic (?), a. Relating to bicycles.

Bicy̆cling (?), n. The use of a bicycle; the act or practice of riding a bicycle.

Bicy̆clism (?), n. The art of riding a bicycle.

Bicy̆clist (?), n. A bicycler.

Bi̇́cycui̇́lar (?), a. Relating to bicycling.

Bid (?), v. t. [imp. Bade (?), Bid, (Obs.) Bad; p. p. Bidden (?), Bid; p. pr. & vb. n. Bidding.] [OE. bidden, prop to ask, beg, AS. biddan; akin to OS. biddian, Icel. bi?ja, OHG. bittan, G. bitten, to pray, ask, request, and E. bead, also perh. to Gr. ? to persuade, L. fidere to trust, E. faith, and bide. But this word was early confused with OE. beden, beoden, AS. beċdan, to offer, command; akin to Icel. bj??a, Goth. biudan (in comp.), OHG. biotan to command, bid, G. bieten, D. bieden, to offer, also to Gr. ? to learn by inquiry, Skr. budh to be awake, to heed, present OSlav. bud?ti to be awake, E. bode, v. The word now has the form of OE. bidden to ask, but the meaning of OE. beden to command, except in ½to bid beads., ?30.]

> To make an offer of; to propose. Specifically : To offer to pay (a certain price, as for a thing put up at auction), or to take (a certain price, as for work to be done under a contract).

> To offer in words; to declare, as a wish, a greeting, a threat, or defiance, etc.; as, to bid one welcome; to bid good morning, farewell, etc.

Neither bid him God speed.
2. John 10.
He bids defiance to the gaping crowd.
Granrille.

> To proclaim; to declare publicly; to make known. [Mostly obs.] ½Our banns thrice bid !‚

Gay.

> To order; to direct; to enjoin; to command.

That Power who bids the ocean ebb and flow.
Pope
Lord, if it be thou, bid me come unto thee.
Matt. xiv.28
I was bid to pick up shells.
D. Jerrold.

To invite; to call in; to request to come.

As many as ye shall find, bid to the marriage.
Matt. xxii. 9

To bid beads, to pray with beads, as the Roman Catholics; to distinguish each bead by a prayer. [Obs.] Ð To bid defiance to , to defy openly; to brave. Ð To bid fair, to offer a good prospect; to make fair promise; to seem likely.

Syn. Ð To offer; proffer; tender; propose; order; command; direct; charge; enjoin.

Bid (?), imp. & p. p. of Bid.

Bid, n. An offer of a price, especially at auctions; a statement of a sum which one will give for something to be received, or will take for something to be done or furnished; that which is offered.

Bid, v. i. [See Bid, v. t.] 1. To pray. [Obs.]
Chaucer.

To make a bid; to state what one will pay or take.

Bidale · (?), n. [Bid + ale.] An invitation of friends to drink ale at some poor man's house, and there to contribute in charity for his relief. [Prov. Eng.]

Biddaïble (?), a. Obedient; docile. [Scot.]

Bidden (?), p. p. of Bid.

Bidder (?), n. [AS. biddere.] One who bids or offers a price.
Burke.

Bidderly ware · (?). [From Beder or Bidar a town in India.] A kind of metallic ware make in India. The material is a composition of Inc, tin, and lead, in which ornaments of gold and silver are inlaid o? damascened. [Spelt also bidry, bidree, bedery, beder.]

Bidding, n. 1. Command; order; a proclamation o? notifying. ½Do thou thy master's bidding.
Shak.

The act or process of making bids; an offer; a proposal of a price, as at an auction.

Bidding prayer · (?). 1. (R. C. Ch.) The prayer for the souls of benefactors, said before the sermon.

(Angl. Ch.) The prayer before the sermon, with petitions for various specified classes of persons.

Biddy (?), n. [Etymology uncertain.] A name used in calling a hen or chicken.

Shak.

Biddy, n. [A familiar form of Bridget.] An Irish serving woman or girl. [Colloq.]

Bide (?), v. i. [imp. & p.p. Bided; p. pr. & vb. n. Biding.] [OE. biden, AS. bÆdan; akin to OHG. bÆtan, Goth. beidan, Icel. bÆ??; perh. orig., to wait with trust, and akin to bid. See Bid, v. t., and cf. Abide.] 1. To dwell; to inhabit; to abide; to stay.

All knees to thee shall bow of them that bide
In heaven or earth, or under earth, in hell.

Milton.

To remain; to continue or be permanent in a place or state; to continue to be.

Shak.

Bide, v. t. 1. To encounter; to remain firm under (a hardship); to endure; to suffer; to undergo.

Poor naked wretches, wheresoe'er you are,
That bide the pelting of this pitiless storm.

Shak.

To wait for; as, I bide my time. See Abide.

Bident (?), n. [L. bidens, ïentis, having two prongs; bis twice + dens a tooth.] An instrument or weapon with two prongs.

Bïdental (?), a. Having two teeth.

Swift.

Bïdentate (?), a. (Bot. & Zo"l.) Having two teeth or two toothlike processes; twoÐtoothed.

Bïdet (?), n. [F. bidet, perh. fr. Celtic; cr. Gael. bideach very little, diminutive, bidein a diminutive animal, W. bidan a weakly or sorry wretch.]

A small horse formerly allowed to each trooper or dragoon for carrying his baggage.

B. Jonson.

A kind of bath tub for sitting baths; a sitz bath.

Bïdigïtate (?), a. [Pref. biï + digitate.] Having two fingers or fingerlike projections.

Biding (?), n. Residence; habitation.

Rowe.

Bield (?), n. A shelter. Same as Beild. [Scot.]

Bield, v. t. To shelter. [Scot.]

Biënnial (?), a. [L. biennalis and biennis, fr. biennium a space of two years; bis twice + annus year. Cf. Annual.] 1. Happening, or taking place, once in two years; as, a biennial election.

(Bot.) Continuing for two years, and then perishing, as plants which form roots and leaves the first year, and produce fruit the second.

Biënnial, n. 1. Something which takes place or appears once in two years; esp. a biennial examination.

(Bot.) A plant which exists or lasts for two years.

Biënnialïly, adv. Once in two years.

Bier (?), n. [OE. b'e, beere, AS. b?r, b?re; akin to D. baar, OHG. b¾ra, G. bahre, Icel barar, D? baare, L. feretrum, Gr. ?, from the same ?? bear to produce. See 1st Bear, and cf. Barrow.] 1. A handbarrow or portable frame on which a corpse is placed or borne to the grave.

(Weaving) A count of forty threads in the warp or chain of woolen cloth.

Knight.

<— p. 144 —>

Bierbalk · (?), n. [See Bier, and Balk, n.] A church road (e. g., a path across fields) for funerals. [Obs.]

Homilies.

Biestings, Beestings (?), n. pl. [OE. bestynge, AS. b?sting, fr. b?st, beost; akin to D. biest, OHG. biost, G. biest; of unknown origin.] The first milk given by a cow after calving.

B. Jonson.

The thick and curdy milk ... commonly called biestings.

Newton. (1574).

Biïfacial (?), a. [Pref. biï + facial.] Having the opposite surfaces alike.

Biïfariïous (?), a. [L. bifarius; bis twice + fari to speak. Cf. Gr. ? twofold; ? twice + ? to say.] 1. Twofold; arranged in two rows.

(Bot.) Pointing two ways, as leaves that grow only on opposite sides of a branch; in two vertical rows.

Biïfariïousïly, adv. In a bifarious manner.

Biferïous (?), a. [L. bifer; bis twice + ferre to bear.] Bearing fruit twice a year.

Biffin (?), n. [Cf. Beaufin.] 1. A sort of apple peculiar to Norfolk, Eng. [Sometimes called beaufin; but properly beefin (it is said), from its resemblance to raw beef.]

Wright.

A baked apple pressed down into a flat, round cake; a dried apple.

Dickens.

Bifid (?), a. [L. bifidus; bis twice + root of findere to cleave or split: cf. F. bifide.] Cleft to the middle or slightly beyond the middle; opening with a cleft; divided by a linear sinus, with straight margins.

Bifĭdate (?), a. [L. bifidatus.] See Bifid.

Bifĭlar (?), a. [Pref. bi + filar.] Two-threaded; involving the use of two threads; as, bifilar suspension; a bifilar balance.

Bifilar micrometer (often called a bifilar), an instrument form measuring minute distances or angles by means of two very minute threads (usually spider lines), one of which, at least, is movable; Ð more commonly called a filar micrometer.

Bi · flaĭbellate (?), a. [Pref. bi + flabellate.] (Zo"l.) Flabellate on both sides.

Bi · flaĭgellate (?), a. [Pref. bi + flagellate.] Having two long, narrow, whiplike appendages.

Bifĭlorate (?), **Bifĭlorous** (?), } a. [L. bis twice + flos, floris, flower.] (Bot.) Bearing two flowers; two-flowered.

Bifold (?), a. [Pref. bi + fold.] Twofold; double; of two kinds, degrees, etc.

Shak.

Bifŏliate (?), a. [Pref. bi + foliate.] (Bot.) Having two leaves; two-leaved.

Bifŏliŏlate (?), a. [Pref. bi + foliolate.] (Bot.) Having two leaflets, as some compound leaves.

Bifŏrate (?), a. [L. bis twice + foratus, p. p. of forare to bore or pierce.] (Bot.) Having two perforations.

Bifŏrine (?), n. [L. biforis, biforus, having two doors; bis twice + foris door.] (Bot.) An oval sac or cell, found in the leaves of certain plants of the order Arace'. It has an opening at each end through which raphides, generated inside, are discharged.

Biforked (?), a. Bifurcate.

Biform (?), a. [L. biformis; bis twice + forma shape: cf. F. biforme.] Having two forms, bodies, or shapes.

Croxall.

Biformed (?), a. [Pref. bi + form.] Having two forms.

Johnson.

Bifŏrmĭty (?), n. A double form.

Bifŏrn (?), prep. & adv. Before. [Obs.]

Bifŏrous (?), a. [L. biforis having two doors; bis twice, two + foris door.] See Biforate.

Bifronted (?), a. [Pref. bi + front.] Having two fronts. ½Bifronted Janus.

Massinger.

Bi̇lfurcate (?), Bi̇lfurcȧted (?), } a. [Pref. bi̇ + furcate.] Twȯlpronged; forked.

Bi̇lfurcate (?), v. i. To divide into two branches.

Bi · furi̇cation (?), n. [Cf. F. bifurcation.] A forking, or division into two branches.

Bi̇lfurcous (?), a. [L. bifurcus; bis twice + furca fork.] See Bifurcate, a. [R.]

Coles.

Big (?), a. [compar. Bigger; superl. Biggest.] [Perh. from Celtic; cf. W. beichiog, beichiawg, pregnant, with child, fr. baich burden, Arm. beac'h; or cf. OE. bygly, Icel. biggiligr, (properly) habitable; (then) magnigicent, excellent, fr. OE. biggen, Icel. byggja, to dwell, build, akin to E. be.] 1. Having largeness of size; of much bulk or magnitude; of great size; large. ½He's too big to go in there.͵

Shak.

<small>Great with young; pregnant; swelling; ready to give birth or produce; Ð often figuratively.</small>

[Day] big with the fate of Cato and of Rome.
Addison.

<small>Having greatness, fullness, importance, inflation, distention, etc., whether in a good or a bad sense; as, a big heart; a big voice; big looks; to look big. As applied to looks, it indicates haughtiness or pride.</small>

God hath not in heaven a bigger argument.
Jer. Taylor.

п Big is often used in selfİexplaining compounds; as, bigi̇boned; bigi̇sounding; bigi̇named; bigi̇voiced.

To talk big, to talk loudly, arrogantly, or pretentiously.

I talked big to them at first.
De Foe.

Syn. Ð Bulky; large; great; massive; gross.

Big, Bigg, n. [OE. bif, bigge; akin to Icel. bygg, Dan. byg, Sw. bjugg.] (Bot.) Barley, especially the hardy fouri̇rowed kind.

½Bear interchanges in local use, now with barley, now with bigg.͵

New English Dict.

Big, Bigg, v. t. [OE. biggen, fr. Icel. byggja to inhabit, to build, b?a (neut.) to dwell (active) to make ready. See Boor, and Bound.] To build. [Scot. & North of Eng. Dial.]

Sir W. Scott.

ØBiga (?), n. [L.] (Antiq.) A twoi̇horse chariot.

Bigam (?), n. [L. bigamus twice married: cf. F. bigame. See Bigamy.] A bigamist. [Obs.]

Bigȧlmist (?), n. [Cf. Digamist.] One who is guilty of bigamy.

Ayliffe.

Bigaˈmous (?), a. Guilty of bigamy; involving bigamy; as, a bigamous marriage.

Bigaˈmy (?), n. [OE. bigamie, fr. L. bigamus twice married; bis twice + Gr. ? marriage; prob. akin to Skt. j¾mis related, and L. gemini twins, the root meaning to bind, join: cf. F. bigamie. Cf. Digamy.] (Law) The offense of marrying one person when already legally married to another.

Wharton.

μ It is not strictly correct to call this offense bigamy: it more properly denominated polygamy, i. e., having a plurality of wives or husbands at once, and in several statutes in the United States the offense is classed under the head of polygamy.

In the canon law bigamy was the marrying of two virgins successively, or one after the death of the other, or once marrying a widow. This disqualified a man for orders, and for holding ecclesiastical offices. Shakespeare uses the word in the latter sense.

Blackstone. Bouvier.

Base declension and loathed bigamy.

Shak.

Big · arˈreau (?), **Big · aˈroon** (?), } n. [F. bigarreau, fr. bigarr, variegated.] (Bot.) The large whiteˈheart cherry.

BigÐbel · lied (?), a. Having a great belly; as, a bigˈbellied man or flagon; advanced in pregnancy.

Biˈgamiˈnate (?), a. [Pref. biˈ + geminate.] (Bot.) Having a forked petiole, and a pair of leaflets at the end of each division; biconjugate; twice paired; Ð said of a decompound leaf.

Biˈgential (?), a. [Pref. biˈ + L. gens, gentis, tribe.] (Zo"l.) Including two tribes or races of men.

Bigeye · (?), n. (Zo"l.) A fish of the genus Priacanthus, remarkable for the large size of the eye.

Bigg (?), n. & v. See Big, n. & v.

Biggen (?), v. t. & i. To make or become big; to enlarge. [Obs. or Dial.]

Steele.

Bigger (?), a., compar. of Big.

Biggest (?), a., superl. of Big.

Biggin (?), n. [F. b,guin, prob. from the cap worn by the B,guines. Cf. Beguine, Biggon.] A child's cap; a hood, or something worn on the head.

An old woman's biggin for a nightcap.

Massinger.

Biggin, n. A coffeepot with a strainer or perforated metallic vessel for holding the ground coffee, through which boiling water is poured; Ð so called from Mr. Biggin, the inventor.

Biggin, Bigging, } n. [OE. bigging. See Big, Bigg, v. t.] A building. [Obs.]

Biggon (?), Biggoninet (?), } n. [F. b,guin and OF. beguinet, dim of b,guin. See Biggin a cap.] A cap or hood with pieces covering the ears.

ØBigha (?), n. A measure of land in India, varying from a third of an acre to an acre.

Bighorn· (?), n. (Zo"l.) The Rocky Mountain sheep (Ovis or Caprovis montana).

Bight (?), n. [OE. bi?t a bending; cf. Sw. & Dan. bugt bend, bay; fr. AS. byht, fr. b?gan. ?88. Cf. Bout, Bought a bend, and see Bow, v.] 1. A corner, bend, or angle; a hollow; as, the bight of a horse's knee; the bight of an elbow.

(Geog.) A bend in a coast forming an open bay; as, the Bight of Benin.

(Naut.) The double part of a rope when folded, in distinction from the ends; that is, a round, bend, or coil not including the ends; a loop.

Biïglanduïlar (?), a. [Pref. biï + glandular.] Having two glands, as a plant.

Bigly (?), adv. [From Big, a.] In a tumid, swelling, blustering manner; haughtily; violently.

He brawleth bigly.

Robynson (More's Utopia.)

Bigness, n. The state or quality of being big; largeness; size; bulk.

Biginoniïa (?), n. [Named from the Abb, Bignon.] (Bot.) A large genus of American, mostly tropical, climbing shrubs, having compound leaves and showy somewhat tubular flowers. B. capreolata is the cross vine of the Southern United States. The trumpet creeper was formerly considered to be of this genus.

Bigino · niïaceous (?), a. (Bot.) Of pertaining to, or resembling, the family of plants of which the trumpet flower is an example.

Bigot (?), n. [F. bigot a bigot or hypocrite, a name once given to the Normans in France. Of unknown origin; possibly akin to Sp. bigote a whisker; hombre de bigote a man of spirit and vigor; cf. It. sïbigottire to terrify, to appall. Wedgwood and others maintain that bigot is from the same source as Beguine, Beghard.]

A hypocrite; esp., a superstitious hypocrite. [Obs.]

A person who regards his own faith and views in matters of religion as unquestionably right, and any belief or opinion opposed to or differing from them as unreasonable or wicked. In an extended sense, a person who is intolerant of opinions which conflict with his own, as in politics or morals; one obstinately and blindly devoted to his own church, party, belief, or opinion.

To doubt, where bigots had been content to wonder and believe.
Macaulay.

Bigot, a. Bigoted. [Obs.]

In a country more bigot than ours.

Dryden.

Bigotĕd, a. Obstinately and blindly attached to some creed, opinion practice, or ritual; unreasonably devoted to a system or party, and illiberal toward the opinions of others. ½Bigoted to strife.

Byron.

Syn. Ð Prejudiced; intolerant; narrowĬminded.

BigotĕdĬly, adv. In the manner of a bigot.

BigotĬry (?), n. [Cf. F. bigoterie.] 1. The state of mind of a bigot; obstinate and unreasoning attachment of one's own belief and opinions, with narrow-minded intolerance of beliefs opposed to them.

The practice or tenets of a bigot.

Bigwig· (?), n. [Big, a. + wig.] A person of consequence; as, the bigwigs of society. [Jocose]

In our youth we have heard him spoken of by the bigwigs with extreme condescension.

Dickens.

BigÐwigged· (?), a. characterized by pomposity of manner. [Eng.]

Bi · hyĬdroguĬret (?), n. [Pref. biĬ + hydroguret.] (Chem.) A compound of two atoms of hydrogen with some other substance. [Obs.]

ØBiĬjou (?), n.; pl. Bijoux (?). [F.; of uncertain origin.] A trinket; a jewel; Ð a word applied to anything small and of elegant workmanship.

BiĬjoutry (?), n. [F. bijouterie. See Bijou.] Small articles of virtu, as jewelry, trinkets, etc.

BijuĬgate (?), a. [L. bis twice + jugatus, p. p. of jugare to join.] (Bot.) Having two pairs, as of leaflets.

BijuĬgous (?), a. [L. bijugus yoked two together; bis twice + jugum yoke, pair.] (Bot.) Bijugate.

Bike (?), n. [Ethymol. unknown.] A nest of wild bees, wasps, or ants; a swarm. [Scot.]

Sir W. Scott.

ØBikh (?), n. [Hind., fr. Skr. visha poison.] (Bot.) The East Indian name of a virulent poison extracted from Aconitum ferox or other species of aconite: also, the plant itself.

BiĬlabiĬate (?), a. [Pref. biĬ + labiate.] (Bot.) Having two lips, as the corols of certain flowers.

Bi · laĬciniĬate (?), a. [Pref. biĬ + laciniate.] Doubly fringed.

ØBiĬlalo (?), n. A twoĬmasted passenger boat or small vessel, used in the bay of Manila.

BiĬlamelĬlate (?), BiĬlamelĬla · ted (?), } a. [Pref. biĬ + lamellate.] (Bot.) Formed of two plates, as the stigma of the Mimulus; also, having two elevated ridges, as in the lip of certain flowers.

BiĬlamiĬnar (?), BiĬlamiĬnate (?), } a. [Pref. biĬ + laminar, laminate.] Formed of, or having, two lamin', or thin plates.

Biland (?), n. A byland. [Obs.] Holland.

Bilan**ï**der (?), n. [D. bijlander; bij by + land land, country.] (Naut.) A small two**ï**masted merchant vessel, fitted only for coasting, or for use in canals, as in Holland.

Why choose we, then, like bilanders to creep
Along the coast, and land in view to keep?
Dryden.

Bi**ï**later**ï**al (?), a. [Pref. bi**ï** + lateral: cf. F. bilat,ral.] 1. Having two sides; arranged upon two sides; affecting two sides or two parties.

(Biol.) Of or pertaining to the two sides of a central area or organ, or of a central axis; as, bilateral symmetry in animals, where there is a similarity of parts on the right and left sides of the body.

Bi**ï**lat · er**ï**ali**ï**ty (?), n. State of being bilateral.

Bilber**ï**ry (?), n.; pl. Bilberries (?). [Cf. Dan. b"lleb'r bilberry, where b"lle is perh. akin to E. ball.] 1. (Bot.) The European whortleberry (Vaccinium myrtillus); also, its edible bluish black fruit.

There pinch the maids as blue as bilberry.
Shak.

(Bot.) Any similar plant or its fruit; esp., in America, the species Vaccinium myrtilloides, V. c'spitosum and V. uliginosum.

Bilbo (?), n.; pl. Bilboes (?). 1. A rapier; a sword; so named from Bilbao, in Spain.
Shak.

pl. A long bar or bolt of iron with sliding shackles, and a lock at the end, to confine the feet of prisoners or offenders, esp. on board of ships.

Methought I lay
Worse than the mutines in the bilboes.
Shak.

ØBilbo**ï**quet (?), n. [F.] The toy called cup and ball.

Bilcock (?), n. (Zo"l.) The European water rail.

ØBildstein (?), n. [G., fr. bild image, likeness + stein stone.] Same as Agalmatolite.

Bile (?), n. [L. bilis: cf. F. bile.] 1. (Physiol.) A yellow, or greenish, viscid fluid, usually alkaline in reaction, secreted by the liver. It passes into the intestines, where it aids in the digestive process. Its characteristic constituents are the bile salts, and coloring matters.

Bitterness of feeling; choler; anger; ill humor; as, to stir one's bile.

Prescott.

μ The ancients considered the bile to be the ½humor, which caused irascibility.

Bile, n. [OE. byle, bule, bele, AS. b?le, b?l; skin to D. buil, G. beule, and Goth. ufbauljan to puff up. Cf. Boil a tumor, Bulge.] A boil. [Obs. or Archaic]

Billection (?), n. (Arch.) That portion of a group of moldings which projects beyond the general surface of a panel; a bolection.

Bilestone · (?), n. [Bile + stone.] A gallstone, or biliary calculus. See Biliary.

E. Darwin.

Bilge (?), n. [A different orthography of bulge, of same origin as belly. Cf. Belly, Bulge.] 1. The protuberant part of a cask, which is usually in the middle.

(Naut.) That part of a ship's hull or bottom which is broadest and most nearly flat, and on which she would rest if aground.

Bilge water.

Bilge free (Naut.), stowed in such a way that the bilge is clear of everything; Ð said of a cask. Ð Bilge pump, a pump to draw the bilge water from the gold of a ship. Ð Bilge water (Naut.), water which collects in the bilge or bottom of a ship or other vessel. It is often allowed to remain till it becomes very offensive. Ð Bilge ways, the timbers which support the cradle of a ship upon the ways, and which slide upon the launching ways in launching the vessel.

<— p. 145 —>

Bilge (?), v. i. [imp. & p.p. Bilged (?); p. pr. & vb. n. Bilging.] 1. (Naut.) To suffer a fracture in the bilge; to spring a leak by a fracture in the bilge.

To bulge.

Bilge, v. t. 1. (Naut.) To fracture the bilge of, or stave in the bottom of (a ship or other vessel).

To cause to bulge.

Bilgy (?), a. Having the smell of bilge water.

Billary (?), a. [L. bilis bile: cf. F. biliaire.] (Physiol.) Relating or belonging to bile; conveying bile; as, biliary acids; biliary ducts.

Biliary calculus (Med.), a gallstone, or a concretion formed in the gall bladder or its duct.

Bil · ilation (?), n. (Physiol.) The production and excretion of bile.

Billiferious (?), a. Generating bile.

Bil·ifuscin (?), n. [L. bilis bile + fuscus dark.] (Physiol.) A brownish green pigment found in human gallstones and in old bile. It is a derivative of bilirubin.

ØBilimbi (?), ØBilimbing (?), } n. [Malay.] The berries of two East Indian species of Averrhoa, of the Oxalide' or Sorrel family. They are very acid, and highly esteemed when preserved or picked. The juice is used as a remedy for skin diseases. [Written also blimbi and blimbing.]

Biliment (?), n. A woman's ornament; habiliment. [Obs.]

Bilin (?), n. [Cf. F. biline, from L. bilis bile.] (Physiol. Chem.) A name applied to the amorphous or crystalline mass obtained from bile by the action of alcohol and ether. It is composed of a mixture of the sodium salts of the bile acids.

Bilinear (?), a. (Math.) Of, pertaining to, or included by, two lines; as, bilinear co"rdinates.

Bilingual (?), a. [L. bilinguis; bis twice + lingua tongue, language.] Containing, or consisting of, two languages; expressed in two languages; as, a bilingual inscription; a bilingual dictionary. Ð Bilingually, adv.

Bilingualism (?), n. Quality of being bilingual.

The bilingualism of King's English.

Earle.

Bilinguar (?), a. See Bilingual.

Bilinguist (?), n. One versed in two languages.

Bilinguous (?), a. [L. bilinguis.] Having two tongues, or speaking two languages. [Obs.]

Bilious (?), a. [L. biliosus, fr. bilis bile.] 1. Of or pertaining to the bile.

Disordered in respect to the bile; troubled with and excess of bile; as, a bilious patient; dependent on, or characterized by, an excess of bile; as, bilious symptoms.

Choleric; passionate; ill tempered. ½A bilious old nabob.

Macaulay.

Bilious temperament. See Temperament.

Biliousness, n. The state of being bilious.

Bil·iprasin (?), n. [L. bilis bile + prasinus green.] (Physiol.) A dark green pigment found in small quantity in human gallstones.

Bil·irubin (?), n. [L. bilis biel + ruber red.] (Physiol.) A reddish yellow pigment present in human bile, and in that from carnivorous and herbivorous animals; the normal biliary pigment.

Biliteral (?), a. [L. bis twice + littera letter.] Consisting of two letters; as, a biliteral root of a Sanskrit verb. Sir W. Jones. Ð n. A word, syllable, or root, consisting of two letters.

Biliteralism (?), n. The property or state of being biliteral.

Bil·iverdin (?), n. [L. bilis bile + viridis green. Cf. Verdure.] (Physiol.) A green pigment present in the bile, formed from bilirubin by oxidation.

Bilk (?), v. t. [imp. & p.p. Bilked (?); p. pr. & vb. n. Bilking.] [Origin unknown. Cf. Balk.] To frustrate or disappoint; to deceive or defraud, by nonfulfillment of engagement; to leave in the lurch; to give the slip to; as, to bilk a creditor.

Thackeray.

Bilk, n. 1. A thwarting an adversary in cribbage by spoiling his score; a balk.

<small>A cheat; a trick; a hoax.</small>

Hudibras.

<small>Nonsense; vain words.</small>

B. Jonson.

<small>A person who tricks a creditor; an untrustworthy, tricky person.</small>

Marryat.

Bill (?), n. [OE. bile, bille, AS. bile beak of a bird, proboscis; cf. Ir. & Gael. bil, bile, mouth, lip, bird's bill. Cf. Bill a weapon.] A beak, as of a bird, or sometimes of a turtle or other animal.

Milton.

Bill, v. i. [imp. & p.p. Billed (?); p. pr. & vb. n. Billing.] 1. To strike; to peck. [Obs.]

<small>To join bills, as doves; to caress in fondness. ½As pigeons bill.</small>

Shak.

To bill and coo, to interchange caresses; Ð said of doves; also of demonstrative lovers.

Thackeray.

Bill, n. The bell, or boom, of the bittern

The bittern's hollow bill was heard.

Wordsworth.

Bill, n. [OE. bil, AS. bill, bil; akin to OS. bil sword, OHG. bill pickax, G. bille. Cf. Bill bea?.] 1. A cutting instrument, with hookĭshaped point, and fitted with a handle; Ð used in pruning, etc.; a billhook. When short, called a hand bill, when long, a hedge bill.

<small>A weapon of infantry, in the 14th and 15th centuries. A common form of bill consisted of a broad, heavy, doubleĭedged, hookĭshaped blade, having a short pike at the back and another at the top, and attached to the end of a long staff.</small>

France had no infantry that dared to face the English bows end bills.

Macaulay.

<small>One who wields a bill; a billman.</small>

Strype.

A pickax, or mattock. [Obs.]

(Naut.) The extremity of the arm of an anchor; the point of or beyond the fluke.

Bill (?), v. t. To work upon (as to dig, hoe, hack, or chop anything) with a bill.

Bill, n. [OE. bill, bille, fr. LL. billa (or OF. bille), for L. bulla anything rounded, LL., seal, stamp, letter, edict, roll; cf. F. bille a ball, prob. fr. Ger.; cf. MHG. bickel, D. bikkel, dice. Cf. Bull papal edict, Billet a paper.]

(Law) A declaration made in writing, stating some wrong the complainant has suffered from the defendant, or a fault committed by some person against a law.

A writing binding the signer or signers to pay a certain sum at a future day or on demand, with or without interest, as may be stated in the document. [Eng.]

μ In the United States, it is usually called a note, a note of hand, or a promissory note.

A form or draft of a law, presented to a legislature for enactment; a proposed or projected law.

A paper, written or printed, and posted up or given away, to advertise something, as a lecture, a play, or the sale of goods; a placard; a poster; a handbill.

She put up the bill in her parlor window.
Dickens.

An account of goods sold, services rendered, or work done, with the price or charge; a statement of a creditor's claim, in gross or by items; as, a grocer's bill.

Any paper, containing a statement of particulars; as, a bill of charges or expenditures; a weekly bill of mortality; a bill of fare, etc.

Bill of adventure. See under Adventure. Ð Bill of costs, a statement of the items which form the total amount of the costs of a party to a suit or action. Ð Bill of credit. (a) Within the constitution of the United States, a paper issued by a State, on the mere faith and credit of the State, and designed to circulate as money. No State shall ½emit bills of credit., U. S. Const. Peters. Wharton. Bouvier (b) Among merchants, a letter sent by an agent or other person to a merchant, desiring him to give credit to the bearer for goods or money. Ð Bill of divorce, in the Jewish law, a writing given by the husband to the wife, by which the marriage relation was dissolved. Jer. iii. 8. Ð Bill of entry, a written account of goods entered at the customhouse, whether imported or intended for exportation. Ð Bill of exceptions. See under Exception. Ð Bill of exchange (Com.), a written order or request from one person or house to another, desiring the latter to pay to some person designated a certain sum of money therein generally is, and, to be negotiable, must be, made payable to order or to bearer. So also the order generally expresses a specified time

301

of payment, and that it is drawn for value. The person who draws the bil is called the drawer, the person on whom it is drawn is, before acceptance, called the drawee, Ð after acceptance, the acceptor; the person to whom the money is directed to be paid is called the payee. The person making the order may himself be the payee. The bill itself is frequently called a draft. See Exchange. Chitty. Ð Bill of fare, a written or printed enumeration of the dishes served at a public table, or of the dishes (with prices annexed) which may be ordered at a restaurant, etc. Ð Bill of health, a certificate from the proper authorities as to the state of health of a ship's company at the time of her leaving port. Ð Bill of indictment, a written accusation lawfully presented to a grand jury. If the jury consider the evidence sufficient to support the accusation, they indorse it ½A true bill,͵ or ½Not found,͵ or ½Ignoramus͵, or ½Ignored.͵ Ð Bill of lading, a written account of goods shipped by any person, signed by the agent of the owner of the vessel, or by its master, acknowledging the receipt of the goods, and promising to deliver them safe at the place directed, dangers of the sea excepted. It is usual for the master to sign two, three, or four copies of the bill; one of which he keeps in possession, one is kept by the shipper, and one is sent to the consignee of the goods. Ð Bill of mortality, an official statement of the number of deaths in a place or district within a given time; also, a district required to be covered by such statement; as, a place within the bills of mortality of London. Ð Bill of pains and penalties, a special act of a legislature which inflicts a punishment less than death upon persons supposed to be guilty of treason or felony, without any conviction in the ordinary course of judicial proceedings. Bouvier. Wharton. Ð Bill of parcels, an account given by the seller to the buyer of the several articles purchased, with the price of each. Ð Bill of particulars (Law), a detailed statement of the items of a plaintiff's demand in an action, or of the defendant's setÏoff. Ð Bill of rights, a summary of rights and privileges claimed by a people. Such was the declaration presented by the Lords and Commons of England to the Prince and Princess of Orange in 1688, and enacted in Parliament after they became king and queen. In America, a bill or declaration of rights is prefixed to most of the constitutions of the several States. Ð Bill of sale, a formal instrument for the conveyance or transfer of goods and chattels. Ð Bill of sight, a form of entry at the customhouse, by which goods, respecting which the importer is not possessed of full information, may be provisionally landed for examination. Ð Bill of store, a license granted at the customhouse to merchants, to carry such stores and provisions as are necessary for a voyage, custom free. Wharton. Ð Bills payable (pl.), the outstanding unpaid notes or acceptances made and issued by an individual or firm. Ð Bills receivable (pl.), the unpaid promissory notes or acceptances held by an individual or firm. McElrath. Ð A true bill, a bill of indictment sanctioned by a grand jury.

Bill, v. t. 1. To advertise by a bill or public notice.

To charge or enter in a bill; as, to bill goods.

Billage (?), n. and v. t. & i. Same as Bilge.

Billard (?), n. (Zo"l.) An English fish, allied to the cod; the coalfish. [Written also billet and billit.]

Bill · beetle (?), or Billbug · (?), n. (Zo"l.) A weevil or curculio of various species, as the corn weevil. See Curculio.

Billboard · (?), n. 1. (Naut.) A piece of thick plank, armed with iron plates, and fixed on the bow or fore channels of a vessel, for the bill or fluke of the anchor to rest on.

Totten.

A flat surface, as of a panel or of a fence, on which bills are posted; a bulletin board.

Bill book · (?). (Com.) A book in which a person keeps an account of his notes, bills, bills of exchange, etc., thus showing all that he issues and receives.

Bill bro · ker (?). One who negotiates the discount of bills.

Billed (?), a. Furnished with, or having, a bill, as a bird; Ð used in composition; as, broadÏbilled.

Billet (?), n. [F. billet, dim. of an OF. bille bill. See Bill a writing.] 1. A small paper; a note; a short letter. ½I got your melancholy billet.͵

Sterne.

A ticket from a public officer directing soldiers at what house to lodge; as, a billet of residence.

Billet, v. t. [imp. & p.p. Billeted; p. pr. & vb. n. Billeting.] [From Billet a ticket.] (Mil.) To direct, by a ticket or note, where to lodge. Hence: To quarter, or place in lodgings, as soldiers in private houses.

Billeted in so antiquated a mansion.

W. Irving.

Billet, n. [F. billette, bille, log; of unknown origin; a different word from bille ball. Cf. Billiards, Billot.] 1. A small stick of wood, as for firewood.

They shall beat out my brains with billets.

Shak.

(Metal.) A short bar of metal, as of gold or iron.

(Arch.) An ornament in Norman work, resembling a billet of wood either square or round.

(Saddlery) (a) A strap which enters a buckle. (b) A loop which receives the end of a buckled strap.

Knight.

(Her.) A bearing in the form of an oblong rectangle.

ØBil · letÐdoux (?), n.; pl. BilletsÐdoux (?). [F. billet note + doux sweet, L. dulcis.] A love letter or note.

A lover chanting out a billet-doux.

Spectator.

Billet׳head (?), n. (Naut.) A round piece of timber at the bow or stern of a whaleboat, around which the harpoon lone is run out when the whale darts off.

Billfish (?), n. (Zo"l.) A name applied to several distinct fishes: (a) The garfish (Tylosurus, or Belone, longirostris) and allied species. (b) The saury, a slender fish of the Atlantic coast (Scomberesox saurus). (c) The Tetrapturus albidus, a large oceanic species related to the swordfish; the spearfish. (d) The American fresh׳water garpike (Lepidosteus osseus).

Billhead (?), n. A printed form, used by merchants in making out bills or rendering accounts.

Bill hold·er (?). 1. A person who holds a bill or acceptance.

A device by means of which bills, etc., are held.

Billhook (?), n. [Bill + hook.] A thick, heavy knife with a hooked point, used in pruning hedges, etc. When it has a short handle, it is sometimes called a hand bill; when the handle is long, a hedge bill or scimiter.

Billiard (?), a. Of or pertaining to the game of billiards. ½Smooth as is a billiard ball.͵

B. Jonson.

Billiards (?), n. [F. billiard billiards, OF. billart staff, cue form playing, fr. bille log. See Billet a stick.] A game played with ivory balls o a cloth׳covered, rectangular table, bounded by elastic cushions. The player seeks to impel his ball with his cue so that it shall either strike (carom upon) two other balls, or drive another ball into one of the pockets with which the table sometimes is furnished.

Billing (?), a. & n. Caressing; kissing.

Billings׳gate (?), n. 1. A market near the Billings gate in London, celebrated for fish and foul language.

Coarsely abusive, foul, or profane language; vituperation; ribaldry.

Billion (?), n. [F. billion, arbitrarily formed fr. L. bis twice, in imitation of million a million. See Million.] According to the French and American method of numeration, a thousand millions, or 1,000,000,000; according to the English method, a million millions, or 1,000,000,000,000. See Numeration.

Billman (?), n.; pl. Billmen (?). One who uses, or is armed with, a bill or hooked ax. ½A billman of the guard.͵

Savile.

ØBil·lon (?), n. [F. Cf. Billet a stick.] An alloy of gold and silver with a large proportion of copper or other base metal, used in coinage.

Billot (?), n. [F. billot, dim. of bille. See Billet a stick.] Bullion in the bar or mass.

Billow (?), n. [Cf. Icel. bylgja billow, Dan. b"lge, Sw. b"lja; akin to MHG. bulge billow, bag, and to E. bulge. See Bulge.] 1. A great wave or surge of the sea or other water, caused usually by violent wind.

Whom the winds waft where'er the billows roll.
Cowper.

A great wave or flood of anything.

Milton.

Billow, v. i. [imp. & p.p. Billowed (?); p. pr. & vb. n. Billowing.] To surge; to rise and roll in waves or surges; to undulate. ½The billowing snow.‚
Prior.

Billowly (?), a. Of or pertaining to billows; swelling or swollen into large waves; full of billows or surges; resembling billows.

And whitening down the manyïtinctured stream,
Descends the billowy foam.
Thomson.

Billpost · er (?), Billsticker (?), } n. One whose occupation is to post handbills or posters in public places.

Billy (?), n. 1. A club; esp., a policeman's club.

(Wool Manuf.) A slubbing or roving machine.

Billyïboy · (?), n. A flatïbottomed river barge or coasting vessel. [Eng.]
Billy goat · (?). A male goat. [Colloq.]
<— p. 146 —>
Billobate (?), a. [Pref. biï + lobate.] Divided into two lobes or segments.
Bilobed (?), a. [Pref. biï + lobe.] Bilobate.
Bi · loïcation (?), n. [Pref. biï + location.] Double location; the state or power of being in two places at the same instant; Ð a miraculous power attributed to some of the saints.
Tylor.

Billocuïlar (?), a. [Pref. biï + locular: cf. F. biloculaire.] Divided into two cells or compartments; as, a bilocular pericarp.
Gray.

Bilsted (?), n. (Bot.) See Sweet gum.
ØBiltong (?), n. [S. African.] Lean meat cut into strips and sunïdried.
H. R. Haggard.

Biïmacuïlate (?), a. [Pref. biï + maculate, a.] Having, or marked with, two spots.

ØBimaïna (?), n. pl. [NL. See Bimanous.] (Zo"l.) Animals having two hands; Ð a term applied by Cuvier to man as a special order of Mammalia.

Bimaïnous (?), a. [L. bis twice + manus hand.] (Zo"l.) Having two hands; twoïhanded.

Bi̇margini̇ate (?), a. [Pref. bi̇ + marginate.] Having a double margin, as certain shells.

Bi̇mastism (?), n. [Pref. bi̇ + Gr. ? breast.] (Anat.) The condition of having two mamm' or teats.

Bi̇medi̇al (?), a. [Pref. bi̇ + medial.] (Geom.) Applied to a line which is the sum of two lines commensurable only in power (as the side and diagonal of a square).

Bi̇membral (?), a. [L. bis twice + membrum member.] (Gram.) Having two members; as, a bimembral sentence.

J. W. Gibbs.

Bi̇mensal (?), a. [Pref. bi̇ + mensal.] See Bimonthly, a. [Obs. or R.]

Bi̇mestri̇al (?), a. [L. bimestris; bis twice + mensis month.] Continuing two months. [R.]

Bi · mei̇tallic (?), a. [Pref. bi̇ + metallic: cf. F. bim,tallique.] Of or relating to, or using, a double metallic standard (as gold and silver) for a system of coins or currency.

Bi̇metali̇lism (?), n. [F. bim,talisme.] The legalized use of two metals (as gold and silver) in the currency of a country, at a fixed relative value; Đ in opposition to monometallism.

μ The words bim,tallisme and monom,tallisme are due to M. Cernuschi [1869].

Littr,.

Bi̇metali̇list (?), n. An advocate of bimetallism.

Bi̇monthly (?), a. [Pref. bi̇ + monthly.] Occurring, done, or coming, once in two months; as, bimonthly visits; bimonthly publications. Đ n. A bimonthly publication.

Bi̇monthly, adv. Once in two months.

Bi̇muscui̇lar (?), a. [Pref. bi̇ + muscular.] (Zo"l.) Having two adductor muscles, as a bivalve mollusk.

Bin (?), n. [OE. binne, AS. binn manager, crib; perh. akin to D. ben, benne, basket, and to L. benna a kind of carriage (a Gallic word), W. benn, men, wain, cart.] A box, frame, crib, or inclosed place, used as a receptacle for any commodity; as, a corn bin; a wine bin; a coal bin.

Bin, v. t. [imp. & p.p. Binned (?); p. pr. & vb. n. Binning.] To put into a bin; as, to bin wine.

Bin. An old form of Be and Been. [Obs.]

Bini̇. A euphonic form of the prefix Bi̇.

Binal (?), a. [See Binary.] Twofold; double. [R.] ½Binal revenge, all this.,

Ford·

Bin · ari̇seni̇ate (?), n. [Pref. bini̇ + arseniate.] (Chem.) A salt having two equivalents of arsenic acid to one of the base.

Graham.

Binai̇ry (?), a. [L. binarius, fr. bini two by two, two at a time, fr. root of bis twice; akin to E. two: cf. F. binaire.] Compounded or consisting of two things or parts; characterized by two (things).

Binary arithmetic, that in which numbers are expressed according to the binary scale, or in which two figures only, 0 and 1, are used, in lieu of ten; the cipher multiplying everything by two, as in common arithmetic by ten. Thus, 1 is one; 10 is two; 11 is three; 100 is four, etc. Davies & Peck. Ð Binary compound (Chem.), a compound of two elements, or of an element and a compound performing the function of an element, or of two compounds performing the function of elements. Ð Binary logarithms, a system of logarithms devised by Euler for facilitating musical calculations, in which 1 is logarithm of 2, instead of 10, as in the common logarithms, and the modulus 1.442695 instead of .43429448. Ð Binary measure (Mus.), measure divisible by two or four; common time. Ð Binary nomenclature (Nat. Hist.), nomenclature in which the names designate both genus and species. Ð Binary scale (Arith.), a uniform scale of notation whose ratio is two. Ð Binary star (Astron.), a double star whose members have a revolution round their common center of gravity. Ð Binary theory (Chem.), the theory that all chemical compounds consist of two constituents of opposite and unlike qualities.

Binaĭry, n. That which is constituted of two figures, things, or parts; two; duality.

Fotherby.

Binate (?), a. [L. bini two and two.] (Bot.) Double; growing in pairs or couples.

Gray.

Binĭaural (?), a. [Pref. binĭ + aural.] Of or pertaining to, or used by, both ears.

Bind (?), v. t. [imp. Bound (?); p. p. Bound, formerly Bounden (?); p. pr. & vb. n. Binding.] [AS. bindan, perfect tense band, bundon, p. p. bunden; akin to D. & G. binden, Dan. binde, Sw. & Icel. binda, Goth. bindan, Skr. bandh (for bhandh) to bind, cf. Gr. ? (for ?) cable, and L. offendix. ?90.] 1. To tie, or confine with a cord, band, ligature, chain, etc.; to fetter; to make fast; as, to bind grain in bundles; to bind a prisoner.

> To confine, restrain, or hold by physical force or influence of any kind; as, attraction binds the planets to the sun; frost binds the earth, or the streams.

He bindeth the floods from overflowing.
Job xxviii. 11.
Whom Satan hath bound, lo, these eighteen years.
Luke xiii. 16.

> To cover, as with a bandage; to bandage or dress; Ð sometimes with up; as, to bind up a wound.

> To make fast (a thing) about or upon something, as by tying; to encircle with something; as, to bind a belt about one; to bind a compress upon a part.

To prevent or restrain from customary or natural action; as, certain drugs bind the bowels.

To protect or strengthen by a band or binding, as the edge of a carpet or garment.

To sew or fasten together, and inclose in a cover; as, to bind a book.

Fig.: To oblige, restrain, or hold, by authority, law, duty, promise, vow, affection, or other moral tie; as, to bind the conscience; to bind by kindness; bound by affection; commerce binds nations to each other.

Who made our laws to bind us, not himself.
Milton.

(Law) (a) To bring (any one) under definite legal obligations; esp. under the obligation of a bond or covenant. Abbott. (b) To place under legal obligation to serve; to indenture; as, to bind an apprentice; Ð sometimes with out; as, bound out to service.

To bind over, to put under bonds to do something, as to appear at court, to keep the peace, etc. Ð To bind to, to contract; as, to bind one's self to a wife. Ð To bind up in, to cause to be wholly engrossed with; to absorb in.

Syn. Ð To fetter; tie; fasten; restrain; restrict; oblige.

Bind (?), v. i. 1. To tie; to confine by any ligature.

They that reap must sheaf and bind.
Shak.

To contract; to grow hard or stiff; to cohere or stick together in a mass; as, clay binds by heat.

Mortimer.

To be restrained from motion, or from customary or natural action, as by friction.

To exert a binding or restraining influence.

Locke.

Bind, n. 1. That which binds or ties.

Any twining or climbing plant or stem, esp. a hop vine; a bine.

(Metal.) Indurated clay, when much mixed with the oxide of iron.

Kirwan.

(Mus.) A ligature or tie for grouping notes.

Binder (?), n. 1. One who binds; as, a binder of sheaves; one whose trade is to bind; as, a binder of books.

Anything that binds, as a fillet, cord, rope, or band; a bandage; Ð esp. the principal piece of timber intended to bind together any building.

Binderly (?), n. A place where books, or other articles, are bound; a bookbinder's establishment.

Bindheimlite (?), n. [From Bindheim, a German who analyzed it.] (Min.) An amorphous antimonate of lead, produced from the alteration of other ores, as from jamesonite.

Binding (?), a. That binds; obligatory.

Binding beam (Arch.), the main timber in double flooring. Ð Binding joist (Arch.), the secondary timber in doubleïframed flooring.

Syn. Ð Obligatory; restraining; restrictive; stringent; astringent; costive; styptic.

Binding, n. 1. The act or process of one who, or that which, binds.

Anything that binds; a bandage; the cover of a book, or the cover with the sewing, etc.; something that secures the edge of cloth from raveling.

pl. (Naut.) The transoms, knees, beams, keelson, and other chief timbers used for connecting and strengthening the parts of a vessel.

Bindingly, adv. So as to bind.

Bindingïness, n. The condition or property of being binding; obligatory quality.

Coleridge.

Bindweed · (?), n. (Bot.) A plant of the genus Convolvulus; as, greater bindweed (C. Sepium); lesser bindweed (C. arvensis); the white, the blue, the Syrian, bindweed. The black bryony, or Tamus, is called black bindweed, and the Smilax aspera, rough bindweed.

The fragile bindweed bells and bryony rings.

Tennyson.

Bine (?), n. [Bind, cf. Woodbine.] The winding or twining stem of a hop vine or other climbing plant.

Biïnervate (?), a. [L. bis twice + nervus sinew, nerve.] 1. (Bot.) Twoïnerved; Ð applied to leaves which have two longitudinal ribs or nerves.

(Zo"l.) Having only two nerves, as the wings of some insects.

Bing (?), n. [Cf. Icel. bingr, Sw. binge, G. beige, beuge. Cf. Prov. E. bink bench, and bench coal the uppermost stratum of coal.] A heap or pile; as, a bing of wood. ½Potato bings.„ Burns. ½A bing of corn.„ Surrey. [Obs. or Dial. Eng. & Scot.]

Binïioïdide (?), n. Same as Diiodide.

Bink (?), n. A bench. [North of Eng. & Scot.]

Binnaïcle (?), n. [For bittacle, corrupted (perh. by influence of bin) fr. Pg. bitacola binnacle, fr. L. habitaculum dwelling place, fr. habitare to dwell. See Habit, and cf. Bittacle.] (Naut.) A case or box placed near the helmsman, containing the compass of a ship, and a light to show it at night.

Totten.

Binny (?), n. (Zo"l.) A large species of barbel (Barbus bynni), found in the Nile, and much esteemed for food.

Binocle (?), n. [F. binocle; L. bini two at a time + oculus eye.] (Opt.) A dioptric telescope, fitted with two tubes joining, so as to enable a person to view an object with both eyes at once; a double-barreled field glass or an opera glass.

Binocular (?), a. [Cf. F. binoculaire. See Binocle.] 1. Having two eyes. ½Most animals are binocular.

Derham.

Pertaining to both eyes; employing both eyes at once; as, binocular vision.

Adapted to the use of both eyes; as, a binocular microscope or telescope.

Brewster.

Binocular (?), n. A binocular glass, whether opera glass, telescope, or microscope.

Binocularly, adv. In a binocular manner.

Binoculate (?), a. Having two eyes.

Binomial (?), n. [L. bis twice + nomen name: cf. F. binome, LL. binomius (or fr. bi + Gr. ? distribution ?). Cf. Monomial.] (Alg.) An expression consisting of two terms connected by the sign plus (+) or minus (Ð); as, a+b, or 7Ð3.

Binomial, a. 1. Consisting of two terms; pertaining to binomials; as, a binomial root.

(Nat. Hist.) Having two names; Ð used of the system by which every animal and plant receives two names, the one indicating the genus, the other the species, to which it belongs.

Binomial theorem (Alg.), the theorem which expresses the law of formation of any power of a binomial.

Binominal (?), a. [See Binomial.] Of or pertaining to two names; binomial.

Binominous (?), a. Binominal. [Obs.]

Binotonous (?), a. [L. bini two at a time + tonus, fr. Gr. ?, tone.] Consisting of two notes; as, a binotonous cry.

Binous (?), a. Same as Binate.

Binoxalate (?), n. [Pref. bin + oxalate.] (Chem.) A salt having two equivalents of oxalic acid to one of the base; an acid oxalate.

Binoxide (?), n. [Pref. bin + oxide.] (Chem.) Same as Dioxide.

ØBintu**rong** (?), n. (Zo"l.) A small Asiatic civet of the genus Arctilis.

Binuclear (?), **Binucleate** (?), } a. [Pref. bi + nuclear, nucleate.] (Biol.) Having two nuclei; as, binucleate cells.

Binucleolate (?), a. [Pref. bi + nucleolus.] (Biol.) Having two nucleoli.

Bioblast (?), n. [Gr. ? life + blast.] (Biol.) Same as Bioplast.

Bi˘ocel˘late (?), a. [L. bis twice + ocellatus. See Ocellated.] (Zo"l.) Having two ocelli (eyelike spots); Ð said of a wing, etc.

Bi · o˘chemis˘try (?), n. [Gr. ? life + E. chemistry.] (Biol.) The chemistry of living organisms; the chemistry of the processes incidental to ? characteristic of, life.

Bi · o˘dy˘namics (?), n. [Gr. ? life + E. dynamics.] (Biol.) The doctrine of vital forces or energy.

Bio˘gen (?), n. [Gr. ? life + ˘gen.] (Biol.) Bioplasm.

Bi · o˘gene˘sis (?), Bi˘oge˘ny (?), } n. [Gr. ? life + ?, ?, birth.] (Biol.) (a) A doctrine that the genesis or production of living organisms can take place only through the agency of living germs or parents; Ð opposed to abiogenesis. (b) Life development generally.

Bi · o˘ge˘netic (?), a. (Biol.) Pertaining to biogenesis.

Bi˘oge˘nist (?), n. A believer in the theory of biogenesis.

ØBi · og˘nosis (?), n. [Gr. ? life + ? investigation.] (Biol.) The investigation of life.

Bi˘ogra˘pher (?), n. One who writes an account or history of the life of a particular person; a writer of lives, as Plutarch.

Bio˘graphic (?), Bi · o˘graphic˘al (?), } a. Of or pertaining to biography; containing biography. Ð Bi · o˘graphic˘al˘ly, adv.

Bi˘ogra˘phize (?), v. t. To write a history of the life of.
Southey.

Bi˘ogra˘phy (?), n.; pl. Biographies (?). [Gr. ?; ? life + ? to write: cf. F. biographie. See Graphic.] 1. The written history of a person's life.

Biographical writings in general.

Bi · o˘llogic (?), Bi · o˘llogic˘al (?), } a. Of or relating to biology. Ð Bi · o˘logic˘al˘ly, adv.

Bi˘olo˘gist (?), n. A student of biology; one versed in the science of biology.

Bi˘olo˘gy (?), n. [Gr. ? life + ˘logy: cf. F. biologie.] The science of life; that branch of knowledge which treats of living matter as distinct from matter which is not living; the study of living tissue. It has to do with the origin, structure, development, function, and distribution of animals and plants.

ØBi˘oly˘sis (?), n. [Gr. ? life + ? a dissolving.] (Biol.) The destruction of life.

Bi · o˘llytic (?), a. [Gr. ? life + ? to destroy.] Relating to the destruction of life.

Bi · o˘mag˘netic (?), a. Relating to biomagnetism.

Bi · o˘magnet˘ism (?), n. [Gr. ? life + E. magnetism.] Animal magnetism.

Bi˘ome˘try (?), n. [Gr. ? life + ˘metry.] Measurement of life; calculation of the probable duration of human life.

Bion (?), n. [Gr. ? living, p. pr. of ? to live.] (Biol.) The physiological individual, characterized by definiteness and independence of function, in distinction from the morphological individual or morphon.

Bi′onoĭmy (?), n. [Gr. ? life + ? law.] Physiology. [R.] Dunglison.

Bi′ŏphor · Bi′ŏphore · } (?), n. [Gr. ? life + ? bearing, fr. ? to bear.] (Biol.) One of the smaller vital units of a cell, the bearer of vitality and heredity. See Pangen, in Supplement.

Bi′oplasm (?), n. [Gr. ? life + ? form, mold, fr. ? to mold.] (Biol.) A name suggested by Dr. Beale for the germinal matter supposed to be essential to the functions of all living beings; the material through which every form of life manifests itself; unaltered protoplasm.

<— p. 147 —>

Bi · oĭplasmic (?), a. Pertaining to, or consisting of, bioplasm.

Bi′oplast (?), n. [Gr. ? life + ? to form.] (Biol.) A tiny mass of bioplasm, in itself a living unit and having formative power, as a living white blood corpuscle; bioblast.

Bi · oĭplastic (?), a. (Biol.) Bioplasmic.

Bi′organ (?), n. [Gr. ? life + E. organ.] (Biol.) A physiological organ; a living organ; an organ endowed with function; Ð distinguished from idorgan.

Bi · oĭstatics (?), n. [Gr. ? life + ?. See Statics.] (Biol.) The physical phenomena of organized bodies, in opposition to their organic or vital phenomena.

Bi · oĭstaĭtistics (?), n. [Gr. ? life + E. statistics.] (Biol.) Vital statistics.

Bi′otax · y (?), n. [Gr. ? life + ? arrangement.] (Biol.) The classification of living organisms according to their structural character; taxonomy.

Bi′otic (?), a. [Gr. ? pert. to life.] (Biol.) Relating to life; as, the biotic principle.

Bi′otite (?), n. [From Biot, a French naturalist.] (Min.) Mica containing iron and magnesia, generally of a black or dark green color; Ð a common constituent of crystalline rocks. See Mica.

Bi′palmate (?), a. [Pref. bi′ + palmate.] (Bot.) Palmately branched, with the branches again palmated.

Bi · paĭrieĭtal (?), a. [Pref. bi′ + parietal.] (Anat.) Of or pertaining to the diameter of the cranium, from one parietal fossa to the other.

Bipa′rous (?), a. [L. bis twice + parere to bring forth.] Bringing forth two at a birth.

Bi′partiĭble (?), a. [Cf. F. bipartible. See Bipartite.] Capable of being divided into two parts.

Bi′partient (?), a. [L. bis twice + partiens, p. pr. of partire to divide.] Dividing into two parts. Ð n. A number that divides another into two equal parts without a remainder.

Bi′partile (?), a. Divisible into two parts.

Bipar′tite (?), a. [L. bipartitus, p. p. of bipartire; bis twice + partire. See Partite.] 1. Being in two parts; having two correspondent parts, as a legal contract or writing, one for each party; shared by two; as, a bipartite treaty.

Divided into two parts almost to the base, as a leaf; consisting of two parts or subdivisions.

Gray.

Bi·parĭtition (?), n. The act of dividing into two parts, or of making two correspondent parts, or the state of being so divided.

Bĭpectĭnate (?), Bĭpectĭna·ted (?), } a. [Pref. bĭ + pectinate.] (Biol.) Having two margins toothed like a comb.

Biped (?), n. [L. bipes; bis twice + pes, pedis, ?oot: cf. F. bipŠde.] A twoĭfooted animal, as man.

Biped, a. Having two feet; twoĭfooted.

By which the man, when heavenly life was ceased,
Became a helpless, naked, biped beast.

Byrom.

Bipeĭdal (?), a. [L. bipedalis: cf. F. bip,dal. See Biped, n.] 1. Having two feet; biped.

Pertaining to a biped.

Bĭpeltate (?), a. [Pref. bĭ + peltate.] Having a shell or covering like a double shield.

Bĭpennate (?), Bĭpennaĭted (?), } a. [Pref. bĭ + pennate: cf. L. bipennis. Cf. Bipinnate.] Having two wings. ½Bipennated insects.‚

Derham.

ØBĭpennis (?), n. [L.] An ax with an edge or blade on each side of the handle.

Bĭpetalĭous (?), a. [Pref. bĭ + petalous.] (Bot.) Having two petals.

ØBi·pinĭnariĭa (?), n. [NL., fr. L. bis twice + pinna feather.] (Zo"l.) The larva of certain starfishes as developed in the freeĭswimming stage.

Bĭpinnate (?), Bĭpinnaĭted (?), } a. [Pref. bĭ + pinnate; cf. F. bipinn,. Cf. Bipennate.] Twice pinnate.

Bi·pinĭnatiĭfid (?), a. [Pref. bĭ + pinnatifid.] (Bot.) Doubly pinnatifid.

A bipinnatifid leaf is a pinnatifid leaf having its segments or divisions also pinnatifid. The primary divisions are pinn' and the secondary pinnules.

Bipliĭcate (?), a. [Pref. bĭ + plicate.] Twice folded together.

Henslow.

Bĭpliciĭty (?), n. The state of being twice folded; reduplication. [R.]

Bailey.

Bĭpolar (?), a. [Pref. bĭ + polar. Cf. Dipolar.] Doubly polar; having two poles; as, a bipolar cell or corpuscle.

Bi·poĭlariĭty (?), n. Bipolar quality.

Bipont (?), Bĭpontine (?), a. (Bibliog.) Relating to books printed at Deuxponts, or Bipontium (Zweibrcken), in Bavaria.

Bĭpunctate (?), a. [Pref. bĭ + punctate.] Having two punctures, or spots.

Bi˘punctu˘al (?), a. Having two points.

Bi˘pupil˘late (?), a. [Pref. bi˘ + pupil (of the eye).] (Zo"l.) Having an eyelike spot on the wing, with two dots within it of a different color, as in some butterflies.

Bi · py˘rami˘dal (?), a. [Pref. bi˘ + pyramidal.] Consisting of two pyramids placed base to base; having a pyramid at each of the extremities of a prism, as in quartz crystals.

Bi˘quadrate (?), n. [Pref. bi˘ + quadrate.] (Math.) The fourth power, or the square of the square. Thus 4x4=16, the square of 4, and 16x16=256, the biquadrate of 4.

Bi · quad˘ratic (?), a. [Pref. bi˘ + quadratic: cf. F. biquadratique.] (Math.) Of or pertaining to the biquadrate, or fourth power.

Biquadratic equation (Alg.), an equation of the fourth degree, or an equation in some term of which the unknown quantity is raised to the fourth power. Ð Biquadratic root of a number, the square root of the square root of that number. Thus the square root of 81 is 9, and the square root of 9 is 3, which is the biquadratic root of 81. Hutton.

Bi · quad˘ratic, n. (Math.) (a) A biquadrate. (b) A biquadratic equation.

Bi˘quintile (?), n. [Pref. bi˘ + quintile: cf. F. biquintile.] (Astron.) An aspect of the planets when they are distant from each other by twice the fifth part of a great circle Ð that is, twice 72 degrees.

Bi˘radi˘ate (?), Bi˘radi˘a · ted (?), } a. [Pref. bi˘ + radiate.] Having two rays; as, a biradiate fin.

Bi˘ramous (?), a. [Pref. bi˘ + ramous.] (Biol.) Having, or consisting of, two branches.

Birch (?), n.; pl. Birches (?). [OE. birche, birk, AS. birce, beorc; akin to Icel. bj"rk, Sw. bj"rk, Dan. birk, D. berk, OHG. piricha, MHG. birche, birke, G. birke, Russ. bereza, Pol. brzoza, Serv. breza, Skr. bh?rja. ?254. Cf. 1st Birk.] 1. A tree of several species, constituting the genus Betula; as, the white or common birch (B. alba) (also called silver birch and lady birch); the dwarf birch (B. glandulosa); the paper or canoe birch (B. papyracea); the yellow birch (B. lutea); the black or cherry birch (B. lenta).

The wood or timber of the birch.

A birch twig or birch twigs, used for flogging.

µ The twigs of the common European birch (B. alba), being tough and slender, were formerly much used for rods in schools. They were also made into brooms.

The threatening twigs of birch.
Shak.

A birch˘bark canoe.

Birch of Jamaica, a species (Bursera gummifera) of turpentine tree. Ð Birch partridge. (Zo"l.) See Ruffed grouse. Ð Birch wine, wine made of the spring sap of the birch. Ð Oil of birch. (a) An oil obtained from the bark of the common European birch (Betula alba), and used in the preparation of genuine (and sometimes of the imitation) Russia leather, to which it gives its peculiar odor. (b) An oil prepared from the black birch (B. lenta), said to be identical with the oil of wintergreen, for which it is largely sold.

Birch, a. Of or pertaining to the birch; birchen.

Birch, v. t. [imp. & p.p. Birched (?); p. pr. & vb. n. Birching.] To whip with a birch rod or twig; to flog.

Birchen (?), a. Of or relating to birch.

He passed where Newark's stately tower
Looks out from Yarrow's birchen bower.
Sir W. Scott.

Bird (?), n. [OE. brid, bred, bird, young bird, bird, AS. bridd young bird. ?92.] 1. Orig., a chicken; the young of a fowl; a young eaglet; a nestling; and hence, a feathered flying animal (see 2).

That ungentle gull, the cuckoo's bird.
Shak.

The brydds [birds] of the aier have nestes.
Tyndale (Matt. viii. 20).

(Zo"l.) A warmĭblooded, feathered vertebrate provided with wings. See Aves.

Specifically, among sportsmen, a game bird.

Fig.: A girl; a maiden.

And by my word! the bonny bird
In danger shall not tarry.
Campbell.

Arabian bird, the phenix. Ð Bird of Jove, the eagle. Ð Bird of Juno, the peacock. Ð Bird louse (Zo"l.), a wingless insect of the group Mallophaga, of which the genera and species are very numerous and mostly parasitic upon birds. Ð Bird mite (Zo"l.), a small mite (genera Dermanyssus, Dermaleichus and allies) parasitic upon birds. The species are numerous. Ð Bird of passage, a migratory bird. Ð Bird spider (Zo"l.), a very large South American spider (Mygale avicularia). It is said sometimes to capture and kill small birds. Ð Bird tick (Zo"l.), a dipterous insect parasitic upon birds (genus Ornithomyia, and allies), usually winged.

Bird (?), v. i. 1. To catch or shoot birds.

Hence: To seek for game or plunder; to thieve. [R.]

B. Jonson.

Birdbolt · (?), n. A short blunt arrow for killing birds without piercing them. Hence: Anything which smites without penetrating.

Shak.

Bird cage, or Birdcage· (?), n. A cage for confining birds.

Birdcall· (?), n. 1. A sound made in imitation of the note or cry of a bird for the purpose of decoying the bird or its mate.

An instrument of any kind, as a whistle, used in making the sound of a birdcall.

Birdcatch · er (?), n. One whose employment it is to catch birds; a fowler.

Birdcatch · ing, n. The art, act, or occupation or catching birds or wild fowls.

Bird cher · ry (?). (Bot.) A shrub (Prunus Padus) found in Northern and Central Europe. It bears small black cherries.

Birder (?), n. A birdcatcher.

BirdÐeyed· (?), a. QuickÏsighted; catching a glance as one goes.

Bird fan · ciÏer (?). 1. One who takes pleasure in rearing or collecting rare or curious birds.

One who has for sale the various kinds of birds which are kept in cages.

Birdie (?), n. A pretty or dear little bird; Ð a pet name.
Tennyson.

BirdiÏkin (?), n. A young bird.
Thackeray.

Birding, n. Birdcatching or fowling.
Shak.

Birding piece, a fowling piece.
Shak.

Birdlet, n. A little bird; a nestling.

Birdlike· (?), a. Resembling a bird.

Birdlime· (?), n. [Bird + lime viscous substance.] An extremely adhesive viscid substance, usually made of the middle bark of the holly, by boiling, fermenting, and cleansing it. When a twig is smeared with this substance it will hold small birds which may light upon it. Hence: Anything which insnares.

Not birdlime or Idean pitch produce
A more tenacious mass of clammy juice.
　Dryden.

μ Birdlime is also made from mistletoe, elder, etc.

Birdlime·, v. t. To smear with birdlime; to catch with birdlime; to insnare.

When the heart is thus birdlimed, then it cleaves to everything it meets with.
Coodwin.

Birdling, n. A little bird; a nestling.

Birdman (?), n. A fowler or birdcatcher.

Bird of paraĭdise (?). (Zo"l.) The name of several very beautiful birds of the genus Paradisea and allied genera, inhabiting New Guinea and the adjacent islands. The males have brilliant colors, elegant plumes, and often remarkable tail feathers.

µ The Great emerald (Paradisea apoda) and the Lesser emerald (P. minor) furnish many of the plumes used as ornaments by ladies; the Red is P. rubra or sanguinea; the Golden is Parotia aurea or sexsetacea; the King is Cincinnurus regius.

The name is also applied to the lingerĭbilled birds of another related group (Epimachin') from the same region. The Twelvewired (Seleucides alba) is one of these. See Paradise bird, and Note under Apod.

Bird pep · per (?). A species of capsicum (Capsicum baccatum), whose small, conical, coralĭred fruit is among the most piquant of all red peppers.

Bird'sÐbeak · (?), n. (Arch.) A molding whose section is thought to resemble a beak.

Birdseed · (?), n. Canary seed, hemp, millet or other small seeds used for feeding caged birds.

Bird'sÐeye · (?), a. 1. Seen from above, as if by a flying bird; embraced at a glance; hence, general? not minute, or entering into details; as, a bird'sÐeye view.

Marked with spots resembling bird's eyes; as, bird'sÐeye diaper; bird'sÐeye maple.

Bird'sÐeye · , n. (Bot.) A plant with a small bright flower, as the Adonis or pheasant's eye, the mealy primrose (Primula farinosa), and species of Veronica, Geranium, etc.

Bird'sÐeye · maple (?). See under Maple.

Bird'sÐfoot · (?), n. (Bot.) A papilionaceous plant, the Ornithopus, having a curved, cylindrical pod tipped with a short, clawlike point.

Bird'sÐfoot trefoil. (Bot.) (a) A genus of plants (Lotus) with clawlike pods. L. corniculatas, with yellow flowers, is very common in Great Britain. (b) the related plant, Trigonella ornithopodioides, is also European.

Bird'sÐmouth · (?), n. (Arch.) An interior a?gle or notch cut across a piece of timber, for the reception of the edge of another, as that in a rafter to be laid on a plate; Ð commonly called crow'sÐfoot in the United States.

Bird's nest · , or Bird'sÐnest (?), n. 1. The nest in which a bird lays eggs and hatches her young.

(Cookery) The nest of a small swallow (Collocalia nidifica and several allied species), of China and the neighboring countries, which is mixed with soups.

µ The nests are found in caverns and fissures of
<— p. 148 —>
cliffs on rocky coasts, and are composed in part of alg'. They are of the size of a goose egg, and in substance resemble isinglass. See Illust. under Edible.

(Bot.) An orchideous plant with matted roots, of the genus Neottia (N. nidus͞lavis.)

Bird's-nest pudding, a pudding containing apples whose cores have been replaces by sugar. Ð Yellow bird's nest, a plant, the Monotropa hypopitys.

Bird's-nest · ing (?), n. Hunting for, or taking, birds' nests or their contents.

Bird's-tongue · (?), n. (Bot.) The knotgrass (Polygonum aviculare).

Bird-wit · ted (?), a. Flighty; passing rapidly from one subject to another; not having the faculty of attention.

Bacon.

Bi · rec͞tangu͞llar (?), a. [Pref. bi͞l + rectangular.] Containing or having two right angles; as, a birectangular spherical triangle.

Bireme (?), n. [L. biremis; bis twice + remus oar: cf. F. birŠme.] An ancient galley or vessel with two banks or tiers of oars.

Bi͞lretta (?), n. Same as Berretta.

Birgan͞Ider (?), n. See Bergander.

Birk (?), n. [See Birch, n.] A birch tree. [Prov. Eng.] ½The silver birk.͵ Tennyson.

Birk, n. (Zo"l.) A small European minnow (Leuciscus phoxinus).

Birken (?), v. t. [From 1st Birk.] To whip with a birch or rod. [Obs.]

Birken, a. Birchen; as, birken groves.

Burns.

Birkie (?), n. A lively or mettlesome fellow. [Jocular, Scot.]

Burns.

Birl (?), v. t. & i. To revolve or cause to revolve; to spin. [Scot.]

Sir W. Scott.

Birl (?), v. t. & i. [AS. byrlian. ?92.] To pour (beer or wine); to ply with drink; to drink; to carouse. [Obs. or Dial.]

Skelton.

Birlaw (?), n. [See By͞Ilaw.] (Law) A law made by husbandmen respecting rural affairs; a rustic or local law or by͞Ilaw. [Written also byrlaw, birlie, birley.]

Bi͞lros · trate (?), Bi͞lrostra͞Ited (?), } a. [Pref. bi͞l + rostrate.] Having a double beak, or two processes resembling beaks.

The capsule is bilocular and birostrated.

Ed. Encyc.

Birr (?), v. i. [imp. & p.p. Birred (?); p. pr. & vb. n. Birring.] [Cf. OE. bur, bir, wind, storm wind, fr. Icel. byrr wind. Perh. imitative.] To make, or move with, a whirring noise, as of wheels in motion.

Birr, n. 1. A whirring sound, as of a spinning wheel.

A rush or impetus; force.

Birrus (?), n. [LL., fr. L. birrus a kind of cloak. See Berretta.] A coarse kind of thick woolen cloth, worn by the poor in the Middle Ages; also, a woolen cap or hood worn over the shoulders or over the head.

Birse (?), n. A bristle or bristles. [Scot.]

Birt (?), n. [OE. byrte; cf. F. bertonneau. Cf. Bret, Burt.] (Zo"l.) A fish of the turbot kind; the brill. [Written also burt, bret, or brut.] [Prov. Eng.]

Birth (?), n. [OE. burth, birth, AS. beor?, gebyrd, fr. beran to bear, bring forth; akin to D. geboorate, OHG. burt, giburt, G. geburt, Icel. bur?r, Skr. bhrti bearing, supporting; cf. Ir. & Gael. beirthe born, brought forth. ?92. See 1st Bear, and cf. Berth.] 1. The act or fact of coming into life, or of being born; Ð generally applied to human beings; as, the birth of a son.

Lineage; extraction; descent; sometimes, high birth; noble extraction.

Elected without reference to birth, but solely for qualifications.
Prescott.

The condition to which a person is born; natural state or position; inherited disposition or tendency.

A foe by birth to Troy's unhappy name.
Dryden.

The act of bringing forth; as, she had two children at a birth. ½At her next birth.

Milton.

That which is born; that which is produced, whether animal or vegetable.

Poets are far rarer births that kings.
B. Jonson.

Others hatch their eggs and tend the birth till it is able to shift for itself.
Addison.

Origin; beginning; as, the birth of an empire.

New birth (Theol.), regeneration, or the commencement of a religious life.
Syn. Ð Parentage; extraction; lineage; race; family.

Birth, n. See Berth. [Obs.]
De Foe.

Birthday· (?), n. 1. The day in which any person is born; day of origin or commencement.

Those barbarous ages past, succeeded next
The birthday of invention.
Cowper.

The day of the month in which a person was born, in whatever succeeding year it may recur; the anniversary of one's birth.

This is my birthday; as this very day
Was Cassius born.
Shak.

Birthday ·, a. Of or pertaining to the day of birth, or its anniversary; as, birthday gifts or festivities.

Birthdom (?), n. [Birth + Ïdom.] The land of one's birth; one's inheritance. [R.]
Shak.

Birthing, n. (Naut.) Anything added to raise the sides of a ship.
Bailey.

Birthless, a. Of mean extraction. [R.]
Sir W. Scott.

Birthmark · (?), n. Some peculiar mark or blemish on the body at birth.
Most part of this noble lineage carried upon their body for a natural birthmark, ... a snake.
Sir T. North.

Birthnight · (?), n. The night in which a person is born; the anniversary of that night in succeeding years.

The angelic song in Bethlehem field,
On thy birthnight, that sung thee Savior born.
Milton.

Birthplace · (?), n. The town, city, or country, where a person is born; place of origin or birth, in its more general sense. ½The birthplace of valor.₃
Burns.

Birthright · (?), n. Any right, privilege, or possession to which a person is entitled by birth, such as an estate descendible by law to an heir, or civil liberty under a free constitution; esp. the rights or inheritance of the first born.

Lest there be any ... profane person, as Esau, who for one morsel of meat sold his birthright.
Heb. xii. 16.

Birthroot · (?), n. (Bot.) An herbaceous plant (Trillium erectum), and its astringent rootstock, which is said to have medicinal properties.

Birthwort · (?), n. A genus of herbs and shrubs (Aristolochia), reputed to have medicinal properties.

Bis (?), adv. [L. bis twice, for duis, fr. root of duo two. See Two, and cf. Bïl.] Twice; Ð a word showing that something is, or is to be, repeated; as a passage of music, or an item in accounts.

Bisï, pref. A form of Bïl, sometimes used before s, c, or a vowel.

Bisa anteïlope (?). (Zo"l.) See Oryx.

Bïlsaccate (?), a. [Pref. bïl + saccate.] (Bot.) Having two little bags, sacs, or pouches.

Bisïcayan (?), a. Of or pertaining to Biscay in Spain. Ðn. A native or inhabitant of Biscay.

Biscoïtin (?), n. [F. biscotin. See Biscuit.] A confection made of flour, sugar, marmalade, and eggs; a sweet biscuit.

Biscuit (?), n. [F. biscuit (cf. It. biscotto, Sp. bizcocho, Pg. biscouto), fr. L. bis twice + coctus, p. p. of coquere to cook, bake. See Cook, and cf. Bisque a kind of porcelain.] 1. A kind of unraised bread, of many varieties, plain, sweet, or fancy, formed into flat cakes, and bakes hard; as, ship biscuit.

According to military practice, the bread or biscuit of the Romans was twice prepared in the oven.
Gibbon.

A small loaf or cake of bread, raised and shortened, or made light with soda or baking powder. Usually a number are baked in the same pan, forming a sheet or card.

Earthen ware or porcelain which has undergone the first baking, before it is subjected to the glazing.

(Sculp.) A species of white, unglazed porcelain, in which vases, figures, and groups are formed in miniature.

Meat biscuit, an alimentary preparation consisting of matters extracted from meat by boiling, or of meat ground fine and combined with flour, so as to form biscuits.

Bïscutate (?), a. [Pref. bi + scutate.] (Bot.) Resembling two bucklers placed side by side.

ØBise (?), n. [F.] A cold north wind which prevails on the northern coasts of the Mediterranean and in Switzerland, etc.; Ð nearly the same as the mistral.

Bise (?), n. (Paint.) See Bice.

Bïsect (?), v. t. [imp. & p.p. Bisected; p. pr. & vb. n. Bisecting.] [L. bis twice + secare, sectum, to cut.] 1. To cut or divide into two parts.

(Geom.) To divide into two equal parts.

Bïsection (?), n. [Cf. F. bissection.] Division into two parts, esp. two equal parts.

Bïsector (?), n. One who, or that which, bisects; esp. (Geom.) a straight line which bisects an angle.

Bïsectrix (?), n. The line bisecting the angle between the optic axes of a biaxial crystal.

Bïsegment (?), n. [Pref. bi + segment.] One of tow equal parts of a line, or other magnitude.

Bïseptate (?), a. [Pref. bi + septate.] With two partitions or septa.
Gray.

Bïserïal (?), Bïserïate (?), } a. [Pref. bi + serial, seriate.] In two rows or series.

Bïserrate (?), a. [Pref. bi + serrate.]

(Bot.) Doubly serrate, or having the serratures serrate, as in some leaves.

(Zo"l.) Serrate on both sides, as some antenn'.

Bi̇setose (?), Bi̇setous (?), } a. [Pref. bi̇ + setose, setous.] Having two bristles.

Bi̇sexous (?), a. [L. bis twice + sexus sex: cf. F. bissexe.] Bisexual. [Obs.]

Sir T. Browne.

Bi̇sexual (?), a. [Pref. bi̇ + sexual.] (Biol.) Of both sexes; hermaphrodite; as a flower with stamens and pistil, or an animal having ovaries and testes.

Bi̇sexulous (?), a. Bisexual.

Bi̇seye (?), p. p. of Besee. [Obs.]

Chaucer.

Evil biseye, ill looking. [Obs.]

Bish (?), n. Same as Bikh.

Bishop (?), n. [OE. bischop, biscop, bisceop, AS. bisceop, biscop, L. episcopus overseer, superintendent, bishop, fr. Gr. ?, ? over + ? inspector, fr. root of ?, ?, to look to, perh. akin to L. specere to look at. See Spy, and cf. Episcopal.]

A spiritual overseer, superintendent, or director.

Ye were as sheep going astray; but are now returned unto the Shepherd and Bishop of your souls.

1 Pet. ii. 25.

It is a fact now generally recognized by theologians of all shades of opinion, that in the language of the New Testament the same officer in the church is called indifferently ½bishop„ (?) and ½elder„ or ½presbyter.„

J. B. Lightfoot.

In the Roman Catholic, Greek, and Anglican or Protestant Episcopal churches, one ordained to the highest order of the ministry, superior to the priesthood, and generally claiming to be a successor of the Apostles. The bishop is usually the spiritual head or ruler of a diocese, bishopric, or see.

Bishop in partibus [infidelium] (R. C. Ch.), a bishop of a see which does not actually exist; one who has the office of bishop, without especial jurisdiction. Shipley. Ð Titular bishop (R. C. Ch.), a term officially substituted in 1882 for bishop in partibus. Ð Bench of Bishops. See under Bench.

In the Methodist Episcopal and some other churches, one of the highest church officers or superintendents.

A piece used in the game of chess, bearing a representation of a bishop's miter; Ð formerly called archer.

A beverage, being a mixture of wine, oranges or lemons, and sugar.

Swift.

An old name for a woman's bustle. [U. S.]

If, by her bishop, or her ½grace, alone,
A genuine lady, or a church, is known.
Saxe.

Bishop, v. t. [imp. & p.p. Bishoped (?); p. pr. & vb. n. Bishoping.] To admit into the church by confirmation; to confirm; hence, to receive formally to favor.

Bishop (?), v. t. [imp. & p.p. Bishoped (?); p. pr. & vb. n. Bishoping.] [From the name of the scoundrel who first practiced it. Youatt.] (Far.) To make seem younger, by operating on the teeth; as, to bishop an old horse or his teeth.

The plan adopted is to cut off all the nippers with a saw to the proper length, and then with a cutting instrument the operator scoops out an oval cavity in the corner nippers, which is afterwards burnt with a hot iron until it is black.

J. H. Walsh.

Bishopĭdom (?), n. Jurisdiction of a bishop; episcopate. ½Divine right of bishopdom.,
Milton.

Bishopĭlike · (?), a. Resembling a bishop; belonging to a bishop.
Fulke.

Bishopĭly, a. Bishoplike; episcopal. [Obs.]

Bishopĭly, adv. In the manner of a bishop. [Obs.]

Bishopĭric (?), n. [AS. bisceoprÆce; bisceop bishop + rÆce dominion. See Ĭric.] 1. A diocese; the district over which the jurisdiction of a bishop extends.

The office of a spiritual overseer, as of an apostle, bishop, or presbyter.

Acts i. 20.

Bishop's cap · (?). (Bot.) A plant of the genus Mitella; miterwort.
Longfellow.

Bishop sleeve · (?). A wide sleeve, once worn by women.

Bishop's length · (?). A canvas for a portrait measuring 58 by 94 inches. The half bishop measures 45 of 56.

BishopÐstool · (?), n. A bishop's seat or see.

Bishop'sÐweed · (?), n. (Bot.) (a) An umbelliferous plant of the genus Ammi. (b) Goutweed (?gopodium podagraria).

Bishop'sÐwort · (?), n. (Bot.) Wood betony (Stachys betonica); also, the plant called fennel flower (Nigella Damascena), or devilĭinĭaĭbush.

Bisie (?), v. t. To busy; to employ. [Obs.]

Biĭsiliĭcate (?), n. (Min. Chem.) A salt of metasilicic acid; Ð so called because the ratio of the oxygen of the silica to the oxygen of the base is as two to one. The bisilicates include many of the most common and important minerals.

Bisk (?), n. [F. bisque.] Soup or broth made by boiling several sorts of flesh together.

King.

Bisk, n. [F. bisque.] (Tennis) See Bisque.

Bismare (?), Bismer (?), n. [AS. bismer.] Shame; abuse. [Obs.]
Chaucer.

Bismer (?), n. 1. A rule steelyard. [Scot.]

(Zo"l.) The fifteenspined (Gasterosteus spinachia).

ØBismillah (?), interj. [Arabic, in the name of God!] An adjuration or exclamation common among the Mohammedans. [Written also Bizmillah.]

Bismite (?), n. (Min.) Bismuth trioxide, or bismuth ocher.

Bismuth (?), n. [Ger. bismuth, wismuth: cf. F. bismuth.] (Chem.) One of the elements; a metal of a reddish white color, crystallizing in rhombohedrons. It is somewhat harder than lead, and rather brittle; masses show broad cleavage surfaces when broken across. It metals at 507? Fahr., being easily fused in the flame of a candle. It is found in a native state, and as a constituent of some minerals. Specific gravity 9.8. Atomic weight 207.5. Symbol Bi.

μ Chemically, bismuth (with arsenic and antimony is intermediate between the metals and nonmetals; it is used in thermoelectric piles, and as an alloy with lead and tin in the fusible alloy or metal. Bismuth is the most diamagnetic substance known.

Bismuth glance, bismuth sulphide; bismuthinite. Ð Bismuth ocher, a native bismuth oxide; bismite.

Bismuthial (?), a. Containing bismuth.

Bismuthic (?), a. (Chem.) Of or pertaining to bismuth; containing bismuth, when this element has its higher valence; as, bismuthic oxide.

Bis · muthiferious (?), a. [Bismuth + Iferous.] Containing bismuth.

Bismuthine (?), Bismuthinlite (?), } n. Native bismuth sulphide; Ð sometimes called bismuthite.

Bismuthious (?), a. Of, or containing, bismuth, when this element has its lower valence.

Bismuthiyl · (?), n. (Min.) Hydrous carbonate of bismuth, an earthy mineral of a dull white or yellowish color. [Written also bismuthite.]

Bison (?), n. [L. bison, Gr. ?, a wild ox; akin to OHG. wisunt, wisant, G. wisent, AS. wesend, Icel. vÆsundr: cf. F. bison.] (Zo"l.) (a) The aurochs or European bison. (b) The American bison buffalo (Bison Americanus), a large, gregarious bovine quadruped with shaggy mane and short black horns, which formerly roamed in herds over most of the temperate portion of North America, but is now restricted to very limited districts in the region of the Rocky Mountains, and is rapidly decreasing in numbers.

<— p. 149 —>

Bi′spinose (?), a. [Pref. bi′ + spinose.] (Zo"l.) Having two spines.

∅Bisque (?), n. [A corruption of biscuit.] Unglazed white porcelain.

Bisque, n. [F.] A point taken by the receiver of odds in the game of tennis; also, an extra innings allowed to a weaker player in croquet.

∅Bisque, n. [F.] A white soup made of crayfish.

Bis′sextile (?), n. [L. bissextilis annus, fr. bissextus (bis + sextus sixth, fr. sex six) the sixth of the calends of March, or twenty′fourth day of February, which was reckoned twice every fourth year, by the intercalation of a day.] Leap year; every fourth year, in which a day is added to the month of February on account of the excess of the tropical year (365 d. 5 h. 48 m. 46 s.) above 365 days. But one day added every four years is equivalent to six hours each year, which is 11 m. 14 s. more than the excess of the real year. Hence, it is necessary to suppress the bissextile day at the end of every century which is not divisible by 400, while it is retained at the end of those which are divisible by 400.

Bis′sextile, a. Pertaining to leap year.

Bisson (?), a. [OE. bisen, bisne, AS. bisen, prob. for bÆs?ne; bi by + s?ne clear, akin to seen to see; clear when near, hence short′sighted. See See.] Purblind; blinding. [Obs.] ½Bisson rheum.

Shak.

Bister, Bistre } (?), n. [F. bistre a color made of soot; of unknown origin. Cf., however, LG. biester frowning, dark, ugly.] (Paint.) A dark brown pigment extracted from the soot of wood.

Bi′stipuled (?), a. [Pref. bi′ + stipule.] (Bot.) Having two stipules.

Bistort (?), n. [L. bis + tortus, p. p. of torquere to twist: cf. F. bistorte.] (Bot.) An herbaceous plant of the genus Polygonum, section Bistorta; snakeweed; adderwort. Its root is used in medicine as an astringent.

Bistou′ry (?), n.; pl. Bistouries (?). [F. bistouri.] A surgical instrument consisting of a slender knife, either straight or curved, generally used by introducing it beneath the part to be divided, and cutting towards the surface.

Bistre (?), n. See Bister.

Bi′sulcate (?), a. [Pref. bi′ + sulcate.]

Having two grooves or furrows.

(Zo"l.) Cloven; said of a foot or hoof.

Bi′sulcous (?), a. [L. bisulcus; bis twice + sulcus furrow.] Bisulcate. Sir T. Browne.

Bi′sulphate (?), n. [Pref. bi′ + sulphate.] (Chem.) A sulphate in which but half the hydrogen of the acid is replaced by a positive element or radical, thus making the proportion of the acid to the positive or basic portion twice what it is in the normal sulphates; an acid sulphate.

Bi‍sulphide (?), n. [Pref. bi‍ + sulphide.] (Chem.) A sulphide having two atoms of sulphur in the molecule; a disulphide, as in iron pyrites, FeS2; Ð less frequently called bisulphuret.

Bi‍sulphite (?), n. (Chem.) A salt of sulphurous acid in which the base replaces but half the hydrogen of the acid; an acid sulphite.

Bi‍sulphu‍ret (?), n. [Pref. bi‍ + sulphuret.] (Chem.) See Bisulphide.

Bit (?), n. [OE. bitt, bite, AS. bite, bite, fr. bÆtan to bite. See Bite, n. & v., and cf. Bit a morsel.] 1. The part of a bridle, usually of iron, which is inserted in the mouth of a horse, and having appendages to which the reins are fastened.

Shak.

The foamy bridle with the bit of gold.

Chaucer.

Fig.: Anything which curbs or restrains.

Bit, v. t. [imp. & p.p. Bitted (?); p. pr. & vb. n. Bitting.] To put a bridle upon; to put the bit in the mouth of.

Bit, imp. & p. p. of Bite.

Bit, n. [OE. bite, AS. bita, fr. bÆtan to bite; akin to D. beet, G. bissen bit, morsel, Icel. biti. See Bite, v., and cf. Bit part of a bridle.] 1. A part of anything, such as may be bitten off or taken into the mouth; a morsel; a bite. Hence: A small piece of anything; a little; a mite.

Somewhat; something, but not very great.

My young companion was a bit of a poet.

T. Hook.

μ This word is used, also, like jot and whit, to express the smallest degree; as, he is not a bit wiser.

A tool for boring, of various forms and sizes, usually turned by means of a brace or bitstock. See Bitstock.

The part of a key which enters the lock and acts upon the bolt and tumblers.

Knight.

The cutting iron of a plane.

Knight.

In the Southern and Southwestern States, a small silver coin (as the real) formerly current; commonly, one worth about 12 1/2 cents; also, the sum of 12 1/2 cents.

Bit my bit, piecemeal.
 Pope.
Bit, 3d sing. pr. of Bid, for biddeth. [Obs.]

Chaucer.

Bi̇take (?), v. t. [See Betake, Betaught.] To commend; to commit. [Obs.] Chaucer.

Bi̇tangent (?), a. [Pref. bi̇ + tangent.] (Geom.) Possessing the property of touching at two points. Ð n. A line that touches a curve in two points.

Bi̇tartrate (?), n. (Chem.) A salt of tartaric acid in which the base replaces but half the acid hydrogen; an acid tartrate, as cream of tartar.

Bitch (?), n. [OE. biche, bicche, AS. bicce; cf. Icel. bikkja, G. betze, peize.] 1. The female of the canine kind, as of the dog, wolf, and fox.

> An opprobrious name for a woman, especially a lewd woman.

Pope.

Bite (?), v. t. [imp. Bit (?); p. p. Bitten (?), Bit; p. pr. & vb. n. Biting.] [OE. biten, AS. bÆtan; akin to D. bijten, OS. bÆtan, OHG. bÆzan, G. beissen, Goth. beitan, Icel. bÆta, Sw. bita, Dan. bide, L. findere to cleave, Skr. bhid to cleave. ?87. Cf. Fissure.]

> To seize with the teeth, so that they enter or nip the thing seized; to lacerate, crush, or wound with the teeth; as, to bite an apple; to bite a crust; the dog bit a man.

Such smiling rogues as these,
Like rats, oft bite the holy cords atwain.
Shak.

> To puncture, abrade, or sting with an organ (of some insects) used in taking food.

> To cause sharp pain, or smarting, to; to hurt or injure, in a literal or a figurative sense; as, pepper bites the mouth. ½Frosts do bite the meads.

Shak.

> To cheat; to trick; to take in. [Colloq.]

Pope.

> To take hold of; to hold fast; to adhere to; as, the anchor bites the ground.

The last screw of the rack having been turned so often that its purchase crumbled, ... it turned and turned with nothing to bite.
Dickens.

To bite the dust, To bite the ground, to fall in the agonies of death; as, he made his enemy bite the dust. Ð To bite in (Etching), to corrode or eat into metallic plates by means of an acid. Ð To bite the thumb at (any one), formerly a mark of contempt, designed to provoke a quarrel; to defy. ½Do you bite your thumb at us ? Shak. Ð To bite the tongue, to keep silence. Shak.

Bite (?), v. i. 1. To seize something forcibly with the teeth; to wound with the teeth; to have the habit of so doing; as, does the dog bite ?

To cause a smarting sensation; to have a property which causes such a sensation; to be pungent; as, it bites like pepper or mustard.

To cause sharp pain; to produce anguish; to hurt or injure; to have the property of so doing.

At the last it [wine] biteth like serpent, and stingeth like an adder.
Prov. xxiii. 32.

To take a bait into the mouth, as a fish does; hence, to take a tempting offer.

To take or keep a firm hold; as, the anchor bites.

Bite, n. [OE. bite, bit, bitt, AS. bite bite, fr. bÆtan to bite, akin to Icel. bit, OS. biti, G. biss. See Bite, v., and cf. Bit.] 1. The act of seizing with the teeth or mouth; the act of wounding or separating with the teeth or mouth; a seizure with the teeth or mouth, as of a bait; as, to give anything a hard bite.

I have known a very good fisher angle diligently four or six hours for a river carp, and not have a bite.
Walton.

The act of puncturing or abrading with an organ for taking food, as is done by some insects.

The wound made by biting; as, the pain of a dog's or snake's bite; the bite of a mosquito.

A morsel; as much as is taken at once by biting.

The hold which the short end of a lever has upon the thing to be lifted, or the hold which one part of a machine has upon another.

A cheat; a trick; a fraud. [Colloq.]

The baser methods of getting money by fraud and bite, by deceiving and overreaching.
Humorist.

A sharper; one who cheats. [Slang]

Johnson.

(Print.) A blank on the edge or corner of a page, owing to a portion of the frisket, or something else, intervening between the type and paper.

Biter (?), n. 1. One who, or that which, bites; that which bites often, or is inclined to bite, as a dog or fish. ½Great barkers are no biters.,
Camden.

One who cheats; a sharper. [Colloq.]

Spectator.

Biternate (?), a. [Pref. bi + ternate.] (Bot.)Doubly ternate, as when a petiole has three ternate leaflets. Ð Biternately, adv.
Gray.

Bithelism (?), n. [Pref. bi + theism.] Belief in the existence of two gods; dualism.

Biting (?), a. That bites; sharp; cutting; sarcastic; caustic. ½A biting affliction., ½A biting jest.,
Shak.

Biting in (?). (Etching.) The process of corroding or eating into metallic plates, by means of an acid. See Etch.
G. Francis.

Bitingly, adv. In a biting manner.

Bitless (?), a. Not having a bit or bridle.

Bitstock · (?), n. A stock or handle for holding and rotating a bit; a brace.

Bitt (?), n. (Naut.) See Bitts.

Bitt (?), v. t. [See Bitts.] (Naut.) To put round the bitts; as, to bitt the cable, in order to fasten it or to slacken it gradually, which is called veering away.
Totten.

Bittacle (?), n. A binnacle. [Obs.]

Bitten (?), p. p. of Bite.

Bitten (?), a. (Bot.) Terminating abruptly, as if bitten off; premorse.

Bitter (?), n. [See Bitts.] (Naut.) AA turn of the cable which is round the bitts.

Bitter end, that part of a cable which is abaft the bitts, and so within board, when the ship rides at anchor.

Bitter (?), a. [AS. biter; akin to Goth. baitrs, Icel. bitr, Dan., Sw., D., & G. bitter, OS. bittar, fr. root of E. bite. See Bite, v. t.] 1. Having a peculiar, acrid, biting taste, like that of wormwood or an infusion of hops; as, a bitter medicine; bitter as aloes.

Causing pain or smart; piercing; painful; sharp; severe; as, a bitter cold day.

Causing, or fitted to cause, pain or distress to the mind; calamitous; poignant.

It is an evil thing and bitter, that thou hast forsaken the Lord thy God.
Jer. ii. 19.

Characterized by sharpness, severity, or cruelty; harsh; stern; virulent; as, bitter reproach.

Husbands, love your wives, and be not bitter against them.
Col. iii. 19.

Mournful; sad; distressing; painful; pitiable.

The Egyptians ... made their lives bitter with hard bondage.

Ex. i. 14.

Bitter apple, Bitter cucumber, Bitter gourd. (Bot.) See Colocynth. Ð Bitter cress (Bot.), a plant of the genus Cardamine, esp. C. amara. Ð Bitter earth (Min.), tale earth; calcined magnesia. Ð Bitter principles (Chem.), a class of substances, extracted from vegetable products, having strong bitter taste but with no sharply defined chemical characteristics. Ð Bitter salt, Epsom salts;; magnesium sulphate. Ð Bitter vetch (Bot.), a name given to two European leguminous herbs, Vicia Orobus and Ervum Ervilia. Ð To the bitter end, to the last extremity, however calamitous.

Syn. Ð Acrid; sharp; harsh; pungent; stinging; cutting; severe; acrimonious.

Bitter (?), n. Any substance that is bitter. See Bitters.

Bitter, v. t. To make bitter.

Wolcott.

Bitterĭbump · (?), n. (Zo"l.) the butterbump or bittern.

Bitterĭful (?), a. Full of bitterness. [Obs.]

Bitterĭing, n. A bitter compound used in adulterating beer; bittern.

Bitterĭish, a. Somewhat bitter.

Goldsmith.

Bitterĭling (?), n. [G.] (Zo"l.) A roachlike European fish (Rhodima amarus).

Bitterĭly, adv. In a bitter manner.

Bittern (?), n. [OE. bitoure, betore, bitter, fr. F. butor; of unknown origin.] (Zo"l.) A wading bird of the genus Botaurus, allied to the herons, of various species.

μ The common European bittern is Botaurus stellaris. It makes, during the brooding season, a noise called by Dryden bumping, and by Goldsmith booming. The American bittern is B. lentiginosus, and is also called stakeĭdriver and meadow hen. See Stakeĭdriver.

The name is applied to other related birds, as the least bittern (Ardetta exilis), and the sun bittern.

Bittern, n. [From Bitter, a.] 1. The brine which remains in salt works after the salt is concreted, having a bitter taste from the chloride of magnesium which it contains.

A very bitter compound of quassia, cocculus Indicus, etc., used by fraudulent brewers in adulterating beer.

Cooley.

Bitterĭness (?), n. [AS. biternys; biter better + Ĭnys = Ĭness.] 1. The quality or state of being bitter, sharp, or acrid, in either a literal or figurative sense; implacableness; resentfulness; severity; keenness of reproach or sarcasm; deep distress, grief, or vexation of mind.

The lip that curls with bitterness.

Percival.

I will complain in the bitterness of my soul.
Job vii. 11.

A state of extreme impiety or enmity to God.

Thou art in the gall of bitterness, and in the bond of iniquity.
Acts viii. 23.

Dangerous error, or schism, tending to draw persons to apostasy.

Looking diligently, ... lest any root of bitterness springing up trouble you.
Heb. xii. 15.

Bitterǐnut, n. (Bot.) The swamp hickory (Carya amara). Its thinǐshelled nuts are bitter.

Bitterǐroot · (?), n. (Bot.) A plant (Lewisia rediviva) allied to the purslane, but with fleshy, farinaceous roots, growing in the mountains of Idaho, Montana, etc. It gives the name to the Bitter Root mountains and river. The Indians call both the plant and the river Sp't'lum.

Bitters (?), n. pl. A liquor, generally spirituous in which a bitter herb, leaf, or root is steeped.

Bitter spar (?). A common name of dolomite Đ so called because it contains magnesia, the soluble salts of which are bitter. See Dolomite.

Bitterǐsweet · (?), a. Sweet and then bitter or bitter and then sweet; esp. sweet with a bitter after taste; hence (Fig.), pleasant but painful.

Bitterǐsweet · , n. 1. Anything which is bittersweet.

A kind of apple so called.

Gower.

(Bot.) (a) A climbing shrub, with oval corallred berries (Solanum dulcamara); woody nightshade. The whole plant is poisonous, and has a taste at first sweetish and then bitter. The branches are the officinal dulcamara. (b) An American woody climber (Celastrus scandens), whose yellow capsules open late in autumn, and disclose the red aril which covers the seeds; Đ also called Roxbury waxwork.

Bitterǐweed · (?), n. (Bot.) A species of Ambrosia (A. artemisi'folia); Roman worm wood.

Gray.

Bitterǐwood · (?), n. A West Indian tree (Picr'na excelsa) from the wood of which the bitter drug Jamaica quassia is obtained.

Bitterǐwort · (?), n. (Bot.) The yellow gentian (Gentiana lutea), which has a very bitter taste.

Bittock (?), n. [See Bit a morsel.] A small bit of anything, of indefinite size or quantity; a short distance. [Scot.]

Sir W. Scott.

Bittor Bittour } (?), n. [See Bittern] (Zo"l.) The bittern. Dryden.

Bitts (?), n. pl. [Cf. F. bitte, Icel. biti, a beam. ?87.] (Naut.) A frame of two strong timbers fixed perpendicularly in the fore part of a ship, on which to fasten the cables as the ship rides at anchor, or in warping. Other bitts are used for belaying (belaying bitts), for sustaining the windlass (carrick bitts, winch bitts, or windlass bitts), to hold the pawls of the windlass (pawl bitts) etc.

Bitume (?), n. [F. See Bitumen.] Bitumen. [Poetic] May.

Bitumed (?), a. Smeared with bitumen. [R.] ½The hatches caulked and bitumed., Shak.

Bitumen (?), n. [L. bitumen: cf. F. bitume. Cf. B,ton.] 1. Mineral pitch; a black, tarry substance, burning with a bright flame; Jew's pitch. ?

<— p. 150 —>

occurs as an abundant natural product in many places, as on the shores of the Dead and Caspian Seas. It is used in cements, in the construction of pavements, etc. See Asphalt. 2. By extension, any one of the natural hydrocarbons, including the hard, solid, brittle varieties called asphalt, the semisolid maltha and mineral tars, the oily petroleums, and even the light, volatile naphthas. Bitumiïnate (?), v. t. [imp. & p.p. Bituminated; p. pr. & vb. n. Bituminating.] [L. bituminatus, p. p. of bituminare to bituminate. See Bitumen.] To treat or impregnate with bitumen; to cement with bitumen. ½Bituminated walls of Babylon., Feltham. Bitu · miïniferïous (?), a. [Bitumen + Iferous.] Producing bitumen. Kirwan. Bitu · miïnilzation (?), n. [Cf. F. bituminisation.] The process of bituminizing. Mantell. Bitumiïnize (?), v. t. [imp. & p.p. Bituminized (?); p. pr. & vb. n. Bituminizing.] [Cf. F. bituminiser.] To prepare, treat, impregnate, or coat with bitumen. Bitumiïnous (?), a. [L. bituminosus: cf. F. bitumineux.] Having the qualities of bitumen; compounded with bitumen; containing bitumen. Near that bituminous lake where Sodom flamed. Milton. Bituminous coal, a kind of coal which yields, when heated, a considerable amount of volatile bituminous matter. It burns with a yellow smoky flame. Ð Bituminous limestone, a mineral of a brown or black color, emitting an unpleasant smell when rubbed. That of Dalmatia is so charged with bitumen that it may be cut like soap. Ð Bituminous shale, an argillaceous shale impregnated with bitumen, often accompanying coal. Biulret (?), n. [Pref. biï + urea.] (Chem.) A white, crystalline, nitrogenous substance, C2O2N3H5, formed by heating urea. It is intermediate between urea and cyanuric acid. Bivaïlenïcy (?), n. (Chem.) The quality of being bivalent. Bivaïlent (?), a. [L. bis twice + valens, p. pr. See Valence.] (Chem.) Equivalent in combining or displacing power to two atoms of hydrogen; dyad. Bivalve (?), n. [F. bivalve; biï (L. bis) + valve valve.] 1. (Zo"l.) A mollusk having a shell consisting of two lateral plates or valves joined together by an elastic ligament at the hinge, which is usually strengthened by prominences called teeth. The shell is closed by the contraction of two transverse muscles attached to the inner surface, as in the clam, Ð or by one, as in the oyster. See Mollusca. 2. (Bot.) A pericarp in which the seed case opens or splits into two parts or valves. Bivalve (?), a. [Pref. biï + valve.] (Zo"l. & Bot.) Having two shells or valves which open and shut, as the oyster and certain seed vessels. Bivalved (?), a. Having two valves, as the oyster and some seed pods; bivalve. Biïvalvous (?), a. Bivalvular. Biïvalvuïlar (?), a. Having two valves. Biïvaulted (?), a. [Pref. biï + vault.] Having two vaults or arches. Biïvector (?), n. [Pref. biï + vector.] (Math.) A term made up of the two parts ? + ?1 ?Ð1, where ? and ?1 are vectors. Biïventral (?), a. [Pref. biï + ventral.] (Anat.) Having two bellies or protuberances; as, a biventral, or digastric, muscle, or the biventral lobe of the cerebellum. Biviïal (?), a. Of or relating to the bivium. Biviïous (?), a. [L. bivius; bis twice + via way.] Having, or leading, two ways. Bivious theorems and Janusïfaced doctrines. Sir T. Browne. ØBiviïum (?), n. [L., a place with two ways. See Bivious.] (Zo"l.) One side of an echinoderm, including a pair of ambulacra, in distinction from the opposite side (trivium), which includes three ambulacra. Bivouac (?), n. [F. bivouac, bivac, prab. fr. G. beiwache, or beiwacht; bei by, near + wachen to watch, wache watch, guard. See By, and Watch.] (Mil.) (a) The watch of a whole army by night, when in danger of surprise or attack. (b) An encampment for the night without tents or covering. Bivouac, v. i. [imp. & p.p. Bivouacked (?); p. pr. & vb. n. Bivouacking.] (Mil.) (a) To watch at night or be on guard, as a whole army. (b) To encamp for the night without tents or covering. Biweek·ly (?), a. [Pref. biï + weekly.] Occurring or appearing once every two weeks; fortnightly. Ð n. A publication issued every two weeks. Ð Biweekly, adv. Biïwreye (?), v. t. To bewray; to reveal. [Obs.] Bizanïtine (?). See Byzantine. Biïzarre (?), a. [F. bizarre odd, fr. Sp. bizarro gallant, brave, liberal, prob. of Basque origin; cf. Basque bizarra beard, whence the meaning manly, brave.] Odd in manner or appearance; fantastic; whimsical; extravagant; grotesque. C. Kingsley. Biïzet (?), n. [Cf. Bezel.] The upper faceted portion of a brilliantïcut diamond, which projects from the setting and occupies the zone between the girdle and the table. See Brilliant, n. Blab (?), v. t. [imp. & p.p. Blabbed (?); p. pr. & vb. n. Blabbing.] [Cf. OE. blaberen, or Dan. blabbre, G. plappern, Gael. blabaran a stammerer; prob. of imitative origin. Cf. also Blubber, v.] To utter or tell unnecessarily, or in a thoughtless manner; to publish (secrets or trifles) without reserve or discretion. Udall. And yonder a vile physician blabbing The case of his patient. Tennyson. Blab, v. i. To talk thoughtlessly or without discretion; to tattle; to tell tales. She must burst or blab. Dryden. Blab, n. [OE. blabbe.] One who blabs; a babbler; a telltale. ½Avoided as a blab., Milton. For who will open himself to a blab or a babbler. Bacon. Blabber (?), n. A tattler; a telltale. Black (?), a. [OE. blak, AS. bl'c; akin to Icel. blakkr dark, swarthy, Sw. bl„ck ink,

Dan. bl'k, OHG. blach, LG. & D. blaken to burn with a black smoke. Not akin to AS. bl¾c, E. bleak pallid. ?98.] 1. Destitute of light, or incapable of reflecting it; of the color of soot or coal; of the darkest or a very dark color, the opposite of white; characterized by such a color; as, black cloth; black hair or eyes. O night, with hue so black! Shak. 2. In a less literal sense: Enveloped or shrouded in darkness; very dark or gloomy; as, a black night; the heavens black with clouds. I spy a black, suspicious, threatening cloud. Shak. 3. Fig.: Dismal, gloomy, or forbidding, like darkness; destitute of moral light or goodness; atrociously wicked; cruel; mournful; calamitous; horrible. ½This day's black fate., ½Black villainy., ½Arise, black vengeance., ½Black day., ½Black despair., Shak. 4. Expressing menace, or discontent; threatening; sullen; foreboding; as, to regard one with black looks. µ Black is often used in selfïexplaining compound words; as, blackïeyed, blackïfaced, blackïhaired, blackïvisaged. Black act, the English statute 9 George I, which makes it a felony to appear armed in any park or warren, etc., or to hunt or steal deer, etc., with the face blackened or disguised. Subsequent acts inflicting heavy penalties for malicious injuries to cattle and machinery have been called black acts. Ð Black angel (Zo"l.), a fish of the West Indies and Florida (Holacanthus tricolor), with the head and tail yellow, and the middle of the body black. Ð Black antimony (Chem.), the black sulphide of antimony, Sb_2S_3, used in pyrotechnics, etc. Ð Black bear (Zo"l.), the common American bear (Ursus Americanus). Ð Black beast. See Bˆte noire. Ð Black beetle (Zo"l.), the common large cockroach (Blatta orientalis). Ð Black and blue, the dark color of a bruise in the flesh, which is accompanied with a mixture of blue. ½To pinch the slatterns black and blue., Hudibras. Ð Black bonnet (Zo"l.), the blackïheaded bunting (Embriza Sch?niclus) of Europe. Ð Black canker, a disease in turnips and other crops, produced by a species of caterpillar. Ð Black cat (Zo"l.), the fisher, a quadruped of North America allied to the sable, but larger. See Fisher. Ð Black cattle, any bovine cattle reared for slaughter, in distinction from dairy cattle. [Eng.] Ð Black cherry. See under Cherry. Ð Black cockatoo (Zo"l.), the palm cockatoo. See Cockatoo. Ð Black copper. Same as Melaconite. Ð Black currant. (Bot.) See Currant. Ð Black diamond. (Min.) See Carbonado. Ð Black draught (Med.), a cathartic medicine, composed of senna and magnesia. Ð Black drop (Med.), vinegar of opium; a narcotic preparation consisting essentially of a solution of opium in vinegar. Ð Black earth, mold; earth of a dark color. Woodward. Ð Black flag, the flag of a pirate, often bearing in white a skull and crossbones; a signal of defiance. Ð Black flea (Zo"l.), a flea beetle (Haltica nemorum) injurious to turnips. Ð Black flux, a mixture of carbonate of potash and charcoal, obtained by deflagrating tartar with half its weight of niter. Brande & C. Ð Black fly. (Zo"l.) (a) In the United States, a small, venomous, twoïwinged fly of the genus Simuliu? of several ?, exceedingly abundant and troublesome in the northern forests. The larv' are aquatic. (b) A black plant louse, as the bean aphis (A. fab'). Ð Black Forest [a translation of G. Schwarzwald], a forest in Baden and Wrtemburg, in Germany; a part of the ancient Hercynian forest. Ð Black game, or Black grouse. (Zo"l.) See Blackcock, Grouse, and Heath grouse. Ð Black grass (Bot.), a grasslike rush of the species Juncus Gerardi, growing on salt marshes, and making good hay. Ð Black gum (Bot.), an American tree, the tupelo or pepperidge. See Tupelo. Ð Black Hamburg (grape) (Bot.), a sweet and juicy variety of dark purple or ½black, grape. Ð Black horse (Zo"l.), a fish of the Mississippi valley (Cycleptus elongatus), of the sucker family; the Missouri sucker. Ð Black lemur (Zo"l.), the Lemurniger of Madagascar; the acoumbo of the natives. Ð Black list, a list of persons who are for some reason thought deserving of censure or punishment; Ð esp. a list of persons stigmatized as insolvent or untrustworthy, made for the protection of tradesmen or employers. See Blacklist, v. t. Ð Black manganese (Chem.), the black oxide of manganese, MnO_2. Ð Black Maria, the close wagon in which prisoners are carried to or from jail. Ð Black martin (Zo"l.), the chimney swift. See Swift. Ð Black moss (Bot.), the common soĺcalled long moss of the southern United States. See Tillandsia. Ð Black oak. See under Oak. Ð Black ocher. See Wad. Ð Black pigment, a very fine, light carbonaceous substance, or lampblack, prepared chiefly for the manufacture of printers' ink. It is obtained by burning common coal tar. Ð Black plate, sheet iron before it is tinned. Knight. Ð Black quarter, malignant anthrax with engorgement of a shoulder or quarter, etc., as of an ox. Ð Black rat (Zo"l.), one of the species of rats (Mus rattus), commonly infesting houses. Ð Black rent. See Blackmail, n., 3. Ð Black rust, a disease of wheat, in which a black, moist matter is deposited in the fissures of the grain. Ð Black sheep, one in a family or company who is unlike the rest, and makes trouble. Ð Black silver. (Min.) See under Silver. Ð Black and tan, black mixed or spotted with tan color or reddish brown; Ð used in describing certain breeds of dogs. Ð Black tea. See under Tea. Ð Black tin (Mining), tin ore (cassiterite), when dressed, stamped and washed, ready for smelting. It is in the form of a black powder, like fine sand. Knight. Ð Black walnut. See under Walnut. Ð Black warrior (Zo"l.), an American hawk (Buteo Harlani). Syn. Ð Dark; murky; pitchy; inky; somber; dusky; gloomy; swart; Cimmerian; ebon; atrocious. Black (?), adv. Sullenly; threateningly; maliciously; so as to produce blackness. Black, n. 1. That which is destitute of light or whiteness; the darkest color, or rather a destitution of all color; as, a cloth has a good black. Black is the badge of hell, The hue of dungeons, and the suit of night. Shak. 2. A black pigment or dye. 3. A negro; a person whose skin is of a black color, or shaded with black; esp. a member or descendant of certain African races. 4. A black garment or dress; as, she wears black pl. (Obs.) Mourning garments of a black color; funereal drapery. Friends weeping, and blacks, and obsequies, and the like show death terrible. Bacon. That was the full time they used to wear blacks for the death of their fathers. Sir T. North. 5. The part of a thing which is distinguished from the rest by being black. The black or sight of the eye. Sir K. Digby. 6. A stain; a spot; a smooch. Defiling her white lawn of chastity with ugly blacks of lust. Rowley. Black and white, writing or print; as, I must have that statement in black and white. Ð Blue black, a pigment of a blue black color. Ð Ivory black, a fine kind of animal charcoal prepared by calcining ivory or bones. When ground it is the chief ingredient of the ink used in copperplate printing. Ð Berlin black. See under Berlin. Black, v. t. [imp. & p.p. Blacked ; p. pr. & vb. n. Blacking.] [See Black, a., and cf. Blacken.]

To make black; to blacken; to soil; to sully. They have their teeth blacked, both men and women, for they say a dog hath his teeth white, therefore they will black theirs. Hakluyt. Sins which black thy soul. J. Fletcher.

To make black and shining, as boots or a stove, by applying blacking and then polishing with a brush. Blackaĭmoor (?), n. [Black + Moor.] A negro or negress. Shak. Black art · (?). The art practiced by conjurers and witches; necromancy; conjuration; magic. µ This name was given in the Middle Ages to necromancy, under the idea that the latter term was derived from niger black, instead of ?, a dead person, and ?, divination. Wright. BlackÐaÐvised · (?), a. Darkĭvisaged; swart. Blackball · (?), n. 1. A composition for blacking shoes, boots, etc.; also, one for taking impressions of engraved work.

A ball of black color, esp. one used as a negative in voting; Ð in this sense usually two words. Blackball ·, v. t. [imp. & p.p. Blackballed (?); p. pr. & vb. n. Blackballing.] 1. To vote against, by putting a black ball into a ballot box; to reject or exclude, as by voting against with black balls; to ostracize. He was blackballed at two clubs in succession. Thackeray.

To blacken (leather, shoes, etc.) with blacking. Blackband · (?), n. (Min.) An earthy carbonate of iron containing considerable carbonaceous matter; Ð valuable as an iron ore. Black bass · (?). (Zo"l.) 1. An edible, freshĭwater fish of the United States, of the genus Micropterus. the smallĭmouthed kind is M. dolomieÆ; the largemouthed is M. salmoides.

The sea bass. See Blackfish, 3. Blackberĭry (?), n. [OE. blakberye, AS. bl'cerie;ȳbl'c black + berie berry.] The fruit of several species of bramble (Rubus); also, the plant itself. Rubus fruticosus is the blackberry of England; R. villosus and R. Canadensis are the high blackberry and low blackberry of the United States. There are also other kinds. Blackbird (?), n. (Zo"l.) In England, a species of thrush (Turdus merula), a singing bird with a fin note; the merle. In America the name is given to several birds, as the Quiscalus versicolor, or crow blackbird; the Agel'us ph?niceus, or redĭwinged blackbird; the cowbird; the rusty grackle, etc. See Redwing. Blackboard · (?), n. A broad board painted black, or any black surface on which writing, drawing, or the working of mathematical problems can be done with chalk or crayons. It is much used in schools. Black book · (?). 1. One of several books of a political character, published at different times and for different purposes; Ð so called either from the color of the binding, or from the character of the contents.

<— p. 151 —>

A book compiled in the twelfth century, containing a description of the court of exchequer of England, an official statement of the revenues of the crown, etc.

A book containing details of the enormities practiced in the English monasteries and religious houses, compiled by order of their visitors under Henry VIII., to hasten their dissolution.

A book of admiralty law, of the highest authority, compiled in the reign of Edw. III.

Bouvier. Wharton.

A book kept for the purpose of registering the names of persons liable to censure or punishment, as in the English universities, or the English armies.

Any book which treats of necromancy.

BlackÐbrowed · (?), a. Having black eyebrows. Hence: Gloomy; dismal; threatening; forbidding.

Shak. Dryden.

BlackÏburniÏan warÏbler (?). [Named from Mrs. Blackburn, an English lady.] (Zo"l.) A beautiful warbler of the United States (Dendroica Blackburni'). The male is strongly marked with orange, yellow, and black on the head and neck, and has an orangeÏyellow breast.

Blackcap · (?), n. 1. (Zo"l.) (a) A small European song bird (Sylvia atricapilla), with a black crown; the mock nightingale. (b) An American titmouse (Parus atricapillus); the chickadee.

(Cookery) An apple roasted till black, to be served in a dish of boiled custard.

The black raspberry.

Blackcoat · (?), n. A clergyman; Ð familiarly so called, as a soldier is sometimes called a redcoat or a bluecoat.

Blackcock · (?), n. (Zo"l.) The male of the European black grouse (Tetrao tetrix, Linn.); Ð so called by sportsmen. The female is called gray hen. See Heath grouse.

Black death · (?). A pestilence which ravaged Europe and Asia in the fourteenth century.

Blacken (?), v. t. [imp. & p.p. Blackened (?); p. pr. & vb. n. Blackening.] [See Black, a., and cf. Black, v. t.] 1. To make or render black.

While the long funerals blacken all the way.

Pope.

To make dark; to darken; to cloud. ½Blackened the whole heavens.

South.

To defame; to sully, as reputation; to make infamous; as, vice blackens the character.

Syn. Ð To denigrate; defame; vilify; slander; calumniate; traduce; malign; asperse.

Blacken, v. i. To grow black or dark.

BlackenÏer (?), n. One who blackens.

BlackÐeyed · (?), a. Having black eyes.

Dryden.

BlackÐfaced · (?), a. Having a black, dark, or gloomy face or aspect.

Blackfeet · (?), n. pl. (Ethn.) A tribe of North American Indians formerly inhabiting the country from the upper Missouri River to the Saskatchewan, but now much reduced in numbers.

337

Blackfin · (?), n. (Zo"l.) See Bluefin.

Blackfish (?), n. 1. (Zo"l.) A small kind of whale, of the genus Globicephalus, of several species. The most common is G. melas. Also sometimes applied to other whales of larger size.

(Zo"l.) The tautog of New England (Tautoga).

(Zo"l.) The black sea bass (Centropristis atrarius) of the Atlantic coast. It is excellent food fish; Ð locally called also black Harry.

(Zo"l.) A fish of southern Europe (Centrolophus pompilus) of the Mackerel family.

(Zo"l.) The female salmon in the spawning season.

µ The name is locally applied to other fishes.

Blackfoot · (?), a. Of or pertaining to the Blackfeet; as, a Blackfoot Indian. Ð n. A Blackfoot Indian.

Black fri · ar (?). (Eccl.) A friar of the Dominican order; Ð called also predicant and preaching friar; in France, Jacobin. Also, sometimes, a Benedictine.

Blackguard (?), n. [Black + guard.] 1. The scullions and lower menials of a court, or of a nobleman's household, who, in a removal from one residence to another, had charge of the kitchen utensils, and being smutted by them, were jocularly called the ½black guard ͺ; also, the servants and hangersion of an army. [Obs.]

A lousy slave, that ... rode with the black guard in the duke's carriage, 'mongst spits and dripping pans.

Webster (1612).

The criminals and vagrants or vagabonds of a town or community, collectively. [Obs.]

A person of stained or low character, esp. one who uses scurrilous language, or treats others with foul abuse; a scoundrel; a rough.

A man whose manners and sentiments are decidedly below those of his class deserves to be called a blackguard.

Macaulay.

A vagrant; a bootblack; a gamin. [Obs.]

Blackguard · , v. t. [imp. & p.p. Blackguarded; p. pr. & vb. n. Blackguarding.] To revile or abuse in scurrilous language.

Southey.

Blackguard, a. Scurrilous; abusive; low; worthless; vicious; as, blackguard language.

Blackguardïsm (?), n. The conduct or language of a blackguard; ruffianism.

Blackguardïly, adv. & a. In the manner of or resembling a blackguard; abusive; scurrilous; ruffianly.

Blackhead · (?), n. (Zo"l.) The scaup duck.

Blackheart · (?), n. A heart-shaped cherry with a very dark-colored skin.

Black-heart · ed, a. Having a wicked, malignant disposition; morally bad.

Black hole · (?). A dungeon or dark cell in a prison; a military lock-up or guardroom; — now commonly with allusion to the cell (the Black Hole) in a fort at Calcutta, into which 146 English prisoners were thrust by the nabob Suraja Dowla on the night of June 20, 17656, and in which 123 of the prisoners died before morning from lack of air.

A discipline of unlimited autocracy, upheld by rods, and ferules, and the black hole.

H. Spencer.

Blacking, n. 1. Any preparation for making things black; esp. one for giving a black luster to boots and shoes, or to stoves.

The act or process of making black.

Blackish, a. Somewhat black.

Black-jack · , n. 1. (Min.) A name given by English miners to sphalerite, or zinc blende; — called also false galena. See Blende.

Caramel or burnt sugar, used to color wines, spirits, ground coffee, etc.

A large leather vessel for beer, etc. [Obs.]

(Bot.) The Quercus nigra, or barren oak.

The ensign of a pirate.

Black · lead (?). Plumbago; graphite. It leaves a blackish mark somewhat like lead. See Graphite.

Black · lead, v. t. To coat or to polish with black lead.

Blackleg · (?), n. 1. A notorious gambler. [Colloq.]

A disease among calves and sheep, characterized by a settling of gelatinous matter in the legs, and sometimes in the neck. [Eng.]

Black let · ter (?). The old English or Gothic letter, in which the Early English manuscripts were written, and the first English books were printed. It was conspicuous for its blackness. See Type.

Black-let · ter, a. 1. Written or printed in black letter; as, a black-letter manuscript or book.

Given to the study of books in black letter; that is, of old books; out of date.

Kemble, a black-letter man!

J. Boaden.

Of or pertaining to the days in the calendar not marked with red letters as saints' days. Hence: Unlucky; inauspicious.

Blacklist · (?), v. t. To put in a black list as deserving of suspicion, censure, or punishment; esp. to put in a list of persons stigmatized as insolvent or untrustworthy, Ð as tradesmen and employers do for mutual protection; as, to blacklist a workman who has been discharged. See Black list, under Black, a.

If you blacklist us, we will boycott you.

John Swinton.

Blackly, adv. In a black manner; darkly, in color; gloomily; threateningly; atrociously. ½Deeds so blackly grim and horrid.ͺ

Feltham.

Blackmail · (?), n. [Black + mail a piece of money.] 1. A certain rate of money, corn, cattle, or other thing, anciently paid, in the north of England and south of Scotland, to certain men who were allied to robbers, or moss troopers, to be by them protected from pillage.

Sir W. Scott.

Payment of money exacted by means of intimidation; also, extortion of money from a person by threats of public accusation, exposure, or censure.

(Eng. Law) Black rent, or rent paid in corn, flesh, or the lowest coin, a opposed to ½white rentͺ, which paid in silver.

To levy blackmail, to extort money by threats, as of injury to one's reputation.

Blackmail ·, v. t. [imp. & p.p. Blackmailed (?); p. pr. & vb. n. Blackmailing.] To extort money from by exciting fears of injury other than bodily harm, as injury to reputation, distress of mind, etc.; as, to blackmail a merchant by threatening to expose an alleged fraud. [U. S.]

Blackmail · er (?), n. One who extorts, or endeavors to extort, money, by black mailing.

Blackmail · ing, n. The act or practice of extorting money by exciting fears of injury other than bodily harm, as injury to reputation.

Black Mon · day (?). 1. Easter Monday, so called from the severity of that day in 1360, which was so unusual that many of Edward III.'s soldiers, then before Paris, died from the cold.

Stow.

Then it was not for nothing that may nose fell a bleeding on Black Monday last.

Shak.

The first Monday after the holidays; Ð so called by English schoolboys.

Halliwell.

Black monk · (?). A Benedictine monk.

Blackmoor (?), n. See Blackamoor.

BlackÐmouthed · (?), a. Using foul or scurrilous language; slanderous.

Blackness, n. The quality or state of being black; black color; atrociousness or enormity in wickedness.

They're darker now than blackness.
Donne.

Blackpoll · (?), n. [Black + poll head.] (Zo"l.) A warbler of the United States (Dendroica striata).

Black pudding (?). A kind of sausage made of blood, suet, etc., thickened with meal.

And fat black puddings, Ð proper food,
For warriors that delight in blood.
Hudibras.

Black Rod · (?). (a) the usher to the Chapter of the Garter, so called from the black rod which he carries. He is of the king's chamber, and also usher to the House of Lords. [Eng.] (b) An usher in the legislature of British colonies.
Cowell.

Committed to the custody of the Black Rod.
Macaulay.

Blackroot · , n. (Bot.) See Colicroot.

Blacks (?), n. pl. 1. The name of a kind of in used in copperplate printing, prepared from the charred husks of the grape, and residue of the wine press.

Soot flying in the air. [Eng.]

Black garments, etc. See Black, n., 4.

Blacksalt · er (?), n. One who, makes crude potash, or black salts.

Black salts · (?). Crude potash.
De Colange.

Blacksmith · (?), n. [Black (in allusion to the color of the metal) + smith. Cf. Whitesmith.] 1. A smith who works in iron with a forge, and makes iron utensils, horseshoes, etc.

The blacksmith may forge what he pleases.
Howell.

(Zo"l.) A fish of the Pacific coast (Chromis, or Heliastes, punctipinnis), of a blackish color.

Black snake · (?) or Blacksnake, n. (Zo"l.) A snake of a black color, of which two species are common in the United States, the Bascanium constrictor, or racer, sometimes six feet long, and the Scotophis Alleghaniensis, seven or eight feet long.

µ %The name is also applied to various other black serpents, as Natrix atra of Jamaica.

Blackstrap · (?), n. 1. A mixture of spirituous liquor (usually rum) and molasses.

No blackstrap toĭnight; switchel, or ginger pop.
Judd.

Bad port wine; any commo wine of the Mediterranean; Đ so called by sailors.

Blacktail · (?), n. [Black + tail.] 1. (Zo"l.) A fish; the ruff or pope.

(Zo"l.) The blackĭtailed deer (Cervus or Cariacus Columbianus) of California and Oregon; also, the mule deer of the Rocky Mountains. See Mule deer.

Blackthorn · (?), n. (Bot.) (a) A spreading thorny shrub or small tree (Prunus spinosa), with blackish bark, and bearing little black plums, which are called sloes; the sloe. (b) A species of Crat'gus or hawthorn (C. tomentosa). Both are used for hedges.

Black vomit (?). (Med.) A copious vomiting of darkĭcolored matter; or the substance so discharged; Đ one of the most fatal symptoms in yellow fever.

Black wash · (?) or Blackwash, n. 1. (Med.) A lotion made by mixing calomel and lime water.

A wash that blackens, as opposed to whitewash; hence, figuratively, calumny.

To remove as far as he can the modern layers of black wash, and let the man himself, fair or foul, be seen.
C. Kingsley.

Blackwood (?), n. A name given to several darkĭcolored timbers. The East Indian black wood is from the tree Dalbergia latifolia.
Balfour.

Blackwork · (?), n. Work wrought by blacksmiths; Đ so called in distinction from that wrought by whitesmiths.
Knight.

Bladder (?), n. [OE. bladder, bleddre, AS. bl?dre, bl?ddre; akin to Icel. bla?ra, SW. bl„ddra, Dan. bl're, D. blaar, OHG. bl¾tara the bladder in the body of animals, G. blatter blister, bustule; all fr. the same root as AS. bl¾wan, E. blow, to puff. See Blow to puff.]

(Anat.) A bag or sac in animals, which serves as the receptacle of some fluid; as, the urinary bladder; the gall bladder; Đ applied especially to the urinary bladder, either within the animal, or when taken out and inflated with air.

Any vesicle or blister, especially if filled with air, or a thin, watery fluid.

(Bot.) A distended, membranaceous pericarp.

Anything inflated, empty, or unsound. ½To swim with bladders of philosophy.„

Rochester.

Bladder nut, or Bladder tree (Bot.), a genus of plants (Staphylea) with bladderlike seed pods. Đ Bladder pod (Bot.), a genus of low herbs (Vesicaria) with inflated seed pods. Đ Bladdor senna (Bot.), a genus of shrubs (Colutea), with membranaceous, inflated pods. Đ Bladder worm (Zo"l.), the larva of any species of tapeworm (T‘nia), found in the flesh or other parts of animals. See Measle, Cysticercus. Ð Bladder wrack (Bot.), the common black rock weed of the seacoast (Fucus nodosus and F. vesiculosus) Ð called also bladder tangle. See Wrack.

Bladder, v. t. [imp. & p.p. Bladdered (?); p. pr. & vb. n. Bladdering.] 1. To swell out like a bladder with air; to inflate. [Obs.]
G. Fletcher.

To put up in bladders; as, bladdered lard.

Bladderïwort · (?), n. (Bot.) A genus (Utricularia) of aquatic or marshy plants, which usually bear numerous vesicles in the divisions of the leaves. These serve as traps for minute animals. See Ascidium.

Bladderïy (?), a. Having bladders; also, resembling a bladder.

Blade (?), n. [OE. blade, blad, AS. bl‘d leaf; akin to OS., D., Dan., & Sw. blad, Icel. bla?, OHG. blat, G. blatt, and perh. to L. folium, Gr. ?. The root is prob. the same as that of AS. bl?wan, E. blow, to blossom. See Blow to blossom, and cf. Foil leaf of metal.]

Properly, the leaf, or flat part of the leaf, of any plant, especially of gramineous plants. The term is sometimes applied to the spire of grasses.

The crimson dulse ... with its waving blade.
Percival.
First the blade, then ear, after that the full corn in the ear.
Mark iv. 28.

The cutting part of an instrument; as, the blade of a knife or a sword.

The broad part of an oar; also, one of the projecting arms of a screw propeller.

The scapula or shoulder blade.

pl. (Arch.) The principal rafters of a roof.

Weale.

pl. (Com.) The four large shell plates on the sides, and the five large ones of the middle, of the carapace of the sea turtle, which yield the best tortoise shell.

De Colange.

A sharpïwitted, dashing, wild, or reckless, fellow; Ð a word of somewhat indefinite meaning.

He saw a turnkey in a trice
Fetter a troublesome blade.
Coleridge.
<— p. 152 —>
Blade (?), v. t. To furnish with a blade.

343

Blade, v. i. To put forth or have a blade.

As sweet a plant, as fair a flower, is faded
As ever in the Muses' garden bladed.
P. Fletcher.

Bladebone · (?), n. The scapula. See Blade, 4.

Bladed (?), a. 1. Having a blade or blades; as a twoïbladed knife.
Decking with liquid pearl the bladed grass.
Shak.

Divested of blades; as, bladed corn.

(Min.) Composed of long and narrow plates, shaped like the blade of a knife.

Bladefish · (?), n. (Zo"l.) A long, thin, marine fish of Europe (Trichiurus lepturus); the ribbon fish.

Bladesmith · (?), n. A sword cutler. [Obs.]

Blady (?), a. Consisting of blades. [R.] ½Blady grass.
Drayton.

Bl' (?), a. [See Blue.] Dark blue or bluish gray; leadïcolored. [Scot.]

Bl'berïry (?), n. [Bl' + berry; akin to Icel bl¾ber, Sw. bl?b„r, D. blaab'r. Cf. Blueberry.] The bilberry. [North of Eng. & Scot.]

ØBlague (?), n. [F.] Mendacious boasting; falcefood; humbug.

Blain (?), n. [OE. blein, bleyn, AS. bl?gen; akin to Dan. blegn, D. blein; perh. fr. the same root as E. bladder. See Bladder.] 1. An inflammatory swelling or sore; a bulla, pustule, or blister.

Blotches and blains must all his flesh emboss.
Milton.

(Far.) A bladder growing on the root of the tongue of a horse, against the windpipe, and stopping the breath.

Blamaïble (?), a. [Cf. F. blfmable.] Deserving of censure; faulty; culpable; reprehensible; censurable; blameworthy. Ð Blamaïbleïness, n. Ð Blamïaïbly (?), adv.

Blame , v. t. [imp. & p.p. Blamed (?); p. pr. & vb. n. Blaming.] [OE. blamen, F. blfr, OF. blasmer, fr. L. blasphemare to blaspheme, LL. also to blame, fr. Gr. ? to speak ill to slander, to blaspheme, fr. ? evil speaking, perh. for ?; ? injury (fr. ? to injure) + ? a saying, fr. ? to say. Cf. Blaspheme, and see Fame.]

To censure; to express disapprobation of; to find fault with; to reproach.

We have none to blame gut ourselves.
Tillotson.

To bring reproach upon; to blemish. [Obs.]

She ... blamed her noble blood.
Spenser.
To blame, to be blamed, or deserving blame; in fault; as, the conductor was to blame for the accident.
You were to blame, I must be plain with you.
Shak.
Blame, n. [OE. blame, fr. F. blfme, OF. blasme, fr. blfmer, OF. blasmer, to blame. See Blame, v.] 1. An expression of disapprobation fir something deemed to be wrong; imputation of fault; censure.
Let me bear the blame forever.
Gen. xiiii. 9.

That which is deserving of censure or disapprobation; culpability; fault; crime; sin.

Holy and without blame before him in love.
Eph. i. 4.

Hurt; injury. [Obs.]

Spenser.
Syn. Ð Censure; reprehension; condemnation; reproach; fault; sin; crime; wrongdoing.
Blameful (?), a. 1. Faulty; meriting blame.
Shak.

Attributing blame or fault; implying or conveying censure; faultfinding; censorious.

Chaucer.
Ð Blamefullly, adv. Ð Blamefullness, n.
Blameless, a. Free from blame; without fault; innocent; guiltless; Ð sometimes followed by of.
A bishop then must be blameless.
1 Tim. iii. 2.
Blameless still of arts that polish to deprave.
Mallet.
We will be blameless of this thine oath.
Josh. ii. 17.
Syn. Ð Irreproachable; sinless; unblemished; inculpable. Ð Blameless, Spotless, Faultless, Stainless. We speak of a thing as blameless when it is free from blame, or the just imputation of fault; as, a blameless life or character. The others are stronger. We speak of a thing as faultless, stainless, or spotless, only when we mean that it is absolutely without fault or blemish; as, a spotless or stainless reputation; a faultless course of conduct. The last three words apply only to the general character, while blameless may be used in reverence to particular points; as, in this transaction he was wholly blameless. We also

apply faultless to personal appearance; as, a faultless figure; which can not be done in respect to any of the other words.

Blamelessily, adv. In a blameless manner.

Blamelessiness, n. The quality or state of being blameless; innocence.

Blamer (?), n. One who blames.

Wyclif.

Blamewor·thy (?), a. Deserving blame; culpable; reprehensible. Ð Blamewor·thiïness, n.

Blancard (?), n. [F., fr. blanc white.] A kind of linen cloth made in Normandy, the thread of which is partly blanches before it is woven.

Blanch (?), v. t. [imp. & p.p. Blanched (?); p. pr. & vb. n. Blanching.] [OE. blanchen, blaunchen, F. blanchir, fr. blanc white. See Blank, a.]

> To take the color out of, and make white; to bleach; as, to blanch linen; age has blanched his hair.

> (Gardening) To bleach by excluding the light, as the stalks or leaves of plants, by earthing them up or tying them together.

> (Confectionery & Cookery) (a) To make white by removing the skin of, as by scalding; as, to blanch almonds. (b) To whiten, as the surface of meat, by plunging into boiling water and afterwards into cold, so as to harden the surface and retain the juices.

> To give a white luster to (silver, before stamping, in the process of coining.).

> To cover (sheet iron) with a coating of tin.

> Fig.: To whiten; to give a favorable appearance to ; to whitewash; to palliate.

Blanch over the blackest and most absurd things.

Tillotson.

Syn. Ð To Blanch, Whiten. To whiten is the generic term, denoting, to render white; as, to whiten the walls of a room. Usually (though not of necessity) this is supposed to be done by placing some white coloring matter in or upon the surface of the object in question. To blanch is to whiten by the removal of coloring matter; as, to blanch linen. So the cheek is blanched by fear, i. e., by the withdrawal of the blood, which leaves it white.

Blanch (?), v. i. To grow or become white; as, his cheek blanched with fear; the rose blanches in the sun.

[Bones] blanching on the grass.

Tennyson.

Blanch, v. t. [See Blench.] 1. To avoid, as from fear; to evade; to leave unnoticed. [Obs.]

Ifs and ands to qualify the words of treason, whereby every man might express his malice and blanch his danger.

Bacon.

I suppose you will not blanch Paris in your way.

Reliq. Wot.

> To cause to turn aside or back; as, to blanch a deer.

Blanch, v. i. To use evasion. [Obs.]

Books will speak plain, when counselors blanch.

Bacon.

Blanch, n. (Mining) Ore, not in masses, but mixed with other minerals.

Blancher (?), n. One who, or that which, blanches or whitens; esp., one who anneals and cleanses money; also, a chemical preparation for this purpose.

Blancher, n. One who, or that which, frightens away or turns aside. [Obs.]

And Gynecia, a blancher, which kept the dearest deer from her.

Sir P. Sidney.

And so even now hath he divers blanchers belonging to the market, to let and stop the light of the gospel.

Latimer.

Blanch hold · ing (?). (Scots Law) A mode of tenure by the payment of a small duty in white rent (silver) or otherwise.

Blanchlimeïter (?), n. [1st blanch + Ïmeter.] An instrument for measuring the bleaching power of chloride of lime and potash; a chlorometer.

Ure.

Blancïmange (?), n. [F. blancmanger, lit. white food; blanc white + manger to eat.] (Cookery) A preparation for desserts, etc., made from isinglass, sea moss, cornstarch, or other gelatinous or starchy substance, with mild, usually sweetened and flavored, and shaped in a mold.

Blancïmanger (?), n. [F. See Blancmange.] A sort of fricassee with white sauce, variously made of capon, fish, etc. [Obs.]

Chaucer.

Bland (?), a. [L. blandus, of unknown origin.]

Mild; soft; gentle; smooth and soothing in manner; suave; as, a bland temper; bland persuasion; a bland sycophant. ½Exhilarating vapor bland.

Milton.

Having soft and soothing qualities; not drastic or irritating; not stimulating; as, a bland oil; a bland diet.

Blanïdation (?), n. [Cf. L. blanditia, blandities, fr. blandus. See Bland.] Flattery. [Obs.]

Blanïdiloïquence (?), n. [L. blandiloquentia; blandus mild + loqui to speak.] Mild, flattering speech.

Blanïdiloïquous (?), Blanïdiïloquiïous (?), } a. Fairïspoken; flattering.

Blandise (?), v. i. [Same word as Blandish.] To blandish any one. [Obs.]

Chaucer.

Blandish (?), v. t. [imp. & p.p. Blandished (?); p. pr. & vb. n. Blandishing.] [OE. blaundisen, F. blandir, fr. L. blandiri, fr. blandus mild, flattering.] 1. To flatter with kind words or affectionate actions; to caress; to cajole.

To make agreeable and enticing.

Mustering all her wiles,
With blandished parleys.
Milton.

Blandishïer (?), n. One who uses blandishments.

Blandishïment (?), n. [Cf. OF. blandissement.] The act of blandishing; a word or act expressive of affection or kindness, and tending to win the heart; soft words and artful caresses; cajolery; allurement.

Cowering low with blandishment.
Milton.

Attacked by royal smiles, by female blandishments.
Macaulay.

Blandly (?), adv. In a bland manner; mildly; suavely.

Blandness, n. The state or quality of being bland.

Blank (?), a. [OE. blank, blonc, blaunc, blaunche, fr. F. blanc, fem. blanche, fr. OHG. blanch shining, bright, white, G. blank; akin to E. blink, cf. also AS. blanc white. ?98. See Blink, and cf. 1st Blanch.]

Of a white or pale color; without color.

To the blank moon
Her office they prescribed.
Milton.

Free from writing, printing, or marks; having an empty space to be filled in with some special writing; Ð said of checks, official documents, etc.; as, blank paper; a blank check; a blank ballot.

Utterly confounded or discomfited.

Adam ... astonied stood, and blank.
Milton.

Empty; void; without result; fruitless; as, a blank space; a blank day.

Lacking characteristics which give variety; as, a blank desert; a blank wall; destitute of interests, affections, hopes, etc.; as, to live a blank existence; destitute of sensations; as, blank unconsciousness.

Lacking animation and intelligence, or their associated characteristics, as expression of face, look, etc.; expressionless; vacant. ½Blank and horrorïstricken faces.

C. Kingsley.
The blank ... glance of a half returned consciousness.
G. Eliot.

Absolute; downright; unmixed; as, blank terror.

Blank bar (Law), a plea put in to oblige the plaintiff in an action of trespass to assign the certain place where the trespass was committed; Ð called also common bar. Ð Blank cartridge, a cartridge containing no ball. Ð Blank deed. See Deed. Ð Blank door, or Blank window (Arch.), a depression in a wall of the size of a door or window, either for symmetrical effect, or for the more convenient insertion of a door or window at a future time, should it be needed. Ð Blank indorsement (Law), an indorsement which omits the name of the person in whose favor it is made; it is usually made by simply writing the name of the indorser on the back of the bill. Ð Blank line (Print.), a vacant space of the breadth of a line, on a printed page; a line of quadrats. Ð Blank tire (Mech.), a tire without a flange. Ð Blank tooling. See Blind tooling, under Blind. Ð Blank verse. See under Verse. Ð Blank wall, a wall in which there is no opening; a dead wall.

Blank (?), n. 1. Any void space; a void space on paper, or in any written instrument; an interval void of consciousness, action, result, etc; a void.

I can not write a paper full, I used to do; and yet I will not forgive a blank of half an inch from you.
Swift.

From this time there ensues a long blank in the history of French legislation.
Hallam.

I was ill. I can't tell how long Ð it was a blank.
G. Eliot.

A lot by which nothing is gained; a ticket in a lottery on which no prize is indicated.

In Fortune's lottery lies
A heap of blanks, like this, for one small prize.
Dryden.

A paper unwritten; a paper without marks or characters a blank ballot; Ð especially, a paper on which are to be inserted designated items of information, for which spaces are left vacant; a bland form.

The freemen signified their approbation by an inscribed vote, and their dissent by a blank.
Palfrey.

A paper containing the substance of a legal instrument, as a deed, release, writ, or execution, with spaces left to be filled with names, date, descriptions, etc.

The point aimed at in a target, marked with a white spot; hence, the object to which anything is directed.

Let me still remain
The true blank of thine eye.
Shak.

Aim; shot; range. [Obs.]

> I have stood ... within the blank of his displeasure
> For my free speech.
>
> Shak.

A kind of base silver money, first coined in England by Henry V., and worth about 8 pence; also, a French coin of the seventeenth century, worth about 4 pence.

Nares.

(Mech.) A piece of metal prepared to be made into something by a further operation, as a coin, screw, nuts.

(Dominoes) A piece or division of a piece, without spots; as, the ½double blank₃; the ½six blank.₃

In blank, with an essential portion to be supplied by another; as, to make out a check in blank.

Blank, v. t. [imp. & p.p. Blanked (?); p. pr. & vb. n. Blanking.] [Cf. 3d Blanch.] 1. To make void; to annul. [Obs.]

Spenser.

To blanch; to make blank; to damp the spirits of; to dispirit or confuse. [Obs.]

> Each opposite that blanks the face of joy.
>
> Shak.

Blanket (?), n. [F. blanchet, OF. also blanket, a woolen waistcoat or shirt, the blanket of a printing press; prop. white woolen stuff, dim. of blanc white; blanquette a kind of white pear, fr. blanc white. See Blank, a.] 1. A heavy, loosely woven fabric, usually of wool, and having a nap, used in bed clothing; also, a similar fabric used as a robe; or any fabric used as a cover for a horse.

(Print.) A piece of rubber, felt, or woolen cloth, used in the tympan to make it soft and elastic.

A streak or layer of blubber in whales.

µ The use of blankets formerly as curtains in theaters explains the following figure of Shakespeare.

Nares.

> Nor heaven peep through the blanket of the dark
> To cry, ½Hold, hold!₃
>
> Shak.

Blanket sheet, a newspaper of folio size. Ð A wet blanket, anything which damps, chills, dispirits, or discour?ges.

Blanket, v. t. [imp. & p.p. Blanketed; p. pr. & vb. n. Blanketing.] 1. To cover with a blanket.

> I'll ... blanket my loins.
>
> Shak.

To toss in a blanket by way of punishment.

We'll have our men blanket 'em i' the hall.
B. Jonson.

To take the wind out of the sails of (another vessel) by sailing to windward of her.

Blanket cattle. See Belted cattle, under Belted.
Blanketing, n. 1. Cloth for blankets.

The act or punishment of tossing in a blanket.

That affair of the blanketing happened to thee for the fault thou wast guilty of.
Smollett.
Blankly (?), adv. 1. In a blank manner; without expression; vacuously; as, to stare blankly.
G. Eliot.

Directly; flatly; point blank.

De Quincey.
Blankness, n. The state of being blank.
ØBlanÏquette (?), n. [F. blanquette, from blanc white.] (Cookery) A white fricassee.
ØBlanÏquillo (?), n. [Sp. blanquillo whitish.] (Zo"l.) A large fish of Florida and the W. Indies (Caulolatilus chrysops). It is red, marked with yellow.
Blare (?), v. i. [imp. & p.p. Blared (?); p. pr. & vb. n. Blaring.] [OE. blaren, bloren, to cry, woop; cf. G. pl„rren to bleat, D. blaren to bleat, cry, weep. Prob. an imitative word, but cf. also E. blast. Cf. Blore.] To sound loudly and somewhat harshly. ½The trumpet blared.¸
Tennyson.
Blare, v. t. To cause to sound like the blare of a trumpet; to proclaim loudly.
To blare its own interpretation.
Tennyson.
Blare, n. The harsh noise of a trumpet; a loud and somewhat harsh noise, like the blast of a trumpet; a roar or bellowing.
With blare of bugle, clamor of men.
Tennyson.
His ears are stunned with the thunder's blare.
J. R. Drake.
Blarney (?), n. [Blarney, a village and castle near Cork.] Smooth, wheedling talk; flattery. [Colloq.]

Blarney stone, a stone in Blarney castle, Ireland, said to make those who kiss it proficient in the use of blarney.

Blarney, v. t. [imp. & p.p. Blarneyed (?); p. pr. & vb. n. Blarneying.] To influence by blarney; to wheedle with smooth talk; to make or accomplish by blarney. ½Blarneyed the landlord.ͺ

Irving.

Had blarneyed his way from Long Island.

S. G. Goodrich.

ØBlaïs, (?), a. [F., p. p. of blaser.] Having the sensibilities deadened by excess or frequency of enjoyment; sated or surfeited with pleasure; used u?

<— p. 153 —>

Blasïpheme (?), v. t. [imp. & p.p. Blasphemed (?); p. pr. & vb. n. Blaspheming.] [OE. blasfem?n, L. blasphemare, fr. Gr. ?: cf. F. blasph,mer. See Blame, v.] 1. To speak of, or address, with impious irreverence; to revile impiously (anything sacred); as, to blaspheme the Holy Spirit. So Dagon shall be magnified, and God, Besides whom is no god, compared with idols, Disglorified, blasphemed, and had in scorn. Milton. How long, O Lord, holy and true, dost thou not judge and avenge thyself on all those who thus continually blaspheme thy great and allïglorious name? Dr. W. Beveridge. 2. Figuratively, of persons and things not religiously sacred, but held in high honor: To calumniate; to revile; to abuse. You do blaspheme the good in mocking me. Shak. Those who from our labors heap their board, Blaspheme their feeder and forget their lord. Pope. Blasïpheme, v. i. To utter blasphemy. He that shall blaspheme against the Holy Ghost hath never forgiveness. Mark iii. 29. Blasïphemer (?), n. One who blasphemes. And each blasphemer quite escape the rod, Because the insult's not on man, but God ? Pope. Blaspheïmous (?), a. [L. blasphemus, Gr. ?.] Speaking or writing blasphemy; uttering or exhibiting anything impiously irreverent; profane; as, a blasphemous person; containing blasphemy; as, a blasphemous book; a blasphemous caricature. ½Blasphemous publications.ͺ Porteus. Nor from the Holy One of Heaven Refrained his tongue blasphemous. Milton. µ Formerly this word was accented on the second syllable, as in the above example. Blaspheïmousïly, adv. In a blasphemous manner. Blaspheïmy (?), n. [L. blasphemia, Gr. ?: cf. OF. blasphemie.] 1. An indignity offered to God in words, writing, or signs; impiously irreverent words or signs addressed to, or used in reference to, God; speaking evil of God; also, the act of claiming the attributes or prerogatives of deity. µ When used generally in statutes or at common law, blasphemy is the use of irreverent words or signs in reference to the Supreme Being in such a way as to produce scandal or provoke violence. 2. Figuratively, of things held in high honor: Calumny; abuse; vilification. Punished for his blasphemy against learning. Bacon. Ïblast (?). [Gr. ? sprout, shoot.] A suffix or terminal formative, used principally in biological terms, and signifying growth, formation; as, bioblast, epiblast, mesoblast, etc. Blast (?), n. [AS. bl?st a puff of wind, a blowing; akin to Icel. bl¾str, OHG.

bl¾st, and fr. a verb akin to Icel. bl¾sa to blow, OHG. blfsan, Goth. bl?san (in comp.); all prob. from the same root as E. blow. See Blow to eject air.] 1. A violent gust of wind. And see where surly Winter passes off, Far to the north, and calls his ruffian blasts; His blasts obey, and quit the howling hill. Thomson. 2. A forcible stream of air from an orifice, as from a bellows, the mouth, etc. Hence: The continuous blowing to which one charge of ore or metal is subjected in a furnace; as, to melt so many tons of iron at a blast. µ The terms hot blast and cold blast are employed to designate whether the current is heated or not heated before entering the furnace. A blast furnace is said to be in blast while it is in operation, and out of blast when not in use. 3. The exhaust steam from and engine, driving a column of air out of a boiler chimney, and thus creating an intense draught through the fire; also, any draught produced by the blast. 4. The sound made by blowing a wind instrument; strictly, the sound produces at one breath. One blast upon his bugle horn Were worth a thousand men. Sir W. Scott. The blast of triumph o'er thy grave. Bryant. 5. A sudden, pernicious effect, as if by a noxious wind, especially on animals and plants; a blight. By the blast of God they perish. Job iv. 9. Virtue preserved from fell destruction's blast. Shak. 6. The act of rending, or attempting to rend, heavy masses of rock, earth, etc., by the explosion of gunpowder, dynamite, etc.; also, the charge used for this purpose. ½Large blasts are often used., Tomlinson. 7. A flatulent disease of sheep. Blast furnace, a furnace, usually a shaft furnace for smelting ores, into which air is forced by pressure. Ð Blast hole, a hole in the bottom of a pump stock through which water enters. Ð Blast nozzle, a fixed or variable orifice in the delivery end of a blast pipe; Ð called also blast orifice. Ð In full blast, in complete operation; in a state of great activity. See Blast, n., 2. [Colloq.] Blast, v. t. [imp. & p.p. Blasted; p. pr. & vb. n. Blasting.] 1. To injure, as by a noxious wind; to cause to wither; to stop or check the growth of, and prevent from fruitÏbearing, by some pernicious influence; to blight; to shrivel. Seven thin ears, and blasted with the east wind. Gen. xii. 6. 2. Hence, to affect with some sudden violence, plague, calamity, or blighting influence, which destroys or causes to fail; to visit with a curse; to curse; to ruin; as, to blast pride, hopes, or character. I'll cross it, though it blast me. Shak. Blasted with excess of light. T. Gray. 3. To confound by a loud blast or din. Trumpeters, With brazen din blast you the city's ear. Shak. 4. To rend open by any explosive agent, as gunpowder, dynamite, etc.; to shatter; as, to blast rocks. Blast, v. i. 1. To be blighted or withered; as, the bud blasted in the blossom. 2. To blow; to blow on a trumpet. [Obs.] Toke his blake trumpe faste And gan to puffen and to blaste. Chaucer. Blasted (?), a. 1. Blighted; withered. Upon this blasted heath. Shak. 2. Confounded; accursed; detestable. Some of her own blasted gypsies. Sir W. Scott. 3. Rent open by an explosive. The blasted quarry thunders, heard remote. Wordsworth. ØBlasÏtema (?), n.; pl. Blastemata (?). [Gr. ? bud, sprout.] (Biol.) The structureless, protoplasmic tissue of the embryo; the primitive basis of an organ yet unformed, from which it grows. Blas̈itemal (?), a. (Biol.) Relating to the blastema; rudimentary. Blas · teïmatic (?), a. (Biol.) Connected with, or proceeding from, the blastema; blastemal. Blaster (?), n. One who, or that which, blasts or destroys. Blastide (?), n. [Gr. ? sprout, fr. ? to grow.] (Biol.) A small, clear space in the segments of the ovum, the precursor of the nucleus. Blasting (?), n. 1. A blast; destruction by a blast, or by some pernicious cause. I have smitten you with blasting and mildew. Amos iv. 9. 2. The act or process of one who, or that which, blasts; the business of one who blasts. Blastment (?), n. A sudden stroke or injury produced by some destructive cause. [Obs.] Shak. Blas · toïcarpous (?), a. [Gr. ? sprout, germ + ? fruit.] (Bot.) Germinating inside the pericarp, as the mangrove. Brande & C. Blastoïc?le (?), n. [Gr. ? sprout + ? hollow.] (Biol.) The cavity of the blastosphere, or segmentation cavity. Blastoïcyst (?), n. [Gr. ? sprout + E. cyst.] (Biol.) The germinal vesicle. Blastoïderm (?), n. [Gr. ? sprout + E. derm.] (Biol.) The germinal membrane in an ovum, from which the embryo is developed. Blas · toïderïmatic (?), Blas · toïdermic (?), } a. Of or pertaining to the blastoderm. Blas · toïgeneïsis (?), n. [Gr. ? sprout + E. genesis.] (Biol.) Multiplication or increase by gemmation or budding. Blastoid (?), n. (Zo"l.) One of the Blastoidea. ØBlasïtoideïa (?), n. pl. [NL., fr. Gr. ? sprout + ïoid.] (Zo"l.) One of the divisions of Crinoidea found fossil in paleozoic rocks; pentremites. They are so named on account of their budlike form. Blastoïmere (?), n. [Gr. ? sprout + ïmere.] (Biol.) One of the segments first formed by the division of the ovum. Balfour. Blas · tophoïral (?), Blas · toïphoric (?), } a. Relating to the blastophore. Blastoïphore (?), n. [Gr. ? sprout + ? to bear.] (Biol.) That portion of the spermatospore which is not converted into spermatoblasts, but carries them. Blastoïpore (?), n. [Gr. ? sprout + E. pore.] (Biol.) The pore or opening leading into the cavity of invagination, or archenteron. [See Illust. of Invagination.] Balfour. Blastoïsphere (?), n. [Gr. ? sprout + E. sphere.] (Biol.) The hollow globe or sphere formed by the arrangement of the blastomeres on the periphery of an impregnated ovum. [See Illust. of Invagination.] Blastoïstyle (?), n. [Gr. ? sprout, bud + ? a pillar.] (Zo"l.) In certain hydroids, an imperfect zooid, whose special function is to produce medusoid buds. See Hydroidea, and Athecata. Blast pipe · (?). The exhaust pipe of a steam engine, or any pipe delivering steam or air, when so constructed as to cause a blast. ØBlastuïla (?), n. [NL., dim. of Gr. ? a sprout.] (Biol.) That stage in the development of the ovum in which the outer cells of the morula become more defined and form the blastoderm. Blastule (?), n. (Biol.) Same as Blastula. Blasty (?), a. 1. Affected by blasts; gusty. 2. Causing blast or injury. [Obs.] Boyle. Blat (?), v. i. To cry, as a calf or sheep; to bleat; to make a senseless noise; to talk inconsiderately. [Low] Blat, v. t. To utter inconsiderately. [Low] If I have anything on my mind, I have to blat it right out. W. D. Howells. Blatanïcy (?), n. Blatant quality. Blatant (?), a. [Cf. Bleat.] Bellowing, as a calf; bawling; brawling; clamoring; disagreeably clamorous; sounding loudly and harshly. ½Harsh and blatant tone.͵ R. H. Dana. A monster, which the blatant beast men call. Spenser. Glory, that blatant word, which haunts some military minds like the bray of the trumpet. W. Irving. Blatantĭly, adv. In a blatant manner. Blatherĭskite (?), n. A blustering, talkative fellow. [Local slang, U. S.] Barllett. Blatter (?), v. i. [imp. & p.p. Blattered (?).] [L. blaterare to babble: cf. F. blat͵rer to bleat.] To prate; to babble; to rail; to make a senseless noise; to patter. [Archaic] ½The rain blattered.͵ Jeffrey. They procured ... preachers to blatter against me, ... so that they had place and time to belie me shamefully. Latimer. Blat · terĭation (?), n. [L. blateratio a babbling.] Blattering. Blatterĭer (?), n. One who blatters; a babbler; a noisy, blustering boaster. Blatterĭing, n. Senseless babble or boasting. Blat · terĭoon (?), n. [L. blatero, ĭonis.] A senseless babbler or boaster. [Obs.] ½I hate such blatteroons.͵ Howell. ØBlaubok (?), n. [D. blauwbok.] (Zo"l.) The blue buck. See Blue buck, under Blue. Blay (?), n. [AS. bl?ge, fr. bl?c, bleak, white; akin to Icel. bleikja, OHG. bleicha, G. bleihe. See Bleak, n. & a.] (Zo"l.) A fish. See Bleak, n. Blaze (?), n. [OE. blase, AS. bl'se, blase; akin to OHG. blass whitish, G. blass pale, MHG. blas torch, Icel. blys torch; perh. fr. the same root as E. blast. Cf. Blast, Bluch, Blink.] 1. A steam of gas or vapor emitting light and heat in the process of combustion; a bright flame. ½To heaven the blaze uprolled.͵ Croly. 2. Intense, direct light accompanied with heat; as, to seek shelter from the blaze of the sun. O dark, dark, dark, amid the blaze of noon ! Milton. 3. A bursting out, or active display of any quality; an outburst; a brilliant display. ½Fierce blaze of riot.͵ ½His blaze of wrath.͵ Shak. For what is glory but the blaze of fame? Milton. 4. [Cf. D. bles; akin to E. blaze light.] A white spot on the forehead of a horse. 5. A spot made on trees by chipping off a piece of the bark, usually as a surveyor's mark. Three blazes in a perpendicular line on the same tree indicating a legislative road, the single blaze a settlement or neighborhood road. Carlton. In a blaze, on fire; burning with a flame; filled with, giving, or reflecting light; excited or exasperated. Ð Like blazes, furiously; rapidly. [Low] ½The horses did along like blazes tear.͵ Poem in Essex dialect. µ In low language in the U. S., blazes is frequently used of something extreme or excessive, especially of something very bad; as, blue as blazes. Neal. Syn. Ð Blaze, Flame. A blaze and a flame are both produced by burning gas. In blaze the idea of light rapidly evolved is prominent, with or without heat; as, the blaze of the sun or of a meteor. Flame includes a stronger notion of heat; as, he perished in the flames. Blaze, v. i. [imp. & p.p. Blazed (?); p. pr. & vb. n. Blazing.] 1. To shine with flame; to glow with flame; as, the fire blazes. 2. To send forth or reflect glowing or brilliant light; to show a blaze. And far and wide the icy summit blazed. Wordsworth. 3. To be resplendent. Macaulay. To blaze away, to discharge a firearm, or to continue firing; Ð said esp. of a number of persons, as a line of soldiers. Also used (fig.) of speech or action. [Colloq.] Blaze, v. t. 1. To mark (a tree) by chipping off a piece of the bark. I found my way by the blazed trees.

Hoffman. 2. To designate by blazing; to mark out, as by blazed trees; as, to blaze a line or path. Champollion died in 1832, having done little more than blaze out the road to be traveled by others. Nott. Blaze, v. t. [OE. blasen to blow; perh. confused with blast and blaze a flame, OE. blase. Cf. Blaze, v. i., and see Blast.] 1. To make public far and wide; to make known; to render conspicuous. On charitable lists he blazed his name. Pollok. To blaze those virtues which the good would hide. Pope. 2. (Her.) To blazon. [Obs.] Peacham. Blazer (?), n. One who spreads reports or blazes matters abroad. ½Blazers of crime., Spenser. Blazing, a. Burning with a blaze; as, a blazing fire; blazing torches. Sir W. Scott. Blazing star. (a) A comet. [Obs.] (b) A brilliant center of attraction. (c) (Bot.) A name given to several plants; as, to Cham'lirium luteum of the Lily family; Liatris squarrosa; and Aletris farinosa, called also colicroot and star grass. Blazon (?), n. [OE. blason, blasoun, shield, fr. F. blason coat of arms, OF. shield, from the root of AS. bl'se blaze, i. e., luster, splendor, MHG. blas torch See Blaze, n.] 1. A shield. [Obs.] 2. An heraldic shield; a coat of arms, or a bearing on a coat of arms; armorial bearings. Their blazon o'er his towers displayed. Sir W. Scott. 3. The art or act of describing or depicting heraldic bearings in the proper language or manner. Peacham. 4. Ostentatious display, either by words or other means; publication; show; description; record. Obtrude the blazon of their exploits upon the company. Collier. Thy tongue, thy face, thy limbs, actions, and spirit, Do give thee fivefold blazon. Shak. Blazon, v. t. [imp. & p.p. Blazoned (?); p. pr. & vb. n. Blazoning (?).] [From blazon, n.; confused with 4th blaze: cf. F. blasonner.] 1. To depict in colors; to display; to exhibit conspicuously; to publish or make public far and wide. Thyself thou blazon'st. Shak. There pride sits blazoned on th' unmeaning brow. Trumbull. To blazon his own worthless name. Cowper. 2. To deck; to embellish; to adorn. She blazons in dread smiles her hideous form. Garth. 3. (Her.) To describe in proper terms (the figures of heraldic devices); also, to delineate (armorial bearings); to emblazon. The coat of , arms, which I am not herald enough to blazon into English. Addison. Blazon, v. i. To shine; to be conspicuous. [R.] Blazoni̇er (?), n. One who gives publicity, proclaims, or blazons; esp., one who blazons coats of arms; a herald. Burke.

<— p. 154 —>

Blazoni̇ment (?), n. The act or blazoning; blazoning; emblazonment.

Blazoni̇ry , n. 1. Same as Blazon, 3.

The principles of blazonry.

Peacham.

A coat of arms; an armorial bearing or bearings.

The blazonry of Argyle.

Lord Dufferin.

Artistic representation or display.

Blea (?), n. The part of a tree which lies immediately under the bark; the alburnum or sapwood.

Bleaberÿry (?), n. (Bot.) See Blaeberry.

Bleach (?), v. t. [imp. & p.p. Bleached (?); p. pr. & vb. n. Bleaching.] [OE. blakien, blechen, v. t. & v. i., AS. bl¾cian, bl?can, to grow pale; akin to Icel. bleikja, Sw. bleka, Dan. blege, D. bleeken, G. bleichen, AS. bl¾c pale. See Bleak, a.] To make white, or whiter; to remove the color, or stains, from; to blanch; to whiten.

The destruction of the coloring matters attached to the bodies to be bleached is effected either by the action of the air and light, of chlorine, or of sulphurous acid.

Ure.

Immortal liberty, whose look sublime
Hath bleached the tyrant's cheek in every varying clime.

Smollett.

Bleach, v. i. To grow white or lose color; to whiten.

Bleached (?), a. Whitened; make white.

Let their bleached bones, and blood's unbleaching stain,
Long mark the battlefield with hideous awe.

Byron.

Bleacher (?), n. One who whitens, or whose occupation is to whiten, by bleaching.

Bleacherÿy (?), n.; pl. Bleacheries (?). A place or an establishment where bleaching is done.

Bleaching, n. The act or process of whitening, by removing color or stains; esp. the process of whitening fabrics by chemical agents.

Ure.

Bleaching powder, a powder for bleaching, consisting of chloride of lime, or some other chemical or chemicals.

Bleak (?), a. [OE. blac, bleyke, bleche, AS. bl¾c, bl?c, pale, wan; akin to Icel. bleikr, Sw. blek, Dan. bleg, OS. bl?k, D. bleek, OHG. pleih, G. bleich; all from the root of AS. blÆcan to shine; akin to OHG. blÆchen to shine; cf. L. flagrare to burn, Gr. ? to burn, shine, Skr. bhr¾j to shine, and E. flame. ?98. Cf. Bleach, Blink, Flame.] 1. Without color; pale; pallid. [Obs.]

When she came out she looked as pale and as bleak as one that were laid out dead.

Foxe.

Desolate and exposed; swept by cold winds.

Wastes too bleak to rear
The common growth of earth, the foodful ear.

Wordsworth.

At daybreak, on the bleak sea beach.

Longfellow.

Cold and cutting; cheerless; as, a bleak blast.

Ð Bleakish, a. Ð Bleakly, adv. Ð Bleakness, n.

Bleak, n. [From Bleak, a., cf. Blay.] (Zo"l.) A small European river fish (Leuciscus alburnus), of the family Cyprinid'; the blay. [Written also blick.]

μ The silvery pigment lining the scales of the bleak is used in the manufacture of artificial pearls.

Baird.

Bleaky (?), a. Bleak. [Obs.]

Dryden.

Blear (?), a. [See Blear, v.] 1. Dim or sore with water or rheum; Ð said of the eyes.

His blear eyes ran in gutters to his chin.

Dryden.

Causing or caused by dimness of sight; dim.

Power to cheat the eye with blear illusion.

Milton.

Blear, v. t. [imp. & p.p. Bleared (?); p. pr. & vb. n. Blearing.] [OE. bleren; cf. Dan. plire to blink, Sw. plira to twinkle, wink, LG. plieren; perh. from the same root as E. blink. See Blink, and cf. Blur.] To make somewhat sore or watery, as the eyes; to dim, or blur, as the sight. Figuratively: To obscure (mental or moral perception); to blind; to hoodwink.

That tickling rheums
Should ever tease the lungs and blear the sight.

Cowper.

To blear the eye of, to deceive; to impose upon. [Obs.]

Chaucer.

Bleared (?), a. Dimmed, as by a watery humor; affected with rheum. Ð BlearedÏness (?), n.

Dardanian wives,
With bleared visages, come forth to view
The issue of the exploit.

Shak.

Bleareye · (?), n. (Med.) A disease of the eyelids, consisting in chronic inflammation of the margins, with a gummy secretion of sebaceous matter.

Dunglison.

BlearÐeyed · (?), a. 1. Having sore eyes; having the eyes dim with rheum; dimÏsighted.

The blearÏeyed Crispin.

Drant.

Lacking in perception or penetration; shortÏsighted; as, a blearÏeyed bigot.

Bleareyed · ness, n. The state of being blearĭeyed.

Bleary (?), a. Somewhat blear.

Bleat (?), v. i. [imp. & p.p. Bleated; p. pr. & vb. n. Bleating.] [OE. bleten, AS. bl?tan; akin to D. blaten, bleeten, OHG. bl¾zan, pl¾zan; prob. of imitative origin.] To make the noise of, or one like that of, a sheep; to cry like a sheep or calf.

Then suddenly was heard along the main,
To low the ox, to bleat the woolly train.
Pope

The ewe that will not hear her lamb when it baas, will never answer a calf when he bleats.
Shak.

Bleat, n. A plaintive cry of, or like that of, a sheep.

The bleat of fleecy sheep.
Chapman's Homer.

Bleater (?), n. One who bleats; a sheep.

In cold, stiff soils the bleaters oft complain
Of gouty ails.
Dyer.

Bleating, a. Crying as a sheep does.

Then came the shepherd back with his bleating flocks from the seaside.
Longfellow.

Bleating, n. The cry of, or as of, a sheep.
Chapman.

Bleb (?), n. [Prov. E. bleb, bleib, blob, bubble, blister. This word belongs to the root of blub, blubber, blabber, and perh. blow to puff.] A large vesicle or bulla, usually containing a serous fluid; a blister; a bubble, as in water, glass, etc.

Arsenic abounds with air blebs.
Kirwan.

Blebby (?), a. Containing blebs, or characterized by blebs; as, blebby glass.

Bleck, Blek (?), v. t. To blacken; also, to defile. [Obs. or Dial.]
Wyclif.

Bled (?), imp. & p. p. of Bleed.

Blee (?), n. [AS. bleo, bleoh.] Complexion; color; hue; likeness; form. [Archaic]

For him which is so bright of blee.
Lament. of Mary Magd.

That boy has a strong blee of his father.
Forby.

Bleed (?), v. i. [imp. & p.p. Bled (?); p. pr. & vb. n. Bleeding.] [OE. bleden, AS. bl?dan, fr. bl?d blood; akin to Sw. bl"da, Dan. bl"de, D. bloeden, G. bluten. See Blood.] 1. To emit blood; to lose blood; to run with blood, by whatever means; as, the arm bleeds; the wound bled freely; to bleed at the nose.

To withdraw blood from the body; to let blood; as, Dr. A. bleeds in fevers.

To lose or shed one's blood, as in case of a violent death or severe wounds; to die by violence. ½C'sar must bleed.

Shak.
The lamb thy riot dooms to bleed toĭday.
Pope.

To issue forth, or drop, as blood from an incision.

For me the balm shall bleed.
Pope.

To lose sap, gum, or juice; as, a tree or a vine bleeds when tapped or wounded.

To pay or lose money; to have money drawn or extorted; as, to bleed freely for a cause. [Colloq.]

To make the heart bleed, to cause extreme pain, as from sympathy or pity.

Bleed, v. t. 1. To let blood from; to take or draw blood from, as by opening a vein.

To lose, as blood; to emit or let drop, as sap.

A decaying pine of stately size, bleeding amber.
H. Miller.

To draw money from (one); to induce to pay; as, they bled him freely for this fund. [Colloq.]

Bleeder (?), n. (Med.) (a) One who, or that which, draws blood. (b) One in whom slight wounds give rise to profuse or uncontrollable bleeding.

Bleeding, a. Emitting, or appearing to emit, blood or sap, etc.; also, expressing anguish or compassion.

Bleeding, n. A running or issuing of blood, as from the nose or a wound; a hemorrhage; the operation of letting blood, as in surgery; a drawing or running of sap from a tree or plant.

Blemish (?), v. t. [imp. & p.p. Blemished (?); p. pr. & vb. n. Blemishing.] [OE. blemissen, blemishen, OF. blemir, blesmir, to strike, injure, soil, F. bl^mir to grow pale, fr. OF. bleme, blesme, pale, wan, F. bl^me, prob. fr. Icel bl¾man the livid color of a wound, fr. bl¾r blue; akin to E. blue. OF. blemir properly signifies to beat one (black and) blue, and to render blue or dirty. See Blue.] 1. To mark with deformity; to injure or impair, as anything which is well formed, or excellent; to mar, or make defective, either the body or mind.

Sin is a soil which blemisheth the beauty of thy soul.
Brathwait.

To tarnish, as reputation or character; to defame.

There had nothing passed between us that might blemish reputation.
Oldys.

Blemish, n.; pl. Blemishes (?). Any mark of deformity or injury, whether physical or moral; anything; that diminishes beauty, or renders imperfect that which is otherwise well formed; that which impairs reputation.

He shall take two he lambs without blemish, and one ewe lamb of the first year without blemish.
Lev. xiv. 10.

The reliefs of an envious man are those little blemishes and imperfections that discover themselves in an illustrious character.
Spectator.

Syn. Ð Spot; speck; flaw; deformity; stain; defect; fault; taint; reproach; dishonor; imputation; disgrace.

Blemishĭless, a. Without blemish; spotless.

A life in all so blemishless.
Feltham.

Blemishĭment (?), n. The state of being blemished; blemish; disgrace; damage; impairment.

For dread of blame and honor's blemishment.
Spenser.

Blench (?), v. i. [imp. & p.p. Blenched (?); p. pr. & vb. n. Blenching.] [OE. blenchen to blench, elude, deceive, AS. blencan to deceive; akin to Icel. blekkja to impose upon. Prop. a causative of blink to make to wink, to deceive. See Blink, and cf. 3d Blanch.] 1. To shrink; to start back; to draw back, from lack of courage or resolution; to flinch; to quail.

Blench not at thy chosen lot.
Bryant.

This painful, heroic task he undertook, and never blenched from its fulfillment.
Jeffrey.

To fly off; to turn aside. [Obs.]

Though sometimes you do blench from this to that.
Shak.

Blench, v. t. 1. To baffle; to disconcert; to turn away; Ð also, to obstruct; to hinder. [Obs.]

Ye should have somewhat blenched him therewith, yet he might and would of likelihood have gone further.
Sir T. More.

To draw back from; to deny from fear. [Obs.]

He now blenched what before he affirmed.
Evelyn.
Blench, n. A looking aside or askance. [Obs.]
These blenches gave my heart another youth.
Shak.
Blench, v. i. & t. [See 1st Blanch.] To grow or make pale.
Barbour.
Blencher (?), n. 1. One who, or that which, scares another; specifically, a person stationed to prevent the escape of the deer, at a hunt. See Blancher. [Obs.]

One who blenches, flinches, or shrinks back.

Blench hold · ing. (Law) See Blanch holding.
Blend (?), v. t. [imp. & p.p. Blended or Blent (?); p. pr. & vb. n. Blending.] [OE. blenden, blanden, AS. blandan to blend, mix; akin to Goth. blandan to mix, Icel. blanda, Sw. blanda, Dan. blande, OHG. blantan to mis; to unknown origin.] 1. To mix or mingle together; esp. to mingle, combine, or associate so that the separate things mixed, or the line of demarcation, can not be distinguished. Hence: To confuse; to confound.
Blending the grand, the beautiful, the gay.
Percival.

To pollute by mixture or association; to spoil or corrupt; to blot; to stain. [Obs.]

Spenser.
Syn. Ð To commingle; combine; fuse; merge; amalgamate; harmonize.
Blend (?), v. i. To mingle; to mix; to unite intimately; to pass or shade insensibly into each other, as colors.
There is a tone of solemn and sacred feeling that blends with our conviviality.
Irving.
Blend, n. A thorough mixture of one thing with another, as color, tint, etc., into another, so that it cannot be known where one ends or the other begins.
Blend, v. t. [AS. blendan, from blind blind. See Blind, a.] To make blind, literally or figuratively; to dazzle; to deceive. [Obs.]
Chaucer.
Blende (?), n. [G., fr. blenden to blind, dazzle, deceive, fr. blind blind. So called either in allusion to its dazzling luster; or (Dana) because, though often resembling galena, it yields no lead. Cf. Sphalerite.] (Min.) (a) A mineral, called also sphalerite, and by miners mock lead, false galena, and blackÏjack. It is a zinc sulphide, but often contains some iron. Its color is

usually yellow, brown, or black, and its luster resinous. (b) A general term for some minerals, chiefly metallic sulphides which have a somewhat brilliant but nonmetallic luster.

Blender (?), n. One who, or that which, blends; an instrument, as a brush, used in blending.

Blending, n. 1. The act of mingling.

(Paint.) The method of laying on different tints so that they may mingle together while wet, and shade into each other insensibly.

Weale.

Blendous (?), a. Pertaining to, consisting of, or containing, blende.

Blendwa·ter (?), n. A distemper incident to cattle, in which their livers are affected.

Crabb.

Blenheim spaniel (?). [So called from Blenheim House, the seat of the duke of Marlborough, in England.] A small variety of spaniel, kept as a pet.

Blenk, v. i. To blink; to shine; to look. [Obs.]

Blennĭoid (?), Blennĭlid (?), } a. [Blenny + Ðoid] (Zo"l.) Of, pertaining to, or resembling, the blennies.

Blenĭnogeĭnous (?), a. [Gr. ? mucus + Ĭgenous.] Generating mucus.

ØBlen·norĭrhea (?), n. [Gr. ? mucus + ? to flow.] (Med.) (a) An inordinate secretion and discharge of mucus. (b) Gonorrhea.

Dunglison.

Blenny (?), n.; pl. Blennies (?). [L. blennius, blendius, blendea, Gr. ?, fr. ? slime, mucus.] (Zo"l.) A marine fish of the genus Blennius or family Blenniid'; Ð so called from its coating of mucus. The species are numerous.

Blent (?), imp. & p. p. of Blend to mingle. Mingled; mixed; blended; also, polluted; stained.

Rider and horse, friend, foe, in one red burial blent.

Byron.

Blent, imp. & p. p. of Blend to blind. Blinded. Also (Chaucer), 3d sing. pres. Blindeth. [Obs.]

ØBlesbok (?), n. [D., fr. bles a white spot on the forehead + bok buck.] (Zo"l.) A South African antelope (Alcelaphus albifrons), having a large white spot on the forehead.

Bless (?), v. t. [imp. & p.p. Blessed (?) or Blest; p. pr. & vb. n. Blessing.] [OE. blessien, bletsen, AS. bletsian, bledsian, bloedsian, fr. bl?d blood; prob. originally to consecrate by sprinkling with blood. See Blood.] 1. To make or pronounce holy; to consecrate

And God blessed the seventh day, and sanctified it.

Gen. ii. 3.

To make happy, blithesome, or joyous; to confer prosperity or happiness upon; to grant divine favor to.

The quality of mercy is ... twice blest;
It blesseth him that gives and him that takes.
Shak.
It hath pleased thee to bless the house of thy servant, that it may continue forever before thee.
1 Chron. xvii. 27 (R. V.)

To express a wish or prayer for the happiness of; to invoke a blessing upon; Ð applied to persons.

Bless them which persecute you.
Rom. xii. 14.

To invoke or confer beneficial attributes or qualities upon; to invoke or confer a blessing on, Ð as on food.

Then he took the five loaves and the two fishes, and looking up to heaven, he blessed them.
Luke ix. 16.

To make the sign of the cross upon; to cross (one's self). [Archaic]

Holinshed.

To guard; to keep; to protect. [Obs.]

To praise, or glorify; to extol for excellences.

Bless the Lord, O my soul: and all that is within me, bless his holy name.
Ps. ciii. 1.

To esteem or account happy; to felicitate.

The nations shall bless themselves in him.
Jer. iv. 3.

To wave; to brandish. [Obs.]

And burning blades about their heads do bless.
Spenser.
Round his armed head his trenchant blade he blest.
Fairfax.
µ This is an old sense of the word, supposed by Johnson, Nares, and others, to have been derived from the old rite of blessing a field by directing the hands to all parts of it. ½In drawing [their bow] some fetch such a compass as though they would turn about and bless all the field.͵
Ascham.
<— p. 155 —>

Bless me! Bless us! an exclamation of surprise. Milton. Ð To bless from, to secure, defend, or preserve from. ½Bless me from marrying a usurer.⸣
Shak.
To bless the doors from nightly harm.
Milton.
ÐTo bless with, To be blessed with, to favor or endow with; to be favored or endowed with; as, God blesses us with health; we are blessed with happiness.

Blessed (?), a. 1. Hallowed; consecrated; worthy of blessing or adoration; heavenly; holy.
O, run; prevent them with thy humble ode,
And lay it lowly at his blessed feet.
Milton.

Enjoying happiness or bliss; favored with blessings; happy; highly favored.

All generations shall call me blessed.
Luke i. 48.
Towards England's blessed shore.
Shak.

Imparting happiness or bliss; fraught with happiness; blissful; joyful. ½Then was a blessed time.⸣ ½So blessed a disposition.⸣

Shak.

Enjoying, or pertaining to, spiritual happiness, or heavenly felicity; as, the blessed in heaven.

Reverenced like a blessed saint.
Shak.
Cast out from God and blessed vision.
Milton.

(R. C. Ch.) Beatified.

Used euphemistically, ironically, or intensively.

Not a blessed man came to set her [a boat] free.
R. D. Blackmore.
Blessedĭly, adv. Happily; fortunately; joyfully.
We shall blessedly meet again never to depart.
Sir P. Sidney.
Blessedĭness, n. The state of being blessed; happiness; felicity; bliss; heavenly joys; the favor of God.
The assurance of a future blessedness.
Tillotson.
Single blessedness, the unmarried state. ½Grows, lives, and dies in single blessedness.⸣

Shak.

Syn. Ð Delight; beatitude; ecstasy. See Happiness.

Blessed thistle (?). See under Thistle.

Blesser (?), n. One who blesses; one who bestows or invokes a blessing.

Blessing, n. [AS. bletsung. See Bless, v. t.] 1. The act of one who blesses.

A declaration of divine favor, or an invocation imploring divine favor on some or something; a benediction; a wish of happiness pronounces.

This is the blessing, where with Moses the man of God blessed the children of Israel.

Deut. xxxiii. 1.

A means of happiness; that which promotes prosperity and welfare; a beneficent gift.

Nature's full blessings would be well dispensed.
Milton.

(Bib.) A gift. [A Hebraism]

Gen. xxxiii. 11.

Grateful praise or worship.

Blest, a. Blessed. ½This patriarch blest.,
Milton.

White these blest sounds my ravished ear assail.
Trumbull.

Blet (?), n. [F. blet, blette, a., soft from over ripeness.] A form of decay in fruit which is overripe.

Bletonïism (?), n. The supposed faculty of perceiving subterraneous springs and currents by sensation; Ð so called from one Bleton, of France.

Bletting (?), n. A form of decay seen in fleshy, overripe fruit.
Lindley.

Blew (?), imp. of Blow.

Bleyme (?), n. [F. bleime.] (Far.) An inflammation in the foot of a horse, between the sole and the bone. [Obs.]

Bleynte (?), imp. of Blench. [Obs.]
Chaucer.

Blickey (?), n. [D. blik tin.] A tin dinner pail. [Local, U. S.]
Bartlett.

Blight (?), v. t. [imp. & p.p. Blighted; p. pr. & vb. n. Blighting.] [Perh. contr. from AS. blÆcettan to glitter, fr. the same root as E. bleak. The meaning ½to blight, comes in that case from to glitter, hence, to be white or pale, grow pale, make pale, bleach. Cf. Bleach, Bleak.] 1. To affect with blight; to blast; to prevent the growth and fertility of.

[This vapor] blasts vegetables, blights corn and fruit, and is sometimes injurious even to man.
Woodward.

Hence: To destroy the happiness of; to ruin; to mar essentially; to frustrate; as, to blight one's prospects.

Seared in heart and lone and blighted.
Byron.

Blight, v. i. To be affected by blight; to blast; as, this vine never blights.

Blight, n. 1. Mildew; decay; anything nipping or blasting; Ð applied as a general name to various injuries or diseases of plants, causing the whole or a part to wither, whether occasioned by insects, fungi, or atmospheric influences.

The act of blighting, or the state of being blighted; a withering or mildewing, or a stoppage of growth in the whole or a part of a plant, etc.

That which frustrates one's plans or withers one's hopes; that which impairs or destroys.

A blight seemed to have fallen over our fortunes.
Disraeli.

(Zo"l.) A downy species of aphis, or plant louse, destructive to fruit trees, infesting both the roots and branches; Ð also applied to several other injurious insects.

pl. A rashlike eruption on the human skin. [U. S.]

Blighting, a. Causing blight.
Blightingly, adv. So as to cause blight.
Blimbi (?), Blimbing (?), n. See Bilimbi, etc.
Blin (?), v. t. & i. [OE. blinnen, AS. blinnan; pref. beï + linnan to cease.] To stop; to cease; to desist. [Obs.]
Spenser.

Blin, n. [AS. blinn.] Cessation; end. [Obs.]

Blind (?), a. [AS.; akin to D., G., OS., Sw., & Dan. blind, Icel. blindr, Goth. blinds; of uncertain origin.] 1. Destitute of the sense of seeing, either by natural defect or by deprivation; without sight.

He that is strucken blind can not forget
The precious treasure of his eyesight lost.
Shak.

Not having the faculty of discernment; destitute of intellectual light; unable or unwilling to understand or judge; as, authors are blind to their own defects.

But hard be hardened, blind be blinded more,
That they may stumble on, and deeper fall.
Milton.

Undiscerning; undiscriminating; inconsiderate.

This plan is recommended neither to blind approbation nor to blind reprobation.
Jay.

Having such a state or condition as a thing would have to a person who is blind; not well marked or easily discernible; hidden; unseen; concealed; as, a blind path; a blind ditch.

Involved; intricate; not easily followed or traced.

The blind mazes of this tangled wood.
Milton.

Having no openings for light or passage; as, a blind wall; open only at one end; as, a blind alley; a blind gut.

Unintelligible, or not easily intelligible; as, a blind passage in a book; illegible; as, blind writing.

(Hort.) Abortive; failing to produce flowers or fruit; as, blind buds; blind flowers.

Blind alley, an alley closed at one end; a cul*i*de*i*sac. Ð Blind axle, an axle which turns but does not communicate motion. Knight. Ð Blind beetle, one of the insects apt to fly against people, esp. at night. Ð Blind cat (Zo"l.), a species of catfish (Gronias nigrolabris), nearly destitute of eyes, living in caverns in Pennsylvania. Ð Blind coal, coal that burns without flame; anthracite coal. Simmonds. Ð Blind door, Blind window, an imitation of a door or window, without an opening for passage or light. See Blank door or window, under Blank, a. Ð Blind level (Mining), a level or drainage gallery which has a vertical shaft at each end, and acts as an inverted siphon. Knight. Ð Blind nettle (Bot.), dead nettle. See Dead nettle, under Dead. Ð Blind shell (Gunnery), a shell containing no charge, or one that does not explode. Ð Blind side, the side which is most easily assailed; a weak or unguarded side; the side on which one is least able or disposed to see danger. Swift. Ð Blind snake (Zo"l.), a small, harmless, burrowing snake, of the family Typhlopid', with rudimentary eyes. Ð Blind spot (Anat.), the point in the retina of the eye where the optic nerve enters, and which is insensible to light. Ð Blind tooling, in bookbinding and leather work, the indented impression of heated tools, without gilding; Ð called also blank tooling, and blind blocking. Ð Blind wall, a wall without an opening; a blank wall.

Blind (?), v. t. [imp. & p.p. Blinded; p. pr. & vb. n. Blinding.] 1. To make blind; to deprive of sight or discernment. ½To blind the truth and me.͵
Tennyson.

A blind guide is certainly a great mischief; but a guide that blinds those whom he should lead is ... a much greater.
South.

To deprive partially of vision; to make vision difficult for and painful to; to dazzle.

Her beauty all the rest did blind.
P. Fletcher.

To darken; to obscure to the eye or understanding; to conceal; to deceive.

Such darkness blinds the sky.
Dryden.
The state of the controversy between us he endeavored, with all his art, to blind and confound.
Stillingfleet.

To cover with a thin coating of sand and fine gravel; as a road newly paved, in order that the joints between the stones may be filled.

Blind (?), n. 1. Something to hinder sight or keep out light; a screen; a cover; esp. a hinged screen or shutter for a window; a blinder for a horse.

Something to mislead the eye or the understanding, or to conceal some covert deed or design; a subterfuge.

[Cf. F. blindes, p?., fr. G. blende, fr. blenden to blind, fr. blind blind.] (Mil.) A blindage. See Blindage.

A halting place. [Obs.]

Dryden.
Blind, Blinde (?), n. See Blende.
Blindage (?), n. [Cf. F. blindage.] (Mil.) A cover or protection for an advanced trench or approach, formed of fascines and earth supported by a framework.
Blinder (?), n. 1. One who, or that which, blinds.

(Saddlery) One of the leather screens on a bridle, to hinder a horse from seeing objects at the side; a blinker.

Blindfish· (?), n. A small fish (Amblyopsis spel'us) destitute of eyes, found in the waters of the Mammoth Cave, in Kentucky. Related fishes from other caves take the same name.
Blindfold· (?), v. t. [imp. & p.p. Blindfolded; p. pr. & vb. n. Blindfolding.] [OE. blindfolden, blindfelden, blindfellen; AS. blind blind + prob. fellan, fyllan, to fell, strike down.] To cover the eyes of, as with a bandage; to hinder from seeing.

And when they had blindfolded him, they struck him on the face.
Luke xxii. 64.

Blindfold·, a. Having the eyes covered; blinded; having the mental eye darkened. Hence: Heedless; reckless; as, blindfold zeal; blindfold fury.

Fate's blindfold reign the atheist loudly owns.
Dryden.

Blinding, a. Making blind or as if blind; depriving of sight or of understanding; obscuring; as, blinding tears; blinding snow.

Blinding, n. A thin coating of sand and fine gravel over a newly paved road. See Blind, v. t., 4.

Blindly, adv. Without sight, discernment, or understanding; without thought, investigation, knowledge, or purpose of one's own.

By his imperious mistress blindly led.
Dryden.

Blindman's buff (?). [See Buff a buffet.] A play in which one person is blindfolded, and tries to catch some one of the company and tell who it is.

Surely he fancies I play at blindman's buff with him, for he thinks I never have my eyes open.
Stillingfleet.

Blind · man's holiľday (?). The time between daylight and candle light. [Humorous]

Blindness (?), n. State or condition of being blind, literally or figuratively.
Darwin.

Color blindness, inability to distinguish certain color. See Daltonism.

Blindsto · ry (?), n. (Arch.) The triforium as opposed to the clearstory.

Blindworm · (?), n. (Zo"l.) A small, burrowing, snakelike, limbless lizard (Anguis fragilis), with minute eyes, popularly believed to be blind; the slowworm; Ð formerly a name for the adder.

Newts and blindworms do no wrong.
Shak.

Blink (?), v. i. [imp. & p.p. Blinked (?); p. pr. & vb. n. Blinking.] [OE. blenken; akin to dan. blinke, Sw. blinka, G. blinken to shine, glance, wink, twinkle, D. blinken to shine; and prob. to D. blikken to glance, twinkle, G. blicken to look, glance, AS. blÆcan to shine, E. bleak. ?98. See Bleak; cf. 1st Blench.]

To wink; to twinkle with, or as with, the eye.

One eye was blinking, and one leg was lame.
Pope

To see with the eyes half shut, or indistinctly and with frequent winking, as a person with weak eyes.

Show me thy chink, to blink through with mine eyne.
Shak.

To shine, esp. with intermittent light; to twinkle; to flicker; to glimmer, as a lamp.

The dew was falling fast, the stars began to blink.
Wordsworth.
The sun blinked fair on pool and stream .

Sir W. Scott.

To turn slightly sour, as beer, mild, etc.

Blink, v. t. 1. To shut out of sight; to avoid, or purposely evade; to shirk; as, to blink the question.

To trick; to deceive. [Scot.]

Jamieson.
Blink, n. [OE. blink. See Blink, v. i.] 1. A glimpse or glance.
This is the first blink that ever I had of him.
Bp. Hall.

Gleam; glimmer; sparkle.

Sir W. Scott.
Not a blink of light was there.
Wordsworth.

(Naut.) The dazzling whiteness about the horizon caused by the reflection of light from fields of ice at sea; ice blink.

pl. [Cf. Blencher.] (Sporting) Boughs cast where deer are to pass, to turn or check them. [Prov. Eng.]

Blinkard (?), n. [Blind + Ïard.] 1. One who blinks with, or as with, weak eyes.
Among the blind the oneÏeyed blinkard reigns.
Marvell.

That which twinkles or glances, as a dim star, which appears and disappears.

Hakewill.
Blink beer · (?). Beer kept unbroached until it is sharp.
Crabb.
Blinker (?), n. 1. One who, or that which, blinks.

A blinder for horses; a flap of leather on a horse's bridle to prevent him from seeing objects as his side hence, whatever obstructs sight or discernment.

Nor bigots who but one way see,
through blinkers of authority.
M. Green.

pl. A kind of goggles, used to protect the eyes form glare, etc.

BlinkÐeyed · (?), a. Habitually winking.
Marlowe.

Blirt (?), n. (Naut.) A gust of wind and rain.

Ham. Nav. Encyc.

Bliss , n.; pl. Blisses (?). [OE. blis, blisse, AS. blis, blÆ?s, fr. blÆ?e blithe. See Blithe.] Orig., blithesomeness; gladness; now, the highest degree of happiness; blessedness; exalted felicity; heavenly joy.

An then at last our bliss
Full and perfect is.
Milton.

Syn. Ð Blessedness; felicity; beatitude; happiness; joy; enjoyment. See Happiness.

Blissful (?), a. Full of, characterized by, or causing, joy and felicity; happy in the highest degree. ½Blissful solitude.¸ Milton. Ð Blissfullly, adv. Ð Blissfullness, n.

Blissless, a. Destitute of bliss.

Sir P. Sidney.

Blissom (?), v. i. [For blithesome: but cf. also Icel. bl?sma of a goat at heat.] To be lustful; to be lascivious. [Obs.]

Blissom, a. Lascivious; also, in heat; Ð said of ewes.

Blister (?), n. [OE.; akin to OD. bluyster, fr. the same root as blast, bladder, blow. See Blow to eject wind.] 1. A vesicle of the skin, containing watery matter or serum, whether occasioned by a burn or other injury, or by a vesicatory; a collection of serous fluid causing a bladderlike elevation of the cuticle.

And painful blisters swelled my tender hands.

Grainger.

Any elevation made by the separation of the film or skin, as on plants; or by the swelling of the substance at the surface, as on steel.

A vesicatory; a plaster of Spanish flies, or other matter, applied to raise a blister.

Dunglison.

Blister beetle, a beetle used to raise blisters, esp. the Lytta (or Cantharis) vesicatoria, called Cantharis or Spanish fly by druggists. See Cantharis. Ð Blister fly, a blister beetle. Ð Blister plaster, a plaster designed to raise a blister; Ð usually made of Spanish flies. Ð Blister steel, crude steel formed from wrought iron by cementation; Ð so called because of its blistered surface. Called also blistered steel. Ð Blood blister. See under Blood.

Blister, v. i. [imp. & p.p. Blistered (?); p. pr. & vb. n. Blistering.] To be affected with a blister or blisters; to have a blister form on.

Let my tongue blister.

Shak.

Blister, v. t. 1. To raise a blister or blisters upon.

My hands were blistered.

Franklin.

To give pain to, or to injure, as if by a blister.

This tyrant, whose sole name blisters our tongue.
Shak.
Blisterly (?), a. Full of blisters.
Hooker.
Blite (?), n. [L. blitum, Gr. ?.] (Bot.) A
<— p. 156 —>
genus of herbs (Blitum) with a fleshy calyx. Blitum capitatum is the strawberry blite.
Blithe (?), a. [AS. blǽ?e blithe, kind; akin to Goth. blei?s kind, Icel. blǼ?r mild, gentle, Dan. & Sw. blid gentle, D. blijd blithe, OHG. blǼdi kind, blithe.] Gay; merry; sprightly; joyous; glad; cheerful; as, a blithe spirit.
The blithe sounds of festal music.
Prescott.
A daughter fair,
So buxom, blithe, and debonair.
Milton.
Blitheful (?), a. Gay; full of gayety; joyous.
Blithely, adv. In a blithe manner.
Blitheness, n. The state of being blithe.
Chaucer.
Blithesome (?), a. Cheery; gay; merry.
The blithesome sounds of wassail gay.
Sir W. Scott.
Ð Blithesomely, adv. Ð Blithesomeness, n.
Blive (?), adv. [A contraction of Belive.] Quickly; forthwith. [Obs.]
Chaucer.
Blizzard (?), n. [Cf. Blaze to flash. Formerly, in local use, a rattling volley; cf. ½to blaze away„ to fire away.] A gale of piercingly cold wind, usually accompanied with fine and blinding snow; a furious blast. [U. S.]
Bloat (?), v. t. [imp. & p.p. Bloated; p. pr. & vb. n. Bloating.] [Cf. Icel. blotna to become soft, blautr soft, wet, Sw. bl"t soft, bl"ta to soak; akin to G. bloss bare, and AS. ble t wretched; or perh. fr. root of Eng. 5th blow. Cf. Blote.] 1. To make turgid, as with water or air; to cause a swelling of the surface of, from effusion of serum in the cellular tissue, producing a morbid enlargement, often accompanied with softness.

To inflate; to puff up; to make vain.

Dryden.
Bloat, v. i. To grow turgid as by effusion of liquid in the cellular tissue; to puff out; to swell.
Arbuthnot.

Bloat, a. Bloated. [R.]
Shak.

Bloat, n. A term of contempt for a worthless, dissipated fellow. [Slang]

Bloat, v. t. To dry (herrings) in smoke. See Blote.

Bloated (?), p. a. Distended beyond the natural or usual size, as by the presence of water, serum, etc.; turgid; swollen; as, a bloated face. Also, puffed up with pride; pompous.

BloatedÏness, n. The state of being bloated.

Bloater (?), n. [See Bloat, Blote.] The common herring, esp. when of large size, smoked, and half dried; Ð called also bloat herring.

Blob (?), n. [See Bleb.] 1. Something blunt and round; a small drop or lump of something viscid or thick; a drop; a bubble; a blister.

Wright.

(Zo"l.) A small freshÏwater fish (Uranidea Richardsoni); the miller's thumb.

Blobber (?), n. [See Blubber, Blub.] A bubble; blubber. [Low]
T. Carew.

Blobber lip, a thick, protruding lip.

His blobber lips and beetle brows commend.

Dryden.

BlobberÐlipped · (?), a. Having thick lips. ½A blobberÐlipped shell.„
Grew.

ØBloÏcage (?), n. [F.] (Arch.) The roughest and cheapest sort of rubblework, in masonry.

Block (?), n. [OE. blok; cf. F. bloc (fr. OHG.), D. & Dan. blok, Sw. & G. block, OHG. bloch. There is also an OHG. bloch, biloh; bi by + the same root as that of E. lock. Cf. Block, v. t., Blockade, and see Lock.]

A piece of wood more or less bulky; a solid mass of wood, stone, etc., usually with one or more plane, or approximately plane, faces; as, a block on which a butcher chops his meat; a block by which to mount a horse; children's playing blocks, etc.

Now all our neighbors' chimneys smoke,
And Christmas blocks are burning.
Wither.

All her labor was but as a block
Left in the quarry.
Tennyson.

The solid piece of wood on which condemned persons lay their necks when they are beheaded.

Noble heads which have been brought to the block.
E. Everett.

The wooden mold on which hats, bonnets, etc., are shaped. Hence: The pattern on shape of a hat.

He wears his faith but as the fashion of his hat; it ever changes with the next block.
Shak.

A large or long building divided into separate houses or shops, or a number of houses or shops built in contact with each other so as to form one building; a row of houses or shops.

A square, or portion of a city inclosed by streets, whether occupied by buildings or not.

The new city was laid out in rectangular blocks, each block containing thirty building lots. Such an average block, comprising 282 houses and covering nine acres of ground, exists in Oxford Street.
Lond. Quart. Rev.

A grooved pulley or sheave incased in a frame or shell which is provided with a hook, eye, or strap, by which it may be attached to an object. It is used to change the direction of motion, as in raising a heavy object that can not be conveniently reached, and also, when two or more such sheaves are compounded, to change the rate of motion, or to exert increased force; Ð used especially in the rigging of ships, and in tackles.

(Falconry) The perch on which a bird of prey is kept.

Any obstruction, or cause of obstruction; a stop; a hindrance; an obstacle; as, a block in the way.

A piece of box or other wood for engravers' work.

(Print.) A piece of hard wood (as mahogany or cherry) on which a stereotype or electrotype plate is mounted to make it type high.

A blockhead; a stupid fellow; a dolt. [Obs.]

What a block art thou !
Shak.

A section of a railroad where the block system is used. See Block system, below.

A block of shares (Stock Exchange), a large number of shares in a stock company, sold in a lump. Bartlett. Ð Block printing. (a) A mode of printing (common in China and Japan) from engraved boards by means of a sheet of paper laid on the linked surface and rubbed with a brush. S. W. Williams. (b) A method of printing cotton cloth and paper hangings with colors, by pressing them upon an engraved surface coated with coloring matter. Ð Block system on railways, a system by which the track is divided into sections of three or four miles, and trains are so run by the guidance of electric signals that no train enters a section or block before the preceding train has left it.

Block (?), v. t. [imp. & p.p. Blocked (?); p. pr. & vb. n. Blocking.] [Cf. F. bloquer, fr. bloc block. See Block, n.] 1. To obstruct so as to prevent passage or progress; to prevent passage from, through, or into, by obstructing the way; Ð used both of persons and things; Ð often followed by up; as, to block up a road or harbor.

With moles ... would block the port.
Rowe.
A city ... besieged and blocked about.
Milton.

To secure or support by means of blocks; to secure, as two boards at their angles of intersection, by pieces of wood glued to each.

To shape on, or stamp with, a block; as, to block a hat.

To block out, to begin to reduce to shape; to mark out roughly; to lay out; as, to block out a plan.

Blockĭade (?), n. [Cf. It. bloccata. See Block, v. t.] 1. The shutting up of a place by troops or ships, with the purpose of preventing ingress or egress, or the reception of supplies; as, the blockade of the ports of an enemy.

μ Blockade is now usually applied to an investment with ships or vessels, while siege is used of an investment by land forces. To constitute a blockade, the investing power must be able to apply its force to every point of practicable access, so as to render it dangerous to attempt to enter; and there is no blockade of that port where its force can not be brought to bear.
Kent.

An obstruction to passage.

To raise a blockade. See under Raise.

Blockĭade, v. t. [imp. & p.p. Blockaded; p. pr. & vb. n. Blockading.] 1. To shut up, as a town or fortress, by investing it with troops or vessels or war for the purpose of preventing ingress or egress, or the introduction of supplies. See note under Blockade, n. ½Blockaded the place by sea.„
Gilpin.

Hence, to shut in so as to prevent egress.

Till storm and driving ice blockade him there.
Wordsworth.

To obstruct entrance to or egress from.

Huge bales of British cloth blockade the door.
Pope.

Blockĭader (?), n. 1. One who blockades.

(Naut.) A vessel employed in blockading.

Blockage (?), n. The act of blocking up; the state of being blocked up.

Block book · (?). A book printed from engraved wooden blocks instead of movable types.

Blockhead · (?), n. [Block + head.] A stupid fellow; a dolt; a person deficient in understanding.

The bookful blockhead, ignorantly read,
With loads of learned lumber in his head.
Pope.

Blockhead · ed, a. Stupid; dull.

Blockheadĭism (?), n. That which characterizes a blockhead; stupidity. Carlyle.

Blockhouse · (?), n. [Block + house: cf. G. blockhaus.] 1. (Mil.) An edifice or structure of heavy timbers or logs for military defense, having its sides loopholed for musketry, and often an upper story projecting over the lower, or so placed upon it as to have its sides make an angle wit the sides of the lower story, thus enabling the defenders to fire downward, and in all directions; Đ formerly much used in America and Germany.

A house of squared logs. [West. & South. U. S.]

Blocking, n. 1. The act of obstructing, supporting, shaping, or stamping with a block or blocks.

Blocks used to support (a building, etc.) temporarily.

Blocking course · (?). (Arch.) The finishing course of a wall showing above a cornice.

Blockish, a. Like a block; deficient in understanding; stupid; dull. ½Blockish Ajax., Shak. Đ Blockishĭly, adv. Đ Blockishĭness, n.

Blocklike · (?), a. Like a block; stupid.

Block tin · (?). See under Tin.

Bloedite (?), n. [From the chemist Bl"de.] (Min.) A hydrous sulphate of magnesium and sodium.

Blomaĭry (?), n. See Bloomery.

Bloncket, Blonket (?), a. [OF. blanquet whitish, dim. of blanc white. Cf. Blanket.] Gray; bluish gray. [Obs.]

Our bloncket liveries been all too sad.
Spenser.

Blond, Blonde (?), a. [F., fair, light, of uncertain origin; cf. AS. blondenĭfeax grayĭhaired, old, prop. blendedĭhaired, as a mixture of white and brown or black. See Blend, v. t.] Of a fair color; lightĭcolored; as, blond hair; a blond complexion.

Blonde (?), n. [F.] 1. A person of very fair complexion, with light hair and light blue eyes. [Written also blond.]

[So called from its color.] A kind of silk lace originally of the color of raw silk, now sometimes dyed; Đ called also blond lace.

Blond met · al (?). A variety of clay ironstone, in Staffordshire, England, used for making tools.

Blondness, n. The state of being blond.

G. Eliot.

Blood (?), n. [OE. blod, blood, AS. bl?d; akin to D. bloed, OHG. bluot, G. blut, Goth, bl??, Sw. & Dan. blod; prob. fr. the same root as E. blow to bloom. See Blow to bloom.] 1. The fluid which circulates in the principal vascular system of animals, carrying nourishment to all parts of the body, and bringing away waste products to be excreted. See under Arterial.

µ The blood consists of a liquid, the plasma, containing minute particles, the blood corpuscles. In the invertebrate animals it is usually nearly colorless, and contains only one kind of corpuscles; but in all vertebrates, except Amphioxus, it contains some colorless corpuscles, with many more which are red and give the blood its uniformly red color. See Corpuscle, Plasma.

Relationship by descent from a common ancestor; consanguinity; kinship.

To share the blood of Saxon royalty.
Sir W. Scott.
A friend of our own blood.
Waller.

Half blood (Law), relationship through only one parent. Ð Whole blood, relationship through both father and mother. In American Law, blood includes both half blood, and whole blood.

Bouvier. Peters.

Descent; lineage; especially, honorable birth; the highest royal lineage.

Give us a prince of blood, a son of Priam.
Shak.
I am a gentleman of blood and breeding.
Shak.

(Stock Breeding) Descent from parents of recognized breed; excellence or purity of breed.

µ In stock breeding half blood is descent showing one half only of pure breed. Blue blood, full blood, or warm blood, is the same as blood.

The fleshy nature of man.

Nor gives it satisfaction to our blood.
Shak.

The shedding of blood; the taking of life, murder; manslaughter; destruction.

So wills the fierce, avenging sprite,
Till blood for blood atones.
Hood.

A bloodthirsty or murderous disposition. [R.]

He was a thing of blood, whose every motion
Was timed with dying cries.
Shak.

Temper of mind; disposition; state of the passions; Ð as if the blood were the seat of emotions.

When you perceive his blood inclined to mirth.
Shak.

µ Often, in this sense, accompanied with bad, cold, warm, or other qualifying word. Thus, to commit an act in cold blood, is to do it deliberately, and without sudden passion; to do it in bad blood, is to do it in anger. Warm blood denotes a temper inflamed or irritated. To warm or heat the blood is to excite the passions. Qualified by up, excited feeling or passion is signified; as, my blood was up.

A man of fire or spirit; a fiery spark; a gay, showy man; a rake.

Seest thou not ... how giddily 'a turns about all the hot bloods between fourteen and five and thirty?
Shak.
It was the morning costume of a dandy or blood.
Thackeray.

The juice of anything, especially if red.

He washed ... his clothes in the blood of grapes.
Gen. xiix. 11.

µ Blood is often used as an adjective, and as the first part of selfïexplaining compound words; as, bloodïbespotted, bloodïbought, bloodïcurdling, bloodïdyed, bloodïred, bloodïspilling, bloodïstained, bloodïwarm, bloodïwon.

Blood baptism (Eccl. Hist.), the martyrdom of those who had not been baptized. They were considered as baptized in blood, and this was regarded as a full substitute for literal baptism. Ð Blood blister, a blister or bleb containing blood or bloody serum, usually caused by an injury. Ð Blood brother, brother by blood or birth. Ð Blood clam (Zo"l.), a bivalve mollusk of the genus Arca and allied genera, esp. Argina pexata of the American coast. So named from the color of its flesh. Ð Blood corpuscle. See Corpuscle. Ð Blood crystal (Physiol.), one of the crystals formed by the separation in a crystalline form of the h'moglobin of the red blood corpuscles; h'matocrystallin. All blood does not yield blood crystals. Ð Blood heat, heat equal to the temperature of human blood, or about 98« ? F hr. Ð Blood horse, a horse whose blood or lineage is derived from the purest and most highly prized origin or stock. Ð Blood money. See in the Vocabulary. Ð

Blood orange, an orange with dark red pulp. Ð Blood poisoning (Med.), a morbid state of the blood caused by the introduction of poisonous or infective matters from without, or the absorption or retention of such as are produced in the body itself; tox'mia. Ð Blood pudding, a pudding made of blood and other materials. Ð Blood relation, one connected by blood or descent. Ð Blood spavin. See under Spavin. Ð Blood vessel. See in the Vocabulary. Ð Blue blood, the blood of noble or aristocratic families, which, according to a Spanish prover , has in it a tinge of blue; Ð hence, a member of an old and aristocratic family. Ð Flesh and blood. (a) A blood relation, esp. a child. (b) Human nature. Ð In blood (Hunting), in a state of perfect health and vigor. Shak. Ð To let blood. See under Let. Ð Prince of the blood, the son of a sovereign, or the issue of a royal family. The sons, brothers, and uncles of the sovereign are styled princes of the blood royal; and the daughters, sisters, and aunts are princesses of the blood royal.

Blood (?), v. t. [imp. & p.p. Blooded; p. pr. & vb. n. Blooding.] 1. To bleed. [Obs.]

Cowper.

<— p. 157 —>

To stain, smear or wet, with blood. [Archaic]

Reach out their spears afar,
And blood their points.
Dryden.

To give (hounds or soldiers) a first taste or sight of blood, as in hunting or war.

It was most important too that his troops should be blooded.
Macaulay.

To heat the blood of; to exasperate. [Obs.]

The auxiliary forces of the French and English were much blooded one against another.

Bacon.

Bloodbird · (?), n. (Zo"l.) An Australian honeysucker (Myzomela sanguineolata); Ð so called from the bright red color of the male bird.

BloodÐbol · tered (?), a. [Blood + Prov. E. bolter to mat in tufts. Cf. Balter.] Having the hair matted with clotted blood. [Obs. & R.]

The bloodÐboltered Banquo smiles upon me.
Shak.

Blooded, a. Having pure blood, or a large admixture or pure blood; of approved breed; of the best stock.

μ Used also in composition in phrases indicating a particular condition or quality of blood; as, coldÐblooded; warmÐblooded.

Bloodflow·er (?), n. [From the color of the flower.] (Bot.) A genus of bulbous plants, natives of Southern Africa, named H'manthus, of the Amaryllis family. The juice of H. toxicarius is used by the Hottentots to poison their arrows.

Bloodguilt·y (?), a. Guilty of murder or bloodshed. ½A bloodguilty life., Fairfax. Ð Bloodguilt·iǐness (?), n. Ð Bloodguilt·less, a.

Bloodhound· (?), n. A breed of large and powerful dogs, with long, smooth, and pendulous ears, and remarkable for acuteness of smell. It is employed to recover game or prey which has escaped wounded from a hunter, and for tracking criminals. Formerly it was used for pursuing runaway slaves. Other varieties of dog are often used for the same purpose and go by the same name. The Cuban bloodhound is said to be a variety of the mastiff.

Bloodiǐly (?), adv. In a bloody manner; cruelly; with a disposition to shed blood.

Bloodiǐness, n. 1. The state of being bloody.

Disposition to shed blood; bloodthirstiness.

All that bloodiness and savage cruelty which was in our nature.
Holland.

Bloodless, a. [AS. bl?dle s.] 1. Destitute of blood, or apparently so; as, bloodless cheeks; lifeless; dead.

The bloodless carcass of my Hector sold.
Dryden.

Not attended with shedding of blood, or slaughter; as, a bloodless victory.

Froude.

Without spirit or activity.

Thou bloodless remnant of that royal blood !
Shak.

Ð Bloodlessǐly, adv. Ð Bloodlessǐness, n.

Bloodlet· (?), v. t. [AS. bl?dl?tan; bl?d blood + l?atan to let.] To bleed; to let blood.

Arbuthnot.

Bloodlet·ter (?), n. One who, or that which, lets blood; a phlebotomist.

Bloodlet·ting, n. (Med.) The act or process of letting blood or bleeding, as by opening a vein or artery, or by cupping or leeches; Ð esp. applied to venesection.

Blood mon·ey (?). 1. Money paid to the next of kin of a person who has been killed by another.

Money obtained as the price, or at the cost, of another's life; Ð said of a reward for supporting a capital charge, of money obtained for betraying a fugitive or for committing murder, or of money obtained from the sale of that which will destroy the purchaser.

Bloodroot · (?), n. (Bot.) A plant (Sanguinaria Canadensis), with a red root and red sap, and bearing a pretty, white flower in early spring; Ð called also puccoon, redroot, bloodwort, tetterwort, turmeric, and Indian paint. It has acrid emetic properties, and the rootstock is used as a stimulant expectorant. See Sanguinaria.

μ In England the name is given to the tormentil, once used as a remedy for dysentery.

Bloodshed · (?), n. [Blood + shed] The shedding or spilling of blood; slaughter; the act of shedding human blood, or taking life, as in war, riot, or murder.

Bloodshed · der (?), n. One who sheds blood; a manslayer; a murderer.

Bloodshed · ding (?), n. Bloodshed.

Shak.

Bloodshot · (?), a. [Blood + shot, p. p. of shoot to variegate.] Red and inflamed; suffused with blood, or having the vessels turgid with blood, as when the conjunctiva is inflamed or irritated.

His eyes were bloodshot, ... and his hair disheveled.

Dickens.

BloodÐshot · ten (?), a. Bloodshot. [Obs.]

Bloodstick (?), n. (Far.) A piece of hard wood loaded at one end with lead, and used to strike the fleam into the vein.

Youatt.

Bloodstone · (?), n. (Min.) (a) A green siliceous stone sprinkled with red jasper, as if with blood; hence the name; Ð called also heliotrope. (b) Hematite, an ore of iron yielding a blood red powder or ½streak.

Bloodstroke (?), n. [Cf. F. coup de sang.] Loss of sensation and motion from hemorrhage or congestion in the brain.

Dunglison.

Bloodsuck · er (?), n. 1. (Zo"l.) Any animal that sucks blood; esp., the leech (Hirudo medicinalis), and related species.

<small>One who sheds blood; a cruel, bloodthirsty man; one guilty of bloodshed; a murderer. [Obs.]</small>

Shak.

<small>A hard and exacting master, landlord, or money lender; an extortioner.</small>

Bloodthirst · y (?), a. Eager to shed blood; cruel; sanguinary; murderous. Ð Bloodthirst · iÏness (?), n.

Bloodulf (?), n. (Zo"l.) The European bullfinch.

Blood ves · sel (?). (Anat.) Any vessel or canal in which blood circulates in an animal, as an artery or vein.

Bloodwite · (?), Bloodwit · (?), } n. [AS. bl?wÆte; bl?d blood, + wÆte wite, fine.] (Anc. Law) A fine or amercement paid as a composition for the shedding of blood; also, a riot wherein blood was spilled.

Bloodwood (?), n. (Bot.) A tree having the wood or the sap of the color of blood.

Norfolk Island bloodwood is a euphorbiaceous tree (Baloghia lucida), from which the sap is collected for use as a plant. Various other trees have the name, chiefly on account of the color of the wood, as Gordonia H'matoxylon of Jamaica, and several species of Australian Eucalyptus; also the true logwood (H'matoxylon Campechianum).

Bloodwort (?), n. (Bot.) A plant, Rumex sanguineus, or bloodyĪveined dock. The name is applied also to bloodroot (Sanguinaria Canadensis), and to an extensive order of plants (H'modorace'), the roots of many species of which contain a red coloring matter useful in dyeing.

Bloody (?), a. [AS. bl?dig.] 1. Containing or resembling blood; of the nature of blood; as, bloody excretions; bloody sweat.

Smeared or stained with blood; as, bloody hands; a bloody handkerchief.

Given, or tending, to the shedding of blood; having a cruel, savage disposition; murderous; cruel.

Some bloody passion shakes your very frame.
Shak.

Attended with, or involving, bloodshed; sanguinary; esp., marked by great slaughter or cruelty; as, a bloody battle.

Infamous; contemptible; Ð variously used for mere emphasis or as a low epithet. [Vulgar]

Thackeray.

Bloody, v. t. [imp. & p.p. Bloodied (?); p. pr. & vb. n. Bloodying.] To stain with blood.

Overbury.

BloodyĪbones (?), n. A terrible bugbear.

Bloody flux (?). The dysentery, a disease in which the flux or discharge from the bowels has a mixture of blood.

Arbuthnot.

Bloody hand (?). 1. A hand stained with the blood of a deer, which, in the old forest laws of England, was sufficient evidence of a man's trespass in the forest against venison.

Jacob.

(Her.) A red hand, as in the arms of Ulster, which is now the distinguishing mark of a baronet of the United Kingdom.

BloodyÐminded (?), a. Having a cruel, ferocious disposition; bloodthirsty.
Dryden.

Bloody sweat (?). A sweat accompanied by a discharge of blood; a disease, called sweating sickness, formerly prevalent in England and other countries.

Bloom (?), n. [OE. blome, fr. Icel. bl?m, bl?mi; akin to Sw. blom, Goth. bl?ma, OS. bl?mo, D. bloem, OHG. bluomo, bluoma, G. blume; fr. the same root as AS. bl?wan to blow, blossom. See Blow to bloom, and cf. Blossom.] 1. A blossom; the flower of a plant; an expanded bud; flowers, collectively.

The rich blooms of the tropics.

Prescott.

The opening of flowers in general; the state of blossoming or of having the flowers open; as, the cherry trees are in bloom. ½Sight of vernal bloom.

Milton.

A state or time of beauty, freshness, and vigor; an opening to higher perfection, analogous to that of buds into blossoms; as, the bloom of youth.

Every successive mother has transmitted a fainter bloom, a more delicate and briefer beauty.

Hawthorne.

The delicate, powdery coating upon certain growing or newlyÏgathered fruits or leaves, as on grapes, plums, etc. Hence: Anything giving an appearance of attractive freshness; a flush; a glow.

A new, fresh, brilliant world, with all the bloom upon it.

Thackeray.

The clouded appearance which varnish sometimes takes upon the surface of a picture.

A yellowish deposit or powdery coating which appears on wellÐtanned leather.

Knight.

(Min.) A popular term for a brightÐhued variety of some minerals; as, the roseÐred cobalt bloom.

Bloom, v. i. [imp. & p.p. Bloomed (?); p. pr. & vb. n. Blooming.] 1. To produce or yield blossoms; to blossom; to flower or be in flower.

A flower which once
In Paradise, fast by the tree of life,
Began to bloom.

Milton.

To be in a state of healthful, growing youth and vigor; to show beauty and freshness, as of flowers; to give promise, as by or with flowers.

A better country blooms to view,
Beneath a brighter sky.

Logan.

Bloom, v. t. 1. To cause to blossom; to make flourish. [R.]

Charitable affection bloomed them.

Hooker.

To bestow a bloom upon; to make blooming or radiant. [R.]

Milton.
While barred clouds bloom the softÐdying day.
Keats.
Bloom, n. [AS. bl?ma a mass or lump, Æsenes bl?ma a lump or wedge of iron.] (Metal.) (a) A mass of wrought iron from the Catalan forge or from the puddling furnace, deprived of its dross, and shaped usually in the form of an oblong block by shingling. (b) A large bar of steel formed directly from an ingot by hammering or rolling, being a preliminary shape for further working.

Bloomaĭry (?), n. See Bloomery.

Bloomer (?), n. [From Mrs. Bloomer, an American, who sought to introduce this style of dress.] 1. A costume for women, consisting of a short dress, with loose trousers gathered round ankles, and (commonly) a broadÐbrimmed hat.

A woman who wears a Bloomer costume.

Bloomerĭy (?), n. (Manuf.) A furnace and forge in which wrought iron in the form of blooms is made directly from the ore, or (more rarely) from cast iron.

Blooming, n. (Metal.) The process of making blooms from the ore or from cast iron.

Blooming, a. 1. Opening in blossoms; flowering.

Thriving in health, beauty, and vigor; indicating the freshness and beauties of youth or health.

Bloomingĭly, adv. In a blooming manner.
Bloomingĭness, n. A blooming condition.
Bloomless, a. Without bloom or flowers.
Shelley.
Bloomy (?), a. 1. Full of bloom; flowery; flourishing with the vigor of youth; as, a bloomy spray.

But all the bloomy flush of life is fled.
Goldsmith.

Covered with bloom, as fruit.

Dryden.
Blooth (?), n. Bloom; a blossoming. [Prov. Eng.]
All that blooth means heavy autumn work for him and his hands.
T. Hardy.
Blore (?), n. [Perh. a variant of blare, v. i.; or cf. Gael. & Ir. blor a loud noise.] The act of blowing; a roaring wind; a blast. [Obs.]

A most tempestuous blore.

Chapman.

Blosmy (?), a. Blossomy. [Obs.]

Chaucer.

Blossom (?), n. [OE. blosme, blostme, AS. bl?sma, bl?stma, blossom; akin to D. bloesem, L. fios, and E. flower; from the root of E. blow to blossom. See Blow to blossom, and cf. Bloom a blossom.] 1. The flower of a plant, or the essential organs of reproduction, with their appendages; florescence; bloom; the flowers of a plant, collectively; as, the blossoms and fruit of a tree; an apple tree in blossom.

μ The term has been applied by some botanists, and is also applied in common usage, to the corolla. It is more commonly used than flower or bloom, when we have reference to the fruit which is to succeed. Thus we use flowers when we speak of plants cultivated for ornament, and bloom in a more general sense, as of flowers in general, or in reference to the beauty of flowers.

Blossoms flaunting in the eye of day.

Longfellow.

A blooming period or stage of development; something lovely that gives rich promise.

In the blossom of my youth.

Massinger.

The color of a horse that has white hairs intermixed with sorrel and bay hairs; Ð otherwise called peach color.

In blossom, having the blossoms open; in bloom.

Blossom, v. i. [imp. & p.p. Blossomed (?); p. pr. & vb. n. Blossoming.] [AS. bl?stmian. See Blossom, n.] 1. To put forth blossoms or flowers; to bloom; to blow; to flower.

The moving whisper of huge trees that branched
And blossomed.

Tennyson.

To flourish and prosper.

Israel shall blossom and bud, and full the face of the world with fruit.

Isa. xxvii. 6.

Blossomĭless, a. Without blossoms.

Blossomĭy (?), a. Full of blossoms; flowery.

Blot (?), v. t. [imp. & p.p. Blotted (?); p. pr. & vb. n. Blotting.] [Cf. Dan. plette. See 3d Blot.]

To spot, stain, or bespatter, as with ink.

The brief was writ and blotted all with gore.

Gascoigne.

To impair; to damage; to mar; to soil.

> It blots thy beauty, as frosts do bite the meads.
> Shak.

To stain with infamy; to disgrace.

> Blot not thy innocence with guiltless blood.
> Rowe.

To obliterate, as writing with ink; to cancel; to efface; Ð generally with out; as, to blot out a word or a sentence. Often figuratively; as, to blot out offenses.

> One act like this blots out a thousand crimes.
> Dryden.

To obscure; to eclipse; to shadow.

> He sung how earth blots the moon's gilded wane.
> Cowley.

To dry, as writing, with blotting paper.

Syn. Ð To obliterate; expunge; erase; efface; cancel; tarnish; disgrace; blur; sully; smear; smutch.

Blot, v. i. To take a blot; as, this paper blots easily.

Blot, n. [Cf. Icel. blettr, Dan. plet.] 1. A spot or stain, as of ink on paper; a blur. ½Inky blots and rotten parchment bonds.¸

Shak.

An obliteration of something written or printed; an erasure.

Dryden.

A spot on reputation; a stain; a disgrace; a reproach; a blemish.

> This deadly blot in thy digressing son.
> Shak.

Blot, n. [Cf. Dan. blot bare, naked, Sw. blott, d. bloot, G. bloss, and perh. E. bloat.] 1. (Backgammon) (a) An exposure of a single man to be taken up. (b) A single man left on a point, exposed to be taken up.

> He is too great a master of his art to make a blot which may be so easily hit.
> Dryden.

A weak point; a failing; an exposed point or mark.

Blotch (?), n. [Cf. OE. blacche in blacchepot blacking pot, akin to black, as bleach is akin to bleak. See Black, a., or cf. Blot a spot.] 1. A blot or spot, as of color or of ink; especially a large or irregular spot. Also Fig.; as, a moral blotch.

Spots and blotches ... some red, others yellow.
Harvey.

(Med.) A large pustule, or a coarse eruption.

Foul scurf and blotches him defile.
Thomson.

Blotched (?), a. Marked or covered with blotches.
To give their blotched and blistered bodies ease.
Drayton.

Blotchy (?), a. Having blotches.

Blote (?), v. t. [imp. & p.p. Bloted; p. pr. & vb. n. Bloting.] [Cf. Sw. bl"tÐfisk soaked fish, fr. bl"ta to soak. See 1st Bloat.] To cure, as herrings, by salting and smoking them; to bloat. [Obs.]

Blotless (?), a. Without blot.

Blotter (?), n. 1. One who, or that which blots; esp. a device for absorbing superfluous ink.

<— p. 158 —>

(Com.) A wastebook, in which entries of transactions are made as they take place.

Blotïtesque (?), a. (Painting) Characterized by blots or heavy touches; coarsely depicted; wanting in delineation.
Ruskin.

Blotting pa · per (?). A kind of thick, bibulous, unsized paper, used to absorb superfluous ink from freshly written manuscript, and thus prevent blots.

Blouse (?), n. [F. blouse. Of unknown origin.] A light, loose overïgarment, like a smock frock, worn especially by workingmen in France; also, a loose coat of any material, as the undress uniform coat of the United States army.

Blow (?), v. i. [imp. Blew (?); p. p. Blown (?); p. pr. & vb. n. Blowing.] [OE. blowen, AS. bl?wan to blossom; akin to OS. bl?jan, D. bloeijen, OHG. pluojan, MHG. bl?ejen, G. blhen, L. florere to flourish, OIr. blath blossom. Cf. Blow to puff, Flourish.] To flower; to blossom; to bloom.

How blows the citron grove.
Milton.

Blow, v. t. To cause to blossom; to put forth (blossoms or flowers).

The odorous banks, that blow
Flowers of more mingled hue.
Milton.

Blow, n. (Bot.) A blossom; a flower; also, a state of blossoming; a mass of blossoms. ½Such a blow of tulips.‚
Tatler.

Blow, n. [OE. blaw, blowe; cf. OHG. bliuwan, pliuwan, to beat, G. bl„uen, Goth. bliggwan.] 1. A forcible stroke with the hand, fist, or some instrument, as a rod, a club, an ax, or a sword.

Well struck ! there was blow for blow.
Shak.

A sudden or forcible act or effort; an assault.

A vigorous blow might win [Hanno's camp].
T. Arnold.

The infliction of evil; a sudden calamity; something which produces mental, physical, or financial suffering or loss (esp. when sudden); a buffet.

A most poor man, made tame to fortune's blows.
Shak.

At a blow, suddenly; at one effort; by a single vigorous act. ½They lose a province at a blow.‚ Dryden. Ð To come to blows, to engage in combat; to fight; Ð said of individuals, armies, and nations.

Syn. Ð Stroke; knock; shock; misfortune.

Blow, v. i. [imp. Blew (?); p. p. Blown (?); p. pr. & vb. n. Blowing.] [OE. blawen, blowen, AS. bl?wan to blow, as wind; akin to OHG. pl?jan, G. bl„hen, to blow up, swell, L. flare to blow, Gr. ? to spout out, and to E. bladder, blast, inflate, etc., and perh. blow to bloom.] 1. To produce a current of air; to move, as air, esp. to move rapidly or with power; as, the wind blows.

Hark how it rains and blows !
Walton.

To send forth a forcible current of air, as from the mouth or from a pair of bellows.

To breathe hard or quick; to pant; to puff.

Here is Mistress Page at the door, sweating and blowing.
Shak.

To sound on being blown into, as a trumpet.

There let the pealing organ blow.
Milton.

To spout water, etc., from the blowholes, as a whale.

To be carried or moved by the wind; as, the dust blows in from the street.

The grass blows from their graves to thy own.
M. Arnold.

389

To talk loudly; to boast; to storm. [Colloq.]

You blow behind my back, but dare not say anything to my face.
Bartlett.

To blow hot and cold (a saying derived from a fable of ?sop's), to favor a thing at one time and treat it coldly at another; or to appear both to favor and to oppose. Ð To blow off, to let steam escape through a passage provided for the purpose; as, the engine or steamer is blowing off. Ð To blow out. (a) To be driven out by the expansive force of a gas or vapor; as, a steam cock or valve sometimes blows out. (b) To talk violently or abusively. [Low] Ð To blow over, to pass away without effect; to cease, or be dissipated; as, the storm and the clouds have blown over. Ð To blow up, to be torn to pieces and thrown into the air as by an explosion of powder or gas or the expansive force of steam; to burst; to explode; as, a powder mill or steam boiler blows up. ½The enemy's magazines blew up.‚

Tatler.

Blow, v. t. 1. To force a current of air upon with the mouth, or by other means; as, to blow the fire.

To drive by a current air; to impel; as, the tempest blew the ship ashore.

Off at sea northeast winds blow
Sabean odors from the spicy shore.
Milton.

To cause air to pass through by the action of the mouth, or otherwise; to cause to sound, as a wind instrument; as, to blow a trumpet; to blow an organ.

Hath she no husband
That will take pains to blow a horn before her?
Shak.

Boy, blow the pipe until the bubble rise,
Then cast it off to float upon the skies.
Parnell.

To clear of contents by forcing air through; as, to blow an egg; to blow one's nose.

To burst, shatter, or destroy by an explosion; Ð usually with up, down, open, or similar adverb; as, to blow up a building.

To spread by report; to publish; to disclose.

Through the court his courtesy was blown.
Dryden.

His language does his knowledge blow.
Whiting.

To form by inflation; to swell by injecting air; as, to blow bubbles; to blow glass.

To inflate, as with pride; to puff up.

Look how imagination blows him.
Shak.

To put out of breath; to cause to blow from fatigue; as, to blow a horse.

Sir W. Scott.

To deposit eggs or larv‘ upon, or in (meat, etc.).

To suffer
The flesh fly blow my mouth.
Shak.

To blow great guns, to blow furiously and with roaring blasts; Ð said of the wind at sea or along the coast. Ð To blow off, to empty (a boiler) of water through the blowĬoff pipe, while under steam pressure; also, to eject (steam, water, sediment, etc.) from a boiler. Ð To blow one's own trumpet, to vaunt one's own exploits, or sound one's own praises. Ð To blow out, to extinguish by a current of air, as a candle. Ð To blow up. (a) To fill with air; to swell; as, to blow up a bladder or bubble. (b) To inflate, as with pride, selfĬconceit, etc.; to puff up; as, to blow one up with flattery. ½Blown up with high conceits engendering pride.¸ Milton. (c) To excite; as, to blow up a contention.(d) To burst, to raise into the air, or to scatter, by an explosion; as, to blow up a fort. (e) To scold violently; as, to blow up a person for some offense. [Colloq.]

I have blown him up well Ð nobody can say I wink at what he does.
G. Eliot.

Ð To blow upon. (a) To blast; to taint; to bring into discredit; to render stale, unsavory, or worthless. (b) To inform against. [Colloq.]

How far the very custom of hearing anything spouted withers and blows upon a fine passage, may be seen in those speeches from [Shakespeare's] Henry V. which are current in the mouths of schoolboys.
C. Lamb.

A lady's maid whose character had been blown upon.
Macaulay.

Blow (?), n. 1. A blowing, esp., a violent blowing of the wind; a gale; as, a heavy blow came on, and the ship put back to port.

The act of forcing air from the mouth, or through or from some instrument; as, to give a hard blow on a whistle or horn; to give the fire a blow with the bellows.

The spouting of a whale.

(Metal.) A single heat or operation of the Bessemer converter.

Raymond.

An egg, or a larva, deposited by a fly on or in flesh, or the act of depositing it.

Chapman.

Blowball· (?), n. The downy seed head of a dandelion, which children delight to blow away.

B. Jonson.

Blowen (?), Blowess (?), } n. A prostitute; a courtesan; a strumpet. [Low]

Smart.

Blower (?), n. 1. One who, or that which, blows.

(Mech.) A device for producing a current of air; as: (a) A metal plate temporarily placed before the upper part of a grate or open fire. (b) A machine for producing an artificial blast or current of air by pressure, as for increasing the draft of a furnace, ventilating a building or shaft, cleansing gram, etc.

A blowing out or excessive discharge of gas from a hole or fissure in a mine.

The whale; Ð so called by seamen, from the circumstance of its spouting up a column of water.

(Zo"l.) A small fish of the Atlantic coast (Tetrodon turgidus); the puffer.

A braggart, or loud talker. [Slang]

Bartlett.

Blowfly· (?), n. (Zo"l.) Any species of fly of the genus Musca that deposits its eggs or young larv' (called flyblows and maggots) upon meat or other animal products.

Blowgun· (?), n. A tube, as of cane or reed, sometimes twelve feet long, through which an arrow or other projectile may be impelled by the force of the breath. It is a weapon much used by certain Indians of America and the West Indies; Ð called also blowpipe, and blowtube. See Sumpitan.

Blowhole· (?), n. 1. A cavern in a cliff, at the water level, opening to the air at its farther extremity, so that the waters rush in with each surge and rise in a lofty jet from the extremity.

A nostril or spiracle in the top of the head of a whale or other cetacean.

µ There are two spiracles or blowholes in the common whales, but only one in sperm whales, porpoises, etc.

A hole in the ice to which whales, seals, etc., come to breathe.

(Founding) An air hole in a casting.

Blown (?), p. p. & a. 1. Swollen; inflated; distended; puffed up, as cattle when gorged with green food which develops gas.

Stale; worthless.

Out of breath; tired; exhausted. ½Their horses much blown.

Sir W. Scott.

Covered with the eggs and larv' of flies; fly blown.

Blown, p. p. & a. Opened; in blossom or having blossomed, as a flower. Shak.

BlowÐoff · (?), n. 1. A blowing off steam, water, etc. Ð Also, adj.; as, a blowÐoff cock or pipe.

An outburst of temper or excitement. [Colloq.]

BlowÐout · (?), n. The cleaning of the flues of a boiler from scale, etc., by a blast of steam.

Blowpipe · (?), n. 1. A tube for directing a jet of air into a fire or into the flame of a lamp or candle, so as to concentrate the heat on some object.

µ It is called a mouth blowpipe when used with the mouth; but for both chemical and industrial purposes, it is often worked by a bellows or other contrivance. The common mouth blowpipe is a tapering tube with a very small orifice at the end to be inserted in the flame. The oxyhydrogen blowpipe, invented by Dr. Hare in 1801, is an instrument in which oxygen and hydrogen, taken from separate reservoirs, in the proportions of two volumes of hydrogen to one of oxygen, are burned in a jet, under pressure. It gives a heat that will consume the diamond, fuse platinum, and dissipate in vapor, or in gaseous forms, most known substances.

A blowgun; a blowtube.

Blowpipe analysis (Chem.), analysis by means of the blowpipe. Ð Blowpipe reaction (Chem.), the characteristic behavior of a substance subjected to a test by means of the blowpipe.

Blowpoint · (?), n. A child's game. [Obs.]

Blowse , n. See Blowze.

Blowth (?), n. [From Blow to blossom: cf. Growth.] A blossoming; a bloom. [Obs. or Archaic] ½In the blowth and bud.¸

Sir W. Raleigh.

Blowtube · (?), n. 1. A blowgun.

Tylor.

A similar instrument, commonly of tin, used by boys for discharging paper wads and other light missiles.

(Glassmaking) A long wrought iron tube, on the end of which the workman gathers a quantity of ½metal¸ (melted glass), and through which he blows to expand or shape it; Ð called also blowing tube, and blowpipe.

Blow valve · (?). (Mach.) See Snifting valve.

Blowy (?), a. Windy; as, blowy weather; a blowy upland.

Blowze (?), n. [Prob. from the same root as blush.] A ruddy, fatÏfaced woman; a wench. [Obs.]

Shak.

Blowzed (?), a. Having high color from exposure to the weather; ruddyÏfaced; blowzy; disordered.

Huge women blowzed with health and wind.

Tennyson.

Blowzy (?), a. Coarse and ruddyÏfaced; fat and ruddy; high colored; frowzy.

Blub (?), v. t. & i. [Cf. Bleb, Blob.] To swell; to puff out, as with weeping. [Obs.]

Blubber (?), n. [See Blobber, Blob, Bleb.]

A bubble.

At his mouth a blubber stood of foam.

Henryson.

The fat of whales and other large sea animals from which oil is obtained. It lies immediately under the skin and over the muscular flesh.

(Zo"l.) A large sea nettle or medusa.

Blubber, v. i. [imp. & p.p. Blubbered (?); p. pr. & vb. n. Blubbering.] To weep noisily, or so as to disfigure the face; to cry in a childish manner.

She wept, she blubbered, and she tore her hair.

Swift.

Blubber, v. t. 1. To swell or disfigure (the face) with weeping; to wet with tears.

Dear Cloe, how blubbered is that pretty face!

Prior.

To give vent to (tears) or utter (broken words or cries); Ð with forth or out.

Blubbered (?), p. p. & a. Swollen; turgid; as, a blubbered lip.

Spenser.

BlubberÏing, n. The act of weeping noisily.

He spake well save that his blubbering interrupted him.

Winthrop.

BlubberÏy (?), a. 1. Swollen; protuberant.

Like blubber; gelatinous and quivering; as, a blubbery mass.

Blucher (?), n. A kind of half boot, named from the Prussian general Blcher.

Thackeray.

Bludgeon (?), n. [Cf. Ir. blocan a little block, Gael. plocan a mallet, W. plocyn, dim. of ploc block; or perh. connected with E. blow a stroke. Cf. Block, Blow a stroke.] A short stick, with one end loaded, or thicker and heavier that the other, used as an offensive weapon.

Blue (?), a. [Compar. Bluer (?); superl. Bluest.] [OE. bla, blo, blew, blue, Sw. bl?, D. blauw, OHG. bl?o, G. blau; but influenced in form by F. bleu, from OHG. bl¾o.] 1. Having the color of the clear sky, or a hue resembling it, whether lighter or darker; as, the deep, blue sea; as blue as a sapphire; blue violets. ½The blue firmament.͵
Milton.

Pale, without redness or glare, Ð said of a flame; hence, of the color of burning brimstone, betokening the presence of ghosts or devils; as, the candle burns blue; the air was blue with oaths.

Low in spirits; melancholy; as, to feel blue.

Suited to produce low spirits; gloomy in prospect; as, thongs looked blue. [Colloq.]

Severe or over strict in morals; gloom; as, blue and sour religionists; suiting one who is over strict in morals; inculcating an impracticable, severe, or gloomy mortality; as, blue laws.

Literary; Ð applied to women; Ð an abbreviation of bluestocking. [Colloq.]

The ladies were very blue and well informed.
Thackeray.
Blue asbestus. See Crocidolite. Ð Blue black, of, or having, a very dark blue color, almost black. Ð Blue blood. See under Blood. Ð Blue buck (Zo"l.), a small South African antelope (Cephalophus pygm‘us); also applied to a larger species (?goceras leucoph‘us); the blaubok. Ð Blue cod (Zo"l.), the buffalo cod. Ð Blue crab (Zo"l.), the common edible crab of the Atlantic coast of the United States (Callinectes hastatus). Ð Blue curls (Bot.), a common plant (Trichostema dichotomum), resembling pennyroyal, and hence called also bastard pennyroyal. Ð Blue devils, apparitions supposed to be seen by persons suffering with delirium tremens; hence, very low spirits. ½Can Gumbo shut the hall door upon blue devils, or lay them all in a red sea of claret?͵ Thackeray. Ð Blue gage. See under Gage, a plum. Ð Blue gum, an Australian myrtaceous tree (Eucalyptus globulus), of the loftiest proportions, now cultivated in tropical and warm temperate regions for its timber, and as a protection against malaria. The essential oil is beginning to be used in medicine. The timber is very useful. See Eucalyptus. Ð Blue jack, Blue stone, blue vitriol; sulphate of copper. Ð Blue jacket, a man′of war's man; a sailor wearing a naval uniform. Ð Blue jaundice. See under Jaundice. Ð Blue laws, a name first used in the eighteenth century to describe certain supposititious laws of extreme rigor reported to have been enacted in New Haven; hence, any puritanical laws. [U. S.] Ð Blue light, a composition which burns with a brilliant blue flame; Ð used in pyrotechnics and as a night signal at sea, and in military operations. Ð Blue mantle (Her.), one of the four pursuivants of the English college of arms; Ð so called from the color of his official robes. Ð Blue mass, a preparation of mercury from which is formed the blue pill. McElrath. Ð Blue mold, or mould, the blue fungus (Aspergillus glaucus) which grows on cheese. Brande & C. Ð Blue Monday, a Monday following a Sunday of

dissipation, or itself given to dissipation (as the Monday before Lent). Ð Blue ointment (Med.), mercurial ointment. Ð Blue Peter (British Marine), a blue flag with a white square in the center, used as a signal for sailing, to recall boats, etc. It is a corruption of blue repeater, one of the British signal flags. Ð Blue pill. (Med.) (a) A pill of prepared mercury, used as an aperient, etc. (b) Blue mass. Ð Blue ribbon. (a) The ribbon worn by

<— p. 159 —>

members of the order of the Garter; Ð hence, a member of that order. (b) Anything the attainment of which is an object of great ambition; a distinction; a prize. ½These [scholarships] were the blue ribbon of the college., Farrar. (c) The distinctive badge of certain temperance or total abstinence organizations, as of the Blue ribbon Army. Ð Blue ruin, utter ruin; also, gin. [Eng. Slang] Carlyle. Ð Blue spar (Min.), azure spar; lazulite. See Lazulite. Ð Blue thrush (Zo"l.), a European and Asiatic thrush (Petrocossyphus cyaneas). Ð Blue verditer. See Verditer. Ð Blue vitriol (Chem.), sulphate of copper, a violet blue crystallized salt, used in electric batteries, calico printing, etc. Ð Blue water, the open ocean. Ð To look blue, to look disheartened or dejected. Ð True blue, genuine and thorough; not modified, nor mixed; not spurious; specifically, of uncompromising Presbyterianism, blue being the color adopted by the Covenanters.

For his religion...
'T was Presbyterian, true blue.
Hudibras.

Blue (?), n. 1. One of the seven colors into which the rays of light divide themselves, when refracted through a glass prism; the color of the clear sky, or a color resembling that, whether lighter or darker; a pigment having such color. Sometimes, poetically, the sky.

A pedantic woman; a bluestocking. [Colloq.]

pl. [Short for blue devils.] Low spirits; a fit of despondency; melancholy. [Colloq.]

Berlin blue, Prussian blue. Ð Mineral blue. See under Mineral. Ð Prussian blue. See under Prussian.

Blue, v. t. [imp. & p.p. Blued (?); p. pr. & vb. n. Bluing.] To make blue; to dye of a blue color; to make blue by heating, as metals, etc.

Blueback· (?), n. (Zo"l.) (a) A trout (Salmo oquassa) inhabiting some of the lakes of Maine. (b) A salmon (Oncorhynchus nerka) of the Columbia River and northward. (c) An American river herring (Clupea 'stivalis), closely allied to the alewife.

Bluebeard (?), n. The hero of a medi'val French nursery legend, who, leaving home, enjoined his young wife not to open a certain room in his castle. She entered it, and found the murdered bodies of his former wives. Ð Also used adjectively of a subject which it is forbidden to investigate.

The Bluebeard chamber of his mind, into which no eye but his own must look.

Carlyle.

Bluebell · (?), n. (Bot.) (a) A plant of the genus Campanula, especially the Campanula rotundifolia, which bears blue bell-shaped flowers; the harebell. (b) A plant of the genus Scilla (Scilla nutans).

Blueberry (?), n. [Cf. Blaeberry.] (Bot.) The berry of several species of Vaccinium, and ericaceous genus, differing from the American huckleberries in containing numerous minute seeds instead of ten nutlets. The commonest species are V. Pennsylvanicum and V. vacillans. V. corymbosum is the tall blueberry.

Bluebill · (?), n. (Zo"l.) A duck of the genus Fuligula. Two American species (F. marila and F. affinis) are common. See Scaup duck.

Bluebird · (?), n. (Zo"l.) A small song bird (Sialia sialis), very common in the United States, and, in the north, one of the earliest to arrive in spring. The male is blue, with the breast reddish. It is related to the European robin.

Pairy bluebird (Zo"l.), a brilliant Indian or East Indian bird of the genus Irena, of several species.

Blue bon · **net** or **Blueïbon** · **net** (?), n. 1. A broad, flat Scottish cap of blue woolen, or one waring such cap; a Scotchman.

(Bot.) A plant. Same as Bluebottle.

(Zo"l.) The European blue titmouse (Parus c?ruleus); the bluecap.

Blue book · (?). 1. A parliamentary publication, so called from its blue paper covers. [Eng.]

The United States official ½Biennial Register.

Bluebot · **tle** (?), n. 1. (Bot.) A plant (Centaurea cyanus) which grows in grain fields. It receives its name from its blue bottleÐshaped flowers.

(Zo"l.) A large and troublesome species of blowfly (Musca vomitoria). Its body is steel blue.

Bluebreast · (?), n. (Zo"l.) (a) A small European bird; the blueÐthroated warbler.

Bluecap · (?), n. 1. (Zo"l.) (a) The bluepoll. (b) The blue bonnet or blue titmouse.

A Scot; a Scotchman; Ð so named from wearing a blue bonnet. [Poetic]

Shak.

Bluecoat · (?), n. One dressed in blue, as a soldier, a sailor, a beadle, etc.

BlueÐeye · (?), a. Having blue eyes.

BlueÐeyed grass (Bot.), a grasslike plant (Sisyrinchium anceps), with small flowers of a delicate blue color.

Bluefin · (?), n. (Zo"l.) A species of whitefish (Coregonus nigripinnis) found in Lake Michigan.

Bluefish · (?), n. (Zo"l.) 1. A large voracious fish (Pomatomus saitatrix), of the family Carangid‘, valued as a food fish, and widely distributed on the American coast. On the New Jersey and Rhode Island coast it is called the horse mackerel, in Virginia saltwater tailor, or skipjack.

<small>A West Indian fish (Platyglossus radiatus), of the family Labrid‘.</small>

μ The name is applied locally to other species of fishes; as the cunner, sea bass, squeteague, etc.

Bluegown · (?), n. One of a class of paupers or pensioners, or licensed beggars, in Scotland, to whim annually on the king's birthday were distributed certain alms, including a blue gown; a beadsman.

Blue grass · (?). (Bot.) A species of grass (Poa compressa) with bluish green stems, valuable in thin gravelly soils; wire grass.

Kentucky blue grass, a species of grass (Poa pratensis) which has running rootstocks and spreads rapidly. It is valuable as a pasture grass, as it endures both winter and drought better than other kinds, and is very nutritious.

Blue jay · (?). (Zo"l.) The common jay of the United States (Cyanocitta, or Cyanura, cristata). The predominant color is bright blue.

BlueÐjohn · (?), n. A name given to fluor spar in Derbyshire, where it is used for ornamental purposes.

Bluely, adv. With a blue color.

Swift.

Blueness, n. The quality of being blue; a blue color.

Boyle.

Bluenose (?), n. A nickname for a Nova Scotian.

Bluepoll · (?), n. [Blue + poll head.] (Zo"l.) A kind of salmon (Salmo Cambricus) found in Wales.

Blueprint. See under Print.

Bluestock · ing (?), n. 1. A literary lady; a female pedant. [Colloq.]

μ As explained in Boswell's ½Life of Dr. Johnson‚, this term is derived from the name given to certain meetings held by ladies, in Johnson's time, for conversation with distinguished literary men. An eminent attendant of these assemblies was a Mr. Stillingfleet, who always wore blue stockings. He was so much distinguished for his conversational powers that his absence at any time was felt to be a great loss, so that the remark became common, ½We can do nothing without the blue stockings.‚ Hence these meetings were sportively called bluestocking clubs, and the ladies who attended them, bluestockings.

<small>(Zo"l.) The American avocet (Recurvirostra Americana).</small>

Bluestock · ingïism (?), n. The character or manner of a bluestocking; female pedantry. [Colloq.]

Bluestone · (?), n. 1. Blue vitriol.

Dunglison.

A grayish blue building stone, as that commonly used in the eastern United States.

Bluethroat · (?), n. (Zo"l.) A singing bird of northern Europe and Asia (Cyanecula Suecica), related to the nightingales; Ð called also blueÐthroated robin and blueÐthroated warbler.

Bluets (?), n. [F. bluet, bleuet, dim. of bleu blue. See Blue, a.] (Bot.) A name given to several different species of plants having blue flowers, as the Houstonia c?rulea, the Centaurea cyanus or bluebottle, and the Vaccinium angustifolium.

BlueÐveined · (?), a. Having blue veins or blue streaks.

Bluewing · (?), n. (Zo"l.) The blueÐwinged teal. See Teal.

Bluey (?), a. Bluish.

Southey.

Bluff (?), a. [Cf. OD. blaf flat, broad, blaffaert one with a broad face, also, a boaster; or G. verblffen to confuse, LG. bluffen to frighten; to unknown origin.] 1. Having a broad, flattened front; as, the bluff bows of a ship. ½Bluff visages.

Irving.

Rising steeply with a flat or rounded front. ½A bluff or bold shore.

Falconer.

Its banks, if not really steep, had a bluff and precipitous aspect.

Judd.

Surly; churlish; gruff; rough.

Abrupt; roughly frank; unceremonious; blunt; brusque; as, a bluff answer; a bluff manner of talking; a bluff sea captain. ½Bluff King Hal.

Sir W. Scott.

There is indeed a bluff pertinacity which is a proper defense in a moment of surprise.

I. Taylor.

Bluff, n. 1. A high, steep bank, as by a river or the sea, or beside a ravine or plain; a cliff with a broad face.

Beach, bluff, and wave, adieu.

Whittier.

An act of bluffing; an expression of selfÐconfidence for the purpose of intimidation; braggadocio; as, that is only bluff, or a bluff.

A game at cards; poker. [U.S.]

Bartlett.

Bluff, v. t. [imp. & p.p. Bluffed (?); p. pr. & vb. n. Bluffing.] 1. (Poker) To deter (an opponent) from taking the risk of betting on his hand of cards, as the bluffer does by betting heavily on his own hand although it may be of less value. [U. S.]

To frighten or deter from accomplishing a purpose by making a show of confidence in one's strength or resources; as, he bluffed me off. [Colloq.]

Bluff, v. i. To act as in the game of bluff.

Bluff-bowed · (?), a. (Naut.) Built with the stem nearly straight up and down.

Bluffness, n. The quality or state of being bluff.

Bluffy (?), a. 1. Having bluffs, or bold, steep banks.

Inclined to bo bluff; brusque.

Bluing (?), n. 1. The act of rendering blue; as, the bluing of steel.
Tomlinson.

Something to give a bluish tint, as indigo, or preparations used by washerwomen.

Bluish (?), a. Somewhat blue; as, bluish veins. ½Bluish mists.„ Dryden. Ð Bluishĭly, adv. Ð Bluishĭness, n.

Blunder (?), v. i. [imp. & p.p. Blundered (?); p. pr. & vb. n. Blundering.] [OE. blunderen, blondren, to stir, confuse, blunder; perh. allied to blend to mix, to confound by mixture.] 1. To make a gross error or mistake; as, to blunder in writing or preparing a medical prescription.
Swift.

To move in an awkward, clumsy manner; to flounder and stumble.

I was never distinguished for address, and have often even blundered in making my bow.
Goldsmith.
Yet knows not how to find the uncertain place,
And blunders on, and staggers every pace.
Dryden.

To blunder on. (a) To continue blundering. (b) To find or reach as if by an accident involving more or less stupidity, Ð applied to something desirable; as, to blunder on a useful discovery.

Blunder, v. t. 1. To cause to blunder. [Obs.] ½To blunder an adversary.„
Ditton.

To do or treat in a blundering manner; to confuse.

He blunders and confounds all these together.
Stillingfleet.

Blunder, n. 1. Confusion; disturbance. [Obs.]

A gross error or mistake, resulting from carelessness, stupidity, or culpable ignorance.

Syn. Đ Blunder, Error, Mistake, Bull. An error is a departure or deviation from that which is right or correct; as, an error of the press; an error of judgment. A mistake is the interchange or taking of one thing for another, through haste, inadvertence, etc.; as, a careless mistake. A blunder is a mistake or error of a gross kind. It supposes a person to flounder on in his course, from carelessness, ignorance, or stupidity. A bull is a verbal blunder containing a laughable incongruity of ideas.

Blunderĭbuss (?), n. [Either fr. blunder + D. bus tube, box, akin to G. bchse box, gun, E. box; or corrupted fr. D. donderbus (literally) thunder box, gun, musket.] 1. A short gun or firearm, with a large bore, capable of holding a number of balls, and intended to do execution without exact aim.

A stupid, blundering fellow.

Blunderĭer (?), n. One who is apt to blunder.
Blunderĭhead · (?), n. [Blunder + head.] A stupid, blundering fellow.
Blunderĭing, a. Characterized by blunders.
Blunderĭingĭly, adv. In a blundering manner.
Blunge (?), v. t. To amalgamate and blend; to beat up or mix in water, as clay.
Blunger (?), n. [Corrupted from plunger.] A wooden blade with a cross handle, used for mi?ing the clay in potteries; a plunger.
Tomlinson.
Blunging (?), n. The process of mixing clay in potteries with a blunger.
Tomlinson.
Blunt (?), a. [Cf. Prov. G. bludde a dull or blunt knife, Dan. blunde to sleep, Sw. & Icel. blunda; or perh. akin to E. blind.] 1. Having a thick edge or point, as an instrument; dull; not sharp.

The murderous knife was dull and blunt.
Shak.

Dull in understanding; slow of discernment; stupid; Đ opposed to acute.

His wits are not so blunt.
Shak.

Abrupt in address; plain; unceremonious; wanting the forms of civility; rough in manners or speech. ½Hiding his bitter jests in blunt behavior.͵ ½A plain, blunt man.͵

Shak.
Hard to impress or penetrate. [R.]

I find my heart hardened and blunt to new impressions.
Pope.

µ Blunt is much used in composition, as bluntĭedged, bluntĭsighted, bluntĭspoken.

Syn. Ð Obtuse; dull; pointless; curt; short; coarse; rude; brusque; impolite; uncivil.

Blunt, v. t. [imp. & p.p. Blunted; p. pr. & vb. n. Blunting.] 1. To dull the edge or point of, by making it thicker; to make blunt.

Shak.

> To repress or weaken, as any appetite, desire, or power of the mind; to impair the force, keenness, or susceptibility, of; as, to blunt the feelings.

Blunt, n. 1. A fencer's foil. [Obs.]

> A short needle with a strong point. See Needle.
>
> Money. [Cant]

Beaconsfield.

Bluntish, a. Somewhat blunt. Ð Bluntishĭness, n.

Bluntly, adv. In a blunt manner; coarsely; plainly; abruptly; without delicacy, or the usual forms of civility.

Sometimes after bluntly giving his opinions, he would quietly lay himself asleep until the end of their deliberations.

Jeffrey.

Bluntness, n. 1. Want of edge or point; dullness; obtuseness; want of sharpness.

The multitude of elements and bluntness of angles.

Holland.

> A bruptness of address; rude plainness. ½Bluntness of speech.

Boyle.

BluntÐwit · ted (?), n. Dull; stupid.

BluntÐwitted lord, ignoble in demeanor!

Shak.

Blur (?), v. t. [imp. & p.p. Blurred (?); p. pr. & vb. n. Blurring.] [Prob. of same origin as blear. See Blear.] 1. To render obscure by making the form or outline of confused and uncertain, as by soiling; to smear; to make indistinct and confused; as, to blur manuscript by handling it while damp; to blur the impression of a woodcut by an excess of ink.

But time hath nothing blurred those lines of favor
Which then he wore.

Shak.

> To cause imperfection of vision in; to dim; to darken.

Her eyes are blurred with the lightning's glare.

J. R. Drake.

> To sully; to stain; to blemish, as reputation.

Sarcasms may eclipse thine own,
But can not blur my lost renown.
Hudibras.
Syn. Ð To spot; blot; disfigure; stain; sully.
<— p. 160 —>
<— p. 160 —>

Blur (?), n. 1. That which obscures without effacing; a stain; a blot, as upon paper or other substance.

As for those who cleanse blurs with blotted fingers, they make it worse.
Fuller.

A dim, confused appearance; indistinctness of vision; as, to see things with a blur; it was all blur.

A moral stain or blot.

Lest she ... will with her railing set a great blur on mine honesty and good name.
Udall.

Blurry (?), a. Full of blurs; blurred.

Blurt (?), v. t. [imp. & p.p. Blurted; p. pr. & vb. n. Blurting.] [Cf. Blare.] To utter suddenly and unadvisedly; to divulge inconsiderately; to ejaculate; Ð commonly with out.

Others ... can not hold, but blurt out, those words which afterward they forced to eat.
Hakewill.

To blurt at, to speak contemptuously of. [Obs.]
Shak.

Blush (?) v. i. [imp. & p.p. Blushed (?); p. pr. & vb. n. Blushing.] [OE. bluschen to shine, look, turn red, AS. blyscan to glow; akin to blysa a torch, ¾bl?sian to blush, D. blozen, Dan. blusse to blaze, blush.]

To become suffused with red in the cheeks, as from a sense of shame, modesty, or confusion; to become red from such cause, as the cheeks or face.

To the nuptial bower
I led her blushing like the morn.
Milton.

In the presence of the shameless and unblushing, the young offender is ashamed to blush.
Buckminster.

He would stroke
The head of modest and ingenuous worth,
That blushed at its own praise.
Cowper.

To grow red; to have a red or rosy color.

The sun of heaven, methought, was loth to set,
But stayed, and made the western welkin blush.
Shak.

To have a warm and delicate color, as some roses and other flowers.

Full many a flower is born to blush unseen.
T. Gray.
Blush, v. t. 1. To suffuse with a blush; to redden; to make roseate. [Obs.]
To blush and beautify the cheek again.
Shak.

To express or make known by blushing.

I'll blush you thanks.
Shak.
Blush, n. 1. A suffusion of the cheeks or face with red, as from a sense of shame, confusion, or modesty.
The rosy blush of love.
Trumbull.

A red or reddish color; a rosy tint.

Light's last blushes tinged the distant hills.
Lyttleton.
At first blush, or At the first blush, at the first appearance or view. ½At the first blush, we thought they had been ships come from France., Hakluyt. This phrase is used now more of ideas, opinions, etc., than of material things. ½All purely identical propositions, obviously, and at first blush, appear., etc. Locke. Đ To put to the blush, to cause to blush with shame; to put to shame.
Blusher (?), n. One that blushes.
Blushet (?), n. A modest girl. [Obs.]
B. Jonson.
Blushful (?), a. Full of blushes.
While from his ardent look the turning Spring
Averts her blushful face.
Thomson.
Blushing, a. Showing blushes; rosy red; having a warm and delicate color like some roses and other flowers; blooming; ruddy; roseate.
The dappled pink and blushing rose.
Prior.
Blushing, n. The act of turning red; the appearance of a reddish color or flush upon the cheeks.
Blushingly, adv. In a blushing manner; with a blush or blushes; as, to answer or confess blushingly.

404

Blushless, a. Free from blushes; incapable of blushing; shameless; impudent.

Vice now, secure, her blushless front shall raise.

Dodsley.

Blushy (?), a. Like a blush; having the color of a blush; rosy. [R.] ½A blushy color.

Harvey.

Bluster (?), v. i. [imp. & p.p. Blustered (?); p. pr. & vb. n. Blustering.] [Allied to blast.]

To blow fitfully with violence and noise, as wind; to be windy and boisterous, as the weather.

And ever͏̆threatening storms
Of Chaos blustering round.
Milton.

To talk with noisy violence; to swagger, as a turbulent or boasting person; to act in a noisy, tumultuous way; to play the bully; to storm; to rage.

Your ministerial directors blustered like tragic tyrants.

Burke.

Bluster, v. t. To utter, or do, with noisy violence; to force by blustering; to bully.

He bloweth and blustereth out ... his abominable blasphemy.

Sir T. More.

As if therewith he meant to bluster all princes into a perfect obedience to his commands.

Fuller.

Bluster, n. 1. Fitful noise and violence, as of a storm; violent winds; boisterousness.

To the winds they set
Their corners, when with bluster to confound
Sea, air, and shore.
Milton.

Noisy and violent or threatening talk; noisy and boastful language.

L'Estrange.

Syn. Ð Noise; boisterousness; tumult; turbulence; confusion; boasting; swaggering; bullying.

Bluster͏̆er (?), n. One who, or that which, blusters; a noisy swaggerer.

Bluster͏̆ling, a. 1. Exhibiting noisy violence, as the wind; stormy; tumultuous.

A tempest and a blustering day.
Shak.

Uttering noisy threats; noisy and swaggering; boisterous. ½A blustering fellow.

L'Estrange.
Blusteringly, adv. In a blustering manner.
Blusterous (?), a. Inclined to bluster; given to blustering; blustering.
Motley.
Blustrous (?), a. Blusterous.
Shak.
Bo (?), interj. [Cf. W. bw, an interj. of threatening or frightening; n., terror, fear, dread.] An exclamation used to startle or frighten. [Spelt also boh and boo.]
Boa (?), n.; pl. Boas. [L. boa a kind of water serpent. Perh. fr. bos an ox.] 1. (Zo"l.) A genus of large American serpents, including the boa constrictor, the emperor boa of Mexico (B. imperator), and the chevalier boa of Peru (B. eques).

µ The name is also applied to related genera; as, the dogÐheaded boa (Xiphosoma caninum).

A long, round fur tippet; Ð so called from its resemblance in shape to the boa constrictor.

Boa conÏstrictor (?). [NL. See Boa, and Constrictor.] (Zo"l.) A large and powerful serpent of tropical America, sometimes twenty or thirty feet long. See Illustration in Appendix.

µ It has a succession of spots, alternately black and yellow, extending along the back. It kills its prey by constriction. The name is also loosely applied to other large serpents which crush their prey, particularly to those of the genus Python, found in Asia and Africa.

Ø Bo · aÏnerges (?). [Gr. ?, fr. Heb. bn? hargem sons of thunder. Ð an appellation given by Christ to two of his disciples (James and John). See Mark iii. 17.] Any declamatory and vociferous preacher or orator.

Boar (?), n. [OE. bar, bor, bore, AS. b¾r; akin to OHG. p?r, MHG. b?r, G. b„r, boar (but not b„r bear), and perh. Russ. borov' boar.] (Zo"l.) The uncastrated male of swine; specifically, the wild hog.

Board (?), n. [OE. bord, AS. bord board, shipboard; akin to bred plank, Icel. bor? board, side of a ship, Goth. f?tuÐbaurd footstool, D. bord board, G. brett, bort. See def. 8. ?92.] 1. A piece of timber sawed thin, and of considerable length and breadth as compared with the thickness, Ð used for building, etc.

µ When sawed thick, as over one and a half or two inches, it is usually called a plank.

A table to put food upon.

µ The term board answers to the modern table, but it was often movable, and placed on trestles.

Halliwell.

Fruit of all kinds ...
She gathers, tribute large, and on the board
Heaps with unsparing hand.

Milton.

Hence: What is served on a table as food; stated meals; provision; entertainment; Ð usually as furnished for pay; as, to work for one's board; the price of board.

A table at which a council or court is held. Hence: A council, convened for business, or any authorized assembly or meeting, public or private; a number of persons appointed or elected to sit in council for the management or direction of some public or private business or trust; as, the Board of Admiralty; a board of trade; a board of directors, trustees, commissioners, etc.

Both better acquainted with affairs than any other who sat then at that board.

Clarendon.

We may judge from their letters to the board.

Porteus.

A square or oblong piece of thin wood or other material used for some special purpose, as, a molding board; a board or surface painted or arranged for a game; as, a chessboard; a backgammon board.

Paper made thick and stiff like a board, for book covers, etc.; pasteboard; as, to bind a book in boards.

pl. The stage in a theater; as, to go upon the boards, to enter upon the theatrical profession.

[In this use originally perh. a different word meaning border, margin; cf. D. boord, G. bord, shipboard, and G. borte trimming; also F. bord (fr. G.) the side of a ship. Cf. Border.] The border or side of anything. (Naut.) (a) The side of a ship. ½Now board to board the rival vessels row.͵ Dryden. See On board, below. (b) The stretch which a ship makes in one tack.

μ Board is much used adjectively or as the last part of a compound; as, fir board, clapboard, floor board, shipboard, sideboard, ironing board, chessboard, cardboard, pasteboard, seaboard; board measure.

The American Board, a shortened form of ½The American Board of Commissioners for Foreign Missions͵ (the foreign missionary society of the American Congregational churches). Ð Bed and board. See under Bed. Ð Board and board (Naut.), side by side. Ð Board of control, six privy councilors formerly appointed to superintend the affairs of the British East Indies. Stormonth. Ð Board rule, a figured scale for finding without calculation the number of square feet in a board. Haldeman. Ð Board of trade, in England, a committee of the privy council appointed to superintend matters relating to trade. In the United States, a body of men appointed for the advancement and protection of their business interests; a chamber of commerce. Ð Board wages. (a) Food and lodging supplied as compensation for services; as, to work hard, and get only board wages. (b) Money wages which are barely sufficient to buy food and lodging. (c) A separate or special allowance of wages for the procurement of food, or food and lodging. Dryden. Ð By the board, over the board, or side. ½The mast went by the board.¸ Totten. Hence (Fig.), To go by the board, to suffer complete destruction or overthrow. Ð To enter on the boards, to have one's name inscribed on a board or tablet in a college as a student. [Cambridge, England.] ½Having been entered on the boards of Trinity college.¸ Hallam. Ð To make a good board (Naut.), to sail in a straight line when closeÐhauled; to lose little to leeward. Ð To make short boards, to tack frequently. Ð On board. (a) On shipboard; in a ship or a boat; on board of; as, I came on board early; to be on board ship. (b) In or into a railway car or train. [Colloq. U. S.] Ð Returning board, a board empowered to canvass and make an official statement of the votes cast at an election. [U.S.]

Board, v. t. [imp. & p.p. Boarded; p. pr. & vb. n. Boarding.] 1. To cover with boards or boarding; as, to board a house. ½The boarded hovel.¸ Cowper.

[Cf. Board to accost, and see Board, n.] To go on board of, or enter, as a ship, whether in a hostile or a friendly way.

You board an enemy to capture her, and a stranger to receive news or make a communication.
Totten.

To enter, as a railway car. [Colloq. U. S.]

To furnish with regular meals, or with meals and lodgings, for compensation; to supply with daily meals.

To place at board, for compensation; as, to board one's horse at a livery stable.

Board (?), v. i. To obtain meals, or meals and lodgings, statedly for compensation; as, he boards at the hotel.

We are several of us, gentlemen and ladies, who board in the same house.
Spectator.

Board, v. t. [F. aborder. See Abord, v. t.] To approach; to accost; to address; hence, to woo. [Obs.]

I will board her, though she chide as loud
As thunder when the clouds in autumn crack.
Shak.

BoardaÏble (?), a. That can be boarded, as a ship.

Boarder (?), n. 1. One who has food statedly at another's table, or meals and lodgings in his house, for pay, or compensation of any kind.

(Naut.) One who boards a ship; one selected to board an enemy's ship.

Totten.

Boarding, n. 1. (Naut.) The act of entering a ship, whether with a hostile or a friendly purpose.

Both slain at one time, as they attempted the boarding of a frigate.
Sir F. Drake.

The act of covering with boards; also, boards, collectively; or a covering made of boards.

The act of supplying, or the state of being supplied, with regular or specified meals, or with meals and lodgings, for pay.

Boarding house, a house in which boarders are kept. Ð Boarding nettings (Naut.), a strong network of cords or ropes erected at the side of a ship to prevent an enemy from boarding it. Ð Boarding pike (Naut.), a pike used by sailors in boarding a vessel, or in repelling an attempt to board it. Totten. Ð Boarding school, a school in which pupils receive board and lodging as well as instruction.

Boarfish · (?), n. (Zo"l.) (a) A Mediterranean fish (Capros aper), of the family Caproid'; Ð so called from the resemblance of the extended lips to a hog's snout. (b) An Australian percoid fish (Histiopterus recurvirostris), valued as a food fish.

Boarish, a. Swinish; brutal; cruel.
In his anointed flesh stick boarish fangs.
Shak.

Boast (?), v. i. [imp. & p.p. Boasted; p. pr. & vb. n. Boasting.] [OE. bosten, boosten, v., bost, boost, n., noise, boasting; cf. G. bausen, bauschen, to swell, pusten, Dan. puste, Sw. pusta, to blow, Sw. p"sa to swell; or W. bostio to boast, bost boast, Gael. bosd. But these last may be from English.] 1. To vaunt one's self; to brag; to say or tell things which are intended to give others a high opinion of one's self or of things belonging to one's self; as, to boast of one's exploits courage, descent, wealth.

? grace are ye saved through faith; and that not of your selves: .. not of works, lest any man should boast.
Eph. ii. 8, 9.

To speak in exulting language of another; to glory; to exult.

In God we boast all the day long.
Ps. xiiv. 8

Syn. Ð To brag; bluster; vapor; crow; talk big.

Boast, v. t. 1. To display in ostentatious language; to speak of with pride, vanity, or exultation, with a view to selfÐcommendation; to extol.

Lest bad men should boast
Their specious deeds.
Milton.

To display vaingloriously.

To possess or have; as, to boast a name.

To boast one's self, to speak with unbecoming confidence in, and approval of, one's self; Ð followed by of and the thing to which the boasting relates. [Archaic]

Boast not thyself of tołmorrow.

Prov. xxvii.?

Boast, v. t. [Of uncertain etymology.] 1. (Masonry) To dress, as a stone, with a broad chisel.

Weale.

(Sculp.) To shape roughly as a preparation for the finer work to follow; to cut to the general form required.

Boast, n. 1. Act of boasting; vaunting or bragging.

Reason and morals? and where live they most,
In Christian comfort, or in Stoic boast!

Byron.

The cause of boasting; occasion of pride or exultation, Ð sometimes of laudable pride or exultation.

The boast of historians.

Macaulay.

Boastance (?), n. Boasting. [Obs.]

Chaucer.

Boaster (?), n. One who boasts; a braggart.

Boaster, n. A stone mason's broadÐfaced chisel.

Boastful (?), a. Given to, or full of, boasting; inclined to boast; vaunting; vainglorious; selfÐpraising. Ð Boastfullly, adv. Ð Boastfullness, n.

Boasting, n. The act of glorying or vaunting; vainglorious speaking; ostentatious display.

When boasting ends, then dignity begins.

Young.

Boastingİly, adv. Boastfully; with boasting. ½He boastingly tells you.„

Burke.

Boastive (?), a. Presumptuous. [R.]

Boastless, a. Without boasting or ostentation.

Boat (?), n. [OE. boot, bat, AS. b¾t; akin to Icel. b¾tr, Sw. b†t, Dan. baad, D.& G. boot. Cf. Bateau.]

A small open vessel, or water craft, usually moved by cars or paddles, but often by a sail.

µ Different kinds of boats have different names; as, canoe, yawl, wherry, pinnace, punt, etc.

Hence, any vessel; usually with some epithet descriptive of its use or mode of propulsion; as, pilot boat, packet boat, passage boat, advice boat, etc. The term is sometimes applied to steam vessels, even of the largest class; as, the Cunard boats.

A vehicle, utensil, or dish, somewhat resembling a boat in shape; as, a stone boat; a gravy boat.

<— p. 161 —>

µ Boat is much used either adjectively or in combination; as, boat builder or boatbuilder; boat building or boatbuilding; boat hook or boathook; boathouse; boat keeper or boatkeeper; boat load; boat race; boat racing; boat rowing; boat song; boatlike; boatÐshaped.

Advice boat. See under Advice. Ð Boat hook (Naut.), an iron hook with a point on the back, fixed to a long pole, to pull or push a boat, raft, log, etc. Totten. Ð Boat rope, a rope for fastening a boat; Ð usually called a painter. Ð In same boat, in the same situation or predicament. [Colloq.]

F. W. Newman.

Boat (?), v. t. [imp. & p.p. Boated; p. pr. & vb. n. Boating.] 1. To transport in a boat; as, to boat goods.

To place in a boat; as, to boat oars.

To boat the oars. See under Oar.
Boat, v. i. To go or row in a boat.
I boated over, ran my craft aground.
Tennyson.
Boataïble (?), a. 1. Such as can be transported in a boat.

Navigable for boats, or small river craft.

The boatable waters of the Alleghany.
J. Morse.
Boatage (?), n. Conveyance by boat; also, a charge for such conveyance.
Boatbill · (?), n. (Zo"l.) 1. A wading bird (Cancroma cochlearia) of the tropical parts of South America. Its bill is somewhat like a boat with the keel uppermost.

A perching bird of India, of the genus Eurylaimus.

Boat bug · (?). (Zo"l.) An aquatic hemipterous insect of the genus Notonecta; Ð so called from swimming on its back, which gives it the appearance of a little boat. Called also boat fly, boat insect, boatman, and water boatman.
Boatful (?), n.; pl. Boatfuls. The quantity or amount that fills a boat.
Boathouse · (?), n. A house for sheltering boats.
Half the latticed boathouse hides.
Wordsworth.
Boating, n. 1. The act or practice of rowing or sailing, esp. as an amusement; carriage in boats.

In Persia, a punishment of capital offenders, by laying them on the back in a covered boat, where they are left to perish.

Boïation (?), n. [L. boatus, fr. boare to roar.] A crying out; a roaring; a bellowing; reverberation. [Obs.]

The guns were heard ... about a hundred Italian miles, in long boations.
Derham.

Boatman (?), n.; pl. Boatmen (?). 1. A man who manages a boat; a rower of a boat.

As late the boatman hies him home.
Percival.

(Zo"l.) A boat bug. See Boat bug.

Boatmanĭship, n. The art of managing a boat.
BoatĐshaped · (?), a. (Bot.) See Cymbiform.
Boat shell · (?). (Zo"l.) (a) A marine gastropod of the genus Crepidula. The species are numerous. It is so named from its form and interior deck. (b) A marine univalve shell of the genus Cymba.

Boatsman (?), n. A boatman. [Archaic]
Boatswain (?), n. [Boat + swain.] 1. (Naut.) An officer who has charge of the boats, sails, rigging, colors, anchors, cables, cordage, etc., of a ship, and who also summons the crew, and performs other duties.

(Zo"l.) (a) The jager gull. (b) The tropic bird.

Boatswain's mate, an assistant of the boatswain.
Totten.

BoatĐtail · (?), n. (Zo"l.) A large grackle or blackbird (Quiscalus major), found in the Southern United States.

Boatwom · an (?), n.; pl. Boatwomen (?). A woman who manages a boat.
Bob (?), n. [An onomatopoetic word, expressing quick, jerky motion; OE. bob bunch, bobben to strike, mock, deceive. Cf. Prov. Eng. bob, n., a ball, an engine beam, bunch, blast, trick, taunt, scoff; as, a v., to dance, to courtesy, to disappoint, OF. bober to mock.] 1. Anything that hangs so as to play loosely, or with a short abrupt motion, as at the end of a string; a pendant; as, the bob at the end of a kite's tail.

In jewels dressed and at each ear a bob.
Dryden.

A knot of worms, or of rags, on a string, used in angling, as for eels; formerly, a worm suitable for bait.

Or yellow bobs, turned up before the plow,
Are chiefest baits, with cork and lead enow.
Lauson.

A small piece of cork or light wood attached to a fishing line to show when a fish is biting; a float.

The ball or heavy part of a pendulum; also, the ball or weight at the end of a plumb line.

A small wheel, made of leather, with rounded edges, used in polishing spoons, etc.

A short, jerking motion; act of bobbing; as, a bob of the head.

(Steam Engine) A working beam.

A knot or short curl of hair; also, a bob wig.

A plain brown bob he wore.
Shenstone.

A peculiar mode of ringing changes on bells.

The refrain of a song.

To bed, to bed, will be the bob of the song.
L'Estrange.

A blow; a shake or jog; a rap, as with the fist.

A jeer or flout; a sharp jest or taunt; a trick.

He that a fool doth very wisely hit,
Doth very foolishly, although he smart,
Not to seem senseless of the bob.
Shak.

A shilling. [Slang, Eng.]

Dickens.

Bob (?), v. t. [imp. & p.p. Bobbed (?); p. pr. & vb. n. Bobbing.] [OE. bobben. See Bob, n.] 1. To cause to move in a short, jerking manner; to move (a thing) with a bob. ½He bobbed his head.
W. Irving.

To strike with a quick, light blow; to tap.

If any man happened by long sitting to sleep... he was suddenly bobbed on the face by the servants.
Elyot.

To cheat; to gain by fraud or cheating; to filch.

Gold and jewels that I bobbed from him.
Shak.

To mock or delude; to cheat.

To play her pranks, and bob the fool,
The shrewish wife began.
Turbervile.

To cut short; as, to bob the hair, or a horse's tail.

Bob, v. i. 1. To have a short, jerking motion; to play to and fro, or up and down; to play loosely against anything. ½Bobbing and courtesying.,
Thackeray.

To angle with a bob. See Bob, n., 2 & 3.

He ne'er had learned the art to bob
For anything but eels.
Saxe.

To bob at an apple, cherry, etc. to attempt to bite or seize with the mouth an apple, cherry, or other round fruit, while it is swinging from a string or floating in a tug of water.

Ø Bobac (?), n. (Zo"l.) The Poland marmot (Arctomys bobac).

Boïbance (?), n. [OF. bobance, F. bombance, boasting, pageantry, fr. L. bombus a humming, buzzing.] A boasting. [Obs.]
Chaucer.

Bobber (?), n. One who, or that which, bobs.

Bobberïy (?), n. [Prob. an AngloÐIndian form of Hindi b¾p re O thou father! (a very disrespectful address).] A squabble; a tumult; a noisy disturbance; as, to raise a bobbery. [Low]
Halliwell.

Bobbin (?), n. [F. bobine; of uncertain origin; cf. L. bombus a humming, from the noise it makes, or Ir. & Gael. baban tassel, or E. bob.] 1. A small pin, or cylinder, formerly of bone, now most commonly of wood, used in the making of pillow lace. Each thread is wound on a separate bobbin which hangs down holding the thread at a slight tension.

A spool or reel of various material and construction, with a head at one or both ends, and sometimes with a hole bored through its length by which it may be placed on a spindle or pivot. It is used to hold yarn or thread, as in spinning or warping machines, looms, sewing machines, etc.

The little rounded piece of wood, at the end of a latch string, which is pulled to raise the latch.

(Haberdashery) A fine cord or narrow braid.

(Elec.) A cylindrical or spoolÐshaped coil or insulated wire, usually containing a core of soft iron which becomes magnetic when the wire is traversed by an electrical current.

Bobbin and fly frame, a roving machine. Ð Bobbin lace, lace made on a pillow with bobbins; pillow lace.

Bob · biÏnet (?), n. [Bobbin + net.] A kind of cotton lace which is wrought by machines, and not by hand. [Sometimes written bobbin net.]

The English machine—made net is now confined to point net, warp net, and bobbin net, so called from the peculiar construction of the machines by which they are produced.

Tomlinsom.

Bobbin‧work · (?), n. Work woven with bobbins.

Bobbish (?), a. Hearty; in good spirits. [Low, Eng.]

Dickens.

Bobby (?), n. A nickname for a policeman; — from Sir Robert Peel, who remodeled the police force. See Peeler. [Slang, Eng.]

Dickens.

Bob—cher · ry (?), n. A play among children, in which a cherry, hung so as to bob against the mouth, is to be caught with the teeth.

Bobfly · (?), n. (Fishing) The fly at the end of the leader; an end fly.

Bobo‧link · (?), n. (Zo"l.) An American singing bird (Dolichonyx oryzivorus). The male is black and white; the female is brown; — called also, ricebird, reedbird, and Boblincoln.

The happiest bird of our spring is the bobolink.

W. Irving.

Bobsled · (?), Bobsleigh · (?), n. A short sled, mostly used as one of a pair connected by a reach or coupling; also, the compound sled so formed. [U. S.]

The long wagon body set on bobsleds.

W. D. Howells.

Bobstay · (?), n. [Bob + stay.] (Naut.) A rope or chain to confine the bowsprit of a ship downward to the stem or cutwater; — usually in the pl.

Bobtail · (?), n. [Bob + tail.] An animal (as a horse or dog) with a short tail.

Rag, tag, and bobtail, the rabble.

Bobtail · , a. Bobtailed. ½Bobtail cur.

Marryat.

Bobtailed · (?), a. Having the tail cut short, or naturally short; curtailed; as, a bobtailed horse or dog; a bobtailed coat.

Bobwhite · (?), n. (Zo"l.) The common qua? of North America (Colinus, or Ortyx, Virginianus); — so called from its note.

Bob wig · (?). A short wig with bobs or short curls; — called also bobtail wig.

Spectator.

Bocal (?), n. [F.] A cylindrical glass vessel, with a large and short neck.

Bo‧cardo (?), n. [A mnemonic word.] 1. (Logic) A form of syllogism of which the first and third propositions are particular negatives, and the middle term a universal affirmative.

Baroko and Bocardo have been stumbling blocks to the logicians.

Bowen.

A prison; Đ originally the name of the old north gate in Oxford, which was used as a prison. [Eng.]

Latimer.

Bocaïsine (?), n. [F. bocassin, boucassin.] A sort of fine buckram.

Ø Bocca (?), n. [It., mouth.] The round hole in the furnace of a glass manufactory through which the fused glass is taken out.

Craig.

Boce (?), n. [L. box, bocis, Gr. ?, ?.] (Zo"l.) A European fish (Box vulgaris), having a compressed body and bright colors; Đ called also box, and bogue.

Bock beer · (?). [G. bockbier; bock a buck + bier beer; Đ said to be so named from its tendency to cause the drinker to caper like a goat.] A strong beer, originally made in Bavaria. [Also written buck beer.]

Bockellet (?), n. (Zo"l.) A kind of longïwinged hawk; Đ called also bockerel, and bockeret. [Obs.]

Bockey (?), n. [D. bokaal.] A bowl or vessel made from a gourd. [Local, New York]

Bartlett.

Bocking, n. A coarse woolen fabric, used for floor cloths, to cover carpets, etc.; Đ so called from the town of Bocking, in England, where it was first made.

Bockland (?), n. See Bookland.

Boddice (?), n. See Bodick.

Bode (?), v. t. [imp. & p.p. Boded; p. pr. & vb. n. Boding.] [OE. bodien, AS. bodian to announce, tell from bod command; akin to Icel. bo?a to announce, Sw. b†da to announce, portend. ?89. See Bid.] To indicate by signs, as future events; to be the omen of; to portend to presage; to foreshow.

A raven that bodes nothing but mischief.

Goldsmith.

Good onset bodes good end.

Spenser.

Bode, v. i. To foreshow something; to augur.

Whatever now
The omen proved, it boded well to you.

Dryden.

Syn. Đ To forebode; foreshadow; augur; betoken.

Bode, n. 1. An omen; a foreshadowing. [Obs.]

The owl eke, that of death the bode bringeth.

Chaucer.

A bid; an offer. [Obs. or Dial.]

Sir W. Scott

Bode, n. [AS. boda; akin to OFries. boda, AS. bodo, OHG. boto. See Bode, v. t.] A messenger; a herald.
Robertson.
Bode, n. [See Abide.] A stop; a halting; delay. [Obs.]
Bode, imp. & p. p. from Bide. Abode.
There that night they bode.
Tennyson.
Bode, p. p. of Bid. Bid or bidden. [Obs.]
Chaucer.
Bodeful (?), a. Portentous; ominous.
Carlyle.
Bodement (?), n. An omen; a prognostic. [Obs.]
This foolish, dreaming, superstitious girl
Makes all these bodements.
Shak.
Bodge (?), n. A botch; a patch. [Dial.]
Whitlock.
Bodge (?), v. t. [imp. & p.p. Bodged (?).] To botch; to mend clumsily; to patch. [Obs. or Dial.]
Bodge, v. i. See Budge.
Bodian (?), n. (Zo"l.) A large food fish (Diagramma lineatum), native of the East Indies.
Bodice (?), n. [This is properly the plural of body, Oe. bodise a pair of bodies, equiv. to a bodice. Cf. Corset, and see Body.] 1. A kind of under waist stiffened with whalebone, etc., worn esp. by women; a corset; stays.

A close-fitting outer waist or vest forming the upper part of a woman's dress, or a portion of it.

Her bodice half way she unlaced.
Prior.
Bodiced (?), a. Wearing a bodice.
Thackeray.
Bodied (?), a. Having a body; Ð usually in composition; as, able-bodied.
A doe ... not altogether so fat, but very good flesh and good bodied.
Hakluyt.
Bodiless (?), a. 1. Having no body.

Without material form; incorporeal.

Phantoms bodiless and vain.
Swift.
Bodiliness (?), n. Corporeality.
Minsheu.

Bodily (?), a. 1. Having a body or material form; physical; corporeal; consisting of matter.

You are a mere spirit, and have no knowledge of the bodily part of us.
Tatler.

Of or pertaining to the body, in distinction from the mind. ½Bodily defects.

L'Estrange.

Real; actual; put in execution. [Obs.]

Be brought to bodily act.
Shak.
Bodily fear, apprehension of physical injury.
Syn. Ð See Corporal.
Bodily, adv. 1. Corporeally; in bodily form; united with a body or matter; in the body.
For in him dwelleth all the fullness of the Godhead bodily.
Col.ii.9

In respect to, or so as to affect, the entire body of

<— p. 162 —>
mass; entirely; all at once; completely; as, to carry away bodily. ½Leapt bodily below. Lowell. Boding (?), a. Foreshowing; presaging; ominous. Ð Bodingly, adv. Boding, n. A prognostic; an omen; a foreboding. Bodkin (?), n. [OE. boydekyn dagger; of uncertain origin; cf. W. bidog hanger, short sword, Ir. bideog, Gael. biodag.] 1. A dagger. [Obs.] When he himself might his quietus make With a bare bodkin. Shak. 2. (Needlework) An implement of steel, bone, ivory, etc., with a sharp point, for making holes by piercing; a ?tiletto; an eyeleteer. 3. (Print.) A sharp tool, like an awl, used for picking ?ut letters from a column or page in making corrections. 4. A kind of needle with a large eye and a blunt point, for drawing tape, ribbon, etc., through a loop or a hem; a tape needle. Wedged whole ages in a bodkin's eye. Pope. 5. A kind of pin used by women to fasten the hair. To sit, ride, or travel bodkin, to sit closely wedged between two persons. [Colloq.] Thackeray. Bodkin, n. See Baudekin. [Obs.] Shirley. Bodle (?), n. A small Scotch coin worth about one sixth of an English penny. Sir W.Scott. Bodleiïan, a. Of or pertaining to Sir Thomas Bodley, or to the celebrated library at Oxford, founded by him in the sixteenth century. Boïdock (?), n. [Corrupt. fr. bois d'arc.] The Osage orange. [Southwestern U.S.] Bodrage (?), n. [Prob. of Celtic origin: cf. Bordrage.] A raid. [Obs.] Body (?), n.; pl. Bodies (?). [OE. bodi, AS. bodig; akin to OHG. botah. ?257. Cf. Bodice.]

> The material organized substance of an animal, whether living or dead, as distinguished from the spirit, or vital principle; the physical person. Absent in body, but present in spirit. 1 Cor. v. 3 For of the soul the body form doth take. For soul is form, and doth the body make. Spenser.

The trunk, or main part, of a person or animal, as distinguished from the limbs and head; the main, central, or principal part, as of a tree, army, country, etc. Who set the body and the limbs Of this great sport together? Shak. The van of the king's army was led by the general; ... in the body was the king and the prince. Clarendon. Rivers that run up into the body of Italy. Addison.

The real, as opposed to the symbolical; the substance, as opposed to the shadow. Which are a shadow of things to come; but the body is of Christ. Col.ii. 17.

A person; a human being; Ð frequently in composition; as, anybody, nobody. A dry, shrewd kind of a body. W. Irving.

A number of individuals spoken of collectively, usually as united by some common tie, or as organized for some purpose; a collective whole or totality; a corporation; as, a legislative body; a clerical body. A numerous body led unresistingly to the slaughter. Prescott.

A number of things or particulars embodied in a system; a general collection; as, a great body of facts; a body of laws or of divinity.

Any mass or portion of matter; any substance distinct from others; as, a metallic body; a moving body; an a‰oriform body. ½A body of cold air., Huxley. By collision of two bodies, grind The air attrite to fire. Milton.

Amount; quantity; extent.

That part of a garment covering the body, as distinguished from the parts covering the limbs.

The bed or box of a vehicle, on or in which the load is placed; as, a wagon body; a cart body.

(Print.) The shank of a type, or the depth of the shank (by which the size is indicated); as, a nonpareil face on an agate body.

(Geom.) A figure that has length, breadth, and thickness; any solid figure.

Consistency; thickness; substance; strength; as, this color has body; wine of a good body. µ Colors bear a body when they are capable of being ground so fine, and of being mixed so entirely with oil, as to seem only a very thick oil of the same color. After body (Naut.), the part of a ship abaft the dead flat. Ð Body cavity (Anat.), the space between the walls of the body and the inclosed viscera; the c'lum; Ð in mammals, divided by the diaphragm into thoracic and abdominal cavities. Ð Body of a church, the nave. Ð Body cloth; pl. Body cloths; a cloth or blanket for covering horses. Ð Body clothes. (pl.) 1. Clothing for the body; esp. underclothing. 2. Body cloths for horses. [Obs.] Addison. Ð Body coat, a gentleman's dress coat. Ð Body color (Paint.), a pigment that has consistency, thickness, or body, in distinction from a tint or wash. Ð Body of a law (Law), the main and operative part. Ð Body louse (Zo"l.), a species of louse (Pediculus vestimenti), which sometimes infests the human body and clothes. See Grayback. Ð Body plan (Shipbuilding), an end elevation, showing the conbour of the sides of a ship at certain points of her length. Ð Body politic, the collective body of a nation or state as politically organized, or as exercising political functions; also, a corporation. Wharton. As to the persons who compose the body politic or associate themselves, they take collectively the name of ½people., or ½nation.. Bouvier. ÐBody servant, a valet. Ð The bodies seven (Alchemy), the metals corresponding to the planets. [Obs.] Sol gold is, and Luna silver we threpe (=call), Mars yren (=iron), Mercurie quicksilver we clepe, Saturnus lead, and Jupiter is tin, and Venus coper. Chaucer. ÐBody snatcher, one who secretly removes without right or authority a dead body from a grave, vault, etc.; a resurrectionist. Ð Body snatching (Law), the unauthorized removal of a dead body from the grave; usually for the purpose of dissection. Body (?), v.t. [imp. & p.p. Bodied (?); p. pr. & vb. n. Bodying.] To furnish with, or as with, a body; to produce in definite shape; to embody. To body forth, to give from or shape to mentally. Imagination bodies forth The forms of things unknown. Shak. Bodyǐguard · (?), n. 1. A guard to protect or defend the person; a lifeguard.

Retinue; attendance; following. Bp. Porteus. B'ĭotian (?), a. [L. Boeotia, Gr. ?, noted for its moist, thick atmosphere, and the dullness and stupidity of its inhabitants.] Of or pertaining to B'otia; hence, stupid; dull; obtuse. Ð n. A native of B'otia; also, one who is dull and ignorant. Ø Boer (?), n. [D., a farmer. See Boor.] A colonist or farmer in South Africa of Dutch descent. Boes (?), 3d sing. pr. of Behove. Behoves or behooves. [Obs.] Chaucer. Bog (?), n. [Ir. & Gael. bog soft, tender, moist: cf. Ir. bogach bog, moor, marsh, Gael. bogan quagmire.]

A quagmire filled with decayed moss and other vegetable matter; wet spongy ground where a heavy body is apt to sink; a marsh; a morass. Appalled with thoughts of bog, or caverned pit, Of treacherous earth, subsiding where they tread. R. Jago.

A little elevated spot or clump of earth, roots, and grass, in a marsh or swamp. [Local, U. S.] Bog bean. See Buck bean. Ð Bog bumper (bump to make a loud noise), Bog blitter, Bog bluiter, or Bog jumper, the bittern. [Prov.] Ð Bog butter, a hydrocarbon of butterlike consistence found in the peat bogs of Ireland. Ð Bog earth (Min.), a soil composed for the most part of silex and partially decomposed vegetable fiber. P. Cyc. Ð Bog moss. (Bot.) Same as Sphagnum. Ð Bog myrtle (Bot.), the sweet gale. Ð Bog ore. (Min.) (a) An ore of iron found in boggy or swampy land; a variety of brown iron ore, or limonite. (b) Bog manganese, the hydrated peroxide of manganese. Ð Bog rush (Bot.), any rush growing in bogs; saw grass. Ð Bog spavin. See under Spavin. Bog, v. t. [imp. & p.p. Bogged (?); p. pr. & vb. n. Bogging.] To sink, as into a bog; to submerge in a bog; to cause to sink and stick, as in mud and mire. At another time, he was bogged up to the middle in the slough of Lochend. Sir W. Scott. Bogber · ry (?), n. (Bot.) The small cranberry (Vaccinium oxycoccus), which grows in boggy places. Bogey (?), n. A goblin; a bugbear. See Bogy. Boggard (?), n. A bogey. [Local, Eng.] Boggle (?), v. i. [imp. & p.p. Boggled (?); p. pr. & vb. n. Boggling (?).] [See Bogle, n.] 1. To stop or hesitate as if suddenly frightened, or in doubt, or impeded by unforeseen difficulties; to take alarm; to exhibit hesitancy and indecision. We start and boggle at every unusual appearance. Glanvill. Boggling at nothing which serveth their purpose. Barrow.

To do anything awkwardly or unskillfully.

To play fast and loose; to dissemble. Howell. Syn. Ð To doubt; hesitate; shrink; stickle; demur. Boggle, v. t. To embarrass with difficulties; to make a bungle or botch of. [Local, U. S.] Boggler (?), n. One who boggles. Bogglish (?), a. Doubtful; skittish. [Obs.] Boggy (?), a. Consisting of, or containing, a bog or bogs; of the nature of a bog; swampy; as, boggy land. Bogie (?), n. [A dialectic word. N. of Eng. & Scot.] A fourÐwheeled truck, having a certain amount of play around a vertical axis, used to support in part a locomotive on a railway track. Bogle (?), n. [Scot. and North Eng. bogle, bogill, bugill, specter; as a verb, to terrify, fr. W. bwgwl threatening, fear, bwg, bwgan, specter, hobgoblin. Cf. Bug.] A goblin; a specter; a frightful phantom; a bogy; a bugbear. [Written also boggle.] Bogsuck · er (?), n. (Zo"l.) The American woodcock; Ð so called from its feeding among the bogs. Bogtrot · ter (?), n. One who lives in a boggy country; Ð applied in derision to the lowest class of Irish. Halliwell. Bogtrot · ting (?), a. Living among bogs. Bogue (?), v. i. (Naut.) To fall off from the wind; to edge away to leeward; Ð said only of inferior craft. Bogue (?), n. (Zo"l.) The boce; Ð called also bogue bream. See Boce. Bogus (?), a. [Etymol. uncertain.] Spurious; fictitious; sham; Ð a cant term originally applied to counterfeit coin, and hence denoting anything counterfeit. [Colloq. U. S.] Bogus, n. A liquor made of rum and molasses. [Local, U. S.] Bartlett. Bogwood · (?), n. The wood of trees, esp. of oaks, dug up from peat bogs. It is of a shining black or ebony color, and is largely used for making ornaments. Bogy (?), n.; pl. Bogies (?). [See Bogle.] A specter; a hobgoblin; a bugbear. ½Death's heads and bogies.¸ J. H. Newman. [Written also bogey.] There are plenty of such foolish attempts at playing bogy in the history of savages. C. Kingsley. Boĭhea (?), n. [From Wuǐli, pronounced by the Chinese bŭi̇, the name of the hills where this kind of tea is grown.] Bohea tea, an inferior kind of black tea. See under Tea. µ The name was formerly applied to superior kinds of black tea, or to black tea in general. Bo̊hemi̇a (?), n. 1. A country of central Europe.

Fig.: The region or community of social Bohemians. See Bohemian, n., 3. She knew every one who was any one in the land of Bohemia. Compton Reade. Bo̊hemi̇an (?), a. 1. Of or pertaining to Bohemia, or to the language of its ancient inhabitants or their descendants. See Bohemian, n., 2.

Of or pertaining to a social gypsy or ½Bohemian, (see Bohemian, n., 3); vagabond; unconventional; free and easy. [Modern] Hers was a pleasant Bohemian life till she was five and thirty. Blackw. Mag. Artists have abandoned their Bohemian manners and customs nowadays. W. Black. Bohemian chatterer, or Bohemian waxwing (Zo"l.), a small bird of Europe and America (Ampelis garrulus); the waxwing. Ð Bohemian glass, a variety of hard glass of fine quality, made in Bohemia. It is of variable composition, containing usually silica, lime, and potash, rarely soda, but no lead. It is often remarkable for beauty of color. Bo̊hemi̇an (?), n. 1. A native of Bohemia.

The language of the Czechs (the ancient inhabitants of Bohemia), the richest and most developed of the dialects of the Slavic family.

A restless vagabond; Ð originally, an idle stroller or gypsy (as in France) thought to have come from Bohemia; in later times often applied to an adventurer in art or literature, of irregular, unconventional habits, questionable tastes, or free morals. [Modern] µ In this sense from the French boh‚mien, a gypsy; also, a person of irregular habits. She was of a wild, roving nature, inherited from father and mother, who were both Bohemians by taste and circumstances. Thackeray. Bo̊hemi̇ani̇sm (?), n. The characteristic conduct or methods of a Bohemian. [Modern] Ø Bohun upas (?). See Upas. Ø Bo̊i̇ar (?), n. See Boyar. Boil (?), v.i. [imp. & p.p. Boiled (?); p. pr. & vb. n. Boiling.] [OE. boilen, OF. boilir, builir, F. bouillir, fr. L. bullire to be in a bubbling motion, from bulla bubble; akin to Gr. ?, Lith. bumbuls. Cf. Bull an edict, Budge, v., and Ebullition.] 1. To be agitated, or tumultuously moved, as a liquid by the generation and rising of bubbles of steam (or vapor), or of currents produced by heating it to the boiling point; to be in a state of ebullition; as, the water boils.

To be agitated like boiling water, by any other cause than heat; to bubble; to effervesce; as, the boiling waves. He maketh the deep to boil like a pot. Job xii. 31.

To pass from a liquid to an a‰riform state or vapor when heated; as, the water boils away.

To be moved or excited with passion; to be hot or fervid; as, his blood boils with anger. Then boiled my breast with flame and burning wrath. Surrey.

To be in boiling water, as in cooking; as, the potatoes are boiling. To boil away, to vaporize; to evaporate or be evaporated by the action of heat. Ð To boil over, to run over the top of a vessel, as liquid when thrown into violent agitation by heat or other cause of effervescence; to be excited with ardor or passion so as to lose selfÐcontrol. Boil, v.t. 1. To heat to the boiling point, or so as to cause ebullition; as, to boil water.

To form, or separate, by boiling or evaporation; as, to boil sugar or salt.

To subject to the action of heat in a boiling liquid so as to produce some specific effect, as cooking, cleansing, etc.; as, to boil meat; to boil clothes. The stomach cook is for the hall, And boileth meate for them all. Gower.

To steep or soak in warm water. [Obs.] To try whether seeds be old or new, the sense can not inform; but if you boil them in water, the new seeds will sprout sooner. Bacon. To boil down, to reduce in bulk by boiling; as, to boil down sap or sirup. Boil, n. Act or state of boiling. [Colloq.] Boil, n. [Influenced by boil, v. See Beal, Bile.] A hard, painful, inflamed tumor, which, on suppuration, discharges pus, mixed with blood, and discloses a small fibrous mass of dead tissue, called the core. A blind boil, one that suppurates imperfectly, or fails to come to a head. Ð Delhi boil (Med.), a peculiar affection of the skin, probably parasitic in origin, prevailing in India (as among the British troops) and especially at Delhi. Boilaïry (?), n. See Boilery. Boiled (?), a. Dressed or cooked by boiling; subjected to the action of a boiling liquid; as, boiled meat; a boiled dinner; boiled clothes. Boiler (?), n. 1. One who boils.

A vessel in which any thing is boiled. ¶ The word boiler is a generic term covering a great variety of kettles, saucepans, clothes boilers, evaporators, coppers, retorts, etc.

(Mech.) A strong metallic vessel, usually of wrought iron plates riveted together, or a composite structure variously formed, in which steam is generated for driving engines, or for heating, cooking, or other purposes. ¶ The earliest steam boilers were usually spheres or sections of spheres, heated wholly from the outside. Watt used the wagon boiler (shaped like the top of a covered wagon) which is still used with low pressures. Most of the boilers in present use may be classified as plain cylinder boilers, flue boilers, sectional and tubular boilers. Barrel of a boiler, the cylindrical part containing the flues. Ð Boiler plate, Boiler iron, plate or rolled iron of about a quarter to a half inch in thickness, used for making boilers and tanks, for covering ships, etc. Ð Cylinder boiler, one which consists of a single iron cylinder. Ð Flue boilers are usually single shells containing a small

<— p. 163 —>

number of large flues, through which the heat either passes from the fire or returns to the chimney, and sometimes containing a fire box inclosed by water. Ð Locomotive boiler, a boiler which contains an inclosed fire box and a large number of small flues leading to the chimney. Ð Multiflue boiler. Same as Tubular boiler, below. Ð Sectional boiler, a boiler composed of a number of sections, which are usually of small capacity and similar to, and connected with, each other. By multiplication of the sections a boiler of any desired capacity can be built up. Ð Tubular boiler, a boiler containing tubes which form flues, and are surrounded by the water contained in the boiler. See Illust. of Steam boiler, under Steam. Ð Tubulous boiler. See under Tubulous. See Tube, n., 6, and 1st Flue.

Boilerÿ (?), n. [Cf. F. bouillerie.] A place and apparatus for boiling, as for evaporating brine in salt making.

Boiling, a. Heated to the point of bubbling; heaving with bubbles; in tumultuous agitation, as boiling liquid; surging; seething; swelling with heat, ardor, or passion.

Boiling point, the temperature at which a fluid is converted into vapor, with the phenomena of ebullition. This is different for different liquids, and for the same liquid under different pressures. For water, at the level of the sea, barometer 30 in., it is 212 ? Fahrenheit; for alcohol, 172.96?; for ether, 94.8?; for mercury, about 675?. The boiling point of water is lowered one degree Fahrenheit for about 550 feet of ascent above the level of the sea. Ð Boiling spring, a spring which gives out very hot water, or water and steam, often ejecting it with much force; a geyser. Ð To be at the boiling point, to be very angry. Ð To keep the pot boiling, to keep going on actively, as in certain games. [Colloq.]

Boiling, n. 1. The act of ebullition or of tumultuous agitation.

Exposure to the action of a hot liquid.

Boilingly, adv. With boiling or ebullition.
And lakes of bitumen rise boiling higher.
Byron.

Ø Bois d'arc (?). [F., bow wood. So called because used for bows by the Western Indians.] (Bot.) The Osage orange (Maclura aurantiaca).
The bois d'arc seems to be the characteristic growth of the black prairies.
U. S. Census (1880).

Ø Bois dur · ci (?). [F., hardened wood.] A hard, highly polishable composition, made of fine sawdust from hard wood (as rosewood) mixed with blood, and pressed.

Boist (?), n. [OF. boiste, F. boŒte, from the same root as E. box.] A box. [Obs.]

Boisterious (?), a. [OE. boistous; of uncertain origin; cf. W. bwyst wild, savage, wildness, ferocity, bwystus ferocious.] 1. Rough or rude; unbending; unyielding; strong; powerful. [Obs.] ½Boisterous sword.¸ ½Boisterous hand.¸
Shak.

Exhibiting tumultuous violence and fury; acting with noisy turbulence; violent; rough; stormy.

The waters swell before a boisterous storm.
Shak.
The brute and boisterous force of violent men.
Milton.

Noisy; rough; turbulent; as, boisterous mirth; boisterous behavior.

I like not that loud, boisterous man.
Addison.

Vehement; excessive. [R.]

The heat becomes too powerful and boisterous for them.
Woodward.

Syn. Ð Loud; roaring; violent; stormy; turbulent; furious; tumultuous; noisy; impetuous; vehement.

Boisteriously, adv. In a boisterous manner.

Boisteriousness, n. The state or quality of being boisterous; turbulence; disorder; tumultuousness.

Boistous (?), a. Rough or rude; coarse; strong; violent; boisterous; noisy. [Obs.] Chaucer. Ð Boistously, adv. Ð Boistousness, n. [Obs.] Chaucer.

Boïjanus organ (?). [From Bojanus, the discoverer.] (Zo"l.) A glandular organ of bivalve mollusca, serving in part as a kidney.

Bokaĭdam · (?), n. (Zo"l.) See Cerberus.

Boke, v. t. & i. To poke; to thrust. [Obs. or Dial.]

Bolar (?), a. [See Bole clay.] Of or pertaining to bole or clay; partaking of the nature and qualities of bole; clayey.

Ø Bolas (?), n. sing. & pl. [Sp.] A kind of missile weapon consisting of one, two, or more balls of stone, iron, or other material, attached to the ends of a leather cord; Ð used by the Gauchos of South America, and others, for hurling at and entangling an animal.

Bold (?), a. [OE. bald, bold, AS. bald, beald; akin to Icel. ballr, OHG. bald, MHG. balt, D. boud, Goth. bal?ei boldness, It. baldo. In Ger. there remains only bald, adv. soon. Cf. Bawd, n.] 1. Forward to meet danger; venturesome; daring; not timorous or shrinking from risk; brave; courageous.

Throngs of knights and barons bold.
Milton.

Exhibiting or requiring spirit and contempt of danger; planned with courage; daring; vigorous. ½The bold design leased highly.ˌ

Milton.

In a bad sense, too forward; taking undue liberties; over assuming or confident; lacking proper modesty or restraint; rude; impudent.

Thou art too wild, too rude and bold of voice.
Shak.

Somewhat overstepping usual bounds, or conventional rules, as in art, literature, etc.; taking liberties in o composition or expression; as, the figures of an author are bold. ½Bold tales.ˌ

Waller.
The cathedral church is a very bold work.
Addison.

Standing prominently out to view; markedly conspicuous; striking the eye; in high relief.

Shadows in painting ... make the figure bolder.
Dryden.

Steep; abrupt; prominent.

Where the bold cape its warning forehead rears.
Trumbull.

Bold eagle (Zo"l.), an Australian eagle (Aquila audax), which destroys lambs and even the kangaroo. Ð To make bold, to take liberties or the liberty; to venture.

Syn. Ð Courageous; daring; brave; intrepid; fearless; dauntless; valiant; manful; audacious; stouthearted; highÏspirited; adventurous; confident; strenuous; forward; impudent.

Bold (?), v. t. To make bold or daring. [Obs.]

Shak.

Bold, v. i. To be or become bold. [Obs.]

Bolden (?), v. t. [imp. & p.p. Boldened (?).] To make bold; to encourage; to embolden.

Ready speakers, being boldened with their present abilities to say more, ... use less help of diligence and study.

Ascham.

BoldÐfaced · (?), a. 1. Somewhat impudent; lacking modesty; as, a boldÐfaced woman.

I have seen enough to confute all the boldÐfaced atheists of this age.

Bramhall.

(Print.) Having a conspicuous or heavy face.

µ This line is boldÐfaced nonpareil.?

Boldly, adv. [AS. bealdlÆce.] In a bold manner.

Boldness, n. The state or quality of being bold.

Syn. Ð Courage; bravery; intrepidity; dauntlessness; hardihood; assurance.

Ø Boldo (?), Ø Boldu (?), } n. (Bot.) A fragrant evergreen shrub of Chili (Peumus Boldus). The bark is used in tanning, the wood for making charcoal, the leaves in medicine, and the drupes are eaten.

Bole (?), n. [OE. bole, fr. Icel. bolr; akin to Sw. b†l, Dan. bul, trunk, stem of a tree, G. bohle a thick plank or board; cf. LG. boll round. Cf. Bulge.] The trunk or stem of a tree, or that which is like it.

Enormous elmÏtree boles did stoop and lean.

Tennyson.

Bole, n. [Etym. doubtful.] An aperture, with a wooden shutter, in the wall of a house, for giving, occasionally, air or light; also, a small closet. [Scot.]

Open the bole wi'speed, that I may see if this be the right Lord Geraldin.

Sir W. Scott.

Bole, n. A measure. See Boll, n., 2.

Mortimer.

Bole, n. [Gr. ? a clod or lump of earth: cf. F. bol, and also L. bolus morsel. Cf. Bolus.] 1. Any one of several varieties of friable earthy clay, usually colored more or less strongly red by oxide of iron, and used to color and adulterate various substances. It was formerly used in medicine. It is composed essentially of hydrous silicates of alumina, or more rarely of magnesia. See Clay, and Terra alba.

A bolus; a dose.

Coleridge.

Armenian bole. See under Armenian. Đ Bole Armoniac, or Armoniak, Armenian bole. [Obs.]

Chaucer.

Boïlection (?), n. (Arch.) A projecting molding round a panel. Same as Bilection.

Gwilt.

Ø Boïlero (?), n. [Sp.] (Mus.) A Spanish dance, or the lively music which accompanies it.

Boïletic (?), a. (Chem.) Pertaining to, or obtained from, the Boletus.

Boletic acid, an acid obtained from the Boletus fomentarius, variety pseudoligniarius. Same as Fumaric acid.

Ø Boïletus (?), n. [L. boletus, Gr. ?.] (Bot.) A genus of fungi having the under side of the pileus or cap composed of a multitude of fine separate tubes. A few are edible, and others very poisonous.

Boley, Bolye (?), n. Same as Booly.

Bolide (?), n. [F. See Bolis.] A kind of meteor; a bolis.

Ø Bolis, n. [L., fr. Gr. ? missile, arrow, fr. ? to throw.] A meteor or brilliant shooting star, followed by a train of light or sparks; esp. one which explodes.

Boïlivilan (?), a. Of or pertaining to Bolivia. Đ n. A native of Bolivia.

Boll (?), n. [OE. bolle boll, bowl, AS. bolla. See Bowl a vessel.] 1. The pod or capsule of a plant, as of flax or cotton; a pericarp of a globular form.

> A Scotch measure, formerly in use: for wheat and beans it contained four Winchester bushels; for oats, barley, and potatoes, six bushels. A boll of meal is 140 lbs. avoirdupois. Also, a measure for salt of two bushels. [Sometimes spelled bole.]

Boll, v. i. [imp. & p.p. Bolled (?).] To form a boll or seed vessel; to go to seed.

The barley was in the ear, and the flax was bolled.

Ex. ix. 31.

Bollandïists (?), n. pl. The Jesuit editors of the ½Acta Sanctorum", or Lives of the Saints; Đ named from John Bolland, who began the work.

Bollard (?), n. [Cf. Bole the stem of a tree, and Pollard.] An upright wooden or iron post in a boat or on a dock, used in veering or fastening ropes.

Bollard timber (Naut.), a timber, also called a knighthead, rising just within the stem in a ship, on either side of the bowsprit, to secure its end.

Bollen (?), a. See Boln, a.

Bolling (?), n. [Cf. Bole stem of a tree, and Poll, v. t.] A tree from which the branches have been cut; a pollard.

Bollworm · (?), n. (Zo"l.) The larva of a moth (Heliothis armigera) which devours the bolls or unripe pods of the cotton plant, often doing great damage to the crops.

Boln (?), v. i. [OE. bolnen, bollen; cf. Dan. bulne. Cf. Bulge.] To swell; to puff.
Holland.
Boln (?), Bollen (?), } a. Swollen; puffed out.
Thin, and boln out like a sail.
B. Jonson.
Bologna (?), n. 1. A city of Italy which has given its name to various objects.

A Bologna sausage.

Bologna sausage [It. salsiccia di Bologna], a large sausage made of bacon or ham, veal, and pork, chopped fine and inclosed in a skin. Đ Bologna stone (Min.), radiated barite, or barium sulphate, found in roundish masses composed of radiating fibers, first discovered near Bologna. It is phosphorescent when calcined. Đ Bologna vial, a vial of unannealed glass which will fly into pieces when its surface is scratched by a hard body, as by dropping into it a fragment of flint; whereas a bullet may be dropped into it without injury.

Boïlo · gnese (?), a. Of or pertaining to Bologna. Đ n. A native of Bologna.

Bolognese school (Paint.), a school of painting founded by the Carracci, otherwise called the Lombard or Eclectic school, the object of which was to unite the excellences of the preceding schools.

Bolognian (?), a. & n. Bolognese.

Bolognian stone. See Bologna stone, under Bologna.

Bolomeïter (?), n. [Gr. ? a stroke, ray + ïmeter.] (Physics) An instrument for measuring minute quantities of radiant heat, especially in different parts of the spectrum; Đ called also actinic balance, thermic balance.
S. P. Langley.

Bolster (?), n. [AS. bolster; akin to Icel. b?lstr, Sw. & Dan. bolster, OHG. bolstar, polstar, G. polster; from the same root as E. bole stem, bowl hollow vessel. Cf. Bulge, Poltroon.] 1. A long pillow or cushion, used to support the head of a person lying on a bed; Đ generally laid under the pillows.

And here I'll fling the pillow, there the bolster,
This way the coverlet, another way the sheets.
Shak.

A pad, quilt, or anything used to hinder pressure, support any part of the body, or make a bandage sit easy upon a wounded part; a compress.

This arm shall be a bolster for thy head.
Gay.

Anything arranged to act as a support, as in various forms of mechanism, etc.

(Saddlery) A cushioned or a piece part of a saddle.

(Naut.) (a) A cushioned or a piece of soft wood covered with tarred canvas, placed on the trestletrees and against the mast, for the collars of the shrouds to rest on, to prevent chafing. (b) Anything used to prevent chafing.

A plate of iron or a mass of wood under the end of a bridge girder, to keep the girder from resting directly on the abutment.

A transverse bar above the axle of a wagon, on which the bed or body rests.

The crossbeam forming the bearing piece of the body of a railway car; the central and principal cross beam of a car truck.

(Mech.) the perforated plate in a punching machine on which anything rests when being punched.

(Cutlery) (a) That part of a knife blade which abuts upon the end of the handle. (b) The metallic end of a pocketknife handle.

G. Francis.

(Arch.) The rolls forming the ends or sides of the Ionic capital.

G. Francis.

(Mil.) A block of wood on the carriage of a siege gun, upon which the breech of the gun rests when arranged for transportation. [See Illust. of Gun carriage.]

Bolster work (Arch.), members which are bellied or curved outward like cushions, as in friezes of certain classical styles.

Bolster, v. t. [imp. & p.p. Bolstered (?); p. pr. & vb. n. Bolstering.] 1. To support with a bolster or pillow.

S. Sharp.

To support, hold up, or maintain with difficulty or unusual effort; Ð often with up.

To bolster baseness.
Drayton.
Shoddy inventions designed to bolster up a factitious pride.
Compton Reade.
Bolstered (?), a. 1. Supported; upheld.

Swelled out.

BolsterÏer (?), n. A supporter.

Bolt (?), n. [AS. bolt; akin to Icel. bolti, Dan. bolt, D. bout, OHG. bolz, G. bolz, bolzen; of uncertain origin.] 1. A shaft or missile intended to be shot from a crossbow or catapult, esp. a short, stout, bluntÐheaded arrow; a quarrel; an arrow, or that which resembles an arrow; a dart.

Look that the crossbowmen lack not bolts.
Sir W. Scott.
A fool's bolt is soon shot.
Shak.

Lightning; a thunderbolt.

A strong pin, of iron or other material, used to fasten or hold something in place, often having a head at one end and screw thread cut upon the other end.

A sliding catch, or fastening, as for a door or gate; the portion of a lock which is shot or withdrawn by the action of the key.

An iron to fasten the legs of a prisoner; a shackle; a fetter. [Obs.]

> Away with him to prison!
> lay bolts enough upon him.
> Shak.

A compact package or roll of cloth, as of canvas or silk, often containing about forty yards.

A bundle, as of oziers.

Bolt auger, an auger of large size; an auger to make holes for the bolts used by shipwrights. Ð Bolt and nut, a metallic pin with a head formed upon one end, and a movable piece (the nut) screwed upon a thread cut upon the other end. See B, C, and D, in illust. above.

See Tap bolt, Screw bolt, and Stud bolt.

Bolt, v. t. [imp. & p.p. Bolted; p. pr. & vb. n. Bolting.] 1. To shoot; to discharge or drive forth.

<— p. 164 —>

To utter precipitately; to blurt or throw out.

> I hate when Vice can bolt her arguments.
> Milton.

To swallow without chewing; as, to bolt food.

(U. S. Politics) To refuse to support, as a nomination made by a party to which one has belonged or by a caucus in which one has taken part.

(Sporting) To cause to start or spring forth; to dislodge, as conies, rabbits, etc.

To fasten or secure with, or as with, a bolt or bolts, as a door, a timber, fetters; to shackle; to restrain.

> Let tenfold iron bolt my door.
> Langhorn.
> Which shackles accidents and bolts up change.
> Shak.

Bolt (?), v. i. 1. To start forth like a bolt or arrow; to spring abruptly; to come or go suddenly; to dart; as, to bolt out of the room.

> This Puck seems but a dreaming dolt, ...
> And oft out of a bush doth bolt.
> Drayton.

To strike or fall suddenly like a bolt.

His cloudless thunder bolted on their heads.
Milton.

To spring suddenly aside, or out of the regular path; as, the horse bolted.

(U.S. Politics) To refuse to support a nomination made by a party or a caucus with which one has been connected; to break away from a party.

Bolt, adv. In the manner of a bolt; suddenly; straight; unbendingly.
[He] came bolt up against the heavy dragoon.
Thackeray.
Bolt upright.   (a) Perfectly upright; perpendicular; straight up; unbendingly erect. Addison. (b) On the back at full length. [Obs.]
Chaucer.
Bolt, n. [From Bolt, v. i.] 1. A sudden spring or start; a sudden spring aside; as, the horse made a bolt.

A sudden flight, as to escape creditors.

This gentleman was so hopelessly involved that he contemplated a bolt to America Ð or anywhere.
Compton Reade.

(U. S. Politics) A refusal to support a nomination made by the party with which one has been connected; a breaking away from one's party.

Bolt, v. t. [imp. & p.p. Bolted; p. pr. & vb. n. Bolting.] [OE. bolten, boulten, OF. buleter, F. bluter, fr. Ll. buletare, buratare, cf. F. bure coarse woolen stuff; fr. L. burrus red. See Borrel, and cf. Bultel.]

To sift or separate the coarser from the finer particles of, as bran from flour, by means of a bolter; to separate, assort, refine, or purify by other means.

He now had bolted all the flour.
Spenser.
Ill schooled in bolted language.
Shak.

To separate, as if by sifting or bolting; Ð with out.

Time and nature will bolt out the truth of things.
L'Estrange.

(Law) To discuss or argue privately, and for practice, as cases at law.

Jacob.
To bolt to the bran, to examine thoroughly, so as to separate or discover everything important.
Chaucer.

This bolts the matter fairly to the bran.

Harte.

The report of the committee was examined and sifted and bolted to the bran.

Burke.

Bolt, n. A sieve, esp. a long fine sieve used in milling for bolting flour and meal; a bolter.

B. Jonson.

Boltel (?), n. See Boultel.

Bolter (?), n. One who bolts; esp.: (a) A horse which starts suddenly aside. (b) A man who breaks away from his party.

Bolter, n. 1. One who sifts flour or meal.

An instrument or machine for separating bran from flour, or the coarser part of meal from the finer; a sieve.

Bolter, n. A kind of fishing line. See Boulter.

Bolthead · (?), n. 1. (Chem.) A long, straightnecked, glass vessel for chemical distillations; Ð called also a matrass or receiver.

The head of a bolt.

Bolting, n. A darting away; a starting off or aside.

Bolting, n. 1. A sifting, as of flour or meal.

(Law) A private arguing of cases for practice by students, as in the Inns of Court. [Obs.]

Bolting cloth, wire, hair, silk, or other sieve cloth of different degrees of fineness; Ð used by millers for sifting flour. McElrath. Ð Bolting hutch, a bin or tub for the bolted flour or meal; (fig.) a receptacle.

Boltonïite (?), n. (Min.) A granular mineral of a grayish or yellowish color, found in Bolton, Massachusetts. It is a silicate of magnesium, belonging to the chrysolite family.

Boltrope · (?), n. (Naut.) A rope stitched to the edges of a sail to strengthen the sail.

Boltsprit · (?), n. [A corruption of bowsprit.] (Naut.) See Bowsprit.

Bolty (?), n. (Zo"l.) An edible fish of the Nile (genus Chromis). [Written also bulti.]

Bolus (?), n.; pl. Boluses (?). [L. bolus bit, morsel; cf. G. ? lump of earth. See Bole, n., clay.] A rounded mass of anything, esp. a large pill.

Bom (?), n. (Zo"l.) A large American serpent, so called from the sound it makes.

Bomb (?), n. [F. bombe bombshell, fr. L. bombus a humming or buzzing noise, Gr. ?.]

A great noise; a hollow sound. [Obs.]

A pillar of iron ... which if you had struck, would make ... a great bomb in the chamber beneath.

Bacon.

(Mil.) A shell; esp. a spherical shell, like those fired from mortars. See Shell.

A bomb ketch.

Bomb chest (Mil.), a chest filled with bombs, or only with gunpowder, placed under ground, to cause destruction by its explosion. Đ Bomb ketch, Bomb vessel (Naut.), a small ketch or vessel, very strongly built, on which mortars are mounted to be used in naval bombardments; Đ called also mortar vessel. Đ Bomb lance, a lance or harpoon with an explosive head, used in whale fishing. Đ Volcanic bomb, a mass of lava of a spherical or pear shape. ½I noticed volcanic bombs.

Darwin.

Bomb, v. t. To bombard. [Obs.]

Prior.

Bomb, v. i. [Cf. Boom.] To sound; to boom; to make a humming or buzzing sound. [Obs.]

B. Jonson.

Bombace (?), n. [OF.] Cotton; padding. [Obs.]

Bombard (?), n. [F. bombarde, LL. bombarda, fr. L. bombus + Ïard. Cf. Bumper, and see Bomb.] 1. (Gun.) A piece of heavy ordnance formerly used for throwing stones and other ponderous missiles. It was the earliest kind of cannon.

They planted in divers places twelve great bombards, wherewith they threw huge stones into the air, which, falling down into the city, might break down the houses.

Knolles.

A bombardment. [Poetic & R.]

J. Barlow.

A large drinking vessel or can, or a leather bottle, for carrying liquor or beer. [Obs.]

Yond same black cloud, yond huge one, looks like a foul bombard that would shed his liquor.

Shak.

pl. Padded breeches. [Obs.]

Bombard phrase, inflated language; bombast. [Obs.]

B. Jonson.

Bombard (?), n. [OE. bombarde, fr. F. bombarde.] (Mus.) See Bombardo. [Obs.]

Bom‧bard (?), v. t. [imp. & p.p. Bombarded; p. pr. & vb. n. Bombarding.] To attack with bombards or with artillery; especially, to throw shells, hot shot, etc., at or into.

Next, she means to bombard Naples.

Burke.

His fleet bombarded and burnt down Dieppe.

Wood.

Bom‧bar‧dier (?), n. [F. bombardier.] (Mil.) (a) One who used or managed a bombard; an artilleryman; a gunner. [Archaic] (b) A noncommissioned officer in the British artillery.

Bombardier beetle (Zo"l.), a kind of beetle (Brachinus crepitans), so called because, when disturbed, it makes an explosive discharge of a pungent and acrid vapor from its anal glands. The name is applied to other related species, as the B. displosor, which can produce ten or twelve explosions successively. The common American species is B. fumans.

Bombard‧man (?), n. One who carried liquor or beer in a can or bombard. [Obs.]

They ... made room for a bombardman that brought bouge for a country lady.

B. Jonson.

Bom‧bardment (?), n. [F. bombardement.] An attack upon a fortress or fortified town, with shells, hot shot, rockets, etc.; the act of throwing bombs and shot into a town or fortified place.

Ø Bom‧bardo (?), Bom‧bardon (?), } n. [It. bombardo.] (Mus.) Originally, a deep‧toned instrument of the oboe or bassoon family; thence, a bass reed stop on the organ. The name bombardon is now given to a brass instrument, the lowest of a saxhorns, in tone resembling the ophicleide.

Grove.

Bom‧bar‧sine (?), n. Same as Bombazine.

Bombast (?), n. [OF. bombace cotton, LL. bombax cotton, bombasium a doublet of cotton; hence, padding, wadding, fustian. See Bombazine.] 1. Originally, cotton, or cotton wool. [Obs.]

A candle with a wick of bombast.

Lupton.

Cotton, or any soft, fibrous material, used as stuffing for garments; stuffing; padding. [Obs.]

How now, my sweet creature of bombast!

Shak.

Doublets, stuffed with four, five, or six pounds of bombast at least.

Stubbes.

Fig.: High‧sounding words; an inflated style; language above the dignity of the occasion; fustian.

Yet noisy bombast carefully avoid.
Dryden.

Bombast, a. High‐sounding; inflated; big without meaning; magniloquent; bombastic.

[He] evades them with a bombast circumstance,
Horribly stuffed with epithets of war.
Shak.

Nor a tall metaphor in bombast way.
Cowley.

Bom·bast (?), v. t. To swell or fill out; to pad; to inflate. [Obs.]

Not bombasted with words vain ticklish ears to feed.
Drayton.

Bom·bastic (?), Bom·bastic·al (?), a. Characterized by bombast; highsounding; inflated. ‐ Bom·bastic·al·ly, adv.

A theatrical, bombastic, windy phraseology.
Burke.

Syn. ‐ Turgid; tumid; pompous; grandiloquent.

Bombast·ry (?), n. Swelling words without much meaning; bombastic language; fustian.

Bombastry and buffoonery, by nature lofty and light, soar highest of all.
Swift.

Ø Bombax (?), n. [LL., cotton. See Bombast, n.] (Bot.) A genus of trees, called also the silkcotton tree; also, a tree of the genus Bombax.

Bom·ba·zet Bom·ba·zette } (?), n. [Cf. Bombazine.] A sort of thin woolen cloth. It is of various colors, and may be plain or twilled.

Bom·ba·zine (?), n. [F. bombasin, LL. bombacinium, bambacinium, L. bombycinus silken, bombycinum a silk or cotton texture, fr. bombyx silk, silkworm, Gr. ?. Cf. Bombast, Bombycinous.] A twilled fabric for dresses, of which the warp is silk, and the weft worsted. Black bombazine has been much used for mourning garments. [Sometimes spelt bombasin, and bombasine.]
Tomlinson.

Bombic (?), a. [L. bombyx silk, silkworm: cf. F. bombique.] Pertaining to, or obtained from, the silkworm; as, bombic acid.

Bombi·llate (?), v. i. [LL. bombilare, for L. bombitare. See Bomb, n.] To hum; to buzz. [R.]

Bom·bil·lation (?), n. A humming sound; a booming.

To ... silence the bombilation of guns.
Sir T. Browne.

Bombi·nate (?), v. i. To hum; to boom.

Bom·bi·nation (?), n. A humming or buzzing.

Bombo·lo (?), n.; pl. Bomboloes (?). [Cf. It. bombola a pitcher.] A thin spheroidal glass retort or flask, used in the sublimation of camphor. [Written also bumbelo, and bumbolo.]

Bombproof· (?), a. Secure against the explosive force of bombs. Đ n. A structure which heavy shot and shell will not penetrate.

Bombshell· (?), n. A bomb. See Bomb, n.

Bomĭbycid (?), a. (Zo"l.) Like or pertaining to the genus Bombyx, or the family Bombycid'.

Bomĭbycĭlnous (?), a. [L. bombycinus. See Bombazine.] 1. Silken; made of silk. [Obs.]

Coles.

<small>Being of the color of the silkworm; transparent with a yellow tint.</small>

E. Darwin.

Bomĭbylĭlous (?), a. [L. bombylius a bumblebee, Gr. ?.] Buzzing, like a bumblebee; as, the bombylious noise of the horse fly. [Obs.]

Derham.

Ø Bombyx (?), n. [L., silkworm. See Bombazine.] (Zo"l.) A genus of moths, which includes the silkworm moth. See Silkworm.

Ø Bon (?), a. [F., fr. L. bonus.] Good; valid as security for something.

BonĐacĭcord (?), n. Good will; good fellowship; agreement. [Scot.]

Ø Bona fide (?). [L.] In or with good faith; without fraud or deceit; real or really; actual or actually; genuine or genuinely; as, you must proceed bona fide; a bona fide purchaser or transaction.

Boĭnair (?), a. [OE., also bonere, OF. bonnaire, Cotgr., abbrev. of debonnaire. See Debonair.] Gentle; courteous; complaisant; yielding. [Obs.]

Boĭnanza (?), n. [Sp., prop. calm., fair weather, prosperity, fr. L. bonus good.] In mining, a rich mine or vein of silver or gold; hence, anything which is a mine of wealth or yields a large income. [Colloq. U. S.]

Bo · naĭparteĭan (?), a. Of or pertaining to Napoleon Bonaparte or his family.

Bonaĭpart · ism (?), n. The policy of Bonaparte or of the Bonapartes.

Bonaĭpart · ist, n. One attached to the policy or family of Bonaparte, or of the Bonapartes.

Ø Bona per · iĭtura (?). [L.] (Law) Perishable goods.

Bouvier.

Ø Bona roba (?). [It., prop. ½good stuff.ͺ] A showy wanton; a courtesan.

Shak

Boĭnasus (?), Boĭnassus (?), n. [L. bonasus, Gr. ?, ?.] (Zo"l.) The aurochs or European bison. See Aurochs.

Ø Bonbon· (?), n. [F. bonbon, fr. bon bon very good, a superlative by reduplication, fr. bon good.] Sugar confectionery; a sugarplum; hence, any dainty.

Bonce (?), n. [Etymol. unknown.] A boy's game played with large marbles.

Ø Bon·chr,·tien (?), n. [F., good Christian.] A name given to several kinds of pears. See Bartlett.

Boncillate (?), n. [Empirical trade name.] A substance composed of ground bone, mineral matters, etc., hardened by pressure, and used for making billiard balls, boxes, etc.

Bond (?), n. [The same word as band. Cf. Band, Bend.] 1. That which binds, ties, fastens,or confines, or by which anything is fastened or bound, as a cord, chain, etc.; a band; a ligament; a shackle or a manacle.

Gnawing with my teeth my bonds in sunder,
I gained my freedom.
Shak.

pl. The state of being bound; imprisonment; captivity, restraint. ½This man doeth nothing worthy of death or of bonds.

Acts xxvi.

A binding force or influence; a cause of union; a uniting tie; as, the bonds of fellowship.

A people with whom I have no tie but the common bond of mankind.
Burke.

Moral or political duty or obligation.

I love your majesty
According to my bond, nor more nor less.
Shak.

(Law) A writing under seal, by which a person binds himself, his heirs, executors, and administrators, to pay a certain sum on or before a future day appointed. This is a single bond. But usually a condition is added, that, if the obligor shall do a certain act, appear at a certain place, conform to certain rules, faithfully perform certain duties, or pay a certain sum of money, on or before a time specified, the obligation shall be void; otherwise it shall remain in full force. If the condition is not performed, the bond becomes forfeited, and the obligor and his heirs are liable to the payment of the whole sum.

Bouvier. Wharton.

An instrument (of the nature of the ordinary legal bond) made by a government or a corporation for purpose of borrowing money; as, a government, city, or railway bond.

The state of goods placed in a bonded warehouse till the duties are paid; as, merchandise in bond.

(Arch.) The union or tie of the several stones or bricks forming a wall. The bricks may be arranged for this purpose in several different ways, as in English or block bond (Fig. 1), where one course consists of bricks with their ends toward the face of the wall, called headers, and the next course of bricks with their lengths parallel to the face of the wall, called stretchers; Flemish bond (Fig.2), where each course consists of headers and stretchers alternately, so laid as always to break joints; Cross bond, which differs from the English by the change of the second stretcher line so that its joints come in the middle of the first, and the same position of stretchers comes back every fifth line; Combined cross and English bond, where the inner part of the wall is laid in the one method, the outer in the other.

<— p. 165 —>

(Chem.) A unit of chemical attraction; s, oxygen has two bonds of affinity. It is often represented in graphic formul' by a short line or dash. See Diagram of Benzene nucleus, and Valence.

Arbitration bond. See under Arbitration. Ð Bond crediter (Law), a creditor whose debt is secured by a bond. Blackstone. Ð Bond debt (Law), a debt contracted under the obligation of a bond. Burrows. Ð Bond (or lap) of a slate, the distance between the top of one slate and the bottom or drip of the second slate above, i. e., the space which is covered with three thicknesses; also, the distance between the nail of the under slate and the lower edge of the upper slate. Ð Bond timber, timber worked into a wall to tie or strengthen it longitudinally.

Syn. Ð Chains; fetters; captivity; imprisonment.

Bond (?), v. t. [imp. & p.p. Bonded; p. pr. & vb. n. Bonding.] 1. To place under the conditions of a bond; to mortgage; to secure the payment of the duties on (goods or merchandise) by giving a bond.

(Arch.) To dispose in building, as the materials of a wall, so as to secure solidity.

Bond, n. [OE. bond, bonde, peasant, serf, AS. bonda, bunda, husband, bouseholder, from Icel. b?ndi husbandman, for b?andi, fr. b?a to dwell. See Boor, Husband.] A xassal or serf; a slave. [Obs. or Archaic]

Bond, a. In a state of servitude or slavery; captive.

By one Spirit are we all baptized .. whether we be Jews or Bentiles, whether we be bond or free.

1 Cor. xii. 13.

Bondage (?), n. [LL. bondagium. See Bond, a.]

The state of being bound; condition of being under restraint; restraint of personal liberty by compulsion; involuntary servitude; slavery; captivity.

The King, when he designed you for my guard,
Resolved he would not make my bondage hard.
Dryden.

Obligation; tie of duty.

He must resolve by no means to be ... brought under the bondage of onserving oaths.

South.

(Old Eng. Law) Villenage; tenure of land on condition of doing the meanest services for the owner.

Syn. Ð Thralldom; bond service; imprisonment.

Bondaïger (?), n. A field worker, esp. a woman who works in the field. [Scot.]

Ø Bondar (?), n. [Native name.] (Zo"l.) A small quadruped of Bengal (Paradoxurus bondar), allied to the genet; Ð called also musk cat.

Bonded (?), a. Placed under, or covered by, a bond, as for the payment of duties, or for conformity to coertain regulations.

Bonded goods, goods placed in a bonded warehouse; goods, for the duties on which bonds are given at the customhouse. Ð Bonded warehouse, a warehouse in which goods on which the duties are unpaid are stored under bond and in the joint custody of the importer, or his agent, and the customs officers.

Bonder (?), n. 1. One who places goods under bond or in a bonded warehouse.

(Masonry) A bonding stone or brick; a bondstone.

Bonder, n. [Norwegian bonde.] A freeholder on a small scale. [Norway] Emerson.

Bondhold · er (?), n. A person who holds the bonds of a public or private corporation for the payment of money at a certain time.

Bondmaid · (?), n. [Bond, a. or n. + maid.] A female slave, or one bound to service without wages, as distinguished from a hired servant.

Bondman (?), n.; pl. Bondmen (?). [Bond, a. or n. + man.] 1. A man slave, or one bound to service without wages. ½To enfranchise bondmen.„ Macaulay.

(Old Eng. Law) A villain, or tenant in villenage.

Bond serv · ant (?). A slave; one who is bound to service without wages.

If thy brother ... be waxen poor, and be sold unto thee; thou shalt not compel him to serve as a bond servant: but as an hired servant.

Lev. xxv. 39, 40.

Bond serv · ice (?). The condition of a bond servant; sevice without wages; slavery.

Their children ... upon those did Solomon levy a tribute of bond service.

1 Kings ix. 21.

Bondslave · (?), n. A person in a state of slavery; one whose person and liberty are subjected to the authority of a master.

Bondsman (?), n.; pl. Bondsmen . [Bond, a. or n. + man.] 1. A slave; a villain; a serf; a bondman.

Carnal, greedy people, without such a precept, would have no mercy upon their poor bondsmen.

Derham.

(Law) A surety; one who is bound, or who gives security, for another.

Bondstone · (?), n. [Bond, n. + stone.] (Masonry) A stone running through a wall from one face to another, to bind it together; a binding stone.

Bondswom · an (?), n. See Bondwoman.

Ø Bonduc (?), n. [F. bonduc, fr. Ar. bunduq hazel nut, filbert nut.] (Bot.) See Nicker tree.

Bondwom · an (?), n.; pl. Bondwomen (?). [Bond, a. or n. + woman.] A woman who is a slave, or in bondage.

He who was of the bondwoman.

Gal. iv. 23.

Bone (?), n. [OE. bon, ban, AS. b¾n; akin to Icel. bein, Sw. ben, Dan. & D. been, G. bein bone, leg; cf. Icel. beinn straight.] 1. (Anat.) The hard, calcified tissue of the skeleton of vertebrate animals, consisting very largely of calcic carbonate, calcic phosphate, and gelatine; as, blood and bone.

μ Even in the hardest parts of bone there are many minute cavities containing living matter and connected by minute canals, some of which connect with larger canals through which blood vessels ramify.

One of the pieces or parts of an animal skeleton; as, a rib or a thigh bone; a bone of the arm or leg; also, any fragment of bony substance. (pl.) The frame or skeleton of the body.

Anything made of bone, as a bobbin for weaving bone lace.

pl. Two or four pieces of bone held between the fingers and struck together to make a kind of music.

pl. Dice.

Whalebone; hence, a piece of whalebone or of steel for a corset.

Fig.: The framework of anything.

A bone of contention, a subject of contention or dispute. Ð A bone to pick, something to investigate, or to busy one's self about; a dispute to be settled (with some one). Ð Bone ash, the residue from calcined bones; Ð used for making cupels, and for cleaning jewelry. Ð Bone black (Chem.), the black, carbonaceous substance into which bones are converted by calcination in close vessels; Ð called also animal charcoal. It is used as a decolorizing material in filtering sirups, extracts, etc., and as a black pigment. See Ivory black, under Black. Ð Bone cave, a cave in which are found bones of extinct or recent animals, mingled sometimes with the works and bones of man. Am. Cyc. Ð Bone dust, ground or pulverized bones, used as a fertilizer. Ð Bone earth (Chem.), the earthy residuum after the calcination of bone, consisting chiefly of phosphate of calcium. Ð Bone lace, a lace made of linen thread, so called because woven with bobbins of bone. Ð Bone oil, an oil obtained by, heating bones (as in the manufacture of bone black), and remarkable for containing the nitrogenous bases, pyridine and quinoline, and their derivatives; Ð also called Dippel's oil. Ð Bone setter. Same as Bonesetter. See in the Vocabulary. Ð Bone shark (Zo"l.), the basking shark. Ð Bone spavin. See under Spavin. Ð Bone turquoise, fossil bone or tooth of a delicate blue color, sometimes used as an imitation of true turquoise. Ð Bone whale (Zo"l.), a right whale. Ð To be upon the bones of, to attack. [Obs.] Ð To make no bones, to make no scruple; not to hesitate. [Low] Ð To pick a bone with, to quarrel with, as dogs quarrel over a bone; to settle a disagreement. [Colloq.]

Bone (?), v. t. [imp. & p.p. Boned (?); p. pr. & vb. n. Boning.] 1. To withdraw bones from the flesh of, as in cookery. ½To bone a turkey.¸

Soyer.

To put whalebone into; as, to bone stays.

Ash.

To fertilize with bone.

To steal; to take possession of. [Slang]

Bone, v. t. [F. bornoyer to look at with one eye, to sight, fr. borgne oneÐeyed.] To sight along an object or set of objects, to see if it or they be level or in line, as in carpentry, masonry, and surveying.

Knight.

Joiners, etc., bone their work with two straight edges. W.

M. Buchanan.

Boneache · (?), n. Pain in the bones.

Shak.

Boneblack · (?), n. See Bone black, under Bone, n.

Boned (?), a. 1. Having (such) bones; Ð used in composition; as, bigÐboned; strongÐboned.

No bigÐboned men framed of the Cyclops' size.

Shak.

Deprived of bones; as, boned turkey or codfish.

Manured with bone; as, boned land.

Bonedog · (?), n. (Zo"l.) The spiny dogfish.

Bonefish · (?), n. (Zo"l.) See Ladyfish.

Boneless, a. Without bones. ½Boneless gums.¸

Shak.

Boneset · (?), n. (Bot.) A medicinal plant, the thoroughwort (Eupatorium perfoliatum). Its properties are diaphoretic and tonic.

Bonesetῐter (?), n. One who sets broken or dislocated bones; Ð commonly applied to one, not a regular surgeon, who makes an occupation of setting bones. Ð **Bonesetῐting**, n.

Boneshaw (?), n. (Med.) Sciatica. [Obs.]

Boῐnetta (?), n. See Bonito.

Sir T. Herbert.

Bonfire · (?), n. [OE. bonefire, banefire, orig. a fire of bones; bone + fire; but cf. also Prov. E. bun a dry stalk.] A large fire built in the open air, as an expression of public joy and exultation, or for amusement.

Full soon by bonfire and by bell,
We learnt our liege was passing well.

Gay.

Bongrace · (?), n. [F. bon good + grfce grace, charm.] A projecting bonnet or shade to protect the complexion; also, a wideÐbrimmed hat. [Obs.]

Ø **Bon** · **hoῐmie**, Ø **Bon** · **homῐmie** (?), n. [F.] good nature; pleasant and easy manner.

Boniῐbell (?), n. See Bonnibel. [Obs.]

Spenser.

Boniῐface (?), n. [From the sleek, jolly landlord in Farquhar's comedy of ½The Beaux' Stratagem.͵] An innkeeper.

Boniῐform (?), a. [L. bonus good + ῐform.] Sensitive or responsive to moral excellence.

Dr. H. More.

Boniῐfy (?), v. t. [L. bonus good + ῐfy: cf. F. bonifier.] To convert into, or make, good.

To bonify evils, or tincture them with good.

Cudworth.

Boniῐness (?), n. The condition or quality of being bony.

Boning, n. [Senses 1 and 2 fr. 1st Bone, sense 3 fr. 3d Bone.] 1. The clearing of bones from fish or meat.

<small>The manuring of land with bones.</small>

<small>A method of leveling a line or surface by sighting along the tops of two or more straight edges, or a range of properly spaced poles. See 3d Bone, v. t.</small>

Boniῐtaῐry (?), a. Beneficial, as opposed to statutory or civil; as, bonitary dominion of land.

Boῐnito (?), n.; pl. **Bonitoes** (?). [Sp. & Pg. bonito, fr. Ar. bainÆt and bainÆth.] [Often incorrectly written bonita.] (Zo"l.) 1. A large tropical fish (Orcynus pelamys) allied to the tunny. It is about three feet long, blue above, with four brown stripes on the sides. It is sometimes found on the American coast.

<small>The skipjack (Sarda Mediterranea) of the Atlantic, an important and abundant food fish on the coast of the United States, and (S. Chilensis) of the Pacific, and other related species. They are large and active fishes, of a blue color with black oblique stripes.</small>

The medregal (Seriola fasciata), an edible fish of the southern of the United States and the West Indies.

The cobia or crab eater (Elacate canada), an edible fish of the Middle and Southern United States.

Ø Bonmot · (?), n.; pl. Bonsmots (?). [F. bon good + mot word.] A witty repartee; a jest.

Ø Bonne (?), n. (F., prop. good woman.) A female servant charged with the care of a young child.

Ø Bonne bouche (?); pl. Bonnes bouches (?). [F. bon, fem. bonne, good + bouche mouth.] A delicious morsel or mouthful; a tidbit.

Bonnet (?), n. [OE. bonet, OF. bonet, bonete. F. bonnet fr. LL. bonneta, bonetum; orig. the name of a stuff, and ? unknown origin.] 1. A headdress for men and boys; a cap. [Obs.]
Milton. Shak.

A soft, ?, very durable cap, made of thick, seamless wool? stuff, and worn by men in Scotland.

And ? and bonnets waving high.
Sir W. Scott.

A covering for the head, worn by women, usually protecting more or less the back and sides of the head, but no part of the forehead. The shape of the bonnet varies greatly at different times; formerly the front part projected, and spread outward, like the mouth of a funnel.

Anything resembling a bonnet in shape or use; as, (a) (Fort.) A small defense work at a salient angle; or a part of a parapet elevated to screen the other part from enfilade fire. (b) A metallic canopy, or projection, over an opening, as a fireplace, or a cowl or hood to increase the draught of a chimney, etc. (c) A frame of wire netting over a locomotive chimney, to prevent escape of sparks. (d) A roofing over the cage of a mine, to protect its occupants from objects falling down the shaft. (e) In pumps, a metal covering for the openings in the valve chambers.

(Naut.) An additional piece of canvas la?ed to the foot of a jib or foresail in moderate winds.

Hakluyt.

The second stomach of a ruminating animal.

An accomplice of a gambler, auctioneer, etc., who entices others to bet or to bid; a decoy. [Cant]

Bonnet head (Zo"l.), a shark (Sphyrna tiburio) of the southern United States and West Indies. Ð Bonnet limpet (Zo"l.), a name given, from their shape, to various species of shells (family Calyptr'id'). Ð Bonnet monkey (Zo"l.), an East Indian monkey (Macacus sinicus), with a tuft of hair on its head; the munga. Ð Bonnet piece, a gold coin of the time of James V. of Scotland, the king's head o? which wears a bonnet. Sir W. Scott. Ð To have a bee in the bonnet. See under Bee. Ð Black bonnet. See under Black. Ð Blue bonnet. See in the Vocabulary.

Bonnet, v. i. To take off the bonnet or cap as a mark of respect; to uncover. [Obs.]

Shak.

Bonnet′ed, a. 1. Wearing a bonnet. ½Bonneted and shawled.₃

Howitt.

(Fort.) Protected by a bonnet. See Bonnet, 4 (a).

Bonnet′less, a. Without a bonnet.

Bonni′bel (?), n. [F. bonne et belle, good and beautiful. Cf. Bellibone.] A handsome girl. [Obs.]

Bonnie (?), a. [Scot.] See Bonny, a.

Bonni′lass · (?), n. [Bonny + lass.] A ½bonny lass₃; a beautiful girl. [Obs.]

Spenser.

Bonni′ly, adv. Gayly; handsomely.

Bonni′ness, n. The quality of being bonny; gayety? handsomeness. [R.]

Bonny (?), a. [Spelled bonnie by the Scotch.] [OE. boni, prob. fr. F. bon, fem. bonne, good, fr. L. bonus good. See Bounty, and cf. Bonus, Boon.] 1. Handsome; beautiful; pretty; attractively lively and graceful.

Till bonny Susan sped across the plain.

Gay.

Far from the bonnie banks of Ayr.

Burns.

Gay; merry; frolicsome; cheerful; blithe.

Be you blithe and bonny.

Shak.

Report speaks you a bonny monk, that would hear the mati?chime ere he quitted his bowl.

Sir W. Scott.

Bonny, n. (Mining) A round and compact bed of ore, or a distinct bed, not communicating with a vein.

Bonny′clab · ber (?), n. [Ir. bainne, baine, milk + clabar mud, mire.] Coagulated sour milk; loppered milk; curdled milk; Ð sometimes called simply clabber.

B. Jonson.

Ø Bon Si · lŠne (?). [F.] (Bot.) A very fragrant tea rose with petals of various shades of pink.

Bonspiel (?), n. [Scot.; of uncertain origin.] A cur?ing match between clubs. [Scot.]

Ø Bonteĭbok (?), n. [D. bont a sort of skin or fur, prop. variegated + bok buck.] (Zo"l.) The pied antelope of South Africa (Alcelaphus pygarga). Its face and rum[are white. Called also nunni.

Ø Bon ton (?). [F., good tone, manner.] The height of the fashion; fashionable society.

Bonus (?), n.; pl. Bonuses (?). [L. bonus good. Cf. Bonny.] 1. (Law) A premium given for a loan, or for a charter or other privilege granted to a company; as the bank paid a bonus for its charter.

Bouvier.

An extra dividend to the shareholders of a joint stock company, out of accumulated profits.

Money paid in addition to a stated compensation.

Ø Bon vi · vant (?); pl. Bons vivants (?). [F. bon good + vivant, p. pr. of vivre to live.] A good fellow; a jovial companion; a free liver.

Bony (?), a. 1. Consisting of bone, or of bones; full of bones; pertaining to bones.

Having large or prominent bones.

Bony fish (Zo"l.), the menhaden. Đ Bony pike (Zo"l.), the gar pike (Lepidosteus).

Bonze (?), n. [Pg. bonzo, fr. Japan bŌzu a Buddhist priest: cf. F. bonze.] A Buddhist or Fohist priest, monk, or nun.

μ The name was given by the Portuguese to the priests of Japan, and has since been applied to the priests of China, Cochin China, and the neighboring countries.

Booby (?), n.; pl. Boobies (?). [Sp. bobe dunce, idiot; cf. L. balbus stammering, E. barbarous.]

A dunce; a stupid fellow.

(Zo"l.) (a) A swimming bird (Sula fiber or S. sula) related to the common gannet, and found in the West

<— p. 166 —>

Indies, nesting on the bare rocks. It is so called on account of its apparent stupidity. The name is also sometimes applied to other species of gannets; as, S. piscator, the redĐfooted booby. (b) A species of penguin of the antarctic seas.

Booby hatch (Naut.), a kind of wooden hood over a hatch, readily removable. Đ Booby hut, a carriage body put upon sleigh runners. [Local, U. S.] Bartlett. Đ Booby hutch, a clumsy covered carriage or seat, used in the eastern part of England. Forby. Đ Booby trap, a schoolboy's practical joke, as a shower bath when a door is opened.

Booby (?), a. Having the characteristics of a booby; stupid.

Boobylish, a. Stupid; dull.

Boodh (?), n. Same as Buddha.
Malcom.

Boodhism (?), n. Same as Buddhism.

Boodhist, n. Same as Buddhist.

Boodle (?), n. [Origin un?tain.] 1. The whole collection or lot; caboodle. [Low, U. S.]
Bartlett.

<small>Money given in payment for votes or political influence; bribe money; swag. [Polit. slang, U. S.]</small>

Boo · hoe (?), v. i. [imp. & p.p. Boohooed (?); p. pr. & vb. n. Boohooing.] [An imitative word.] To bawl; to cry loudly. [Low]
Bartlett.

Boohoo · (?), n. (Zo"l.) The sailfish; Ð called also woohoo.

Book (?), n. [OE. book, bok, AS. b?c; akin to Goth. b?ka a letter, in pl. book, writing, Icel. b?k, Sw. bok, Dan. bog, OS. b?k, D. boek, OHG. puoh, G. buch; and fr. AS. b?c, b?ce, beech; because the ancient Saxons and Germans in general wrote runes on pieces of beechen board. Cf. Beech.] 1. A collection of sheets of paper, or similar material, blank, written, or printed, bound together; commonly, many folded and bound sheets containing continuous printing or writing.

µ When blank, it is called a blank book. When printed, the term often distinguishes a bound volume, or a volume of some size, from a pamphlet.

µ It has been held that, under the copyright law, a book is not necessarily a volume made of many sheets bound together; it may be printed on a single sheet, as music or a diagram of patterns.
Abbott.

<small>A composition, written or printed; a treatise.</small>

A good book is the precious life blood of a master spirit, embalmed and treasured up on purpose to a life beyond life.
Milton.

<small>A part or subdivision of a treatise or literary work; as, the tenth book of ½Paradise Lost.</small>

<small>A volume or collection of sheets in which accounts are kept; a register of debts and credits, receipts and expenditures, etc.</small>

<small>Six tricks taken by one side, in the game of whist; in certain other games, two or more corresponding cards, forming a set.</small>

µ Book is used adjectively or as a part of many compounds; as, book buyer, bookrack, book club, book lore, book sale, book trade, memorandum book, cashbook.

Book account, an account or register of debt or credit in a book. Ð Book debt, a debt for items charged to the debtor by the creditor in his book of accounts. Ð Book learning, learning acquired from books, as distinguished from practical knowledge. ½Neither does it so much require book learning and scholarship, as good natural sense, to distinguish true and false.¸ Burnet. Ð Book louse (Zo"l.), one of several species of minute, wingless insects injurious to books and papers. They belong to the Pseudoneuroptera. Ð Book moth (Zo"l.), the name of several species of moths, the larv' of which eat books. Ð Book oath, an oath made on The Book, or Bible. Ð The Book of Books, the Bible. Ð Book post, a system under which books, bulky manuscripts, etc., may be transmitted by mail. Ð Book scorpion (Zo"l.), one of the false scorpions (Chelifer cancroides) found among books and papers. It can run sidewise and backward, and feeds on small insects. Ð Book stall, a stand or stall, often in the open air, for retailing books. Ð Canonical books. See Canonical. Ð In one's books, in one's favor. ½I was so much in his books, that at his decease he left me his lamp.¸ Addison. Ð To bring to book. (a) To compel to give an account. (b) To compare with an admitted authority. ½To bring it manifestly to book is impossible.¸ M. Arnold. Ð To course by bell, book, and candle. See under Bell. Ð To make a book (Horse Racing), to lay bets (recorded in a pocket book) against the success of every horse, so that the bookmaker wins on all the unsuccessful horses and loses only on the winning horse or horses. Ð To speak by the book, to speak with minute exactness. Ð Without book. (a) By memory. (b) Without authority.

Book, v. t. [imp. & p.p. Booked (?); p. pr. & vb. n. Booking.] 1. To enter, write, or register in a book or list.

Let it be booked with the rest of this day's deeds.

Shak.

To enter the name of (any one) in a book for the purpose of securing a passage, conveyance, or seat; as, to be booked for Southampton; to book a seat in a theater.

To mark out for; to destine or assign for; as, he is booked for the valedictory. [Colloq.]

Here I am booked for three days more in Paris.

Charles Reade.

Bookbind · er (?), n. One whose occupation is to bind books.

Bookbind · erÏy (?), n. A bookbinder's shop; a place or establishment for binding books.

Bookbind · ing, n. The art, process, or business of binding books.

Bookcase · (?), n. A case with shelves for holding books, esp. one with glazed doors.

Bookcraft · (?), n. Authorship; literary skill.

Booked (?), a. 1. Registered.

On the way; destined. [Colloq.]

Booker (?), n. One who enters accounts or names, etc., in a book; a bookkeeper.

Bookful (?), n. As much as will fill a book; a book full. Shak. Ð a. Filled with book learning. [R.] ½The bookful blockhead.͵ Pope.

Bookhold·er (?), n. 1. A prompter at a theater. [Obs.] Beau & Fl.

A support for a book, holding it open, while one reads or copies from it.

Booking clerk· (?). A clerk who registers passengers, baggage, etc., for conveyance, as by railway or steamship, or who sells passage tickets at a booking office.

Booking of·fice (?). 1. An office where passengers, baggage, etc., are registered for conveyance, as by railway or steamship.

An office where passage tickets are sold. [Eng.]

Bookish, a. 1. Given to reading; fond of study; better acquainted with books than with men; learned from books. ½A bookish man.͵ Addison. ½Bookish skill.͵ Bp. Hall.

Characterized by a method of expression generally found in books; formal; labored; pedantic; as, a bookish way of talking; bookish sentences.

Ð Bookishĭly, adv. Ð Bookishĭness, n.

Bookkeep·er (?), n. One who keeps accounts; one who has the charge of keeping the books and accounts in an office.

Bookkeep·ing, n. The art of recording pecuniary or business transactions in a regular and systematic manner, so as to show their relation to each other, and the state of the business in which they occur; the art of keeping accounts. The books commonly ? are a daybook, cashbook, journal, and ledger. See Daybook, Cashbook, Journal, and Ledger.

Bookkeeping by single entry, the method of keeping books by carrying the record of each transaction to the debit or credit of a single account. Ð Bookkeeping by double entry, a mode of bookkeeping in which two entries of every transaction are carried to the ledger, one to the Dr., or left hand, side of one account, and the other to the Cr., or right hand, side of a corresponding account, in order tha? the one entry may check the other; Ð sometimes called, from the place of its origin, the Italian method.

Bookland· (?), Bockland· (?), n. [AS. b?cland; b?c book + land land.] (O. Eng. Law) Charter land held by deed under certain rents and free services, which differed in nothing from free socage lands. This species of tenure has given rise to the modern freeholds.

BookÐlearned· (?), a. Versed in books; having knowledge derived from books. [Often in a disparaging sense.]

Whate'er these bookÐlearned blockheads say,
Solon's the veriest fool in all the play.
Dryden.

Bookless, a. Without books; unlearned.
Shenstone.

Booklet (?), n. A little book.
T. Arnold.

Bookmak · er (?), n. 1. One who writes and publishes books; especially, one who gathers his materials from other books; a compiler.

(Horse Racing) A betting man who ½makes a book., See To make a book, under Book, n.

Bookman (?), n.; pl. Bookmen (?). A studious man; a scholar.
Shak.

Bookmark · (?), n. Something placed in a book to guide in finding a particular page or passage; also, a label in a book to designate the owner; a bookplate.

Bookmate · (?), n. [Book + mate.] A schoolfellow; an associate in study.

Bookmon · ger (?), n. A dealer in books.

Book mus · lin (?). 1. A kind of muslin used for the covers of books.

A kind of thin white muslin for ladies' dresses.

Bookplate · (?), n. A label, placed upon or in a book, showing its ownership or its position in a library.

Booksell · er (?), n. One who sells books.

Booksell · ing (?), n. The employment of selling books.

Bookshelf · (?), n.; pl. Bookshelves (?). A shelf to hold books.

Bookshop · (?), n. A bookseller's shop. [Eng.]

Bookstall · (?), n. A stall or stand where books are sold.

Bookstand · (?), n. 1. A place or stand for the sale of books in the streets; a bookstall.

A stand to hold books for reading or reference.

Bookstore · (?), n. A store where books are kept for sale; Ð called in England a bookseller's shop.

Bookwork · (?), n. 1. Work done upon a book or books (as in a printing office), in distinction from newspaper or job work.

Study; application to books.

Bookworm · (?), n. 1. (Zo"l.) Any larva of a beetle or moth, which is injurious to books. Many species are known.

A student closely attached to books or addicted to study; a reader without appreciation.

I wanted but a black gown and a salary to be as mere a bookworm as any there.
Pope.

Booky (?), a. Bookish.

Booly (?), n.; pl. Boolies (?). [Ir. buachail cowherd; bo cow + giolla boy.] A company of Irish herdsmen, or a single herdsman, wandering from place to place with flocks and herds, and living on their milk, like the Tartars; also, a place in the mountain pastures inclosed for the shelter of cattle or their keepers. [Obs.] [Written also boley, bolye, bouillie.]
Spenser.

Boom (?), n. [D. boom tree, pole, beam, bar. See Beam.] 1. (Naut.) A long pole or spar, run out for the purpose of extending the bottom of a particular sail; as, the job boom, the studdingsail boom, etc.

(Mech.) A long spar or beam, projecting from the mast of a derrick, from the outer end of which the body to be lifted in suspended.

A pole with a conspicuous top, set up to mark the channel in a river or harbor. [Obs.]

(Mil. & Naval) A strong chain cable, or line of spars bound together, extended across a river or the mouth of a harbor, to obstruct navigation or passage.

(Lumbering) A line of connected floating timbers stretched across a river, or inclosing an area of water, to keep saw logs, etc., from floating away.

Boom iron, one of the iron rings on the yards through which the studding-sail booms traverse. — The booms, that space on the upper deck of a ship between the foremast and mainmast, where the boats, spare spars, etc., are stowed.
Totten.

Boom (?), v. t. (Naut.) To extend, or push, with a boom or pole; as, to boom out a sail; to boom off a boat.

Boom (?), v. i. [imp. & p.p. Boomed (?), p. pr. & vb. n. Booming.] [Of imitative origin; cf. OE. bommen to hum, D. bommen to drum, sound as an empty barrel, also W. bwmp a hollow sound; aderyn y bwmp, the bird of the hollow sound, i. e., the bittern. Cf. Bum, Bump, v. i., Bomb, v. i.] 1. To cry with a hollow note; to make a hollow sound, as the bittern, and some insects.

At eve the beetle boometh
Athwart the thicket lone.
Tennyson.

To make a hollow sound, as of waves or cannon.

Alarm guns booming through the night air.
W. Irving.

To rush with violence and noise, as a ship under a press of sail, before a free wind.

She comes booming down before it.
Totten.

To have a rapid growth in market value or in popular favor; to go on rushingly.

Boom, n. 1. A hollow roar, as of waves or cannon; also, the hollow cry of the bittern; a booming.

A strong and extensive advance, with more or less noisy excitement; Ð applied colloquially or humorously to market prices, the demand for stocks or commodities and to political chances of aspirants to office; as a boom in the stock market; a boom in coffee. [Colloq. U. S.]

Boom, v. t. To cause to advance rapidly in price; as, to boom railroad or mining shares; to create a ½boom‸ for; as to boom Mr. C. for senator. [Colloq. U. S.]

Ø **Boomdas** (?), n. [D. boom tree + das badger.] (Zo"l.) A small African hyracoid mammal (Dendrohyrax arboreus) resembling the daman.

Boomer (?), n. 1. One who, or that which, booms.

(Zo"l.) A North American rodent, so named because ? is said to make a booming noise. See Sewellel.

(Zo"l.) A large male kangaroo.

One who works up a ½boom‸. [Slang, U. S.]

Boomerïang (?), n. A very singular missile weapon used by the natives of Australia and in some parts of India. It is usually a curved stick of hard wood, from twenty to thirty inches in length, from two to three inches wide, and half or three quarters of an inch thick. When thrown from the hand with a quick rotary motion, it describes very remarkable curves, according to the shape of the instrument and the manner of throwing it, often moving nearly horizontally a long distance, then curving upward to a considerable height, and finally taking a retrograde direction, so as to fall near the place from which it was thrown, or even far in the rear of it.

Booming, a. 1. Rushing with violence; swelling with a hollow sound; making a hollow sound or note; roaring; resounding.

O'er the seaÐbeat ships the booming waters roar.

Falcone.

Advancing or increasing amid noisy excitement; as, booming prices; booming popularity. [Colloq. U. S.]

Booming, n. The act of producing a hollow or roaring sound; a violent rushing with heavy roar; as, the booming of the sea; a deep, h?llow sound; as, the booming of bitterns.

Howitt.

Boomkin (?), n. (Naut.) Same as Bumkin.

Ø **Boomoïrah** (?), n. [Native name.] (Zo"l.) A small West African chevrotain (Hy'moschus aquaticus), resembling the musk deer.

Ø Boomslangĭe (?), n. [D. boom tree + slang snake.] (Zo"l.) A large South African tree snake (Bucephalus Capensis). Although considered venomous by natives, it has no poison fangs.

Boon (?), n. [OE. bone, boin, a petition, fr. Icel. b?n; akin to Sw. & Dan. b?n, AS. b?n, and perh. to E. ban; but influenced by F. bon good, fr. L. bonus. ?86. See 2d Ban, Bounty.] 1. A prayer or petition. [Obs.]

For which to God he made so many an idle boon.
Spenser.

That which is asked or granted as a benefit or favor; a gift; a benefaction; a grant; a present.

Every good gift and every perfect boon is from above.
James i. 17 (Rev. Ver.).

Boon, a. [F. bon. See Boon, n.] 1. Good; prosperous; as, boon voyage. [Obs.]

Kind; bountiful; benign.

Which ... Nature boon
Poured forth profuse on hill, and dale, and plain.
Milton.

Gay; merry; jovial; convivial.

A boon companion, loving his bottle.
Arbuthnot.

Boon, n. [Scot. boon, bune, been, Gael. & Ir. bunach coarse tow, fr. bun root, stubble.] The woody portion flax, which is separated from the fiber as refuse matter by retting, braking, and scutching.

Boor (?), n. [D. boer farmer, boor; akin to AS. geb?r countryman, G. bauer; fr. the root of AS. b?an to inhabit, and akin to E. bower, be. Cf. Neighbor, Boer, and Big to build.] 1. A husbandman; a peasant; a rustic; esp. a clownish or unrefined countryman.

A Dutch, German, or Russian peasant; esp. a Dutch colonist in South Africa, Guiana, etc.: a boer.

A rude illĭbred person; one who is clownish in manners.

Boorish, a. Like a boor; clownish; uncultured; unmannerly. Đ Boorishĭly, adv. Đ Boorishĭness, n.

Which is in truth a gross and boorish opinion.
Milton.

Boort (?), n. See Bort.

Boose (?), n. [AS. bÓs, bÓsig; akin to Icel. b¾ss, Sw. b†s, Dan. baas, stall, G. banse, Goth. bansts barn, Skr. bh¾sas stall. û252.] A stall or a crib for an ox, cow, or other animal. [Prov. Eng.]

Halliwell.

Boose (?), v. i. To drink excessively. See Booze.

Booser (?), n. A toper; a guzzler. See Boozer.

Boost (?), v. t. [imp. & p.p. Boosted; p. pr. & vb. n. Boosting.] [Cf. Boast, v. i.] To lift or push

<— p. 167 —>

from behind (one who is endeavoring to climb); to push up; hence, to assist in overcoming obstacles, or in making advancement. [Colloq. U. S.] Boost (?), n. A push from behind, as to one who is endeavoring to climb; help. [Colloq. U. S.] Boot (?), n. [OE. bot, bote, adbantage, amends, cure, AS. b?t; akin to Icel. b?t, Sw. bot, Dan. bod, Goth. b?ta, D. boete, G. busse; prop., a making good or better, from the root of E. better, adj. ?255.] 1. Remedy; relief; amends; reparation; hence, one who brings relief. He gaf the sike man his boote. Chaucer. Thou art boot for many a bruise And healest many a wound. Sir W. Scott. Next her Son, our soul's best boot. Wordsworth. 2. That which is given to make an exchange equal, or to make up for the deficiency of value in one of the things exchanged. I'll give you boot, I'll give you three for one. Shak. 3. Profit; gain; advantage; use. [Obs.] Then talk no more of flight, it is no boot. Shak. To boot, in addition; over and above; besides; as a compensation for the difference of value between things bartered. Helen, to change, would give an eye to boot. Shak. A man's heaviness is refreshed long before he comes to drunkenness, for when he arrives thither he hath but changed his heaviness, and taken a crime to boot. Jer. Taylor. Boot, v. t. [imp. & p.p. Booted; p. pr. & vb. n. Booting.] 1. To profit; to advantage; to avail; Ð generally followed by it; as, what boots it? What booteth it to others that we wish them well, and do nothing for them? Hooker. What subdued To change like this a mind so far imbued With scorn of man, it little boots to know. Byron. What boots to us your victories? Southey. 2. To enrich; to benefit; to give in addition. [Obs.] And I will boot thee with what gift beside Thy modesty can beg. Shak. Boot, n. [OE. bote, OF. bote, F. botte, LL. botta; of uncertain origin.] 1. A covering for the foot and lower part of the leg, ordinarily made of leather. 2. An instrument of torture for the leg, formerly used to extort confessions, particularly in Scotland. So he was put to the torture, which in Scotland they call the boots; for they put a pair of iron boots close on the leg, and drive wedges between them and the leg. Bp. Burnet. 3. A place at the side of a coach, where attendants rode; also, a low outside place before and behind the body of the coach. [Obs.] 4. A place for baggage at either end of an oldÐfashioned stagecoach. 5. An apron or cover (of leather or rubber cloth) for the driving seat of a vehicle, to protect from rain and mud. 6. (Plumbing) The metal casing and flange fitted about a pipe where it passes through a roof. Boot catcher, the person at an inn whose business it was to pull off boots and clean them. [Obs.] Swift. Ð Boot closer, one who, or that which, sews the uppers of boots. Ð Boot crimp, a frame or device used by bootmakers for drawing and shaping the body of a boot. Ð Boot hook, a hook with a handle, used for pulling on boots. Ð Boots and ?addles (Cavalry Tactics), the trumpet call which is the first signal for mounted drill. Ð Sly boots. See Slyboots, in the Vocabulary. Boot, v. t. [imp. & p.p. Booted; p. pr. & vb. n. Booting.] 1. To put boots on, esp. for riding. Coated and booted for it. B. Jonson. 2. To punish by kicking with a booted foot. [U. S.] Boot, v. i. To boot one's self; to put on one's boots. Boot, n. Booty; spoil. [Obs. or R.] Shak. Bootblack· (?), n. One who blacks boots. Booted (?), a. 1. Wearing boots, especially boots with long tops, as for riding; as, a booted squire. 2. (Zo"l.) Having an undivided, horny, bootlike covering; Ð said of the tarsus of some birds. Bootĭee (?), n. A half boot or short boot. Ø Boï"tes (?), n. [L. Bootes, Gr. ? herdsman, fr. ?, gen. ?, ox, cow.] (Astron.) A northern constellation, containing the bright star Arcturus. Booth (?), n. [OE. bothe; cf. Icel. b?, Dan. & Sw. bod, MHG. buode, G. bude, baude; from the same root as AS. b?an to dwell, E. boor, bower, be; cf. Bohem. bauda, Pol. buda, Russ. budka, Lith. buda, W. bwth, pl. bythod, Gael. buth, Ir. both.] 1. A house or shed built of boards, boughs, or other slight materials, for temporary occupation. Camden. 2. A covered stall or temporary structure in a fair or market, or at a polling place. Boothale· (?), v. t. & i. [Boot, for booty + hale.] To forage for booty; to plunder. [Obs.] Beau. & Fl. Boothose· (?), n. 1. Stocking hose, or spatterdashes, in lieu of boots. Shak. 2. Hose made to be worn with boots, as by travelers on horseback. Sir W. Scott. Boothy (?), n. See Bothy. Bootiľkin (?), n. [Boot + ĭkin.] 1. A little boot, legging, or gaiter. 2. A covering for the foot or hand, worn as a cure for the gout. H. Walpole. Booting, n. Advantage; gain; gain by plunder; booty. [Obs.] Sir. J. Harrington. Booting, n. 1. A kind of torture. See Boot, n., 2. 2. A kicking, as with a booted foot. [U. S.] Bootjack· (?), n. A device for pulling off boots. Bootless (?), a. [From Boot profit.] Unavailing; unprofitable; useless; without advantage or success. Chaucer. I'll follow him no more with bootless prayers. Shak. ÐBootlessĭly, adv. Ð Bootlessĭness, n. Bootlick· (?), n. A toady. [Low, U. S.] Bartlett. Bootmak·er (?), n. One who makes boots. Ð Bootmak·ing, n. Boots (?), n. A servant at a hotel or elsewhere, who cleans and blacks the boots and shoes. Boottop·ping (?), n. 1. (Naut.) The act or process of daubing a vessel's bottom near the surface of the water with a mixture of tallow, sulphur, and resin, as a temporary protection against worms, after the slime, she?ls, etc., have been scraped off. 2. (Naut.) Sheathing a vessel with planking over felt. Boottree· (?), n. [Boot + tree wood, timber.] An instrument to stretch and widen the log of a boot, consisting of two pieces, together shaped like a leg, between which, when put into the boot, a wedge is driven. The pretty boots trimly stretched on boottrees. Thackeray. Booty (?), n. [Cf. Icel. b?ti exchange, barter, Sw. byte barter, booty, Dan. bytte; akin to D. buit booty, G. beute, and fr. Icel. byta, Sw. byta, Dan. bytte, to distribute, exchange. The Scandinavian word was influenced in English by boot profit.] That which is seized by violence or obtained by robbery, especially collective spoil taken in war; plunder; pillage. Milton. To play booty, to play dishonestly, with an intent to lose; to allow one's adversary to win at cards at first, in order to induce him to continue playing and victimize him afterwards. [Obs.] L'Estrange. Booze (?), v. i. [imp. & p.p. Boozed (?); p. pr. & vb. n. Boozing.] [D. buizen; akin to G. bausen, and perh. fr. D. buis tube, channel, bus box, jar.] To drink greedily or immoderately, esp. alcoholic liquor; to tipple. [Written also bouse, and boose.] Landor. This is better than boozing in public houses. H. R. Haweis. Booze, n. A carouse; a drinking. Sir W. Scott. Boozer (?), n. One who boozes; a toper; a guzzler of alcoholic liquors; a bouser. Boozy (?), a. A little intoxicated; fuddled; stupid with liquor; bousy. [Colloq.] C. Kingsley. Boïpeep (?), n. [Bo + peep.] The act of looking out suddenly, as from behind a screen, so as to startle some one (as by children in play), or of looking out and drawing suddenly back, as if frightened. I for sorrow sung, That such a king should play bopeep, And go the fools among. Shak. Boraïble (?), a. Capable of being bored. [R.] Boïrachte (?), n. [Sp. borracha a leather bottle for wine, borracho drunk, fr. borra a lamb.] A large leather bottle for liquors, etc., made of the skin of a goat or other animal. Hence: A drunkard. [Obs.] You're an absolute borachio. Congreve. Boïracic (?), a. [Cf. F. boracique. See Borax.] Pertaining to, or produced from, borax; containing boron; boric; as, boracic acid. Boraïcite (?), n. (Min.) A mineral of a white or gray color occurring massive and in isometric crystals; in composition it is a magnesium borate with magnesium chloride. Boraïcous (?), a. (Chem.) Relating to, or obtained from, borax; containing borax. Borage (?), n. [OE. borage (cf. F. bourrache, It. borraggine, borrace, LL. borago, borrago, LGr. ?), fr. LL. borra, F. bourre, hair of beasts, flock; so called from its hairy leaves.] (Bot.) A mucilaginous plant of the genus Borago (B. officinalis), which is used, esp. in France, as a demulcent and diaphoretic. Borageïwort · (?), n. Plant of the Borage family. Boïrag · iïnaceous (?), a. (Bot.) Of, pertaining to, or resembling, a family of plants (Boraginace‘) which includes the borage, heliotrope, beggar's lice, and many pestiferous plants. Bor · aïgineïous (?), a. (Bot.) Relating to the Borage tribe; boraginaceous. Boraïmez (?), n. See Barometz. Borate (?), n. [From Boric.] (Chem.) A salt formed by the combination of boric acid with a base or positive radical. Borax (?), n. [OE. boras, fr. F. borax, earlier spelt borras; cf. LL. borax, Sp. borraj; all fr. Ar. b?rag, fr. Pers. b?rah.] A white or gray crystalline salt, with a slight alkaline taste, used as a flux, in soldering metals, making enamels, fixing colors on porcelain, and as a soap. It occurs native in certain mineral springs, and is made from the boric acid of hot springs in Tuscany. It was originally obtained from a lake in Thibet, and was sent to Europe under the name of tincal. Borax is a pyroborate or tetraborate of sodium, $Na_2B_4O_7 \cdot 10H_2O$. Borax bead. (Chem.) See Bead, n., 3. Borboïrygm (?), n. [F. borborygme, fr. Gr. ?, fr. ? to rumble in the bowels.] (Med.) A rumbling or gurgling noise produced by wind in the bowels. Dunglison. Bord (?), n. [See Board, n.] 1.

A board; a table. [Obs.] Chaucer. 2. (Mining) The face of coal parallel to the natural fissures. Bord (?), n. See Bourd. [Obs.] Spenser. Bordage (?), n. [LL. bordagium.] The base or servile tenure by which a bordar held his cottage. Bordar (?), n. [LL. bordarius, fr. borda a cottage; of uncertain origin.] A villein who rendered menial service for his cottage; a cottier. The cottar, the bordar, and the laborer were bound to aid in the work of the home farm. J. R. Green. Borĭdeaux (?), a. Pertaining to Bordeaux in the south of France. Đ n. A claret wine from Bordeaux. Bordel (?), Borĭdello (?), } n. [F. bordel, orig. a little hut, OF. borde hut, cabin, of German origin, and akin to E. board, n. See. Board, n.] A brothel; a bawdyhouse; a house devoted to prostitution. [Obs.] B. Jonson. Ø Bor · dellais (?), a. [F.] Of or pertaining to Bordeaux, in France, or to the district around Bordeaux. Bordelĭler (?), n. A keeper or a frequenter of a brothel. [Obs.] Gower. Border (?), n. [OE. bordure, F. bordure, fr. border to border, fr. bord a border; of German origin; cf. MHG. borte border, trimming, G. borte trimming, ribbon; akin to E. board in sense 8. See Board, n., and cf. Bordure.] 1. The outer part or edge of anything, as of a garment, a garden, etc.; margin; verge; brink. Upon the borders of these solitudes. Bentham. In the borders of death. Barrow. 2. A boundary; a frontier of a state or of the settled part of a country; a frontier district. 3. A strip or stripe arranged along or near the edge of something, as an ornament or finish. 4. A narrow flower bed. Border land, land on the frontiers of two adjoining countries; debatable land; Đ often used figuratively; as, the border land of science. Đ The Border, The Borders, specifically, the frontier districts of Scotland and England which lie adjacent. Đ Over the border, across the boundary line or frontier. Syn. Đ Edge; verge; brink; margin; brim; rim; boundary; confine. Border, v. i. [imp. & p.p. Bordered (?); p. pr. & vb. n. Bordering.] 1. To touch at the edge or boundary; to be contiguous or adjacent; Đ with on or upon as, Connecticut borders on Massachusetts. 2. To approach; to come near to; to verge. Wit which borders upon profaneness deserves to be branded as folly. Abp. Tillotson. Border, v. t. 1. To make a border for; to furnish with a border, as for ornament; as, to border a garment or a garden. 2. To be, or to have, contiguous to; to touch, or be touched, as by a border; to be, or to have, near the limits or boundary; as, the region borders a forest, or is bordered on the north by a forest. The country is bordered by a broad tract called the ½hot region., Prescott. Shebah and Raamah ... border the sea called the Persian gulf. Sir W. Raleigh. 3. To confine within bounds; to limit. [Obs.] That nature, which contemns its origin, Can not be bordered certain in itself. Shak. Borderĭer (?), n. One who dwells on a border, or at the extreme part or confines of a country, region, or tract of land; one who dwells near to a place or region. Borderers of the Caspian. Dyer. Bordland · (?), n. [Bordar (or perh. bord a board) + land.] (O. Eng. Law) Either land held by a bordar, or the land which a lord kept for the maintenance of his board, or table. Spelman. Bordlode · (?), n. [Bordar (or perh. bord a board) + lode leading.] (O. Eng. Law) The service formerly required of a tenant, to carry timber from the woods to the lord's house. Bailey. Mozley & W. Bordman (?), n. [Bordar (or perh. bord a board) + man.] A bordar; a tenant in bordage. Bordrag (?), Bordra · ging (?), } n. [Perh. from OE. bord, for border + raging. Cf. Bodrage.] An incursion upon the borders of a country; a raid. [Obs.] Spenser. Bord serv · ice (?). [Bordar (or perh. bord a board) + service.] (O. Eng. Law) Service due from a bordar; bordage. Bordure (?), n. [F. bordure. See Border, n.] (Her.) A border one fifth the width of the shield, surrounding the field. It is usually plain, but may be charged. Bore (?), v. t. [imp. & p.p. Bored (?); p. pr. & vb. n. Boring.] [OE. borien, AS. borian; akin to Icel. bora, Dan. bore, D. boren, OHG. por?n, G. bohren, L. forare, Gr. ? to plow, Zend bar. ?91.] 1. To perforate or penetrate, as a solid body, by turning an auger, gimlet, drill, or other instrument; to make a round hole in or through; to pierce; as, to bore a plank. I'll believe as soon this whole earth may be bored. Shak. 2. To form or enlarge by means of a boring instrument or apparatus; as, to bore a steam cylinder or a gun barrel; to bore a hole. Short but very powerful jaws, by means whereof the insect can bore, as with a centerbit, a cylindrical passage through the most solid wood. T. W. Harris. 3. To make (a passage) by laborious effort, as in boring; as, to bore one's way through a crowd; to force a narrow and difficult passage through. ½What bustling crowds I bored.ˎ Gay. 4. To weary by tedious iteration or by dullness; to tire; to trouble; to vex; to annoy; to pester. He bores me with some trick. Shak. Used to come and bore me at rare intervals. Carlyle. 5. To befool; to trick. [Obs.] I am abused, betrayed; I am laughed at, scorned, Baffled and bored, it seems. Beau. & Fl. Bore, v. i. 1. To make a hole or perforation with, or as with, a boring instrument; to cut a circular hole by the rotary motion of a tool; as, to bore for water or oil (i. e., to sink a well by boring for water or oil); to bore with a gimlet; to bore into a tree (as insects). 2. To be pierced or penetrated by an instrument that cuts as it turns; as, this timber does not bore well, or is hard to bore. 3. To push forward in a certain direction with laborious effort. They take their flight ... boring to the west. Dryden.

<— p. 168 —>

(Ma??) To shoot out the nose or toss it in the air; ? said of a horse. Crabb. Bore (?), n. 1. A hole made by boring; a perforation.

The internal cylindrical cavity of a gun, cannon, pistol, or other firearm, or of a pipe or tube. The bores of wind instruments. Bacon. Love's counselor should fill the bores of hearing. Shak.

The size of a hole; the interior diameter of a tube or gun barrel; the caliber.

A tool for making a hole by boring, as an auger.

Caliber; importance. [Obs.] Yet are they much too light for the bore of the matter. Shak.

A person or thing that wearies by prolixity or dullness; a tiresome person or affair; any person or thing which causes ennui. It is as great a bore as to hear a poet read his own verses. Hawthorne. Bore, n. [Icel. b¾ra wave: cf. G. empor upwards, OHG. bor height, burren to lift, perh. allied to AS. beran, E. 1st bear. ?92.] (Physical Geog.) (a) A tidal flood which regularly or occasionally rushes into certain rivers of peculiar configuration or location, in one or more waves which present a very abrupt front of considerable height, dangerous to shipping, as at the mouth of the Amazon, in South America, the Hoogly and Indus, in India, and the TsienÐtang, in China. (b) Less properly, a very high and rapid tidal flow, when not so abrupt, such as occurs at the Bay of Fundy and in the British Channel. Bore, imp. of 1st & 2d Bear. Boreïal (?), a. [L. borealis: cf. F. bor,al. See Boreas.] Northern; pertaining to the north, or to the north wind; as, a boreal bird; a boreal blast. So from their own clear north in radiant streams, Bright over Europe bursts the boreal morn. Thomson. Ø Boreïas (?), n. [L. boreas, Gr. ?.] The north wind; Ð usually a personification. Borecole · (?), n. [Cf. D. boerenkool (lit.) husbandman's cabbage.] A brassicaceous plant of many varieties, cultivated for its leaves, which are not formed into a compact head like the cabbage, but are loose, and are generally curled or wrinkled; kale. Boredom (?), n. 1. The state of being bored, or pestered; a state of ennui. Dickens.

The realm of bores; bores, collectively. Boïree (?), n. Same as Bourr,. [Obs.] Swift. Borel (?), n. See Borrel. Boreïle (?), n. (Zo"l.) The smaller twoÐhorned rhinoceros of South Africa (Atelodus bicornis). Borer (?), n. 1. One that bores; an instrument for boring.

(Zo"l.) (a) A marine, bivalve mollusk, of the genus Teredo and allies, which burrows in wood. See Teredo. (b) Any bivalve mollusk (Saxicava, Lithodomus, etc.) which bores into limestone and similar substances. (c) One of the larv‘ of many species of insects, which penetrate trees, as the apple, peach, pine, etc. See Apple borer, under Apple. (d) The hagfish (Myxine). Boric (?), a. (Chem.) Of, pertaining to, or containing, boron. Boric acid, a white crystalline substance B(OH)3, easily obtained from its salts, and occurring in solution in the hot lagoons of Tuscany. Boride (?), n. (Chem.) A binary compound of boron with a more positive or basic element or radical; Ð formerly called boruret. Boring (?), n. 1. The act or process of one who, or that which, bores; as, the boring of cannon; the boring of piles and ship timbers by certain marine mollusks. One of the most important applications of boring is in the formation of artesian wells. Tomlinson.

A hole made by boring.

pl. The chips or fragments made by boring. Boring bar, a revolving or stationary bar, carrying one or more cutting tools for dressing round holes. Ð Boring tool (Metal Working), a cutting tool placed in a cutter head to dress round holes. Knight. Born (?), p. p. & a. [See Bear, v. t.] 1. Brought forth, as an animal; brought into life; introduced by birth. No one could be born into slavery in Mexico. Prescott.

Having from birth a certain character; by or from birth; by nature; innate; as, a born liar. ½A born matchmaker., W. D. Howells. Born again (Theol.), regenerated; renewed; having received spiritual life. ½Except a man be born again, he can not see the kingdom of God., John iii. 3. Ð Born days, days since one was born; lifetime. [Colloq.] Borne (?), p. p. of Bear. Carried; conveyed;; supported; defrayed. See Bear, v. t. Borneïol (?), n. [Borneo + ïol.] (Chem.) A rare variety of camphor, C10H17.OH, resembling ordinary camphor, from which it can be produced by reduction. It is said to occur in the camphor tree of Borneo and Sumatra (Dryobalanops camphora), but the natural borneol is rarely found in European or American commerce, being in great request by the Chinese. Called also Borneo camphor, Malay camphor, and camphol. Bornite (?), n. [Named after Von Born, a mineralogist.] (Min.) A valuable ore of copper, containing copper, iron, and sulphur; Ð also called purple copper ore (or erubescite), in allusion to the colors shown upon the slightly tarnished surface. Bo · roïfluorïide (?), n. [Boron + fluoride.] (Chem.) A double fluoride of boron and hydrogen, or some other positive element, or radical; Ð called also fluoboride, and formerly fluoborate. Boroïglycerïide (?), n. [Boron + glyceride.] (Chem.) A compound of boric acid and glycerin, used as an antiseptic. Boron (?), n. [See Borax.] (Chem.) A nonmetallic element occurring abundantly in borax. It is reduced with difficulty to the free state, when it can be obtained in several different forms; viz., as a substance of a deep olive color, in a semimetallic form, and in colorless quadratic crystals similar to the diamond in hardness and other properties. It occurs in nature also in boracite, datolite, tourmaline, and some other minerals. Atomic weight 10.9. Symbol B. Boroĭsiliĭcate (?), n. [Boron + silicate.] (Chem.) A double salt of boric and silicic acids, as in the natural minerals tourmaline, datolite, etc. Borough (?), n. [OE. burgh, burw, boru, port, town, burrow, AS. burh, burg; akin to Icel., Sw., & Dan. borg, OS. & D. burg, OHG. puruc, purc, MHG. burc, G. burg, Goth. baɼrgs; and from the root of AS. beorgan to hide, save, defend, G. bergen; or perh. from that of AS. beorg hill, mountain. ?95. See Bury, v. t., and cf. Burrow, Burg, Bury, n., Burgess, Iceberg, Borrow, Harbor, Hauberk.] 1. In England, an incorporated town that is not a city; also, a town that sends members to parliament; in Scotland, a body corporate, consisting of the inhabitants of a certain district, erected by the sovereign, with a certain jurisdiction; in America, an incorporated town or village, as in Pennsylvania and Connecticut. Burrill. Erskine.

The collective body of citizens or inhabitants of a borough; as, the borough voted to lay a tax. Close borough, or Pocket borough, a borough having the right of sending a member to Parliament, whose nomination is in the hands of a single person. Ð Rotten borough, a name given to any borough which, at the time of the passage of the Reform Bill of 1832, contained but few voters, yet retained the privilege of sending a member to Parliament. Borough, n. [See Borrow.] (O. Eng. Law) (a) An association of men who gave pledges or sureties to the king for the good behavior of each other. (b) The pledge or surety thus given. Blackstone. Tomlins. BoroughÐEnglish (?), n. (Eng. Law) A custom, as in some ancient boroughs, by which lands and tenements descend to the youngest son, instead of the eldest; or, if the owner have no issue, to the youngest brother. Blackstone. Boroughĭhead · (?), n. See Headborough. [Obs.] Boroughĭholder (?), n. A headborough; a borsholder. Boroughĭmaster (?), n. [Cf. Burgomaster.] The mayor, governor, or bailiff of a borough. Boroughĭmonger (?), n. One who buys or sells the parliamentary seats of boroughs. Boroughĭmongerĭing, Boroughĭmongerĭy (?), n. The practices of a boroughmonger. Borĭracho (?), n. See Borachio. [Obs.] Borrage (?), n., Borĭrag · iĭnaceous (?), a., etc. See Borage, n., etc. Borrel (?), n. [OF. burel a kind of coarse woolen cloth, fr. F. bure drugget. See Bureau. Rustic and common people dressed in this cloth, which was prob. so called from its color.] 1. Coarse woolen cloth; hence, coarse clothing; a garment. [Obs.] Chaucer.

A kind of light stuff, of silk and wool. Borrel, a. [Prob. from Borrel, n.] Ignorant, unlearned; belonging to the laity. [Obs.] Chaucer. Borrow (?), v. t. [imp. & p.p. Borrowed (?); p. pr. & vb. n. Borrowing.] [OE. borwen, AS. borgian, fr. borg, borh, pledge; akin to D. borg, G. borg; prob. fr. root of AS. beorgan to protect. ?95. See 1st Borough.] 1. To receive from another as a loan, with the implied or expressed intention of returning the identical article or its equivalent in kind; Ð the opposite of lend.

(Arith.) To take (one or more) from the next higher denomination in order to add it to the next lower; Ð a term of subtraction when the figure of the subtrahend is larger than the corresponding one of the minuend.

To copy or imitate; to adopt; as, to borrow the style, manner, or opinions of another. Rites borrowed from the ancients. Macaulay. It is not hard for any man, who hath a Bible in his hands, to borrow good words and holy sayings in abundance; but to make them his own is a work of grace only from above. Milton.

To feign or counterfeit. ½Borrowed hair.¸ Spenser. The borrowed majesty of England. Shak.

To receive; to take; to derive. Any drop thou borrowedst from thy mother. Shak. To borrow trouble, to be needlessly troubled; to be overapprehensive. Borrow, n. 1. Something deposited as security; a pledge; a surety; a hostage. [Obs.] Ye may retain as borrows my two priests. Sir W. Scott.

The act of borrowing. [Obs.] Of your royal presence I'll adventure The borrow of a week. Shak. Borrowĭer (?), n. One who borrows. Neither a borrower nor a lender be. Shak. Borshold·er (?), n. [OE. borsolder; prob. fr. AS. borg, gen. borges, pledge + ealdor elder. See Borrow, and Elder, a.] (Eng. Law) The head or chief of a tithing, or borough (see 2d Borough); the headborough; a parish constable. Spelman. Bort (?), n. Imperfectly crystallized or coarse diamonds, or fragments made in cutting good diamonds which are reduced to powder and used in lapidary work. Boruĭret (?), n. (Chem.) A boride. [Obs.] Borwe (?), n. Pledge; borrow. [Obs.] Chaucer. Ø Bos (?), n. [L., ox, cow.] (Zo"l.) A genus of ruminant quadrupeds, including the wild and domestic cattle, distinguished by a stout body, hollow horns, and a large fold of skin hanging from the neck. Ø Bosa (?), n. [Ar. b?za, Pers. b?zah: cf. F. bosan.] A drink, used in the East. See Boza. Boscage (?), n. [OF. boscage grove, F. bocage, fr. LL. boscus, buscus, thicket, wood. See 1st Bush.] 1. A growth of trees or shrubs; underwood; a thicket; thick foliage; a wooded landscape.

(O. Eng. Law) Food or sustenance for cattle, obtained from bushes and trees; also, a tax on wood. Bosh (?), n. [Cf. G. posse joke, trifle; It. bozzo a rough stone, bozzetto a rough sketch, sĭbozzo a rough draught, sketch.] Figure; outline; show. [Obs.] Bosh, n. [Turk.] Empty talk; contemptible nonsense; trash; humbug. [Colloq.] Bosh, n.; pl. Boshes (?). [Cf. G. b"schung a slope.]

One of the sloping sides of the lower part of a blast furnace; also, one of the hollow iron or brick sides of the bed of a puddling or boiling furnace.

pl. The lower part of a blast furnace, which slopes inward, or the widest space at the top of this part.

In forging and smelting, a trough in which tools and ingots are cooled. Ø Boshbok (?), n. [D. bosch wood + bok buck.] (Zo"l.) A kind of antelope. See Bush buck. Ø Boshvark (?), n. [D. bosch wood + varken pig.] (Zo"l.) The bush hog. See under Bush, a thicket. Ø Bosjesĭman (?), n.; pl. Bosjesmans. [D. boschjesman.] See Bushman. Bosk (?), n. [See Bosket.] A thicket; a small wood. ½Through bosk and dell. Sir W. Scott. Boskage (?), n. Same as Boscage. Thridding the somber boskage of the wood. Tennyson. Bosket, Bosquet (?), n. [F. bosquet a little wood, dim. fr. LL. boscus. See Boscage, and cf. Bouquet.] (Gardening) A grove; a thicket; shrubbery; an inclosure formed by branches of trees, regularly or irregularly disposed. Boskiĭness (?), n. Boscage; also, the state or quality of being bosky. Bosky (?), a. [Cf. Bushy.] 1. Woody or bushy; covered with boscage or thickets. Milton.

Caused by boscage. Darkened over by long bosky shadows. H. James. Bosom (?), n. [AS. b?sm; akin to D. bozem, Fries. b?sm, OHG. puosum, G. busen, and prob. E. bough.] 1. The breast of a human being; the part, between the arms, to which anything is pressed when embraced by them. You must prepare your bosom for his knife. Shak.

The breast, considered as the seat of the passions, affections, and operations of the mind; consciousness; se??et thoughts. Tut, I am in their bosoms, and I know Wherefore they do it. Shak. If I covered my transgressions as Adam, by hiding my iniquity in my bosom. Job xxxi. 33.

Embrace; loving or affectionate inclosure; fold. Within the bosom of that church. Hooker.

Any thing or place resembling the breast; a supporting surface; an inner recess; the interior; as, the bosom of the earth. ½The bosom of the ocean. Addison.

The part of the dress worn upon the breast; an article, or a portion of an article, of dress to be worn upon the breast; as, the bosom of a shirt; a linen bosom. He put his hand into his bosom: and when he took it out, behold, his hand was leprous as snow. Ex.iv. 6.

Inclination; desire. [Obs.] Shak.

A depression round the eye of a millstone. Knight. Bosom, a. 1. Of or pertaining to the bosom.

Intimate; confidential; familiar; trusted; cherished; beloved; as, a bosom friend. Bosom, v. t. [imp. & p.p. Bosomed (?); p. pr. & vb. n. Bosoming.] 1. To inclose or carry in the bosom; to keep with care; to take to heart; to cherish. Bosom up my counsel, You'll find it wholesome. Shak.

To conceal; to hide from view; to embosom. To happy convents bosomed deep in vines. Pope. Bosomed (?), a. Having, or resembling, bosom; kept in the bosom; hidden. Bosomly (?), a. Characterized by recesses or sheltered hollows. Boson (?), n. See Boatswain. [Obs.] Dryden. Bosĭporĭlan (?), a. [L. Bosporus, G. ?, lit., oxĭford, the ox's or heifer's ford, on account of Io's passage here as a heifer; fr. ? ox, heifer + ? ford.] Of or pertaining to the Thracian or the Cimmerian Bosporus. The Alans forced the Bosporian kings to pay them tribute and exterminated the Taurians. Tooke. Bospoĭrus (?), n. [L.] A strait or narrow sea between two seas, or a lake and a seas; as, the Bosporus (formerly the Thracian Bosporus) or Strait of Constantinople, between the Black Sea and Sea of Marmora; the Cimmerian Bosporus, between the Black Sea and Sea of Azof. [Written also Bosphorus.] Bosquet (?), n. See Bosket. Boss (?), n.; pl. Bosses (?). [OE. boce, bose, boche, OF. boce, boche, bosse, F. bosse, of G. origin; cf. OHG. bŏzo tuft, bunch, OHG. bŏzan, MHG. b"zen, to beat. See Beat, and cf. Botch a swelling.] 1. Any protuberant part; a round, swelling part or body; a knoblike process; as, a boss of wood.

A protuberant ornament on any work, either of different material from that of the work or of the same, as

<— p. 169 —>
upon a buckler or bridle; a stud; a knob; the central projection of a shield. See Umbilicus.

(Arch.) A projecting ornament placed at the intersection of the ribs of ceilings, whether vaulted or flat, and in other situations.

[Cf. D. bus box, Dan. b"sse.] A wooden vessel for the mortar used in tiling or masonry, hung by a hook from the laths, or from the rounds of a ladder.

Gwilt.

(Mech.) (a) The enlarged part of a shaft, on which a wheel is keyed, or at the end, where it is coupled to another. (b) A swage or die used for shaping metals.

A head or reservoir of water. [Obs.]

Boss (?), v. t. [imp. & p.p. Bossed (?); p. pr. & vb. n. Bossing.] [OE. bocen, fr. OF. bocier. See the preceding word.] To ornament with bosses; to stud.

Boss, n. [D. baas master.] A master workman or superintendent; a director or manager; a political dictator. [Slang, U. S.]

Bossage (?), n. [F. bossage, fr. bosse. See Boss a stud.] 1. (Arch.) A stone in a building, left rough and projecting, to be afterward carved into shape.

Gwilt.

(Arch.) Rustic work, consisting of stones which seem to advance beyond the level of the building, by reason of indentures or channels left in the joinings.

Gwilt.

Bossed (?), a. Embossed; also, bossy.

Bosset (?), n. [Cf. Boss a stud.] (Zo"l.) A rudimental antler of a young male of the red deer.

Bossism (?), n. The rule or practices of bosses, esp. political bosses. [Slang, U. S.]

Bossy (?), a. Ornamented with bosses; studded.

Bossy, n. [Dim. fr. Prov. E. boss in bossÐcalf, bussÐcalf, for booseÐcalf, prop., a calf kept in the stall. See 1st Boose.] A cor or calf; Ð familiarly so called. [U. S.]

Boston (?), n. A game at cards, played by four persons, with two packs of fiftyÐtwo cards each; Ð said to be so called from Boston, Massachusetts, and to have been invented by officers of the French army in America during the Revolutionary war.

Bosİwellilan (?), a. Relating to, or characteristic of, Boswell, the biographer of Dr. Johnson.

Boswelllism (?), n. The style of Boswell.

Bot (?), n. (Zo"l.) See Bots.

Boİtanic (?), **Boİtanicİal** (?), } a. [Cf. F. botanique. See Botany.] Of or pertaining to botany; relating to the study of plants; as, a botanical system, arrangement, textbook, expedition. Ð Botanicİalİly, adv.

Botanic garden, a garden devoted to the culture of plants collected for the purpose of illustrating the science of botany. Ð **Botanic physician**, a physician whose medicines consist chiefly of herbs and roots.

Botaİnist (?), n. [Cf. F. botaniste.] One skilled in botany; one versed in the knowledge of plants.

Botaİnize (?), v. i. [imp. & p.p. Botanized (?); p. pr. & vb. n. Botanizing (?).] [Cf. F. botaniser.] To seek after plants for botanical investigation; to study plants.

Botaİnize, v. t. To explore for botanical purposes.

Botaİni · zer (?), n. One who botanizes.

Bot · aİnoloİger (?), n. A botanist. [Obs.]

Bot · aİnoloİgy (?), n. [Botany + İlogy: cf. F. botanologie.] The science of botany. [Obs.]

Bailey.

Botaİnoİman · cy (?), n. [Botany + İmancy: cf. F. botanomantie.] An ancient species of divination by means of plants, esp. sage and fig leaves.

Botaİny (?), n.; pl. Botanies (?). [F. botanique, a. & n., fr. Gr. ? botanic, fr. ? herb, plant, fr. ? to feed, graze.] 1. The science which treats of the structure of plants, the functions of their parts, their places of growth, their classification, and the terms which are employed in their description and denomination. See Plant.

A book which treats of the science of botany.

µ Botany is divided into various departments; as, Structural Botany, which investigates the structure and organic composition of plants; Physiological Botany, the study of their functions and life; and Systematic Botany, which has to do with their classification, description, nomenclature, etc.

Botaĭny Bay (?). A harbor on the east coast of Australia, and an English convict settlement there; Ð so called from the number of new plants found on its shore at its discovery by Cook in 1770.

Hence, any place to which desperadoes resort.

Botany Bay kino (Med.), an astringent, reddish substance consisting of the inspissated juice of several Australian species of Eucalyptus. Ð Botany Bay resin (Med.), a resin of reddish yellow color, resembling gamboge, the product of different Australian species of Xanthorrh'a, esp. the grass three (X. hastilis.)

Boĭtargo (?), n. [It. bottarga, bottarica; or Sp. botarga; a kind of large sausages, a sort of wide breeches: cf. F. boutargue.] A sort of cake or sausage, made of the salted roes of the mullet, much used on the coast of the Mediterranean as an incentive to drink.

Botch (?), n.; pl. Botches (?). [Same as Boss a stud. For senses 2 & 3 cf. D. botsen to beat, akin to E. beat.] 1. A swelling on the skin; a large ulcerous affection; a boil; an eruptive disease. [Obs. or Dial.]

Botches and blains must all his flesh emboss.
Milton.

A patch put on, or a part of a garment patched or ?ended in a clumsy manner.

Work done in a bungling manner; a clumsy performance; a piece of work, or a place in work, marred in the doing, or not properly finished; a bungle.

To leave no rubs nor botches in the work.
Shak.

Botch, v. t. [imp. & p.p. Botched (?); p. pr. & vb. n. Botching.] [See Botch, n.] 1. To mark with, or as with, botches.

Young Hylas, botched with stains.
Garth.

To repair; to mend; esp. to patch in a clumsy or imperfect manner, as a garment; Ð sometimes with up.

Sick bodies ... to be kept and botched up for a time.
Robynson (More's Utopia).

To put together unsuitably or unskillfully; to express or perform in a bungling manner; to spoil or mar, as by unskillful work.

For treason botched in rhyme will be thy bane.
Dryden.

Botchedĭly (?), adv. In a clumsy manner.

Botcher (?), n. 1. One who mends or patches, esp. a tailor or cobbler. Shak.

A clumsy or careless workman; a bungler.

(Zo"l.) A young salmon; a grilse.

Botcherĭly, a. Bungling; awkward. [R.]

Botcherĭy (?), n. A botching, or that which is done by botching; clumsy or careless workmanship.

Botchy (?), a. Marked with botches; full of botches; poorly done. ½This botchy business.ͺ
Bp. Watson.

Bote (?), n. [Old form of boot; Đ used in composition. See 1st Boot.] (Law) (a) Compensation; amends; satisfaction; expiation; as, man bote, a compensation or a man slain. (b) Payment of any kind. Bouvier. (c) A privilege or allowance of necessaries.

μ This word is still used in composition as equivalent to the French estovers, supplies, necessaries; as, housebote, a sufficiency of wood to repair a house, or for fuel, sometimes called firebote; so plowbote, cartbote, wood for making or repairing instruments of husbandry; haybote or hedgebote, wood for hedges, fences, etc. These were privileges enjoyed by tenants under the feudal system.

Burrill. Bouvier. Blackstone.

Boteless, a. Unavailing; in vain. See Bootless.

Botfly · (?), n. (Zo"l.) A dipterous insect of the family (Estrid‘, of many different species, some of which are particularly troublesome to domestic animals, as the horse, ox, and sheep, on which they deposit their eggs. A common species is one of the botflies of the horse (Gastrophilus equi), the larv‘ of which (bots) are taken into the stomach of the animal, where they live several months and pass through their larval states. In tropical America one species sometimes lives under the human skin, and another in the stomach. See Gadfly.

Both (?), a. or pron. [OE. bothe, ba?e, fr. Icel. b¾?ir; akin to Dan. baade, Sw. b†da, Goth. baj??s, OHG. beid?, b?d?, G. & D. beide, also AS. begen, b¾, b?, Goth. bai, and Gr. ?, L. ambo, Lith. ab..., OSlav. oba, Skr. ubha. ?310. Cf. AmbÐ.] The one and the other; the two; the pair, without exception of either.

μ It is generally used adjectively with nouns; as, both horses ran away; but with pronouns, and often with nous, it is used substantively, and followed by of.

It frequently stands as a pronoun.

She alone is heir to both of us.
Shak.

Abraham took sheep and oxen, and gave them unto Abimelech; and both of them made a covenant.
Gen. xxi. 27.

He will not bear the loss of his rank, because he can bear the loss of his estate; but he will bear both, because he is prepared for both.
Bolingbroke.

It is often used in apposition with nouns or pronouns.

Thy weal and woe are both of them extremes.
Shak.

This said, they both betook them several ways.
Milton.

Both now always precedes any other attributive words; as, both their armies; both our eyes.

Both of is used before pronouns in the objective case; as, both of us, them, whom, etc.; but before substantives its used is colloquial, both (without of) being the preferred form; as, both the brothers.

Both, conj. As well; not only; equally.

Both precedes the first of two co"rdinate words or phrases, and is followed by and before the other, both ... and ...; as well the one as the other; not only this, but also that; equally the former and the latter. It is also sometimes followed by more than two co"rdinate words, connected by and expressed or understood.

To judge both quick and dead.
Milton.

A masterpiece both for argument and style.
Goldsmith.

To whom bothe heven and erthe and see is sene.
Chaucer.

Both mongrel, puppy, whelp, and hound.
Goldsmith.

He prayeth well who loveth well
Both man and bird and beast.
Coleridge.

Bother (?), v. t. [imp. & p.p. Bothered (?); p. pr. & vb. n. Bothering.] [Cf. Ir. buaidhirt trouble, buaidhrim I vex.] To annoy; to trouble; to worry; to perplex. See Pother.

µ The imperative is sometimes used as an exclamation mildly imprecatory.

Bother, v. i. To feel care or anxiety; to make or take trouble; to be troublesome.

Without bothering about it.
H. James.

Bother, n. One who, or that which, bothers; state of perplexity or annoyance; embarrassment; worry; disturbance; petty trouble; as, to be in a bother.

Both · erĭation (?), n. The act of bothering, or state of being bothered; cause of trouble; perplexity; annoyance; vexation. [Colloq.]

Botherĭer (?), n. One who bothers.

Botherĭsome (?), a. Vexatious; causing bother; causing trouble or perplexity; troublesome.

BothĐhands · (?), n. A factotum. [R.]

He is his master's bothĐhands, I assure you.

B. Jonson.

Bothie (?), n. Same as Bothy. [Scot.]

Bothniĭan (?), Bothnic (?), } a. Of or pertaining to Bothnia, a country of northern Europe, or to a gulf of the same name which forms the northern part of the Baltic sea.

Ø Bothĭrenchyĭma (?), n. [Gr. ? pit + ? something poured in. Formed like parenchyma.] (Bot.) Dotted or pitted ducts or vessels forming the pores seen in many kinds of wood.

Bothy (?) Boothy (?) n.; pl. ĭies (?) [Scottish. Cf. Booth.] A wooden hut or humble cot, esp. a rude hut or barrack for unmarried farm servants; a shepherd's or hunter's hut; a booth. [Scot.]

Ø Bo · toĭcudos (?), n. pl. [Pg. botoque stopple. So called because they wear a wooden plug in the pierced lower lip.] A Brazilian tribe of Indians, noted for their use of poisons; Đ also called Aymbor,s.

Bo tree · (?). (Bot.) The peepul tree; esp., the very ancient tree standing at Anurajahpoora in Ceylon, grown from a slip of the tree under which Gautama is said to have received the heavenly light and so to have become Buddha.

The sacred bo tree of the Buddhists (Ficus religiosa), which is planted close to every temple, and attracts almost as much veneration as the status of the god himself ....It differs from the banyan (Ficus Indica) by sending down no roots from its branches.

Tennent.

Botryĭoĭgen (?), n. [Gr. ? cluster of grapes + ĭgen.] (Min.) A hydrous sulphate of iron of a deep red color. It often occurs in botryoidal form.

Botryĭoid (?), Bot · ryĭoidal (?), } a. [Gr. ? cluster of grapes + ĭoid.] Having the form of a bunch of grapes; like a cluster of grapes, as a mineral presenting an aggregation of small spherical or spheroidal prominences.

Botryĭoĭlite (?), n. [Gr. ? cluster of grapes + ĭlite.] (Min.) A variety of datolite, usually having a botryoidal structure.

Botryĭose · (?), a. (Bot.) (a) Having the form of a cluster of grapes. (b) Of the racemose or acropetal type of inflorescence.

Gray.

Bots (?), n. pl. [Cf. Gael. botus belly worm, boiteag maggot.] (Zo"l.) The larv' of several species of botfly, especially those larv' which infest the stomach, throat, or intestines of the horse, and are supposed to be the cause of various ailments. [Written also botts.] See Illust. of Botfly.

Botĭtine (?), n. [F. See Boot (for the foot.).]

A small boot; a lady's boot.

An appliance resembling a small boot furnished with straps, buckles, etc., used to correct or prevent distortions in the lower extremities of children.

Dunglison.

Bottle (?), n. [OE. bote, botelle, OF. botel, bouteille, F. bouteille, fr. LL. buticula, dim. of butis, buttis, butta, flask. Cf. Butt a cask.] 1. A hollow vessel, usually of glass or earthenware (but formerly of leather), with a narrow neck or mouth, for holding liquids.

The contents of a bottle; as much as a bottle contains; as, to drink a bottle of wine.

Fig.: Intoxicating liquor; as, to drown one's reason in the bottle.

µ Bottle is much used adjectively, or as the first part of a compound.

Bottle ale, bottled ale. [Obs.] Shak. Ð Bottle brush, a cylindrical brush for cleansing the interior of bottles. Ð Bottle fish (Zo"l.), a kind of deepÐsea eel (Saccopharynz ampullaceus), remarkable for its baglike gullet, which enables it to swallow fishes two or three times its won size. Ð Bottle flower. (Bot.) Same as Bluebottle. Ð Bottle glass, a coarse, green glass, used in the manufacture of bottles. Ure. Ð Bottle gourd (Bot.), the common gourd or calabash (Lagenaria Vulgaris), whose shell is used for bottles, dippers, etc. Ð Bottle grass (Bot.), a nutritious fodder grass (Setaria glauca and S. viridis); Ð called also foxtail, and green foxtail. Ð Bottle tit (Zo"l.), the European longÐtailed titmouse; Ð so called from the shape of its nest. Ð Bottle tree (Bot.), an Australian tree (Sterculia rupestris), with a bottleÐshaped, or greatly swollen, trunk. Ð Feeding bottle, Nursing bottle, a bottle with a rubber nipple (generally with an intervening tubve), used in feeding infants.

Bottle, v. t. [imp. & p.p. Bottled (?) p. pr. & vb. n. Bottling (?).] To put into bottles; to inclose in, or as in, a bottle or bottles; to keep or restrain as in a bottle; as, to bottle wine or porter; to bottle up one's wrath.

Bottle, n. [OE. botel, OF. botel, dim. of F. botte; cf. OHG. bozo bunch. See Boss stud.] A bundle, esp. of hay. [Obs. or Prov. Eng.]

Chaucer. Shak.

Bottled (?), a. 1. Put into bottles; inclosed in bottles; pent up in, or as in, a bottle.

Having the shape of a bottle; protuberant.

Shak.

Bottle green · (?). A dark shade of green, like that of bottle glass. Đ BottleĐgreen · , a.

Bottlehead · (?), n. (Zo"l.) A cetacean allied to the grampus; Đ called also bottlenosed whale<— bottle-nosed dolphin?—>.

μ There are several species so named, as the pilot whales, of the genus Globicephalus, and one or more species of Hypero"don (H. bidens, etc.), found on the European coast. See Blackfish, 1.

Bottlehold·er (?), n. 1. One who attends a pugilist in a prize fight; Đ so called from the bottle of water of which he has charge.

> One who assists or supports another in a contest; an abettor; a backer. [Colloq.]

Lord Palmerston considered himself the bottleholder of oppressed states.
The London Times.

BottleĐnose · (?), a. Having the nose bottleshaped, or large at the end.
Dickens.

Bottler (?), n. One who bottles wine, beer, soda water, etc.

Bottlescrew · (?) n. A corkscrew.
Swift.

Bottling (?) n. The act or the process of
<— p. 170 —>
? anything into bottles (as beer, mineral water, etc., and corking the bottles.

Bottom (?), n. [OE. botum, botme, AS. botm; ?akin to OS. bodom, D. bodem, OHG. podam, G. boden, Icel. botn, Sw. botten, Dan. bund (for budn), L. fundus (for fudnus), Gr.? (for ?), Skr. budhna (for ?hudhna), and Ir. bonn sole of the foot, W. bon stem, ?base. + 257. Cf. 4th Found, Fund, n.]

> The lowest part of anything; the foot; as, the bottom of a tree or well; the bottom of a hill, a lane, or a page.

Or dive into the bottom of the deep.

Shak.

> The part of anything which is beneath the contents and supports them, as the part of a chair on which a person sits, the circular base or lower head of a cask or tub, or the plank floor of a ship's hold; the under surface.

Barrels with the bottom knocked out.

Macaulay.

No two chairs were alike; such high backs and low backs and
      leather bottoms and worsted bottoms.
W.Irving.

> That upon which anything rests or is founded, in a literal or a figurative sense; foundation; groundwork.

The bed of a body of water, as of a river, lake, sea.

The fundament; the buttocks.

An abyss. [Obs.]

Dryden.

Low land formed by alluvial deposits along a river; low—lying ground; a dale; a valley. —The bottoms and the high grounds.

Stoddard.

(Naut.) The part of a ship which is ordinarily under water; hence, the vessel itself; a ship.

My ventures are not in one bottom trusted.
Shak.
Not to sell the teas, but to return them to London in the same bottoms in which they were shipped.
Bancroft.
Full bottom, a hull of such shape as permits carrying a large amount of merchandise.

Power of endurance; as, a horse of a good bottom.

Dregs or grounds; lees; sediment.

Johnson.

At bottom, At the bottom, at the foundation or basis; in reality. —He was at the bottom a good man.

J.F.Cooper.

— To be at the bottom of, to be the cause or originator of; to be the source of. [Usually in an opprobrious sense.]
J.H.Newman.

He was at the bottom of many excellent counsels.

Addison.

—To go to the bottom, to sink; esp. to be wrecked. — To touch bottom, to reach the lowest point; to find something on which to rest.

Bottom, a. Of or pertaining to the bottom; fundamental; lowest; under; as, bottom rock; the bottom board of a wagon box; bottom prices.

Bottom glade, a low glade or open place; a valley; a dale.

Milton.

—Bottom grass, grass growing on bottom lands.— Bottom land. See 1st Bottom, n., 7.?

Bottom, v.t. [imp. & p.p. Bottomed (?); p. pr. & vb. n. Bottoming.]

To found or build upon; to fix upon as a support; — followed by on or upon.

Action is supposed to be bottomed upon principle.

Atterbury.

Those false and deceiving grounds upon which many bottom their eternal state.

South.

To furnish with a bottom; as, to bottom a chair.

To reach or get to the bottom of.

Smiles.

Bottom, v. i.

To rest, as upon an ultimate support; to be based or grounded; Ð usually with on or upon.

Find on what foundation any proposition bottoms.

Locke.

To reach or impinge against the bottom, so as to impede free action, as when the point of a cog strikes the bottom of a space between two other cogs, or a piston the end of a cylinder.

Bottom, n. [OE. botme, perh. corrupt. for button. See Button.] A ball or skein of thread; a cocoon. [Obs.]

Silkworms finish their bottoms in ... fifteen days.

Mortimer.

Bottom, v. t. To wind round something, as in making a ball of thread. [Obs.]

As you unwind her love from him,
Lest it should ravel and be good to none,
You must provide to bottom it on me.

Shak.

Bottomed (?), a. Having at the bottom, or as a bottom; resting upon a bottom; grounded; Ð mostly,? in composition; as, sharpÐbottomed; wellÐbottomed.

Bottomless, a. Without a bottom; hence, fathomless; baseless; as, a bottomless abyss. ½Bottomless speculations.¸

Burke.

Buttomry (?), n. [From 1st Bottom in sense 8: cf.D. bodemerij. Cf. Bummery.] (Mar.Law) A contract in the nature of a mortgage, by which the owner of a ship, or the master as his agent, hypothecates and binds the ship (and sometimes the accruing freight) as security for the repayment of money advanced or lent for the use of the ship, if she terminates her voyage successfully. If the ship is lost by perils of the sea, the lender loses the money; but if the ship arrives safe, he is to receive the money lent, with the interest or premium stipulated, although it may, and usually does, exceed he legal rate of interest. See Hypothecation.

Bottonly (?), Bottoin, (?),} a. [F. boutonn,, fr. boutonner to bud, button.] (Her.) Having a bud or button, or a kind of trefoil, at the end; furnished with knobs or buttons.

Cross bottony (Her.), a cross having each arm
terminating in three rounded lobes, forming a sort of
trefoil.

Botts (?), n. pl. (Zo"l.) See Bots.

Botuliliform · (?), a. [L. botulus sausage + Ð form.] (Bot.) Having the shape of a sausage.

Henslow.

ØBouche (?), n. [F.] Same as Bush, a lining.

Bouche, v.t. Same as Bush, to line.

ØBouche, Bouch } (?), n. [F. bouche mouth, victuals.]

A mouth. [Obs.]

An allowance of meat and drink for the tables of inferior officers or servants in a nobleman's palace or at court. [Obs.]

ØBou · ch,es (?), n. pl. [F., morsels, mouthfuls, fr. bouche mouth.] (Cookery) Small patties.

Boud (?), n. A weevil; a worm that breeds in malt, biscuit, etc. [Obs.]

Tusser.

ØBoudoir (?), n. [F., fr. bouder to pout, be sulky.] A small room, esp. if pleasant, or elegantly furnished, to which a lady may retire to be alone, or to receive intimate friends; a lady's (or sometimes a gentleman's) private room.

Cowper.

ØBouffe (?), n. [F., buffoon.] Comic opera. See Opera Bouffe.

ØBou · gainIvilIl' · a (?), n. [Named from Bougainville, the French navigator.] (Bot.) A genus of plants of the order Nyctoginace', from tropical South America, having the flowers surrounded by large bracts.

Bouge (?), v. i. [imp. & p. p. Bouged (?)] [Variant of bulge. Cf. Bowge.]

To swell out. [Obs.]

To bilge. [Obs.] ½Their ship bouged.,

Hakluyt.

Bouge, v. t. To stave in; to bilge. [Obs.]

Holland.

Bouge, n. [F. bouche mouth, victuals.] Bouche (see Bouche, 2?); food and drink; provisions. [Obs.]

[They] made room for a bombardman that brought bouge for a
country lady or two, that fainted ... with fasting.

B.Jonson.

Bouget (?), n. [Cf. F. bougette sack, bag. Cf. Budget.] (Her.) A charge representing a leather vessel for carrying water; Ð also called water bouget.

Bough (?), n. [OE. bogh, AS. b"?g, b"h?, bough, shoulder; akin to Icel. b"?gr shoulder, bow of a ship, Sw. bog, Dan. bov, OHG. buog, G. bug, and to Gr.? (for ?)

forearm, Skr. b„?hu (for bh„?ghu) arm. ?88, 251. Cf. Bow of a ship.]

An arm or branch of a tree, esp. a large arm or main branch.

A gallows. [Archaic]

Spenser.

Bought (?), n. [Cf. Dan. bugt bend, turning, Icel. bug?a. Cf. Bight, Bout, and see Bow to bend.]

A flexure; a bend; a twist; a turn; a coil, as in a rope; as the boughts of a serpent. [Obs.]

Spenser.

The boughts of the fore legs.

Sir T.Browne.

The part of a sling that contains the stone. [Obs.]

Bought (?), imp & p.p. of Buy.
Bought, p.a. Purchased; bribed.
Boughten (?), a. Purchased; not obtained or produced at home.

Coleridge.

Boughty (?), a. Bending. [Obs.] Sherwood. ØBouïgie (?), n. [F. bougie wax candle, bougie, fr. Bougie, Bugia, a town of North Africa, from which these candles were first imported into Europe.]

(Surg.) A long, flexible instrument, that is introduced into the urethra, esophagus, etc., to remove obstructions, or for the other purposes. It was originally made of waxed linen rolled into cylindrical form.

(Pharm.) A long slender rod consisting of gelatin or some other substance that melts at the temperature of the body. It is impregnated with medicine, and designed for introduction into urethra, etc. ØBou·illi (?), n. [F., fr. bouillir to boil.] (Cookery) Boiled or stewed meat; beef boiled with vegetables in water from which its gravy is to be made; beef from which bouillon or soup has been made. ØBou·illon (?), n. [F., fr. bouillir to boil.]

A nutritious liquid food made by boiling beef, or other meat, in water; a clear soup or broth.

(Far.) An excrescence on a horse's frush or frog. Bouk (?), n. [AS. bc? belly; akin to G. bauch, Icel. b?kr body.]

The body. [Obs.] Chaucer.

Bulk; volume. [Scot.] Boul (?), n. A curved handle. Sir W.Scott. Bouïlangerïite (?), n. [From Boulanger, a French mineralogist.] (Min.) A mineral of a bluish gray color and metallic luster, usually in plumose masses, also compact.It is sulphide of antimony and lead. Bulder (?), n. Same as Bowlder. Boulderïy (?), a. Characterized by bowlders. Boule (?), Boulework· (?), n. Same as Buhl, Buhlwork. ØBouleïvard· (?), n. [F. boulevard, boulevart, fr. G. bollwerk. See Bulwark.]

Originally, a bulwark or rampart of fortification or fortified town.

A public walk or street occupying the site of demolished fortifications. Hence: A broad avenue in or around a city. ØBoule · verse · ment (?), n. [F., fr. bouleverser to overthrow.] Complete overthrow; disorder; a turning upside down. Buolt (?), n. Corrupted form Bolt. Boultel (?), Boultin (?), n. (Arch.) (a) A molding, the convexity of which is one fourth of a circle, being a member just below the abacus in the Tuscan and Roman Doric capital; a torus; an ovolo. (b) One of the shafts of a clustered column. [Written also bowtel, boltel, boultell, etc.] Boulter (?), n. [Etymol. uncertain.] A long, stout fishing line to which many hooks are attached. Boun (?), a. [See Bound ready.] Ready; prepared; destined; tending. [Obs.] Chaucer. Boun, v.t. To make or get ready. Sir W.Scott. Bounce (?), v.i. [imp. & p.p. Bounced (?); p.pr. & vb. n. Bouncing (?).] [OE. bunsen; cf. D. bonzen to strike, bounce, bons blow, LG. bunsen to knock; all prob. of imitative origin.]

To strike or thump, so as to rebound, or to make a sudden noise; a knock loudly. Another bounces as hard as he can knock. Swift. Against his bosom bounced his heaving heart. Dryden.

To leap or spring suddenly or unceremoniously; to bound; as, she bounced into the room. Out bounced the mastiff. Swift. Bounced off his arm+chair. Thackeray.

To boast; to talk big; to bluster. [Obs.] Bounce, v.t.

To drive against anything suddenly and violently; to bump; to thump. Swift.

To cause to bound or rebound; sometimes, to toss.

To eject violently, as from a ?room; to discharge unceremoniously, as from employment. [Collog. U. S.]

To bully; to scold. [Collog.] J.Fletcher. Bounce (?), n.

A sudden leap or bound; a rebound.

A heavy, sudden, and often noisy, blow or thump. The bounce burst open the door. Dryden.

An explosion, or the noise of one. [Obs.]

Bluster; brag; untruthful boasting; audacious exaggeration; an impudent lie; a bouncer. Johnson. De Quincey.?

(Zo"l.) A dogfish of Europe (Scyllium catulus). Bounce, adv. With a sudden leap; suddenly. This impudent puppy comes bounce in upon me. Bickerstaff. Bouncer (?), n.

One who bounces; a large, heavy person who makes much noise in moving.

A boaster; a bully. [Collog.] Johnson.

A bold lie; also, a liar. [Collog.] Marryat.

Something big; a good stout example of the kind. The stone must be a bouncer. De Quincey. Bouncing (?), a.

Stout; plump and healthy; lusty; buxom. Many tall and bouncing young ladies. Thackeray.

Excessive; big. ½A bouncing reckoning., B. & Fl.? Bouncing Bet (Bot.), the common soapwort (Saponaria officinalis). Harper's Mag. Bouncingly, adv. With a bounce. Bound (?), n. [OE. bounde, bunne, OF. bonne, bonde, bodne, F. borne, fr. LL. bodina, bodena, bonna; prob. of Celtic origin; cf. Arm. bonn boundary, limit, and boden, bod, a tuft or cluster of trees, by which a boundary or limit could be marked. Cf. Bourne.] The external or limiting line, either real or imaginary, of any object or space; that which limits or restrains, or within which something is limited or restrained; limit; confine; extent; boundary. He hath compassed the waters with bounds. Job xxvi. 10. On earth's remotest bounds. Campbell. And mete the bounds of hate and love.

Tennyson. To keep within bounds, not to exceed or pass beyond assigned limits; to act with propriety or discretion. Syn. Ð See Boundary. Bound, v.t. [imp. & p.p. Bounded; p.pr. & vb. n. Bounding.]

To limit; to terminate; to fix the furthest point of extension of; Ð said of natural or of moral objects; to lie along, or form, a boundary of; to inclose; to circumscribe; to restrain; to confine. Where full measure only bounds excess. Milton. Phlegethon ... Whose fiery flood the burning empire bounds. Dryden.

To name the boundaries of; as, to bound France. Bound, v.i. [F. bondir to leap, OF. bondir, bundir, to leap, resound, fr. L. bombitare to buzz, hum?, fr. bombus a humming, buzzing. See Bomb.]

To move with a sudden spring or leap, or with a succession of springs or leaps; as the beast bounded from his den; the herd bounded across the plain. Before his lord the ready spaniel bounds. Pope. And the waves bound beneath me as a steed That knows his rider. Byron.

To rebound, as an elastic ball. Bound, v.t.

To make to bound or leap; as, to bound a horse. [R.] Shak.

To cause to rebound; to throw so that it will rebound; as, to bound a ball on the floor. [Collog.] Bound, n.

A leap; an elastic spring; a jump. A bound of graceful hardihood. Wordsworth.

Rebound; as, the bound of a ball. Johnson.

(Dancing) Spring from one foot to the other. Bound, imp. & p. p. of Bind. Bound, p. p. & a.

Restrained by a hand, rope, chain, fetters, or the like.

Inclosed in a binding or cover; as, a bound volume.

Under legal or moral restraint or obligation.

Constrained or compelled; destined; certain; Ð followed by the infinitive; as, he is bound to succeed; he is bound to fail.

Resolved; as, I am bound to do it. [Collog. U. S.]

Constipated; costive. µ Used also in composition; as, icebound, windbound, hidebound, etc. Bound bailiff (Eng. Law), a sheriff's officer who serves writs, makes arrests, etc. The sheriff being answerable for the bailiff's misdemeanors, the bailiff is usually under bond for the faithful discharge of his trust. Ð Bound up in, entirely devoted to; inseparable from. Bound, a. [Past p. of OE. bounen to prepare, fr. boun ready, prepared, fr. Icel. b?inn, p. p. of ba? to dwell, prepare; akin to E. boor and bower. See Bond, a., and cf. Busk, v.] Ready or intending to go; on the way toward; going; Ð with to or for, or with an adverb of motion; as, a ship is bound to Cadiz, or for Cadiz. ½The mariner bound homeward., Cowper. Boundaïry (?), n.; pl. Boundaries (?) [From Bound a limit; cf. LL. bonnarium piece of land with fixed limits.] That which indicates or fixes a limit or extent, or marks a bound, as of a territory; a bounding or separating line; a real or imaginary limit. But still his native country lies Beyond the boundaries of the skies. N.Cotton. That bright and tranquil stream, the boundary of Louth and Meath. Macaulay. Sensation and reflection are the boundaries of our thoughts. Locke. Syn. Ð Limit; bound; border; term; termination; barrier; verge; confines; precinct. Bound, Boundary. Boundary, in its original and strictest sense, is a visible object or mark indicating a limit. Bound is the limit itself. But in ordinary usage the two words are made interchangeable. Bounden (?), p.p & a. [Old. p. p. of bind.]

Bound; fastened by bonds. [Obs.]

<— p. 171 —>

Under obligation; bound by some favor rendered; obliged; beholden. This holy word, that teacheth us truly our bounden duty toward our Lord God in every point. Ridley.

Made obligatory; imposed as a duty; binding. I am much bounden to your majesty. Shak. Bounder (?), n. One who, or that which, limits; a boundary. Sir T.Herbert. Bounding, a. Moving with a bound or bounds. The bounding pulse, the languid limb. Montgomery. Boundless, a. Without bounds or confines; illimitable; vast; unlimited. ½The boundless sky. Bryant. ½The boundless ocean. Dryden. ½Boundless rapacity. ½Boundless prospect of gain. Macaulay. Syn. Ð Unlimited; unconfined; immeasurable; illimitable; infinite. Ð Boundlessĭly, adv. Ð BoundlessÐness, n. Bountĕous (?), a. [OE. bountevous, fr. bounte bounty.] Liberal in charity; disposed to give freely; generously liberal; munificent; beneficent; free in bestowing gifts; as, bounteous production. But O, thou bounteous Giver of all good. Cowper. Ð Bountĕousĭly, adv. Ð Bountĕousĭness, n. Bountĭful (?), a.

Free in giving; lib??ral in bestowing gifts and favors. God, the bountiful Author of our being. Locke.

Plentiful; abundant; as, a bountiful supply of food. Syn. Ð Liberal; munificent; generous; bounteous. Ð Bountĭfulĭly, adv. Ð Bountĭfulĭness, n. Bountĭhead (?), BountyĬhood (?), } n. Goodness; generosity. [Obs.] Spenser. Bounty, n.; pl. Bounties (?). [OE. bounte goodness, kindness, F. bont,, fr. L. bonitas, fr. bonus good, for older duonus; cf. Skr. duvas honor, respect.]

Goodness, kindness; virtue; worth. [Obs.] Nature set in her at once beauty with bounty. Gower.

Liberality in bestowing gifts or favors; gracious or liberal giving; generosity; munificence. My bounty is as boundless as the sea. Shak.

That which is given generously or liberally. ½Thy morning bounties. Cowper.

A premium offered or given to induce men to enlist into the public service; or to encourage any branch of industry, as husbandry or manufactures. Bounty jumper, one who, during the latter part of the Civil War, enlisted in the United States service, and deserted as soon as possible after receiving the bounty. [Colloq.] Ð Queen Anne's bounty (Eng. Hist.), a provision made in Queen Anne's reign for augmenting poor clerical livings. Syn. Ð Munificence; generosity; beneficence. Bouĭquet (?), n. [F. bouquet bunch, bunch of flowers, trees, feathers, for bousquet, bosquet, thicket, a little wood, dim. of LL. boscus. See Bush thicket, and cf. Bosket, Busket.]

A nosegay; a bunch of flowers.

A perfume; an aroma; as, the bouquet of wine. ØBou · queĭtin (?), n. [F.] (Zo"l.) The ibex. Bour (?), n. [See Bower a chamber.] A chamber or a cottage. [Obs.] Chaucer. Bourbon (?), n. [From the castle and seigniory of Bourbon in central France.]

A member of a family which has occupied several European thrones, and whose descendants still claim throne of France.

A politician who is behind the age; a ruler or politician who neither forgets nor learns anything; an obstinate conservative. Bourbonĭism (?), n. The principles of those adhering to the house of Bourbon; obstinate conservatism. Bourbonĭist, n. One who adheres to the house of Bourbon; a legitimist. Bourbon whisky. See under Whisky. Bourd (?), n. [F. bourde fib, lie, OF. borde, bourde, jest, joke.] A jest. [Obs.] Chaucer. Bourd (?), v.i. To jest. [Obs.] Chaucer. Bourder (?), n. A jester. [Obs.] Bourdon (?), n. [F., fr. L. burdo mule, esp. one used for carrying litters. Cf. Sp. muleta a young she mule; also, crutch, prop.] A pilgrim's staff. ØBourdon · (?), n. [F. See Burden a refrain.] (Mus.) (a) A drone bass, as in a bagpipe, or a hurdyÐgurdy. See Burden (of a song.) (b) A kind of organ stop. Bourĭgeois (?), n. [From a French type founder named Bourgeois, or fr. F. bourgeois of the middle class; hence applied to an intermediate size of type between brevier and long primer: cf. G. bourgeois, borgis.

Cf. Burgess.] (Print.) A size of type between long primer and brevier. See Type. µ This line is printed in bourgeois type.? ØBourǐgeois (?), n. [F., fr. bourg town; of German origin. See Burgess.] A man of middle rank in society; one of the shopkeeping class. [France.] Đ? a. Characteristic of the middle class, as in France. Bourǐgeoiǐsie ?, n. [F.] The French middle class, particularly such as are concerned in, or dependent on, trade. Bourgeon (?), v.i. [OE. burjoun a bud, burjounen to bud, F. bourgeon a bud, bourgeonner to bud; cf. OHG. burjan to raise.] To sprout; to put forth buds; to shoot forth, as a branch. Gayly to bourgeon and broadly to grow. Sir W.Scott. ØBouri (?), n. [Native name.] (Zo"l.) A mullet (Mugil capito) found in the rivers of Southern Europe and in Africa. Bourn, Bourne } (?), n. [OE. burne, borne, AS. burna; akin to OS. brunno spring, G. born, ? unnen, OHG. prunno, Goth. brunna, Icel. brunn?r and perh. to Gr. ?. The root is prob. that of burn, v., because the source of a stream seems to issue forth bubbling and boiling from the earth. Cf. Torrent, and see Burn, v.] A stream or rivulet; a burn. My little boat can safely pass this perilous bourn. Spenser. Bourn, Bourne } (?), n. [F. borne. See Bound a limit.] A bound; a boundary; a limit. Hence: Point aimed at; goal. Where the land slopes to its watery bourn. Cowper. The undiscovered country, from whose bourn No traveler returns. Shak. Sole bourn, sole wish, sole object of my song. Wordsworth. To make the doctrine ... their intellectual bourne. Tyndall. Bournless, a. Without a bourn or limit. Bournonǐite (?), n. [Named after Count? Bournon, a mineralogist.] (Min.) A mineral of a steelgray to black color and metallic luster, occurring crystallized, often in twin crystals shaped like cogwheels (wheel ore), also massive. It is a sulphide of antimony, lead, and copper. Bourǐnous (?), n. See Burnoose. ØBourǐr,e (?), n. [F.] (Mus.) An old French dance tune in common time. ØBourse (?), n. [F. bourse purse, exchange, LL. bursa, fr. Gr.? skin, hide, of which a purse was usually made. Cf. Purse, Burse.] An exchange, or place where merchants, bankers, etc., meet for business at certain hours; esp., the ?Stock Exchange of Paris.? Bouse (?), v.i. To drink immoderately; to carouse; to booze. See Booze. Bouse, n. Drink, esp. alcoholic drink; also, a carouse; a booze. ½A good bouse of liquor., Carlyle. Bouser (?), n. A toper; a boozer. ØBou · stroǐphedon (?), n. [Gr. ? turning like oxen in plowing; ? to turn.] An ancient mode of writing, in alternate directions, one line from left to right, and the next from right to left (as fields are plowed), as in early Greek and Hittite. Bouǐstroph · eǐdonic (?), a. Relating to the boustrophedon made of writing. Bouǐstorphic (?), a. [Gr. ? ?oxĐguiding.] Boustrophedonic. Bousy (?), a. Drunken; sotted; boozy. In his cups the bousy poet songs. Dryden. Bout (?), n. [A different spelling and application of bought bend.]

As much of an action as is performed at one time; a going and returning, as of workmen in reaping, mowing, etc.; a turn; a round. In notes with many a winding bout Of linked sweetness long drawn out. Milton. The prince ... has taken me in his train, so that I am in no danger of starving for this bout. Goldsmith.

A conflict; contest; attempt; trial; a setĐto at anything; as, a fencing bout; a drinking bout. The gentleman will, for his honor's sake, have one bout with you; he can not by the duello avoid it. Shak. Bouǐtade (?), n. [F., fr. bouter to thrust. See Butt.] An outbreak; a caprice; a whim. [Obs.] Boutefeu (?), n. [F.; bouter to thrust, ?put+feu fire.] An incendiary; an inciter of quarrels. [Obs.] Animated by ... John ... Chamber, a very boutefeu, ... they entered into open rebellion. Bacon. ØBou · ton · niŠre (?), n. [F., buttonhole.] A bouquet worn in a buttonhole. ØBouts · Iriǐm,s (?), n. pl. [F. bout ?end+rim, rhymed.] Words that rhyme, proposed as the ends of verses, to be filled out by the ingenuity of the person to whom they are offered. Bovate (?), n. [LL. bovata, fr. bos, bovis, ox.] (O.Eng.Law.) An oxgang, or as much land as an ox can plow in a year; an ancient measure of land, of indefinite quantity, but usually estimated at fifteen acres. Bovey coal · (?). (Min.) A kind of mineral coal, or brown lignite, burning with a weak flame, and generally a disagreeable odor; Đ found at Bovey Tracey, Devonshire, England. It is of geological age of the o"lite, and of the true coal era. Bovid (?), a. [L. bos, bovis, ox, cow.] (Zo"l.) Relating to that tribe of ruminant mammals of which the genus Bos is the type. Boviǐform (?), a. [L. bos, bovis, ox +?Đform.] Resembling an ox in form; oxÐshaped. [R.] Bovine (?), a. [LL. bovinus, fr.L. bos, bovis, ox, cow: cf. F. bovine. See Cow.]

(Zo"l.) of or pertaining to the genus Bos; relating to, or resembling, the ox or cow; oxlike; as, the bovine genus; a bovine antelope.

Having qualities characteristic of oxen or cows; sluggish and patient; dull; as, a bovine temperament. The bovine gaze of gaping rustics. W.Black. Bow (?), v.t. [imp. & p.p. Bowed (?); p. pr. & vb. n. Bowing.] [OE. bowen, bogen, bugen, AS. b?gan (generally v.i.); akin to D. buigen, OHG. biogan, G. biegen, beugen, Icel. boginn bent, beygja to bend, Sw. b"ja, Dan. b"ie, bugne, Coth. biugan; also to L. fugere to flee, Gr. ?, and Skr. bhuj to bend. ?88. Cf. Fugitive.]

To cause to deviate from straightness; to bend; to inflect; to make crooked or curved. We bow things the contrary way, to make them come to their natural straightness. Milton. The whole nation bowed their necks to the worst kind of tyranny. Prescott.

To exercise powerful or controlling influence over; to bend, figuratively; to turn; to incline. Adversities do more bow men's minds to religion. Bacon. Not to bow and bias their opinions. Fuller.

To bend or incline, as the head or body, in token of respect, gratitude, assent, homage, or condescension. They came to meet him, and bowed themselves to the ground before him. 2 Kings ii. 15.

To cause to bend down; to prostrate; to depress,;? to crush; to subdue. Whose heavy hand hath bowed you to the grave. Shak.

To express by bowing; as, to bow one's thanks. Bow (?), v.i. 1. To bend; to curve. [Obs.]

To stop. [Archaic] They stoop, they bow down together. Is.xlvi.2?

To bend the head, knee, or body, in token of reverence or submission; Ð often with down. O come, let us worship and bow down: let us kneel before the Lord our maker. Ps.xcv.6.

To incline the head in token of salutation, civility, or assent; to make bow. Admired, adored by all circling crowd, For wheresoe'er she turned her face, they bowed. Dryden. Bow (?), n. An inclination of the head, or a bending of the body, in token of reverence, respect, civility, or submission; an obeisance; as, a bow of deep humility. Bow (?), n. [OE. bowe, boge, AS. boga, fr. AS. b?gan to bend; akin to D. boog, G. bogen, Icel. bogi. See Bow, v.t.]

Anything bent, or in the form of a curve, as the rainbow. I do set my bow in the cloud. Gen.ix.13.

A weapon made of a strip of wood, or other elastic material, with a cord connecting the two ends, by means of which an arrow is propelled.

An ornamental knot, with projecting lops, formed by doubling a ribbon or string.

The ?UÐshaped piece which embraces the neck of an ox and fastens it to the yoke.

(Mus.) An appliance consisting of an elastic rod, with a number of horse hairs stretched from end to end of it, used in playing on a stringed instrument.

An acrograph.

(Mech. & Manuf.) Any instrument consisting of an elastic rod, with ends connected by a string, employed for giving reciprocating motion to a drill, or for preparing and arranging the hair, fur, etc., used by hatters.

(Naut.) A rude sort of quadrant formerly used for taking the sun's altitude at sea.

(Saddlery) sing. or pl. Two pieces of wood which form the arched forward part of a saddletree. Bow bearer (O. Eng. Law), an under officer of the forest who looked after trespassers. Ð Bow drill, a drill worked by a bow and string. Ð Bow instrument (Mus.), any stringed instrument from which the tones are produced by the bow. Ð Bow window (Arch.) See Bay window. Ð To draw a long bow, to lie; to exaggerate. [Collog.] Bow (?), v. i. [imp. & p. p. Bowed (?); p. pr. & vb. n. Bowing.] To play (music) with a bow. Ð v.i. To manage the bow. Bow (?), n. [Icel. b"?gr shoulder, bow of a ship. See Bough.]

(Naut.) The bending or rounded part of a ship forward; the stream or prow.

(Naut.) One who rows in the forward part of a boat; the bow oar. Bow chaser (Naut.), a gun in the bow for firing while chasing another vessel. Totten. Ð Bow piece, a piece of ordnance carried at the bow of a ship. Ð On the bow (Naut.), on that part of the horizon whithin 45? on either side of the line ahead. Totten. Bowaĭble (?), a. Capable of being bowed or bent; flexible; easily influenced; yielding. [Obs.] Bowbell· (?), n. One born within hearing distance of BowÐbells; a cockney. Halliwell. Bowĭbells· (?), n. pl. The bells of Bow Church in London; cockneydom. People born within the sound of BowÐbells are usually called cockneys. Murray's Handbook of London. Bowbent· (??), a. Bent, like a bow. Milton. BowÐcom· pass (?), n.; pl. BowÐcompasses (?).

An arcograph.

A small pair of compasses, one leg of which carries a pencil, or a pen, for drawing circles. Its legs are often connected by a bowÐshaped spring, instead of by a joint.

A pair of compasses, with a bow or arched plats riveted to one of the legs, and passing through the other. Bowel (?), n. [OE. bouel, bouele, OF. boel, boele, F. boyau, fr. L. botellus a small sausage, in LL. also intestine, dim. of L. botulus sausage.]

One of the intestines of an animal; an entrail, especially of man; a gut; Ð generally used in the plural. He burst asunder in the midst, and all his bowels gushed out. Acts i.18.

pl. Hence, figuratively: The interior part of anything; as, the bowels of the earth. His soldiers ... cried out amain, And rushed into the bowels of the battle. Shak.

pl. The seat of pity or kindness. Hence: Tenderness; compassion. ½Thou thing of no bowels., Shak. Bloody Bonner, that corpulent tyrant, full (as one said) of guts, and empty of bowels. Fuller.

pl. Offspring. [Obs.] Shak. Bowel, v.t. [imp. & p. p. Boweled or Bowelled (?); p.pr.& vb.n. Boweling or Bowelling.] To take out the bowels of; to eviscerate; to disembowel. Boweled (?), a. [Written also bowelled.] Having bowels; hollow. ½The boweled cavern., Thomson. Bowellless, a. Without pity. Sir T.Browne. Bowenlite (?), n. [From G.T.Bowen, who analyzed it in 1822.] (Min.) A hard, compact variety of serpentine found in Rhode Island. It is of a ligth green color and resembles jade. Bower (?), n. [From Bow, v. & n.]

One who bows or bends.

(Naut.) An anchor carried at the bow of a ship.

A muscle that bends a limb, esp. the arm. [Obs.] His rawbone arms, whose mighty brawned bowers Were wont to rive steel plates and helmets hew. Spenser. Best bower, Small bower. See the Note under Anchor.

<— p. 172 —>

Bower (?), n. [G. bauer a peasant. So called from the figure sometimes used for the knave in cards. See Boor.] One of the two highest cards in the pack commonly used in the game of euchre.

Right bower, the knave of the trump suit, the highest card (except the ½Joker‚) in the game. Ð Left bower, the knave of the other suit of the same color as the trump, being the next to the right bower in value. Ð Best bower or? Joker, in some forms of euchre and some other games, an extra card sometimes added to the pack, which takes precedence of all others as the highest card.

Bower, n. [OE. bour, bur, room, dwelling, AS. b?r, fr. the root of AS. ?ban to dwell; akin to Icel. br? chamber, storehouse, Sw. br? cage, Dan. buur, OHG. pr? room, G. bauer cage, bauer a peasant. ?97 Cf.Boor, Byre.]

Anciently, a chamber; a lodging room; esp., a lady's private apartment.

Give me my lute in bed now as I lie,
And lock the doors of mine unlucky bower.
Gascoigne.

A rustic cottage or abode; poetically, an attractive abode or retreat.

Shenstone. B.Johnson.

A shelter or covered place in a garden, made with boughs of trees or vines, etc., twined together; an arbor; a shady recess.

Bower, v.t. To embowar; to inclose.
Shak.
Bower, v.i. To lodge. [Obs.]
Spenser.
Bower, n. [From Bough, cf. Brancher.] (Falconry) A young hawk, when it begins to leave thenest. [Obs.]

Bower bird · (?). (Zo"l.) An Australian bird (Ptilonorhynchus violaceus or holosericeus), allied to the starling, which constructs singular bowers or playhouses of twigs and decorates them with brightcolored objects; the satin bird.

µ The name is also applied to other related birds of the same region, having similar habits; as, the spotted bower bird (Chalmydodera maculata), and the regent bird (Sericulus melinus).

Bowerly (?), a. Shading, like a bower; full of bowers.

A bowery maze that shades the purple streams.
Trumbull.

Bowerly, n.; pl. Boweries (?) [D. bouwerij.] A farm or plantation with its buildings. [U.S.Hist.]

The emigrants [in New York] were scattered on boweries or plantetions; and seeing the evils of this mode of living widely ?apart, they were advised, in 1643 and 1646, by the Dutch authorities, to gather into ½villages, towns, and hamlets, as the English were in the habit of doing.‚
Bancroft.

Bowerly, a. Characteristic of the street called the ?Bowery, in New York city; swaggering; flashy.

Bowess (?), n. (Falconry) Same as Bower. [Obs.]

Bowfin · (?), n. (Zo"l.) A voracious ganoid fish (Amia calva) found in the fresh waters of the United States; the mudfish; Ð called also Johnny Grindle, and dogfish.

Bowge (?), v. i. To swell out. See Bouge. [Obs.]

Bowge, v. t. To cause to leak. [Obs.] See Bouge.

Bowgrace · (?), n. (Naut.) A frame or fender of rope or junk, laid out at the sides or bows of a vessel to secure it from injury by floating ice.

Bow hand · (?). 1. (Archery) The hand that holds the bow, i.e., the left hand.

Surely he shoots wide on the bow hand.
Spenser.

(Mus.) The hand that draws the bow, i.e., the right hand.

Bowhead · (?), n. (Zo"l.) The great Arctic or Greenland whale. (Bal'na mysticetus). See Baleen, and Whale.

Bowie knife · (?). A knife with a strong blade from ten to fifteen inches long, and doubleÐedged near the point; Ð used as a hunting knife, and formerly as a weapon in the southwestern part of the United States. It was named from its inventor, Coolnel James Bowie. Also, by extension, any large sheath knife.

Bowing (?), n. (Mus.) 1. The act or art of managing the bow in playing on stringed instruments.

Bowing constitutes a principal part of the art of the violinist, the violist, etc.
J.W.Moore.

In hatmaking, the act or process of separating and distributing the fur or hair by means of a bow, to prepare it for felting.

Bowingly (?), adv. In a bending manner.

Bowknot · (?), n. A knot in which a portion of the string is drawn through in the form of a loop or bow, so as to be readily untied.

Bowl (?), n. [OE. bolle, AS. bolla; akin to Icel. bolli, Dan. bolle, G. bolle, and perh. to E. boil a tumor. Cf. Boll.]

A concave vessel of various forms (often approximately hemispherical), to hold liquids, etc.

Brought them food in bowls of basswood.
Longfellow.

Specifically, a drinking vessel for wine or other spirituous liquors; hence, convival drinking.

The contents of a full bowl; what a bowl will hold.

The bollow part of a thing; as, the bowl of a spoon.

Bowl (?), n. [F. boule, fr. L. bulla bubble, stud. Cf. Bull an edict, Bill a writing.]

A ball of wood or other material used for rolling on a level surface in play; a ball of hard wood having one side heavier than the other, so as to give it a bias when rolled.

pl. An ancient game, popular in Great Britain, played with biased balls on a level plat of greensward.

Like an uninstructed bowler, ... who thinks to attain the jack by delivering his bowl straightforward upon it.
Sir W.Scott.

pl. The game of tenpins or bowling. [U.S.]

Bowl (?), v.t. [imp. & p. p. Bowledÿ(?); p. pr. & vb. n. Bowling.] 1. To roll, as a bowl or cricket ball.

Break all the spokes and fellies from her wheel,
And bowl the round nave down the hill of heaven.
Shak.

To roll or carry smoothly on, or as on, wheels; as, we were bowled rapidly along the road.

To pelt or strike with anything rolled.

Alas, I had rather be set quick i' the earth,
And bowled to death with turnips?
Shak.

To bowl (a player) out ?, in cricket, to put out a striker by knocking down a bail or a stump in bowling.

Bowl, v. i.

To play with bowls.

To roll a ball on a plane, as at cricket, bowls, etc.

To move rapidly, smoothly, and like a ball; as, the carriage bowled along.

Bowlder, Boulder (?), n. [Cf. Sw. bullra to roar, rattle, Dan. buldre, dial. Sw. bullersteen larger kind of pebbles; perh. akin to E. bellow.]

A large stone, worn smooth or rounded by the action of water; a large pebble.

(Geol.) A mass of any rock, whether rounded or not, that has been transported by natural agencies from its native bed. See Drift.

Bowlder clay, the unstratified clay deposit of the Glacial or Drift epoch, often containing large numbers of bowlders. Ð Bowlder wall, a wall constructed of large stones or bowlders.

Bowlderly (?), a. Characterized by bowlders.

Bowleg · (?), n. A crooked leg.

Jer.Taylor.

BowlÐlegged · (?), a. Having crooked legs, esp. with the kness bent outward.

Johnson.

Bowler (?), n. One who plays at bowls, or who rolls the ball in cricket or any other game.

Bowless, a. Destitute of a bow.

Bowline (?), n. [Cf. D. boelijn, Icel. b"gl‹na?, Dan. bovline; properly the line attached to the shoulder or side of the sail. See Bow (of a ship), and Line.] (Naut.) A rope fastened near the middle of the leech or perpendicular edge of the square sails, by subordinate ropes, called bridles, and used to keep the weather edge of the sail tight forward, when the ship is closehauled.

Bowline bridles, the ropes by which the bowline is fastened to the leech of the sail. Ð Bowline knot. See Illust. under Knot. Ð On a bowline, closeÐhauled or sailing close to the wind; Ð said of a ship.

Bowling (?), n. The act of playing at or rolling bowls, or of rolling the ball at cricket; the game of bowls or of tenpins.

Bowling alley, a covered place for playing at bowls or tenpins. Ð Bowling green, a level piece of greensward or smooth ground for bowling, as the small park in lower Broadway, New York, where the Dutch of New Amsterdam played this game.?

Bowls (?), n. pl. See Bowl, a ball, a game.

Bowman (?), n.; pl. Bowmen (?). A man who uses a bow; an archer.

The whole city shall flee for the noise of the horsemen and bowmen.
Jer.iv.29.

Bowman's root. (Bot.) See Indian physic, under Indian.

Bowman (?), n. (Naut.) The man who rows the foremost oar in a boat; the bow oar.

Bowne (?), v.t. [See Boun.] To make ready; to prepare; to dress. [Obs.]
We will all bowne ourselves for the banquet.
Sir W.Scott.

Bow net · (?).

A trap for lobsters, being a wickerwork cylinder with a funnelÐshaped entrance at one end.

A net for catching birds.

J.H.Walsh.

Bow oar · (?).

The oar used by the bowman.

One who rows at the bow of a boat.

BowÐpen· (?), n. BowÐcompasses carrying a drawing pen. See BowÐcompass.

BowÐpen·cil (?), n. BowÐcompasses, one leg of which carries a pencil.

BowÐsaw· (?), n. A saw with a thin or narrow blade set in a strong frame.

Bowse (?), v.i. [See Booze, and Bouse.]

To carouse; to bouse; to booze.

De Quincey.

(Naut.) To pull or haul; as, to bowse upon a tack; to bowse away, i.e., to pull all together.

Bowse, n. A carouse; a drinking bout; a booze.

Bowshot· (?), n. The distance traversed by an arrow shot from a bow.

Bowsprit· (?), n. [Bow + sprit; akin to D.boegspriet; boeg bow of a ship + spriet, E. sprit, also Sw. bogspr"t, G. bugspriet.] (Naut.) A large boom or spar, which project over the stem of a ship or other vessel, to carry sail forward.

Bowssen (?), v.t. To drench; to soak; especially, to immerse (in water believed to have curative properties). [Obs.]

There were many bowssening places, for curing of mad men.

...If there appeared small amendment he was bowssened again and again.

Carew.

Bowstring· (?), n.

The string of a bow.

A string used by the Turks for strangling offenders.

Bowstring bridge, a bridge formed of an arch of timber or iron, often braced, the thrust of which is resisted by a tie forming a chord of the arch. Ð Bowstring girder, an arched beam strengthened by a tie connecting its two ends. Ð Bowstring hemp (Bot.), the tenacious fiber of the Sanseviera Zeylanica, growing in India and Africa, from which bowstrings are made.

Balfour.

Bowstring· (?), v.t. [imp. & p.p.] Bowstringed (?) or

Bowstrung (?); p.pr. & vb.n. Bowstringing.] To strangle with a bowstring.

Bowstringed· (?), p.a. 1. Furnished with bowstring.

Put to death with a bowstring; strangled.

Bowtel (?), n. See Boultel.

Bowwow · (?), n. An onomatopoetic name for a dog or its bark. Ð a. Onomatopoetic; as, the bowwow theory of language; a bowwow word.

[Jocose.]

Bowyer (?), n. [From Bow, like lawyer from law.]

An archer; one who uses bow.

One who makes or sells bows.

Box (?), n. [As. box, L. buxus, fr. Gr. ?. See Box a case.] (Bot.) A tree or shrub, flourishing in different parts of the world. The common box (Buxus sempervirens) has two varieties, one of which, the dwaft box (B.suffruticosa), is much used for borders in gardens. The wood of the tree varieties, being very hard and smooth, is extensively used in the arts, as by turners, engravers, mathematical instrument makers, etc.

Box elder, the ashÐleaved maple (Negundo aceroides), of North America. Ð Box holly, the butcher's broom (Russus aculeatus). Ð Box thorn, a shrub (Lycium barbarum). Ð Box tree, the tree variety of the common box.

Box, n.pl. Boxes (?) [As. box a small case or vessel with a cover; akin to OHG. buhsa box, G. bchse; fr. L. buxus boxwood, anything made of boxwood. See Pyx, and cf. Box a tree, Bushel.]

A receptacle or case of any firm material and of various shapes.

The quantity that a box contain.

A space with a few seats partitioned off in a theater, or other place of public amusement.

Laughed at by the pit, box, galleries, nay, stage.
Dorset.
The boxes and the pit are sovereign judges.
Dryden.

A chest or any receptacle for the deposit of money; as, a poor box; a contribution box.

Yet since his neighbors give, the churl unlocks,
Damning the poor, his trippleÐbolted box.
J.Warton.

A small country house. ½A shooting box.

Wilson.
Tight boxes neatly sashed.
Cowper.

A boxlike shed for shelter; as, a sentry box.

(Mach) (a) An axle box, journal box, journal bearing, or bushing. (b) A chamber or section of tube in which a valve works; the bucket of a lifting pump.

The driver's seat on a carriage or coach.

A present in a box; a present; esp. a Christmas box or gift. ½A Christmas box.,

Dickens.

(Baseball) The square in which the pitcher stands.

(Zo"l.) A Mediterranean food fish; the bogue.

μ Box is much used adjectively or in composition; as box lid, box maker, box circle, etc.; also with modifying substantives; as money box, letter box, bandbox, hatbox or hat box, snuff box or snuffbox.

Box beam (Arch.), a beam made of metal plates so as to have the form of a long box. Ð Box car (Railroads), a freight car covered with a roof and inclosed on the sides to protect its contents. Ð Box chronometer, a ship's chronometer, mounted in gimbals, to preserve its proper position. Ð Box coat, a thick overcoat for driving; sometimes with a heavy cape to carry off the rain. Ð Box coupling, a metal collar uniting the ends of shafts or other parts in machinery. Ð Box crab (Zo"l.), a crab of the genus Calappa, which, when at rest with the legs retracted, resembles a box. Ð Box drain (Arch.), a drain constructed with upright sides, and with flat top and bottom. Ð Box girder (Arch.), a box beam. Ð Box groove (Metal Working), a closed groove between two rolls, formed by a collar on one roll fitting between collars on another.

R.W.Raymond.

Ð Box metal, an alloy of copper and tin, or of zinc, lead, and antimony, for the bearings of journals, etc. Ð Box plait, a plait that doubles both to the rigth and the left. Ð Box turtle or Box tortoise (Zo"l.), a land tortoise or turtle of the genera Cistudo and Emys; Ð so named because it can withdraw entirely within its shell, which can be closed by hinged joints in the lower shell. Also, humorously, an exceedingly reticent person.

Emerson.

Ð In a box, in a perplexity or an embarrassing position; in difficulty. (Colloq.) Ð In the wrong box, out of one's place; out of one's element; awkwardly situated. (Colloq.)

Ridley (1554)?

Box, v.t. [imp. & p.p. Boxed (?); p.pr. & vb.n. Boxing.]

To inclose in a box.

To furnish with boxes, as a wheel.

(Arch.) To inclose with boarding, lathing, etc., so as to bring to a required form.

To box a tree, to make an incision or hole in a tree for the purpose of procuring the sap. Ð To box off, to divide into tight compartments. Ð To box up. (a) To put into a box in order to save; as, he had boxed up twelve score pounds. (b) To confine; as, to be boxed up in narrow quarters.

Box, n. [Cf.Dan. baske to slap, bask slap, blow. Cf. Pash.] A blow on the head or ear with the hand.

A goodÐhumored box on the ear.

W.Irving.

Box, v.i. To fight with the fist; to combat with, or as with, the hand or fist; to spar.

Box, v.t. To strike with the hand or fist, especially to strike on the ear, or on the side of the head.

Box, v.t. [Cf.Sp. boxar, now spelt bojar.] To boxhaul.

To box off (Naut.), to turn the head of a vessel either way by bracing the headyards aback. Ð To box the compass (Naut.), to name the thirtyÐtwo points of the compass in their order.

Boxber · ry (?), n. (Bot.) The wintergreern. (Gaultheria procumbens). [Local, U.S.]

<— p. 173 —>

Boxen (?), a. Made of boxwood; pertaining to, or resembling, the box (Buxus). [R.]

The faded hue of sapless boxen leaves.

Dryden.

Boxer (?),n. One who packs boxes.

Boxer ,n. One who boxes; a pugilist.

Boxfish · ÿ(?), n. (Zo"l.) The trunkfish.

Boxhaul· (?), v. t. [imp. & p. p. Boxhauled (?).] (Naut.) To put (a vessel) on the other tack by veering her short round on her heel; Ð so called from the circumstance of bracing the head yards abox (i. e., sharp aback, on the wind).

Totten.

Boxhaul · ing, n. (Naut.) A method of going from one tack to another. See Boxhaul.

Boxing, n. 1. The act of inclosing (anything) in a box, as for storage or transportation.

Material used in making boxes or casings.

Any boxlike inclosure or recess; a casing.

(Arch.) The external case of thin material used to bring any member to a required form.

Boxing, n. The act of fighting with the fist; a combat with the fist; sparring.

Blackstone.

Boxing glove, a large padded mitten or glove used in sparring for exercise or amusement.

BoxÐi · ronÿ(?), n. A hollow smoothing iron containing a heater within.

Boxkeep · er (?), n. An attendant at a theater who has charge of the boxes.

Boxthorn · (?), n. (Bot.) A plant of the genus Lycium, esp. Lycium barbarum.

Boxwood · (?), n. The wood of the box (Buxus).

Boy (?), n. [Cf. D. boef, Fries. boi, boy; akin to G. bube, Icel. bofi rouge.] A male child, from birth to the age of puberty; a lad; hence, a son.

My only boy fell by the side of great Dundee.

Sir W. Scott.

µBoy is often used as a term of comradeship, as in college, or in the army or navy. In the plural used colloquially of members of an assosiaton, fraternity, or party.

Boy bishop, a boy (usually a chorister) elected bishop, in old Christian sports, and invested with robes and other insignia. He practiced a kind of mimicry of the ceremonies in which the bishop usually officiated. The Old Boy, the Devil. [Slang] Ð Yellow boys, guineas. [Slang, Eng.] Ð Boy's love, a popular English name of Southernwood (Artemisia abrotonum);) Ð called also lad's love. Ð Boy's play, childish amusements; anything trifling.

Boy, v. t. To act as a boy; Ð in allusion to the former practice of boys acting women's parts on the stage.

I shall see

Some squeaking Cleopatra boy my greatness.

Shak.

BoÐyar (?), BoÐyard (?), n. [Russ. boi rin'.] A member of a Russian aristocratic order abolished by Peter the Great. Also, one of a privileged class in Roumania.

µ English writers sometimes call Russian landed proprietors boyars.

Ø Boyau (?), n.; pl. Boyaux or Boyaus (?). [F. boyau gut, a long and narrow place, and (of trenches) a branch. See Bowel.] (Fort.) A winding or zigzag trench forming a path or communication from one siegework to another, to a magazine, etc.

Boycott · (?), v. t. [imp. & p. p. Boycotted; p. pr. & vb. n. Boycotting.] [From Captain Boycott, a land agent in Mayo, Ireland, so treated in 1880.] To combine against (a landlord, tradesman, employer, or other person), to withhold social or business relations from him, and to deter other from holding such relations; to subject to a boycott.

Boycott, n. The process, fact, or pressure of boycotting; a combining to withhold or prevent dealing or social intercourse with a tradesman, employer, etc.; social and business interdiction for the purpose of coercion.

Boycott · er (?), n. A participant in boycotting.

BoycottÐism (?), n. Methods of boycotters.

BoydeÐkin (?), n. A dagger; a bodkin. [Obs.]

Boyer (?), n. [D. boeijer; Ð so called because these vessels were employed for laying the boeijen, or buoys: cf. F. boyer. See Buoy.] (Naut.) A Flemish sloop with a castle at each end.

Sir W. Raleigh.

Boyhood (?), n. [Boy + Ðhood.] The state of being a boy; the time during which one is a boy.

Hood.

Boyish, a. Resembling a boy in a manners or opinions; belonging to a boy; childish; trifling; puerile.

A boyish, odd conceit.

Baillie.

BoyishÐly, adv. In a boyish manner; like a boy.

BoyishÐness, n. The manners or behavior of a boy.

Boyism (?), n 1. Boyhood. [Obs.]

T.Warton.

The nature of a boy; childishness.

Dryden.

Boyle's law · ÿ(?). See under Law.

Ø Boza (?), n. [See Bosa.] An acidulated fermented drink of the Arabs and Egyptians, made from millet seed and various astringent substances; also, an intoxicating beverage made from hemp seed, darnel meal, and water. [Written also bosa, bozah, bouza.]

BraÐbantine (?), a. Pertaining to Brabant, an ancient province of the Netherlands.

Brabble (?), v.i. [D. brabbelen to talk confusedly. ?95. Cf. Blab, Babble.] To clamor; to contest noisily. [R.]

Brabble, n. A broil; a noisy contest; a wrangle.

This petty brabble will undo us all.

Shak.

BrabbleÐment (?), n. A brabble. [r.]

Holland.

Brabblerÿ3, n. A clamorous, quarrelsome, noisy fellow; a wrangler. [R]

Shak.

Braccate (?), a.[L. bracatus wearing breeches, fr. bracae breeches.] (Zo"l.) Furnished with feathers which conceal the feet.

Brace (?), n. [OF. brace, brasse, the two arms, embrace, fathom, F. brasse fathom, fr. L. bracchia the arms (stretched out), pl. of bracchium arm; cf. Gr. ?.] 1. That which holds anything tightly or supports it firmly; a bandage or a prop.

A cord, ligament, or rod, for producing or maintaining tension, as a cord on the side of a drum.

The little bones of the ear drum do in straining and relaxing it as the braces of the war drum do in that.

Derham.

The state of being braced or tight; tension.

The laxness of the tympanum, when it has lost its brace or tension.
Holder.

(Arch. & Engin.) A piece of material used to transmit, or change the direction of, weight or pressure; any one of the pieces, in a frame or truss, which divide the structure into triangular parts. It may act as a tie, or as a strut, and serves to prevent distortion of the structure, and transverse strains in its members. A boiler brace is a diagonal stay, connecting the head with the shell.

(Print.) A vertical curved line connecting two or more words or lines, which are to be taken together; thus, boll, bowl; or, in music, used to connect staves.

6. (Naut.) A rope reeved through a block at the end of a yard, by which the yard is moved horizontally; also, a rudder gudgeon.

(Mech.) A curved instrument or handle of iron or wood, for holding and turning bits, etc.; a bitstock.

A pair; a couple; as, a brace of ducks; now rarely applied to persons, except familiarly or with some contempt. ½A brace of greyhounds.

Shak.
He is said to have shot...fifty brace of pheasants.
Addison.
A brace of brethren, both bishops, both eminent for learning and religion, now appeared in the church.
Fuller.
But you, my brace of lords.
Shak.

9. pl. Straps or bands to sustain trousers; suspenders.
I embroidered for you a beautiful pair of braces.
Thackeray.

Harness; warlike preparation. [Obs.]

For that it stands not in such warlike brace.
Shak.

Armor for the arm; vantbrace.

(Mining) The mouth of a shaft. [Cornwall]

Angle brace. See under Angle.
Braceÿ(?), v. t. [imp. & p. p. Braced (?); p. pr. & vb. n. Bracing.] 1. To furnish with braces; to support; to prop; as, to brace a beam in a building.

To draw tight; to tighten; to put in a state of tension; to strain; to strengthen; as, to brace the nerves.

And welcome war to brace her drums.
Campbell.

To bind or tie closely; to fasten tightly.

The women of China, by bracing and binding them from their infancy, have very little feet.
Locke.
Some who spurs had first braced on.
Sir W. Scott.

To place in a position for resisting pressure; to hold firmly; as, he braced himself against the crowd.

A sturdy lance in his right hand he braced.
Fairfax.
(Naut.) To move around by means of braces; as, to brace the yards.

To brace about (Naut.), to turn (a yard) round for the contrary tack. Ð To brace a yard (Naut.), to move it horizontally by means of a brace. Ð To brace in (Naut.), to turn (a yard) by hauling in the weather brace. Ð To brace one's self, to call up one's energies. ½He braced himself for an effort which he was little able to make.

J.D.Forbes.Ð To brace to (Naut.), to turn (a yard) by checking or easing off the lee brace, and hauling in the weather one, to assist in tacking. Ð To brace up (Naut.), to bring (a yard) nearer the direction of the keel by hauling in the lee brace. Ð To brace up sharp (Naut.), to turn (a yard) as far forward as the rigging will permit.

Brace, v.i. To get tone or vigor; to rouse one's energies; Ðwith up. [Colloq.]

Bracelet (?), n. [F. bracelet, dim. of OF. bracel armlet, prop. little arm, dim. of bras arm, fr. L. bracchium. See Brace,n.] 1. An ornamental band or ring, for the wrist or the arm; in modern times, an ornament encircling the wrist, worn by women or girls.

A piece of defensive armor for the arm.

Johnson.

Bracer (?), n. 1. That which braces, binds, or makes firm; a band or bandage.

A covering to protect the arm of the bowman from the vibration of the string; also, a brassart.

Chaucer.

A medicine, as an astringent or a tonic, which gives tension or tone to any part of the body.

Johnson.

Brach (?), n. [OE. brache a kind of scenting hound or setting dog, OF. brache, ? braque, fr. OHG. braccho, G. bracke; possibly akin to E. fragrant, fr. L. fragrare to smell.] A bitch of the hound kind.

Shak.

Ø BrachƉelyƉtra (?), n. pl. [NL., fr. Gr. (?) short + ? a covering.] (Zo"l.) A group of beetles having short elytra, as the rove beetles.

ØBrachiƉa (?), n. pl. See Brachium.

BrachiƉal (?) or (?), a. [L. brachialis (bracchƉ), from bracchium (bracchƉ) arm: cf. F. brachial.] 1. (Anat.) Pertaining or belonging to the arm; as, the brachial artery; the brachial nerve.

Of the nature of an arm; resembling an arm.

Ø Brach · iƉata (?), n. pl. [See Brachiate.] (Zo"l.) A division of the Crinoidea, including those furnished with long jointed arms. See Crinoidea.

BrachiƉateÿ(?), a. [L. brachiatus (bracchƉ) with boughs or branches like arms, from brackium (bracchƉ) arm.] (Bot.) Having branches in pairs, decussated, all nearly horizontal, and each pair at right angles with the next, as in the maple and lilac.

Brach · iƉogaƉnoid (?), n. One of the Brachioganoidei.

Ø Brach · iƉoƉgaƉnoideƉi (?), n. pl.[NL., from L. brachium (bracchƉ) arm + NL. ganoidei.] (Zo"l.) An order of ganoid fishes of which the bichir of Africa is a living example. See Crossopterygii.

Ø Brach · iƉoƉlariƉaÿ(?), n. pl. [NL., fr. L. brachiolum (bracchƉ), dim. of brachium (bracchƉ) arm.] (Zo"l.) A peculiar early larval stage of certain starfishes, having a bilateral structure, and swimming by means of bands of vibrating cilia.

BrachiƉoƉpodÿ(?), n. [Cf.F. brachiopode.] (Zo"l.) One of the Brachiopoda, or its shell.

Ø Brach · iƉopoƉda (?), n. [NL., from Gr. ? arm + Ɖpoda.] (Zo"l.) A class of Molluscoidea having a symmetrical bivalve shell, often attached by a fleshy peduncle.

µ Within the shell is a pair of ½arms,, often long and spirally coiled, bearing rows of ciliated tentacles by which a current of water is made to flow into the mantle cavity, bringing the microscopic food to the mouth between the bases of the arms. The shell is both opened and closed by special muscles. They form two orders; Lyopoma, in which the shell is thin, and without a distinct hinge, as in Lingula; and Arthropoma, in which the firm calcareous shell has a regular hinge, as in Rhynchonella. See Arthropomata.

Ø BrachiƉum (?), n.; pl. Bracchiaÿ(?). [L. brachium or bracchium, arm.] (Anat.) The upper arm; the segment of the fore limb between the shoulder and the elbow.

Brachmanÿ(?), n. [L. Brachmanae, pl., Gr. ?.] See Brahman. [Obs.]

490

Brach·yDcat·aDlecticÿ(?), n. [Gr. ?; ? short + ? to leave off; cf. ? incomplete.] (Gr.& Last. Pros.) A verse wanting two syllables at its termination.

Brach·yDceDphalic (?), Brach·yDcephaDlous (?)}, a. [Gr. ? short + ? head.] (Anat.) Having the skull short in proportion to its breadth; shortheaded; D in distinction from dolichocephalic.

Brach·yDcephaDly (?), Brach·yDcephaDlism (?)}, n. [Cf. F. Brachyc,phalie]. (Anat.) The state or condition of being brachycephalic; shortness of head.

BraDchycerDal (?), a. [Gr. ? short + ? horn.] (Zo"l.) Having short antenn', as certain insects.

Brach·yDdiDagoDnal (?), a. [Gr. ? short + E. diagonal.] Pertaining to the shorter diagonal, as of a rhombic prism.

Brachydiagonal axis, the shorter lateral axis of an orthorhombic crystal.

Brach·yDdiDagoDnal, n. The shorter of the diagonals in a rhombic prism.

Brach·yDdomeÿ(?), n. [Gr. ? short + E. dome.] (Crystallog.) A dome parallel to the shorter lateral axis. See Dome.

BraDchygraDpher (?), n. A writer in short hand; a stenographer.

He asked the brachygrapher whether he wrote the notes of the sermon. Gayton.

BraDchygraDphyÿ(?), n. [Gr. ? short + Dgraphy: cf. F. brachygraphie.] Stenograhy.

B.Jonson.

BraDchyloDgyÿ(?), n. [Gr. ? :? short + ? discourse: cf. F. brachylogie.] (Rhet.) Conciseness of expression; brevity.

Brach·yDpinaDcoid (?), n. [Gr. ? short + E. pinacoid.] (Crytallog.) A plane of an orthorhombic crystal which is parallel both to the vertical axis and to the shorter lateral (brachydiagonal) axis.

Ø BraDchypteDraÿ(?), n. pl. [NL., fr. Gr. ? shortDwinged; short + ? feather, wing.] (Zo"l.) A group of Coleoptera having short wings; the rove beetles.

Ø BraDchypteDres (?), n.pl. [NL. See Brachyptera.] (Zo"l.) A group of birds, including auks, divers, and penguins.

BraDchypterDous (?), a. [Gr. ? :cf. F. brachyptŠre.] (Zo"l.) Having short wings.

BraDchystoDchrone (?), n. [Incorrect for brachistochrone, fr. Gr. ? shortest (superl. of ? short) + ? time : cf. F. brachistochrone.] (Math.) A curve, in which a body, starting from a given point, and descending solely by the force of gravity, will reach another given point in a shorter time than it could by any other path. This curve of quickest descent, as it is sometimes called, is, in a vacuum, the same as the cycloid.

BrachyDty·pous (?), a. [Gr. ? short + ? stamp, form.] (Min.) Of a short form.

Ø Brach·yÐuraÿ(?), n. pl. [NL., fr. Gr. ? short + ? tail.] (Zo"l.) A group of decapod Crustacea, including the common crabs, characterized by a small and short abdomen, which is bent up beneath the large cephaloÐthorax. [Also spelt Brachyoura.] See Crab, and Illustration in Appendix.

Brach·yÐuralÿ(?), Brach·yÐurous (?)}, a. [Cf. F. brachyure.] (Zo"l.) Of or pertaining to the Brachyura.

Brach·yÐuran (?), n. One of the Brachyura.

Bracing (?), a. Imparting strength or tone; strengthening; invigorating; as, a bracing north wind.

Bracing (?), n. 1. The act of strengthening, supporting, or propping, with a brace or braces; the state of being braced.

> (Engin.) Any system of braces; braces, collectively; as, the bracing of a truss.

<— p. 174 —>

Brack (?), n. [Cf.D. braak, Dan. br'k, a breaking, Sw. & Isel. brak a crackling, creaking. Cf. Breach.]

An opening caused by the parting of any solid body; a crack or breach; a flaw.

Stain or brack in her sweet reputation.

J.Fletcher.

Brack, n. [D. brak, adj., salt; cf. LG. wrak refuse, G. brack.] Salt or brackish water. [Obs.]

Drayton.

Bracken (?), n. [OE. braken, AS. bracce. See 2d Brake, n.] A brake or fern.

Sir W.Scott.

Bracket (?), n. [Cf.OF. braguette codpiece, F. brayette, Sp. bragueta, also a projecting mold in architecture; dim. fr.L. bracae breeches; cf. also, OF. bracon beam, prop, support; of unknown origin. Cf. Breeches.]

> (Arch.) An architectural member, plain or ornamental, projecting from a wall or pier, to support weight falling outside of the same; also, a decorative feature seeming to discharge such an office.

µ This is the more general word. See Brace, Cantalever, Console, Corbel, Strut.

> (Engin. & Mech.) A piece or combination of pieces, usually triangular in general shape, projecting from, or fastened to, a wall, or other surface, to support heavy bodies or to strengthen angles.

> (Naut.) A shot, crooked timber, resembling a knee, used as a support.

> (Mil.) The cheek or side of an ordnance carriage.

> (Print.) One of two characters [ ]?, used to inclose a reference, explanation, or note, or a part to be excluded from a sentence, to indicate an interpolation, to rectify a mistake, or to supply an omission, and for certain other purposes; Ð called also crotchet.

> A gas fixture or lamp holder projecting from the face of a wall, column, or the like.

Bracket light, a gas fixture or a lamp attached to a wall, column, etc.

Bracket, v.t. [imp. & p.p. Bracketed; p.pr. & vb.n. Bracketing] To place within brackets; to connect by brackets; to furnish with brackets.

Bracketing, n. (Arch.) A series or group of brackets; brackets, collectively.

Brackish (?), a. [See Brack salt water.] Saltish, or salt in a moderate degree, as water in saline soil.

Springs in deserts found seem sweet, all brackish though they be.
Byron.

Brackishiness, n. The quality or state of being brackish, or somewhat salt.

Bracky (?), a. Brackish.
Drayton.

Bract (?), n. [See Bractea.] (Bot.) (a) A leaf, usually smaller than the true leaves of a plant, from the axil of which a flower stalk arises. (b) Any modified leaf, or scale, on a flower stalk or at the base of a flower.

µ Bracts are often inconspicuous, but sometimes large and showy, or highly colored, as in many cactaceous plants. The spathes of aroid plants are conspicuous forms of bracts.

ØBractela (?), n. [L., a thin plate of metal or wood, gold foil.] (Bot.) A bract.

Bractelal (?), a. [Cf.F. bract,al.] Having the nature or appearance of a bract.

Bracteiate (?), a. [Cf.L. bracteatus covered with gold plate.] (Bot.) Having a bract or bracts.

Bracted (?), a. (Bot.) Furnished with bracts.

Bracteollate (?), a. (Bot.) Furnished with bracteoles or bractlets.

Bracteiole (?), n. [L. bracteola, dim. of bractea. See Bractea.] (Bot.) Same as Bractlet.

Bractless, a. (Bot.) Destitute of bracts.

Bractlet (?), n. [Bract + Ðlet] (Bot.) A bract on the stalk of a single flower, which is itself on a main stalk that support several flowers.
Gray.

Brad (?), n. [Cf.OE. brod, Dan. braad prick, sting, brodde ice spur, frost nail, Sw. brodd frost nail, Icel. broddr any pointed piece of iron or stell; akin to AS. brord point, spire of grass, and perh. to E. bristle. See Bristle, n.]

A thin nail, usually small, with a slight projection at the top on one side instead of a head; also, a small wire nail, with a flat circular head; sometimes, a small, tapering, squareÐbodied finishing nail, with a countersunk head.

Brad awl · (?). A straight awl with chisel edge, used to make holes for brads, etc.
Weale.

Braidoon (?), n. Same as Bridoon.

ØBrae (?), n. [See Bray a hill.] A hillside; a slope; a bank; a hill. [Scot.]
Burns.

Brag (?), v.i. [imp. & p. p. Bragged (?); p. pr. & vb. n. Bragging.] [OE. braggen to resound, blow, boast (cf. F. braguer to lead a merry life, flaunt, boast, OF. brague merriment), from Icel. braka to creak, brak noise, fr. the same root as E. break; properly then, to make a noise, boast. ?95.] To talk about one's self, or things pertaining to one's self, in a manner intended to excite admiration, envy, or wonder; to talk boastfully; to boast; Ð often followed by of; as, to brag of one's exploits, courage, or money, or of the great things one intends to do.

Coinceit, more rich in matter than in words,
Brags of his substance, not of ornament.
Shak.

Syn. Ð To swagger; boast; vapor; bluster; vaunt; flourish; talk big.

Brag, v.t. To boast of. [Obs.]
Shak.

Brag, n.

A boast or boasting; bragging; ostentatious pretense or self glorification.

C'sar ... made not here his brag
Of ½came,, and ½saw,, and ½overcame.,
Shak.

The thing which is boasted of.

Beauty is Nature's brag.
Milton.

A game at cards similar to bluff.

Chesterfield.

Brag (?), a. [See Brag, v.i.] Brisk; full of spirits; boasting; pretentious; conceited. [Arhaic]

A brag young fellow.
B.Jonson.

Brag, adv. Proudly; boastfully. [Obs.]
Fuller.

Brag · galdocio (?), n. [From Braggadocchio, a boastful character in Spenser's ½Fa‰rie Queene.,]

A braggart; a boaster; a swaggerer.

Dryden.

Empty boasting; mere brag; pretension.

Braggardïism (?), n. [See Braggart.] Boastfulness; act of bragging.
Shak.

Braggart (?), n. [OF. bragard flaunting, vain, bragging. See Brag, v.i.] A boaster.

O, I could play the woman with mine eyes,
And braggart with my tongue.
Shak.

Braggart, a. Boastful.Ð Braggartĭly, adv.

Bragger (?), n. One who brags; a boaster.

Bragget (?), n. [OE. braket, bragot, fr. W. bragawd, bragod, fr. brag malt.] A liquor made of ale and honey fermented, with spices, etc. [Obs.]
B.Jonson.

Bragging · ly (?), adv. Boastingly.

Bragless, a. Without bragging. [R.]
Shak.

Bragly, adv. In a manner to be bragged of; finely; proudly. [Obs.]
Spenser.

Brahma (?), n. [See Brahman.]

(Hindoo Myth.) The One First Cause; also, one of the triad of Hindoo gods. The triad consists of Brahma, the Creator, Vishnu, the Preserver, and Siva, the Destroyer.

µ According to the Hindoo religious books, Brahma (with the final a short), or Brahm, is the Divine Essence, the One First Cause, the All in All, while the personal gods, Brahm (with the final a long), Vishnu, and Siva, are emanations or manifestations of Brahma the Divine Essence.

(Zo"l.) A valuable variety of large, domestic fowl, peculiar in having the comb divided lengthwise into three parts, and the legs well feathered. There are two breeds, the dark or penciled, and the light; Ð called also Brahmapootra.

Brahman (?), Brahmin (?), } n.; pl. Brahmans, Brahmins. [Skr. Br¾hmana (cf. Brahman 0worship, holiness; the God Brahma, also Brahman): cf. F. Brahmane, Brachmane, Bramine, L. Brachmanae, Ðmanes, Ðmani, pl., Gr. ?, pl.] A person of the highest or sacerdotal caste among the Hindoos.

Brahman bull (Zo"l.), the male of a variety of the zebu, or Indian ox, considered sacred by the Hindoos.

Brahmanĭess (?), n. A Brahmani.

Brahmanĭi (?), n. [Fem. of Brahman.] Any Brahman woman. [Written also Brahmanee.]

Brahĭmanic (?), ĭicĭal (?), Brahĭminĭic (?),ĭicĭal (?), a. Of or pertaining to the Brahmans or to their doctrines and worship.

Brahmanĭism (?), Brahminĭism (?), } n. The religion or system of doctrines of the Brahmans; the religion of Brahma.

Brahmanĭist (?), Brahminĭist (?), } n. An adherent of the religion of the Brahmans.

Brahmoĭism (?), n. The religious system of BrahmoÐsomaj.

Balfour.

Brah · moÐsoĬmaj (?), n. [Bengalese, a wor?hiping assembly.] A modern reforming theistic sect among the Hindos. [Written also BrahmaÐsamaj.]

Braid (?), v.t. [imp. &. p.p. Braided; p. pr. & vb. n. Braiding.] [OE. braiden, breiden, to pull, reach, braid, AS. bregdan to move to and fro, to weave; akin. to Icel. breg?a, D. breiden to knit, OS. bregdan to weave, OHG. brettan to brandish. Cf. Broid.]

To weave, interlace, or entwine together, as three or more strands or threads; to form into a braid; to plait.

Braid your locks with rosy twine.
Milton.

To mingle, or to bring to a uniformly soft consistence, by beating, rubbing, or straining, as in some culinary operations.

To reproach. [Obs.] See Upbraid.

Shak.

Braid (?), n. 1. A plait, band, or narrow fabric formed by intertwining or weaving together different strands.

A braid of hair composed of two different colors twined together.
Scott.

A narrow fabric, as of wool, silk, or linen, used for binding, trimming, or ornamenting dresses, etc.

Braid, n. [Cf.Icel. breg?a to move quickly.]

A quick motion; a start. [Obs.]

Sackville.

A fancy; freak; caprice. [Obs.]

R.Hyrde.

Braid v.i. To start; to awake. [Obs.]

Chaucer.

Braid, a. [AS. br'd, bred, deceit; akin to Icel. brag? trick, AS. bredan, bregdan, to braid, knit, (hence) to knit a net, to draw into a net, i.e., to deceive. See Braid, v.t.] Deceitful. [Obs.]

Since Frenchmen are so braid,
Marry that will, I live and die a maid.
Shak.

Braiding, n. 1. The act of making or using braids.

Braids, collectively; trimming.

A gentleman enveloped in mustachios, whiskers, fur collars, and braiding. Thackeray.

Brail (?), n. [OE. brayle furling rope, OF. braiol a band placed around the breeches, fr.F. braies, pl., breeches, fr.L. braca, bracae, breeches, a Gallic word; cf. Arm. bragez. Cf. Breeches.]

(Falconry) A thong of soft leather to bind up a hawk's wing.

pl. (Naut.) Ropes passing through pulleys, and used to haul in or up the leeches, bottoms, or corners of sails, preparatory to furling.

A stock at each end of a seine to keep it stretched.

Brail, v.t. (Naut.) To haul up by the brails; Ð used with up; as, to brail up a sail.

Brain (?), n. [OE. brain, brein, AS. bragen, br'gen; akin to LG. br„gen, bregen, D. brein, and perh. to Gr. ?, the upper part of head, if ? =? ? 95.]

(Anat.) The whitish mass of soft matter (the center of the nervous system, and the seat of consciousness and volition) which is inclosed in the cartilaginous or bony cranium of vertebrate animals. It is simply the anterior termination of the spinal cord, and is developed from three embryonic vesicles, whose cavities are connected with the central canal of the cord; the cavities of the vesicles become the central cavities, or ventricles, and the walls thicken unequally and become the three segments, the foreÐ, midÐ, and hindÐbrain.

µ In the brain of man the cerebral lobes, or largest part of the forebrain, are enormously developed so as to overhang the cerebellum, the great lobe of the hindbrain, and completely cover the lobes of the midbrain. The surface of the cerebrum is divided into irregular ridges, or convolutions, separated by grooves (the soÐcalled fissures and sulci), and the two hemispheres are connected at the bottom of the longitudinal fissure by a great transverse band of nervous matter, the corpus callosum, while the two halves of the cerebellum are connected on the under side of the brain by the bridge, or pons Varolii.

(Zo"l.) The anterior or cephalic ganglion in insects and other invertebrates.

The organ or seat of intellect; hence, the understanding. ½ My brain is too dull.

Sir W.Scott.

µ In this sense, often used in the plural.

The affections; fancy; imagination. [R.]

Shak.

To have on the brain, to have constantly in one's thoughts, as a sort of monomania. [Low]

Brain box or case, the bony on cartilaginous case inclosing the brain. Ð Brain coral, Brain stone coral (Zo"l), a massive reefÐbuilding coral having the surface covered by ridges separated by furrows so as to resemble somewhat the surface of the brain, esp. such corals of the genera M'andrina and Diploria. Ð Brain fag (Med.), brain weariness. See Cerebropathy.Ð Brain fever (Med.), fever in which the brain is specially affected; any acute cerebral affection attended by fever. Ð Brain sand, calcareous matter found in the pineal gland.

Brain (?), v.t. [imp. & p.p. Brained (?); p.pr. & vb.n. Braining.]

To dash out the brains of; to kill by beating out the brains. Hence, Fig.: To destroy; to put an end to; to defeat.

There thou mayst brain him.
Shak.
It was the swift celerity of the death ...
That brained my purpose.
Shak.

To conceive; to understand. [Obs.]

?T is still a dream, or else such stuff as madmen
Tongue, and brain not.
Shak.
Brained (?), p.a. Supplied with brains.
If th' other two be brained like us.
Shak.
Brainish, a. HotÐheaded; furious. [R.]
Shak.
Brainless, a. Without understanding; silly; thougthless; witless. Ð Brainlessĭness, n.

Brainpan · (?), n. [Brain + pan.] The bones which inclose the brain; the skull; the cranium.

Brainsick · (?), a. Disordered in the understanding; giddy; thoughtless. Ð Brainsickĭness, a.

Brainsick · ly, adv. In a brainsick manner.

Brainy (?), a. Having an active or vigorous mind. [Colloq.]

Braise, Braize (?), n. [So called from its iridescent colors.] (Zo"l.) A European marine fish (Pagrus vulgaris) allied to the American scup; the becker. The name is sometimes applied to the related species. [Also written brazier.]

Braise, Braize, n. [F.] 1. Charcoal powder; breeze.

(Cookery) Braised meat.

Braise, v.t. [F. braiser, fr. braise coals.] (Cookery) To stew or broil in a covered kettle or pan.

A braising kettle has a deep cover which holds coals; consequently the cooking is done from above, as well as below.
Mrs. Henderson.

Braiser (?), n. A kettle or pan for braising.

Brait (?), n. [Cf.W. braith variegated, Ir. breath, breagh, fine, comely.] A rough diamond.

Braize (?), n. See Braise.

Brake (?), imp. of Break. [Arhaic]
Tennyson.

Brake, n. [OE. brake fern; cf. AS. bracce fern, LG. brake willow bush, Da. bregne fern, G. brach fallow; prob. orig. the growth on rough, broken ground, fr. the root of E. break. See Break, v.t., cf. Bracken, and 2d Brake, n.]

(Bot.) A fern of the genus Pteris, esp. the P. aquilina, common in almost all countries. It has solitary stems dividing into three principal branches. Less properly: Any fern.

A thicket; a place overgrown with shrubs and brambles, with undergrowth and ferns, or with canes.

Rounds rising hillocks, brakes obscure and rough,
To shelter thee from tempest and from rain.
Shak.
He stayed not for brake, and he stopped not for stone.
Sir W.Scott.
Cane brake, a thicket of canes. See Canebrake.
<— p. 175 —>
Brake (?), n. [OE. brake; cf. LG. brake an instrument for breaking flax, G. breche, fr. the root of E. break. See Break, v. t., and cf. Breach.] 1. An instrument or machine to break or bruise the woody part of flax or hemp so that it may be separated from the fiber. 2. An extended handle by means of which a number of men can unite in working a pump, as in a fire engine. 3. A baker's kneading though. Johnson. 4. A sharp bit or snaffle. Pampered jades...which need nor break nor bit. Gascoigne. 5. A frame for confining a refractory horse while the smith is shoeing him; also, an inclosure to restrain cattle, horses, etc. A horse... which Philip had bought... and because of his fierceness kept him within a brake of iron bars. J. Brende. 6. That part of a carriage, as of a movable battery, or engine, which enables it to turn. 7. (Mil.) An ancient engine of war analogous to the crossbow and ballista. 8. (Agric.) A large, heavy harrow for breaking clods after plowing; a drag. 9. A piece of mechanism for retarding or stopping motion by friction, as of a carriage or railway car, by the pressure of rubbers against the wheels, or of clogs or ratchets against the track or roadway, or of a pivoted lever against a wheel or drum in a machine. 10. (Engin.) An apparatus for testing the power of a steam engine, or other motor, by weighing the amount of friction that the motor will overcome; a friction brake. 11. A cart or carriage without a body, used in breaking in horses. 12. An ancient instrument of torture. Holinshed. Air brake. See Air brake, in the Vocabulary. Ð Brake beam or Brake bar, the beam that connects the brake blocks of opposite wheels. Ð

Brake block. (a) The part of a brake holding the brake shoe. (b) A brake shoe. Ð Brake shoe or Brake rubber, the part of a brake against which the wheel rubs. Ð Brake wheel, a wheel on the platform or top of a car by which brakes are operated. Ð Continuous brake . See under Continuous. Brakeman (?), n.; pl. Brakemen (?).

(Railroads) A man in charge of a brake or brakes.

(Mining) The man in charge of the winding (or hoisting) engine for a mine. Braky (?), a. Full of brakes; abounding with brambles, shrubs, or ferns; rough; thorny. In the woods and braky glens. W.Browne. Brama (?), n. See Brahma. Bramah press · (?). A hydrostatic press of immense power, invented by Joseph Bramah of London. See under Hydrostatic. Bramble (?), n. [OE. brembil, AS.br?mbel, br?mbel (akin to OHG. bramal), fr. the same root as E. broom, As. br?m. See Broom.] 1. (Bot.) Any plant of the genus Rubus, including the raspberry and blackberry. Hence: Any rough, prickly shrub. The thorny brambles, and embracing bushes. Shak.

(Zo"l.) The brambling or bramble finch. Bramble bush · (?). (Bot.) The bramble, or a collection of brambles growing together. He jumped into a bramble bush And scratched out both his eyes. Mother Goose. Brambled (?), a. Overgrown with brambles. Forlorn she sits upon the brambled floor. T.Warton. Bramble net · (?). A net to catch birds. Brambling (?), n. [OE. bramline. See Bramble, n.] (Zo"l.) The European mountain finch (Fringilla montifringilla); Ð called also bramble finch and bramble. Brambly (?), a. Pertaining to, resembling, or full of, brambles. ½In brambly wildernesses.¸ Tennyson. Brame (?), n. [Cf. Breme.] Sharp passion; vexation. [Obs.] HeartÐburning brame. Spenser. Bramin (?), Braĭminic (?), etc. See Brahman, Brachmanic, etc. Bran (?), n. [OE. bren, bran, OF. bren, F. bran, from Celtic; cf. Armor. brenn, Ir. bran, bran, chaff.] 1. The broken coat of the seed of wheat, rye, or other cereal grain, separated from the flour or meal by sifting or bolting; the coarse, chaffy part of ground grain.

(Zo"l.) The European carrion crow. Brancard (?), n. [F.] A litter on which a person may be carried. [Obs.] Coigrave. Branch (?), n.; pl. Branchesÿ(?). [OE. braunche, F. branche, fr. LL. branca claw of a bird or beast of prey; cf. Armor. brank branch, bough.] 1. (Bot.) A shoot or secondary stem growing from the main stem, or from a principal limb or bough of a tree or other plant.

Any division extending like a branch; any arm or part connected with the main body of thing; ramification; as, the branch of an antler; the branch of a chandelier; a branch of a river; a branch of a railway. Most of the branches , or streams, were dried up. W.Irving.

Any member or part of a body or system; a distinct article; a section or subdivision; a department. ½Branches of knowledge.¸ Prescott. It is a branch and parcel of mine oath. Shak.

(Geom.) One of the portions of a curve that extends outwards to an indefinitely great distance; as, the branches of an hyperbola.

A line of family descent, in distinction from some other line or lines from the same stock; any descendant in such a line; as, the English branch of a family. His father, a younger branch of the ancient stock. Carew.

(Naut.) A warrant or commission given to a pilot, authorizing him to pilot vessels in certain waters. Branches of a bridle, two pieces of bent iron, which bear the bit, the cross chains, and the curb. Ð Branch herring. See Alewife.Ð Root and branch , totally, wholly. Syn. Ð Bough; limb; shoot; offshoot; twig; sprig. Branch (?), a. Diverging from, or tributary to, a main stock, line, way, theme, etc.; as, a branch vein; a branch road or line; a branch topic; a branch store. Branch, v. i. [imp. & p. p. Branchedÿ(?); p .pr. & vb. n. Branching.] 1. To shoot or spread in branches; to separate into branches; to ramify.

To divide into separate parts or subdivision. To branch off, to form a branch or a separate part; to diverge. Đ To branch out, to speak diffusively; to extend one's discourse to other topics than the main one; also, to enlarge the scope of one's business, etc. To branch out into a long disputation. Spectator. Branch, v. t. 1. To divide as into branches; to make subordinate division in.

To adorn with needlework representing branches, flowers, or twigs. The train whereof loose far behind her strayed, Branched with gold and pearl, most richly wrought. Spenser. Brancher (?), n. 1. That which shoots forth branches; one who shows growth in various directions.

(Falconry) A young hawk when it begins to leave the nest and take to the branches. Brancherĭy (?), n. A system of branches. Ø Branchiĭa (?), n.; pl. Branchi?y̆(?). [L., fr. Gr. ?, pl. of ?.] (Anat.) A gill; a respiratory organ for breathing the air contained in water, such as many aquatic and semiaquatic animals have. Branchiĭal (?), a. (Anat.) Of or pertaining to branchi'; or gills. Branchial arches, the bony or cartilaginous arches which support the gills on each side of the throat of fishes and amphibians. See Illustration in Appendix. Đ Branchial clefts, the openings between the branchial arches through which water passes. Branchiĭate (?), a. (Anat.) Furnished with branchi'; as branchiate segments. Branĭchiferĭous (?), a. (Anat.) Having gills; branchiate; as, branchiferous gastropods. Branchiĭness (?), n. Fullness of branches. Branching, a. Furnished with branches; shooting our branches; extending in a branch or branches. Shaded with branching palm. Milton. Branching, n. The act or state of separation into branches; division into branches; a division or branch. The sciences, with their numerous branchings. L.Watts. Ø Bran · chiĭoĭgasĭtropoĭda (?), n. pl. [NL., from Gr. ? gill + E. gastropoda.] (Zo"l.) Those Gastropoda that breathe by branchi'; including the Prosobranchiata and Opisthobranchiata. Bran · chiĭomerĭism (?), n. [Gr. ? gill + Đmere.] (Anat.) The state of being made up of branchiate segments. R. Wiedersheim. Branchiĭoĭpod (?), n. One of the Branchiopoda. Ø Branchiĭoĭpoda (?), n. pl. [Gr. ? gill + Đpoda: cf. F. branchiopode.] (Zo"l.) An order of Entomostraca; Đ so named from the feet of branchiopods having been supposed to perform the function of gills. It includes the freshĐwater genera Branchipus, Apus, and Limnadia, and the genus Artemia found in salt lakes. It is also called Phyllopoda. See Phyllopoda, Cladocera. It is sometimes used in a broader sense. Bran · chiĭosteĭgal (?), a. [Gr. ? gill + ? to cover: cf. F. branchiostŠge.] (Anat.) Pertaining to the membrane covering the gills of fishes. Đ n. (Anat.) A branchiostegal ray. See Illustration of Branchial arches in Appendix. μ This term was formerly applied to a group of fishes having boneless branchi'. But the arrangement was artificial, and has been rejected. Bran · chiĭostege (?), (Anat.) The branchiostegal membrane. See Illustration in Appendix. Bran · chiĭosteĭgous (?), a. (Anat.) Branchiostegal. Ø Bran · chiĭostoĭma (?), n. [NL., fr., Gr. ? gill + ? mouth.] (Zo"l.) The lancelet. See Amphioxus. Ø Branchiĭura (?), n. pl. [NL., fr., Gr. ? gill + ? tail.] (Zo"l.) A group of Entomostraca, with suctorial mouths, including species parasitic on fishes, as the carp lice (Argulus). Branchless (?), a. Destitute of branches or shoots; without any valuable product; barren; naked. Branchlet (?), n. [Branch + Đlet.] A little branch; a twig. Branch pi · lot (?). A pilot who has a branch or commission, as from Trinity House, England, for special navigation. Branchy (?), a. Full of branches; having wideĐspreading branches; consisting of branches. Beneath thy branchy bowers of thickest gloom. J.Scott. Brand (?), n. [OE. brand, brond, AS. brand brond brand, sword, from byrnan, beornan, to burn; akin to D., Dan., Sw., & G. brand brand, Icel. brandr a brand, blade of a sword. ?32. See Burn, v. t., and cf. Brandish.] 1. A burning piece of wood; or a stick or piece of wood partly burnt, whether burning or after the fire is extinct. Snatching a live brand from a wigwam, Mason threw it on a matted roof. Palfrey.

A sword, so called from its glittering or flashing brightness. [Poetic] Tennyson. Paradise, so late their happy seat, Waved over by that flaming brand. Milton.

A mark made by burning with a hot iron, as upon a cask, to designate the quality, manufacturer, etc., of the contents, or upon an animal, to designate ownership; Ð also, a mark for a similar purpose made in any other way, as with a stencil. Hence, figuratively: Quality; kind; grade; as, a good brand of flour.

A mark put upon criminals with a hot iron. Hence: Any mark of infamy or vice; a stigma. The brand of private vice. Channing.

An instrument to brand with; a branding iron.

(Bot.) Any minute fungus which produces a burnt appearance in plants. The brands are of many species and several genera of the order Puccini'i. Brand (?), v.t [imp. & p.p. Branded; p. pr. & vb. n. Branding.]. 1. To burn a distinctive mark into or upon with a hot iron, to indicate quality, ownership, etc., or to mark as infamous (as a convict).

To put an actual distinctive mark upon in any other way, as with a stencil, to show quality of contents, name of manufacture, etc.

Fig.: To fix a mark of infamy, or a stigma, upon. The Inquisition branded its victims with infamy. Prescott. There were the enormities, branded and condemned by the first and most natural verdict of common humanity. South.

To mark or impress indelibly, as with a hot iron. As if it were branded on my mind. Geo. Eliot. Brander (?), n. 1. One who, or that which, brands; a branding iron.

A gridiron. [Scot.] Brand goose · (?). [Prob. fr. 1st brand + goose: cf. Sw. brandgțs. Cf. Brant.] (Zo"l.) A species of wild goose (Branta bernicla) usually called in America brant. See Brant. Brandied (?), a. Mingled with brandy; made stronger by the addition of brandy; flavored or treated with brandy; as, brandied peaches. Branding i · Iron (?). An iron to brand with. Brand i · ron. 1. A branding iron.

A trivet to set a pot on. Huloet.

The horizontal bar of an andiron. Brandish (?), v. t. [imp. & p.p. Brandishedÿ(?); p. pr. & vb. n. Brandishing.] [OE. braundisen, F. brandir, fr. brand a sword, fr. OHG. brant brand. See Brand, n.] 1. To move or wave, as a weapon; to raise and move in various directions; to shake or flourish. The quivering lance which he brandished bright. Drake.

To play with; to flourish; as, to brandish syllogisms. Brandish, n. A flourish, as with a weapon, whip, etc. ½Brandishes of the fan., Tailer. BrandishÐer (?), n. One who brandishes. Brandle (?), v. t. & i. [F. brandiller.] To shake; to totter. [Obs.] Brandling (?), Brandlin (?) }, n. (Zo"l.) Same as Branlin, fish and worm. BrandÐnew (?), a. [See Brand, and cf. Brannew.] Quite new; bright as if fresh from the forge. Brand spore · (?). (Bot.) One of several spores growing in a series or chain, and produced by one of the fungi called brand. Brandy (?), n.; pl. Brandiesÿ(?). [From older brandywine, brandwine, fr. D. brandewijn, fr. p. p. of branden to burn, distill + wijn wine, akin to G. branntwein. See Brand.] A strong alcoholic liquor distilled from wine. The name is also given to spirit distilled from other liquors, and in the United States to that distilled from cider and peaches. In northern Europe, it is also applied to a spirit obtained from grain. Brandy fruit, fruit preserved in brandy and sugar. BrandyÏwine · (?), n. Brandy. [Obs.] Wiseman. Brangle (?), n. [Prov. E. brangled confused, entangled, Scot. brangle to shake, menace; probably a variant of wrangle, confused with brawl. ?95.] A wrangle; a squabble; a noisy contest or dispute. [R.] A brangle between him and his neighbor. Swift. Brangle, v.i [imp. & p. p. Brangledÿ(?); p.pr. & vb. n. Branglingÿ(?).] To wrangle; to dispute contentiously; to squabble. [R.] BrangleÏment (?), n. Wrangle; brangle. [Obs.] Brangler (?), n. A quarrelsome person. Brangling (?), n. A quarrel. [R.] Whitlock. Brank (?), n. [Prov. of Celtic origin; cf. L. brance, brace, the Gallic name of a particularly white kind of corn.] Buckwheat. [Local, Eng.] Halliwell. Brank, Branks,} n. [Cf. Gael. brangus, brangas, a sort of pillory, Ir. brancas halter, or D. pranger fetter.] 1. A sort of bridle with wooden side pieces. [Scot. & Prov. Eng.] Jamieson.

A scolding bridle, an instrument formerly used for correcting scolding women.It was an iron frame surrounding the head and heaving a triangular piece entering the mouth of the scold. Brank, v. i. 1. To hold up and toss the head; Ð applied to horses as spurning the bit. [Scot. & Prov. Eng.]

To prance; to caper. [Scot.] Jamieson. Brankurĭsine (?), n. [F. brancÐursine, branchÐursine, fr. LL. branca claw + L. ursinus belonging to a bear (fr. ursus bear), i .e., bear's claw, because its leaves resemble the claws of a bear. Cf. Branch.] (Bot.) Bear'sÐbreech, or Acanthus. Branlin (?), n. [Scot. branlie fr. brand.] (Zo"l.) A young salmon or parr, in the stage in which it has transverse black bands, as if burned by a gridiron. Branlin, n. [See Brand.] A small red worm or larva, used as bait for small freshÐwater fish; Ð so called from its red color. BranÐnew (?), a. See BrandÐnew. Branny (?), a. Having the appearance of bran; consisting of or containing bran. Wiseman. Bransle (?), n. [See Brawl a dance.] A brawl or dance. [Obs.] Spenser.

<— p. 176 —>

Brant (?), n. [Cf.Brand goose, Brent, Brenicle.] (Zo"l.) A species of wild goose (Branta bernicla)Ð called also brent and brand goose. The name is also applied to other related species.

Brant, a. [See Brent.] Steep. [Prov. Eng.]

Brantail · (?), n. (Zo"l.) The European redstart; Ð so called from the red color of its tail.

Brantĭfox · (?), n. [For brandÐfox; cf. G. brandfuchs, Sw. bradr„f. So called from its yellowish brown and somewhat black color. See Brand.] (Zo"l.) A kind of fox found in Sweden (Vulpes alopex), smaller than the common fox (V. vulgaris), but probably a variety of it.

Branuïlar (?), a. Relating to the brain; cerebral.

I.Taylor.

Brasen (?), a. Same as Brazen.

Brash (?), a. [Cf. Gael. bras or G. barsch harsh, sharp, tart, impetuous, D. barsch, Sw. & Dan. barsk.] Hasty in temper; impetuous.

Grose.

Brash, a. [Cf. Amer. bresk, brusk, fragile, brittle.] Brittle, as wood or vegetables. [Colloq., U. S.]

Bartlett.

Brash, n. [See Brash brittle.] 1. A rash or eruption; a sudden or transient fit of sickness.

Refuse boughs of trees; also, the clippings of hedges. [Prov. Eng.]

Wright.

(Geol.) Broken and angular fragments of rocks underlying alluvial deposits.

Lyell.

Broken fragments of ice.

Kane.

Water brash (Med.), an affection characterized by a spasmodic pain or hot sensation in the stomach with a rising of watery liquid into the mouth; pyrosis. Ð Weaning brash (Med.), a severe form of diarrhea which sometimes attacks children just weaned.

Brasier, Brazier (?), n. [OE. brasiere, F. braise live coals. See Brass.] An artificer who works in brass.

Franklin.

Brasier, Brazier, n. [F. brasier, braisjer, fr. braise live coals. See Brass.] A pan for holding burning coals.

Brass (?), n.; pl. Brasses (?). [OE. bras, bres, AS. br's; akin to Icel. bras cement, solder, brasa to harden by fire, and to E. braze, brazen. Cf. 1st & 2d Braze.] 1. An alloy (usually yellow) of copper and zinc, in variable proportion, but often containing two parts of copper to one part of zinc. It sometimes contains tin, and rarely other metals.

> (Mach.) A journal bearing, so called because frequently made of brass. A brass is often lined with a softer metal, when the latter is generally called a white metal lining. See Axle box, Journal Box, and Bearing.

> Coin made of copper, brass, or bronze. [Obs.]

Provide neither gold, nor silver, nor brass in your purses, nor scrip for your journey.

Matt. x. 9.

> Impudence; a brazen face. [Colloq.]

> pl. Utensils, ornaments, or other articles of brass.

The very scullion who cleans the brasses.
Hopkinson.

> A brass plate engraved with a figure or device. Specifically, one used as a memorial to the dead, and generally having the portrait, coat of arms, etc.

> pl. (Mining) Lumps of pyrites or sulphuret of iron, the color of which is near to that of brass.

μ The word brass as used in Sculpture language is a translation for copper or some kind of bronze.

μ Brass is often used adjectively or in selfÐexplaining compounds; as, brass button, brass kettle, brass founder, brass foundry or brassfoundry.

Brass band (Mus.), a band of musicians who play upon wind instruments made of brass, as trumpets, cornets, etc. Ð Brass foil, Brass leaf, brass made into very thin sheets; Ð called also Dutch gold.

Brassage (?), n. {F.] A sum formerly levied to pay the expense of coinage; Ð now called seigniorage.

Brassart (?), n. [F. brassard, fr. bras arm. See Brace, n.] Armor for the arm; Ð generally used for the whole arm from the shoulder to the wrist, and consisting, in the 15th and 16th centuries, of many parts.

Brasse (?), n. [Perh. a transposition of barse; but cf. LG. brasse the bream, G. brassen Cf. Bream.] (Zo"l.) A spotted European fish of the genus Lucioperca, resembling a perch.

Brassets (?), n. See Brassart.

Ø Brassilca (?), n. [L., cabbage.] (Bot.) A genus of plants embracing several species ad varieties differing much in appearance and qualities: such as the common cabbage (B. oleracea), broccoli, cauliflowers, etc.; the wild turnip (B. campestris); the common turnip (B. rapa); the rape of coleseed (B. napus), etc.

Bras · silcaceous (?), a. [L. brassica cabbage.] (Bot.) Related to, or resembling, the cabbage, or plants of the Cabbage family.

Brassilness (?), n. The state, conditions, or quality of being brassy. [Colloq.]

BrassIvisaged (?), a. Impudent; bold.

Brassy (?), a. 1. Of or pertaining to brass; having the nature, appearance, or hardness, of brass.

Impudent; impudently bold. [Colloq.]

Brast (?), v. t. & i. [See Burst.] To burst. [Obs.]
And both his y‰on braste out of his face.
Chaucer.
Dreadfull furies which their chains have brast.
Spenser.

Brat (?), n. [OE. bratt coarse garnment, AS. bratt cloak, fr. the Celtic; cf. W. brat clout, rag, Gael. brat cloak, apron, raf, Ir. brat cloak; properly then, a child's bib or clout; hence, a child.] 1. A coarse garnment or cloak; also, coarse clothing, in general. [Obs.]
Chaucer.

A coarse kind of apron for keeping the clothes clean; a bib. [Prov. Eng. & Scot.]

Wright.

A child; an offspring; Ð formerly used in a good sense, but now usually in a contemptuous sense. ½This brat is none of mine.„

Shak.
½A beggar's brat.„
Swift.
O Israel? O household of the Lord?
O Abraham's brats? O brood of blessed seed?
Gascoigne.

The young of an animal. [Obs.]

L'Estrange.

Brat (?), n. (Mining) A thin bed of coal mixed with pyrites or carbonate of lime.

Ø Bratsche (?), n. [G., fr. It. viola da braccio viola held on the arm.] The tenor viola, or viola.

Brattice (?), n. [See Brettice.] (Mining) (a) A wall of separation in a shaft or gallery used for ventilation. (b) Planking to support a roof or wall.

Brattishĭing (?), n. 1. See Brattice, n.

(Arch.) Carved openwork, as of a shrine, battlement, or parapet.

Braunite (?), n. (Min.) A native oxide of manganese, of dark brownish black color. It was named from a Mr. Braun of Gotha.

Braïvade (?), n. Bravado. [Obs.]

Fanshawe.

Braïvado (?), n., pl. Bravadoesÿ(?). [Sp. bravada, bravata, boast, brag: cf. F. bravade. See Brave.] Boastful and threatening behavior; a boastful menace.

In spite of our host's bravado.

Irving.

Brave (?), a. [Compar. Braver; superl. Bravest.] [F. brave, It. or Sp. bravo, (orig.) fierce, wild, savage, prob. from. L. barbarus. See Barbarous, and cf. Bravo.]

Bold; courageous; daring; intrepid; Đ opposed to cowardly; as, a brave man; a brave act.

Having any sort of superiority or excellence; Đ especially such as in conspicuous. [Obs. or Archaic as applied to material things.]

Iron is a brave commodity where wood aboundeth.

Bacon.

It being a brave day, I walked to Whitehall.

Pepys.

Making a fine show or display. [Archaic]

Wear my dagger with the braver grace.

Shak.

For I have gold, and therefore will be brave.

In silks I'll rattle it of every color.

Robert Greene.

Frog and lizard in holiday coats

And turtle brave in his golden spots.

Emerson.

Syn. Ð Courageous; gallant; daring; valiant; valorous; bold; heroic; intrepid; fearless; dauntless; magnanimous; highÐspirited; stoutÐhearted. See Gallant.

Brave (?), n. 1. A brave person; one who is daring.

The starÐspangled banner, O,long may it wave
O'er the land of the free and the home of the brave.
F.S.Key.

Specifically, an Indian warrior.

A man daring beyond discretion; a bully.

Hot braves like thee may fight.
Dryden.

A challenge; a defiance; bravado. [Obs.]

Demetrius, thou dost overween in all;
And so in this, to bear me down with braves.
Shak.

Brave, v. t. [imp. & p. p. Bravedÿ(?); p. pr. & vb. n. Braving.] 1. To encounter with courage and fortitude; to set at defiance; to defy; to dare.

These I can brave, but those I can not bear.
Dryden.

To adorn; to make fine or showy. [Obs.]

Thou [a tailor whom Grunio was browbeating] hast braved meny men; brave not me; I'll neither be faced or braved.
Shak.]

Bravely (?), adv. 1. In a brave manner; courageously; gallantly; valiantly; splendidly; nobly.

Finely; gaudily; gayly; showily.

And [she] decked herself bravely to allure the eyes of all men that should see her.
Judith. x. 4.

Well; thrivingly; prosperously. [Colloq.]

Braveness, n. The quality of state or being brave.

Braverly (?), n. [Cf. F. braverie.] 1. The quality of being brave; fearless; intrepidity.

Remember, sir, my liege, ...
The natural bravery of your isle.
Shak.

The act of braving; defiance; bravado. [Obs.]

Reform, then, without bravery or scandal of former times and persons.

Splendor; magnificence; showy appearance; ostentation; fine dress.

With scarfs and fans and double change of bravery.
Shak.
Like a stately ship...
With all her bravery on, and tackle trim.
Milton.

A showy person; a fine gentleman; a beau. [Obs.]

A man that is the bravery of his age.
Beau. & Fl.
Syn. Ð Courage; heroism; interpidity; gallantry; valor; fearlessness; dauntlessness; hardihood; manfulness. See Courage, and Heroism.

Braving (?), n. A bravado; a boast.
With so proud a strain
Of threats and bravings.
Chapman.

Bravingly (?), adv. In a defiant manner.

Bravo (?), n.; pl. Bravoesÿ(?). [I. See Brave, a.] A daring villain; a bandit; one who sets law at defiance; a professional assassin or murderer.

Safe from detection, seize the unwary prey.
And stab, like bravoes, all who come this way.
Churchill.

Bravo (?), interj. [It. See Brave.] Well done? excellent? an exclamation expressive of applause.

Ø Braḯvura (?), n. [It., (properly) bravery, spirit, from bravo. See Brave.] (Mus.) A florid, brilliant style of music, written for effect, to show the range and flexibility of a singer's voice, or the technical force and skill of a performer; virtuoso music.

Aria di bravura (?) [It.], a florid air demanding brilliant execution.

Brawl (?), v. i. [imp. & p.p. Brawled (?); p. pr. & vb. n. Brawling.] [OE. braulen to quarrel, boast, brallen to cry, make a noise; cf. LG. brallen to brag, MHG. pr?ulen, G. prahlen, F. brailler to cry, shout, Pr. brailar, braillar, W. bragal to vociferate, brag, Armor. bragal to romp, to strut, W. broliaw to brag, brawl boast. ?95.] 1. To quarrel noisily and outrageously.

Let a man that is a man consider that he is a fool that brawleth openly with his wife.
Golden Boke.

To complain loudly; to scold.

To make a loud confused noise, as the water of a rapid stream running over stones.

Where the brook brawls along the painful road.
Wordsworth.

Syn. Ð To wrangle; squabble; contend.

Brawl (?), n. A noisy quarrel; loud, angry contention; a wrangle; a tumult; as, a drunken brawl.

His sports were hindered by the brawls.
Shak.

Syn. Ð Noise; quarrel; uproar; row; tumult.

Brawler (?), n. One that brawls; wrangler.

Common brawlers (Law), one who disturbs a neighborhood by brawling (and is therefore indictable at common law as a nuisance).
Wharton.

Brawling, a. 1. Quarreling; quarrelsome; noisy.

She is an irksome brawling scold.
Shak.

Making a loud confused noise. See Brawl, v. i., 3.

A brawling stream.
J.S. Shairp.

Brawlingïly, adv. In a brawling manner.

Brawn (?), n. [OF. braon fleshy part, muscle, fr. HG. br?to flesh, G. braten roast meat; akin to Icel. br?? flesh, food of beasts, AS. br?de roast meat, br?dan to roast, G. braten, and possibly to E. breed.] 1. A muscle; flesh. [Obs.]

Formed well of brawns and of bones.
Chaucer.

Full, strong muscles, esp. of the arm or leg, muscular strength; a protuberant muscular part of the body; sometimes, the arm.

Brawn without brains is thine.
Dryden.

It was ordained that murderers should be brent on the brawn of the left hand.
E. Hall.

And in my vantbrace put this withered brawn.
Shak.

The flesh of a boar; also, the salted and prepared flesh of a boar.

The best age for the boar is from two to five years, at which time it is best to geld him, or sell him for brawn.
Mortimer.

A boar. [Obs.]

Beau. & Fl.

Brawned (?), a. Brawny; strong; muscular. [Obs.]
Spenser.

Brawner (?), n. A boor killed for the table.

Brawniness (?), n. The quality or state of being brawny.

Brawny (?), a. Having large, strong muscles; muscular; fleshy; strong.
½Brawny limbs.
W.Irving.

Syn. Ð Muscular; fleshy; strong; bulky; sinewy; athletic; stalwart; powerful; robust.

Braxy (?), n. [Cf. AS. breac rheum, broc sickness, Ir. bracha corruption. Jamieson.] 1. A disease of sheep. The term is variously applied in different localities. [Scot.]

A diseased sheep, or its mutton.

Bray (?), v. t. [imp. & p. p. Brayed (?); p. pr. & vb. n. Braying.] [OE. brayen, OF. breier, F. broyer to pound, grind, fr. OHG. brehhan to break. See Break.] To pound, beat, rub, or grind small or fine.

Though thou shouldest bray a fool in a mortar, ... yet will not his foolishness depart from him.
Prov. xxvii. 22.

Bray, v. i. [OE brayen, F. braire to bray, OF. braire to cry, fr. LL. bragire to whinny; perh. fr. the Celtic and akin to E. break; or perh. of imitative origin.]

To utter a loud, harsh cry, as an ass.

Laugh, and they
Return it louder than an ass can bray.
Dryden.

To make a harsh, grating, or discordant noise.

Heard ye the din of battle bray?
Gray.

Bray, v. t. To make or utter with a loud, discordant, or harsh and grating sound.

Arms on armor clashing, brayed
Horrible discord.
MIlton.

And varying notes the war pipes brayed.
Sir W.Scott.

Bray, n. The harsh cry of an ass; also, any harsh, grating, or discordant sound.

The bray and roar of multitudinous London.

Jerrold.

Bray, n. [OE. braye, brey, brew, eyebrow, brow of a hill, hill, bank, Scot. bra, brae, bray, fr. AS. br?w eyebrow, influenced by the allied Icel. br? eyebrow, bank, also akin to AS. br? yebrow. See Brow.] A bank; the slope of a hill; a hill. See Brae, which is now the usual spelling. [North of Eng. & Scot.]

Fairfax.

Brayer (?), n. An implement for braying and spreading ink in hand printing.

Brayer, n. One that brays like an ass.

Pope.

Braying, a. Making a harsh noise; blaring, ½Braying trumpets.

Shak.

Braze (?), v. i.[imp. & p. p. Brazedÿ(?); p. pr & vb. n. Brazing.][F. braser to solder, fr. Icel. brasa to harden by fire. Cf. Brass.] 1. To solder with hard solder, esp. with an alloy of copper and zinc; as, to braze the seams of a copper pipe.

To harden. ½Now I am brazes to it.

Shak.

Braze (?), v. t. [AS. br'sian, fr. br's brass. See Brass.] To cover or ornament with brass.

Chapman.

Brazen (?), a.[OE. brasen, AS. br'sen. See Brass.] 1. Pertaining to, made of, or resembling, brass.

Sounding harsh and loud, like resounding brass.

Impudent; immodest; shameless; having a front like brass; as, a brazen countenance.

Brazen age. (a) (Muth.) The age of war and lawlessness which succeeded the silver age. (b) (Arch'ol.)ÿSee under Bronze. Ð Brazen sea (Jewish Antiq.), a large laver of brass, placed in Solomon's temple for the use of the priests.

Brazen, v. t. [imp. & p. p. Brazened (?); p. pr. & vb. n. Brazening.] To carry through impudently or shamelessly; as, to brazen the matter through.

Sabina brazened it out before Mrs. Wygram, but inwardly she was resolved to be a good deal more circumspect.

W.Black.

BrazenÏbrowed · (?), a. Shamelessly impudent.

Sir T.Browne.

BrazenÏface · (?), n. An impudent of shameless person. ½Well said, brazenface; hold it out.

Shak.

BrazenÏfaced · (?), a. Impudent; shameless.

BrazenÏly (?), adv. In a bold, impudent manner.

<— p. 177 —>

Brazen**i**ness (?), n. The quality or state of being brazen. Johnson.

Brazier (?), n. Same as Brasier.

ØBraz · i**l**letto (?), n. [Cf. Pg. & Sp. brasilete, It. brasiletto.] See Brazil wood.

Bra**i**zilian (?), a. Of or pertaining to Brasil. Ð n. A native or an inhabitant of Brazil.

Brazilian pebble. See Pebble, n., 2.

Brazi**l**lin (?), n. [Cf. F. br‚siline. See Brazil.] (Chem.) A substance contained in both Brazil wood and Sapan wood, from which it is extracted as a yellow crystalline substance which is white when pure. It is colored intensely red by alkalies. [Written also brezilin.]

Bra**i**zil nut · (?). (Bot.) An oily, threeÐsided nut, the seed of the Bertholletia excelsa; the cream nut.

µ From eighteen to twentyÐfour of the seed or ½nuts‚ grow in a hard and nearly globular shell.

Bra**i**zil wood · (?). [OE. brasil, LL. brasile (cf. Pg. & Sp. brasil, Pr. bresil, Pr. bresil); perh. from Sp. or Pg. brasa a live coal (cf. Braze, Brasier); or Ar. vars plant for dyeing red or yellow. This name was given to the wood from its color; and it is said that King Emanuel, of Portugal, gave the name Brazil to the country in South America on account of its producing this wood.]

> The wood of the oriental C'salpinia Sapan; Ð so called before the discovery of America.

> A very heavy wood of a reddish color, imported from Brazil and other tropical countries, for cabinetÐwork, and for dyeing. The best is the heartwood of C'salpinia echinata, a leguminous tree; but other trees also yield it. An interior sort comes from Jamaica, the timber of C. Braziliensis and C. crista. This is often distinguished as Braziletto , but the better kind is also frequently so named.

Breach (?), n. [OE. breke, breche, AS. brice, gebrice, gebrece (in comp.), fr. brecan to break; akin to Dan. br'k, MHG. breche, gap, breach. See Break, and cf. Brake (the instrument), Brack a break]. 1. The act of breaking, in a figurative sense.

> Specifically: A breaking or infraction of a law, or of any obligation or tie; violation; nonÐfulfillment; as a breach of contract; a breach of promise.

> A gap or opening made made by breaking or battering, as in a wall or fortification; the space between the parts of a solid body rent by violence; a break; a rupture.

Once more unto the breach, dear friends, once more;
Or close the wall up with our English dead.
Shak.

> A breaking of waters, as over a vessel; the waters themselves; surge; surf.

The Lord hath broken forth upon mine enemies before me, as the breach of waters.
2 Sam. v. 20?
A clear breach implies that the waves roll over the vessel without breaking. Đ A clean breach implies that everything on deck is swept away.
Ham. Nav. Encyc.

A breaking up of amicable relations; rupture.

There's fallen between him and my lord
An unkind breach.
Shak.

A bruise; a wound.

Breach for breach, eye for eye.
Lev. xxiv.20?

(Med.) A hernia; a rupture.

A breaking out upon; an assault.

The Lord had made a breach upon Uzza.
1.Chron.xiii.11?
Breach of faith, a breaking, or a failure to keep, an expressed or implied promise; a betrayal of confidence or trust. Đ Breach of peace, disorderly conduct, disturbing the public peace. Đ Breach of privilege, an act or default in violation of the privilege or either house of Parliament, of Congress, or of a State legislature, as, for instance, by false swearing before a committee.
Mozley. Abbott.
Đ Breach of promise, violation of one's plighted word, esp. of a promise to marry. Đ Breach of trust, violation of one's duty or faith in a matter entrusted to one.
Syn. Đ Rent; cleft; chasm; rift; aperture; gap; break; disruption; fracture; rupture; infraction; infringement; violation; quarrel; dispute; contention; difference; misunderstanding.
Breach, v. t. [imp. & p.p. Breached (?) ; p. pr. & vb. n. Breaching.] To make a breach or opening in; as, to breach the walls of a city.
Breach, v. i. To break the water, as by leaping out; Đ said of a whale.
Breachy (?),a. Apt to break fences or to break out of pasture; unruly; as, breachy cattle.
Bread (?), v. t. [AS. br'dan to make broad, to spread. See Broad, a.] To spread. [Obs.]
Ray.
Bread (?), n. [AS. bre d; akin to OFries. br¾d, OS. br?d, D. brood, G. brod, brot, Icel. brau?, Sw. & Dan. br"d. The root is probably that of

E. brew. ? See Brew.] 1. An article of food made from flour or meal by moistening, kneading, and baking.

μ Raised bread is made with yeast, salt, and sometimes a little butter or lard, and is mixed with warm milk or water to form the dough, which, after kneading, is given time to rise before baking. Ð Cream of tartar bread is raised by the action of an alkaline carbonate or bicarbonate (as saleratus or ammonium bicarbonate) and cream of tartar (acid tartrate of potassium) or some acid. ÐUnleavened bread is usually mixed with water and salt only.

A‰crated bread. See under A?rated. Bread and butter (fig.), means of living. Ð Brown bread, Indian bread, Graham bread, Rye and Indian bread. See Brown bread, under Brown. Ð Bread tree. See Breadfruit.

Food; sustenance; support of life, in general.

Give us this day our daily bread.
Matt. vi. 11?

Bread, v. t. (Cookery) To cover with bread crumbs, preparatory to cooking; as, breaded cutlets.

Breadbas · ket (?), n. The stomach. [Humorous]
S. Foote.

Breadcorn · (?). Corn of grain of which bread is made, as wheat, rye, etc.

Breaded, a. Braided [Obs.]
Spenser.

Breaden (?), a. Made of bread. [R.]

Breadfruit · (?), n. (Bot.) 1. The fruit of a tree (Artocarpus incisa) found in the islands of the Pacific, esp. the South Sea islands. It is of a roundish form, from four to six or seven inches in diameter, and, when baked, somewhat resembles bread, and is eaten as food, whence the name.

(Bot.) The tree itself, which is one of considerable size, with large, lobed leaves. Cloth is made from the bark, and the timber is used for many purposes. Called also breadfruit tree and bread tree.

Breadless, a. Without bread; destitude of food.
Plump peers and breadless bards alike are dull.
P.Whitehead.

Bread · root (?), n. (Bot.) The root of a leguminous plant (Psoralea esculenta), found near the Rocky Mountains. It is usually oval in form, and abounds in farinaceous matter, affording sweet and palatable food.

μ It is the Pomme blanche of Canadian voyageurs.

Breadstuff (?), n. Grain, flour, or meal of which bread is made.

Breadth (?), n. [OE. brede, breede, whence later bredette, AS. br?du, fr. br¾d broad. See Broad, a.]

Distance from side to side of any surface or thing; measure across, or at right angles to the length; width.

(Fine Arts) The quality of having the colors and shadows broad and massive, and the arrangement of objects such as to avoid to great multiplicity of details, producing an impression of largeness and simple grandeur; Ð called also breadth of effect.

Breadth of coloring is a prominent character in the painting of all great masters.
Weale.
Breadthless, a. Without breadth.
Breadthways (?), ads. Breadthwise.
Whewell.
Breadthwise (?), ads. In the direction of the breadth.
Breadthwin · ner (?), n. The member of a family whose labor supplies the food of the family; one who works for his living.
H. Spencer.
Breakÿ(?), v. t. [imp. broke (?), (Obs. Brake); p.p. Broken (?), (Obs. Broke); p. pr. & vb. n. Breaking.] [OE. breken, AS. brecan; akin to OS. brekan, D. breken, OHG. brehhan, G. brechen, Icel.braka to creak, Sw. braka, br„kka to crack, Dan. br‘kke to break, Goth. brikan to break, L. frangere. Cf. Bray to pound, Breach, Fragile.] 1. To strain apart; to sever by fracture; to divide with violence; as, to break a rope or chain; to break a seal; to break an axle; to break rocks or coal; to break a lock.
Shak.

To lay open as by breaking; to divide; as, to break a package of goods.

To lay open, as a purpose; to disclose, divulge, or communicate.

Katharine, break thy mind to me.
Shak.

To infringe or violate, as an obligation, law, or promise.

Out, out, hyena ? these are thy wonted arts...
To break all faith, all vows, deceive, betray.
Milton

To interrupt; to destroy the continuity of; to dissolve or terminate; as, to break silence; to break one's sleep; to break one's journey.

Go, release them, Ariel;
My charms I'll break, their senses I'll restore.
Shak.

To destroy the completeness of; to remove a part from; as, to break a set.

To destroy the arrangement of; to throw into disorder; to pierce; as, the cavalry were not able to break the British squares.

To shatter to pieces; to reduce to fragments.

The victim broke in pieces the musical instruments with which he had solaced the hours of captivity.
Prescott.

To exchange for other money or currency of smaller denomination; as, to break a five dollar bill.

To destroy the strength, firmness, or consistency of; as, to break flax.

To weaken or impair, as health, spirit, or mind.

An old man, broken with the storms of state.
Shak.

To diminish the force of; to lessen the shock of, as a fall or blow.

I'll rather leap down first, and break your fall.
Dryden.

To impart, as news or information; to broach; Ð with to, and often with a modified word implying some reserve; as, to break the news gently to the widow; to break a purpose cautiously to a friend.

To tame; to reduce to subjection; to make tractable; to discipline; as, to break a horse to the harness or saddle. ½To break a colt.¸

Spenser.
Why, then thou canst not break her to the lute?
Shak.

To destroy the financial credit of; to make bankrupt; to ruin.

With arts like these rich Matho, when he speaks,
Attracts all fees, and little lawyers breaks.
Dryden.

To destroy the official character and standing of; to cashier; to dismiss.

I see a great officer broken.
Swift.

With prepositions or adverbs: Ð

To break down. (a) To crush; to overwhelm; as, to break down one's strength; to break down opposition. (b) To remove, or open a way through, by breaking; as, to break down a door or wall. Ð To break in. (a) To force in; as, to break in a door. (b) To train; to discipline; as, a horse well broken in. ÐTo break of, to rid of; to cause to abandon; as, to break one of a habit.Ð To break off. (a) To separate by breaking; as, to break off a twig.(b) To stop suddenly; to abandon. ½Break off thy sins by righteousness.¸

Dan. iv.27.

Ð To break open, to open by breaking. ½Open the door, or I will break it open.¸

Shak.

Ð To break out, to take or force out by breaking; as, to break out a pane of glass. Ð To break out a cargo, to unstow a cargo, so as to unload it easily. Ð To break through. (a) To make an opening through, as, as by violence or the force of gravity; to pass violently through; as to break through the enemy's lines; to break through the ice. (b) To disregard; as, to break through the ceremony. Ð To break up. (a) To separate into parts; to plow (new or fallow ground). ½Break up this capon.͵

Shak.

½Break up your fallow ground.͵

Jer. iv. 3?

(b) To dissolve; to put an end to. ½Break up the court.͵

Shak.

To break (one) all up, to unsettle or disconcert completely; to upset. [Colloq.]

With an immediate object: Ð

To break the back. (a) To dislocate the backbone; hence, to disable totally. (b) To get through the worst part of; as, to break the back of a difficult undertaking. Ð To break bulk, to destroy the entirety of a load by removing a portion of it; to begin to unload; also, to transfer in detail, as from boats to cars. ÐTo break cover, to burst forth from a protecting concealment, as game when hunted. Ð To break a deer or stag, to cut it up and apportion the parts among those entitled to a share. Ð To break fast, to partake of food after abstinence. See Breakfast. Ð To break ground. (a) To open the earth as for planting; to commence excavation, as for building, siege operations, and the like; as, to break ground for a foundation, a canal, or a railroad. (b) Fig.: To begin to execute any plan. (c) (Naut.) To release the anchor from the bottom. Ð To break the heart, to crush or overwhelm (one) with grief. Ð To break a house (Law), to remove or set aside with violence and a felonious intent any part of a house or of the fastenings provided to secure it. Ð To break the ice, to get through first difficulties; to overcome obstacles and make a beginning; to introduce a subject. Ð To break jail, to escape from confinement in jail, usually by forcible means. Ð To break a jest, to utter a jest. ½Patroclus...the livelong day break scurril jests.͵

Shak.

Ð To break joints, to lay or arrange bricks, shingles, etc., so that the joints in one course shall not coincide with those in the preceding course. Ð To break a lance, to engage in a tilt or contest. Ð To break the neck, to dislocate the joints of the neck. Ð To break no squares, to create no trouble. [Obs.] Ð To break a path, road, etc., too open a way through obstacles by force or labor. Ð To break upon a wheel, to execute or torture, as a criminal by stretching him upon a wheel, and breaking his limbs with an iron bar; Ð a mode of punishment formerly employed in some countries. Ð To break wind, to give vent to wind from the anus.

Syn. Đ To dispart; rend; tear; shatter; batter; violate; infringe; demolish; destroy; burst; dislocate.

Break (?), v. i. 1. To come apart or divide into two or more pieces, usually with suddenness and violence; to part; to burst asunder.

To open spontaneously, or by pressure from within, as a bubble, a tumor, a seed vessel, a bag.

Else the bottle break, and the wine runneth out.
Math. ix. 17.?

To burst forth; to make its way; to come to view; to appear; to dawn.

The day begins to break, and night is fied.
Shak.
And from the turf a fountain broke,
and gurgled at our feet.
Wordswoorth.

To burst forth violently, as a storm.

The clouds are still above; and, while I speak,
A second deluge o'er our head may break.
Shak.

To open up. to be scattered; t be dissipated; as, the clouds are breaking.

At length the darkness begins to break.
Macawlay.

To become weakened in constitution or faculties; to lose health or strength.

See how the dean begins to break;
Poor gentleman ? he droops apace.
Swift.

To be crushed, or overwhelmed with sorrow or grief; as, my heart is breaking.

To fall in business; to become bankrupt.

He that puts all upon adventures doth oftentimes break, and come to poverty.
Bacn.

To make an abrupt or sudden change; to change the gait; as, to break into a run or gallop.

To fail in musical quality; as, a singer's voice breaks when it is strained beyond its compass and a tone or note is not completed, but degenerates into an unmusical sound instead. Also, to change in tone, as a boy's voice at puberty.

To fall out; to terminate friendship.

To break upon the score of danger or expense is to be mean and narrow-spirited.

Collier.

With prepositions or adverbs:

To break away, to disengage one's self abruptly; to come or go away against resistance.

Fear me not, man; I will not break away.

Shak.

To break down. (a) To come down by breaking; as, the coach broke down. (b) To fail in any undertaking.

He had broken down almost at the outset.

Thackeray.

To break forth, to issue; to come out suddenly, as sound, light, etc. ½Then shall thy light break forth as the morning.

Isa. lviii. 8;

often with into in expressing or giving vent to one's feelings. ½Break forth into singing, ye mountains.

Isa. xliv. 23.

To break from, to go away from abruptly.

This radiant from the circling crowd he broke.

Dryden.

To break into, to enter by breaking; as, to break into a house. To break in upon, to enter or approach violently or unexpectedly. ½This, this is he; softly awhile; let us not break in upon him.

Milton.

To break loose. (a) To extricate one's self forcibly. ½Who would not, finding way, break loose from hell?

Milton.

(b) To cast off restraint, as of morals or propriety. To break off. (a) To become separated by rupture, or with suddenness and violence. (b) To desist or cease suddenly. ½Nay, forward, old man; do not break off so.

Shak.

To break off from, to desist from; to abandon, as a habit. To break out. (a) To burst forth; to escape from restraint; to appear suddenly, as a fire or an epidemic. ½For in the wilderness

<— p. 178 —>

shall waters break out, and stream in the desert. Isa. xxxv. 6

(b) To show itself in cutaneous eruptions; said of a disease. (c) To have a rash or eruption on the akin; said of a patient. To break over, to overflow; to go beyond limits. To break up. (a) To become separated into parts or fragments; as, the ice break up in the rivers; the wreck will break up in the next storm. (b) To disperse.½The company breaks up.

I.Watts.

Ð To break upon, to discover itself suddenly to; to dawn upon. Ð To break with. (a) To fall out; to sever one's relations with; to part friendship. ½It can not be the Volsces dare break with us.‚

Shak.

Ð ½If she did not intend to marry Clive, she should have broken with him altogether.‚

Thackeray.

(b) To come to an explanation; to enter into conference; to speak [Obs.] ½I will break with her and with her father.‚

Shak.

Break (?), n. [See Break, v. t., and cf. Brake (the instrument), Breach, Brack a crack.] 1. An opening made by fracture or disruption.

An interruption of continuity; change of direction; as , a break in a wall; a break in the deck of a ship. Specifically: (a) (Arch.) A projection or recess from the face of a building. (b) (Elec.) An opening or displacement in the circuit, interrupting the electrical current.

An interruption; a pause; as, a break in friendship; a break in the conversation.

An interruption in continuity in writing or printing, as where there is an omission, an unfilled line, etc.

All modern trash is
Set forth with numerous breaks and dashes.
Swift.

The first appearing, as of light in the morning; the dawn; as, the break of day; the break of dawn.

A large fourÐwheeled carriage, having a straight body and calash top, with the driver's seat in front and the footman's behind.

A device for checking motion, or for measuring friction. See Brake, n. 9 & 10.

(Teleg.) See Commutator.

Breaka˙ble (?), a. Capable of being broken.

Breakage (?), n. 1. The act of breaking; a break; a breaking; also, articles broken.

An allowance or compensation for things broken accidentally, as in transportation or use.

Breakbone · fe · ver (?). (Med.) See Dengue.

Break˙cir · cuit (?), n.(Elec.) A key or other device for breaking an electrical circuit.

Breakdown · (?), n. 1. The act or result of breaking down, as of a carriage; downfall.

(a) A noisy, rapid, shuffling dance engaged in competitively by a number of persons or pairs in succession, as among the colored people of the Southern United States, and so called, perhaps, because the exercise is continued until most of those who take part in it break down. (b) Any rude, noisy dance performed by shuffling the feet, usually by one person at a time. [U.S.]

Don't clear out when the quadrilles are over, for we are going to have a breakdown to wind up with.
New Eng. Tales.
Breaker (?), n. 1. One who, or that which, breaks.
I'll be no breaker of the law.
Shak.

Specifically: A machine for breaking rocks, or for breaking coal at the mines; also, the building in which such a machine is placed.

(Naut.) A small water cask.

Totten.

A wave breaking into foam against the shore, or against a sand bank, or a rock or reef near the surface.

The breakers were right beneath her bows.
Longfellow.
Breakfast (?), n. [Break + fast.] 1. The first meal in the day, or that which is eaten at the first meal.
A sorry breakfast for my lord protector.
Shak.

A meal after fasting, or food in general.

The wolves will get a breakfast by my death.
Dryden.
Breakfast, v. i. [imp. & p. p. breakfasted; p. pr. & vb. n. Breakfasting.] To break one's fast in the morning; too eat the first meal in the day.
First, sir, I read, and then I breakfast.
Prior.
Breakfast, v. t. To furnish with breakfast.
Milton.
Breakman (?), n. See Brakeman.
Breakneck· (?), n. 1. A fall that breaks the neck.

A steep place endangering the neck.

Breakneck· (?), a. Producing danger of a broken neck; as, breakneck speed.
BreakĬup· (?), n. Disruption; a separation and dispersion of the parts or members; as, a breakÐup of an assembly or dinner party; a breakÐup of the government.
Breakwa·ter (?), n. Any structure or contrivance, as a mole, or a wall at the mouth of a harbor, to break the force of waves, and afford protection from their violence.

Breamÿ(?), n. [OE. breme, brem, F. brˆme, OF. bresme, of German origin; cf. OHG. brahsema, brahsina, OLG. bressemo, G. brassen. Cf. Brasse.]

(Zo"l) A European freshÐwater cyprinoid fish of the genus Abramis, little valued as food. Several species are known.

(Zo"l) An American freshÐwater fish, of various species of Pomotis and allied genera, which are also called sunfishes and pondfishes. See Pondfish.

(Zo"l) A marine sparoid fish of the genus Pagellus, and allied genera. See Sea Bream.

Bream, v. t. [imp. & p. p. Breamed (?); p. pr. & vb. n. Breaming.] [Cf. Broom, and G. ein schiff brennen.] (Naut.) To clean, as a ship's bottom of adherent shells, seaweed, etc., by the application of fire and scraping.

Breast (?), n. [OE. brest, breost, As. breċst; akin to Icel. brj?st, Sw. br"st, Dan. bryst, Goth. brusts, OS. briost, D. borst, G. brust.] 1. The fore part of the body, between the neck and the belly; the chest; as, the breast of a man or of a horse.

Either one of the protuberant glands, situated on the front of the chest or thorax in the female of man and of some other mammalia, in which milk is secreted for the nourishment of the young; a mammma; a teat.

My brother, that sucked the breasts of my mother.
Cant. viii. 1.

Anything resembling the human breast, or bosom; the front or forward part of anything; as, a chimney breast; a plow breast; the breast of a hill.

Mountains on whose barren breast
The laboring clouds do often rest.
Milton.

(Mining) (a) The face of a coal working. (b) The front of a furnace.

The seat of consciousness; the repository of thought and selfÐconsciousness, or of secrets; the seat of the affections and passions; the heart.

He has a loyal breast.
Shak.

The power of singing; a musical voice; Ð so called, probably, from the connection of the voice with the lungs, which lie within the breast. [Obs.]

By my troth, the fool has an excellent breast.
Shak.

Breast drill, a portable drilling machine, provided with a breastplate, for forcing the drill against the work. Ð Breast pang. See Angina pectoris, under Angina. Ð To make a clean breast, to disclose the secrets which weigh upon one; to make full confession.

Breast, v. t. [imp. & p. p.Breasted; p. pr. & vb. n. Breasted.] To meet, with the breast; to struggle with or oppose manfully; as, to breast the storm or waves.

The court breasted the popular current by sustaining the demurrer.

Wirt.

To breast up a hedge, to cut the face of it on one side so as to lay bare the principal upright stems of the plants.

Breastband · (?), n. A band for the breast. Specifically: (Naut.) A band of canvas, or a rope, fastened at both ends to the rigging, to support the man who heaves the lead in sounding.

Breastbeam · (?), n. (Mach.) The front transverse beam of a locomotive.

Breastbone · (?), n. The bone of the breast; the sternum.

Breast‡deep · (?), a. Deep as from the breast to the feet; as high as the breast.

See him breast‐deep in earth, and famish him.

Shak.

Breasted, a. Having a breast; ‐ used in composition with qualifying words, in either a literal or a metaphorical sense; as, a single‐breasted coat.

The close minister is buttoned up, and the brave officer open‐breasted, on these occasions.

Spectator.

Breastfast · (?), n. (Naut.) A large rope to fasten the midship part of a ship to a wharf, or to another vessel.

Breastheight · (?), n. The interior slope of a fortification, against which the garnison lean in firing.

Breast‡high · (?), a. High as the breast.

Breasthook · ÿ(?), n. (Naut.) A thick piece of timber in the form of a knee, placed across the stem of a ship to strengthen the fore part and unite the bows on each side.

Totten.

Breasting, n. (Mach.) The curved channel in which a breast wheel turns. It is closely adapted to the curve of the wheel through about a quarter of its circumference, and prevents the escape of the water until it has spent its force upon the wheel. See Breast wheel.

Breastknot · (?), n. A pin worn of the breast for a fastening, or for ornament; a brooch.

Breastplate · (?), n. 1. A plate of metal covering the breast as defensive armor.

Before his old rusty breastplate could be scoured, and his cracked headpiece mended.

Swift.

A piece against which the workman presses his breast in operating a breast drill, or other similar tool.

A strap that runs across a horse's breast.

Ash.

(Jewish Antiq.) A part of the vestment of the high priest, worn upon the front of the ephod. It was a double piece of richly embroidered stuff, a span square, set with twelve precious stones, on which were engraved the names of the twelve tribes of Israel. See Ephod.

Breatplow·, Breastplough· (?), n. A kind of plow, driven by the breast of the workman; Ð used to cut or pare turf.

Breastrall· (?), n. The upper rail of any parapet of ordinary height, as of a balcony; the railing of a quarterÐdeck, etc.

Breastrope· (?), n. See Breastband.

Breastsum·merÿ3, n. (Arch.) A summer or girder extending across a building flush with, and supporting, the upper part of a front or external wall; a long lintel; a girder; Ð used principally above shop windows. [Written also brestsummer and bressummer.]

Breastwheel·ÿ(?), n. A water wheel, on which the stream of water strikes neither so high as in the overshot wheel, nor so low as in the undershot, but generally at about half the height of the wheel, being kept in contact with it by the breasting. The water acts on the float boards partly by impulse, partly by its weight.

Breastwork· (?), n. 1. (Fort.) A defensive work of moderate height, hastily thrown up, of earth or other material.

(Naut.) A railing on the quarterÐdeck and forecastle.

Breathÿ(?), n. [OE. breth, breeth, AS. br?? odor, scent, breath; cf. OHG. br¾dam steam, vapor, breath, G. brodem, and possibly E. Brawn, and Breed.] 1. The air inhaled and exhaled in respiration, air which, in the process of respiration, has parted with oxygen and has received carbonic acid, aqueous vapor, warmth, etc.

Melted as breath into the wind.
Shak.

The act of breathing naturally or freely; the power or capacity to breathe freely; as, I am out of breath.

The power of respiration, and hence, life.

Hood.
Thou takest away their breath, they die.
Ps. civ. 29.

Time to breathe; respite; pause.

Give me some breath, some little pause.
Shak.

A single respiration, or the time of making it; a single act; an instant.

He smiles and he frowns in a breath.
Dryden.

Fig.: That which gives or strengthens life.

The earthquake voice of victory,
To thee the breath of life.
Byron.

A single word; the slightest effort; a triffle.

A breath can make them, as a breath has made.
Goldsmith.

A very slight breeze; air in gentle motion.

Calm and unruffled as a summer's sea,
When not a breath of wind flies o'er its surface.
Addison.

Fragrance; exhalation; odor; perfume.

Tennison.
The breath of flowers.
Bacon.

Gentle exercise, causing a quicker respiration.

An after dinner's breath.
Shak.

Out of breath, breathless, exhausted; breathing with difficulty. Ð Under one's breath, in low tones.

Breathaïbleÿ(?), a. Such as can be breathed.

Breathaïbleïness, n. State of being breathable.

Breathe (?),v. i. [imp. & p. p Breathed (?); p. pr. & vb. n. Breathing.] [From Breath.]

To respire; to inhale and exhale air; hence;, to live. ½I am in health, I breathe.

Shak.
Breathes there a man with soul so dead?
Sir W. Scott.

To take breath; to rest from action.

Well? breathe awhile, and then to it again?
Shak.

To pass like breath; noiselessly or gently; to exhale; to emanate; to blow gently.

The air breathes upon us here most sweetly.
Shak.
There breathes a living fragrance from the shore.
Byron.
Breathe, v. t. 1. To inhale and exhale in the process of respiration; to respire.
To view the light of heaven, and breathe the vital air.
Dryden.

To inject by breathing; to infuse; Ð with into.

Able to breathe life into a stone.
Shak.
And the Lord God formed man of the dust of the ground, and breathed into his nostrils the breath of life.
Gen. ii. 7.

To emit or utter by the breath; to utter softly; to whisper; as, to breathe a vow.

He softly breathed thy name.
Dryden.
Or let the church, our mother, breathe her curse,
A mother's curse, on her revolting son.
Shak.

To exhale; to emit, as breath; as, the flowers breathe odors or perfumes.

To express; to manifest; to give forth.

Others articles breathe the same severe spirit.
Milner.

To act upon by the breath; to cause to sound by breathing. ½They breathe the flute.,

Prior.

To promote free respiration in; to exercise.

And every man should beat thee. I think thou wast created for men to breathe themselves upon thee.
Shak.

To suffer to take breath, or recover the natural breathing; to rest; as, to breathe a horse.

A moment breathed his panting steed.
Sir W. Scott.

To put out of breath; to exhaust.

Mr. Tulkinghorn arrives in his turret room, a little breathed by the journey up.
Dickens.

(Phonetics) To utter without vocality, as the nonvocal consonants.

The same sound may be pronounces either breathed, voiced, or whispered.
H. Sweet.

Breathed elements, being already voiceless, remain unchanged [in whispering].
H. Sweet.

To breathe again, to take breath; to feel a sense of relief, as from danger, responsibility, or press of business. Ð To breathe one's last, to die; to expire. Ð To breathe a vein, to open a vein; to let blood.
Dryden.

Breatherÿ(?), n. 1. One who breathes. Hence: (a) One who lives. (b) One who utters. (c) One who animates or inspires.

That which puts one out of breath, as violent exercise. [Colloq.]

Breathful (?), a. Full of breath; full of odor; fragrant. [Obs.]
Breathingÿ(?), n. 1. Respiration; the act of inhaling and exhaling air.
Subject to a difficulty of breathing.
Melmoth.

Air in gentle motion.

Any gentle influence or operation; inspiration; as, the breathings of the Spirit.

Aspiration; secret prayer. ½Earnest desires and breathings after that blessed state.

Tillotson.

Exercising; promotion of respiration.

Here is a lady that wants breathing too;
And I have heard, you knights of Tyre
Are excellent in making ladies trip.
Shak.

Utterance; communication or publicity by words.

I am sorry to give breathing to my purpose.
Shak.

Breathing place; vent.

Dryden.

Stop; pause; delay.

You shake the head at so long a breathing.
Shak.

Also, in a wider sense, the sound caused by the

<— p. 179 —>
? friction of the outgoing breath in the throat, mouth, etc., when the glottis is wide open; aspiration; the sound expressed by the letter h.

(Gr. Gram.) A mark to indicate aspiration or its absence. See Rough breathing, Smooth breathing, below.

Breathing place. (a) A pause. ½That c'sura, or breathing place, in the midst of the verse., Sir P.Sidney. (b) A vent. Ð Breathing time, pause; relaxation. Bp. Hall. Ð Breathing while, time sufficient for drawing breath; a short time. Shak. Ð Rough breathing (spiritus asper) (?). See 2d Asper, n. Ð Smooth breathing (spiritus lenis), a mark (') indicating the absence of the sound of h, as in ? (ienai).

Breathless (?), a. 1. Spent with labor or violent action; out of breath.

Not breathing; holdingÿthe breath, on account of fear, expectation, or intense interest; attended with a holding of the breath; as, breathless attention.

But breathless, as we grow when feeling most.
Byron.

Dead; as, a breathless body.

Breathlessïly, adv. In a breathless manner.
Breathlessïness, n. The state of being breathless or out of breath.
ØBreccia (?), n. [It., breach, pebble, fragments of stone, fr. F. brŠche; of German origin. See Breach.] (Geol.) A rock composed of angular fragments either of the same mineral or of different minerals, etc., united by a cement, and commonly presenting a variety of colors.

Bone breccia, a breccia containing bones, usually fragmentary. Ð Coin breccia, a breccia containing coins.

Brecciïa · ted (?), a. Consisting of angular fragments cemented together; resembling breccia in appearance.

The brecciated appearance of many specimens [of meteorites].
H.A.Newton.

Bred (?), imp. & p.p. of Breed.

Bred out, degenerated. ½The strain of man's bred out into baboon and monkey., Shak. Ð Bred to arms. See under Arms. Ð Well bred. (a) Of a good family; having a good pedigree. ½A gentleman well bred and of good name., Shak. [Obs., except as applied to domestic animals.] (b) Well brought up, as shown in having good manners; cultivated; refined; polite.

Brede, or Breede (?), n. Breadth. [Obs.]

Chaucer.

Brede (?), n. [See Braid woven cord.] A braid. [R.]

Half lapped in glowing gauze and golden brede.

Tennyson.

Breech (?), n. [See Breeches.] 1. The lower part of the body behind; the buttocks.

Breeches. [Obs.]

Shak.

The hinder part of anything; esp., the part of a cannon, or other firearm, behind the chamber.

(Naut.) The external angle of knee timber, the inside of which is called the throat.

Breech, v.t. [imp. & p.p. Breeched (?); p.pr. & vb.n. Breeching (?).] 1. To put into, or clothe with, breeches.

A great man ... anxious to know whether the blacksmith's ?oungest boy was breeched.

Macaulay.

To cover as with breeches. [Poetic]

THeir daggers unmannerly breeched with gore.

Shak.

To fit or furnish with a breech; as, to breech a gun.

To whip on the breech. [Obs.]

Had not a courteous serving man conveyed me away, whilst he went to fetch whips, I think, in my conscience, he would have breeched me.

Old Play.

To fasten with breeching.

Breechblock (?), n. The movable piece which closes the breech of a breechÐloading firearm, and resists the backward force of the discharge. It is withdrawn for the insertion of a cartridge, and closed again before the gun is fired.

Breechcloth · (?), n. A cloth worn aroundÿthe breech.

Breeches (?), n. pl. [OE. brech, brek, AS. brÇk, pl. of brÓc breech, breeches; akin to Icel. brÓk breeches, ODan. brog, D. broek, G. bruch; cf. L. bracae, braccae, which is of Celtic origin. Cf. Brail.] 1. A garment worn by men, covering the hips and thighs; smallclothes.

His jacket was red, and his breeches were blue.

Coleridge.

Trousers; pantaloons. [Colloq.]

Breeches buoy, in the lifeÐsaving service, a pair of canvas breeches depending from an annular or beltlike life buoy which is usually of cork. This contrivance, inclosing the person to be rescued, is hung by short ropes from a block which runs upon the hawser stretched from the ship to the shore, and is drawn to land by hauling lines. Ð Breeches pipe, a forked pipe forming two branches united at one end. Ð Knee breeches, breeches coming to the knee, and buckled or fastened there; smallclothes. Ð To wear the breeches, to usurp the authority of the husband; Ð said of a wife. [Colloq.]

Breeching (?), n. 1. A whipping on the breech, or the act of whipping on the breech.

I view the prince with Aristarchus' eyes,
Whose looks were as a breeching to a boy.
Marlowe.

That part of a harness which passes round the breech of a horse, enabling him to hold back a vehicle.

(Naut.) A strong rope rove through the cascabel of a cannon and secured to ringbolts in the ship's side, to limit the recoil of the gun when it is discharged.

The sheet iron casing at the end of boilers to convey the smoke from the flues to the smokestack.

Breechload · er (?), n. A firearm which receives its load at the breech.
For cavalry, the revolver and breechloader will supersede the saber.
Rep. Sec. War (1860).

BreechÐload · ing, a. Receiving the charge at the breech instead of at the muzzle.

Breech pin · (?), Breech screw · (?). A strong iron or steel plug screwed into the breech of a musket or other firearm, to close the bottom of the bore.

Breech sight · (?). A device attached to the breech of a firearm, to guide the eye, in conjunction with the front sight, in taking aim.

Breed (?), v.t. [imp. & p.p. Bred (?); p.pr. & vb.n. Breeding.] [OE. breden, AS. brÇdanÿto nourish, cherish, keep warm, from brÓd brood; akin to D. broedenÿto brood, OHG. bruoten, G. brten. See Brood.] 1. To produce as offspring; to bring forth; to bear; to procreate; to generate; to beget; to hatch.

Yet every mother breeds not sons alike.
Shak.
If the sun breed maggots in a dead dog.
Shak.

To take care of in infancy, and through the age of youth; to bring up; to nurse and foster.

To bring thee forth with pain, with care to breed.
Dryden.
Born and bred on the verge of the wilderness.

Everett.

To educate; to instruct; to form by education; to train; Ð sometimes followed by up.

But no care was taken to breed him a Protestant.
Bp. Burnet.
His farm may not remove his children too far from him, or the trade he breeds them up in.
Locke.

To engender; to cause; to occasion; to originate; to produce; as, to breed a storm; to breed disease.

Lest the place
And my quaint habits breed astonishment.
Milton.

To give birth to; to be the native place of; as, a pond breeds fish; a northern country breeds stout men.

To raise, as any kind of stock.

To produce or obtain by any natural process. [Obs.]

Children would breed their teeth with less danger.
Locke.
Syn. - To engender; generate; beget; produce; hatch; originate; bring up; nourish; train; instruct.
Breed, v.i. 1. To bear and nourish young; to reproduce or multiply itself; to be pregnant.
That they breed abundantly in the earth.
Gen.viii.17.
The mother had never bred before.
Carpenter.
Ant. Is your gold and silver ewes and rams?
Shy. I can not tell. I make it breed as fast.
Shak.

To be formed in the parent or dam; to be generated, or to grow, as young before birth.

To have birth; to be produced or multiplied.

Heavens rain grace
On that which breeds between them.
Shak.

To raise a breed; to get progeny.

The kind of animal which you wish to breed from.
Gardner.
To breed in and in, ÿ to breed from animals of the same stock that are closely related.

Breed, n. 1. A race or variety of men or other animals (or of plants), perpetuating its special or distinctive characteristics by inheritance.

Twice fifteen thousand hearts of England's breed.
Shak.
Greyhounds of the best breed.
Carpenter.

<small>Class; sort; kind; Ð of men, things, or qualities.</small>

Are these the breed of wits so wondered at?
Shak.
This courtesy is not of the right breed.
Shak.

<small>A number produced at once; a brood. [Obs.]</small>

μ Breed is usually applied to domestic animals; species or variety to wild animals and to plants; and race to men.

Breedbate (?), n. One who breeds or originates quarrels. [Obs.] ½No telltale nor no breedbate.
Shak.

Breeder (?), n. 1. One who, or that which, breeds, produces, brings up, etc.

She was a great breeder.
Dr. A. Carlyle.
Italy and Rome have been the best breeders of worthy men.
Ascham.

<small>A cause. ½The breeder of my sorrow.</small>

Shak.
Breeding (?), n. 1. The act or process of generating or bearing.

<small>The raising or improving of any kind of domestic animals; as, farmers should pay attention to breeding.</small>

<small>Nurture; education; formation of manners.</small>

She had her breeding at my father's charge.
Shak.

<small>Deportment or behavior in the external offices and decorums of social life; manners; knowledge of, or training in, the ceremonies, or polite observances of society.</small>

Delicacy of breeding, or that polite deference and respect which civility obliges us either to express or counterfeit towards the persons with whom we converse.
Hume.

<small>Descent; pedigree; extraction. [Obs.]</small>

Honest gentlemen, I know not your breeding.
Shak.

Close breeding, In and in breeding, breeding from a male and female from the same parentage. Ð Cross breeding, breeding from a male and female of different lineage. Ð Good breeding, politeness; genteel deportment.

Syn. - Education; instruction; nurture; training; manners. See Education.

Breeze (?), n., Breeze fly · (?). [OE. brese, AS. briɔsa; perh. akin to OHG. brimissa, G. breme, bremse, D. brems, which are akin to G. brummen to growl, buzz, grumble, L. fremereÿto murmur; cf. G. brausen, Sw. brusa, Dan. bruse, to roar, rush.] (Zo"l.) A fly of various species, of the family Tabanid‘, noted for buzzing about animals, and tormenting them by sucking their blood; Ð called also horsefly, and gadfly. They are among the largest of twoÐwinged or dipterous insects. The name is also given to different species of botflies. [Written also breese and brize.]

Breeze, n. [F. brise; akin to It. brezza breeze, Sp. briza, brisa, a breeze from northeast, Pg. briza northeast wind; of uncertain origin; cf. F. bise, Pr. bisa, OHG. bisa, north wind, Arm. biz northeast wind.] 1. A light, gentle wind; a fresh, softÐblowing wind.

Into a gradual calm the breezes sink.
Wordsworth.

<small>An excited or ruffed state of feeling; a flurry of excitement; a disturbance; a quarrel; as, the discovery produced a breeze. [Colloq.]</small>

Land breeze, a wind blowing from the land, generally at night. Ð Sea breeze, a breeze or wind blowing, generally in the daytime, from the sea.

Breeze (?), n. [F. braise cinders, live coals. See Brasier.] 1. Refuse left in the process of making coke or burning charcoal.

<small>(Brickmaking) Refuse coal, coal ashes, and cinders, used in the burning of bricks.</small>

Breeze, v.i. To blow gently. [R.]
J.Barlow.
To breeze upÿ(Naut.), to blow with increasing freshness.
Breezeless, a. Motionless; destitute of breezes.
A stagnant, breezeless air becalms my soul.
Shenstone.
Breeziïness (?), n. State of being breezy.

Breezy (?), a. 1. Characterized by, or having, breezes; airy. ½A breezy day in May.

Coleridge.

'Mid lawns and shades by breezy rivulets fanned.

Wordsworth.

Fresh; brisk; full of life. [Colloq.]

ØBregma (?), n. [Gr. ? the front part of the head: cf. F. bregma.] (Anat.) The point of junction of the coronal and sagittal sutures of the skull.

Bregĭmatic (?), a. (Anat.) Pertaining to the bregma.

Brehon (?), n. [Ir. breitheamh judge.] An ancient Irish or Scotch judge.

Brehon laws, the ancient Irish laws, Đ unwritten, like the common law of England. They were abolished by statute of Edward III.

Breme (?), a. [OE. breme, brime, fierce, impetuous, glorious, AS. brÇme, br?me, famous. Cf. Brim, a.] 1. Fierce; sharp; severe; cruel. [Obs.]

Spenser.

From the septentrion cold, in the breme freezing air.

Drayton.

Famous; renowned; well known.

Wright.

[Written also brim and brimme.]

Bren (?), Brenne (?), } v.t. & i. [imp. & p.p. Brent (?); p.pr. & vb.n. Brenning.] [See Burn.] To burn. [Obs.]

Chaucer.

Consuming fire brent his shearing house or stall.

W.Browne.

Bren, n. Bran. [Obs.]

Chaucer.

Brennage (?), n. [OF. brenage; cf. LL. brennagium, brenagium.ÿSee Bran.] (Old Eng. Law) A tribute which tenants paid to their lord, in lieu of bran, which they were obliged to furnish for his hounds.

BrenningÏly, adv. Burningly; ardently. [Obs.]

Brent (?), Brant (?), a. [AS. brant; akin to Dan. brat, Icel. brattr, steep.] 1. Steep; high. [Obs.]

Grapes grow on the brant rocks so wonderfully that ye will marvel how any man dare climb up to them.

Ascham.

Smooth; unwrinkled. [Scot.]

Your bonnie brow was brent.

Burns.

Brent, imp. & p.p. of Bren. Burnt. [Obs.]

Brent, n. [Cf. Brant.] A brant. See Brant.

Brequet chain · (?). A watchÐguard.

Brere (?), n. A brier. [Archaic]
Chaucer.

Brest (?), 3d sing.pr. for Bursteth. [Obs.]

Brest, Breast (?), n. (Arch.) A torus. [Obs.]

Breste (?), v.t. & i. [imp. Brast; p.p. Brusten, Borsten, Bursten.] To burst. [Obs.]
Chaucer.

Brestsum · mer (?), n. See Breastsummer.

Bret (?), n. (Zo"l.) See Birt.

Bretful (?), a. [OE. also brerdful, fr. brerd top, brim, AS. brerd.] Brimful. [Obs.]
Chaucer.

Brethren (?), n.; pl. of Brother.

µ This form of the plural is used, for the most part, in solemn address, and in speaking of religious sects or fraternities, or their members.

Breton (?), a. [F. breton.] Of or relating to Brittany, or Bretagne, in France. Ð n. A native or inhabitant of Brittany, or Bretagne, in France; also, the ancient language of Brittany; Armorican.

Brett (?), n. Same as Britzska.

Brettice (?), n.; pl. Brettices (?). [OE. bretasce, bretage, parapet, OF. bretesche wooden tower, F. bretŠche, LL. breteschia, bertresca, prob. fr. OHG. bret, G. brett board; akin to E. board. See Board, n., and cf. Bartizan.] The wooden boarding used in supporting the roofs and walls of coal mines. See Brattice.

Bretwal˘da (?), n. [AS. Bretwalda, br?ten walda, a powerful ruler.] (Eng. Hist.) The official title applied to that one of the AngloÐSaxon chieftains who was chosen by the other chiefs to lead them in their warfare against the British tribes.
Brande & C.

Bretzel (?), n. [G.] See Pretzel.

Breve (?), n. [It. & (in sense 2) LL. breve, fr. L. brevis short. See Brief.] 1. (Mus.) A note or character of time, equivalent to two semibreves or four minims. When dotted, it is equal to three semibreves. It was formerly of a square figure (as thus: ?), but is now made oval, with a line perpendicular to the staff on each of its sides; Ð formerly much used for choir service.
Moore.

(Law) Any writ or precept under seal, issued out of any court.

(Print.) A curved mark [?] used commonly to indicate the short quantity of a vowel.

(Zo"l.) The great ant thrush of Sumatra (Pitta gigas), which has a very short tail.

Brĕvet (?), n. [F. brevet, LL. brevetum, fr. L. brevis short. See Brief.] 1. A warrant from the government, granting a privilege, title, or dignity. [French usage].

(Mil.) A commission giving an officer higher rank than that for which he receives pay; an honorary promotion of an officer.

μ In the United States army, rank by brevet is conferred, by and with the advice and consent of the Senate, for ½gallant actions or meritorious services., A brevet rank gives no right of command in the particular corps to which the officer brevetted belongs, and can be exercised only by special assignment of the President, or on court martial, and detachments composed of different corps, with pay of the brevet rank when on such duty.

<— p. 180 —>
<— p. 180 —>

Brĕvet (?), v.t. [imp. & p.p. Brevetted (?); p.pr. & vb.n. Brevetting.] (Mil.) To confer rank upon by brevet.

Brĕvet, a. (Mil.) Taking or conferring rank by brevet; as, a brevet colonel; a brevet commission.

Brĕvetcy (?), n.; pl. Brevetcies (?). (Mil.)ÿThe rank or conditionÿof a brevet officer.

Brevĭa̅ry (?), n.; pl. Breviaries (?). [F. br,viarie, L. breviarium summary, abridgment, neut. noun fr. breviarius abridged, fr. brevis short. See Brief, and cf. Brevier.] 1. An abridgment; a compend; an epitome; a brief account or summary.

A book entitled the abridgment or breviary of those roots that are to be cut up or gathered.

Holland.

A book containing the daily public or canonical prayers of the Roman Catholic or of the Greek Church for the seven canonical hours, namely, matins and lauds, the first, third, sixth, and ninth hours, vespers, and compline; Ð distinguishedÿfrom the missal.

Brevĭa̅te (?), n. [L. breviatus, p.p. of breviareÿto shorten, brevis short.] 1. A short compend; a summary; a brief statement.

I omit in this breviate to rehearse.

Hakluyt.

The same little breviates of infidelity have ... been published and dispersed with great activity.

Bp. Porteus.

A lawyer's brief. [R.]

Hudibras.

Brevĭa̅te (?), v.t. To abbreviate. [Obs.]

Brevĭa̅ture (?), n. An abbreviature; an abbreviation. [Obs.]

Johnson.

Bre′vier (?), n. [Prob. from being originally used in printing a breviary. See Breviary.] (Print.) A size of type between bourgeous and minion.

¶ This line is printed in brevier type. ?

Bre′vilo′quence (?), n. [L. breviloquentia.] A brief and pertinent mode of speaking. [R.]

Brevi′ped (?), a. [L. brevis short + pes, pedis, foot: cf. F. br,vipŠde.] (Zo"l.) Having short legs. Ð n. A breviped bird.

Brevi′pen (?), n. [L. brevis short + penna wing: cf. F. br,vipenne.] (Zo"l.) A brevipennate bird.

Brev · i′pennate (?), a. [L. brevis short + E. pennate.] (Zo"l.) ShortÐwinged; Ð applied to birds which can not fly, owing to their short wings, as the ostrich, cassowary, and emu.

Brev · i′rostral (?), Brev · i′rostrate (?), } a. [L. brevis short + E. rostral, rostrate.] (Zo"l.) ShortÐbilled; having a short beak.

Brevi′ty (?), n.; pl. Brevities (?). [L. brevitas, fr. brevis short: cf. F. briŠvit,. See Brief.] 1. Shortness of duration; briefness of time; as, the brevity of human life.

Contraction into few words; conciseness.

Brevity is the soul of wit.
Shak.

This argument is stated by St. John with his usual elegant brevity and simplicity.
Bp. Porteus.

Syn. - Shortness; conciseness; succinctness; terseness.

Brew (?), v.t. [imp. & p.p. Brewed (?); p.pr. & vb.n. Brewing.] [OE. brewen, AS. breŵwan; akin to D. brouwen, OHG. priuwan, MHG. briuwen, br?wen, G. brauen, Icel. brugga, Sw. brygga, Dan. brygge, and perh. to L. defrutum must boiled down, Gr. ? (for ??) a kind of beer. The original meaning seems to have been to prepare by heat. û93.ÿCf. Broth, Bread.] 1. To boil or seethe; to cook. [Obs.]

To prepare, as beer or other liquor, from malt and hops, or from other materials, by steeping, boiling, and fermentation. ½She brews good ale.

Shak.

To prepare by steeping and mingling; to concoct.

Go, brew me a pottle of sack finely.
Shak.

To foment or prepare, as by brewing; to contrive; to plot; to concoct; to hatch; as, to brew mischief.

Hence with thy brewed enchantments, foul deceiver!

Milton.

Brew (?), v.i. 1. To attend to the business, or go through the processes, of brewing or making beer.

I wash, wring, brew, bake, scour.

Shak.

To be in a state of preparation; to be mixing, forming, or gathering; as, a storm brews in the west.

There is some ill a-brewing towards my rest.

Shak.

Brew (?), n. The mixture formed by brewing; that which is brewed.

Bacon.

Brewage (?), n. Malt liquor; drink brewed. ½Some well-spiced brewage.

Milton.

A rich brewage, made of the best Spanish wine.

Macaulay.

Brewer (?), n. One who brews; one whose occupation is to prepare malt liquors.

Brewerly (?), n. A brewhouse; the building and apparatus where brewing is carried on.

Brewhouse · (?), n. A house or building appropriated to brewing; a brewery.

Brewing (?), n. 1. The act or process of preparing liquors which are brewed, as beer and ale.

The quantity brewed at once.

A brewing of new beer, set by old beer.

Bacon.

A mixing together.

I am not able to avouch anything for certainty, such a brewing and sophistication of them they make.

Holland.

(Naut.) A gathering or formingÿof a storm or squall, indicated by thick, dark clouds.

Brewis (?), n. [OE. brewis, brouwys, browesse, brewet, OF. brouet, ĭs being the OF. ending of the nom. sing. and acc. pl.; dim. of OHG. brod. û93. See Broth, and cf. Brose.] 1. Broth or pottage. [Obs.]

Let them of their Bonner's ½beef, and ½broth, make what brewis they please for their credulous guests.

Bp. Hall.

Bread soaked in broth, drippings of roast meat, milk, or water and butter.

Brewsterlite (?), n. [Named after Sir David Brewster.] A rare zeolitic mineral occurring in white monolitic crystals with pearly luster. It is a hydrous silicate of aluminia, baryta, and strontia.

Brezillin (?), n. See Brazilin.

Briar (?), n. Same as Brier.

Briarean (?), a. [L. Briareius, fr. Briareus a mythological hundredÐhanded giant, Gr. ?, fr. ? strong.] Pertaining to, or resembling, Briareus, a giant fabled to have a hundred hands; hence, hundredÐhanded or manyÐhanded.

Bribable (?), a. Capable of being bribed.

A more bribable class of electors.

S.Edwards.

Bribe (?), n. [F. bribe a lump of bread, scraps, leavings of meals (that are generally given to a beggar), LL. briba scrap of bread; cf. OF. briber, brifer, to eat gluttonously, to beg, and OHG. bilibi food.] 1. A gift begged; a present. [Obs.]

Chaucer.

A price, reward, gift, or favor bestowed or promised with a view to prevent the judgment or corrupt the conduct of a judge, witness, voter, or other person in a position of trust.

Undue rewardÿfor anything against justice is a bribe.

Hobart.

That which seduces; seduction; allurement.

Not the bribes of sordid wealth can seduce to leave these ever?blooming sweets.

Akenside.

Bribe, v.t. [imp. & p.p. Bribed (?); p.pr. & vb.n. Bribing.] 1. To rob or steal. [Obs.]

Chaucer.

To give or promise a reward or consideration to (a judge, juror, legislator, voter, or other person in a position of trust) with a view to prevent the judgment or corrupt the conduct; to induce or influence by a bribe; to give a bribe to.

Neither is he worthy who bribes a man to vote against his conscience.

F.W.Robertson.

To gain by a bribe; of induce as by a bribe.

Bribe, v.i. 1. To commit robbery or theft. [Obs.]

To give a bribe to a person; to pervert the judgment or corrupt the action of a person in a position of trust, by some gift or promise.

An attempt to bribe, though unsuccessful, has been holden to be criminal, and the offender may be indicted.

Bouvier.

The bard may supplicate, but cannot bribe.

Goldsmith.

Bribeless, a. Incapable of being bribed; free from bribes.

From thence to heaven's bribeless hall.

Sir W.Raleigh.

Bribeer (?), n. 1. A thief. [Obs.]

Lydgate.

One who bribes, or pays for corrupt practices.

That which bribes; a bribe.

His service ... were a sufficient briber for his life.

Shak.

BribeerÏy (?), n.; pl. Briberies (?). [OE. brybery rascality, OF. briberie. See Bribe, n.] 1. Robbery; extortion. [Obs.]

The act or practice of giving or taking bribes; the act of influencing the official or political action of another by corrupt inducements.

Bribery oath, an oath taken by a person that he has not been bribed as to voting. [Eng.]

BricÐa brac · (?), n. [F.] Miscellaneous curiosities and works of decorative art, considered collectively.

A piece of bricÐaÐbrac, any curious or antique article of virtu, as a piece of antiquated furniture or metal work, or an odd knickknack.

Brick (?), n. [OE. brik, F. brique; of Ger. origin; cf. AS. brice a breaking, fragment, Prov. E. brique piece, brique de pain, equiv. to AS. hl¾fes brice, fr. the root of E. break. See Break.] 1. A block or clay tempered with water, sand, etc., molded into a regular form, usually rectangular, and sunÐdried, or burnt in a kiln, or in a heap or stack called a clamp.

The Assyrians appear to have made much less use of bricks baked in the furnace than the Babylonians.

Layard.

Bricks, collectively, as designating that kind of material; as, a load of brick; a thousand of brick.

Some of Palladio's finest examples are of brick.

Weale.

Any oblong rectangular mass; as, a brick of maple sugar; a penny brick (of bread).

A good fellow; a merry person; as, you 're a brick. [Slang] ½He 's a dear little brick.

Thackeray.

To have a brick in one's hat, to be drunk. [Slang]

μ Brick is used adjectively or in combination; as, brick wall; brick clay; brick color; brick red.

Brick clay, clay suitable for, or used in making, bricks. Ð Brick dust, dust of pounded or broken bricks. Ð Brick earth, clay or earth suitable for, or used in making, bricks. Ð Brick loaf, a loaf of bread somewhat resembling a brick in shape. Ð Brick noggingÿ(Arch.), rough brickwork used to fill in the spaces between the uprights of a wooden partition; brick filling. Ð Brick tea, tea leaves and young shoots, or refuse tea, steamed or mixed with fat, etc., and pressed into the form of bricks. It is used in Northern and Central Asia. S.W.Williams. Ð Brick trimmer (Arch.), a brick arch under a hearth, usually within the thickness of a wooden floor, to guard against accidents by fire. Ð Brick trowel. See Trowel. Ð Brick works, a place where bricks are made. Ð Bath brick. See under Bath, a city. Ð Pressed brick, bricks which, before burning, have been subjected to pressure, to free them from the imperfections of shape and texture which are common in molded bricks.

Brick, v.t. [imp. & p.p. Bricked (?); p.pr. & vb.n. Bricking.] 1. To lay or pave with bricks; to surround, line, or construct with bricks.

To imitate or counterfeit a brick wall on, as by smearing plaster with red ocher, making the joints with an edge tool, and pointing them.

To brick up, to fill up, inclose, or line, with brick.

Brickbat · (?), n. A piece or fragment of a brick. See Bat, 4.

Bacon.

Brickkiln · (?), n. A kiln, or furnace, in which bricks are baked or burnt; or a pile of green bricks, laid loose, with arches underneath to receive the wood or fuel for burning them.

Bricklay · er (?), n. [Brick + lay.] One whose pccupation is to build with bricks.

Bricklayer's itch. See under Itch.

Bricklay · ing, n. The art of building with bricks, or of uniting them by cement or mortar into various forms; the act or occupation of laying bricks.

Brickle (?), a. [OE. brekil, brokel, bruchel, fr. AS. brecan, E. break. Cf. Brittle.] Brittle; easily broken. [Obs. or Prov.]

Spenser.

As stubborn steel excels the brickle glass.

Turbervile.

Brickleïness, n. Brittleness. [Obs.]

Brickmak · er (?), n. One whose occupation is to make bricks. Ð Brickmakïing, n.

Brickwork · (?), n. 1. Anything made of bricks.

Niches in brickwork form the most difficult part of the bricklayer's art.

Tomlinson.

The act of building with or laying bricks.

Bricky (?), a. Full of bricks; formed of bricks; resembling bricks or brick dust. [R.]
Spenser.

Brickyard· (?), n. A place where bricks are made, especially an inclosed place.

ØBri̇cole (?), n. [F.] (Mil.) A kind of traces with hooks and rings, with which men drag and maneuver guns where horses can not be used.

Brid (?), n. A bird. [Obs.]
Chaucer.

Bridal (?), a. [From Bride. Cf. Bridal, n.] Of or pertaining to a bride, or to wedding; nuptial; as, bridal ornaments; a bridal outfit; a bridal chamber.

Bridal, n. [OE. bridale, brudale, AS. br?dealo brideale, bridal feast. See Bride, and Ale, 2.] A nuptia; festival or ceremony; a marriage.

Sweet day, so cool, so calm, so bright,
The bridal of the earth and sky.
Herbert.

Bridalı̇ty (?), n. Celebration of the nuptial feast. [Obs.] ½In honor of this bridalty.„
B.Jonson.

Bride (?), n. [OE. bride, brid, brude, brud, burd, AS. br?d; akin to OFries. breid, OSax. br?d, D. bruid, OHG. pr?t, br?t, G. braut, Icel. br??r, Sw. & Dan. brud, Goth. br33s; cf. Armor. pried spouse, W. priawd a married person.] 1. A woman newly married, or about to be married.

Has by his own experience tried
How much the wife is dearer than the bride.
Lyttleton.

I will show thee the bride, the Lamb's wife.
Rev.xxi.9.

Fig.: An object ardently loved.

Bride of the sea, the city of Venice.

Bride, v.t. To make a bride of. [Obs.]

Brideḯale· (?), n. [See Bridal.] A rustic wedding feast; a bridal. See Ale.

The man that 's bid to brideÐale, if he ha' cake,
And drink enough, he need not fear his stake.
B.Jonson.

Bridebed· (?), n. The marriage bed. [Poetic]

Bridecake· (?), n. Rich or highly ornamented cake, to be distributed to the guests at a wedding, or sent to friends after the wedding.

Bridecham·ber (?), n. The nuptial appartment.
Matt.ix.15.

Bridegroom · (?), n. [OE. bridegome, brudgume, AS. br?dguma (akin to OS. br?digumo, D. bruidegom, bruigom, OHG. pr?tigomo, MHG. briutegome, G. br„utigam); AS. br?dÿbride + guma man, akin to Goth. guma, Icel. gumi, OHG. gomo, L. homo; the insertion of r being caused by confusion with groom. See Bride, and cf. Groom, Homage.] A man newly married, or just about to be married.

Brideknot · (?), n. A knot of ribbons worn by a guest at a wedding; a wedding favor. [Obs.]

Bridemaid · (?), n., Brideman (?), n. See Bridesmaid, Bridesman.

Bridesmaid · (?), n. A female friend who attends on a bride at her wedding.

Bridesman (?), n.; pl. Bridesmen (?). A male friend who attends upon a bridegroom and bride at their marriage; the ½best man.

Sir W.Scott.

Bridestake · (?), n. A stake or post set in the ground, for guests at a wedding to dance round.

Divide the broad bridecake
Round about the bridestake.
B.Jonson.

Bridewell (?), n. A house of correction for the confinement of disorderly persons; Ð so called from a hospital built in 1553 near St. Bride's (or Bridget's) well, in London, which was subsequently a penal workhouse.

Bridge (?), n. [OE. brig, brigge, brug, brugge, AS. brycg, bricg; akin to Fries. bregge, D. brug, OHG. bruccu, G. brcke, Icel. bryggja pier, bridge, Sw. brygga, Dan. brygge, and prob. Icel. br?ÿbridge, Sw. & Dan. broÿbridge, pavement, and possibly to E. brow.] 1. A structure, usually of wood, stone, brick, or iron, erected over a river or other water course, or over a chasm, railroad, etc., to make a passageway from one bank to the other.

> Anything supported at the ends, which serves to keep some other thing from resting upon the object spanned, as in engraving, watchmaking, etc., or which forms a platform or staging over which something passes or is conveyed.

> (Mus.) The small arch or bar at right angles to the strings of a violin, guitar, etc., serving of raise them and transmit their vibrations to the body of the instrument.

> (Elec.) A device to measure the resistance of a wire or other conductor forming part of an electric circuit.

> A low wall or vertical partition in the fire chamber of a furnace, for deflecting flame, etc.; Ð usually called a bridge wall.

Aqueduct bridge. See Aqueduct. Ð Asses' bridge, Bascule bridge, Bateau bridge. See under Ass, Bascule, Bateau. Ð Bridge of a steamerÿ(Naut.), a narrow platform across the deck, above the rail, for the convenience of the officer in charge of the ship; in paddlewheel vessels it connects the paddle boxes. Ð Bridge of the nose, the upper, bony part of the nose. Ð Cantalever bridge. See under Cantalever. Ð Draw bridge. See Drawbridge. Ð Flying bridge, a temporary bridge suspended or floating, as for the passage of armies; also, a floating structure connected by a cable with an anchor or pier up stream, and made to pass from bank to bank by the action of the current or other means. Ð Girder bridgeÿor Truss bridge, a bridge formed by girders, or by trusses resting upon abutments or piers. Ð Lattice bridge, a bridge formed by lattice girders. Ð Pontoon bridge, Ponton bridge. See under Pontoon. Ð Skew bridge, a bridge built obliquely from bank to bank, as sometimes required in railway engineering. Ð Suspension bridge. See under Suspension. Ð Trestle bridge, a bridge formed of a series of short, simple girders resting on trestles. Ð Tubular bridge, a bridge in the form of a hollow trunk or rectangular tube, with cellular walls made of iron plates riveted together, as the Britannia bridge over the Menai Strait, and the Victoria bridge at Montreal. Ð Wheatstone's bridge (Elec.), a device for the measurement of resistances, so called because the balance between the resistances to be measured is indicated by the absence of a current in a certain wire forming a bridge or connection between two points of the apparatus; Ð invented by Sir Charles Wheatstone.

<— p. 181 —>

Bridge (?), v.t. [imp. & p.p. Bridged (?); p.pr. & vb.n. Bridging.] 1. To build a bridge or bridges on or over; as, to bridge a river. Their simple engineering bridged with felled trees the streams which could not be forded. Palfrey. 2. To open or make a passage, as by a bridge. Xerxes ... over Hellespont Bridging his way, Europe with Asia joined. Milton. 3. To find a way of getting over, as a difficulty; Ð generally with over. Bridgeboard · (?), n. 1. (Arch.) A notched board to which the treads and risers of the steps of wooden stairs are fastened. 2. A board or plank used as a bridge. Bridgehead · (?), n. A fortification commanding the extremity of a bridge nearest the enemy, to insure the preservation and usefulness of the bridge, and prevent the enemy from crossing; a tˆteÐdeÐpont. Bridgeless, a. Having no bridge; not bridged. Bridgepot · (?), n. (Mining) The adjustable socket, or step, of a millstone spindle. Knight. Bridgetree · (?), n. [Bridge + tree a beam.] (Mining) The beam which supports the spindle socket of the runner in a grinding mill. Knight. BridgeÐward · (?), n. 1. Aÿbridge keeper; a warden or a guard for a bridge. [Obs.] Sir W.Scott. 2. The principal ward of a key. Knight. Bridgeing (?), n. (Arch.) The system of bracing used between floor or other timbers to distribute the weight. Bridging joist. Same as Binding joist. Bridgey (?), a. Full of bridges. [R.] Sherwood. Bridle (?), n. [OE. bridel, AS. bridel; akin to OHG. britil, brittil, D. breidel, and possibly to E. braid. Cf. Bridoon.] 1. The head gear with which a horse is governed and restrained, consisting of a headstall, a bit, and reins, with other appendages. 2. A restraint; a curb; a check. I.Watts. 3. (Gun.) The piece in the interior of a gun lock, which holds in place the timbler, sear, etc. 4. (Naut.) (a) A span of rope, line, or chain made fast as both ends, so that another rope, line, or chain may be attached to its middle. (b) A mooring hawser. Bowline bridle.

See under Bowline. Đ Branches of a bridle. See under Branch. Đ Bridle cable (Naut.), a cable which is bent to a bridle. See 4, above. Đ Bridle hand, the hand which holds the bridle in riding; the left hand. Đ Bridle path, Bridle way, a path or way for saddle horses and pack horses, as distinguished from a road for vehicles. Đ Bridle port (Naut.), a porthole or opening in the bow through which hawsers, mooring or bridle cables, etc., are passed. Đ Bridle rein, a rein attached to the bit. Đ Bridle road. (a) Same as Bridle path. Lowell. (b) A road in a pleasure park reserved for horseback exercise. Đ Bridle track, a bridle path. Đ Scolding bridle. See Branks, 2. Syn. - A check; restrain. Bridle, v.t. [imp. & p.p. Bridled (?); p.pr. & vb.n. Bridling (?).] 1. To put a bridle upon; to equip with a bridle; as, to bridle a horse. He bridled her mouth with a silkweed twist. Drake. 2. To restrain, guide, or govern, with, or as with, a bridle; to check, curb, or control; as, to bridle the passions; to bridle a muse. Addison. Savoy and Nice, the keys of Italy, and the citadel in her hands to bridle Switzerland, are in that consolidation. Burke. Syn. - To check; restrain; curb; govern; control; repress; master; subdue. Bridle, v.i. To hold up the head, and draw in the chin, as an expression of pride, scorn, or resentment; to assume a lofty manner; Đ usually with up. ½His bridling neck., Wordsworth. By her bridling up I perceived she expected to be treated hereafter not as Jenny Distaff, but Mrs. Tranquillus. Tatler. Bridle i · ron (?). (Arch.) A strong flat bar of iron, so bent as to support, as in a stirrup, one end of a floor timber, etc., where no sufficient bearing can be had; Đ called also stirrupÿand hanger. Bridler (?), n. One who bridles; one who restrains and governs, as with a bridle. Milton. BriÏdoon (?), n. [F. bridon, from bride; of German origin. See Bridle, n.] (Mil.) The snaffle and rein of a military bridle, which acts independently of the bit, at the pleasure of the rider. It is used in connection with a curb bit, which has its own rein. Campbell. Brief (?), a. [OE. bref, F. brief, bref, fr. L. brevis; akin to Gr. ? short, and perh. to Skr. barhÿto tear. Cf. Breve.] 1. Short in duration. How brief the life of man. Shak. 2. Concise; terse; succinct. The brief style is that which expresseth much in little. B.Jonson. 3. Rife; common; prevalent. [Prov. Eng.] In brief. See under Brief, n. Syn. - Short; concise; succinct; summary; compenduous; condensed; terse; curt; transistory; shortĐlived. Brief, adv. 1. Briefly. [Obs. or Poetic] Adam, faltering long, thus answered brief. Milton. 2. Soon; quickly. [Obs.] Shak. Brief (?), n. [See Brief, a., and cf. Breve.] 1. A short concise writing or letter; a statement in few words. Bear this sealed brief, With winged hastle, to the lord marshal. Shak. And she told me In a sweet, verbal brief. Shak. 2. An epitome. Each woman is a briefÿof womankind. Overbury. 3. (Law) An abridgment or concise statement of a client's case, made out for the instruction of counsel in a trial at law. This word is applied also to a statement of the heads or points of a law argument. It was not without some reference to it that I perused many a brief. Sir J.Stephen. µ In England, the brief is prepared by the attorney; in the United States, counsel generally make up their own briefs. 4. (Law) A writ; a breve.

See Breve, n., 2. 5. (Scots Law) A writ issuing from the chancery, directed to any judge ordinary, commanding and authorizing that judge to call a jury to inquire into the case, and upon their verdict to pronounce sentence. 6. A letter patent, from proper authority, authorizing a collection or charitable contribution of money in churches, for any public or private purpose. [Eng.] Apostolical brief, a letter of the pope written on fine parchment in modern characters, subscribed by the secretary of briefs, dated ½a die Nativitatis, i.e., ½from the day of the Nativity, and sealed with the ring of the fisherman. It differs from a bull, in its parchment, written character, date, and seal. See Bull. Ð Brief of title, an abstract or abridgment of all the deeds and other papers constituting the chain of title to any real estate. Ð In brief, in a few words; in short; briefly. ½Open the matter in brief. Shak. Brief, v.t. To make an abstract or abridgment of; to shorten; as, to brief pleadings. Briefless (?), a. Having no brief; without clients; as, a briefless barrister. Briefly (?), adv. Concisely; in few words. Briefman (?), n. 1. One who makes a brief. 2. A copier of a manuscript. Briefness (?), n. The quality of being brief; brevity; conciseness in discourse or writing. Brier, Briar (?), n. [OE. brere, brer, AS. brÇr, br'r; cf. Ir. briar prickle, thorn, brier, pin, Gael. preas bush, brier, W. prys, prysg.] 1. A plant with a slender woody stem bearing stout prickles; especially, species of Rosa, Rubus, and Smilax. 2. Fig.: Anything sharp or unpleasant to the feelings. The thorns and briers of reproof. Cowper. Brier root, the root of the southern Smilax laurifolia and S. Walleri; Ð used for tobacco pipes. Ð Cat brier, Green brier, several species of Smilax (S. rotundifolia, etc.) Ð Sweet brier (Rosa rubiginosa). See Sweetbrier. Ð Yellow brier, the Rosa Eglantina. Briered (?), a. Set with briers. Chatterton. Brierïy (?), a. Full of briers; thorny. Brierïy, n. A place where briers grow. Huloet. Brig (?), n. A bridge. [Scot.] Burns. Brig, n. [Shortened from Brigantine.] (Naut.) A twoÐmasted, squareÐrigged vessel. Hermaphrodite brig, a twoÐmasted vessel squareÐrigged forward and schoonerÐrigged aft. See Illustration in Appendix. Brïgade (?), n. [F. brigade, fr. It. brigata troop, crew, brigade, originally, a contending troop, fr. briga trouble, quarrel. See Brigand.] 1. (Mil.) A body of troops, whether cavalry, artillery, infantry, or mixed, consisting of two or more regiments, under the command of a brigadier general. µ Two or more brigades constitute a division, commanded by a major general; two or more divisions constitute an army corps, or corps d'arm,e. [U.S.] 2. Any body of persons organized for actingÿor marching together under authority; as, a fire brigade. Brigade inspector, an officer whose duty is to inspect troops in companies before they are mustered into service. Ð Brigade major, an officer who may be attached to a brigade to assist the brigadier in his duties. Brïgade, v.t. [imp. & p.p. Brigaded; p.pr. & vb.n. Brigading.] (Mil.) To form into a brigade, or into brigades. Brig · aïdier generïal (?). [F. brigadier, fr. brigade.] (Mil.) An officer in rank next above a colonel, and below a major general. He commands a brigade, and is sometimes called, by a shortening of his title, simple a brigadier. Brigand (?), n. [F. brigand, OF. brigant lightDarmed soldier, fr. LL. brigans lightDarmed soldier (cf. It. brigante.) fr. brigare to strive, contend, fr. briga quarrel; prob. of German origin, and akin to E. break; cf. Goth. brikanÿto break, brakja strife. Cf. Brigue.] 1. A lightDarmed, irregular foot soldier. [Obs.] 2. A lawless fellow who lives by plunder; one of a band of robbers; especially, one of a gang living in mountain retreats; a highwayman; a freebooter. Giving them not a little the air of brigands or banditti. Jeffery. BrigandÏage (?), n. [F. brigandage.] Life and practice of brigands; highway robbery; plunder. BrigandÏdine (?), n. [F. brigandine (cf. It. brigantina), fr. OF. brigant. See Brigand.] A coast of armor for the body, consistingÿof scales or plates, sometimes overlappingÿeach other, generally of metal, and sewed to linen or other material. It was worn in the Middle Ages. [Written also brigantine.] Jer.xlvi.4. Then put on all thy gorgeous arms, thy helmet, And brigandine of brass. Milton. BrigandÏish (?), a. Like a brigand or freebooter; robberlike. BrigandÏism (?), n. Brigandage. BrigandÏtine (?), n. [F. brigantin, fr. It. brigantino, originally, a practical vessel. See Brigand, and cf. Brig] 1. A practical vessel. [Obs.] 2. A twoDmasted, squareDrigged vessel, differing from a brig in that she does not carry a square mainsail. 3. See Brigandine. Brigge (?), n. A bridge. [Obs.] Chaucer. Bright (?), v.i. See Brite, v.i. Bright (?), a. [OE. briht, AS. beorht, briht; akin to OS. berht, OHG. beraht, Icel. bjartr, Goth. baȷrhts. û94.] 1. Radiating or reflecting light; shedding or having much light; shining; luminous; not dark. The sun was bright o'erhead. Longfellow. The earth was dark, but the heavens were bright. Drake. The public places were as bright as at noonday. Macaulay. 2. Transmitting light; clear; transparent. From the brightest wines He 'd turn abhorrent. Thomson. 3. Having qualities that render conspicuous or attractive, or that affect the mind as light does the eye; resplendent with charms; as, bright beauty. Bright as an angel newDdropped from the sky. Parnell. 4. Having a clear, quick intellect; intelligent. 5. Sparkling with wit; lively; vivacious; shedding cheerfulness and joy around; cheerful; cheery. Be bright and jovial among your guests. Shak. 6. Illustrious; glorious. In the brightest annals of a female reign. Cotton. 7. Manifest to the mind, as light is to the eyes; clear; evident; plain. That he may with more ease, with brighter evidence, and with surer success, draw the bearner on. I.Watts. 8. Of brilliant color; of lively hue or appearance. Here the bright crocus and blue violet grew. Pope. µ Bright is used in composition in the sense of brilliant, clear, sunny, etc.; as, brightDeyed, brightDhaired, brightDhued. Syn. - Shining; splending; luminous; lustrous; brilliant; resplendent; effulgent; refulgent; radiant; sparkling; glittering; lucid; beamy; clear; transparent; illustrious; witty; clear; vivacious; sunny. Bright, n. Splendor; brightness. [Poetic] Dark with excessive bright thy skirts appear. Milton. Bright, adv. Brightly. Chaucer. I say it is the moon that shines so bright. Shak. Brighten, v.t. [imp. & p.p. Brightened (?); p.pr. & vb.n. Brightening.] From Bright, a.] 1. To make bright or brighter; to make to shine; to increase the luster of;

to give a brighter hue to. 2. To make illustrious, or more distinguished; to add luster or splendor to. The present queen would brighten her character, if she would exert her authority to instill virtues into her people. Swift. 3. To improve or relieve by dispelling gloom or removing that which obscures and darkens; to shed light upon; to make cheerful; as, to brighten one's prospects. An ecstasy, which mothers only feel, Plays round my heart and brightens all my sorrow. Philips. 4. To make acute or witty; to enliven. Johnson. Brighten, v.i. [AS. beorhtan.] To grow bright, or more bright; to become less dark or gloomy; to clear up; to become bright or cheerful. And night shall brighten into day. N.Cotton. And, all his prospects brightening to the last, His heaven commences ere world be past. Goldsmith. BrightÐhar · nessed (?), a. Having glittering armor. [Poetic] Milton. Brightly, adv. 1. Brilliantly; splendidly; with luster; as, brightly shining armor. 2. With lively intelligence; intelligently. Looking brightly into the mother's face. Hawthorne. Brightness, n. [AS. beorhines. See Bright.] 1. The quality or state of being bright; splendor; luster; brilliancy; clearness. A sudden brightness in his face appear. Crabbe. 2. Acutenessÿ(of the faculties); sharpness 9wit. The brightness of his parts ... distinguished him. Prior. Syn. - Splendor; luster; radiance; resplendence; brilliancy; effulgence; glory; clearness. Bright's disIease (?). [From Dr. Bright of London, who first described it.] (Med.) An affection of the kidneys, usually inflammatory in character, and distinguished by the occurrence of albumin and renal casts in the urine. Several varieties of Bright's disease are now recognized, differing in the part of the kidney involved, and in the intensity and course of the morbid process. Brightsome (?), a. Bright; clear; luminous; brilliant. [R.] Marlowe. BriÏgose (?), a. [LL. brigosus, It. brigoso. See Brigue, n.] Contentious; quarrelsome. [Obs.] Puller. Brigue (?), n. [F. brigue, fr. LL. briga quarrel. See Brigand.] A cabal, intrigue, faction, contention, strife, or quarrel. [Obs.] Chesterfield. Brigue, v.i. [F. briguer. See Brigue, n.] To contend for; to canvass; to solicit. [Obs.] Bp. Hurd. Brike (?), n. [AS. brice.] A breach; ruin; downfall; peril. [Obs.] Chaucer. Brill (?), n. [Cf. Corn. brilli mackerel, fr. brith streaked, speckled.] (Zo"l.) A fish allied to the turbot (Rhombus levis), much esteemed in England for food; Ð called also bret, pearl, prill. See Bret. ØBrilÏlante (?), adv. [It. See Brilliant, a.] (Mus.) In a gay, showy, and sparkling style. Brillance (?), n. Brilliancy. Tennyson. BrillanIcy (?), n. [See Brilliant.] The quality of being brilliant; splendor; glitter; great brighness, whether in a literal or figurative sense. With many readers brilliancy of style passes for affluence of thought. Longfellow.

<— p. 182 —>

Brilliant (?), a. [F. brillant, p.pr. of brilleryto shine or sparkle (cf. Pr. & Sp. brillar, It. brillare), fr. L. beryllus a precious stone of seaÐgreen color, Prov. It. brill. See Beryl.] 1. Sparklingÿwith luster; glittering; very bright; as, a brilliant star.

Distinguished by qualities which excite admiration; splended; shining; as, brilliant talents.

Washington was more solicitous to avoid fatal mistakes than to perform brilliant exploits.
Fisher Ames.
Syn. - See Shining.
Brilliant, n. [F. brillant. See Brilliant, a.] 1. A diamond or other gem of the finest cut, formed into faces and facets, so as to reflect and refract the light, by which it is rendered nore brilliant. It has at the middle, or top, a principal face, called the table, which is surrounded by a number of sloping facets forming a bizet; below, it has a small face or collet, parallel to the table, connected with the gridle by a pavilion of elongated facets. It is thus distinguished from the rose diamond, which is entirely covered with facets on the surface, and is flat below.
This snuffbox Ð on the hinge see brilliants shine.
Pope.

(Print.) The small size of type used in England printing.

µ This line is printed in the type called Brilliant. ??

A kind of kotton goods, figured on the weaving.

Brilliantĭly, adv. In a brilliant manner.
Brilliantĭness, n. Brilliancy; splendor; glitter.
Brills (?), n. pl. [CF. G. brille spectacles, D. bril, fr. L. berillus. See Brilliant.] The hair on the eyelids of a horse.
Bailey.
Brim (?), n. [OE. brim, brimme, AS. brymme edge, border; akin to Icel. barmr, Sw. br„m, Dan. brʻmme, G. brame, br„me. Possibly the same word as AS. brim surge, sea, and properly meaning, the line of surf at the border of the sea, and akin to L. fremere to roar, murmur. Cf. Breeze a fly.] 1. The rim, border, or upper sdge of a cup, dish, or any hollow vessel used for holding anything.
Saw I that insect on this goblet's brim
I would remove it with an anxious pity.
Coleridge.

The edgeÿor margin, as of a fountain, or of the water contained in it; the brink; border.

The feet of the priest that bare the ark were dipped in the brim of the water.
Josh.iii.15.

The rim of a hat.

Wordsworth.

Brim, v.i. [imp. & p.p. Brimmed (?); p.pr. & vb.n. Brimming.] To be full to the brim. "The brimming stream."

Milton.

To brim over (literally or figuratively), to be so full that some of the contents flows over the brim; as, cup brimming over with wine; a man brimming over with fun.

Brim, v.t. To fill to the brim, upper edge, or top.

Arrange the board and brim the glass.

Tennyson.

Brim, a. Fierce; sharp; cold. See Breme. [Obs.]

Brimful (?), a. Full to the brim; completely full; ready to overflow. "Her brimful eyes."

Dryden.

Brimless, a. Having no brim; as, brimless caps.

Brimmed (?), a. 1. Having a brim; — usually in composition. "Broad-brimmed hat."

Spectator.

Full to, or level with, the brim.

Milton.

Brimmer (?), n. A brimful bowl; a bumper.

Brimming, a. Full to the brim; overflowing.

Brimstone (?), n. [OE. brimston, bremston, bernston, brenston; cf. Icel. brennistein. See Burn, v.t., and Stone.] Sulphur; See Sulphur.

Brimstone, a. Made of, or pertaining to, brimstone; as, brimstone matches.

From his brimstone bed at break of day
A-walking the devil has gone.

Coleridge.

Brimsto·ny (?), a. Containing or resembling brimstone; sulphurous.

B.Jonson.

Brin (?), n. [F.] One of the radiating sticks of a fan. The outermost are larger and longer, and are called panaches.

Knight.

Brinded (?), a. [Cf. Icel. br"ndÓttr brindled, fr. brandr brand; and OE. bernen, brinnen, to burn. See Brand, Burn.] Of a gray or tawny color with streaks of darker hue; streaked; brindled. "Three brinded cows," Dryden. "The brinded cat." Shak.

Brindle (?), n. [See Brindled.] 1. The state of being brindled.

A brindled color; also, that which is brindled.

Brindle, a. Brindled.

Brindled (?), a. [A dim. form of brinded.] Having dark streaks or spots on a gray or tawny ground; brinded. ½With a brindled lion played.,
Churchill.

Brine (?), n. [AS. bryne a burning, salt liquor, brine, fr. brinnan, brynnan, to burn. See Burn.] 1. Water saturated or strongly inpregnated with salt; pickle; hence, any strong saline solution; also, the saline residue or strong mother liquor resultingÿfrom the evaporation of natural or artificial waters.

The ocean; the water of an ocean, sea, or salt lake.

Not long beneath the whelming brine ... he lay.
Cowper.

Tears; Đ so called from their saltness.

What a deal of brine
Hath washed thy sallow cheecks for
Rosaline!
Shak.

Brine flyÿ(Zo"l.), a fly of the genus Ephydra, the larv' of which live in artificial brines and in salt lakes. Đ Brine gauge, an instrument for measuring the saltnessÿof a liquid. Đ Brine pan, a pit or pan of salt water, where salt is formed by cristallization. Đ Brine pit, a salt spring or well, from which water is taken to be boiled or evaporated for making salt. Đ Brine pump (Marine Engin.), a pump for changing the water in the boilers, so as to clear them of the brine which collects at the bottom. Đ Brine shrimp, Brine wormÿ(Zo"l.), a phyllopod crustacean of the genus Artemia, inhabiting the strong brines of salt works and natural salt lakes. See Artemia. Đ Brine spring, a spring of salt water. Đ Leach brine (Saltmaking), brineÿwhich drops from granulated salt in drying, and is preserved to be boiled again.

Brine (?), v.t. 1. To steep or saturate in brine.

To sprinkle with salt or brine; as, to brine hay.

Bring (?), v.t. [imp. & p.p. Brought (?); p.pr. & vb.n. Bringing.] [OE. bringen, AS. bringan; akin to OS. brengian, D. brengen, Fries. brenga, OHG. bringan, G. bringen, Goth. briggan.] 1. To convey to the place where the speaker is or is to be; to bear from a more distant to a nearer place; to fetch.

And as she was going to fetch it, he called to her, and said, Bring me, I pray thee, a morsel of bread.
1 Kings xvii.11.

To France shall we convey you safe,
And bring you back.
Shak.

To cause the accession or obtaining of; to procure; to make to come; to produce; to draw to.

There is nothing will bring you more honor ... than to do what right in justice you may.
Bacon.

<small>To convey; to move; to carry or conduct.</small>

In distillation, the water ... brings over with it some part of the oil of vitriol.
Sir I.Newton.

<small>To persuade; to induce; to draw; to lead; to guide.</small>

It seems so preposterous a thing ... that they do not easily bring themselves to it.
Locke.
The nature of the things ... would not suffer him to think otherwise, how, or whensoever, he is brought to reflect on them.
Locke.

<small>To produce in exchange; to sell for; to fetch; as, what does coal bring per ton?</small>

To bring about, to bring to pass; to effect; to accomplish. Ð To bring back. (a) To recall. (b) To restore, as something borrowed, to its owner. Ð To bring by the lee (Naut.), to incline so rapidly to leeward of the course, when a ship sails large, as to bring the lee side suddenly to the windward, any by laying the sails aback, expose her to danger of upsetting. Ð To bringÿdown. (a) To cause to come down. (b) To humble or abase; as, to bring down high looks. Ð To bring down the house, to cause tremendous applause. [Colloq.] Ð To bring forth. (a) To produce, as young fruit. (b) To bring to light; to make manifest. Ð To bring forward (a) To exhibit; to introduce; to produce to view. (b) To hasten; to promote; to forward. (c) To propose; to adduce; as, to bring forward arguments. Ð Toÿbring home. (a) To bring to one's house. (b) To prove conclusively; as, to bring home a charge of treason. (c) To cause one to feel or appreciate by personal experience. (d) (Naut.) To lift of its place, as an anchor. Ð To bring in. (a) To fetch from without; to import. (b) To introduce, as a bill in a deliberative assembly. (c) To return or repot to, or lay before, a court or other body; to render; as, to bring in a verdict or a report. (d) To take to an appointed place of deposit or collection; as, to bring in provisions or money for a specified object. (e) To produce, as income. (f) To induce to join. Ð To bring off, to bear or convey away; to clear from condemnation; to cause to escape. Ð To bring on. (a) To cause to begin. (b) To originate or cause to exist; as, to bring on a disease. Ð Toÿbring one on one's way, to accompany, guide, or attend one. Ð Toÿbring out, to expose; to detect; to bring to light from concealment. Ð To bring over. (a) To fetch or bear across. (b) To convert by persuasion or other means; to cause to change sides or an opinion. Ð Toÿbring to. (a) To resuscitate; to bring back to consciousness, or life, as a fainting person. (b) (Naut.) To check the course of, as of a ship, by dropping the anchor, or by counterbracing the sails so as to keep her nearly stationary (she is then said to lie to). (c) To cause (a vessel) to lie to, as by firing across her course. (d) To apply a rope to the capstan. — To bring to light, to disclose; to discover; to make clear; to reveal. — To bring a sail to (Naut.), to bend it to the yard. — To bring to pass, to accomplish to effect. ½Trust also in Him; and He shall bring it to pass., Ps. xxxvii.5. — To bring under, to subdue; to restrain; to reduce to obedience. — To bring up. (a) To carry upward; to nurse; to rear; to educate. (b) To cause to stop suddenly. (c) [v.i. by dropping the reflexive pronoun] To stop suddenly; to come to a standstill. [Colloq.] — To bring up (any one) with a round turn, to cause (any one) to stop abruptly. [Colloq.] — To be brought to bed. See under Bed.

Syn. - To fetch; bear; carry; convey; transport; import; procure; produce; cause; adduce; induce.

Bringer (?), n. One who brings.

Yet the first bringer of unwelcome news
Hath but a losing office.
Shak.

Bringer in, one who, or that which, introduces.

Brininess (?), n. The state or quality of being briny; saltness; brinishness.

Brinish (?), a. Like brine; somewhat salt; saltish. ½Brinish tears.,
Shak.

Brinishiness, n. State or quality of being brinish.

ØBrinjaIree · (?), n. [Native name.] (Zo"l.) A rough-haired East Indian variety of the greyhound.

Brink (?), n. [Dan. brink edge, verge; akin to Sw. brink declivity, hill, Icel. brekka; cf. LG. brink a grassy hill, W. bryn hill, bryncyn hillock.] The edge, margin, or border of a steep place, as of a precipice; a bank or edge, as of a river or pit; a verge; a border; as, the brink of a chasm. Also Fig. ½The brink of vice., Bp. Porteus. ½The brink of ruin., Burke.

The plashy brink of weedy lake.
Bryant.

Briny (?), a. [From Brine.] Of or pertaining to brine, or to the sea; partaking of the nature of brine; salt; as, a briny taste; the briny flood.

Briolny (?), n. See Bryony.
Tennyson.

Brisk (?), a. [Cf. W. brysg, fr. brys haste, Gael. briosg quick, lively, Ir. broisg a start, leap, jerk.] 1. Full of liveliness, and activity; characterized by quickness of motion or action; lively; spirited; quick.

Cheerily, boys; be brick awhile.
Shak.

Brick toil alternating with ready ease.
Wordworth.

Full of spirit of life; effervesc?ng, as liquors; sparkling; as, brick cider.

Syn. - Active; lively; agile; alert; nimble; quick; sprightly; vivacious; gay; spirited; animated.

Brisk (?), v.t. & i. [imp. & p.p. Bricked (?); p.pr. & vb.n. Bricking.] To make or become lively; to enliven; to animate; to take, or cause to take, an erect or bold attitude; Ð usually with up.

Brisket (?), n. [OE. bruskette, OF. bruschet, F. br,chet, brichet; prob. of Celtic origin; cf. W. bryscedÿthe breast of a slain animal, brisket, Corn. vrys breast, Armor. brusk, bruched, the front of the chest, Gael. brisgein the cartilaginous part of a bone.] That part of the breast of an animal which extends from the fore legs back beneath the ribs; also applied to the fore part of a horse, from the shoulders to the bottom of the chest. [See Illust. of Beef.]

Briskly (?), adv. In a brisk manner; nimbly.

Briskness, n. Liveliness; vigor in action; quickness; gayety; vivacity; effervescence.

Bristle (?), n. [OE. bristel, brustel, AS. bristl, byrst; akin to D. borstel, OHG. burst, G. borste, Icel. burst, Sw. borst, and to Skr. bh?shti edge, point, and prob, L. fastigium extremity, Gr. ? stern of a ship, and E. brush, burr, perh. to brad. û96.] 1. A short, stiff, coarse hair, as on the back of swine.

(Bot.) A stiff, sharp, roundish hair.

Gray.

Bristle, v.t. [imp. & p.p. Bristled (?); p.pr. & vb.n. Bristling (?).] 1. To erect the bristles of; to cause to stand up, as the bristles of an angry hog; Ð sometimes with up.

Now for the bareÐpicked bone of majesty
Doth dogged war bristle his angry crest.
Shak.
Boy, bristle thy courage up.
Shak.

To fix a bristle to; as, to bristle a thread.

Bristle, v.i. 1. To rise or stand erect, like bristles.
His hair did bristle upon his head.
Sir W.Scott.

To appear as if covered with bristles; to have standing, thick and erect, like bristles.

The hill of L? Haye Sainte bristling with ten thousand bayonets.
Thackeray.
Ports bristling with thousands of masts.
Macaulay.

To show defiance or indignation.

To bristle up, to show anger or defiance.

Bristle‑point‧ed (?), a. (Bot.) Terminating in a very fine, sharp point, as some leaves.

Bristle‑shaped‧ (?), a. Resembling a bristle in form; as, a bristle‑shaped leaf.

Bristle‑tail‧ (?), n. (Zo"l.) An insect of the genera Lepisma, Campodea, etc., belonging to the Thysanura.

Bristliness (?), n. The quality or state of having bristles.

Bristly (?), a. THick set with bristles, or with hairs resembling bristles; rough.

The leaves of the black mulberry are somewhat bristly.

Bacon.

Bristol (?), n. A seaport city in the west of England.

Bristol board, a kind of fine pasteboard, made with a smooth but usually unglazed surface. Ð Bristol brick, a brick of siliceous matter used for polishing cultery; Ð originally manufactured at Bristol. Ð Bristol stone, rock crystal, or brilliant crystals of quartz, found in the mountain limestone near Bristol, and used in making ornaments, vases, etc. When polished, it is called Bristol diamond.

Brisure (?), n. [F.] 1. (Fort.) Any part of a rampart or parapet which deviates from the general direction.

(Her.) A mark of cadency or difference.

Brit, Britt (?), n. (Zo"l.) (a) The young of the common herring; also, a small species of herring; the sprat. (b) The minute marine animals (chiefly Entomostraca) upon which the right whales feed.

Britannia (?), n. [From L. Britannia Great Britain.] A white‑metal alloy of tin, antimony, bismuth, copper, etc. It somewhat resembles silver, and isused for table ware. Called also Britannia metal.

Britannic (?), a. [L. Britannicus, fr. Britannia Great Britain.] Of or pertaining to Great Britain; British; as, her Britannic Majesty.

Brite, Bright (?), v.t. To be or become overripe, as wheat, barley, or hops. [Prov. Eng.]

Briticism (?), n. A word, phrase, or idiom peculiar to Great Britain; any manner of using a word or words that is peculiar to Great Britain.

British (?), a. [AS. Brittisc, Bryttisc.] Of or pertaining to Great Britain or to its inhabitants; Ð sometimes restrict to the original inhabitants.

British gum, a brownish substance, very soluble in cold water, formed by heating dry starch at a temperature of about 600ø Fahr. It corresponds, in its properties, to dextrin, and is used, in solution, as a substitute for gum in stiffering goods. Ð British lion, the national emblem of Great Britain. Ð British seas, the four seas which surround Great Britain.

British, n. pl. People of Great Britain.

Britishĭer, n. An Englishman; a subjectÿor inhabitant of Great Britain, esp. one in the British military or naval service. [Now used jocosely]

Briton (?), a. [AS. bryten Britain.] British. [Obs.] Spenser.Ð n. A native of Great Britain.

Brittle (?), a. [OE. britel, brutel, AS. bryttian to dispense, fr. breċtanÿto break; akin to Icel. brytja, Sw. bryta, Dan. bryde. Cf. Brickle.] Easily broken; apt to break; fragile; not tough or tenacious<— contrast to flexible; usually hard —>.

Farewell, thou pretty, brittle piece

Of fineÐcut crystal.

Cotton.

Brittle silver ore, the mineral stephanite.

Brittleĭly, adv. In a brittle manner.

Sherwood.

Brittleĭness, n. Aptness to break; fragility.

<— p. 183 —>

Brittle star · (?). Any speciesÿof ophiuran starfishes. See Ophiuroidea.

Britzska (?), n. [Russ. britshka; cf. Pol. bryczka, dim. of bryka freight wagon.] A long carriage, with a calash top, so constructed as to give space for recliningÿat night, when used on a journey.

Brize (?), n. The breeze fly. See Breeze.

Shak.

Broach (?), n. [OE. broche, F. broche, fr. LL. brocca; prob. of Celtic origin; cf. W. proc thrust, stab, Gael. brog awl. Cf. Brooch.] 1. A spit. [Obs.]

He turned a broach that had worn a crown.

Bacon.

An awl; a bodkin; also, a wooden rod or pin, sharpened at each end, used by thatchers. [Prov. Eng.]

Forby.

(Mech.) (a) A tool of steel, generally tapering, and of a polygonal form, with from four to eight cutting edges, for smoothing or enlarging holes in metal; sometimes made smooth or without edges, as for burnishing pivot holes in watches; a reamer. The broach for gun barrels is commonly square and without taper. (b) A straight tool with file teeth, made of steel, to be pressed through irregular holes in metal that cannot be dressed by revolving tools; a drift.

(Masonry) A broad chisel for stonecutting.

(Arch.) A spire rising from a tower. [Local, Eng.]

A clasp for fastening a garment. See Brooch.

A spitlike start, on the head of a young stag.

The stick from which candle wicks are suspended for dipping.

Knight.

The pin in a lock which enters the barrel of the key.

Broach, v.t. [imp. & p.p. Broached (?); p.pr. & vb.n. Broaching.] [F. brocher, fr. broche. See Broach, n.] 1. To spit; to pierce as with a spit.
I'll broach the tadpole on my rapier's point.
Shak.

To tap; to pierce, as a cask, in order to draw the liquor. Hence: To let out; to shed, as blood.

Whereat with blade, with bloody blameful blade,
He bravely broached his boiling bloody breast.
Shak.

To open for the first time, as stores.

You shall want neither weapons, victuals, nor aid; I will open the old armories, I will broach my store, and will bring forth my stores.
Knolles.

To make public; to utter; to publish first; to put forth; to introduce as a topic of conversation.

Those very opinions themselves had broached.
Swift.

To cause to begin or break out. [Obs.]

Shak.

(Masonry) To shape roughly, as a block of stone, by chiseling with a coarse tool. [Scot. & North of Eng.]

To enlarge or dress (a hole), by using a broach.

To broach to (Naut.), to incline suddenly to windward, so as to lay the sails aback, and expose the vessel to the danger of oversetting.
Broacher (?), n. 1. A spit; a broach.
On five sharp broachers ranked, the roast they turned.
Dryden.

One who broaches, opens, or utters; a first publisher or promoter.

Some such broacher of heresy.

Atterbury.

Broad (?), a. [Compar. Broader (?); superl. Broadest.] [OE. brod, brad, AS. brǣd; akin to OS. brÇd, D. breed, G. breit, Icel. brei?r, Sw. & Dan. bred, Goth. braids. Cf. Breadth.] 1. Wide; extend in breadth, or from side to side; Ð opposed to narrow; as, a broad street, a broad table; an inch broad.

Extending far and wide; extensive; vast; as, the broad expanse of ocean.

Extended, in the sense of diffused; open; clear; full. ½Broad and open day.

Bp. Porteus.

Fig.: Having a large measure of any thing or quality; not limited; not restrained; Ð applied to any subject, and retaining the literal idea more or less clearly, the precise meaning depending largely on the substantive.

A broad mixture of falsehood.

Locke.

Hence: Ð

Comprehensive; liberal; enlarged.

The words in the Constitution are broad enough to include the case.

D.Daggett.

In a broad, statesmanlike, and masterly way.

E.Everett.

Plain; evident; as, a broad hint.

Free; unrestrained; unconfined.

As broad and general as the casing air.

Shak.

(Fine Arts) Characterized by breadth. See Breadth.

Cross; coarse; indelicate; as, a broad compliment; a broad joke; broad humor.

Strongly marked; as, a broad Scotch accent.

µ Broad is often used in compounds to signify wide, large, etc.; as, broadÐchested, broadÐshouldered, broadÐspreading, broadÐwinged.

Broad acres. See under Acre. Ð Broad arrow, originally a pheon. See Pheon, and Broad arrow under Arrow. Ð As broad as long, having the length equal to the breadth; hence, the same one way as another; coming to the same result by different ways or processes.

It is as broad as long, whether they rise to others, or bring others down to them.

L'Estrange.

Ð Broad pennant. See under Pennant.

Syn. - Wide; large; ample; expanded; spacious; roomy; extensive; vast; comprehensive; liberal.

Broad, n. 1. The broad part of anything; as, the broad of an oar.

The spread of a river into a sheet of water; a flooded fen. [Local, Eng.]

Southey.

A lathe tool for turning down the insides and bottoms of cylinders.

Knight.

Broadax · Broadaxe · } (?), n. 1. An ancient military weapon; a battleÐax.

An ax with a broad edge, for hewingÿtimber.

Broadbill · (?), n. 1. (Zo"l.) A wild duck (Aythya, or Fuligula, marila), which appears in large numbers on the eastern coast of the United States, in auntum; Ð called also bluebill, blackhead, raft duck, and scaup duck. See Scaup duck.

(Zo"l.) The shoveler. See Shoveler.

Broadbrim · (?), n. 1. A hat with a very broad brim, like those worn by men of the society of Friends.

A member of the society of Friends; a Quaker. [Sportive]

BroadÐbrimmed · (?), a. Having a broad brim.

A broadÐbrimmed flat silver plate.

Tatler.

Broadcast · (?), n. (Agric.) A casting or throwing seed in all directions, as from the hand in sowing.

Broadcast ·, a. 1. Cast or dispersed in all directions, as seed from the hand in sowing; widely diffused.

Scattering in all directions (as a method of sowing); Ð opposed to planting in hills, or rows.

Broadcast ·, adv. So as to scatter or be scattered in all directions; so as to spread widely, as seed from the hand in sowing, or news from the press.

Broad Church · (?). (Eccl.) A portion of the Church of England, consisting of persons who claim to hold a position, in respect to doctrine and fellowship, intermediate between the High Church party and the Low Church, or evangelical, party. The term has been applied to otherbodies of men holding liberal or comprehensive views of Christian doctrine and fellowship.

Side by side with these various shades of High and Low Church, another party of a different character has always existed in the Church of England.

It is called by different names: Moderate, Catholic, or Broad Church, by its friends; Latitudinarian or Indifferent, by its enemies. Its distinctive character is the desire of comprehension. Its watch words are charity and toleration.

Conybeare.

Broadcloth (?), n. A fine smooth-faced woolen cloth for men's garments, usually of double width (i.e., a yard and a half); — so called in distinction from woolens three quarters of a yard wide.

Broaden (?), v.t. [imp. & p.p. Broadened (?); p.pr. & vb.n. Broadening (?).] [From Broad, a.] To grow broad; to become broader or wider.

The broadening sun appears.

Wordsworth.

Broaden, v.t. To make broad or broader; to render more broad or comprehensive.

Broad gauge · (?). (Railroad) A wider distance between the rails than the standard gauge of four feet eight inches and a half. See Gauge.

Broad-horned · (?), a. Having horns spreading widely.

Broadish, a. Rather broad; moderately broad.

Broadleaf · (?), n. (Bot.) A tree (Terminalia latifolia) of Jamaica, the wood of which is used for boards, scantling, shingles, etc; — sometimes called the almond tree, from the shape of its fruit.

Broad-leaved · (?), Broad-leafed · (?), a. Having broad, or relatively broad, leaves.

Keats.

Broadly, adv. In a broad manner.

Broadmouth · (?), n. (Zo"l.) One of the Eurylaimid‘, a family of East Indian passerine birds.

Broadness, n. [AS. brádnes.] The condition or quality of being broad; breadth; coarseness; grossness.

Broadpiece · (?), n. An old English gold coin, broader than a guinea, as a Carolus or Jacobus.

Broad seal · (?). The great seal of England; the public seal of a country or state.

Broadseal · , v.t. To stamp with the broad seal; to make sure; to guarantee or warrant. [Obs.]

Thy presence broadseals our delights for pure.

B.Jonson.

Broadside · (?), n. 1. (Naut.) The side of a ship above the water line, from the bow to the quarter.

A discharge of or from all the guns on one side of a ship, at the same time.

A volley of abuse or denunciation. [Colloq.]

(Print.) A sheet of paper containing one large page, or printed on one side only; — called also broadsheet.

Broadspread· (?), a. Widespread.

Broadspread·ing, a. Spreading widely.

Broadsword· (?), n. A sword with a broad blade and a cutting edge; a claymore.

I heard the broadsword's deadly clang.

Sir W.Scott.

Broadwise· (?), adv. Breadthwise. [Archaic]

Brob (?), n. [Cf. Gael. brog, E. brog, n.] (Carp.) A peculiar bradÐshaped spike, to be driven alongside the end of an abutting timber to prevent its slipping.

Brob·dingĭnagiĭan (?), a. [From Brobdingnag, a country of giants in ½Gulliver's Travels.ˌ] Colossal' of extraordinary height; gigantic. Ð n. A giant. [Spelt often Brobdignagian.]

Broĭcade (?), n. [Sp. brocado (cf. It. broccato, F. brocart), fr. LL. brocare *prick, to figure (textile fabrics), to emboss (linen), to stitch. See Broach.] Silk stuff, woven with gold and silver threads, or ornamented with raised flowers, foliage, etc.; Ð also applied to other stuffs thus wrought and enriched.

A gala suit of faded brocade.

W.Irving.

Broĭcaded (?), a. 1. Woven or worked, as brocade, with gold and silver, or with raised flowers, etc.

Brocaded flowers o'er the gay mantua shine.

Gay.

Dressed in brocade.

Brocage (?), n. See Brokkerage.

Brocard (?), n. [Perh. fr. Brocardica, Brocardicorum opus, a collection of ecclesiastical canons by Burkhard, Bishop of Worms, called, by the Italians and French, Brocard.] An elementary principle or maximum; a short, proverbial rule, in law, ethics, or metaphysics.

The legal brocard, ½Falsus in uno, falsus in omnibus,ˌ is a rule not more applicable to other witness than to consciousness.

Sir W.Hamilton.

Brocaĭtel (?), n. [F. brocatelle, fr. It. brocatello: cf. Sp. brocatel. See Brocade.] 1. A kind of coarse brocade, or figured fabric, used chiefly for tapestry, linings for carriages, etc.

A marble, clouded and veined with white, gray, yellow, and red, in which the yellow usually prevails. It is also called Siena marble, from its locality.

Bro·caĭtello (?), n. Same as Brocatel.

Broccoĭli (?), n. [It. broccoli, pl. of broccolo sprout, cabbage sprout, dim. of brocco splinter. See Broach, n.] (Bot.) A plant of the Cabbage species

(Brassica oleracea) of many varieties, resembling the cauliflower. The ½curd, or flowering head, is the part used for food.

Brochantite (?), n. [From Brochant de Villiers, a French mineralogist.] (Min.) A basic sulphate of copper, occurring in emerald-green crystals.

ØBro · ch, (?), a. [F.] Woven with a figure; as, broch. goods.

ØBroche (?), n. [F.] See Broach, n.

ØBroïchure (?), n. [F., fr. brocher to stitch. See Broach, v.t.] A printed and stitched book containing only a few leaves; a pamphlet.

Brock (?), n. [AS. broc, fr. W. broch; akin to Ir. & Gael. broc, Corn. & Armor. broch; cf. Ir. & Gael. breac speckled.] (Zo"l.) A badger.

Or with pretense of chasing thence the brock.
B.Jonson.

Brock, n. [See Brocket.] (Zo"l.) A brocket.
Bailey.

Brocker (?), n. [OE. broket, F. broquart fallow deer a year old, fr. the same root as E. broach, meaning point (hence tine of a horn).] 1. (Zo"l.) A male red deer two years old; Ð sometimes called brock.

(Zo"l.) A small South American deer, of several species (Coassus superciliaris, C. rufus, and C. auritus).

Brockish, a. Beastly; brutal. [Obs.]
Bale.

Brodekin (?), n. [F. brodequin, OE. brossequin, fr. OD. broseken, brosekin, dim. of broos buskin, prob. fr. LL. byrsa leather, Gr. ? skin, hide. Cf. Buskin.] A buskin or halfÐboot. [Written also brodequin.] [Obs.]

Brog (?), n. [Gael. Cf. Brob.] A pointed instrument, as a joiner's awl, a brad awl, a needle, or a small ship stick.

Brog, v.t. To prod with a pointed instrument, as a lance; also, to broggle. [Scot. & Prov.]
Sir W.Scott.

Brogan (?), n. A stout, coarse shoe; a brogue.

Broggle (?), v.i. [Dim. of Prov. E. brog to broggle. Cf. Brog, n.] To sniggle, or fish with a brog. [Prov. Eng.]
Wright.

Brogue (?), n. [Ir. & Gael. brog shoe, hoof.] 1. A stout, coarse shoe; a brogan.

µ In the Highlands of Scotland, the ancient brogue was made of horsehide or deerskin, untanned or tenned with the hair on, gathered round the ankle with a thong. The name was afterward given to any shoe worn as a part of the Highland costume.

Clouted brogues, patched brogues; also, brogues studded with nails. See under Clout, v.t.

A dialectic pronunciation; esp. the Irish manner of pronouncing English.

Or take, Hibernis, thy still ranker brogue.
Lloyd.

Brogues (?), n. pl. [Cf. Breeches.] Breeches. [Obs.]
Shenstone.

Broid (?), v.t. To braid. [Obs.]
Chaucer.

Broider (?), v.t. [imp. & p.p. Broidered (?).] [OE. broiden, brouden, F. broder, confused with E. braid; F. broder is either the same word as border to border (see Border), or perh. of Celtic origin; cf. W. brathu to sting, stab, Ir. & Gael. brod goad, prickle, OE. brod a goad; and also Icel. broddr a spike, a sting, AS. brord a point.] To embroider. [Archaic]

They shall make a broidered coat.
Ex.xxviii.4.

Broiderïer (?), n. One who embroiders. [Archaic]

Broiderïy (?), n. Embroidery. [Archaic]

The golden broidery tender Milkah wove.
Tickell.

Broil (?), n. [F. brouiller to disorder, from LL. brogilus, broilus, brolium, thicket, wood, park; of uncertain origin; cf. W. brog a swelling out, OHG. prÓil marsh, G. brhl, MHG. brogen to rise. The meaning tumult, confusion, comes apparently from tangled undergrowth, thicket, and this possibly from the meaning to grow, rise, sprout.] A tumult; a noisy quarrel; a disturbance; a brawl; contention; discord, either between individuals or in the state.

I will own that there is a haughtiness and fierceness in human nature which will which will cause innumerable broils, place men in what situation you please.
Burke.

Syn. - Contention; fray; affray; tumult; altercation; dissension; discord; contest; conflict; brawl; uproar.

Broil, v.t. [imp. & p.p. Broiled (?); p.pr. & vb.n. Broiling.] [OE. broilen, OF. bruillir, fr. bruirÿto broil, burn; of Ger. origin; cf. MHG. brejen, G. brhen, to scald, akin to E. brood.] 1. To cook by direct exposure to heat over a fire, esp. upon a gridiron over coals.

To subject to great (commonly direct) heat.

Broil, v.i. To be subjected to the action of heat, as meat over the fire; to be greatly heated, or to be made uncomfortable with heat.

The planets and comets had been broiling in the sun.
Cheyne.

Broiler (?), n. One who excites broils; one who engages in or promotes noisy quarrels.

What doth he but turn broiler, ... make new libels against the church?
Hammond.

Broiler, n. 1. One who broils, or cooks by broiling.

A gridiron or other utensil used in broiling.

A chicken or other bird fit for broiling. [Colloq.]

Broiling, a. Excessively hot; as, a broiling sun. Ð n. The act of causing anything to broil.

Brokage (?), n. See Brokerage.

Broke (?), v.i. [See Broker, and cf. Brook.] 1. To transact business for another. [R.]

Brome.

To act as procurer in love matters; to pimp. [Obs.]

We do want a certain necessary woman to broke between them, Cupid said.

Fanshawe.

And brokes with all that can in such a suit
Corrupt the tender honor of a maid.

Shak.

<— p. 184 —>

Broke (?), imp. p.p. of Break. Broken (?), a. [From Break, v.t.] 1. Separated into parts or pieces by violence; divided into fragments; as, a broken chain or rope; a broken dish. 2. Disconnected; not continuous; also, rough; uneven; as, a broken surface. 3. Fractured; cracked; disunited; sundered; strained; apart; as, a broken reed; broken friendship. 4. Made infirm or weak, by disease, age, or hardships. The one being who remembered him as he been before his mind was broken. G.Eliot. The broken soldier, kindly bade to stay, Sat by his fire, and talked the night away. Goldsmith. 5. Subdued; humbled; contrite. The sacrifices of God are a broken spirit. Ps.li.17. 6. Subjugated; trained for use, as a horse. 7. Crushed and ruined as by something that destroys hope; blighted. ½Her broken love and life.ₓ G.Eliot. 8. Not carried into effect; not adhered to; violated; as, a broken promise, vow, or contract; a broken law. 9. Ruined financially; incapable of redeeming promises made, or of paying debts incurred; as, a broken bank; a broken tradesman. 10. Imperfectly spoken, as by a foreigner; as, broken English; imperfectly spoken on account of emotion; as, to say a few broken words at parting. Amidst the broken words and loud weeping of those grave senators. Macaulay. Broken ground. (a) (Mil.) Rough or uneven ground; as, the troops were retarded in their advance by broken ground. (b) Ground recently opened with the plow. Ð Broken line (Geom.), the straight lines which join a number of given points taken in some specified order. Ð Broken meat, fragments of meat or other food. Ð Broken number, a fraction. Ð Broken weather, unsettled weather. BrokenÐbacked · (?), a. 1. Having a broken back; as, a brokenÐbacked chair. 2. (Naut.) Hogged; so weakened in the frame as to droop at each end; Ð said of a ship. Totten. BrokenÐbel · lied (?), a. Having a ruptured belly. [R.] BrokenÐheart · ed (?), a. Having the spirits depressed or crushed by grief or despair. She left her husband almost brokenÐhearted. Macaulay. Syn. - Disconsolable; heartÐbroken; inconsolable; comfortless; woeÐbegone; forlorn. BrokenÏly, adv. In a broken, interrupted manner; in a broken state; in broken language. The pagans worship God ... as it were brokenly and by piecemeal. Cudworth. BrokenÏness, n. 1. The state or quality of being broken; unevenness. Macaulay. 2. Contrition; as, brokenness of heart. Broken wind · (?). (Far.) The heaves. BrokenÐwind · ed, a. (Far.) Having short breath or disordered respiration, as a horse. Broker (?), n. [OE. brocour, from a word akin to broken, bruken, to use, enjoy, possess, digest, fr. AS. br?canÿto use, enjoy; cf. Fries. broker, F. brocanteur. See Brook, v.t.] 1. One who transacts business for another; an agent. 2. (Law) An agent employed to effect bargains and contracts, as a middleman or negotiator, between other persons, for a compensation commonly called brokerage. He takes no possession, as broker, of the subject matter of the negotiation. He generally contracts in the names of those who employ him, and not in his own. Story. 3. A dealer in money, notes, bills of exchange, etc. 4. A dealer in secondhand goods. [Eng.] 5. A pimp or procurer. [Obs.] Shak. Bill broker, one who buys and sells notes and bills of exchange. Ð Curbstone broker or Street broker, an operator in stocks (not a member of the Stock Exchange) who executes orders by running from office to office, or by transactions on the street. [U.S.] Ð Exchange broker, one who buys and sells uncurrent money, and deals in exchanges relating to money. Ð Insurance broker, one who is agent in procuring insurance on vessels, or against fire. Ð Pawn broker. See Pawnbroker. Ð Real estate broker, one who buys and sells lands, and negotiates loans, etc., upon mortgage. Ð Ship broker, one who acts as agent in buying and selling ships, procuring freight, etc. Ð Stock broker. See Stockbroker. BrokerÏage (?), n. 1. The businessÿor employment of a broker. Burke. 2. The fee, reward, or commission, given or changed for transacting business as a broker. BrokerÏly, a. Mean; servile. [Obs.] B.Jonson. BrokerÏy (?), n. The businessÿof a broker. [Obs.] And with extorting, cozening, forfeiting, And tricks belonging unto brokery. Marlowe. Broking (?), a. Of or pertaining to a broker or brokers, or to brokerage. [Obs.] Redeem from broking pawn the blemished crown. Shak. Broma (?), n. [NL., fr. Gr. ? food, ? to eat.] 1. (Med.) Aliment; food. Dunglison. 2. A light form of prepared cocoa (or cacao), or the drink made from it. Bromal (?), n. [Bromine + aldehyde.] (Chem.) An oily, colorless fluid, $CBr?.COH$, related to bromoform, as chloral is to chloroform, and obtained by the action of bromine on alcohol. Bromate (?), n. (Chem.) A salt of bromic acid. Bromate (?), v.t. (Med.) To combine or impregnate with bromine; as, bromated camphor. Bro · maÏtoloÏgist (?), n. One versed in the scienceÿof foods. Bro · maÏtoloÏgy (?), n. [Gr. ?, ?, food + Ïlogy.] The science of aliments. Dunglison. ØBrome (?), n. [F.] (Chem.) See Bromine. Brome grass · (?). [L. bromos a kind of oats, Gr. ?.] (Bot.) A genus (Bromus) of grasses, one speciesÿof which is the chess or cheat. Bromelilaceous (?), a. [Named after Olaf Bromel, a Swedish botanist.] (Bot.) Pertaining to, or resembling, a family of endogenous and mostly epiphytic or saxicolous plants of which the genera Tillandsia and Billbergia are examples. The pineapple, though terrestrial, is also of this family. Bromic (?), a. (Chem.) Of, pertaining to, or containing, bromine; Ð said of those compounds of bromine in which this element has a valence of five, or the next to its highest; as, bromic acid. Bromide (?), n. (Chem.) A compound ÿof bromine with a positive radical. Bromïnate (?), v.t. See Bromate, v.t. Bromine (?), n. [Gr. ? bad smell, stink. Cf. Brome.] (Chem.) One of the elements, related in its chemical qualities to chlorine and iodine. Atomic weight 79.8. Symbol Br. It is a deep reddish brown liquid of a very disagreeable odor, emitting a brownish vapor at the ordinary temperature. In combination it is found in minute quantities in sea water, and in many saline springs. It occurs also in the mineral bromyrite. Bromism (?), n. (Med.) A diseased conditionÿproduced by the excessive use of bromine or one of its compounds. It is characterized by mental dullnessÿand muscular weakness. Bromize (?), v.t. (Photog.) To prepare or treat with bromine; as, to bromize a silvered plate. Bromlife (?), n. [From Bromley Hill, near Alston, Cumberland, England.] (Min.) A carbonate of baryta and lime, intermediate between witherite and strontianite; Ð called also alstonite. Bromoïform (?), n. [Bromine + formyl.] (Chem.) A colorless liquid, CHBr?, having an agreeable odor and sweetish taste. It is produced by the simultaneous action of bromine and caustic potash upon wood spirit, alcohol, or acetone, as also by certain other reactions. In composition it is the same as chloroform, with the substitution of bromine for chlorine. It is somewhat similar to chloroform in its effects. Watts. Bromïpicrin (?), n. [G. brompikrin; brom bromine + pikrins„ure picric acid.] (Chem.) A pungent colorless explosive liquid, CNO?Br?, analogous to and resembling chlorpicrin. [Spelt also brompikrin.] Bromuïret (?), n. See Bromide. [Obs.] Bromyïrite (?), n. [Bromine + Gr. ? silver.] (Min.) Silver bromide, a rare mineral; Ð called also bromargyrite. ØBronchi (?), n. pl. (Anat.) See Bronchus. ØBronchiïa (?), n. pl. [L. , pl. Cf. Bronchus.] (Anat.) The bronchial tubes which arise from the branching of the trachea, esp. the subdivision of the bronchi. Dunglison. Bronchiïal (?), a. [Cf. F. bronchial. See Bronchia.] (Anat.) Belonging to the bronchi and their ramifications in the lungs. Bronchial arteries, branchÿof the descending aorta, accompanying the bronchia in all their ramifications. Ð Bronchial cells, the air cells terminating the bronchia. Ð Bronchial glands, glands whose functions are unknown, seated along the bronchia. Ð Bronchial membrane, the mucous membrane lining the bronchia. Ð Bronchial tube, the bronchi, or the bronchia. Bronchic (?), a. (Anat.) Bronchial. Bronchiïole (?), n. (Anat.) A minute bronchial tube. Bronïchitic (?), a. Of or pertaining to bronchitis; as, bronchitic inflammation. Bronïchitis (?), n. [Bronchus + ïitis.] (Med.) Inflammation, acute or chronic, of the bronchial tubes or any part of them. Broncho (?), n. [Sp. bronco rough, wild.] A native or a Mexican horse of small size. [Western U.S.] Bronchoïcele (?), n. [Gr. ?; ? windpipe + ? tumor.] (Med.) See Goiter. Bronïchophoïny (?), n. [Gr. ? windpipe + ? sound.] A modification of the voice sounds, by which they are intensified and heightened in pitch; Ð observed in auscultation of the chest in certain cases of introÐthroacic disease. Bron · choÐpneuïmoniïa (?), n. [Bronchus + pneumonia.] (Med.) Inflammation of the bronchi and lungs; catarrhal pneumonia. Bronchoïtome (?), n. [Gr. ? windpipe + ? to cut.] (Surg.) An instrument for cutting into the bronchial tubes. Bronïchotoïmy (?), n. (Surg.) An incision into the windpipe or larynx, including the operations of tracheotomy and laryngotomy. ØBronchus (?), n.; pl. Bronchi (?). [NL., fr. Gr. ? windpipe. Cf. Bronchia.] (Anat.) One of the subdivisions of the trachea or windpipe; esp. one of the two primary divisions. Bronco (?), n. Same as Broncho. Brond (?), n. [See Brand.] A sword. [Obs.] Brontoïlite (?), Brontoïlith (?), } n. [Gr. ? + Ïlite, Ïlith.] An a‰rolite. [R.] Bronïtoloïgy (?), n. [Gr. ? thunder + Ïlogy.] A treatise upon thunder. ØBron · toïsaurus (?), n. [NL., fr. Gr. ? thunder + ? lizard.] (Paleon.) A genus of American jurassic dinosaurs. A length of sixty feet is believed to have been attained by these reptiles. ØBron · toïtheriïum (?), n. [NL., fr. Gr. ? thunder + ? beast.] (Paleon.) A genus of large extinct mammals from the moicene strata of western North America. They were allied to the rhinoceros, but the skull bears a pair of powerful horn cores in front of the orbits, and the fore feet were fourÐtoed. See Illustration in Appendix. ØBron · toïzoum (?), n. [NL., fr. Gr. ? thunder + ? animal.] (Paleon.) An extinct animal of large size, known from its threeÐtoed footprints in Mesozoic sandstone. µ The tracks made by these reptiles are found eighteen inches in length, and were formerly referred to gigantic birds; but the discovery of large bipedal threeÐtoed dinosaurs has suggested that they were made by those reptiles. Bronze (?), n. [F. bronze, fr. It. bronzo brown, fr. OHG. br?n, G. braun. See Brown, a.] 1. An alloy of copper and tin, to which small proportions of other metals, especially zinc, are sometimes added. It is hard and sonorous, and is used for statues, bells, cannon, etc., the proportions of the ingredients being varied to suit the particular purposes. The varieties containing the higher proportions of tin are brittle, as in bell metal and speculum metal. 2. A statue, bust, etc., cast in bronze. A print, a bronze, a flower, a root. Prior. 3. A yellowish or reddish brown, the color of bronze; also, a pigment or powder for imitating bronze. 4. Boldness; impudence; ½brass., Imbrowned with native bronze, lo! Henley stands. Pope. Aluminium bronze. See under Aluminium. Ð Bronze age, an age of the world which followed the stone age, and was characterized by the use of implements and ornaments of copper or bronze. Ð Bronze powder, a metallic powder, used with size or in combination with painting, to give the appearance of bronze, gold, or other metal, to any surface. Ð Phosphor bronze and Silicious or Silicium bronze are made by adding phosphorus and silicon respectively to ordinary bronze, and are characterized by great tenacity. Bronze, v.t. [imp. & p.p. Bronzed (?); p.pr. & vb.n. Bronzing.] [Cf. F.

bronzer. See Bronze, n.] 1. To give an appearance of bronzeto, by a coating of bronze powder, or by other means; to make of the color of bronze; as, to bronze plaster casts; to bronze coins or medals. The tall bronzed blackÐeyed stranger. W.Black. 2. To make hard or unfeeling; to brazen. The lawer who bronzes his bosom instead of his forefead. Sir W.Scott. Bronzed skin disease. (Pathol.) See Addison's disease. Bronzewing · (?), n. (Zo"l.) An Australian pigeon of the genus Phaps, of several species; Ð so called from its bronze plumage. Bronzine (?), n. A metal so prepared as to have the appearance of bronze. Ð a. Made of bron?ine; resembling bronze; bronzelike. Bronzing, n. 1. The act or art of communicating to articles in metal, wood, clay, plaster, etc., the appearance of bronze by means of bronze powders, or imitative painting, or by chemical processes. Tomlinson. 2. A material for bronzing. Bronzist, n. One who makes, imitates, collects, or deals in, bronzes. Bronzite (?), n. [Cf. F. bronzite.] (Min.) A variety of enstatite, often having a bronzelike luster. It is a silicate of magnesia and iron, of the pyroxene family. Bronzy (?), a. Like bronze. Brooch (?), n. [See Broach, n.] 1. An ornament, in various forms, with a tongue, pin, or loop for attaching it to a garment; now worn at the breast by women; a breastpin. Formerly worn by men on the hat. Honor 's a good brooch to wear a man's hat. B.Jonson. 2. (Paint.) A painting all of one color, as a sepia painting, or an India painting. Brooch, v.t. [imp. & p.p. Brooched (?).] To adorn as with a brooch. [R.] Brood (?), n. [OE. brod, AS. brÓd; akin to D. broed, OHG. bruot, G. brut, and also to G. brhe broth, MHG. breje, and perh. to E. brawn, breath. Cf. Breed, v.t.] 1. The young birds hatched at one time; a hatch; as, a brood of chicken. As a hen doth gather her brood under her wings. Luke xiii.34. A hen followed by a brood of ducks. Spectator. 2. The young from the same dam, whether produced at the same time or not; young children of the same mother, especially if nearly of the same age; offspring; progeny; as, a woman with a brood of children. The lion roars and gluts his tawny brood. Wordsworth. 3. That which is bred or produced; breed; species. Flocks of the airy brood, (Cranes, geese or longÐnecked swans). Chapman. 4. (Mining) Heavy waste in tin and copper ores. To sit on brood, to ponder. [Poetic] Shak. Brood, a. 1. Sitting or inclined to sit on eggs. 2. Kept for breeding from; as, a brood mare; brood stock; having young; as, a brood sow. Brood (?), v.i. [imp. & p.p. Brooded (?); p.pr. & vb.n. Brooding.] 1. To sit on and cover eggs, as a fowl, for the purpose of warming them and hatching the young; or to sit over and cover young, as a hen her chickens, in order to warm and protect them; hence, to sit quitely, as if brooding. Birds of calm sir brooding on the charmed wave. Milton. 2. To have the mind dwell continuously or moodily on a subject; to think long and anxiously; to be in a state of gloomy, serious thought; Ð usually followed by over or on; as, to brood over misfortunes. Brooding on unprofitable gold. Dryden. Brooding over all these matters, the mother felt like one who has evoked a spirit. Hawthorne. When with downcast eyes we muse and brood. Tennyson.

<— p. 185 —>

Brood (?), v.t. 1. To sit over, cover, and cherish; as, a hen broods her chickens.

<small>To cherish with care. [R.]</small>

<small>To think anxiously or moodily upon.</small>

You'll sit and brood your sorrows on a throne.
Dryden.
Broody (?), a. Inclined to brood.
Ray.
Brook (?), n. [OE. brok, broke, brook, AS. brÓc; akin to D. broek, LG. brÓk, marshy ground, OHG. pruoh, G. bruch marsh; prob. fr. the root of E. break, so as that it signifies water breaking through the earth, a spring or brook, as well as a marsh. See Break, v.t.] A natural stream of water smaller than a river or creek.

The Lord thy God bringeth thee into a good land, a land of brooks of water.
Deut.viii.7.
Empires itself, as doth an inland brook
Into the main of waters.
Shak.
Brook, v.t. [imp. & p.p. Brooked (?); p.pr. & vb.n. Brooking.] [OE. broken, bruken, to use, enjoy, digest, AS. br?can; akin to D. gebruiken to use, OHG. pr?hhan, G. brauchen, gebrauchen, Icel. br?ka, Goth. br?kjan, and L. frui, to enjoy. Cf. Fruit, Broker.] 1. To use; to enjoy. [Obs.]
Chaucer.

<small>To bear; to endure; to put up with; to tolerate; as, young men can not brook restraint.</small>

Spenser.
Shall we, who could not brook one lord,
Crouch to the wicked ten?
Macaulay.

<small>To deserve; to earn. [Obs.]</small>

Sir J.Hawkins.
Brookite (?), n. [Named from the English mineralogist, H.J.Brooke.] (Min.) A mineral consisting of titanic oxide, and hence identical with rutile and octahedrite in composition, but crystallizing in the orthorhombic system.
Brooklet (?), n. A small brook.
Brooklime · (?), n. (Bot.) A plant (Veronica Beccabunga), with flowers, usually blue, in axillary racemes. The American species is V. Americana. [Formerly written broklempe or broklympe.]

Brook mint · (?). (Bot.) See Water mint.

Brookside · (?), n. The bank of a brook.

Brookweed · (?), n. (Bot.) A small whiteÐflowered herb (Samolus Valerandi) found usually in wet places; water pimpernel.

Broom (?), n. [OE. brom, brome, AS. brÓm; akin to LG. bram, D. brem, OHG. br¾mo broom, thorn?bush, G. brombeere blackberry. Cf. Bramble, n.] 1. (Bot.) A plant having twigs suitable for makingÿbrooms to sweep with when bound together; esp., the Cytisus scoparius of Western Europe, which is a low shrub with long, straight, green, angular branches, mintue leaves, and large yellow flowers.

No gypsy cowered o'er fires of furze and broom.

Wordsworth.

An implement for sweeping floors, etc., commonly made of the panicles or tops of broom corn, bound together or attached to a long wooden handle; Ð so called because originally made of the twigs of the broom.

Butcher's broom, a plant (Ruscus aculeatus) of the Smilax family, used by butchers for brooms to sweep their blocks; Ð called also knee holly. See Cladophyll. Ð Dyer's broom, a species of mignonette (Reseda luteola), used for dyeing yellow; dyer's weed; dyer's rocket. Ð Spanish broom. See under Spanish.

Broom, v.t. (Naut.) See Bream.

Broom corn · (?). (Bot.) A variety of Sorghum vulgare, having a joined stem, like maize, rising to the height of eight or ten feet, and bearing its seeds on a panicle with long branches, of which brooms are made.

Broom rape · (?). (Bot.) A genus (Orobanche) of parasitic plants of Europe and Asia. They are destitute of chlorophyll, have scales instead of leaves, and spiked flowers, and grow attached to the roots of other plants, as furze, clover, flax, wild carrot, etc. The name is sometimes applied to other plants related to this genus, as Aphyllon uniflorumand A. Ludovicianum.

Broomstaff · (?), n. A broomstick. [Obs.]

Shak.

Broomstick · (?), n. A stick used as a handle of a broom.

Broomy (?), a. Of or pertaining to broom; overgrowing with broom; resembling broom or a broom.

If land grow mossy or broomy.

Mortimer.

Brose (?), n. [CF. Gael. brothas. Cf. Brewis, Broth.] Pottage made by pouring some boilingÿliquid on meal (esp. oatmeal), and stirring it. It is called beef brose, water brose, etc., according to the name of the liquid (beef broth, hot water, etc.) used. [Scot.]

Brotel (?), a. Brittle. [Obs.]

Chaucer.

Brotelïness, n. Brittleness. [Obs.]

Chaucer.

Broth (?), n. [AS. bro?; akin to OHG. brod, brot; cf. Ir. broth, Gael. brot. û93. Cf. Brewis, Brew.] Liquid in which flesh (and sometimes other substances, as barley or rice) has been boiled; thin or simple soup.

I am sure by your unprejudiced discourses that you love broth better than soup.

Addison.

Brothel (?), n. [OE. brothel, brodel, brethel, a prostitute, a worthless fellow, fr. AS. berc?an to ruin, destroy; cf. AS. brectan to break, and E. brittle. The term brothel house was confused with bordel brothel. CF. Bordel.] A house of lewdness or ill fame; a house frequented by prostitutes; a bawdyhouse.

Brotheller (?), n. One who frequents brothels.

Brothellry (?), n. Lewdness; obscenity; a brothel.

B.Jonson.

Brother (?), n.; pl. Brothers (?) or Brethren (?). See Brethren. [OE. brother, AS. brÓ?or; akin to OS. brothar, D. broeder, OHG. pruodar, G. bruder, Icel. brÓ?ir, Sw. & Dan. broder, Goth. brÓ?ar, Ir. brathair, W. brawd, pl. brodyr, Lith. brolis, Lett. brahlis, Russ. brat', Pol. & Serv. brat, OSlav. brat?, L. frater, Skr. bhr¾t?, Zend. bratar brother, Gr. ?, ?, a clansman. The common plural is Brothers; in the solemn style, Brethren, OE. pl. brether, bretheren, AS. dat. sing. brÇ?er, nom. pl. brÓ?or, brÓ?ru. û258. Cf. Frair, Fraternal.] 1. A male person who has the same father and mother with another person, or who has one of them only. In the latter case he is more definitely called a half brother, or brother of the half blood.

Two of us in the churchyard lie,
My sister and my brother.
Wordsworth.

One related or closely united to another by some common tie or interest, as of rank, profession, membership in a society, toil, suffering, etc.; Ð used among judges, clergymen, monks, physicians, lawers, professors of religion, etc. ½A brother of your order.

Shak.

We few, we happy few, we band of brothers,
For he toÐdday that sheds his blood with me
Shall be my brother.
Shak.

One who, or that which, resembles another in distinctive qualities or traits of character.

He also that is slothful in his work is brother to him that is a great waster.
Prov.xviii.9.
That April morn
Of this the very brother.

Wordsworth.

μ In Scripture, the term brother is applied to a kinsman by blood more remote than a son of the same parents, as in the case of Abraham and Lot, Jacob and Laban. In a more general sense, brother or brethren is used for fellow-man or fellow-men.

For of whom such massacre
Make they but of their brethren, men of men?
Milton.

Brother Jonathan, a humorous designation for the people of the United States collectively. The phrase is said to have originated from Washington's referring to the patriotic Jonathan Trumbull, governor of Connecticut, as ½Brother Jonathan., Ð Blood brother. See under Blood.

Brother (?), v.t. [imp. & p.p. Brothered (?).] To make a brother of; to call or treat as a brother; to admit to a brotherhood.

Sir W.Scott.

Brother german (?). (Law) A brother by both the father's and mother's side, in contradistinction to a uterine brother, one by the mother only.

Bouvier.

Brotherİhood (?), n. [Brother + İhood.] 1. The state of being brothers or a brother.

An association for any purpose, as a society of monks; a fraternity.

The whole body of persons engaged in the same business, Ð especially those of the same profession; as, the legal or medical brotherhood.

Persons, and, poetically, things, of a like kind.

A brotherhood of venerable trees.
Wordsworth.

Syn. - Fraternity; association; fellowship; sodality.

BrotherÐinÐlaw · (?), n.; pl. BrothersÐinÏlaw (?). The brother of one's husband or wife; also, the husband of one's sister; sometimes, the husband of one's wife's sister.

BrotherÏliÏness (?), n. The state or quality of being brotherly.

BrotherÏly (?), a. Of or pertaining to brothers; such as is natural for brothers; becoming to brothers; kind; affectionate; as, brotherly love.

Syn. - Fraternal; kind; affectionate; tender.

BrotherÏly, adv. Like a brother; affectionately; kindly. ½I speak but brotherly of him.,

Shak.

Brouded (?), p.a. Braided; broidered. [Obs.]
Alle his clothes brouded up and down.
Chaucer.

Brougham (?), n. A light, close carriage, with seats inside for two or four, and the fore wheels so arranged as to turn short.

Brow (?), n. [OE. browe, bruwe, AS. br?; akin to AS. br?w, bre w, eyelid, OFries. brÇ, D. braauw, Icel. br¾, br?n, OHG. pr¾wa, G. braue, OSlav. br?v?, Russ. brove, Ir. brai, Ir. & Gael. abhra, Armor. abrant, Gr. ?, Skr. bhr?. Cf. Bray a bank, Bridge.] 1. The prominent ridge over the eye, with the hair that covers it, forming an arch above the orbit.

And his arched brow, pulled o'er his eyes,
With solemn proof proclaims him wise.
Churchill.

The hair that covers the brow (ridge over the eyes); the eyebrow.

'T is not your inky brows, your brack silk hair.
Shak.

The forehead; as, a feverish brow.

Beads of sweat have stood upon thy brow.
Shak.

The general air of the countenance.

To whom thus Satan with contemptuous brow.
Milton.
He told them with a masterly brow.
Milton.

The edge or projecting upper aprt of a steep place; as, the brow of a precipice; the brow of a hill.

To bend the brow, To knit the brows, to frown; to scowl.
Brow, v.t. To boundÿto limit; to be at, or form, the edge of. [R.]
Tending my flocks hard by i' the hilly crofts
That brow this bottom glade.
Milton.

Browbeat· (?), v.t. [imp. Browbeat; p.p. Browbeaten (?); p.pr. & vb.n. Browbeating.] To depress or bear down with haughty, stern looks, or with arrogant speech and dogmatic assertions; to abash or disconcert by impudent or abusive words or looks; to bully; as, to browbeat witnesses.

My grandfather was not a man to be browbeaten.
W.Irving.

Browbeat·ing, n. The act of bearing down, abashing, or disconcerting, with stern looks, suspercilious manners, or confident assertions.

The imperious browbeating and scorn of great men.
L'Estrange.

Browbound· (?), a. Crowned; having the head encircled as with a diadem.
Shak.

Browdyng (?), n. Embroidery. [Obs.]

Of goldsmithrye, of browdying, and of steel.

Chaucer.

Browed (?), a. Having (such) a brow; Đ used in composition; as, darkĐbrowed, sternĐbrowed.

Browless (?), a. Without shame.

L.Addison.

Brown (?), a. [Compar. Browner (?); superl. Brownest.] [OE. brun, broun, AS. br?n; akin to D. bruin, OHG. br?n, Icel. br?nn, Sw. brun, Dan. bruun, G. braun, Lith. brunas, Skr. babhru. û93, 253. Cf. Bruin, Beaver, Burnish, Brunette.] Of a dark color, of various shades between black and red or yellow.

Cheeks brown as the oak leaves.

Longfellow.

Brown Bess, the old regulation flintlock smoothbore musket, with bronzed barrel, formerly used in the British army. Đ Brown bread. (a) Dark colored bread; esp. a kind made of unbolted wheat flour, sometimes called in the United States Graham bread. ½He would mouth with a beggar though she smelt brown bread and garlic., Shak. (b) Dark colored bread made of rye meal and Indian meal, or of wheat and rye or Indian; rye and Indian bread. [U.S.] Đ Brown coal, wood coal. See Lignite. Đ Brown hematitre or Brown iron ore (Min.), the hydrous iron oxide, limonite, which has a brown streak. See Limonite. Đ Brown holland. See under Holland. Đ Brown paper, dark colored paper, esp. coarse wrapping paper, made of unbleached materials. Đ Brown sparÿ(Min.), a ferruginous variety of dolomite, in part identical with ankerite. Đ Brown stone. See Brownstone. Đ Brown stout, a strong kind of proter or malt liquor. Đ Brown study, a state of mental abstraction or serious reverie.

W.Irving.

Brown, n. A dark color inclining to red or yellow, resulting from the mixture of red and black, or of red, black, and yellow; a tawny, dusky hue.

Brown, v.t. [imp. & p.p. Browned (?); p.pr. & vb.n. Browning.] 1. To make brown or dusky.

A trembling twilight o'er welkin moves,

Browns the dim void and darkens deep the groves.

Barlow.

To make brown by scorching slightly; as, to brown meat or flour.

To give a bright brown color to, as to gun barrels, by forming a thin coat of oxide on their surface.

Ure.

Brown, v.i. To become brown.

Brownback· (?), n. (Zo"l.) The dowitcher or redĐbreasted snipe. See Dowitcher.

Brown bill · (?). [Brown + bill cuttingÿtool.] A bill or halberd of the 16th and 17th centuries. See 4th Bill.

Many time, but for a sallet, my brainp?n had been cleft with a brown bill.
Shak.

μ The black, or as it is sometimes called, the brown bill, was a kind of halberd, the cutting part hooked like a woodman's bill, from the back of which projected a spike, and another from the head.
Grose.

Brownïan (?), a. Pertaining to Dr. Robert Brown, who first demonstrated (about 1827) the commonness of the motion described below.

Brownian movement, the peculiar, rapid, vibratory movement exhibited by the microscopic particles of substances when suspended in water or other fluids.

Brownie (?), n. [So called from its supposed tawny or swarthy color.] An imaginary goodÐnatured spirit, who was supposed often to perform important services around the house by night, such as thrashing, churning, sweeping. [Scot.]

Browning, n. 1. The act or operation of giving a brown color, as to gun barrels, etc.

(Masonry) A smooth coat of brown mortar, usually the second coat, and the preparation for the finishing coat of plaster.

Brownish, a. Somewhat brown.

Brownism (?), n. (Eccl. Hist.) The views or teachings of Robert Brown of the Brownists.
Milton.

Brownism, n. (Med.) The doctrines of the Brunonian system of medicine. See Brunonian.

Brownist, n. (Eccl. Hist.) A follower of Robert Brown, of England, in the 16th century, who taught that every church is complete and independent in itself when organized, and consists of members meeting in one place, having full power to elect and depose its officers.

Brownist, n. (Med.) One who advocates the Brunonian system of medicine.

Brownness, n. The quality or state of being brown.

Now like I brown (O lovely brown thy hair);
Only in brownness beauty dwelleth there.
Drayton.

Brownstone · (?), n. A dark variety of sandstone, much used for building purposes.

Brown thrush (?). (Zo"l.) A common American singing bird (Harporhynchus rufus), allied to the mocking bird; Ð also called brown thrasher.

Brownwort · (?), n. (Bot.) A species 9figwort or Scrophularia (S. vernalis), and otherÿspecies of the same genus, mostly perennials with inconspicuous coarse flowers.

Browny (?), a. Brownÿor, somewhat brown. ½Browny locks.˳ Shak.

Browpost · (?), n. (Carp.) A beam that goes across a building.

Browse (?), n. [OF. brost, broust, sprout, shoot, F. brout browse, browsewood, prob. fr. OHG. burst, G. borste, bristle; cf. also Armor. broustaÿto browse. See Bristle, n., Brush, n.] The tender branches or twigs of trees and shrubs, fit for the food of cattle and other animals; green food.

Spenser.

Sheep, goats, and oxen, and the nobler steed,
On browse, and corn, and flowery meadows feed.

Dryden.

Browse, v.t. [imp. & p.p. Browsed (?); p.pr. & vb.n. Browsing.] [For broust, OF. brouster, bruster, F. brouter. See Browse, n., and cf. Brut.] 1. To eat or nibble off, as the tender branches of trees, shrubs, etc.; Ð said of cattle, sheep, deer, and some other animals.

Yes, like the stag, when snow the plasture sheets,
The barks of trees thou browsedst.

Shak.

_{To feed on, as pasture; to pasture on; to graze.}

Fields ... browsed by deepÐuddered kine.

Tennyson.

<— p. 186 —>

Browse (?), v.i. 1. To feed on the tender branches or shoots of shrubs or trees, as do cattle, sheep, and deer. 2. To pasture; to feed; to nibble. Shak. Browser (?), n. An animal that browses. Browsewood · (?), n. Srubs and bushes upon which animals browse. Browsing, n. Browse; also, a place abounding with shrubs where animals may browse. Browsings for the deer. Howell. Browspot · (?), n. (Zo"l.) A rounded organ between the eyes of the frog; the interocular gland. ØBruÏang (?), n. [Native name.] (Zo"l.) The Malayan sun bear. Brucine (?), n. [Cf. F. brucine, fr. James Bruce, a Scottish traveler.] (Chem.) A poweful vegetable alkaloid, found, associated with strychnine, in the seeds of different species of Strychnos, especially in the ux vomica. It is powerful than strychnine. Called also bruciaÿand brucina. Brucite (?), n. [Named after Dr. A.Bruce of New York.] (Min.) (a) A white, pearly mineral, occurring thin and foliated, like talc, and also fibrous; a native magnesium hydrate. (b) The mineral chondrodite. [R.] Bruckeled (?), a. Wet and dirty; begrimed. [Obs. or Dial.] Herrick. ØBruh (?), n. (Zo"l.) [Native name.] The rhesus monkey. See Rhesus. Bruin (?), n. [D. bruin brown. In the epic poem of ½Reynard the Fox˳ the bear is so called from his color. See

Brown, a.] A bear; Ð so called in popular tales and fables. Bruise (?), v.t. [imp. & p.p. Bruised (?); p.pr. & vb.n. Bruising.] [OE. brusen, brisen, brosen, bresen, AS. br?sanÿor fr. OF. bruiser, bruisier, bruser, to break, shiver, perh. from OHG. brochisÓn. Cf. Break, v.t.] 1. To injure, as by a blow or collision, without laceration; to contuse; as, to bruise one's finger with a hammer; to bruise the bark of a tree with a stone; to bruise an apple by letting it fall. 2. To break; as in a mortar; to bray, as minerals, roots, etc.; to crush. Nor bruise her flowerets with the armed hoofs. Shak. Syn. - To pulverize; bray; triturate; pound; contuse. Bruise, v.i. To fight with the fists; to box. Bruising was considered a fine, manly, old English custom. Thackeray. Bruise, n. An injury to the flesh of animals, or to plants, fruit, etc., with a blunt or heavy instrument, or by collision with some other body; a contusion; as, a bruise on the head; bruises on fruit. From the sole of the foot even unto the head there is no soundness in it; but wounds, and bruises. Isa.i.6. Bruiser (?), n. 1. One who, or that which, bruises. 2. A boxer; a pugilist. R.Browning. Like a new bruiser on Broughtonic aand, Amid the lists our hero takes his stand. T.Warton. 3. A concave tool used in grinding lenses or the speculums of telescopes. Knight. Bruisewort · (?), n. A plant supposed to heal bruises, as the true daisy, the soapwort, and the comfrey. Bruit (?), n. [OE. bruit, brut, noise, bruit, F. bruit, fr. LL. brugitus; cf. L. rugireÿto roar; perh. influenced by the source of E. bray to make a harsh noise, Armor. brud bruit.] 1. Report; rumor; fame. The bruit thereof will bring you many friends. Shak. 2. [French pron. ?.] (Med.) An abnormal sound of several kinds, heard on auscultation. Bruit, v.t. [imp. & p.p. Bruited; p.pr. & vb.n. Bruiting.] To report; to noise abroad. I find thou art no less than fame hath bruited. Shak. ØBru · maire (?), n. [F., fr. L. bruma winter.] The second month of the calendar adopted by the first French republic. It began thirty days after the autumnal equinox. See Vendemiaire. Brumal (?), a. [L. brumalis, fr. bruma winter: cf. F. brumal.] Of or pertaining to winter. ½The brumal solstice.͵ Sir T.Browne. Brume (?), n. [F. brume winter season, mist, L. bruma winter.] Mist; fog; vapors. ½The drifting brume.͵ Longfellow. Brummaïgem (?), a. [Birmingham (formerly Bromwycham), Eng., ½the great mart and manufactory of gilt toys, cheap jewelry,͵ etc.] Counterfeit; gaudy but worthless; sham. [Slang] ½These Brummagem gentry.͵ Lady D.Hardy. Brumous (?), a. Foggy; misty. Brun (?), n. [See Broun a brook.] Same as Brun, a brook. [Scot.] BruÏnette (?), n. [F. brunet, brunette, brownish, dim. of brun, brune, brown, fr. OHG. br?n. See Brown, a.] A girl or woman with a somewhat brown or dark complexion. Ð a. Having a dark tint. Brunion (?), n. [F. brugnon (cf. It. brugna, prugna), fr. L. prunum. See Prune, n.] A nectarine. BruÏnoniÏan (?), a. Pertaining to, or invented by, Brown; Ð a term applied to a system of medicine promulgated in the 18th century by John Brown, of Scotland, the fundamental doctrine of which was, that life is a state of excitation produced by the normal action of external agents upon the body, and that disease consists in excess or deficiency of excitation. Brunswick black · (?). See Japan black. Brunswick green · (?). [G. Braunschweiger grn, first made at Brunswick, in Germany.] An oxychloride 9copper, used as a green pigment; also, a carbonate of copper similarly employed. Brunt (?), n. [OE. brunt, bront, fr. Icel. brunaÿto rush; cf. Icel. brennaÿto burn. Cf. Burn, v.t.] 1. The heat, or utmost violence, of an onset; the strength or greatest fury of any contention; as, the brunt of a battle. 2. The force of a blow; shock; collision. ½And heavy brunt of cannon ball.ˬ Hudibras. It is instantly and irrecoverably scattered by our first brunt with some real affair of common life. I.Taylor. Brush (?), n. [OE. brusche, OF. broche, broce, brosse, brushwood, F. brosseÿbrush, LL. brustia, bruscia, fr. OHG. brusta, brust, bristle, G. borste bristle, brste brush. See Bristle, n., and cf. Browse.] 1. An instrument composed of bristles, or other like material, set in a suitable back or handle, as of wood, bone, or ivory, and used for various purposes, as in removing dust from clothes, laying on colors, etc. Brushes have different shapes and names according to their use; as, clothes brush, paint brush, tooth brush, etc. 2. The bushy tail of a fox. 3. (Zo"l.) A tuft of hair on the mandibles. 4. Branchesÿof trees lopped off; brushwood. 5. A thicket of shrubs or small trees; the shrubs and small trees in a wood; underbrush. 6. (Elec.) A bundle of flexible wires or thin plates of metal, used to conduct an electrical currentÿto or from the commutator of a dynamo, electric motor, or similar apparatus. 7. The act of brushing; as, to give one's clothes a brush; a rubbing or grazing with a quick motion; a light touch; as, we got a brush from the wheel as it passed. [As leaves] have with one winter's brush Fell from their boughts. Shak. 8. A skirmish; a slight encounter; a shock or collision; as, to have a brush with an enemy. Let grow thy sinews till their knots be strong, And tempt not yet the brushes of the war. Shak. 9. A shoer contest, or trial, of speed. Let us enjoy a brush across the country. Cornhill Mag. Electrical brush, a form of the electric discharge characterized by a brushlike appearance of luminous rays diverging from an electrified body. Brush, v.t. [imp. & p.p. Brushed (?); p.pr. & vb.n. Brushing.] [OE. bruschen; cf. F. brosser. See Brush, n.] 1. To apply a brush to, according to its particular use; to rub, smooth, clean, paint, etc., with a brush. ½A' brushes his hat o' mornings.ˬ Shak. 2. To touch in passing, or to pass lightly over, as with a brush. Some spread their sailes, some with strong oars sweep The waters smooth, and brush the buxom wave. Fairfax. Brushed with the kiss of rustling wings. Milton. 3. To remove or gather by brushing, or by an act like that of brushing, or by passing lightly over, as wind; Ð commonly with off. As wicked dew as e'er my mother brushed With raven's feather from unwholesome fen. Shak. And from the boughts brush off the evil dew. Milton. To brush aside, to remove from one's way, as with a brush. Ð To brush away, to remove, as with a brush or brushing motion. Ð To brush up, to paint, or make clean or bright with a brush; to cleanse or improve; to renew. You have commissioned me to paint your shop, and I have done my best to brush you up like your neighbors. Pope. Brush, v.i. To move nimbly in haste; to move so lightly as scarcely to be perceived; as, to brush by. Snatching his hat, he brushed off like the wind. Goldsmith. Brusher (?), n. One who, or that which, brushes. Brushiľness (?), n. The quality of resembling a brush; brushlike condition; shagginess. Dr. H.More. Brushing, a. 1. Constructed or used to brush with; as a brushing machine. 2. Brisk; light; as, a brushing gallop. Brushite (?), n. [From George J.Brush, an American mineralogist.] (Min.) A white or gray crystalline mineral consisting of the acid phosphate of calcium. Brush tur · key (?). (Zo"l.) A large, edible, gregarious bird of Australia (Talegalla Lathami) of the family Megapodidː. Also applied to several allied species of New Guinea. µ The brush turkeys live in the ½brush,͵ and construct a common nest by collecting a large heap of decaying vegetable matter, which generates heat sufficient to hatch the numerous eggs (sometimes half a bushel) deposited in it by the females of the flock. Brush wheel · (?). 1. A wheel without teeth, used to turn a similar one by the friction of bristles or something brushlike or soft attached to the circumference. 2. A circular revolving brush used by turners, lapidaries, silversmiths, etc., for polishing. Brushwood (?), n. 1. Brush; a thicket or coppice of small trees and shrubs. 2. Small branches of trees cut off. Brushy, a. Resembling a brush; shaggy; rough. Brusk (?), a. Same as Brusque. Brusque (?), a. [F. brusque, from It. bruscoÿbrusque, tart, sour, perh. fr. L. (vitis) labrusca wild (vine); or cf. OHG. bruttisc grim, fr. brutti terror.] Rough and prompt in manner; blunt; abrupt; hluff; as, a brusque man; a brusque style. Brusqueness, n. Quality of beingÿbrusque; roughness joined with promptness; blutness. Brit. Quar. Brussels (?), n. A city of Belgium, giving its name to a kind of carpet, a kind of lace, etc. Brussels carpet, a kind of carpet made of worsted yarn fixed in a foundation web of strong linen thread. The worsted, which alone shows on the upper surface in drawn up in loops to form the pattern. Ð Brussels ground, a name given to the handmade ground of real Brussels lace. It is very costly because of the extreme finenessÿof the threads. Ð Brussels lace, an expensive kind of lace of several varieties, originally made in Brussels; as, Brussels point, Brussels ground, Brussels wire ground. Ð Brussels net, an imitation of Brussels ground, made by machinery. Ð Brussels point. See Point lace. Ð Brussels sproutsÿ(Bot.), a plant of the Cabbage family, which produces, in the axils of the upright stem, numerous small green heads, or ½sprouts,͵ each a cabbage in miniature, of one or two inches in diameter; the thousandÐheaded cabbage. Ð Brussels wire ground, a ground for lace, made of silk, with meshes partly straight and partly arched. Brustle (?), v.i. [imp. & p.p. Brustled (?); p.pr. & vb.n. Brustling (?).] [OE. brustlien and brastlien, AS. brastlian, fr. berstan to burst, akin to G. prasselnÿto crackle. See Burst, v.i.] 1. To crackle; to rustle, as a silk garment. [Obs.] Gower. 2. To make a show of firecenessÿor defiance; to bristle. [Obs.] To brustle up, to bristle up. [Obs.] Otway. Brustle, n. A bristle. [Obs. or Prov.] Chaucer. Brut (?), v.i. [F. brouter, OF. brouster. See Browse, n.] To browse. [Obs.] Evelyn. Brut, n. (Zo"l.) See Birt. ØBruta (?), n. [NL., neuter pl., fr. L. brutus heavy, stupid.] (Zo"l.) See Edentata. Brutal (?), a. [Cf. F.

brutal. See Brute, a.] 1. Of or pertaining to a brute; as, brutal nature. ½Above the rest of brutal kind., Milton. 2. Like a brute; savage; cruel; inhuman; brutish; unfeeling; merciless; gross; as, brutal manners. ½Brutal intemperance., Macaulay. Brutalïism (?), n. Brutish quality; brutality. Bruïtalïïty (?), n.; pl. Brutalities (?). [Cf. F. brutalit,.] 1. The quality of beingÿbrutal; inhumanity; savageness; pitilessness. 2. An inhuman act. The ... brutalities exercised in war. Brougham. Bru · talïïïzation (?), n. The act or processÿof making brutal; state of being brutalized. Brutalïize (?), v.t. [imp. & p.p. Brutalized (?); p.pr. & vb.n. Brutalizing.] [Cf. F. brutaliser.] To make brutal; beasty; unfeeling; or inhuman. Brutalïize, v.i. To become brutal, inhuman, barbarous, or coarse and beasty. [R.] He mixed ... with his countrymen, brutalized with them in their habits and manners. Addison. Brutalïly, adv. In a brutal manner; cruelly. Brute (?), a. [F. brut, nasc., brute, fem., raw, rough, rude, brutish, L. brutus stupid, irrational: cf. It. & Sp. bruto.] 1. Not having sensation; senseless; inanimate; unconscious; without intelligence or volition; as, the brute earth; the brute powers of nature. 2. Not possessing reason, irrational; unthinking; as, a brute beast; the brute creation. A creature ... not prone And brute as other creatures, but endued With sanctity of reason. Milton. 3. Of, pertaining to, or characteristic of, a brute beast. Hence: Brutal; cruel; fierce; ferocious; savage; pitiless; as, brute violence. Macaulay. The influence of capital and mere brute labor. Playfair. 4. Having the physical powers predominating over the mental; coarse; unpolished; unintelligent. A great brute farmer from Liddesdale. Sir W.Scott. 5. Rough; uncivilized; unfeeling. [R.] Brute, n. 1. An animal destitute of human reason; any animal not human; esp. a quadruped; a beast. Brutes may be considered as either a‰oral, terrestrial, aquatic, or amphibious. Locke. 2. A brutal person; a savage in heart or manners; as unfeeling or coarse person. An illÐnatured brute of a husband. Franklin. Syn. - See Beast. Brute, v.t. [For bruit.] To report; to bruit. [Obs.] Brutely, adv. In a rude or violent manner. Bruteness, n. 1. Brutality. [Obs.] Spenser. 2. Insensibility. ½The bruteness of nature., Emerson. Brutïïfy (?), v.t. [imp. & p.p. Brutified (?); p.pr. & vb.n. Brutifying.] [Brute + Ïfy: cf. F. brutifier.] To make like a brute; to make senseless, stupid, or unfeeling; to brutalize. Any man not quite brutified and void of sense. Barrow. Brutish (?), a. Pertaining to, or resembling, a brute or brutes; of a cruel, gross, and stupid nature; coarse; unfeeling; unintelligent. O, let all provocation Take every brutish shape it can devise. Leigh Hunt. Man may ... render himself brutish, but it is in vain that he would seek to take the rank and density of the brute. I.Taylor. Syn. - Insensible; stupid; unfeeling; savage; cruel; brutal; barbarous; inhuman; ferocious; gross; carnal; sensual; bestial. Ð Brutishïly, adv. Ð Brutishïness, n. Brutism (?), n. The nature or characteristic qualities or actions of a brute; extreme stupidity, or beastly vulgarity. Bruting (?), n. Browsing. [Obs.] Evelyn. Bryïoïlogiïcal (?), a. Relating to bryology; as, bryological studies. Bryïoloïgist (?), n. One versed in bryology. Bryӗolоӗgy (?), n. [Gr. ? moss + ӗlogy.] That part of botany which relates to mosses. Bryoӗnin (?), n. (Chem.) A bitter principle obtained from the root of the bryony (Bryonia alba and B. dioica). It is a white, or slightly colored, substance, and is emetic and cathartic.

<— p. 187 —>

Bryoӗny (?), n. [L. bryonia, Gr. ?, fr. ? to swell, esp. of plants.] (Bot.) The commonname of several cucurbitaceous plants of the genus Bryonia. The root of B. alba (rough or white bryony) and of B. dioica is a strong, irritating cathartic.

Black bryony, a plant (Tamus communis) so named from its dark glossy leaves and black root; black bindweed.

ØBryӗophyӗta (?), n. pl. See Cryptogamia.

ØBry · oӗzoa (?), n. pl. [NL., fr. Gr. ? moss + ? animal.] (Zo"l.) A class of Molluscoidea, including minute animals which by budding form compound colonies; Đ called also Polyzoa.

μ̇ They are often coralike in form and appearance, each small cell containing an individual zooid. Other species grow in delicate, flexible, branched forms, resembling moss, whence the name. Some are found in fresh water, but most are marine. The three principal divisions are Ectoprocta, Entoprocta, and Pterobranchia. See Cyclostoma, Chilostoma, and Phylactolema.

Bry · oӗzoan (?), a. (Zo"l.) Of or pertaining to the Bryozoa. Đ n. One of the Bryozoa.

ØBry · oӗzoum (?), n. [NL. See Bryozoa.] (Zo"l.) An individual zooid of a bryozoan coralline, of which there may be two or more kinds in a single colony. The zoÒcia usually have a wreath of tentacles around the mouth, and a well developed stomach and intestinal canal; but these parts are lacking in the otherzooids (Avicularia, OÒcia, etc.).

ØBu · anӗsuah (?), n. [Native name.] (Zo"l.) The wild dog of northern India (Cuon prim'vus), supposed by some to be an ancestral species of the domsetic dog.

ØBuat (?), n. [Scot., of uncertain origin.] A lantern; also, the moon. [Scot.]

Sir W.Scott.

Bub (?), n. Strong malt liquor. [Cant]

Prior.

Bub, n. [Cf. 2d Bubby.] A young brother; a little boy; Đ a familiar term of address of a small boy.

Bub, v.t. [Abbrev. from Bubble.] To throw out in bubbles; to bubble. [Obs.]

Sackville.

Bubaӗle (?), n. [Cf. F. bubale. See Buffalo, n.] (Zo"l.) A large antelope (Alcelaphus bubalis) of Egypt and the Desert of Sahara, supposed by some to be the fallow deer of the Bible.

Buba**i**line (?), a. (Zo"l.) Resembling a buffalo.

Bubaline antelope (Zo"l.), the bubale.

Bubble (?), n. [Cf. D. bobbel, Dan. boble, Sw. bubbla. Cf. Blob, n.] 1. A thin film of liquid inflated with air or gas; as, a soap bubble; bubbles on the surface of a river.

Beads of sweat have stood upon thy brow,
Like bubbles in a late disturbed stream.
Shak.

A small quantity of air or gas within a liquid body; as, bubbles rising in champagne or aërated waters.

A globule of air, or globular vacuum, in a transparent solid; as, bubbles in window glass, or in a lens.

A small, hollow, floating bead or globe, formerly used for testing the strength of spirits.

The globule of air in the spirit tube of a level.

Anything that wants firmness or solidity; that which is more specious than real; a false show; a cheat or fraud; a delusive scheme; an empty project; a dishonest speculation; as, the South Sea bubble.

Then a soldier ...
Seeking the bubble reputation
Even in the cannon's mouth.
Shak.

A person deceived by an empty project; a gull. [Obs.] ½Ganny's a cheat, and I'm a bubble.

Prior.

Bubble, v.i. [imp. & p.p. Bubbled (?); p.pr. & vb.n. Bubbling (?).] [Cf. D. bobbelen, Dan. boble.ÿSee Bubble, n.] 1. To rise in bubbles, as liquids when boiling or agitated; to contain bubbles.

The milk that bubbled in the pail.
Tennyson.

To run with a gurdling noise, as if forming bubbles; as, a bubbling stream.

Pope.

To sing with a gurgling or warbling sound.

At mine ear
Bubbled the nightingale and heeded not.
Tennyson.

Bubbler, v.t. To cheat; to deceive.

She has bubbled him out of his youth.
Addison.

The great Locke, who was seldom outwitted by false sounds, was nevertheless bubbled here.

Sterne.

Bubbler (?), n. 1. One who cheats.

All the Jews, jobbers, bubblers, subscribers, projectors, etc.

Pope.

(Zo"l.) A fish of the Ohio river; Ð so called from the noise it makes.

Bubble shell · (?). (Zo"l.) A marine univalve shell of the genus Bulla and allied genera, belonging to the Tectibranchiata.

Bubbling Jock · (?) (Zo"l.) The male wild turkey, the gobbler; Ð so called in allusion to its notes.

Bubbly (?), a. Abounding in bubbles; bubbling.

Nash.

Bubby (?), n. [Cf. Prov. G. bbbi, or It. poppa, Pr. popa, OF. poupe, a woman's breast.] A woman's breast. [Low]

Bubby, n. [A corruption of brother.] Bub; Ð a term of familiar or affectionate address to a small boy.

Bubo (?), n.; pl. **Buboes** (?). [LL. buboÿthe groin, a swelling in the groin, Gr. ?.] (Med.) An inflammation, with enlargement, of a limphatic gland, esp. in the groin, as in syphilis.

Buḯbonic (?), a. Of or pertaining to a bubo or buboes; characterized by buboes.

Buḯbonoïcele (?), n. [Gr. ? groin + ? tumor: cf. F. bubonocŠle.] (Med.) An inguinal hernia; esp. that incomplete variety in which the hernial pouch descends only as far as the groin, forming a swelling there like a bubo.

Bubuïkle (?), n. A red pimple. [R.]

Shak.

Buccal (?), a. [L. bucca cheek: cf. F. buccal.] (Anat.) Of or pertaining to the mouth or cheeks.

Buc · caïneer (?), n. [F. boucanier, fr. boucanerÿto smoke or broil meat and fish, to hunt wild beasts for their skins, boucan a smoking placeÿfor meat or fish, gridiron for smoking: a word of American origin.] A robber upon the sea; a pirate; Ð a term applied especially to the piratical adventurers who made depredations on the Spaniards in America in the 17th and 18th centuries. [Written also bucanier.]

µ Primarily, one who dries and smokes flesh or fish after the manner of the Indians. The name was first given to the French settlers in Hayti or Hispaniola, whose business was to hunt wild cattle and swine.

Buc · caïneer, v.i. To act the part of a buccaneer; to live as a piratical adventurer or sea robber.

Buc · caïneerish, a. Like a buccaneer; piratical.

Bucciïnal (?), a. [L. bucina a crooked horn or trumpet.] Shaped or sounding like a trumpet; trumpetlike.

ØBuc·ciĭnator (?), n. [L., a trumpeter, fr. bucinare to sound the trumpet.] (Anat.) A muscle of the cheek; Ð so called from its use in blowing wind instruments.

Bucciĭnoid (?), a. [Buccinum + ĭoid.] (Zo"l.) Resembling the genus Buccinum, or pertaining to the Buccinid', a family of marine univalve shells. See Whelk, and Prosobranchiata.

ØBucciĭnum (?), n. [L., a trumpet, a trumpet shell.] (Zo"l.) A genus of large univalve mollusks abundant in the arctic seas. It includes the common whelk (B. undatum).

Buĭcentaur (?), n. [Gr. ?; ox + ? centaur.] 1. A fabulous monster, half ox, half man.

[It. bucentoro.] The state barge of Venice, used by the doge in the ceremony of espousing the Adriatic.

ØBuceĭros (?), n. [Gr. ? horned like an ox; ? ox + ? horn.] (Zo"l.) A genus of large perching birds; the hornbills.

Bucholĭzite (?), n. [So called from Bucholz, a German chemist.] (Min.) Same as Fibrolite.

Buchu (?), n. (Bot.) A South African shrub (Barosma) with small leaves that are dotted with oil dlands; also, the leaves themselves, which are used in medicine for diseases of the urinary organs, etc. Several species furnish the leaves.

Buck (?), n. [Akin to LG. bke, Dan. byg, Sw. byk, G. bauche: cf. It. bucato, Prov. Sp. bugada, F. bu,e.] 1. Lye or suds in which cloth is soaked in the operation of bleaching, or in which clothes are washed.

The cloth or clothes soaked or washed. [Obs.]

Shak.

Buck, v.t. [imp. & p.p. Bucked (?); p.pr. & vb.n. Bucking.] [OE. bouken; akin to LG. bken, Dan. byge, Sw. byka, G. bauchen, beuchen; cf. OF. buer. Cf. the preceding noun.] 1. To soak, steep, or boil, in lye or suds; Ð a process in bleaching.

TO wash (clothes) in lye or suds, or, in later usage, by beating them on stones in running water.

(Mining) To break up or pulverize, as ores.

Buck, n. [OE. buk, bucke, AS. bucca, bua, heÐgoat; akin to D. bok, OHG. pocch, G. bock, Ir. boc, W. bwch, Corn. byk; cf. Zend b?za, Skr. bukka. û256. Cf. Butcher, n.] 1. The male of deer, especially fallow deer and antelopes, or of goats, sheep, hares, and rabbits.

µ A male fallow deer is called a fawn in his first year; a pricket in his second; a sorel in his third; a sore in his fourth; a buck of the first head in his fifth; and a great buck in his sixth. The female of the fallow deer is termed a

doe. The male of the red deer is termed a stag or hart and not a buck, and the female is called a hind.
Brande & C.

A gay, dashing young fellow; a fop; a dandy.

The leading bucks of the day.
Thackeray.

A male Indian or negro. [Colloq. U.S.]

µ The word buck is much used in composition for the names of antelopes; as, bush buck, spring buck.

Blue buck. See under Blue. — Water buck, a South African variety of antelope (Kobus ellipsiprymnus). See Illust. of Antelope.

Buck (?), v.i. 1. To copulate, as bucks and does.

To spring with quick plunging leaps, descending with the fore legs rigid and the head held as low down as possible; — said of a vicious horse or mule.

Buck, v.t. 1. (Mil.) To subject to a mode of punishment which consists in tying the wrists together, passing the arms over the bent knees, and putting a stick across the arms and in the angle formed by the knees.

To throw by bucking. See Buck, v.i., 2.

The brute that he was riding had nearly bucked him out of the saddle.
W.E.Norris.

Buck, n. A frame on which firewood is sawed; a sawhorse; a sawbuck.

Buck saw, a saw set in a frame and used for sawing wood on a sawhorse.

Buck, n. [See Beech, n.] The beech tree. [Scot.]

Buck mast, the mast or fruit of the beech tree.
Johnson.

Buck-bas·ket (?), n. [See 1st Buck.] A basket in which clothes are carried to the wash.
Shak.

Buck bean· (?). (Bot.) A plant (Menyanthes trifoliata) which grows in moist and boggy places, having racems of white or reddish flowers and intensely bitter leaves, sometimes used in medicine; marsh trefoil; — called also bog bean.

Buckboard· (?), n. A four-wheeled vehicle, having a long elastic board or frame resting on the bolsters or axletrees, and a seat or seats placed transversely upon it; — called also buck wagon.

Bucker (?), n. (Mining) 1. One who bucks ore.

A broad-headed hammer used in bucking ore.

Bucker, n. A horse or mule that bucks.

Bucket (?), n. [OE. boket; cf. AS. buc pitcher, or Corn. buket tub.] 1. A vessel for drawing up water from a well, or for catching, holding, or carrying water, sap, or other liquids.

The old oaken bucket, the iron-bound bucket,
The moss-covered bucket, which hung in the well.
Wordsworth.

A vessel (as a tub or scoop) for hoisting and conveying coal, ore, grain, etc.

(Mach.) One of the receptacles on the rim of a water wheel into which the water rushes, causing the wheel to revolve; also, a float of a paddle wheel.

The valved piston of a lifting pump.

Fire bucket, a bucket for carrying water to put out fires. -- To kick the bucket, to die. [Low]

Bucket shop · (?). An office or a place where facilities are given for betting small sums on current prices of stocks, petroleum, etc. [Slang, U.S.]

Bucketly (?), n. [A corruption of buckwheat.] Paste used by weavers to dress their webs.
Buchanan.

Buckeye · (?), n. 1. (Bot.) A name given to several American trees and shrubs of the same genus ('sculus) as the horse chestnut.

The Ohio buckeye, or Fetid buckeye, is 'sculus glabra. -- Red buckeye is '. Pavia. -- Small buckeye is '. paviflora. -- Sweet buckeye, or Yellow buckeye, is '. flava.

A cant name for a native in Ohio. [U.S.]

Buckeye State, Ohio; -- so called because buckeye trees abound there.

Buck-eyed · (?), a. Having bad or speckled eyes. ½A buck-eyed horse.
James White.

Buckhound · (?), n. A hound for hunting deer.

Master of the buckhounds, an officer in the royal house hold. [Eng.]

Buckie (?), n. (Zo"l.) A large spiral marine shell, esp. the common whelk. See Buccinum. [Scot.]

Deil's buckie, a perverse, refractory youngster. [Slang]

Bucking, n. 1. The act or process of soaking or boiling cloth in an alkaline liquid in the operation of bleaching; also, the liquid used.
Tomlinson.

A washing.

The process of breaking up or pulverizing ores.

Bucking iron (Mining), a broad-faced hammer, used in bucking or breaking up ores. -- Bucking kier (Manuf.), a large circular boiler, or kier, used in bleaching. -- Bucking stool, a washing block.

Buckish, a. Dandified; foppish.

Buckle (?), n. [OE. bocleÿbuckle, boss of a shield, OF. bocle, F. boucle, boss of a shield, ring, fr. L. buccula a little cheek or mouth, dim. of bucca cheek; this boss or knob resembling a cheek.] 1. A device, usually of metal, consisting of a frame with one more movable tongues or catches, used for fastening things together, as parts of dress or harness, by means of a strap passing through the frame and pierced by the tongue.

A distortion bulge, bend, or kink, as in a saw blade or a plate of sheet metal.

Knight.

A curl of hair, esp. a kind of crisp curl formerly worn; also, the state of being curled.

Earlocks in tight buckles on each side of a lantern face.
W.Irving.
Lets his wig lie in buckle for a whole half year.
Addison.

A contorted expression, as of the face. [R.]

'Gainst nature armed by gravity,
His features too in buckle see.
Churchill.

Buckle (?), v.t. [imp. & p.p. Buckled (?); p.pr. & vb.n. Buckling.] [OE. boclen, F. boucler. See Buckle, n.] 1. To fasten or confine with a buckle or buckles; as, to buckle a harness.

To bend; to cause to kink, or to become distorted.

To prepare for action; to apply with vigor and earnestness; Ð generally used reflexively<— buckle down —>.

Cartwright buckled himself to the employment.
Fuller.

To join in marriage. [Scot.]

Sir W.Scott.
<— p. 188 —>
Buckle (?), v.i. 1. To bend permanently; to become distorted; to bow; to curl; to kink.

Buckled with the heat of the fire like parchment.
Pepys.

To bend out of a true vertical plane, as a wall.

To yield; to give way; to cease opposing. [Obs.]

The Dutch, as high as they seem, do begin to buckle.
Pepys.

To enter upon some labor or contest; to join in close fight; to struggle; to contend.

The bishop was as able and ready to buckle with the Lord Protector as he was with him.
Latimer.
In single combat thou shalt buckle with me.
Shak.
To buckle to, to bend to; to engage with zeal.
To make our sturdy humor buckle thereto.
Barrow.
Before buckling to my winter's work.
J.D.Forbes.

Buckler (?), n. [OE. bocler, OF. bocler, F. bouclier, a shield with a boss, from OF. bocle, boucle, boss. See Buckle, n.] 1. A kind of shield, of various shapes and sizes, worn on one of the arms (usually the left) for protecting the front of the body.

µ In the sword and buckler play of the Middle Ages in England, the buckler was a small shield, used, not to cover the body, but to stop or parry blows.

(Zo"l.) (a) One of the large, bony, external plates found on many ganoid fishes. (b) The anterior segment of the shell of trilobites.

(Naut.) A block of wood or plate of iron made to fit a hawse hole, or the circular opening in a halfÐport, to prevent water from entering when the vessel pitches.

Blind bucklerÿ(Naut.), a solid buckler. Ð Buckler mustardÿ(Bot.), a genus of plants (Biscutella) with small bright yellow flowers. The seed vessel on bursting resembles two bucklers or shields. Ð Buckler thorn, a plant with seed vessels shaped like a buckler. See Christ's thorn. Ð Riding bucklerÿ(Naut.), a buckler with a hole for the passage of a cable.

Buckler, v.t. To shield; to defend. [Obs.]
Can Oxford, that did ever fence the right,
Now buckler falsehood with a pedigree?
Shak.

BucklerÐhead · ed (?), a. Having a head like a buckler.

Buckling (?), a. Wavy; curling, as hair.
Latham.

Buckra (?), n. [In the languageÿof the Calabar coast, buckra means ½demon, a powerful and superior being., J.L.Wilson.] A white man; Ð a term used by negroes of the African coast, West Indies, etc.

Buckra, a. White; white man's; strong; good; as, buckra yam, a white yam.

Buckram (?), n. [OE. bokeram, bougeren, OF. boqueran, F. bougran, MHG. buckeram, LL. buchiranus, boquerannus, fr. MHG. boc, G. bock, goat (as being made of goat's hair), or fr. F. bouracan, by transposing the letter r. See Buck, Barracan.] 1. A coarse cloth of linen or hemp, stiffened with size or glue, used in garments to keep them in the form intended, and for wrappers to cover merchandise.

µ Buckram was formerly a very different material from that now known by the name. It was used for wearing apparel, etc.

Beck (Draper's Dict.).

(Bot.) A plant. See Ramson.

Dr. Prior.
Buckram, a. 1. Made of buckram; as, a buckram suit.

Stiff; precise. ½Buckram dames.

Brooke.
Buckram, v.t. To strengthen with buckram; to make stiff.
Cowper.
Buck'sĐhorn · (?), n. (Bot.) A plant with leaves branched somewhat like a buck's horn (Plantago Coronopus); also, Lobelia coronopifolia.

Buckshot · (?), n. A coarse leaden shot, larger than swan shot, used in hunting deer and large game.

Buckskin · (?), n. 1. The skin of a buck.

A soft strong leather, usually yellowish or grayish in color, made of deerskin.

A person clothed in buckskin, particularly an American soldier of the Revolutionary war.

Cornwallis fought as lang's he dought,
An' did the buckskins claw, man.
Burns.

pl. Breeches made of buckskin.

I have alluded to his buckskin.
Thackeray.
Buckstall · (?), n. A toil or net to take deer.
Buckthorn · (?), n. (Bot.) A genus (Rhamnus) of shrubs or trees. The shorter branches of some species terminate in long spines or thorns. See Rhamnus.

Sea buckthorn, a plant of the genus Hippopha‰.

Bucktooth · (?), n. Any tooth that juts out.
When he laughed, two white buckteeth protruded.
Thackeray.
Buckwheat · (?), n. [Buck a beech tree + wheat; akin to D. boekweit, G. buchweizen.] 1. (Bot.) A plant (Fagopyrum esculentum) of the Polygonum family, the seed of which is used for food.

The triangular seed used, when ground, for griddle cakes, etc.

Bu̅colic (?), a. [L. bucolicus, Gr. ?, fr. ? cowherd, herdsman; ? ox + (perh.) ? race horse; cf. Skr. kalÿto drive: cf. F. bucolique. See Cow the animal.] Of or pertaining to the life and occupation of a shepherd; pastoral; rustic.

Bu̅colic, n. [L. Bucolic"n po‰ma.] A pastoral poem, representing rural affairs, and the life, manners, and occupation of shepherds; as, the Bucolics of Theocritus and Virgil.

Dryden.

Bu̅colic̅al (?), a. Bucolic.

ØBu̅crani̅um (?), n.; pl. L. Bucrania (?). [L., fr. Gr. ? ox head.] A sculptured ornament, representing an ox skull adorned with wreaths, etc.

Bud (?), n. [OE. budde; cf. D. bot, G. butze, butz, the core of a fruit, bud, LG. butte in hagebutte, hainbutte, a hip of the dogÐrose, or OF. boton, F. bouton, bud, button, OF. boter to bud, push; all akin to E. beat. See Button.] 1. (Bot.) A small protuberance on the stem or branches of a plant, containing the rudiments of future leaves, flowers, or stems; an undeveloped branchÿor flower.

(Biol.) A small protuberance on certain low forms of animals and vegetables which develops into a new organism, either free or attached. See Hydra.

Bud moth (Zo"l.), a lepidopterous insect of several species, which destroys the buds of fruit trees; esp. Tmetocera ocellanaÿand Eccopsis malana on the apple tree.

Bud, v.i. [imp. & p.p. Budded; p.pr. & vb.n. Budding.] 1. To put forth or produce buds, as a plant; to grow, as a bud does, into a flower or shoot.

To begin to grow, or to issue from a stock in the manner of a bud, as a horn.

To be like a bud in respect to youth and freshness,ÿor growth and promise; as, a budding virgin.

Shak.

Syn. - To sprout; germinate; blossom.

Bud, v.t. To graft, as a plant with another or into another, by inserting a bud from the one into an opening in the bark of the other, in order to raise, upon the budded stock, fruit different from that which it would naturally bear.

The apricot and the nectarine may be, and usually are, budded upon the peach; the plum and the peach are budded on each other.

Farm. Dict.

Buddha (?), n. [Skr. buddha wise, sage, fr. budhÿto know.] The title of an incarnation of selfÐabnegation, virtue, and wisdom, or a deified religious teacher of the Buddhists, esp. Gautama Siddartha or Sakya Sinha (or Muni), the founder of Buddhism.

Buddhism (?), n. The religion based upon the doctrine originally taught by the Hindoo sage Gautama Siddartha, surnamed Buddha, ½the awakened or enlightened,͵ in the sixth century b.c., and adopted as a religion by the greater part of the inhabitants of Central and Eastern Asia and the Indian Islands. Buddha's teaching is believed to have been atheistic; yet it was characterized by elevated humanity and morality. It presents release from existence (a beatific enfranchisement, Nirvfna) as the greatest good. Buddhists believe in transmigration of souls through all phases and forms of life. Their number was estimated in 1881 at 470,000,000.

Buddhist (?), n. One who accepts the teachings of Buddhism.

Buddhist, a. Of or pertaining to Buddha, Buddhism, or the Buddhists.

BudÏdhistic (?), a. Same as Buddhist, a.

Budding (?), n. 1. The act or process of producing buds.

(Biol.) A processÿof asexual reproduction, in which a new organism or cell is formed by a protrusion of a portion of the animal or vegetable organism, the bud thus formed sometimes remaining attached to the parent stalk or cell, at other times becoming free; gemmation. See Hydroidea.

The act or processÿof ingrafting one kind of plant upon another stock by inserting a bud under the bark.

Buddle (?), n. [Prov. E., to cleanse ore, also a vessel for this purpose; cf. G. buttelnÿto shake.] (Mining) An apparatus, especially an inclined trough or vat, in which stamped ore is concentrated by subjecting it to the action of rynning water so as to wash out the lighter and less valuable portions.

Buddle, v.i. (Mining) To wash ore in a buddle.

Bude burn · er (?). [See Bude light.] A burner consisting of two or more concentric Argand burnes (the inner rising aboveÿthe outer) and a central tube by which oxygen gas or common air is supplied.

Bude light · (?). [From Bude, in Cornwall, the residence of Sir G.Gurney, the inventor.] A light in which high illuminating power is obtained by introducing a jet of oxygen gas or of common air into the center of a flame fed with coal gas or with oil.

Budge (?), v.i. [imp. & p.p. Budged (?); p.pr. & vb.n. Budging.] [F. bouger to stir, move (akin to Pr. bojar, bolegar, to stir, move, It. bulicare to boil, bubble), fr. L. bullire. See Boil, v.i.] To move off; to stir; to walk away.

I'll not budge an inch, boy.
Shak.

The mouse ne'er shunned the cat as they did budge
From rascals worse than they.
Shak.

Budge, a. [See Budge, v.] Brisk; stirring; jocund. [Obs.]
South.

Budge, n. [OE. bouge bag, OF. boge, bouge, fr. L. bulga a leathern bag or knapsack; a Gallic word; cf. OIr. bolc, Gael. bolg. Cf. Budge, n.] A kind of fur prepared from lambskin dressed with the wool on; Ð used formerly as an edging and ornament, esp. of scholastic habits.

Budge, a. 1. Lined with budge; hence, scholastic. ½Budge gowns.ͺ
Milton.

<small>Austere or stiff, like scholastics.</small>

Those budge doctors of the stoic fur.
Milton.

Budge bachelor, one of a company of men clothed in long gowns lined with budge, who formerly accompanied the lord mayor of London in his inaugural procession. Ð Budge barrel (Mil.), a small copperÐhooped barrel with only one head, the other end being closed by a piece of leather, which is drawn togetherÿwith strings like a purse. It is used for carrying powder from the magazine to the battery, in siege or seacoast service.

Budgeness (?), n. Sternness; severity. [Obs.]

A Sara for goodness, a great Bellona for budgeness.
Stanyhurst.

Budger (?), n. One who budges.
Shak.

Øbudgeïrow (?), n. [Hindi bajr¾.] A large and commodious, but generally cumbrous and sluggish boat, used for journeys on the Ganges.

Budget (?), n. [OE. bogett, bouget, F. bougette bag, wallet, dim. of OF. boge, bouge, leather bag. See Budge, n., and cf. Bouget.] 1. A bag or sack with its contents; hence, a stock or store; an accumulation; as, a budget of inventions.

<small>The annual financial statement which the British chancellor of the exchequer makes in the House of Commons. It comprehends a general view of the finances of the country, with the proposed plan of taxation for the ensuing year. The term is sometimes applied to a similar statement in other countries.</small>

To open the budget, to lay before a legislative body the financial estimates and plans of the executive government.

Budgy, a. [From Budge, n.] Consisting of fur. [Obs.]

Budlet (?), n. [Bud + ïlet.] A little bud springing from a parent bud.

We have a criterion to distinguish one bud from another,ÿor the parent bud from the numerous budlets which are its offspring.
E.Darwin.

Buff (?), n. [OE. buff, buffe, buff, buffalo, F. buffleÿbuffalo. See Buffalo.] 1. A sort of leather, prepared from the skin of the buffalo, dressed with oil, like chamois; also, the skins of oxen, elks, and other animals, dressed in like manner. ½A suit of buff.ͺ
Shak.

The color to buff; a light yellow, shading toward pink, gray, or brown.

A visage rough,
Deformed, unfeatured, and a skin of buff.
Dryden.

A military coat, made of buff leather.

Shak.

(Med.) ÿThe grayish viscid substance constituting the buffy coat. See Buffy coat, under Buffy, a.

(Mech.) A wheel covered with buff leather, and used in polishing cutlery, spoons, etc.

The bare skin; as, to strip to the buff. [Colloq.]

To be in buff is equivalent to being naked.
Wright.
Buff, a. 1. Made of buff leather.
Goldsmith.

Of the color of buff.

Buff coat, a close, military outer garment, with short sleeves, and laced tightly over the chest, made of buffalo skin, or other thick and elastic material, worn by soldiers in the 17th century as a defensive covering. Ð Buff jerkin, originally, a leather waistcoat; afterward, one of cloth of a buff color. [Obs.] Nares. Ð Buff stick (Mech.), a strip of wood covered with buff leather, used in polishing.

Buff, v.t. To polish with a buff. See Buff, n., 5.

Buff, v.t. [OF. bufer to cuff, buffet. See Buffet a blow.] To strike. [Obs.] B.Jonson.

Buff, n. [See Buffet.] A buffet; a blow; Ð obsolete except in the phrase ½Blindman's buff.

Nathless so sore a buff to him it lent
That made him reel.
Spenser.

Buff, a. [Of uncertain etymol.] Firm; sturdy.

And for the good old cause stood buff,
'Gainst many a bitter kick and cuff.
Hudibras.

ØBuffa (?), n.fem. (Mus.) [It. See Buffoon.] The comic actress in an opera. Ð a. Comic, farcical.

Aria buffa, a droll or comic air. Ð Opera buffa, a comic opera. See Opera bouffe.

Buffaïlo (?), n.; pl. Buffaloes (?). [Sp. bufalo (cf. It. bufalo, F. buffle), fr. L. bubalus, bufalus, a kind of African stag or gazelle; also, the buffalo or wild ox, fr. Gr. ? buffalo, prob. fr. ? ox. See Cow the animal, and cf. Buff the color, and Bubale.] 1. (Zo"l.) A species of the genus Bos or Bubalus (B. bubalus), originallyÿfrom India, but now found in most of the warmer countries of the eastern continent. It is larger and less docile than the common ox, and is fond of marshy places and rivers.

(Zo"l.) A very large and savage species of the same genus (B. Caffer) found in South Africa; Ð called also Cape buffalo.

(Zo"l.) Any speciesÿof wild ox.

(Zo"l.) The bison of North America.

A buffalo robe. See Buffalo robe, below.

(Zo"l.) The buffalo fish. See Buffalo fish, below.

Buffalo berryÿ(Bot.), a shrub of the Upper Missouri (Sherherdia argentea) with acid edible red berries. Ð Buffalo bird (Zo"l.), an African bird of the genus Buphaga, of two species. These birds perch upon buffaloes and cattle, in search of parasites. Ð Buffalo bug, the carpet beetle. See under Carpet. Ð Buffalo chips, dry dung of the buffalo, or bison, used for fuel. [U.S.] Ð Buffalo cloverÿ(Bot.), a kind of clover (Trifolium reflexum and T.soloniferum) found in the ancient grazing grounds of the American bison. Ð Buffalo cod (Zo"l.), a large, edible, marine fish (Ophiodon elongatus) of the northern Pacific coast; Ð called also blue cod, and cultus cod. Ð Buffalo fish (Zo"l.), one of several large freshÐwater fishes of the family Catostomid', of the Mississippi valley. The redÐmouthed or brown (Ictiobus bubalus), the bigÐmouthed or black (Bubalichthys urus), and the smallÐmouthed (B. altus), are among the more important species used as food. Ð Buffalo fly, or Buffalo gnat (Zo"l.), a small dipterous insect of the genus Simulium, allied to the black fly of the North. It is often extremely abundant in the lower part of the Mississippi valley and does great injury to domestic animals, often killing large numbers of cattle and horses. In Europe the Columbatz fly is a species with similar habits. Ð Buffalo grassÿ(Bot.), a species of short, sweet grass (Buchlo‰ dactyloides), from two to four inches high, covering the prairies on which the buffaloes, or bisons, feed. [U.S.] Ð Buffalo nut (Bot.), the oily and drupelike fruit of an American shrub (Pyrularia oleifera); also, the shrub itself; oilnut. Ð Buffalo robe, the skin of the bison of North America, prepared with the hair on; Ð much used as a lap robe in sleighs.

<— p. 189 —>

Buffel duck (?). [See Buffalo.] (Zo"l.) A small duck (Charitonetta albeola); the spirit duck, or butterball. The head of the male is covered with numerous elongated feathers, and thus appears large. Called also bufflehead.

Buffer (?), n. [Prop a striker. See Buffet a blow.] 1. (Mech.) (a) An elastic apparatus or fender, for deadening the jar caused by the collision of bodies; as, a buffer at the end of a railroad car. (b) A pad or cushion forming the end of a fender, which recieves the blow; Ð sometimes called buffing apparatus.

One who polishes with a buff.

A wheel for buffing; a buff.

A goodDhumored, slowDwitted fellow; Ð usually said of an elderly man. [Colloq.]

Dickens.

BufferIhead · (?), n. The head of a buffer, which recieves the concussion, in railroad carriages.

BufIfet (?), n. [F. buffet, LL. bufetum; of uncertain origin; perh. fr. the same source as E. buffet a blow, the root meaningÿto puff, hence (cf. puffed up) the idea of ostentation or display.] 1. A cupboard or set of shelves, either movable or fixed at one side of a room, for the display of plate, china, etc., a sideboard.

Not when a gilt buffet's reflected pride
Turns you from sound philosophy aside.
Pope.

A counter for refreshments; a restaurant at a railroad station, or place of public gathering.

Buffet (?), n. [OE. buffet, boffet, OF. buffet a slap in the face, a pair of bellows, fr. buffe blow, cf. F. bouffer to blow, puff; prob. akin to E. puff. For the meaning slap, blow, cf. F. soufflet a slap, souffler to blow. See Puff, v.i., and cf. Buffet sidebroad, Buffoon] 1. A blow with the hand; a slap on the face; a cuff.

When on his cheek a buffet fell.
Sir W.Scott.

A blow from any source, or that which affects like a blow, as the violence of winds or waves; a stroke; an adverse action; an affliction; a trial; adversity.

Those planks of tough and hardy oak that used for yeas to brave the buffets of the Bay of Biscay.
Burke.

Fortune's buffets and rewards.
Shak.

A small stool; a stool for a buffet or counter.

Go fetch us a light buffet.
Townely Myst.

Buffet, v.t. [imp. & p.p. Buffeted; p.pr. & vb.n. Buffeting.] [OE. buffeten, OF. buffeter. See the preceding noun.] 1. To strike with the hand or fist; to box; to beat; to cuff; to slap.

They spit in his face and buffeted him.
Matt.xxvi.67.

To affect as with blows; to strike repeatedly; to strive with or contend against; as, to buffet the billows.

The sudden hurricane in thunder roars,
Buffets the bark, and whirls it from the shores.
Broome.
You are lucky fellows who can live in a dreamland of your own, instead of being buffeted about the world.
W.Black.

[Cf. Buffer.] To deaden the sound of (bells) by muffling the clapper.

Buffet, v.i. 1. To exercise or play at boxing; to strike; to smite; to strive; to contend.

If I might buffet for my love, or bound my horse for her favors, I could lay on like a butcher.
Shak.

To make one's way by blows or struggling.

Strove to buffet to land in vain.
Tennyson.
Buffetĭer (?), n. One who buffets; a boxer.
Jonson.
Buffetĭing, n. 1. A striking with the hand.

A succession of blows; continued violence, as of winds or waves; afflictions; adversity.

He seems to have been a plant of slow growth, but ... fitted to endure the buffeting on the rudest storm.
Wirt.
Buffin (?), n. [So called from resembling buff ?eather.] A sort of coarse stuff; as, buffin gowns. [Obs.]

Buffing ap · paĭratus (?). See Buffer, 1.

Buffle (?), n. [OE., from F. buffle. See Buffalo.] The buffalo. [Obs.]
Sir T.Herbert.

Buffle, v.i. To puzzle; to be at a loss. [Obs.]
Swift.

Bufflehead · (?), n. [Buffle + head.] 1. One who has a large head; a heavy, stupid fellow. [Obs.]

What makes you stare so, bufflehead?
Plautus (trans. 1694).

(Zo"l.) The buffel duck. See Buffel duck.

BuffleĐhead · ed, a. Having a large head, like a buffalo; dull; stupid; blundering. [Obs.]

So fell this buffleĐheaded giant.

Gayton.

ØBuffo (?), n.masc. [It. See Buffoon.] (Mus.) The comic actor in an opera.

Buffoon (?), n. [F. bouffon (cf. It. buffone, buffo, buffa, puff of wind, vanity, nonsense, trick), fr. bouffer to puff out, because the buffoons puffed out their cheeks for the amusement of the spectators. See Buffet a blow.] A man who makes a practice of amusing others by low tricks, antic gestures, etc.; a droll; a mimic; a harlequin; a clown; a merryĐandrew.

Buffoon (?), a. Characteristic of, or like, a buffoon. ½Buffoon stories.

Macaulay.

To divert the audience with buffoon postures and antic dances.

Melmoth.

Buffoon, v.i. To act the part of a buffoon. [R.]

Buffoon, v.t. To treat with buffoonery.

Glanwill.

Buffooner̈ly (?), n.; pl. Buffooneries (?). [F. bouffonnerie.] The arts and practices of a buffoon, as low jests, ridiculous pranks, vulgar tricks and postures.

Nor that it will ever constitute a wit to conclude a tart piece of buffoonery with a ½What makes you blush?

Spectator.

Buffoonish, a. Like a buffoon; consisting in low?jests or gestures.

Blair.

Buffoonism (?), n. The practices of a buffoon; buffoonery.

Buffoonly, a. Low; vulgar. [R.]

Apish tricks and buffoonly discourse.

Goodman.

Buffy (?), a. (Med.)ÿResembling, or characterized by, buff.

Buffy coat, the coagulated plasma of blood when the red corpuscles have so settled out that the coagulum appears nearky colorless. This is common in diseased conditions where the corpuscles run together more rapidly and in denser masses than usual.

Huxley.

ØBufo (?), n. [L. bufo a toad.] (Zo"l.) A genus of Amphibia including various species of toads.

Bufonl̈ite (?), n. [L. bufo toad: cf. F. bufonite.] (Paleon.) An old name for a fossil consisting of the petrified teeth and palatal bones of fishes belonging to the family of Pycnodonts (thick teeth), whose remains occur in the o"lite and chalk formations; toadstone; Đ so named from a notion that it was originally formed in the head of a toad.

597

Bug (?), n. [OE. bugge, fr. W. bwg, bwgan, hobgoblin, scarecrow, bugbear. Cf. Bogey, Boggle.] 1. A bugbear; anything which terrifies. [Obs.]
Sir, spare your threats:
The bug which you would fright me with I seek.
Shak.

(Zo"l.) A general name applied to various insects belonging to the Hemiptera; as, the squash bug; the chinch bug, etc.

(Zo"l.) An insect of the genus Cimex, especially the bedbug (C. lectularius). See Bedbug.

(Zo"l.) One of various species of Coleoptera; as, the ladybug; potato bug, etc.; loosely, any beetle.

(Zo"l.) One of certain kinds of Crustacea; as, the sow bug; pill bug; bait bug; salve bug, etc.

µ According to present popular usage in England, and among housekeepers in America, bug, when not joined with some qualifying word, is used specifically for bedbug. As a general term it is used very loosely in America, and was formerly used still more loosely in England. ½God's rare workmanshipÿin the ant, the poorest bug that creeps.„ Rogers (Naaman). ½This bug with gilded wings.„ Pope.

Bait bug. See under Bait. Ð Bug word, swaggering or threatening language. [Obs.]
Beau. & Fl.

Bug · aïboo (?), Bugbear · (?), n. [See Bug.] Something frightful, as a specter; anything imaginary that causes needless fright; something used to excite needless fear; also, something really dangerous, used to frighten children, etc. ½Bugaboos to fright ye.„
Lloyd.

But, to the world no bugbear is so great
As want of figure and a small estate.
Pope.

The bugaboo of the liberals is the church pray.
S.B.Griffin.

The great bugaboo of the birds is the owl.
J.Burroughs.

Syn. - Hobgoblin; goblin; specter; ogre; scarecrow.

Bugbane · (?), n. (Bot.) A perennial whiteÐflowered herb of the order Ranunculace‘ and genus Cimiciguga; bugwort. There are several species.

Bugbear · (?), n. Same as Bugaboo. Ð a. Causing needless fright.
Locke.

Bugbear · , v.t. To alarm with idle phantoms.

Bugfish · (?), n. (Zo"l.) The menhaden. [U.S.]

Bugger (?), n. [F. bougre, fr. LL. Bulgarus, a Bulgarian, and also a heretic; because the inhabitants of Bulgaria were infected with heresy. Those guilty of the crime of buggery were called heretics, because in the eyes of their adversaries there was nothing more heinous than heresy, and it was therefore thought that the origin of such a vice could only be owing to heretics.] 1. One guilty of buggery or unnatural vice; a sodomite.

A wretch; Đ sometimes used humorously or in playful disparagement. [Low]

Buggerly (?), n. [OF. bougrerie, bogrerie, heresy. See Bugger.] Unnatural sexual intercourse; sodomy.

Bugginess (?), n. [From Buggy, a.] The state of being infested with bugs.

Buggy (?), a. [From Bug.] Infested or abounding with bugs.

Buggy, n.; pl. Buggies. 1. A light one horse twoĐwheeled vehicle. [Eng.] Villebeck prevailed upon Flora to drive with him to the race in a buggy. Beaconsfield.

A light, fourĐwheeled vehicle, usually with one seat, and with or without a calash top. [U.S.]

Buggy cultivator, a cultivator with a seat for the driver. Đ Buggy plow, a plow, or set of plows, having a seat for the driver; Đ called also sulky plow.

Bugle (?), n. [OE. bugle buffalo, buffalo's horn, OF. bugle, fr. L. buculus a young bullock, steer, dim. of bos ox. See Cow the animal.] A sort of wild ox; a buffalo.

E.Phillips.

Bugle, n. [See Bugle a wild ox.] 1. A horn used by hunters.

(Mus.) A copper instrument of the horn quality of tone, shorter and more conical that the trumpet, sometimes keyed; formerly much used in military bands, very rarely in the orchestra; now superseded by the cornet; Đ called also the Kent bugle.

Bugle, n. [LL. bugulus a woman's ornament: cf. G. bgel a bent piece of metal or wood, fr. the same root as G. biegenÿto bend, E. bow to bend.] An elingated glass bead, of various colors, though commonly black.

Bugle, a. [From Bugle a bead.] Jet black. ½Bugle eyeballs.,

Shak.

Bugle, n. [F. bugle; cf. It. bugola, L. bugillo.] (Bot.) A plant of the genus Ajuga of the Mint family, a native of the Old World.

Yellow bugle, the Ajuga cham'pitys.

Bugled (?), a. Ornamented with bugles.

Bugle horn · (?). 1. A bugle.

One blast upon his bugle horn
Were worth a thousand men.
Sir W.Scott.

A drinking vessel made of horn. [Obs.]

And drinketh of his bugle horn the wine.
Chaucer.

Bugler (?), n. One who plays on a bugle.

Bugleïweed · (?), n. (Bot.) A plant of the Mint family and genus Lycopus; esp. L. Virginicus, which has mild narcotic and astringent properties, and is sometimes used as a remedy for hemorrhage.

Bugloss (?), n.; pl. Buglosses (?). [F. buglosse, L. buglossa, buglossus, fr. Gr. ? oxtongue ? ox + ? tongue.] (Bot.) A plant of the genus Anchusa, and especially the A. officinalis, sometimes called alkanet; oxtongue.

Small wild bugloss, the Asperugo procumbensÿand the Lycopsis arvensis. Đ Viper's bugloss, a species of Echium.

Bugwort · (?), n. (Bot.) Bugbane.

Buhl (?), Buhlwork (?), n. [From A.Ch.Boule, a French carver in wood.] Decorative woodwork in which tortoise shell, yellow metal, white metal, etc., are inlaid, forming scrolls, cartouches, etc. [Written also boule, boulework.]

Buhlbuhl (?), n. (Zo"l.) See Bulbul.

Buhrstone · (?), n. [OE. bur a whetstone for scythes.] (Min.) A cellular, flinty rock, used for mill stones. [Written also burrstone.]

Build (?), v.t. [imp. & p.p. Built (?); p.pr. & vb.n. Building. The regular imp. & p.p. Builded is antiquated.] [OE. bulden, bilden, AS. byldanÿto build, fr. bold house; cf. Icel. bÓl farm, abode, Dan. bol small farm, OSw. bol, b"le, house, dwelling, fr. root of Icel. b?a to dwell; akin to E. be, bower, boor. û97.] 1. To erect or construct, as an edifice or fabric of any kind; to form by uniting materials into a regular structure; to fabricate; to make; to raise.

Nor aught availed him now
To have built in heaven high towers.
Milton.

To raise or place on a foundation; to form, establish, or produce by using appropriate means.

Who builds his hopes in air of your good looks.
Shak.

To increase and strengthen; to increase the power and stability of; to settle, or establish, and preserve; Đ frequently with up; as, to build up one's constitution.

I commend you to God, and to the word of his grace, which is able to build you up.
Acts xx.32.

Syn. - To erect; construct; raise; found; frame.

Build (?), v.i. 1. To exercise the art, or practice the business, of building.

To rest or depend, as on a foundation; to ground one's self or one's hopes or opinions upon something deemed reliable; to rely; as, to build on the opinions or advice of others.

Build, n. Form or mode of construction; general figure; make; as, the build of a ship.

Builder (?), n. One who builds; one whose occupation is to build, as a carpenter, a shipwright, or a mason.

In the practice of civil architecture, the builder comes between the architect who designs the work and the artisans who execute it.
Eng. Cyc.

Building, n. 1. The act of constructing, erecting, or establishing.

Hence it is that the building of our Sion rises no faster.
Bp. Hall.

The art of constructing edifices, or the practice of civil architecture.

The execution of works of architecture necessarily includes building; but building is frequently employed when the result is not architectural.
Hosking.

That which is built; a fabric or edifice constructed, as a house, a church, etc.

Thy sumptuous buildings and thy wife's attire
Have cost a mass of public treasury.
Shak.

Built (?), n. Shape; build; form of structure; as, the built of a ship. [Obs.] Dryden.

Built, a. Formed; shaped; constructed; made; Ð often used in composition and preceded by the word denotingÿthe form; as, frigateÐbuilt, clipperÐbuilt, etc.

Like the generality of Genoese countrywomen, strongly built.
Landor.

Buke muslin (?). See Book muslin.

ØBukshish (?), n. See Backsheesh.

ØBulau (?), n. [Native name.] (Zo"l.) An East Indian insectivorous mammal (Gymnura Rafflesii), somewhat like a rat in appearance, but allied to the hedgehog.

<— p. 190 —>

Bulb (?), n. [L. bulbus, Gr. ?: cf. F. bulbe.] 1. (Bot.) A spheroidal body growing from a plant either above or below the ground (usually below), which is strictly a bud, consisting of a cluster of partially developed leaves, and producing, as it grows, a stem above, and roots below, as in the onion, tulip, etc. It differs from a corm in not being solid.

(Anat.) A name given to some parts that resemble in shape certain bulbous roots; as, the bulb of the aorta.

Bulb of the eye, the eyeball. Ð Bulb of a hair, the ½root,, or part whence the hair originates. Ð Bulb of the spinal cord, the medulla oblongata, often called simply bulb. Ð Bulb of a tooth, the vascular and nervous papilla contained in the cavity of the tooth.

An expansion or protuberance on a stem or tube, as the bulb of a thermometer, which may be of any form, as spherical, cylindrical, curved, etc.

Tomlinson.

Bulb, v.i. To take the shape of a bulb; to swell.

Bulĭbaceous (?), a. [L. bulbaceus. See Bulb, n.] Bulbous.

Jonson.

Bulbar (?), a. Of or pertaining to bulb; especially, in medicine, pertaining to the bulb of the spinal cord, or medulla oblongata; as, bulbar paralysis.

Bulbed (?), a. Having a bulb; roundÐheaded.

Bulbel (?), n. [Dim., fr. bulb, n.] (Bot.) A separable bulb formed on some flowering plants.

Bulĭbiferĭous (?), a. [Bulb, n. + Ĭferous: cf. F. bulbifŠre.] (Bot.) Producing bulbs.

Bulblet (?), n. [Bulb, n. + Ĭlet.] (Bot.) A small bulb, either produced on a larger bulb, or on some a‰rial part of a plant, as in the axils of leaves in the tiger lily, or replacing the flowers in some kinds of onion.

Bulĭbose (?), a. Bulbous.

BulboÐtu · ber (?), n. [Bulb, n. + tuber.] (Bot.) A corm.

Bulbous (?), a. [L. bulbosus: cf. F. bulbeux. See Bulb, n.] Having or containing bulbs, or a bulb; growing from bulbs; bulblike in shape or structure.

ØBulbul (?), n. [Per.] (Zo"l.) The Persian nightingale (Pycnonotus jocosus). The name is also applied to several other Asiatic singing birds, of the family Timaliidæ. The green bulbuls belong to the Chloropsis and allied genera. [Written also buhlbuhl.]

Bulbule (?), n. [L. bulbulus, dim. of bulbus. See Bulb, n.] A small bulb; a bulblet.

Bulchin (?), n. [Dim. of bull.] A little bull.

Bulge (?), n. [OE. bulge a swelling; cf. AS. belganÿto swell, OSw. bulgja, Icel. bÓlginn swollen, OHG. belganÿto swell, G. bulge leathern sack, Skr. b?hÿto be large, strong;ÿthe root meaning to swell. Cf. Bilge, Belly, Billow, Bouge, n.] 1. The bilge or protuberant part of a cask.

A swelling, protuberant part; a bending outward, esp. when caused by pressure; as, a bulge in a wall.

(Naut.) The bilge of a vessel. See Bilge, 2.

Bulge ways. (Naut.) See Bilge ways.

Bulge, v.i. [imp. & p.p. Bulged (?); p.pr. & vb.n. Bulging.] 1. Toÿswell or jut out; to bend outward, as a wall when it yields to pressure; to be protuberant; as, the wall bulges.

To bilge, as a ship; to founder.

And scattered navies bulge on distant shores.

Broome.

Bulgy (?), a. Bulged; bulging; bending, or tending to bend, outward. [Colloq.]

ØBuḯlimiḯa (?), **Buliḯmy** (?), } n. [NL. bulimia, fr. Gr. ?, lit., oxÐhunger; ? ox + ? hunger: cf. F. boulimie.] (Med.) A disease in which there is a perpetual and insatiable appetite for food; a diseased and voracious appetite.

ØBuḯlimus (?), n. [L. bulimusÿhunger. See Bulimy.] (Zo"l.) A genus of land snails having an elongated spiral shell, often of large size. The species are numerous ingabundant in tropical America.

Bulk (?), n. [OE. bulke, bolke, heap; cf. Dan. bulk lump, clod, OSw. bolk crowd, mass, Icel. b?lkast to be bulky. Cf. Boll, n., Bile a boil, Bulge, n.] 1. Magnitude of material substance; dimensions; mass; size; as, an ox or ship of great bulk.

Against these forces there were prepared near one hundred ships; not so great of bulk indeed, but of a more nimble motion, and more serviceable.

Bacon.

<small>The main mass or body; the largest or principal portion; the majority; as, the bulk of a debt.</small>

The bulk of the people must labor, Burke told them, ½to obtain what by labor can be obtained.

J.Morley.

<small>(Naut.) The cargo of a vessel when stowed.</small>

<small>The body. [Obs.]</small>

Shak.

My liver leaped within my bulk.

Turbervile.

Barrel bulk. See under Barrel. Ð To break bulk (Naut.), to begin to unload or more the cargo. Ð In bulk, in a mass; loose; not inclosed in separate packages or divided into separate parts; in such shape that any desired quantity may be taken or sold. Ð Laden in bulk, Stowed in bulk, having the cargo loose in the hold or not inclosed in boxes, bales, or casks. Ð Sale by bulk, a sale of goods as they are, without weight or measure.

Syn. - Size; magnitude; dimension; volume; bigness; largeness; massiveness.

Bulk (?), v.i. [imp. & p.p. Bulked (?); p.pr. & vb.n. Bulking.] To appear or seem to be, as to bulk or extent; to swell.

The fame of Warburton possibly bulked larger for the moment.

Leslie Stephen.

Bulk, n. [Icel. b¾lkr a beam, partition. Cf. Balk, n. & v.] A projecting part of a building. [Obs.]

Here, stand behind this bulk.

603

Shak.

Bulker (?), n. (Naut.) A person employed to ascertain the bulk or size of goods, in order to fix the amount of freight or dues payable on them.

Bulkhead · (?), n. [See Bulk part of a building.] 1. (Naut.) A partition in a vessel, to separate apartments on the same deck.

A structure of wood or stone, to resist the pressure of earth or water; a partition wall or structure, as in a mine; the limiting wall along a water front.

Bulked line, a line beyond which a wharf must not project; Ð usually, the harbor line.

Bulkiness (?), n. Greatness in bulk; size.

Bulky (?), a. Of great bulk or dimensions; of great size; large; thick; massive; as, bulky volumes.

A bulky digest of the revenue laws.

Hawthorne.

Bull (?), n. [OE. bule, bul, bole; akin to D. bul, G. bulle, Icel. boli, Lith. bullus, Lett. bollis, Russ. vol'; prob. fr. the root of AS. bellan, E. bellow.] 1. (Zo"l.) The male of any species of cattle (Bovid'); hence,ÿthe male of any large quadruped, as the elephant; also, the male of the whale.

µ The wild bullÿof the Old Testament is thought to be the oryx, a large speciesÿof antelope.

One who, or that which, resembles a bull in character or action.

Ps.xxii.12.

(Astron.) (a) Taurus, the second of the twelve signs of the zodiac. (b) A constellation of the zodiac between Aries and Gemini. It contains the Pleiades.

At last from Aries rolls the bounteous sun,
And the bright Bull receives him.
Thomson.

(Stock Exchange) One who operates in expectation of a rise in the price of stocks, or in order to effect such a rise. See 4th Bear, n., 5.

Bull baiting, the practice of baiting bulls, or rendering them furious, as by setting dogs to attack them. Ð John Bull, a humorous name for the English, collectively; also, an Englishman. ½GoodÐlooking young John Bull. W.D.Howells. Ð To take the bullÿby the horns, to grapple with a difficulty instead of avoiding it.

Bull, a. Of or pertaining to a bull; resembling a bull; male; large; fierce.

Bull batÿ(Zo"l.), the night hawk; Ð so called from the loud noise it makes while feeding on the wing, in the evening. Ð Bull calf. (a) A stupid fellow. Ð Bull mackerel (Zo"l.), the chub mackerel. Ð Bull pump (Mining), a direct singleÐacting pumping engine, in which the steam cylinder is placedÿaboveÿthe pump. Ð Bull snakeÿ(Zo"l.), the pine snake of the United States. Ð Bull stag, a castrated bull. See Stag. Ð Bull wheel, a wheel, or drum, on which a rope is woundÿfor lifting heavy articles, as logs, the tools in well boring, etc.

Bull, v.i. To be in heat; to manifest sexual desire as cows do. [Colloq.]

Bull, v.t. (Stock Exchange) To endeavor to raise the market price of; as, to bull railroad bonds; to bull stocks; to bull Lake Shore; to endeavor to raise prices in; as, to bull the market. See 1st Bull, n., 4.

Bull, n. [OE. bulle, fr. L. bulla bubble, stud, knob, LL., a seal or stamp: cf. F. bulle. Cf. Bull a writing, Bowl a ball, Boil, v.i.] 1. A seal. See Bulla.

A letter, edict, or respect, of the pope, written in Gothic characters on rough parchment, sealed with a bulla, and dated ½a die Incarnationis, i.e., ½from the day of the Incarnation. See Apostolical brief, under Brief.

A fresh bull of Leo's had declared how inflexible the court of Rome was in the point of abuses.

Atterbury.

A grotesque blunder in language; an apparent congruity, but real incongruity, of ideas, contained in a form of expression; so called, perhaps, from the apparent incongruity between the dictatorial nature of the pope's bulls and his professions of humility.

And whereas the papist boasts himself to be a Roman Catholic, it is a mere contradiction, one of the pope's bulls, as if he should say universal particular; a Catholic schimatic.

Milton.

The Golden Bull, an edict or imperial constitution made by the emperor Charles IV. (1356), containing what became the fundamental law of the German empire; Ð so called from its golden seal.

Syn. - See Blunder.

ØBulla (?), n.; pl. Bull' (?). [L. bulla bubble. See Bull an edict.] 1. (Med.) A bleb; a vesicle, or an elevation of the cuticle, containing a transparent watery fluid.

(Anat.) The ovoid prominence below the opening of the ear in the skulls of many animals; as, the tympanic or auditory bulla.

A leaden seal for a document; esp. the round leaden seal attached to the papal bulls, which has on one side a representation of St. Peter and St. Paul, and on the other the name of the pope who uses it.

(Zo"l.) A genus of marine shells. See Bubble shell.

Bullace (?), n. [OE. bolas, bolace, OF. beloce; of Celtic origin; cf. Arm. bolos, polos, Gael. bulaistear.] (Bot.) (a) A small European plum (Prunus communis, var. insitita). See Plum. (b) The bully tree.

Bullantic (?), a. [See Bull an edict.] Pertaining to, or used in, papal bulls.

Fry.

Bullantic letters, Gothic letters used in papal bulls.

Bullaīry (?), n. [LL. bullarium: cf. F. bullairie. See Bull an edict.] A collection of papal bulls.

Bullaīry, n.; pl. Bullaries (?). [Cf. Boilary.] A place for boiling or preparating salt; a boilery.

Crabb.

And certain salt fats or bullaries.

Bills in Chancery.

Bullate (?), a. [L. bullatus, fr. bulla bubble.] (Biol.) Appearing as if blistered; inflated; puckered.

Bullate leafÿ(Bot.), a leaf, the membranous part of which rises between the veins puckered elevations convex on one side and concave on the other.

Bullbeg · gar (?), n. Something used or suggested to produce terror, as in children or persons of weak mind; a bugbear.

And being an illÐlooked fellow, he has a pension from the church wardens for being bullbeggar to all the forward children in the parish.

Mountfort (1691).

Bull bri · er (?). (Bot.) A speciesÿof Smilax (S. PseudoÐChina) growing from New Jersey to the Gulf of Mexico, which has very large tuberous and farinaceous rootstocks, formerly used by the Indians for a sort of bread, and by the negroes as an ingredient in making beer; Ð called also bamboo brier and China brier.

Bullcombīer (?), n. (Zo"l.) A scaraboid beetle; esp. the Typh'us vulgarisÿof Europe.

Bulldog · (?), n. 1. (Zo"l.) A variety of dog, of remarkable ferocity, courage, and tenacity of grip; Ð so named, probably, from being formerly employed in baiting bulls.

(Metal.) A refractory material used as a furnace lining, obtained by calcining the cinder or slag from the puddling furnace of a rolling mill.

Bulldog · , a. Characteristic of, or like, a bulldog; stubborn; as, bulldog courage; bulldog tenacity.

Bulldog batÿ(Zo"l.), a bat of the genus Nyctinomus; Ð so called from the shape of its face.

Bulldoze · (?), v.t. [imp. & p.p. Bulldozed (?); p.pr. & vb.n. Bulldozing.] To intimidate; to restrain or coerce by intimidation or violence; Ð used originally of the intimidation of negro voters, in Louisiana. [Slang, U.S.]

Bulldo · zer (?), n. One who bulldozes. [Slang]

Bulled (?), a. [Cf. Boln.] Swollen. [Obs.]

ØBullenÐbullen (?), n. [Native Australian name, from its cry.] (Zo"l.) The lyre bird.

BullenÐnail · (?), n. [Bull large, having a large head + nail.] A nail with a round head and short shank, tinned and lacquered.

Bullet (?), n. [F. boulet, dim. of boule ball. See Bull an edict, and cf. Boulet.] 1. A small ball.

A missile, usually of lead, and round or elongated in form, to be discharged from a rifle, musket, pistol, or other small firearm.

A cannon ball. [Obs.]

A ship before Greenwich ... shot off her ordnance, one piece being charged with a bullet of stone.
Stow.

The fetlock of a horse. [See Illust. under Horse.]

Bullet-proof · (?), a. Capable of resisting the force of a bullet.
Bullet tree. See Bully tree. — Bullet wood, the wood of the bullet tree.
Bulletin (?), n. [F. bulletin, fr. It. bullettino, dim. of bulletta, dim. of bulla, bolla, an edict of the pope, from L. bulla bubble. See Bull an edict.] 1. A brief statement of facts respecting some passing event, as military operations or the health of some distinguished personage, issued by authority for the information of the public.

Any public notice or announcement, especially of news recently received.

A periodical publication, especially one containing the proceeding of a society.

Bulletin board, a board on which announcements are put, particularly at newsrooms, newspaper offices, etc.
Bullfaced · (?), a. Having a large face.
Bullfeast · (?), n. See Bullfight. [Obs.]
Bullfight · (?), **Bullfight** · ing, n. A barbarous sport, of great antiquity, in which men torment, and fight with, a bull or bulls in an arena, for public amusement, — still popular in Spain. — Bullfight · er (?), n.
Bullfinch · (?), n. (Zo"l.) A bird of the genus Pyrrhula and other related genera, especially the P. vulgaris or rubicilla, a bird of Europe allied to the grosbeak, having the breast, cheeks, and neck, red.

¶ As a cage bird it is highly valued for its remarkable power of learning to whistle correctly various musical airs.

Crimson-fronted bullfinch. (Zo"l.) See Burion. — Pine bullfinch, the pine finch.
Bullfist (?), **Bullfice** (?), n. [Cf. G. bofist, AS. wulfes fist puffball, E. fizz, foist.] (Bot.) A kind of fungus. See Puffball.
Bull fly · or **Bullfly** · (?), n. (Zo"l.) Any large fly troublesome to cattle, as the gadflies and breeze flies.
Bullfrog · (?), n. (Zo"l.) A very large species of frog (Rana Catesbiana), found in North America; — so named from its loud bellowing in spring.
Bullhead · (?), n. 1. (Zo"l.) (a) A fresh-water fish of many species, of the genus Uranidea, esp. U. gobio of Europe, and U. Richardsoni of the

United States; Ð called also miller's thumb. (b) In America, several species of Amiurus; Ð called also catfish, horned pout, and bullpout. (c) A marine fish of the genus Cottus; the sculpin.

(Zo"l.) (a) The blackÐbellied plover (Squatarola helvetica); Ð called also beetlehead. (b) The golden plover.

A stupid fellow; a lubber. [Colloq.]

Jonson.

(Zo"l.) A small black water insect.

E.Phillips.
Bullhead whiting (Zo"l.), the kingfish of Florida (Menticirrus alburnus).
<— p. 191 —>
Bullhead · ed (?), a. Having a head like that of a bull. Fig.: Headstrong; obstinate; dogged.

Bullion (?), n. [Cf. OE. bullyon a hook used for fastening the dress, a button, stud, an embossed ornament of various kinds, e.g., on the cover of a book, on bridles or poitrels, for purses, for breeches and doublets, LL. bullio the swelling of boiling water, a mass of gold or silver, fr. L. bulla boss, stud, bubble (see Bull an edict), or perh. corrupted fr. ?. billon base coin, LL. billioÿbullion. Cf. Billon, Billet a stick.] 1. Uncoined gold or silver in the mass.

µ Properly, the precious metals are called bullion, when smelted and not perfectly refined, or when refined, but in bars, ingots or in any form uncoined, as in plate. The word is often often used to denote gold and silver, both coined and uncoined, when reckoned by weight and in mass, including especially foreign, or uncurrent, coin.

Base or uncurrent coin. [Obs.]

And those which eld's strict doom did disallow,
And damm for bullion, go for current now.
Sylvester.

Showy metallic ornament, as of gold, silver, or copper, on bridles, saddles, etc. [Obs.]

The clasps and bullions were worth a thousand pound.
Skelton.

Heavy twisted fringe, made of fine gold or silver wire and used for epaulets; also, any heavy twisted fringe whose cords are prominent.

Bullionïist, n. An advocate for a metallic currency, or a paper currency always convertible into gold.

Bullirag (?), v.t. [Cf. bully, n. & v., and rag to scold, rail. Cf. Ballarag.] To intimidate by bullying; to rally contemptuously; to badger. [Low]

Bullish (?), a. Partaking of the nature of a bull, or a blunder.

Let me inform you, a toothless satire is as improper as a toothed sleek stone, and as bullish.

Milton.

Bullist, n. [F. bulliste. See Bull an edict.] A writer or drawer up of papal bulls. [R.]

Harmar.

Bullition (?), n. [L. bullire, bullitum, to boil. See Boil, v.i.] The action of boiling; boiling. [Obs.] See Ebullition.

Bacon.

BullÐnecked · (?), a. Having a short and thick neck like that of a bull.

Sir W.Scott.

Bullock (?), n. [AS. bulluc a young bull. See Bull.] 1. A young bull, or any male of the ox kind.

Take thy father's young bullock, even the second bullock of seven years old.

Judges vi.25.

An ox, steer, or stag.

Bullock, v.t. To bully. [Obs.]

She shan't think to bullock and domineer over me.

Foote.

Bullock'sÐeye · (?), n. See Bull'sÐeye, 3.

ØBullon (?), n. (Zo"l.) A West Indian fish (Scarus Croicensis).

Bullpout · (?), n. (Zo"l.) See Bullhead, 1 (b).

Bull'sÐeye · (?), n. 1. (Naut.) A small circular or oval wooden block without sheaves, having a groove around it and a hole through it, used for connecting rigging.

A small round cloud, with a ruddy center, supposed by sailors to portend a storm.

A small thick disk of glass inserted in a deck, roof, floor, ship's side, etc., to let in light.

A circular or oval opening for air or light.

A lantern, with a thick glass lens on one side for concentrating the light on any object; also, the lens itself.

Dickens.

(Astron.) Aldebaran, a bright star in the eye of Taurus or the Bull.

(Archery & Gun.) The center of a target.

A thick knob or protuberance left on glass by the end of the pipe through which it was blown.

A small and thick oldÐfashioned watch. [Colloq.]

Bull's‐nose· (?), n. (Arch.) An external angle when obtuse or rounded.

Bull terrier (?). (Zoöl.) A b?eed of dogs obtained by crossing the bulldog and the terrier.

Bull trout· (?). (Zoöl.) (a) In England, a large salmon trout of ??? species, as Salmo ??? and S. Cambricus, which ascend rivers; Ð called also sea trout. (b) Salvelinus malma of California and Oregon; Ð called also Dolly Varden troutÿand redÐspotted trout. (c) The huso or salmon of the Danube.

Bullweed· (?), n. [Bole a stem + weed.] (Bot.) Knapweed.

Prior.

Bullwort· (?), n. (Bot.) See Bishop's‐weed.

Bully (?), n.; pl. Bullies (?). [Cf. LG. bullerjaan, bullerb„k, bullerbrook, a blusterer, D. bulderaar a bluster, bulderen to bluster; prob. of imitative origin; or cf. MHG. buole lover, G. buhle.] 1. A noisy, blustering fellow, more insolent than courageous; one who is threatening and quarrelsome; an insolent, tyrannical fellow.

Bullies seldom execute the threats they deal in.

Palmerston.

A brisk, dashing fellow. [Slang Obs.]

Shak.

Bully (?), a. 1. Jovial and blustering; dashing. [Slang] ½Bless thee, bully doctor.¸

Shak.

Fine; excellent; as, a bully horse. [Slang, U.S.]

Bully, v.t. [imp. & p.p. Bullied (?); p.pr. & vb.n. Bullying.] To intimidate with threats and by an overbearing, swaggering demeanor; to act the part of a bully toward.

For the last fortnight there have been prodigious shoals of voluntrees gone over to bully the French, upon hearing the peace was just singing.

Tatler.

Syn. - To bluster; swagger; hector; domineer.

Bully, v.i. To act as a bully.

Bully‐rag (?), v.t. Same as Bullirag.

Bully‐rock· (?), n. A bully. [Slang Obs.]

Shak.

Bully tree· (?). (Bot.) The name of several West Indian trees of the order Sapotace‘, as Dipholis nigraÿand species of SapotaÿandMimusops. Most of them yield a substance closely resembling guttaÐpercha.

Bulrush· (?), n. [OE. bulrysche, bolroysche; of uncertain origin, perh. fr. bole stem + rush.] (Bot.) A kind of large rush, growing in wet land or in water.

µ The name bulrush is applied in England especially to the catÐtail (Typha latifolia and T. angustifolia) and to the lake clubÐrush (Scirpus lacustris); in America, to the Juncus effusus, and also to species of Scirpus or clubÐrush.

ØBulse (?), n. A purse or bag in which to carry or measure diamonds, etc. [India]

Macaulay.

Bultel (?), n. [LL. bultellus. See Bolt to sift.] A bolter or bolting cloth; also, bran. [Obs.]

Bulti (?), n. (Zo"l.) Same as Bolty.

Bultow · (?), n. A trawl; a boulter; the mod? of fishing with a boulter or spiller.

Bulwark (?), n. [Akin to D. bolwerk, G. bollwerk, Sw. bolwerk, Dan. bolv„rk, bulv„rk, rampart; akin to G. bohle plank, and werk work, defense. See Bole stem, and Work, n., and cf. Boulevard.] 1. (Fort.) A rampart; a fortification; a bastion or outwork.

> That which secures against an enemy, or defends from attack; any means of defense or protection.

> The royal navy of England hath ever been its greatest defense, ... the floating bulwark of our island.
> Blackstone.

pl. (Naut.) The sides of a ship above the upper deck.

Syn. - See Rampart.

Bulwark, v.t. [imp. & p.p. Bulwarked (?); p.pr. & vb.n. Bulwarking.] To fortify with, or as with, a rampart or wall; to secure by fortification; to protect.

> Of some proud city, bulwarked round and armed
> With rising towers.
> Glover.

Bum (?), n. [Contr. fr. bottom in this sense.] The buttock. [Low]

Shak.

Bum, v.i. [imp. & p.p. Bummed (?); p.pr. & vb.n. Bumming (?).] [See Boom, v.i., to roar.] To make murmuring or humming sound.

Jamieson.

Bum, n. A humming noise.

Halliwell.

Bumbailiff (?), n. [A corruption of bound bailiff.] [Low, Eng.] See Bound bailiff, under Bound, a.

Bumbard (?). See Bombard.ÿ[Obs.]

Bumbarge · (?), n. See Bumboat.

Carlyle.

Bumbast (?). See Bombast. [Obs.]

Bumbello (?), n.; pl. Bumbeloes (?). [It. bombola.] A glass used in subliming camphor. [Spelled also bombolo and bumbolo.]

Bumble (?), n. [See Bump to boom.] (Zo"l.) The bittern. [Local, Eng.]

Bumble, v.i. To make a hollow or humming noise, like that of a bumblebee; to cry as a bittern.

As a bittern bumbleth in the mire.

Chaucer.

Bumblebee · (?), n. [OE. bumblen to make a humming noise (dim. of bum, v.i.) + bee. Cf. Humblebee.] (Zo"l.) A large bee of the genus Bombus, sometimes called humblebee; Ð so named from its sound.

μ There are many species. All gather honey, and store it in the empty cocoons after the young have come out.

Bumboat · (?), n. [From bum the buttocks, on account of its clumsy form; or fr. D. bun a box for holding fish in a boat.] (Naut.) A clumsy boat, used for conveying provisions, fruit, etc., for sale, to vessels lying in port or off shore.

Bumkin (?), n. [Boom a beam + Ikin. See Bumpkin.] (Naut.) A projecting beam or boom; as: (a) One projecting from each bow of a vessel, to haul the fore tack to, called a tack bumpkin. (b) Onr from each quarter, for the mainÐbrace blocks, and called brace bumpkin. (c) A small outrigger over the stern of a boat, to extend the mizzen. [Written also boomkin.]

ØBummallo (?), n. [Native name.] (Zo"l.) A small marine Asiatic fish (Saurus ophidon) used in India as a relish; Ð called also Bombay duck.

Bummer (?), n. An idle, worthless fellow, who is without any visible means of support; a dissipated sponger. [Slang, U.S.]

Bummelry (?), n. See Bottomery. [Obs.]

There was a scivener of Wapping brought to hearing for relief against a bummery bond.

R.North.

Bump (?), v.t. [imp. & p.p. Bumped (?); p.pr. & vb.n. Bumping.] [Cf. W. pwmp round mass, pwmpiaw to thump, bang, and E. bum, v.i., boom to roar.] To strike, as with or against anything large or solid; to thump; as, to bump the head against a wall.

Bump, v.i. To come in violent contact with something; to thump. ½Bumping and jumping.„

Southey.

Bump (?), n. [From Bump to strike, to thump.] 1. A thump; a heavy blow.

A swelling or prominence, resulting from a bump or blow; a protuberance.

It had upon its brow
A bump as big as a young cockerel's stone.
Shak.

(Phren.) One of the protuberances on the cranium which are associated with distinct faculties or affections of the mind; as, the bump of ½veneration;, the bump of ½acquisitiveness., [Colloq.]

The act of striking the stern of the boat in advance with the prow of the boat following. [Eng.]

Bump, v.i. [See Boom to roar.] To make a loud, heavy, or hollow noise, as the bittern; to boom.

As a bittern bumps within a reed.
Dryden.

Bump, n. The noise made by the bittern.

Bumper (?), n. [A corruption of bumbard, bombard, a large drinking vessel.] 1. A cup or glass filled to the brim, or till the liquor runs over, particularly in drinking a health or toast.

He frothed his bumpers to the brim.
Tennyson.

A covered house at a theater, etc., in honor of some favorite performer. [Cant]

Bumper (?), n. 1. That which bumps or causes a bump.

Anything which resists or deadens a bump or shock; a buffer.

Bumpkin (?), n. [The same word as bumkin, which Cotgrave defines thus: ½Bumkin, Fr. chicambault, the luffeÐblock, a long and thick piece of wood, whereunto the foreÐsayle and spritÐsayle are fastened, when a ship goes by the winde., Hence, a clumsy man may easily have been compared to such a block of wood; cf. OD. boomken a little tree. See Boom a pole.] An awkward, heavy country fellow; a clown; a country lout. ½Bashful country bumpkins.,
W.Irving.

Bumptious (?), a. SelfÐconceited; forward; pushing. [Colloq.]
Halliwell.

BumptiousÏness, n. Conceitedness. [Colloq.]

Bun, Bunn (?), n. [Scot. bun, bunn, OE. bunne, bonne; fr. Celtic; cf. Ir. bunna, Gael. bonnach, or OF. bugne tumor, Prov. F. bugne a kind of pancake; akin to OHG. bungo bulb, MHG. bunge, Prov. E. bung heap, cluster, bunny a small swelling.] A slightly sweetened raised cake or bisquit with a glazing of sugar and milk on the top crust.

Bunch (?), n. [Akin to OSw. & Dan. bunke heap, Icel. bunki heap, pile, bunga tumor, protuberance; cf. W. pwng cluster. Cf. Bunk.] 1. A protuberance; a hunch; a knob or lump; a hump.

They will carry ... their treasures upon the bunches of camels.
Isa.xxx.6.

A collection, cluster, or tuft, properly of things of the same kind, growing or fastened together; as, a bunch of grapes; a bunch of keys.

(Mining) A small isolated mass of ore, as distinguished from a continuous vein.

Page.

Bunch, v.i. [imp. & p.p. Bunched (?); p.pr. & vb.n. Bunching.] To swell out into a bunch or protuberance; to be protuberant or round.

Bunching out into a large round knob at one end.
Woodward.

Bunch, v.t. To form into a bunch or bunches.

BunchÐbacked· (?), a. Having a bunch on the back; crooked. ½BunchÐbacked toad.

Shak.

Bunchber·ry (?), n. (Bot.) The dwarf cornel (Cornus Canadensis), which bears a dense cluster of bright red, edible berries.

Bunch grass· (?). (Bot.) A grass growing in bunches and affording pasture. In California, Atropis tenuifolia, Festuca scabrella, and several kinds of Stipa are favorite bunch grasses. In Utah, Eriocoma cuspidata is a good bunch grass.

Bunchiïness (?), n. The quality or condition of being bunchy; knobbiness.

Bunchy (?), a. 1. Swelling out in bunches.

An unshapen, bunchy spear, with bark unpiled.
Phaer.

Growing in bunches, or resembling a bunch; having tufts; as, the bird's bunchy tail.

(Mining) Yielding irregularly; sometimes rich, sometimes poor; as, a bunchy mine.

Page.

Buncombe, Bunkum (?), n. [Buncombe a country of North Carolina.] SpeechÐmaking for the gratification of constituents, or to gain public applause; flattering talk for a selfish purpose; anything said for mere show. [Cant or Slang, U.S.]

All that flourish about right of search was bunkum Ð all that brag about hanging your Canada sheriff was bunkum ... slavery speeches are all bunkum.
Haliburton.

To speak for Buncombe, to speak for mere show, or popularly.

µ ½The phrase originated near the close of the debate on the famous 'Missouri Question,' in the 16th Congress. It was then used by Felix Walker Ð a na‹ve old mountaineer, who resided at Waynesville, in Haywood, the most western country of North Carolina, near the border of the adjacent country of Buncombe, which formed part of his district. The old man rose to speak, while the house was impatiently calling for the 'Question,' and several members gathered round him, begging him to desist. He preserved, however, for a while, declaring that the people of his district expected it, and that he was bound to 'make a speech for Buncombe.'

W.Darlington.

ØBund (?), n. [G.] League; confederacy; esp. the confederation of German states.

ØBund (?), n. [Hindi band.] An embankment against inundation. [India] S. Wells Williams.

ØBunder (?), n. [Pers. bandar a landing place, pier.] A boat or raft used in the East Indies in the landing of passengers and goods.

<— p. 192 —>

ØBundesİrath · (?), n. [G., from bund (akin to E. bond) confederacy + rath council, prob. akin to E. read.] The federal council of the German Empire. In the Bundesrath and the Reichstag are vested the legislative functions. The federal council of Switzerland is also so called.

μ The Bundesrath of the German empire is presided over by a chancellor, and is composed of sixtyÐtwo members, who represent the different states of the empire, being appointed for each session by their respective governments.

By this united congress, the highest tribunal of Switzerland, Ð the Bundesrath Ð is chosen, and the head of this is a president.

J.P.Peters (Trans.Mller's Pol. Hist.).

Bundle (?), n. [OE. bundel, AS. byndel; akin to D. bondel, bundel, G. bndel, dim. of bund bundle, fr. the root of E. bind. See Bind.] A number of things bound together, as by a cord or envelope, into a mass or package convenient for handling or conveyance; a loose package; a roll; as, a bundle of straw or of paper; a bundle of old clothes.

The fable of the rods, which, when united in a bundle, no strength could bend.

Goldsmith.

Bundle pillar (Arch.), a column or pier, with others of small dimensions attached to it.

Weale.

Bundle, v.t. [imp. & p.p. Bundled (?); p.pr. & vb.n. Bundling (?).] 1. To tie or bind in a bundle or roll.

To send off abruptly or without ceremony.

They unmercifully bundled me and my gallant second into our own hackney coach.

T.Hook.

To bundle off, to send off in a hurry, or without ceremony. Ð To bundle one's self up, to wrap one's self up warmly or cumbrously.

Bundle, v.i. 1. To prepare for departure; to set off in a hurry or without ceremony.

To sleep on the same bed without undressing; Ð applied to the custom of a man and woman, especially lovers, thus sleeping.

Bartlett.

Van Corlear stopped occasionally in the villages of eat pumpkin pies, dance at country frolics, and bundle with the Yankee lasses.

W.Irving.

Bung (?), n. [Cf. W. bwng orfice, bunghole, Ir. buinne tap, spout, OGeal. buine.] 1. The large spotter of the orfice in the bilge of a cask.

The orfice in the bilge of a cask through which it is filled; bunghole.

A sharper or pickpocket. [Obs. & Low]

You gilthy bung, away.

Shak.

Bung, v.t. [imp. & p.p. Bunged (?); p.pr. & vb.n. Bunging (?).] To stop, as the orfice in the bilge of a cask, with a bung; to close; Ð with up.

To bung up, to use up, as by bruising or over exertion; to exhaust or incapacitate for action. [Low]

He had bunged up his mouth that he should not have spoken these three years.

Shelton (Trans. Don Quixote).

Bungaïlow (?), n. [Bengalee b¾ngl¾] A thatched or tiled house or cottage, of a single story, usually surrounded by a veranda. [India]

ØBungaÏrum (?), n. [Bungar, the native name.] (Zo"l.) A venomous snake of India, of the genus Bungarus, allied to the cobras, but without a hood.

Bunghole · (?), n. See Bung, n., 2.

Shak.

Bungle (?), v.i. [imp. & p.p. Bungled (?); p.pr. & vb.n. Bungling (?).] [Prob. a diminutive from, akin to bang; cf. Prov. G. bungen to beat, bang, OSw. bunga.ÿSee Bang.] The act or work in a clumsy, awkward manner.

Bungle, v.t. To make or mend clumsily; to manage awkwardly; to botch; Ð sometimes with up.

I always had an idea that it would be bungled.

Byron.

Bungle (?), n. A clumsy or awkward performance; a botch; a gross blunder.

Those errors and bungles which are committed.

Cudworth.

Bungler (?), n. A clumsy, awkward workman; one who bungles.

If to be a dunce or a bungler in any profession be shameful, how much more ignominious and infamous to a scholar to be such!

Barrow.

Bungling (?), a. Unskillful; awkward; clumsy; as, a bungling workman.

Swift.

They make but bungling work.

Dryden.

Bunglingly, adv. Clumsily; awkwardly.

Bungo (?), n. (Naut.) A kind of canoe used in Central and South America; also, a kind of boat used in the Southern United States. Bartlett.

Bunion (?), n. (Med.) Same as Bunyon.

Bunk (?), n. [Cf. OSw. *bunke* heap, also boaring, flooring. Cf. Bunch.] 1. A wooden case or box, which serves for a seat in the daytime and for a bed at night. [U.S.]

One of a series of berths or bed places in tiers.

A piece of wood placed on a lumberman's sled to sustain the end of heavy timbers. [Local, U.S.]

Bunk, v.i. [imp. & p.p. Bunked (?); p.pr. & vb.n. Bunking.] To go to bed in a bunk; Ð sometimes with *in*. [Colloq. U.S.] Bartlett.

Bunker (?), n. [Scot. *bunker, bunkart*, a bench, or low chest, serving for a seat. Cf. Bunk, Bank, Bench.] 1. A sort of chest or box, as in a window, the lid of which serves for a seat. [Scot.] Jamieson.

A large bin or similar receptacle; as, a coal bunker.

Bunko (?), n. [Sf. Sp. *banco* bank, *banca* a sort of game at cards. Cf. Bank (in the commercial sense).] A kind of swindling game or scheme, by means of cards or by a sham lottery. [Written also *bunco*.]

Bunko steerer, a person employed as a decoy in bunko. [Slang, U.S.]

Bunkum (?), n. See Buncombe.

Bunn (?), n. See Bun.

Bunnian (?), n. See Bunyon.

Bunny (?), n. (Mining) A great collection of ore without any vein coming into it or going out from it.

Bunny, n. A pet name for a rabbit or a squirrel.

Ø**Bu · noÏdonta** (?), **BunoÏdonts** (?), } n. pl. [NL. *bunodonta*, fr. Gr. ? hill, heap + ?, ?, a tooth.] (Zo"l.) A division of the herbivorous mammals including the hogs and hippopotami; Ð so called because the teeth are tuberculated.

Bunsen's battery (?), **Bunsen's burn·er** (?). See under Battery, and Burner.

Bunt (?), n. (Bot.) A fungus (*Ustilago fÒtida*) which affects the ear of cereals, filling the grains with a fetid dust; Ð also called *pepperbrand*.

Bunt, n. [Cf. Sw. *bunt* bundle, Dan. *bundt*, G. *bund*, E. *bundle*.] (Naut.) The middle part, cavity, or belly of a sail; the part of a furled sail which is at the center of the yard. Totten.

Bunt, v.i. (Naut.) To swell out; as, the sail bunts.

Bunt, v.t. & i. To strike or push with the horns or head; to butt; as, the ram bunted the boy.

Bunter (?), n. A woman who picks up rags in the streets; hence, a low, vulgar woman. [Cant]

Her ... daughters, like bunters in stuff gowns.

Goldsmith.

Bunting (?), n. [Scot. buntlin, cornÐbuntlin, OE. bunting, buntyle; of unknown origin.] (Zo"l.) A birdÿof the genus Emberiza, or of an allied genus, related to the finches and sparrows (family Fringillid').

µ Among European species are the common or corn bunting (Emberiza miliaria); the ortolan (E. hortulana); the cirl (E. cirlus); and the blackÐheaded (Granitivora melanocephala). American species are the bayÐwinged or grass (Po"c'tes or PoÒcetes gramineus); the blackÐthroated (Spiza Americana); the towhee bunting or chewink (Pipilo); the snow bunting (Plectrophanax nivalis); the rice bunting or bobolink, and others. See Ortolan, Chewick, Snow bunting, Lark bunting.

Bunting, Buntine (?), n. [Prov. E. bunting sifting flour, OE. bontenÿto sift, hence prob. the material used for that purpose.] A thin woolen stuff, used chiefly for flags, colors, and ships' signals.

Buntline (?), n. [2d bunt + line.] (Naut.) One of the ropes toggled to the footrope of a sail, used to haul up to the yard the body of the sail when taking it in.

Totten.

Bunyon, Bunion (?), n. [Cf. Prov. E. bunny a small swelling, fr. OF. bugne, It. bugna, bugnone. See Bun.] (Med.) An enlargement and inflammation of a small membranous sac (one of the burs' muscos'), usually occurring on the first joint of the great toe.

Buoy (?), n. [D. boei buoy, fetter, fr. OF. boie, buie, chain, fetter, F. bou‚e a buoy, from L. boia. ½Boiae genus vinculorum tam ferreae quam ligneae.¸ Festus. So called because chained to its place.] (Naut.) A float; esp. a floating object moored to the bottom, to mark a channel or to point out the position of something beneath the water, as an anchor, shoal, rock, etc.

Anchor buoy, aÿbuoy attached to, or marking the position of, an anchor. Ð Bell buoy, a large buoy on which a bell is mounted, to be rung by the motion of the waves. Ð Breeches buoy. See under Breeches. Ð Cable buoy, an empty cask employed to buoy up the cable in rocky anchorage. Ð Can buoy, a hollow buoy made of sheet or boiler iron, usually conical or pearÐshaped. Ð Life buoy, a float intended to support persons who have fallen into the water, until a boat can be dispatched to save them. Ð Nut or Nun buoy, a buoy large in the middle, and tapering nearly to a point at each end. Ð To stream the buoy, to let the anchor buoy fall by the ship's side into the water, before letting go the anchor. Ð Whistling buoy, aÿbuoy fitted with a whistle that is blown by the action of the waves.

Buoy, v.t. [imp. & p.p. Buoyed (?); p.pr. & vb.n. Buoying.] 1. To keep from sinking in a fluid, as in water or air; to keep afloat; Ð with up.

To support or sustain; to preserve from sinking into ruin or despondency.

Those old prejudices, which buoy up the ponderous mass of his nobility, wealth, and title.
Burke.

To fix buoys to; to mark by a buoy or by buoys; as, to buoy an anchor; to buoy or buoy off a channel.

Not one rock near the surface was discovered which was not buoyed by this floating weed.
Darwin.

Buoy, v.i. To float; to rise like a buoy. ½Rising merit will buoy up at last.„
Pope.

Buoyage (?), n. Buoys, taken collectively; a series of buoys, as for the guidance of vessels into or out of port; the providing of buoys.

Buoyance (?), n. Buoyancy. [R.]

Buoyancy (?), n.; pl. Buoyancies (?). 1. The property of floating on the surface of a liquid, or in a fluid, as in the atmosphere; specific lightness, which is inversely as the weight compared with that of an equal volume of water.

(Physics) The upward pressure exerted upon a floating body by a fluid, which is equal to the weight of the body; hence, also, the weight of a floating body, as measured by the volume of fluid displaced.

Such are buoyancies or displacements of the different classes of her majesty's ships.
Eng. Cyc.

Cheerfulness; vivacity; liveliness; sprightliness; Ð the opposite of heaviness; as, buoyancy of spirits.

Buoyant (?), a. [From Buoy, v.t. & i.] 1. Having the quality of rising or floating in a fluid; tending to rise or float; as, iron is buoyant in mercury. ½Buoyant on the flood.„
Pope.

Bearing up, as a fluid; sustaining another body by being specifically heavier.

The water under me was buoyant.
Dryden.

LightÐhearted; vivacious; cheerful; as, a buoyant disposition; buoyant spirits. Ð Buoyantly, adv.

Buĭprestiĭdan (?), n. [L. buprestis, Gr. ?, a poisonous beetle, which, being eaten by cattle in the grass, caused them to swell up and and die; ? ox, cow + ? to blow up, swell out.] (Zo"l.) One of a tribe of beetles, of the genus Buprestis and allied genera, usually with brilliant metallic colors. The larv' are usually bores in timber, or beneath bark, and are often very destructive to trees.

Bur, Burr (?), n. [OE. burre burdock; cf. Dan. borre, OSw. borra, burdock, thistle; perh. akin to E. bristle (burrĭ for burzĭ), or perh. to F. bourre hair, wool, stuff; also, according to Cotgrave, ½the downe, or hairie coat, wherewith divers herbes, fruits, and flowers, are covered, fr. L. burrae trifles, LL. reburrus rough.] 1. (Bot.) Any rough or prickly envelope of the seeds of plants, whether a pericarp, a persistent calyx, or an involucre, as of the chestnut and burdock. Also, any weed which bears burs.

Amongst rude burs and thistles.
Milton.
Bur and brake and brier.
Tennyson.

The thin ridge left by a tool in cutting or shaping metal. See Burr, n., 2.

A ring of iron on a lance or spear. See Burr, n., 4.

The lobe of the ear. See Burr, n., 5.

The sweetbread.

A clinker; a partially vitrified brick.

(Mech.) (a) A small circular saw. (b) A triangular chisel. (c) A drill with a serrated head larger than the shank; Ð used by dentists.

[Cf. Gael. borr, borra, a knob, bunch.] (Zo"l.) The round knob of an antler next to a deer's head. [Commonly written burr.]

Bur oakÿ(Bot.), a useful and ornamental species of oak (Quercus macrocarpa) with ovoid acorns inclosed in deep cups imbricated with pointed scales. It grows in the Middle and Western United States, and its wood is tough, closeÐgrained, and durable. Ð Bur reed (Bot.), a plant of the genus Sparganium, having long ribbonlike leaves.

Burbolt · (?), n. A birdbolt. [Obs.]
Ford.

Burbot (?), n. [F. barbote, fr. barbe beard. See 1st Barb.] (Zo"l.) A freshÐwater fish of the genus Lota, having on the nose two very small barbels, and a larger one on the chin. [Written also burbolt.]

μ The fish is also called an eelpout or ling, and is allied to the codfish. The Lota vulgaris is a common European species. An American species (L. maculosa) is found in New England, the Great Lakes, and farther north.

Bur · deĭlais (?), n. [F. bourdelais, prob. fr. bordelais. See Bordelais.] A sort of grape.
Jonson.

Burden (?), n. [Written also burthen.] [OE. burden, burthen, birthen, birden, AS. byr$en; akin to Icel. byr?i, Dan. byrde, Sw. b"rda, G. brde, OHG. burdi, Goth. ba£r?ei, fr. the root of E. bear, AS. beran, Goth. bairan. û92. See 1st Bear.] 1. That which is borne or carried; a load.

Plants with goodly burden bowing.
Shak.

That which is borne with labor or difficulty; that which is grievous, wearisome, or oppressive.

Deaf, giddy, helpless, left alone,
To all my friends a burden grown.
Swift.

The capacity of a vessel, or the weight of cargo that she will carry; as, a shipÿof a hundred tons burden.

(Mining) The tops or heads of streamÐwork which lie over the stream of tin.

(Metal.) The proportion of ore and flux to fuel, in the charge of a blast furnace.

Raymond.

A fixed quantity of certain commodities; as, a burden of gad steel, 120 pounds.

A birth. [Obs. & R.]

Shak.

Beast of burden, an animal employed in carrying burdens. Ð Burden of proof [L. onus probandi] (Law), the duty of proving a particular position in a court of law, a failure in the performance of which duty calls for judgment against the party on whom the duty is imposed.

Syn. - Burden, Load. A burden is, in the literal sense, a weight to be borne; a load is something laid upon us to be carried. Hence, when used figuratively, there is usually a difference between the two words. Our burdens may be of such a nature that we feel bound to bear them cheerfully or without complaint. They may arise from the nature of our situation; they may be allotments of Providence; they may be the consequences of our errors. What is upon us, as a load, we commonly carry with greater reluctance or sense of oppression. Men often find the charge of their own families to be a burden; but if to this be added a load of care for others, the pressure is usually serve and irksome.

Burden, v.t. [imp. & p.p. Burdened (?); p.pr. & vb.n. Burdening (?).] 1. To encumber with weight (literal or figurative); to lay a heavy load upon; to load.

I mean not that other men be eased, and ye burdened.
2 Cor.viii.13.

To oppress with anything grievous or trying; to overload; as, to burden a nation with taxes.

My burdened heart would break.
Shak.

To impose, as a load or burden; to lay or place as a burden (something heavy or objectionable). [R.]

It is absurd to burden this act on Cromwell.
Coleridge.
Syn. - To load; encumber; overload; oppress.
<— p. 193 —>
Burden (?), n. [OE. burdoun the bass in music, F. bourdon; cf. LL. burdo drone, a long organ pipe, a staff, a mule. Prob. of imitative origin. Cf. Bourdon.] 1. The verse repeated in a song, or the return of the theme at the end of each stanza; the chorus; refrain. Hence: That which is often repeated or which is dwelt upon; the main topic; as, the burden of a prayer.
I would sing my song without a burden.
Shak.

The drone of a bagpipe.

Ruddiman.
Burden, n. [See Burdon.] A club. [Obs.]
Spenser.
Burdenïer (?), n. One who loads; a oppressor.
Burdenïous (?), a. Burdensome. [Obs.] ½Burdenous taxations.„
Shak.
Burdenïsome (?), a. Grievous to be borne; causing uneasiness or fatigue; oppressive.
The debt immense of endless gratitude
So burdensome.
Milton.
Syn. - Heavy; weighty; cumbersome; onerous; grievous; oppressive; troublesome.
Ð Burdenïsomeïly, adv. Ð Burdenïsomeïness, n.
Burdock (?), n. [Bur + dock the plant.] (Bot.) A genus of coarse biennial herbs (Lappa), bearing small burs which adhere tenaciously to clothes, or to the fur or wool of animals.
µ The common burdock is the Lappa officinalis.
Burdon (?), n. [See Bourdon.] A pilgrim's staff. [Written also burden.]
Rom. of R.
Bureau (?), n.; pl. E. Bureaus (?), F. Bureaux (?). [F. bureau a writing table, desk, office, OF., drugget, with which a writing table was often covered, equiv. to F. bure, and fr. OF. buire dark brown, the stuff being named from its color, fr. L. burrus red, fr. Gr. ? flameÐcolored, prob. fr. ? fire. See

Fire, n., and cf. Borel, n.] 1. Originally, a desk or writing table with drawers for papers.
Swift.

The place where such a bureau is used; an office where business requiring writing is transacted.

Hence: A department of public business requiring a force of clerks; the body of officials in a department who labor under the direction of a chief.

µ On the continent of Europe, the highest departments, in most countries, have the name of bureaux; as, the Bureau of the Minister of Foreign Affairs. In Englandÿand America, the term is confined to inferior and subordinate departments; as, the ½Pension Bureau, a subdepartment of the Department of the Interior. [Obs.] In Spanish, bureo denotes a court of justice for the trial of persons belonging to the king's household.

A chest of drawers for clothes, especially when made as an ornamental piece of furniture. [U.S.]

Bureau system. See Bureaucracy. Ð Bureau Veritas, an institution, in the interest of maritime underwriters, for the survey and rating of vessels all over the world. It was founded in Belgium in 1828, removed to Paris in 1830, and re‰stablished in Brussels in 1870.

BuĬreaucraĬcy (?), n. [Bureau + Gr. ? to be strong, to govern, ? strength: cf. F. bureaucratie.] 1. A system of carrying on the business of government by means of departments or bureaus, each under the control of a chief, in contradiction to a system in which the officers of government have an associated authority and responsibility; also, government conducted on this system.

Government officials, collectively.

BuĬreaucrat (?), n. An official of a bureau; esp. an official confirmed in a narrow and arbitrary routine.
C.Kingsley.

Bu · reauĬcratic (?), Bu · reauĬcraticĬal (?), } a. [Cf. F. bureaucratique.] Of, relating to, or resembling, a bureaucracy.

BuĬreaucraĬtist (?), n. An advocate for, or supporter of, bureaucracy.

Burel (?), n. & a. Same as Borrel.

ØBuĬrette (?), n. [F., can, cruet, dim. of buire flagon.] (Chem.) An apparatus for delivering measured quantities of liquid or for measuring the quantity of liquid or gas received or discharged. It consists essentially of a graduated glass tube, usually furnished with a small aperture and stopcock.

Bur fish · (?). (Zo"l.) A spinose, plectognath fish of the Allantic coast of the United States (esp. Chilo mycterus geometricus) having the power of distending its body with water or air, so as to resemble a chestnut bur; Ð called also ball fish, balloon fish, and swellfish.

Burg (?), n. [AS. burh, burg, cf. LL. burgus. See 1st Borough.] 1. A fortified town. [Obs.]

A borough. [Eng.] See 1st Borough.

Burgage (?), n. [From Burg: cf. F. bourgage, LL. burgagium.] (Eng. Law) A tenure by which houses or lands are held of the king or other lord of a borough or city; at a certain yearly rent, or by services relating to trade or handicraft.

Burrill.

Burgall (?), n. (Zo"l.) A small marine fish; Ð also called cunner.

Burgalmot (?), n. See Bergamot.

Burgainet (?), n. See Burgonet.

Burgee (?), n. 1. A kind of small coat.

(Naut.) A swallowÐtailed flag; a distinguishing pen?ant, used by cutters, yachts, and merchant vessels.

Burǐgeois (?), n. (Print.) See 1st Bourgeous.

ØBurǐgeois (?), n. A burgess; a citizen. See 2d Bourgeois. [R.]

Addison.

Burgeon (?), v.i. To bud. See Bourgeon.

Burgess (?), n. [OE. burgeis, OF. burgeis, fr. burcfortified town, town, F. bourg village, fr. LL. burgus fort, city; from the German; cf. MHG. burc, G. burg. See 1st Borough, and cf. 2d Bourgeois.] 1. An inhabitant of a borough or walled town, or one who possesses a tenement therein; a citizen or freeman of a borough.

Blackstone.

µ ½A burgess of a borough corresponds with a citizen of a city.‚

Burrill.

One who represents a borough in Parliament.

A magistrate of a borough.

An inhabitant of a Scotch burgh qualified to vote for municipal officers.

µ Before the Revolution, the representatives in the popular branchÿof the legislature of Virginia were called burgesses; they are now called delegates.

Burgess oath. See Burgher, 2.

BurgessÐship (?), n. The state of privilege of a burgess.

South.

Burggrave (?), n. [G. burggraf; burg fortress + graf count: cf. D. burggraaf, F. burgrave. See Margrave.] (Gremany) Originally, one appointed to the command of a burg (fortress or castle); but the title afterward became hereditary, with a domain attached.

Burgh (?), n. [OE. See Burg.] A borough or incorporated town, especially, one in Scotland. See Borough.

Burghal (?), a. Belonging of a burgh.

Burghbote· (?), n. [Burgh + bote.] (Old Law) A contribution toward the building or repairing of castles or walls for the defense of a city or town.

Burghbrech· (?), n. [Burgh + F. brŠche, equiv. to E. breach.] (AS. Law) The offense of violating the pledge given by every inhabitant of a tithing to keep the peace; breach of the peace.

Burrill.

Burgher (?), n. [From burgh; akin to D. burger, G. brger, Dan. borger, Sw. borgare. See Burgh.] 1. A freeman of a burgh or borough, entitled to enjoy the privileges of the place; any inhabitant of a borough.

> (Eccl. Hist.) A member of that party, among the Scotch seceders, which asserted the lawfulness of the burgess oath (in which burgesses profess ½the true religion professed within the realm.), the opposite party being called antiburghers.

μ These parties arose among the Presbyterians of Scotland, in 1747, and in 1820 reunited under the name of the ½United Associate Synod of the Secession Church.

Burgherĭmas· ter (?), n. See Burgomaster.

Burgherĭship (?), n. The state or privileges of a burgher.

Burghmas· ter (?), n. 1. Aÿburgomaster.

> (Mining) An officer who directs and lays out the meres or boundaries for the workmen; Đ called also bailiff, and barmaster. [Eng.]

Burghmote· (?), n. (AS. Law) [Burgh + mote meeting.] A court or meeting of a burgh or borough; a borough court held three times yearly.

Burglar (?), n. [OE. burg town, F. bourg, fr. LL. burgus (of German origin) + OF. lere thief, fr. L. latro. See Borough, and Larceny.] (Law) One guilty of the crime of burglary.

Burglar alarm, a device for giving alarm if a door or window is opened from without.

Burglarĭer (?), n. A burglar. [Obs.]

Burĭglarĭĭous (?), a. Pertaining to burglary; constituting the crime of burglary.

To come down a chimney is held a burglarious entry.

Blackstone.

Burĭglarĭĭousĭly, adv. With an intent to commit burglary; in the manner of a burglar.

Blackstone.

Burglaĭry (?), n.; pl. Burglaries (?). [Fr. Burglar; cf. LL. burglaria.] (Law) Breaking and entering the dwelling house of another, in the nighttime, with intent to commit a felony therein, whether the felonious purpose be accomplished or not.

Wharton. Burrill.

µ By statute law in some of the United States, burglary includes the breaking with felonious intent into a house by day as well as by night, and into other buildings than dwelling houses. Various degrees of the crime are established.

Burgoïmas · ter (?), n. [D. burgemeester; burgÿborough + meester master; akin to G. burgemeister, brgermeister. See 1st Borough, and Master.] 1. A chief magistrate of a municipal town in Holland, Flanders, and Germany, corresponding to mayor in Englandÿand the United States; a burghmaster.

(Zo"l.) An aquatic bird, the glaucous gull (Larus glaucus), common in arctic regions.

Burgoïnet (?), n. [F. bouruignotte, because the Burgundians, F. Bouruignons, first used it.] A kind of helmet. [Written also burganet.]

Shak.

Burgoo (?), n. [Prov. E. burgood yeast, perh. fr. W. burym yeast + cawl cabbage, gruel.] A kind of oatmeal pudding, or thick gruel, used by seamen. [Written also burgout.]

Burgrass · (?), n. (Bot.) Grass of the genus Cenchrus, growing in sand, and having burs for fruit.

Burgrave (?), n. [F.] See Burggrave.

Burgunïdy (?), n. 1. An old province of France (in the eastern central part).

A richly flavored wine, mostly red, made in Burgundy, France.

Burgundy pitch, a resinous substance prepared from the exudation of the Norway spruce (Abies excelsa) by melting in hot water and straining through cloth. The genuine Burgundy pitch, supposed to have been first prepared in Burgundy, is rare, but there are many imitations. It has a yellowish brown color, is translucent and hard, but viscous. It is used in medicinal plasters.

Burh (?), n. See Burg. [Obs.]

Burhel, Burrhel } (?), n. (Zo"l.) The wild Himalayan, or blue, sheep (Ovis burrhel).

Buriïal (?), n. [OE. buriel, buriels, grave, tomb, AS. byrgels, fr. byrgan to bury, and akin to OS. burgisli sepulcher.] 1. A grave; a tomb; a place of sepulture. [Obs.]

The ert?e schook, and stoones weren cloven, and biriels weren opened.
Wycliff [Matt.xxvii.51, 52].

The act of burying; depositing a dead body in the earth, in a tomb or vault, or in the water, usually with attendant ceremonies; sepulture; interment. ½To give a public burial.

Shak.
Now to glorious burial slowly borne.

Tennyson.

Burial case, a form of coffin, usually of iron, made to close air‐tight, for the preservation of a dead body. Ð Burial ground, a piece of ground selected and set apart for a placeÿof buriials, and consecrated to such use by religious ceremonies. Ð Burial place, any place where burials are made. Ð Burial service. (a) The religious service performed at the interment of the dead; a funeral service. (b) That portion of a liturgy which is read at an interment; as, the English burial service.

Syn. - Sepulture; interment; inhumation.

Buriĺer (?), n. One who, or that which, buries.

Till the buriers have buried it.

Ezek.xxxix.15.

And darkness be the burier of the dead.

Shak.

Burin (?), n. [F. burin, cf. It. burino, bulino; prob. from OHG. bora borer, borÓn to bore, G. bohren. See 1st Bore.] 1. The cutting tool of an engraver on metal, used in line engraving. It is made of tempered steel, one end being ground off obliquely so as to produce a sharp point, and the other end inserted in a handle; a graver; also, the similarly shaped tool used by workers in marble.

The manner or style of execution of an engraver; as, a soft burin; a brilliant burin.

Burinĺist, n. One who works with the burin.

For. Quart. Rev.

Buriĺon (?), n. (Zo"l.) The red‐breasted house sparrow of California (Carpodacus frontalis); Ð called also crimson‐fronted bullfinch. [Written also burrion.]

Burke (?), v.t. [imp. & p.p. Burked (?); p.pr. & vb.n. Burking.] [From one Burke of Edinburgh, who committed the crime in 1829.] 1. To murder by suffocation, or so as to produce few marks of violence, for the purpose of obtaining a body to be sold for dessection.

To dispose of quietly or indirectly; to suppress; to smother; to shelve; as, to burke a parliamentary question.

The court could not burke an inquiry, supported by such a mass of a affidavits.

C.Reade.

Burkism (?), n. The practice of killing persons for the purpose of selling their bodies for dissection.

Burl (?), v.t. [imp. & p.p. Burled (?); p.pr. & vb.n. Burling.] [OE. burle stuffing, or a knot in cloth; cf. F. bourlet, bourrelet, OF. bourel, a wreath or a roll of cloth, linen, or leather, stuffed with flocks, etc., dim. of bourre. û92.

See Bur.] To dress or finish up (cloth); to pick knots, burs, loose threads, etc., from, as in finishing cloth.

Burling iron, a peculiar kind of nippers or tweezers used in burling woolen cloth.

Burl, n. 1. A knot or lump in thread or cloth.

> An overgrown knot, or an excrescence, on a tree; also, veneer made from such excrescences.

Burlap (?), n. A coarse fabric, made of jute or hemp, used for bagging; also, a finer variety of similar material, used for curtains, etc. [Written also burlaps.]

Burler (?), n. One who burls or dresses cloth.

Burlesque (?), a. [F. burlesque, fr. It. burlesco, fr. burla jest, mockery, perh. for burrula, dim. of L. burrae trifles. See Bur.] Tending to excite laughter or contempt by extravagant images, or by a contrast between the subject and the manner of treating it, as when a trifling subject is treated with mock gravity; jocular; ironical.

It is a dispute among the critics, whether burlesque poetry runs best in heroic verse, like that of the Dispensary, or in doggerel, like that of Hudibras.

Addison.

Burlesque (?), n. 1. Ludicrous representation; exaggerated parody; grotesque satire.

Burlesque is therefore of two kinds; the first represents mean persons in the accouterments of heroes, the other describes great persons acting and speaking like the basest among the people.

Addison.

> An ironical or satirical composition intended to excite laughter, or to ridicule anything.

The dull burlesque appeared with impudence,
And pleased by novelty in spite of sense.
Dryden.

> A ludicrous imitation; a caricature; a travesty; a gross perversion.

Who is it that admires, and from the heart is attached to, national representative assemblies, but must turn with horror and disgust from such a profane burlesque and abominable perversion of that sacred institute?

Burke.

Syn. - Mockery; farce; travesty; mimicry.

Burlesque (?), v.t. [imp. & p.p. Burlesqued (?); p.pr. & vb.n. Burlesquing (?).] To ridicule, or to make ludicrous by grotesque representation in action or in language.

They burlesqued the prophet Jeremiah's words, and turned the expression he used into ridicule.

Stillingfleet.

Burlesque, v.i. To employ burlesque.

Burlesquer (?), n. One who burlesques.

<— p. 194 —>

ØBurletta (?), n. [It., dim. of burla mockery. See Burlesque, a.] (Mus.) A comic operetta; a music farce.

Byron.

Burliness (?), n. Quality of being burly.

Burly (?), a. [OE. burlichÿstrong, excellent; perh. orig. fit for a lady's bower, hence handsome, manly, stout. Cf. Bower.] 1. Having a large, strong, or gross body; stout; lusty; Ð now used chiefly of human beings, but formerly of animals, in the sense of stately or beautiful, and of inanimate things that were huge and bulky. ½Burly sacks.„

Drayton.

In his latter days, with overliberal diet, [he was] somewhat corpulent and burly.

Sir T.More.

Burly and big, and studious of his ease.

Cowper.

Coarse and rough; boisterous.

It was the orator's own burly way of nonsense.

Cowley.

Burman (?), n.; pl. Burmans (?). [½The softened modern M'yanÐma, M'yanÐma [native name], is the source of the European corruption Burma.„ Balfour.] (Ethnol.) A member of the Burman family, one of the four great families Burmah; also, sometimes, any inhabitant of Burmah; a Burmese. Ð a. Of or pertaining to the Burmans or to Burmah.

Bur marigold (?). See Beggar's ticks.

Bur · mese (?), a. Of or pertaining to Burmah, or its inhabitants. Ð n.sing. & pl. A native or the natives of Burmah. Also (sing.), the languageÿof the Burmans.

Burn (?), v.t. [imp. & p.p. Burned (?) or Burnt (?); p.pr. & vb.n. Burning.] [OE. bernen, brennen, v.t., early confused with beornen, birnen, v.i., AS. b'rnan, bernan, v.t.; birnan, v.i.; akin to OS. brinnan, OFries. barna, berna, OHG. brinnan, brennan, G. brennen, OD. bernen, D. branden, Dan. br'nde, Sw. br„nna, brinna, Icel. brenna, Goth. brinnan, brannjan (in comp.), and possibly to E. fervent.] 1. To consume with fire; to reduce to ashes by the action of heat or fire; Ð frequently intensified by up: as, to burn up wood. ½We'll burn his body in the holy place.„

Shak.

To injure by fire or heat; to change destructively some property or properties of, by undue exposure to fire or heat; to scorch; to scald; to blister; to singe; to char; to sear; as, to burn steel in forging; to burn one's face in the sun; the sun burns the grass.

To perfect or improve by fire or heat; to submit to the action of fire or heat for some economic purpose; to destroy or change some property or properties of, by exposure to fire or heat in due degree for obtaining a desired residuum, product, or effect; to bake; as, to burn clay in making bricks or pottery; to burn wood so as to produce charcoal; to burn limestone for the lime.

To make or produce, as an effect or result, by the application of fire or heat; as, to burn a hole; to burn charcoal; to burn letters into a block.

To consume, injure, or change the condition of, as if by action of fire or heat; to affect as fire or heat does; as, to burn the mouth with pepper.

This tyrant fever burns me up.
Shak.
This dry sorrow burns up all my tears.
Dryden.
When the cold north wind bloweth, ... it devoureth the mountains, and burneth the wilderness, and consumeth the ??ass as fire.
Ecclus.xliii.20, 21.

(Surg.) To apply a cautery to; to cauterize.

(Chem.) To cause to combine with oxygen or other active agent, with evolution of heat; to consume; to oxidize; as, a man burns a certain amount of carbon at each respiration; to burn iron in oxygen.

To burn, To burn together, as two surfaces of metal (Engin.), to fuse and unite them by pouring over them a quantity of the same metal in a liquid state. Ð To burn a bowl (Game of Bowls), to displace it accidentally, the bowl so displaced being said to be burned. Ð To burn daylight, to light candles before it is dark; to waste time; to perform superfluous actions. Shak. Ð To burn one's fingers, to get one's self into unexpected trouble, as by interfering the concerns of others, speculation, etc. Ð To burn out, to destroy or obliterate by burning. ½Must you with hot irons burn out mine eyes?ͺ Shak. Ð To be burned out, to suffer loss by fire, as the burning of one's house, store, or shop, with the contents. Ð To burn up, To burn down, to burn entirely.

Burn, v.i. 1. To be of fire; to flame. ½The mount burned with fire.ͺ
Deut.ix.15.

To suffer from, or be scorched by, an excess of heat.

Your meat doth burn, quoth I.
Shak.

To have a condition, quality, appearance, sensation, or emotion, as if on fire or excessively heated; to act or rage with destructive violence; to be in a state of lively emotion or strong desire; as, the face burns; to burn with fever.

Did not our heart burn within us, while he talked with us by the way?
Luke xxiv.32.

The barge she sat in, like a burnished throne,
Burned on the water.
Shak.
Burning with high hope.
Byron.
The groan still deepens, and the combat burns. Pope. The parching air Burns frore, and cold performs the effect of fire. Milton. 4. (Chem.) To combine energetically, with evolution of heat; as, copper burns in chlorine. 5. In certain games, to approach near to a concealed object which is sought. [Colloq.] To burn out, to burn till the fuel is exhausted. Ð To burn up, To burn down, to be entirely consumed. Burn, n. 1. A hurt, injury, or effect caused by fire or excessive or intense heat. 2. The operation or result of burning or baking, as in brickmaking; as, they have a good burn. 3. A disease in vegetables. See Brand, n., 6. Burn, n. [See 1st Bourn.] A small stream. [Scot.] Burnaïble (?), a. Combustible. Cotgrave. Burned (?), p.p. & a. See Burnt. Burned (?), p.p. Burnished. [Obs.] Chaucer. Burner (?), n. 1. One who, or that which, burns or sets fire to anything. 2. The part of a lamp, gas fixture, etc., where the flame is produced. Bunsen's burnerÿ(Chem.), a kind of burner, invented by Professor Bunsen of Heidelberg, consisting of a straight tube, four or five inches in length, having small holes for the entrance of air at the bottom. Illuminating gas being also admitted at the bottom, a mixture of gas and air is formed which burns at the top with a feebly luminous but intensely hot flame. Ð Argand burner, Rose burner, etc. See under Argand, Rose, etc. Burnet (?), n. [OE. burnet burnet; also, brownish (the plant perh. being named from its color), fr. F. brunet, dim. of brun brown; cf. OF. brunete a sort of flower. See Brunette.] (Bot.) A genus of perennial herbs (Poterium); especially, P.Sanguisorba, the common, or garden, burnet. Burnet moth (Zo"l.), in England, a handsome moth (Zyg'na filipendula), with crimson spots on the wings. Ð Burnet saxifrage. (Bot.) See Saxifrage. Ð Canadian burnet, a marsh plant (Poterium Canadensis). Ð Great burnet, Wild burnet, Poterium (or Sanguisorba) oficinalis. Burnettĭize (?), v.t. [imp. & p.p. Burnettized (?); p.pr. & vb.n. Burnettizing.] (Manuf.) To subject (wood, fabrics, etc.) to a process of saturation in a solution of chloride of zinc, to prevent decay; Ð a process invented by Sir William Burnett. Burnie (?), n. [See 4th Burn.] A small brook. [Scot.] Burns. Burnieïbee· (?), n. The ladybird. [Prov. Eng.] Burning, a. 1. That burns; being on fire; excessively hot; fiery. 2. Consuming; intense; inflaming; exciting; vehement; powerful; as, burning zeal. Like a young hound upon a burning scent. Dryden. Burning bush (Bot.), an ornamental shrub (Eunoymus atropurpureus), bearing a crimson berry. Burning, n. The act of consuming by fire or heat, or of subjecting to the effect of fire or heat; the state of being on fire or excessively heated. Burning fluid, any volatile illuminating oil, as the lighter petroleums (naphtha, benzine), or oil of turpentine (camphine), but esp. a mixture of the latter with alcohol. Ð Burning glass, a conxex lens of considerable size,

used for producing an intense heat by converging the sun's rays to a focus. Ð Burning houseÿ(Metal.), the furnace in which tin ores are calcined, to sublime the sulphur and arsenic from the pyrites. Weale. Ð Burning mirror, a concave mirror, or a combination of plane mirrors, used for the same purpose as a burning glass. Syn. - Combustion; fire; conflagration; flame; blaze. Burnish (?), v.t. [imp. & p.p. Burnished (?); p.pr. & vb.n. Burnishing.] [OE. burnischen, burnissen, burnen, OF. burnir, brunir, to make brown, polish, F. brunir, fr. F. brun brown, fr. OHG. br?n; cf. MHG. briunen 8make brown, polish. See Brown, a.] To cause to shine; to make smooth and bright; to polish; specifically, to polish by rubbing with something hard and smooth; as, to burnish brass or paper. The frame of burnished steel, that east a glare From far, and seemed to thaw the freezing air. Dryden. Now the village windows blaze, Burnished by the setting sun. Cunningham. Burnishing machine, a machine for smoothing and polishing by compression, as in making paper collars. Burnish, v.i. To shine forth; to brighten; to become smooth and glossy, as from swelling or filling out; hence, to grow large. A slender poet must have time to grow, And spread and burnish as his brothers do. Dryden. My thoughts began to burnish, sprout, and swell. Herbert. Burnish, n. The effect of burnishing; gloss; brightness; luster. Crashaw. BurnishÏer (?), n. 1. One who burnishes. 2. A tool with a hard, smooth, rounded end or surface, as of steel, ivory, or agate, used in smoothing or polishing by rubbing. It has a variety of forms adapted to special uses. Burnoose, Burnous (?), n. [Ar. burnus a kind of highÐcrowned cap: cf. F. bournous, burnous, Sp. alÐbornoz, a sort of upper garment, with a hood attached.] 1. A cloaklike garment and hood woven in one piece, worn by Arabs. 2. A combination cloak and hood worn by women. [Variously written bournous, bernouse, bornous, etc.] Burnstic · kle (?), n. (Zo"l.) A stickle?back (Gasterosteus aculeatus). Burnt (?), p.p. & a. Consumed with, or as with, fire; scorched or dried, as with fire or heat; baked or hardened in the fire or the sun. Burnt ear, a black, powdery fungus which destroys grain. See Smut. Ð Burnt offering, something offered and burnt on an altar, as an atonement for sin; a sacrifice. The offerings of the Jews were a clean animal, as an ox, a calf, a goat, or a sheep; or some vegetable substance, as bread, or ears of wheat or barley. Called also burnt sacrifice. [2 Sam.xxiv.22.] Burr (?), n. [See Bur.] (Bot.) 1. A prickly seed vessel. See Bur, 1. 2. The thin edge or ridge left by a tool in cutting or shaping metal, as in turning, engraving, pressing, etc.; also, the rough neck left on a bullet in casting. The graver, in plowing furrows in the surface of the copper, raises corresponding ridges or burrs. Tomlinson. 3. A thin flat piece of metal, formed from a sheet by punching; a small washer put on the end of a rivet before it is swaged down. 4. A broad iron ring on a tilting lance just below the gripe, to prevent the hand from slipping. 5. The lobe or lap of the ear. 6. [Probably of imitative origin.] A guttural pronounciation of the letter r, produced by trilling the extremity of the soft palate against the back part of the tongue; rotacism; Ð often called the Newcastle, Northumberland, or

Tweedside, burr. 7. The knot at the bottom of an antler. See Bur, n., 8. Burr (?), v.i. [imp. & p.p. Burred (?); p.pr. & vb.n. Burring.] To speak with burr; to make a hoarse or guttural murmur. Mrs. Browning. Burrel (?), n. [Cf. OF. burel reddish (cf. Borel, n.), or F. beurr, butter pear, fr. beurre butter. Cf. Butter.] A sort of pear, called also the red butter pear, its smooth, delicious, soft pulp. Burrel, n. Same as Borrel. Burrel fly · (?). [From its reddish color. See 1st Burrel.] (Zo"l.) The botfly or gadfly of cattle (Hypoderma bovis). See Gadfly. Burrel shot · (?). [Either from annoying the enemy like a burrel fly, or, less probably, fr. F. bourrelerÿto sting, torture.] (Gun.) A mixture of shot, nails, stones, pieces of old iron, etc., fired from a cannon at short range, in an emergency. [R.] Burring maĭchine (?). A machine for cleansing wool of burs, seeds, and otherÿsubstances. Burr millstone · (?). See Buhrstone. Burro (?), n. [Sp., an ass.] (Zo"l.) A donkey. [Southern U.S.] Burrock (?), n. [Perh. from AS. burg, burh, hill + Ĭock.] A small weir or dam in a river to direct the stream to gaps where fish traps are placed. Knight. Burrow (?), n. [See 1st Borough.] 1. An incorporated town. See 1st Borough. 2. A shelter; esp. a hole in the ground made by certain animals, as rabbits, for shelter and habitation. 3. (Mining) A heap or heaps of rubbish or refuse. 4. A mound. See 3d Barrow, and Camp, n., 5. Burrow, v.i. [imp. & p.p. Burrowed (?); p.pr. & vb.n. Burrowing.] 1. To excavate a hole to lodge in, as in the earth; to lodge in a hole excavated in the earth, as conies or rabbits. 2. To lodge, or take refuge, in any deep or concealed place; to hide. Sir, this vermin of court reporters, when they are forced into day upon one point, are sure to burrow in another. Burke. Burrowing owlÿ(Zo"l.), a small owl of the western part of North America (Speotyto cunicularia), which lives in holes, often in company with the prairie dog. BurrowĬer (?), n. One who, or that which, burrows; an animal that makes a hole under groundÿand lives in it. Burrstone · , n. See Buhrstone. Burry (?), a. Abounding in burs, or containing burs; resembling burs; as, burry wool. ØBursa (?), n.; pl. Burs' (?). [L. See Burse.] (Anat.) Any sac or saclike cavity; especially, one of the synovial sacs, or small spaces, often lined with synovial membrane, interposed between tendons and bony prominences. Bursal (?), a. (Anat.) Of or pertaining to a bursa or to burs'. Bursar (?), n. [LL. bursarius, fr. bursa purse. See Burse, and cf. Purser.] 1. A treasurer, or cash keeper; a purser; as, the bursar of a college, or of a monastery. 2. A student to whom a stipend or bursary is paid for his complete or partial support. BursarĬship, n. The office of a bursar. BursaĬry (?), n.; pl. Ĭries (?). [LL. bursaria. See Bursar.] 1. The treasury of a college or monastery. 2. A scholarship or charitable foundation in a university, as in scotland; a sum given to enable a student to pursue his studies. ½No woman of rank or fortune but would have a bursary in her gift., Southey. ØBursch (?), n.; pl. Burschen (?). [G., ultimately fr. LL. bursa. See Burse.] A youth; especially, a student in a german university. Burse (?), n. [LL. bursa, or F. bourse. See Bourse, and cf. Bursch, Purse.] 1. A purse; also, a vesicle; a pod; a hull. [Obs.] Holland. 2. A fund or foundation for the maintenance of needy scholars in their studies; also, the sum given to the beneficiaries. [Scot.] 3. (Eccl.) An ornamental case of hold the corporal when not in use. Shipley. 4. An exchange, for merchants and bankers, in the cities of continental Europe. Same as Bourse. 5. A kind of bazaar. [Obs.] She says she went to the burse for patterns. Old Play. Burĭsicŭllate (?), a. [See Burse.] (Bot.) Bursiform. Bursĭlform (?), a. [LL. bursa purse + Ĭform.] Shaped like a purse. ØBurĭsitis (?), n. [NL., fr. E. bursa + Ĭitis.] (Med.) Inflammation of a bursa. Burst (?), v.i. [imp. & p.p. Burst; p.pr. & vb.n. Bursting. The past participle bursten is obsolete.] [OE. bersten, bresten, AS. berstan (pers. sing. berste, imp. sing. b'rst, imp. pl. burston, p.p. borsten); akin to D. bersten, G. bersten, OHG. brestan, OS. brestan, Icel. bresta, Sw. brista, Dan. briste. Cf. Brast, Break.] 1. To fly apart or in pieces; of break open; to yield to force or pressure, especiallyÿto a sudden and violent exertion of force, or to pressure from within; to explode; as, the boiler had burst; the buds will burst in spring. From the egg that soon Bursting with kindly rupture, forth disclosed Their callow young. Milton. Often used figuratively, as of the heart, in reference to a surcharge of passion, grief, desire, etc. No, no, my heart will burst, an if I speak: And I will speak, that so my heart may burst. Shak. 2. To exert force or pressure by which something is made suddenly to give way; to break through obstacles or limitations; hence, to appear suddenly and unexpecedly or unaccountably, or to depart in such manner; Ð usually with some qualifying adverb or preposition, as forth, out, away, into, upon, through, etc. Tears, such as angels weep, burst forth. Milton. And now you burst (ah cruel!) from my arms. Pope. A resolved villain Whose bowels suddenly burst out. Shak. We were the first that ever burst Into that silent sea. Coleridge. To burst upon him like an earthquake. Goldsmith.

<— p. 195 —>

Burst (?), v.t. 1. To break or rend by violence, as by an overcharge or by strain or pressure, esp. from within; to force open suddenly; as, to burst a cannon; to burst a blood vessel; to burst open the doors. My breast I'll burst with straining of my courage. Shak. 2. To break. [Obs.] You will not pay for the glasses you have burst? Shak. He burst his lance against the sand below. Fairfax (Tasso). 3. To produce as an effect of bursting; as, to burst a hole through the wall. Bursting charge. See under Charge. Burst, n. 1. A sudden breaking forth; a violent rending; an explosion; as, a burst of thunder; a burst of applause; a burst of passion; a burst of inspiration. Bursts of foxÐhunting melody. W.Irving. 2. Any brief, violent evertion or effort; a spurt; as, a burst of speed. 3. A sudden opening, as of landscape; a stretch; an expanse. [R.] ½A fine burst of country.¸ Jane Austen. 4. A rupture of hernia; a breach. Bursten (?), p.p. of Burst, v.i. [Obs.] Burster (?), n. One that bursts. Burstwort · (?), n. (Bot.) A plant (Herniaria glabra) supposed to be valuable for the cure of hernia or rupture. Burt (?), n. (Zo"l.) See Birt. [Prov. Eng.] Burthen (?), n. & v.t. See Burden. [Archaic] Burton (?), n. [Cf. OE. & Prov. E. bortÿto press or indent anything.] (Naut.) A peculiar tackle, formed of two or more blocks, or pulleys, the weight being suspended of a hook block in the bight of the running part. Bury (?), n. [See 1st Borough.] 1. A borough; a manor; as, the Bury of St. Edmond's; Ð used as a termination of names of places; as, Canterbury, Shrewsbury. 2. A manor house; a castle. [Prov. Eng.] To this very day, the chief house of a manor, or the lord's seat, is called bury, in some parts of England. Miege. Bury (?), v.t. [imp. & p.p. Buried (?); p.pr. & vb.n. Burying (?).] [OE. burien, birien, berien, AS. byrgan; akin to beorgan to protect, OHG. bergan, G. bergen, Icel. bjarga, Sw. berga, Dan. bierge, Goth. baj̧rgan. û95. Cf. Burrow.] 1. To cover out of sight, either by heaping something over, or by placing within something, as earth, etc.; to conceal by covering; to hide; as, to bury coals in ashes; to bury the face in the hands. And all their confidence Under the weight of mountains buried deep. Milton. 2. Specifically: To cover out of sight, as the body of a deceased person, in a grave, a tomb, or the ocean; to deposit (a corpse) in its resting place,ÿwith funeral ceremonies; to inter; to inhume. Lord, suffer me first to go and bury my father. Matt.viii.21. I'll bury thee in a triumphant grave. Shak. 3. To hide in oblivion; to put away finally; to abandon; as, to bury strife. Give me a bowl of wine In this I bury all unkindness, Cassius. Shak. Burying beetleÿ(Zo"l.), the general name of many species of beetles, of the tribe Necrophaga; the sexton beetle; Ð so called from their habit of burying small dead animals by digging away the earth beneath them. The larv‘ frrd upon decaying flesh, and are useful scavengers. Ð To bury the hatchet, to lay aside the instruments of war, and make peace; Ð a phrase used in allusion to the custom observed by the North American Indians, of burying a tomahawk when they conclude a peace. Syn. - To intomb; inter; inhume; inurn; hide; cover; conceal; overwhelm; repress. Burying ground · , Burying place. The ground or place for burying the dead; burial place. Bus (?), n. [Abbreviated from omnibus.] An omnibus. [Colloq.] Busby (?), n.; pl. Busbies (?). (Mil.) A military headdress or cap, used in the British army. It is of fur, with a bag, of the same color as the facings of the regiment, hanging from the top over the right shoulder. ØBuscon (?), n. [Sp., a searcher, fr. buscar to search.] One who searches for ores; a prospector. [U.S.] Bush (?), n. [OE. bosch, busch, buysch, bosk, busk; akin to D. bosch, OHG. busc, G. busch, Icel. b?skr, b?ski, Dan. busk, Sw. buske, and also to LL. boscus, buscus, Pr. bosc, It. bosco, Sp. & Pg. bosque, F. bois, OF. bos. Whether the LL. or G. form i? the original is uncertain; if the LL., it is perh. from the same source as E. box a case. Cf. Ambush, Boscage, Bouquet, Box a case.] 1. A thicket, or place abounding in trees or shrubs; a wild forest. µ This was the original sense of the word, as in the Dutch bosch, a wood, and was so used by Chaucer. In this sense it is extensively used in the British colonies, especially at the Cape of Good Hope, and also in Australia and Canada; as, to live or settle in the bush. 2. A shrub; esp., a shrub with branches rising from or near the root; a thick shrub or a cluster of shrubs. To bind a bush of thorns among sweetÐsmelling flowers. Gascoigne.

3. A shrub cut off, or a shrublike branch of a tree; as, bushes to support pea vines. 4. A shrub or branch, properly, a branchÿof ivy (as sacred to Bacchus), hung out at vintners' doors, or as a tavern sign; hence, a tavern sign, and symbolically, the tavern itself. If it be true that good wine needs no bush, 't is true that a good play needs no epilogue. Shak. 5. (Hunting) The tail, or brush, of a fox. To beat about the bush, to approach anything in a roundÐabout manner, instead of coming directly to it; Ð a metaphor taken from hunting. Ð Bush beanÿ(Bot.), a variety of bean which is low and requires no support (Phaseolus vulgaris, variety nanus). See Bean, 1. Ð Bush buck, or Bush goat (Zo"l.), a beautiful South African antelope (Tragelaphus sylvaticus); Ð so called because found mainly in wooden localities. The name is also applied to otherÿspecies. Ð Bush cat (Zo"l.), the serval. See Serval. Ð Bush chat (Zo"l.), a bird of the genus Pratincola, of the Thrush family. Ð Bush dog. (Zo"l.) See Potto. Ð Bush hammer. See Bushhammer in the Vocabulary. Ð Bush harrow (Agric.) See under Harrow. Ð Bush hog (Zo"l.), a South African wild hog (PotamochÒrus Africanus); Ð called also bush pig, and water hog. Ð Bush master (Zo"l.), a venomous snake (Lachesis mutus) of Guinea; Ð called also surucucu. Ð Bush pea (Bot.), a variety of pea that needs to be bushed. Ð Bush shrike (Zo"l.), a bird of the genus Thamnophilus, and allied genera; Ð called also batarg. Many species inhabit tropical America. Ð Bush titÿ(Zo"l.), a small bird of the genus Psaltriparus, allied to the titmouse. P. minimus inhabits California. Bush (?), v.i. To branch thickly in the manner of a bush. ½The bushing alders., Pope. Bush, v.t. [imp. & p.p. Bushed (?); p.pr. & vb.n. Bushing.] 1. To set bushes for; to support with bushes; as, to bush peas. 2. To use a bush harrow on (land), for covering seeds sown; to harrow with a bush; as, to bush a piece of land; to bush seeds into the ground. Bush, n. [D. bus a box, akin to E. box; or F. boucher to plug.] 1. (Mech.) A lining for a hole to make it smaller; a thimble or ring of metal or wood inserted in a plate or other part of machinery to receive the wear of a pivot or arbor. Knight. µ In the larger machines, such a piece is called a box, particularly in the United States. 2. (Gun.) A piece of ??pper, screwed into a gun, through which the venthole is bored. Farrow. Bush, v.t. To furnish with a bush, or lining; as, to bush a pivot hole. Bushboy (?), n. See Bushman. Bushel (?), n. [OE. buschel, boischel, OF. boissel, bussel, boistel, F. boisseau, LL. bustellus; dim. of bustia, buxida (OF. boiste), fr. pyxida, acc. of L. pyxis box, Gr. ?. Cf. Box.] 1. A dry measure, containing four pecks, eight gallons, or thirtyÐtwo quarts. µ The Winchester bushel, formerly used in England, contained 2150.42 cubic inches, being the volume of a cylinder 18? inches in internal diameter and eight inches in depth. The standard bushel measures, prepared by the United States Government and distributed to the States, hold each 77.6274 pounds of distilled water, at 39.8ø Fahr. and 30 inches atmospheric pressure, being the equivalent of the Winchester bushel. The imperial bushel now in use in England is larger than the Winchester bushel, containing 2218.2 cubic inches,

or 80 pounds of water at 62ø Fahr. 2. A vessel of the capacity of a bushel, used in measuring; a bushel measure. Is a candle brought to be put under a bushel, or under a bed, and not to be set on a candlestick? Mark iv.21. 3. A quantity that fills a bushel measure; as, a heap containing ten bushels of apples. μ In the United States a large number of articles, bought and sold by the bushel, are measured by weighing, the number of pounds that make a bushel being determined by State law or by local custom. For some articles, as apples, potatoes, etc., heaped measure is required in measuring a bushel. 4. A large indefinite quantity. [Colloq.] The worthies of antiquity bought the rarest pictures with bushels of gold, without counting the weight or the number of the pieces. Dryden. 5. The iron lining in the nave of a wheel. [Eng.] In the United States it is called a box. See 4th Bush. Bushellage (?), n. A duty payable on commodities by the bushel. [Eng.] Bushellman (?), n. A tailor's assistant for repairing garments; Đ called also busheler. [Local, U.S.] Bushet (?), n. [See Bosket.] A small bush. Bushfight · er (?), n. One accustomed to bushfighting. Parkman. Bushfight · ing (?), n. Fighting in the bush, or from behind bushes, trees, or thickets. Bushham · mer (?), n. A hammer with a head formed of a bundle of square bars, with pyramidal points, arranged in rows, or a solid head with a face cut into a number of rows of such points; Đ used for dressing stone. Bushham · mer, v.t. To dress with bushhammer; as, to bushhammer a block of granite. Bushiĭness (?), n. The condition or quality of being bushy. Bushing, n. [See 4th Bush.] 1. The operation of fitting bushes, or linings, into holes or places where wear is to be received, or friction diminished, as pivot holes, etc. 2. (Mech.) A bush or lining; Đ sometimes called ? thimble. See 4th Bush. Bushless (?), a. Free from bushes; bare. O'er the long backs of the bushless downs. Tennyson. Bushman (?), n.; pl. Bushmen (?). [Cf. D. boschman, boschjesman. See 1st Bush.] 1. A woodsman; a settler in the bush. 2. (Ethnol.) One of a race of South African nomads, living principally in the deserts, and not classified as allied in race or language to any other people. Bushment (?), n. [OE. bussshement ambush, fr. bush.] 1. A thicket; a cluster of bushes. [Obs.] Raleigh. 2. An ambuscade. [Obs.] Sir T.More. Bushran · ger (?), n. One who roams, or hides, among the bushes; especially, in Australia, an escaped criminal living in the bush. Bushwhack · er (?), n. 1. One accustomed to beat about, or travel through, bushes. [U.S.] They were gallant bushwhackers, and hunters of raccoons by moonlight. W.Irving. 2. A guerrilla; a marauding assassin; one who pretends to be a peaceful citizen, but secretly harasses a hostile force or its sympathizers. [U.S.] Farrow. Bushwhack · ing, n. 1. Traveling, or working a way, through bushes; pulling by the bushes, as in hauling a boat along the bushy margin of a stream. [U.S.] T.Flint. 2. The crimes or warfare of bushwhackers. [U.S.] Bushy (?), a. [From 1st Bush.] 1. Thick and spreading, like a bush. ½Bushy eyebrows., Irving. 2. Full of bushes; overgrowing with shrubs. Dingle, or bushy dell, of this wild wood. Milton. Busiĭly (?), adv. In a busy manner. Business (?), n.; pl. Businesses (?). [From

Busy.] 1. That which busies one, or that which engages the time, attention, or labor of any one, as his principal concern or interest, whether for a longer or shorter time; constant employment; regular occupation; as, the business of life; business before pleasure. Wist ye not that I must be about my Father's business? Luke ii.49. 2. Any particular occupation or employment engaged in for livelihood or gain, as agriculture, trade, art, or a profession. ½The business of instruction., Prescott. 3. Financial dealings; buying and selling; traffic in general; mercantile transactions. It seldom happens that men of a studious turn acquire any degree of reputation for their knowledge of business. Bp. Popteus. 4. That which one has to do or should do; special service, duty, or mission. The daughter of the King of France, On serious business, craving quick despatch, Importunes personal conference. Shak. What business has the tortoise among the clouds? L'Estrange. 5. Affair; concern; matter; Ð used in an indefinite sense, and modified by the connected words. It was a gentle business, and becoming The action of good women. Shak. Bestow Your needful counsel to our business. Shak. 6. (Drama) The position, distribution, and order of persons and properties on the stage of a theater, as determined by the stage manager in rehearsal. 7. Care; anxiety; diligence. [Obs.] Chaucer. To do one's business, to ruin one. [Colloq.] Wycherley. Ð To make (a thing) one's business, to occupy one's self with a thing as a special charge or duty. [Colloq.] Ð To mean business, to be earnest. [Colloq.] Syn. - Affairs; concern; transaction; matter; engagement; employment; calling; occupation; trade; profession; vocation; office; duty. BusinessÏlike · (?), a. In the manner of one transacting business wisely and by right methods. Busk (?), n. [F. busc, perh. fr. the hypothetical older form of E. bois wood, because the first busks were made of wood. See Bush, and cf. OF. busche, F. b–che, a piece or log of wood, fr. the same root.] A thin, elastic strip of metal, whalebone, wood, or other material, worn in the front of a corset. Her long slit sleeves, stiff busk, puff verdingall, Is all that makes her thus angelical. Marston. Busk, v.t. & i. [imp. & p.p. Busked (?).] [OE. busken, fr. Icel. b?ask to make one's self ready, rexlexive of b?a to prepare, dwell. Cf. 8th Bound.] 1. To prepare; to make ready; to array; to dress. [Scot. & Old Eng.] Busk you, busk you, my bonny, bonny bride. Hamilton. 2. To go; to direct one's course. [Obs.] Ye might have busked you to Huntly banks. Skelton. Busked (?), a. Wearing a busk. Pollok. Busket (?), n. [See Bosket, Bouquet.] 1. A small bush; also, a sprig or bouquet. [Obs.] Spenser. 2. A part of a garden devoted to shrubs. [R.] Buskin (?), n. [Prob. from OF. brossequin, or D. broosken. See Brodekin.] 1. A strong, protecting covering for the foot, coming some distance up the leg. The hunted red deer's undressed hide Their hairy buskins well supplied. Sir W.Scott. 2. A similar covering for the foot and leg, made with very thick soles, to give an appearance of elevation to the stature; Ð worn by tragic actors in ancient Greece and Rome. Used as a symbol of tragedy, or the tragic drama, as distinguished from comedy. Great Fletcher never treads in buskins here, No greater Jonson dares in socks appear. Dryden. Buskined

(?), a. 1. Wearing buskins. Her buskined virgins traced the dewy lawn. Pope. 2. Trodden by buskins; pertaining to tragedy. ½The buskined stage., Milton. Busky (?), a. See Bosky, and 1st Bush, n. Shak. Buss (?), n. [OE. basse, fr. L. basium; cf. G. bus (Luther), Prov. G. busserl, dim. of bus kiss, bussen to kiss, Sw. puss kiss, pussa to kiss, W. & Gael. bus lip, mouth.] A kiss; a rude or playful kiss; a smack. Shak.

<— p. 196 —>

Buss (?), v.t. [imp. & p.p. Bussed (?); p.pr. & vb.n. Bussing.] To kiss; esp. to kiss with a snImack, or rudely. ½Nor bussed the milking maid.,

Tennyson.

Kissing and bussing differ both in this,
We buss our wantons, but our wives we kiss.

Herrick.

Buss, n. [Cf. OF. busse, Pr. bus, LL. bussa, busa, G. bse, D. buis.] (Naut.) A small strong vessel with two masts and two cabins; Ð used in the herring fishery.

The Dutch whalers and herring busses.

Macaulay.

Bust (?), n. [F. buste, fr. It. busto; cf. LL. busta, bustula, box, of the same origin as E. box a case; cf., for the change of meaning, E. chest. See Bushel.] 1. A piece of sculpture representing the upper part of the human figure, including the head, shoulders, and breast.

Ambition sighed: she found it vain to trust
The faithless column, and the crumbling bust.

Pope.

The portion of the human figure included between the head and waist, whether in statuary or in the person; the chest or thorax; the upper part of the trunk of the body.

Bustard (?), n. [OF. & Prov. F. bistarde, F. outarde, from L. avis tarda, lit., slow bird. Plin. 10, 22; ½proxim' its sunt, quas Hispania aves tardas appellat, Gr'cia ?.,] (Zo"l.) A birdÿof the genus Otis.

µ The great or bearded bustard (Otis tarda) is the largest game bird in Europe. It inhabits the temperate regions of Europe and Asia, and was formerly common in Great Britain. The little bustard (O. tetrax) inhabits eastern Europe and Morocco. Many otherÿspecies are known in Asia and Africa.

Buster (?), n. Something huge; a roistering blade; also, a spree. [Slang, U.S.]

Bartlett.

Bustle (?), v.i. [imp. & p.p. Bustled (?); p.pr. & vb.n. Bustling (?).] [Cf. OE. buskle, perh. fr. AS. bysig busy, bysgÐianÿto busy + the verbal termination Île; or Icel. bustla to splash, bustle.] To move noisily; to be rudely active; to move in a way to cause agitation or disturbance; as, to bustle through a crowd.

And leave the world for me to bustle in.
Shak.

Bustle, n. Great stir; agitation; tumult from stirring or excitement.

A strange bustle and disturbance in the world.
South.

Bustle, n. A kind of pad or cushion worn on the back below the waist, by women, to give fullness to the skirts; Ð called also bishop, and tournure.

Bustler (?), n. An active, stirring person.

Bustling (?), a. Agitated; noisy; tumultuous; characterized by confused activity; as, a bustling crowd. ½A bustling wharf.
Hawthorne.

ØBusto (?), n.; pl. Bustoes (?). [It.] A bust; a statue.

With some antick bustoes in the niches.
Ashmole.

Busy (?), a. [OE. busi, bisi, AS. bysig; akin to D. bezig, LG. besig; cf. Skr. bh?shÿto be active, busy.] 1. Engaged in some business; hard at work (either habitually or only for the time being); occupied with serious affairs; not idle nor at leisure; as, a busy merchant.

Sir, my mistress sends you word
THat she is busy, and she can not come.
Shak.

Constantly at work; diligent; active.

Busy hammers closing rivets up.
Shak.

Religious motives ... are so busy in the heart.
Addison.

Crowded with business or activities; Ð said of places and times; as, a busy street.

ToÐmorrow is a busy day.
Shak.

Officious; meddling; foolish active.

On meddling monkey, or on busy ape.
Shak.

Careful; anxious. [Obs.]

Chaucer.

Syn. - Diligent; industrious; assiduous; active; occupied; engaged.

Busy (?), v.t. [imp. & p.p. Busied (?); p.pr. & vb.n. Busying.] [AS. bysgian.] To make or keep busy; to employ; to engage or keep engaged; to occupy; as, to busy one's self with books.

Be it thy course to busy giddy minds
With foreign quarrels.
Shak.

Bus‍y‍Ibod · y (?), n.; pl. Busybodies (?). One who officiously concerns himself with the affairs of others; a meddling person.

And not only idle, but tattlers also and busybodies, speaking things which they ought not.
1 Tim.v.13.

But (?), prep., adv. & conj. [OE. bute, buten, AS. b?tan, without, on the outside, except, besides; pref. beÏ + ?tan outward, without, fr. ?t out. Primarily, b?tan, as well as ?t, is an adverb. û198. See By, Out; cf. About.]
1. Except with; unless with; without. [Obs.]

So insolent that he could not go but either spurning equals or ?ampling on his inferiors.
Fuller.

Touch not the cat but a glove.
Motto of the Mackintoshes.

Except; besides; save.

Who can it be, ye gods! but perjured Lycon?
E.Smith.

µ In this sense, but is often used with other particles, as, but for, without, had it not been for. ½Uncre?ted but for love divine.
Young.

Excepting or excluding the fact that; save that; were it not that; unless; Ð elliptical, for but that.

And but my noble Moor is true of mind ... it were enough to put him to ill thinking.
Shak.

Otherwise than that; that not; Ð commonly, after a negative, with that.

It cannot be but nature hatj some director, of infinite power, to guide her in all her ways.
Hooker.

There is no question but the king of Spain will reform most of the abuses.
Addison.

Only; solely; merely.

Observe but how their own principles combat one another.
Milton.

If they kill us, we shall but die.

2 Kings vii.4.
A formidable man but to his friends.
Dryden.

On the contrary; on the other hand; only; yet; still; however; nevertheless; more; further; Ð as connective of sentences or clauses of a sentence, in a sense more or less exceptive or adversative; as, the House of Representatives passed the bill, but the Senate dissented; our wants are many, but quite of another kind.

Now abideth faith hope, charity, these three; but the greatest of these is charity.
1 Cor.xiii.13.
When pride cometh, then cometh shame; but with the lowly is wisdom.
Prov.xi.2.
All but. See under All. Ð But and if, but if; an attempt on the part of King James's translators of the Bible to express the conjunctive and adversative force of the Greek ?.
But and if that servant say in his heart, My lord delayeth his coming; ... the lord of that servant will come in a day when he looketh not for him.
Luke xii.45, 46.
Ð But if, unless. [Obs.]
Chaucer.
But this I read, that but if remedy
Thou her afford, full shortly I her dead shall see.
Spenser.
Syn. - But, However, Still. These conjunctions mark opposition in passing from one thought or topic to another. But marks the opposition with a medium degree of strength; as, this is not winter, but it is almost as cold; he requested my assistance, but I shall not aid him at present. However is weaker, and throws the opposition (as it were) into the background; as, this is not winter; it is, however, almost as cold; he required my assistance; at present, however, I shall not afford him aid. The plan, however, is still under consideration, and may yet be adopted. Still is stronger than but, and marks the opposition more emphatically; as, your arguments are weighty; still they do not convince me. See Except, However.

μ ½The chief error with but is to use it where and is enough; an error springing from the tendency to use strong words without sufficient occasio,.͵
Bain.
But (?), n. [Cf. But, prep., adv. & conj.] The outer apartment or kitchen of a twoÐroomed house; Ð opposed to ben, the inner room. [Scot.]
But, n. [See 1st But.] 1. A limit; a boundary.

The end; esp. the larger or thicker end, or the blunt, in distinction from the sharp, end. See 1st Butt.

But end, the larger or thicker end; as, the but end of a log; the but end of a musket. See Butt, n.

But, v.i. [imp. & p.p. Butted; p.pr. & vb.n. Butting.] See Butt, v., and Abut, v.

Butane (?), n. [L. butyrum butter. See Butter.] (Chem.) An inflammable gaseous hydrocarbon, C?H?, of the marsh gas, or paraffin, series.

Butcher (?), n. [OE. bochere, bochier, OF. bochier, F. boucher, orig., slaughterer of buck goats, fr. OF. boc, F. bouc, a buck goat; of German or Celtic origin. See Buck the animal.] 1. One who slaughters animals, or dresses their flesh for market; one whose occupation it is to kill animals for food.

A slaughterer; one who kills in large numbers, or with unusual cruelty; one who causes needless loss of life, as in battle. ½Butcher of an innocent child.

Shak.

Butcher bird (Zo"l.), a species of shrike of the genus Lanius.

µ The Lanius excubitor is the common butcher birdÿof Europe. In England, the bearded tit is sometimes called the lesser butcher bird. The American species are L.borealis, or northernbutcher bird, and L. Ludovicianus or loggerhead shrike. The name butcher birdis derived from its habit of suspending its prey impaled upon thorns, after killing it.

Ð Butcher's meat, such flesh of animals slaughtered for food as is sold for that purpose by butchers, as beef, mutton, lamb, and pork.

Butcher, v.t. [imp. & p.p. Butchered (?); p.pr. & vb.n. Butchering.] 1. To kill or slaughter (animals) for food, or for market; as, to butcher hogs.

To murder, or kill, especially in an unusually bloody or barbarous manner.

Macaulay.
[Ithocles] was murdered, rather butchered.
Ford.
Butcherĭing, n. 1. The business of a butcher.

The act of slaughtering; the act of killing cruelly and needlessly.

That dreadful butchering of one another.
Addison.
Butcherĭlĭiness (?), n. Butchery quality.
Butcherĭly, a. Like a butcher; without compunction; savage; bloody; inhuman; fell. ½The victim of a butcherly murder.
D.Webster.
What stratagems, how fell, how butcherly,
This deadly quarrel daily doth beget!
Shak.

Butcher's broom · (?). (Bot.) A genus of plants (Ruscus); esp. R. aculeatus, which has large red berries and leaflike branches. See Cladophyll.

Butcherly (?), n. [OE. bocherie shambles, fr. F. boucherie. See Butcher, n.] 1. The business of a butcher. [Obs.]

Murder or manslaughter, esp. when committed with unusual barbarity; great or cruel slaughter.

Shak.
The perpetration of human butchery.
Prescott.

A slaughterhouse; the shambles; a place where blood is shed. [Obs.]

Like as an ox is hanged in the butchery.
Fabyan.
Syn. - Murder; slaughter; carnage. See Massacre.

Butler (?), n. [OE. boteler, F. bouteillier a bottleÐbearer, a cupbearer, fr. LL. buticularius, fr. buticula bottle. See Bottle a hollow vessel.] An officer in a king's or a nobleman's household, whose principal business it is to take charge of the liquors, plate, etc.; the head servant in a large house.

The butler and the baker of the king of Egypt.
Gen.xl.5.
Your wine locked up, your butler strolled abroad.
Pope.

Butlerage (?), n. (O. Eng. Law) A duty of two shillings on every tun of wine imported into England by merchant strangers; Ð so called because paid to the king's butler for the king.
Blackstone.

Butlership, n. The office of a butler.

Butment (?), n. [Abbreviation of Abutment.] 1. (Arch.) A buttress of an arch; the supporter, or that part which joins it to the upright pier.

(Masonry) The mass of stone or solid work at the end of a bridge, by which the extreme arches are sustained, or by which the end of a bridge without arches is supported.

Butment cheek (Carp.), the part of a mortised timber surrounding the mortise, and against which the shoulders of the tenon bear.
Knight.

Butt, But (?), n. [F. but butt, aim (cf. butte knoll), or bout, OF. bot, end, extremity, fr. boter, buter, to push, butt, strike, F. bouter;ÿof German origin; cf. OHG. bÓzan, akin to E. beat. See Beat, v.t.] 1. A limit; a bound; a goal; the extreme bound; the end.

Here is my journey's end, here my butt
And very sea mark of my utmost sail.
Shak.

µ As applied to land, the word is nearly synonymous with mete, and signifies properly the end line or boundary; the abuttal.

The thicker end of anything. See But.

A mark to be shot at; a target.

Sir W.Scott.
The groom his fellow groom at butts defies,
And bends his bow, and levels with his eyes.
Dryden.

A person at whom ridicule, jest, or contempt is directed; as, the butt of the company.

I played a sentence or two at my butt, which I thought very smart.
Addison.

A push, thrust, or sudden blow, given by the head of an animal; as, the butt of a ram.

A thrust in fencing.

To prove who gave the fairer butt,
John shows the chalk on Robert's coat.
Prior.

A piece of land left unplowed at the end of a field.

The hay was growing upon headlands and butts in cornfields.
Burrill.

(Mech.) (a) A joint where the ends of two objects come squarely together without scrafing or chamfering; Ð also called butt joint. (b) The end of a connecting rod or other like piece, to which the boxing is attached by the strap, cotter, and gib. (c) The portion of a half?coupling fastened to the end of a hose.

(Shipbuilding) The joint where two planks in a strake meet.

(Carp.) A kind of hinge used in hanging doors, etc.; Ð so named because fastened on the edge of the door, which butts against the casing, instead of on its face, like the strap hinge; also called butt hinge.

(Leather Trade) The thickest and stoutest part of tanned oxhides, used for soles of boots, harness, trunks.

The hut or shelter of the person who attends to the targets in rifle practice.

Butt chain (Saddlery), a short chain attached to the end of a tug. Ð Butt end. The thicker end of anything. See Butt end, under 2d But.
Amen; and make me die a good old man!
That's the butt end of a mother's blessing.
Shak.
A butt's length, the ordinary distance from the placeÿof shooting to the butt, or mark. Ð Butts and bounds (COnveyancing), abuttals and

boundaries. In lands of the ordinary rectangular shape, butts are the lines at the ends (F. bouts), and bounds are those on the sides, or sidings, as they were formerly termed. Burrill. Ð Bead and butt. See under Bead. Ð Butt and butt, joining end to end without overlapping, as planks. Ð Butt weld (Mech.), a butt joint, made by welding together the flat ends, or edges, of a piece of iron or steel, or of separate pieces, without having them overlap. See Weld. Ð Full butt, headfirst with full force. [Colloq.] ½The corporal ... ran full butt at the lieutenant., Marryat.

Butt, v.i. [imp. & p.p. Butted; p.pr. & vb.n. Butting.] [OE. butten, OF. boterÿto push, F. bouter. See Butt an end, and cf. Boutade.] 1. To join at the butt, end, or outward extremity; to terminate; to be bounded; to abut. [Written also but.]

And Barnsdale there doth butt on Don's wellÐwatered ground.
Drayton.

To thrust the head forward; to strike by thrusting the head forward, as an ox or a ram. [See Butt, n.]

A snowÐwhite steer before thine altar led,
Butts with his threatening brows.
Dryden.

Butt, v.t. To strike by thrusting the head against; to strike with the head.
Two harmless lambs are butting one the other.
Sir H.Wotton.

Butt, n. [F. botte, boute, LL. butta. Cf. Bottle a hollow vessel.] A large cask or vessel for wine or beer. It contains two hogsheads.

µ A wine butt contains 126 wine gallons (= 105 imperial gallons, nearly); a beer butt 108 ale gallons (= about 110 imperial gallons).

Butt, n. (Zo"l.) The common English flounder.

ØButte (?), n. [F. See Butt a bound.] A detached low mountain, or high rising abruptly from the general level of the surrounding plain; Ð applied to peculiar elevations in the Rocky Mountain region.

The creek ... passes by two remarkable buttes of red conglomerate.
Ruxton.

<— p. 197 —>

Butter (?), n. [OE. botere, butter, AS. butere, fr. L. butyrum, Gr. ?; either fr. ? ox, cow + ? cheese; or, perhaps, of Scythian origin. Cf. Cow.] 1. An oily, unctuous substance obtained from cream or milk by churning.

Any substance resembling butter in degree of consistence, or other qualities, especially, in old chemistry, the chloridess, as butter of antimony, sesquichloride of antimony; also, certain concrete fat oils remaining nearly solid at ordinary temperatures, as butter of cacao, vegetable butter, shea butter.

Butter and eggs (Bot.), a name given to several plants having flowers of two shades of yellow, as Narcissus incomparabilis, and in the United States to the toadflax (Linaria vulgaris). — Butter boat, a small vessel for holding melted butter at table. — Butter flower, the buttercup, a yellow flower. — Butter print, a piece of carved wood used to mark pats of butter; — called also butter stamp. Locke. — Butter tooth, either of the two middle incisors of the upper jaw. — Butter tree (Bot.), a tree of the genus Bassia, the seeds of which yield a substance closely resembling butter. The butter tree of India is the B. butyracea; that of Africa is the Shea tree (B. Parkii). See Shea tree. — Butter trier, a tool used in sampling butter. — Butter wife, a woman who makes or sells butter; — called also butter woman. [Obs. or Archaic]

Butter, v.t. [imp. & p.p. Buttered (?); p.pr. & vb.n. Buttering.] 1. To cover or spread with butter.

I know what's what. I know on which side
My bread is buttered.
Ford.

To increase, as stakes, at every throw or every game. [Cant]

Johnson.

Butter (?), n. One who, or that which, butts.

But′ter·ball· (?), n. (Zo̲ö̲l.) The buffel duck.

But′ter·bird· (?), n. (Zo̲ö̲l.) The rice bunting or bobolink; — so called in the island of Jamaica.

But′ter·bump· (?), n. [OE. butturȳthe bittern + 5th bump.] (Zo̲ö̲l.) The European bittern.

Johnson.

But′ter·bur· (?), n. (Bot.) A broad-leaved plant (Petasites vulgaris) of the Composite family, said to have been used in England for wrapping up pats of butter.

But′ter·cup· (?), n. (Bot.) A plant of the genus Ranunculus, or crowfoot, particularly R. bulbosus, with bright yellow flowers; — called also butterflower, golden cup, and kingcup. It is the cuckoobud of Shakespeare.

Butter—fin·gered (?), a. Apt to let things fall, or to let them slip away; slippery; careless.

But′ter·fish· (?), n. (Zo̲ö̲l.) A name given to several different fishes, in allusion to their slippery coating of mucus, as the Stromateus triacanthus of the Atlantic coast, the Epinephelus punctatus of the southern coast, the rock eel, and the kelpfish of New Zealand.

But′ter·fly· (?), n.; pl. Butterflies (?). [Perh. from the color of a yellow species. AS. buter-flíge, buttor-fleoge; cf. G. butterfliege, D. botervlieg. See Butter, and Fly.] (Zo̲ö̲l.) A general name for the numerous species of diurnal Lepidoptera. [See Illust. under Aphrodite.]

Asclepias butterfly. See under Asclepias. — Butterfly fish (Zo̲ö̲l.), the ocellated blenny (Blennius ocellaris) of Europe. See Blenny. The term is also applied to the flying gurnard. — Butterfly shell (Zo̲ö̲l.), a shell of the genus

Voluta. Ð Butterfly valve (Mech.), a kind of double clack valve, consisting of two semicircular clappers or wings hinged to a cross rib in the pump bucket. When open it somewhat resembles a butterfly in shape.

Butterĭine (?), n. A substance prepared from animal fat with some other ingredients intermixed, as an imitation of butter.

The manufacturers ship large quantities of oleomargarine to England, Holland, and other countries, to be manufactured into butter, which is sold as butterine or suine.

Johnson's Cyc.

Butterĭis (?), n. [The same word as buttress, noun, in a different application, F. bouter to push.] (Far.) A steel cutting instrument, with a long bent shank set in a handle which rests against the shoulder of the operator. It is operated by a thrust movement, and used in paring the hoofs of horses.

Butterĭman · (?), n.; pl. Buttermen (?). A man who makes or sells butter.

Butterĭmilk · (?), n. The milk that mains after the butter is separated from the cream.

Butterĭnut · (?), n. 1. (Bot.) An American tree (Juglans cinerea) of the Walnut family, and its edible fruit; Ð so called from the oil contained in the latter. Sometimes called oil nutÿand white walnut.

(Bot.) The nut of the Caryocar butyrosumÿand C. nuciferum, of S. America; Ð called also Souari nut.

ButterÐscotch · (?), n. A kind of candy, mainly composed of sugar and butter. [Colloq.]

Dickens.

Butterĭweed · (?), n. (Bot.) An annual composite plant of the Mississippi valley (Senecio lobatus).

Butterĭweight · (?), n. Over weight.

Swift.

µ Formerly it was a custom to give 18 ounces of butter for a pound.

Butterĭwort · (?), n. (Bot.) A genus of low herbs (Pinguicula) having simple leaves which secrete from their glandular upper surface a viscid fluid, to which insects adhere, after which the margin infolds and the insects are digested by the plant. The species are found mostly in the North Temperate zone.

Butterĭy (?), a. Having the qualities, consistence, or appearance, of butter.

Butterĭy, n.; pl. Butteries (?). [OE. botery, botry; cf. LL. botaria wine vessel; also OE. botelerie, fr. F. bouteillerie, fr. boutellie bottle. Not derived from butter. See Bottle a hollow vessel, Butt a cask.] 1. An apartment in a house where butter, milk and other provisions are kept.

All that need a cool and fresh temper, as cellars, pantries, and butteries, to the north.

Sir H.Wotton.

A room in some English colleges where liquors, fruit, and refreshments are kept for sale to the students.

And the major Oxford kept the buttery bar.
E. Hall.

A cellar in which butts of wine are kept.

Weale.
Buttery hatch, a half door between the buttery or kitchen and the hall, in old mansions, over which provisions were passed.
Wright.
Butt hinge · (?). See 1st Butt, 10.
ButÐthorn · (?), n. (Zo"l.) The common European starfish (Asterias rubens).
Butting (?), n. An abuttal; a boundary.
Without buttings or boundings on any side.
Bp. Beveridge.
Butting joint · . A joint between two pieces of timber or wood, at the end of one or both, and either at right angles or oblique to the grain, as the joints which the struts and braces form with the truss posts; Ð sometimes called abutting joint.
Butt joint · (?). A joint in which the edges or ends of the pieces united come squarely together instead of overlapping. See 1st Butt, 8.
Buttock (?), n. [From Butt an end.] 1. The part at the back of the hip, which, in man, forms one of the rounded protuberances on which he sits; the rump.

(Naut.) The convexity of a ship behind, under the stern.

Mar. Dict.
Button (?), n. [OE. boton, botoun, F. bouton button, bud, prop. something pushing out, fr. bouterÿ to push. See Butt an end.] 1. A knob; a small ball; a small, roundish mass.

A catch, of various forms and materials, used to fasten together the different parts of dress, by being attached to one part, and passing through a slit, called a buttonhole, in the other; Ð used also for ornament.

A bud; a germ of a plant.

Shak.

A piece of wood or metal, usually flat and elongated, turning on a nail or screw, to fasten something, as a door.

A globule of metal remaining on an assay cupel or in a crucible, after fusion.

Button hook, a hook for catching a button and drawing it through a buttonhole, as in buttoning boots and gloves. Ð Button shellÿ(Zo"l.), a small, univalve marine shell of the genus Rotella. Ð Button snakeroot. (Bot.) (a) The American composite genus Liatris, having rounded buttonlike heads of flowers. (b) An American umbelliferous plant with rigid, narrow leaves, and flowers in dense heads. Ð Button tree (Bot.), a genus of trees (Conocarpus), furnishing durable timber, mostly natives of the West Indies. Ð To hold by the button, to detain in conversation to weariness; to bore; to buttonhole.

Button, v.t. [imp. & p.p. Buttoned (?); p.pr. & vb.n. Buttoning (?).] [OE. botonen, OF. botoner, F. boutonner. See Button, n.] 1. To fasten with a button or buttons; to inclose or make secure with buttons; Ð often followed by up.

He was a tall, fat, longÐbodied man, buttoned up to the throat in a tight green coat.

Dickens.

To dress or clothe. [Obs.]

Shak.

Button, v.i. To be fastened by a button or buttons; as, the coat will not button.

ButtonÏball· (?), n. (Bot.) See Buttonwood.

ButtonÏbush· (?), n. (Bot.) A shrub (Cephalanthus occidentalis) growing by the waterside; Ð so called from its globular head of flowers. See Capitulum.

ButtonÏhole· (?), n. The hole or loop in which a button is caught.

ButtonÏhole·, v.t. To hold at the button or buttonhole; to detain in conversation to werariness; to bore; as, he buttonholed me a quarter of an hour.

ButtonÏmold· (?), n. A disk of bone, wood, or other material, which is made into a button by covering it with cloth. [Written also buttonmould.]

Fossil buttonmolds, joints of encrinites. See Encrinite.

Buttons (?), n. A boy servant, or page, Ð in allusion to the buttons on his livry. [Colloq.]

Dickens.

ButtonÏweed· (?), n. (Bot.) The name of several plants of the genera Spermacoce and Diodia, of the Madder family.

ButtonÏwood· (?), n. (Bot.) The Platanus occidentalis, or American plane tree, a large tree, producing rough balls, from which it is named; Ð called also buttonball tree, and, in some parts of the United States, sycamore. The California buttonwood is P. racemosa.

ButtonÏy (?), a. Ornamented with a large number of buttons. ½The buttony boy.¸ Thackeray. ½My coat so blue and buttony.¸

W.S.Gilbert.

Buttress (?), n. [OE. butrasse, boterace, fr. F. bouterÿto push; cf. OF. bouteret (nom. sing. and acc. pl. bouterez) buttress. See Butt an end, and cf. Butteris.] 1. (Arch.) A projecting mass of masonry, used for resisting the thrust of an arch, or for ornament and symmetry.

μ When an external projection is used merely to stiffen a wall, it is a pier.

Anything which supports or strengthens. ½The ground pillar and buttress of the good old cause of nonconformity.

South.

Flying buttress. See Flying buttress.

Buttress (?), v.t. [imp. & p.p. Buttressed (?); p.pr. & vb.n. Buttressing.] To support with a buttress; to prop; to brace firmly.

To set it upright again, and to prop and buttress it up for duration.
Burke.

Butt shaft · (?) An arrow without a barb, for shooting at butts; an arrow. [Also but shaft.]

Shak.

Butt weld · (?). See Butt weld, under Butt.

Buttweld ·, v.t. To unite by a butt weld.

Butty (?), n. (Mining) One who mines by contract, at so much per ton of coal or ore.

Butyl (?), n. [L. butyrum butter + ĭyl. See Butter.] (Chem.) A compound radical, regarded as butane, less one atom of hydrogen.

Butylene (?), n. [From Butyl.] (Chem.) Any one of three metameric hydrocarbons, C?H?, of the ethylene series. They are gaseous or easily liquefiable.

Bu · tyĭraceous (?), a. [L. butyrum butter. See Butter.] Having the qualities of butter; resembling butter.

Butyĭrate (?), n. (Chem.) A salt of butyric acid.

Buĭtyric (?), a. (Chem.) Pertaining to, or derived from, butter.

Butyric acid, C?H?.CO?H, an acid found in butter; an oily, limpid fluid, having the smell of rancid butter, and an acrid taste, with a sweetish aftertaste, like that of ether. There are two metameric butyric acids, called in distinction the normalĭ and isoÐbutyric acid. The normal butyric acid is the one common in rancid butter.

Butyĭrin (?), n. (Physiol. Chem.) A butyrate of glycerin; a fat contained in small quantity in milk, which helps to give to butter its peculiar flavor.

Bu · tyĭromeĭter (?), n. [L. butyrum butter + ĭmeter.] An instrument for determining the amount of fatty matter or butter contained in a sample of milk.

Butyĭrone (?), n. [Butyric + ĭone.] (Chem.) A liquid ketone obtained by heating calcium butyrate.

Butyĭrous (?), a. Butyraceous.

Buxeĭous (?), a. [L. buxeus, fr. buxusỹthe box tree.] Belonging to the box tree.

Buxine (?), n. (Chem.) An alkaloid obtained from the Buxus sempervirens, or common box tree. It is identical with bebeerine; Ð called also buxina.

Buxom (?), a. [OE. buxum, boxom, buhsum, pliable, obedient, AS. bÓcsum, b?hsum (akin to D. buigzaam blexible, G. biegsam); b?gan to bow, bend + Ïsum, E. Ïsome. See Bowÿto bend, and Ïsome.] 1. Yielding; pliable or compliant; ready to obey; obedient; tractable; docile; meek; humble. [Obs.]

So wild a beast, so tame ytaught to be,
And buxom to his bands, is joy to see.
Spenser.

I submit myself unto this holy church of Christ, to be ever buxom and obedient to the ordinance of it.
Foxe.

Having the characteristics of health, vigor, and comeliness, combined with a gay, lively manner? stout and rosy; jolly; frolicsome.

A daughter fair,
So buxom, blithe, and debonair.
Milton.

A parcel of buxom bonny dames, that were laughing, singing, dancing, and as merry as the day was long.
Tatler.

Ð BuxomÏly, adv. Ð BuxomÏness, n.

Buy (?), v.t. [imp. & p.p. Bought (?); p.pr. & vb.n. Buying (?).] [OE. buggen, buggen, bien, AS. bycgan, akin to OS. buggean, Goth. bugjan.] 1. To acquire the ownership of (property) by giving an accepted price or consideration therefor, or by agreeing to do so; to acquire by the payment of a price or value; to purchase; Ð opposed to sell.

Buy what thou hast no need of, and ere long thou wilt sell thy necessaries.
B.Franklin.

To acquire or procure by something given or done in exchange, literally or figuratively; to get, at a cost or sacrifice; to buy pleasure with pain.

Buy the truth and sell it not; also wisdom, and instruction, and understanding.
Prov.xxiii.23.

To buy again. See Againbuy. [Obs.] Chaucer.Ð To buy off. (a) To influence to compliance; to cause to bend or yield by some consideration; as, to buy off conscience. (b) To detach by a consideration given; as, to buy off one from a party. Ð To buy out. (a) To buy off, or detach from. Shak. (b) To purchase the share or shares of in a stock, fund, or partnership, by which the seller is separated from the company, and the purchaser takes his place; as, A buys out B. (c) To purchase the entire stock in trade and the good will of a business. Ð To buy in, to purchase stock in any fund or partnership. Ð To buy on credit, to purchase, on a promise, in fact or in law, to make payment at a future day. Ð To buy the refusal (of anything), to give a consideration for the right of purchasing, at a fixed price, at a future time.

Buy, v.i. To negotiate or treat about a purchase.

I will buy with you, sell with you.

Shak.

Buyer (?), n. One who buys; a purchaser.

Buz (?), v. & n. See Buzz. [Obs.]

Buzz (?), v.i. [imp. & p.p. Buzzed (?); p.pr. & vb.n. Buzzing.] [An onomatopÒia.] To make a low, continuous, humming or sibilant sound, like that made by bees with their wings. Hence: To utter a murmuring sound; to speak with a low, humming voice.

Like a wasp is buzzed, and stung him.

Longfellow.

However these disturbers of our peace

Buzz in the people's ears.

Shak.

Buzz, v.t. 1. To sound forth by buzzing.

Shak.

To whisper; to communicate, as tales, in an under tone; to spread, as report, by whispers, or secretly.

I will buzz abroad such prophecies

That Edward shall be fearful of his life.

Shak.

To talk to incessantly or confidentially in a low humming voice. [Colloq.]

(Phonetics) To sound with a ½buzz‚.

H.Sweet.

Buzz, n. 1. A continuous, humming noise, as of bees; a confused murmur, as of general conversation in low

<— p. 198 —>

tones, or of a general expression of surprise or approbation. ½The constant buzz of a fly.‚

Macaulay.

I found the whole room in a buzz of politics.

Addison.

There is a buzz all around regarding the sermon.

Thackeray.

A whisper; a report spread secretly or cautiously.

There's a certain buzz
Of a stolen marriage.
Massinger.

(Phonetics) The audible friction of voice consonants.

H. Sweet.

Buzzard(?),n.[O.E.busard,bosard,F. busard, fr. buse, L.buteo, a kind of falcon or hawk.]

(Zo"l.) A bird of prey of the Hawk family, belonging to the genus Buteo and related genera.

µ The Buteo vulgaris is the common buzzard of Europe. The American species (of which the most common are B.borealis, B.Pennsylvanicus, and B.lineatus) are usually called hen hawks.Ð The roughÐlegged buzzard, or bee hawk, of Europe (Pernis apivorus) feeds on bees and their larv', with other insects, and reptiles.Ð The moor buzzard of Europe is Circus 'ruginosus. See Turkey buzzard, and Carrion buzzard.

Bald buzzard, the fishhawk or osprey. See Fishhawk.

A blockhead; a dunce.

It is common, to a proverb, to call one who can not be taught, or who continues obstinately ignorant, a buzzard.

Goldsmith.

Buzzard, a. Senseless; stupid. [R.& Obs.]

Milton.

BuzzardÏet · (?), n. (Zo"l.) A hawk resembling the buzzard, but with legs relatively longer.

Buzzer (?), n. One who, or that which, buzzes; a whisperer; a talebearer.
And wants not buzzers to infect his ear
With pestilent speeches of his father's death.
Shak.

BuzzingÏly (?), adv. In a buzzing manner; with a buzzing sound.

Buzzsaw · (?) A circular saw; Ð so called from the buzzing it makes when running at full speed.

By (?), prep. [OE. bi, AS. bÆ, big, near to, by, of, from, after, according to; akin to OS.& OFries. bi, be, D. bij, OHG. bÆ, G. bie, Goth. bi, and perh. Gr.?. E. prefix beÐ is orig.the same word. ? See pref. BeÐ.]

In the neighborhood of; near or next to; not far from; close to; along with; as, come and sit by me.

By foundation or by shady rivulet
He sought them both.
Milton.

On; along; in traversing. Compare 5.

Long labors both by sea and land he bore.
Dryden.
By land, by water, they renew the charge.
Pope.

Near to, while passing; hence, from one to the other side of; past; as, to go by a church.

Used in specifying adjacent dimensions; as, a cabin twenty feet by forty.

Against. [Obs.]

Tyndale [1.Cor.iv.4]?

With, as means, way, process, etc.; through means of; with aid of; through; through the act or agency of; as, a city is destroyed by fire; profit is made by commerce; to take by force.

To the meaning of by, as denoting means or agency, belong, more or less closely, most of the following uses of the word: (a) It points out the author and producer; as, ½Waverley, a novel by Sir W.Scott; a statue by Canova; a sonata by Beethoven. (b) In an oath or adjuration, it indicates the being or thing appealed to as sanction; as, I affirm to you by all that is sacred; he swears by his faith as a Christian; no, by Heaven. (c) According to; by direction, authority, or example of; after; Ð in such phrases as, it appears by his account; ten o'clock by my watch; to live by rule; a model to build by. (d) At the rate of; according to the ratio or proportion of; in the measure or quantity of; as, to sell cloth by the yard, milk by the quart, eggs by the dozen, meat by the pound; to board by the year. (e) In comparison, it denotes the measure of excess or deficiency; when anything is increased or diminished, it indicates the measure of increase or diminution; as, larger by a half; older by five years; to lessen by a third. (f) It expresses continuance or duration; during the course of; within the period of; as, by day, by night. (g) As soon as; not later than; near or at; Ð used in expressions of time; as, by this time the sun had risen; he will be here by two o'clock.

In boxing the compass, by indicates a pint nearer to, or towards, the next cardinal point; as, north by east, i.e., a point towards the east from the north; northeast by east, i.e., on point nearer the east than northeast is.

μ With is used instead of by before the instrument with which anything is done; as, to beat one with a stick; the board was fastened by the carpenter with nails. But there are many words which may be regarded as means or processes, or, figuratively, as instruments; and whether with or by shall be used with them is a matter of arbitrary, and often, of unsettled usage; as, to a reduce a town by famine; to consume stubble with fire; he gained his purpose by flattery; he entertained them with a story; he distressed us with or by a recital of his sufferings. see With.

By all means, most assuredly; without fail; certainly.

— By and by. (a) Close together (of place). [Obs.] ½Two yonge knightes liggyng [lying] by and by., Chaucer. (b) Immediately; at once. [Obs.] ½When ... persecution ariseth because of the word, by and by he is offended., Matt. xiii.21. (c) Presently; pretty soon; before long. In this phrase, by seems to be used in the sense of nearness in time, and to be repeated for the sake of emphasis, and thus to be equivalent to ,soon, and soon,, that is instantly; hence, — less emphatically, — pretty soon, presently. — By one's self, with only one's self near; alone; solitary.— By the bye. See under Bye. — By the head (Naut.), having the bows lower than the stern; —said of a vessel when her head is lower in the water than her stern. If her stern is lower, she is by the stern.— By the lee, the situation of a vessel, going free, when she has fallen off so much as to bring the wind round her stern, and to take her sails aback on the other side. — By the run, to let go by the run, to let go altogether, instead of slacking off. — By the way, by the bye; — used to introduce an incidental or secondary remark or subject. —Day by day, One by one, Piece by piece, etc., each day, each one, each piece, etc., by itself singly or separately; each severally. — To come by, to get possession of; to obtain.— To do by, to treat, to behave toward. — To set by, to value, to esteem. — To stand by, to aid, to support.

µ The common phrase good—by is equivalent to farewell, and would be better written good—bye, as it is a corruption of God be with you (b'w'ye).

By (?), adv. 1. Near; in the neighborhood; present; as, there was no person by at the time.

Passing near; going past; past; beyond; as, the procession has gone by; a bird flew by.

Aside; as, to lay by; to put by.

By (?), a. Out of the common path; aside; — used in composition, giving the meaning of something aside, secondary, or incidental, or collateral matter, a thing private or avoiding notice; as, by—line, by—place, by—play, by—street. It was formerly more freely used in composition than it is now; as, by—business, by—concernment, by—design, by—interest, etc.

Byard (?), n. A piece of leather crossing the breast, used by the men who drag sledges in coal mines.

By˙ïbid · der (?), n. One who bids at an auction in behalf of the auctioneer or owner, for the purpose of running up the price of articles. [U.S.]

By˙ïblow · (?), n. 1. A side or incidental blow; an accidental blow.

With their by—blows they did split the very stones in pieces.

Bunyan.

An illegitimate child; a bastard.

The Aga speedily ... brought her [his disgraced slave] to court, together with her pretty by—blow, the present Padre Ottomano.

Evelyn.

By′cor · ner (?), n. A private corner.

Britain being a byÐcorner, out of the road of the world.

Fuller.

By′deĬpend · ence (?), n. An appendage; that which depends on something else, or is distinct from the main dependence; an accessory.

Shak.

By′drink · ing, n. A drinking between meals. [Obs.]

Bye (?), n. 1. A thing not directly aimed at; something which is a secondary object of regard; an object by the way, etc.; as in on or upon the bye, i.e., in passing; indirectly; by implication. [Obs. except in the phrase by the bye.]

The Synod of Dort condemneth upon the bye even the discipline of the Church of England.

Fuller.

(Cricket) A run made upon a missed ball; as, to steal a bye.

T.Hughes.

By the bye, in passing; by way of digression; apropos to the matter in hand. [Written also by the by.]

Bye (?) n. [AS.b?; cf. Icel. byg? dwelling, byggia, b?a, to dwell ? 97.]

A dwelling.

Gibson.

In certain games, a station or place of an individual player.

Emerson.

By′eĬlection (?), n. An election held by itself, not at the time of a general election.

By′end · (?), n. Private end or interest; secret purpose; selfish advantage. [Written also byeÐend.]

½Profit or some other byÐend.⸜

L'Estrange.

Bygone · (?), a. Past; gone by.

½Bygone fooleries.⸜

Shak

Bygone · (?), n. Something gone by or past; a past event.

½Let old bygones be⸜

Tennyson.

Let bygones be bygones, let the past be forgotten.

By′in · terĬest (?), n. SelfÐinterest; private advantage.

Atterbury.

Byland(?), n. A peninsula. [Obs.]

Bylandïer(?), n. See Bilander.[Obs.]

Byïlane · (?), n. A private lane, or one opening out of the usual road.

Byïlaw · (?), n. [Cf.Sw.bylag, D.bylov, Icel.b?arl"g, fr.Sw.& Dan. by town, Icel. b'r, byr (fr. b–a to dwell)+the word for law; hence, a law for one town, a special law. Cf.Birlaw and see Law.] 1. A local or subordinate law; a private law or regulation made by a corporation for its own government.

There was likewise a law to restrain the byÐlaws, or ordinances of corporations.

Bacon.

The law or institution; to which are added two byÐlaws, as a comment upon the general law.

Addison.

A law that is less important than a general law or constitutional provision, and subsidiary to it; a rule relating to a matter of detail; as, civic societies often adopt a constitution and byÐlaws for the government of their members. In this sense the word has probably been influenced by by, meaning secondary or aside.

Byïname · (?), n. A nickname.

Camden.

Byname · , v.t. To give a nickname to.

Camden.

Byïpass(?), n. (Mech.) A byÐpassage, for a pipe, or other channel, to divert circulation from the usual course.

Byïpas · sage (?), n. A passage different from the usual one; a byway.

Byïpast(?), a. Past; gone by ½ByÐpast perils.‚

Shak.

Bypath · (?), n.; pl. Bypaths(?). A private path; an obscure way; indirect means.

God known, my son,
By what bypaths, and indirect crooked ways,
I met this crown.

Shak.

Byïplace · (?), n. A retired or private place.

Byplay (?), n. Action carried on aside, and commonly in dumb show, while the main action proceeds.

Byïprod · uct (?), n. A secondary or additional product; something produced, as in the course of a manufacture, in addition to the principal product.

Byre (?), n. [Cf, Icel. br pantry, Sw. bur cage,Dan. buur, E.bower.] A cow house. [N. of Eng.& Scot.]

Byïreïspect · (?), n. Private end or view; byÐinterest. [Obs.]

Dryden.

Byroad · (?), n. A private or obscure road. ½Through slippery byroads‚

Swift.

Byĭron · ic(?), a. Pertaining to, or in the style of, Lord Byron.
With despair and Byronic misanthropy.
Thackeray

Byĭroom · (?), n. A private room or apartment ½Stand in some byÐroom,
Shak.

Byĭsmot · terĭed(?), p.a. [See Besmut.] Bespotted with mud or dirt. [Obs.]
Chaucer.

Byĭspeech · (?), n. An incidental or casual speech, not directly relating to the point. ½To quote byÐspeeches.,
Hooker.

Byĭspell · (?), n. [AS. bigspell.] A proverb. [Obs.]

Byss (?), n. See Byssus, n.,1.

Bysĭsaceous(?), a. [From Byssus.] (Bot.) Byssuslike; consisting of fine fibers or threads, as some very delicate filamentous alg'.

Bysĭsiferĭous(?), a. [Byssus + Ðferous.] Bearing a byssus or tuft.

Byssin (?), n. See Byssus, n,1.

Byssine (?), a. [L. byssinus made of byssus, Gr.? See Byssus.] Made of silk; having a silky or flaxlike appearance.
Coles.

Byssoid(?), a. [Byssus + Ðoid.] Byssaceous.

Byssoĭlite(?), n [Gr.? See flax + Ðlite.] (Min.) An oliveÐgreen fibrous variety of hornblende.

ØByssus(?), n.; pl. E. Byssuses(?); L. Byssi.(?) [L. byssus fine flax, fine linen or cotton, Gr. ? .]

A cloth of exceedingly fine texture, used by the ancients. It is disputed whether it was of cotton, linen, or silk. [Written also byss and byssin.]

2.(Zo"l.) A tuft of long, tough filaments which are formed in a groove of the foot, and issue from between the valves of certain bivalve mollusks, as the Pinna and Mytilus, by which they attach themselves to rocks, etc.

(Bot.) An obsolete name for certain fungi composed of slender threads.

Asbestus.

Bystand · er (?), n. [By + stander, equiv. to standerÐby; cf. AS. bigÐstandan to stand by or near.] One who stands near; a spectator; one who has no concern with the business transacting.

He addressed the bystanders and scattered pamphlets among them.
Palfrey.

Syn.ÐLooker on; spectator; beholder; observer.

Byĭstreet · (?), n. A separate, private, or obscure street; an out of the way or cross street.

He seeks byÐstreets, and saves the expensive coach.
Gay.

By′stroke · (?), n. An accidental or a slyly given stroke.

By′turn · ing(?), n. An obscure road; a way turning from the main road. Sir P.Sidney.

By′view · (?), n. A private or selfish view; self-interested aim or purpose. No by-views of his own shall mislead him.
Atterbury.

By′walk · (?), n. A secluded or private walk.
He moves afterward in by-walks.
Dryden.

By′wash · (?), n. ÿThe outlet from a dam or reservoir; also, a cut to divert the flow of water.

Byway · (?), n. A secluded, private, or obscure way; a path or road aside from the main one. ½ Take no byways.
Herbert.

By′wipe · (?), n. A secret or side stroke, as of raillery or sarcasm.
Milton.

Byword · (?), n. [AS.b‹word; b‹, E.by+word.] 1. A common saying; a proverb; a saying that has a general currency.

I knew a wise man that had it for a byword.
Bacon.

The object of a contemptuous saying.

Thou makest us a byword among the heathen.
Ps.x?iv.14

Bywork (?), n. Work aside from regular work; subordinate or secondary business.

Byzant(?), Byzan′tine (?) n.} [OE. besant, besaunt, F. besant, fr. LL. Byzantius, Byzantinus, fr. Byzantium.] (Numis.) A gold coin, so called from being coined at Byzantium. See Bezant.

Bi′zantian (?), a.& n. See Byzantine.

By′zantine (?), a. Of or pertaining to Byzantium. Ð n. A native or inhabitant of Byzantium, now Constantinople; sometimes, applied to an inhabitant of the modern city of Constantinople. [Written also Bizantine.]

Byzantine church, the Eastern or Greek church, as distinguished from the Western or Roman or Latin church.See under Greek.Ð Byzantine empire, the Eastern Roman or Greek empire from A.D. 364 or A.D. 395 to the capture of Constantinople by the Turks, A.D. 1453. Ð Byzantine historians, historians and writers (Zonaras, Procopius, etc.) who lived in the Byzantine empire.
P.Cyc.

Ð Byzantine style (Arch.), a style of architecture developed in the Byzantine empire. Its leading forms are the round arch, the dome, the pillar, the circle, and the cross. The capitals of the pillars are the endless variety, and full of invention. The mosque of St.Sophia, Constantinople, and the church of St.Mark, Venice, are prominent examples of Byzantine architecture.

<— p. 199 —>
<— p. 199 —>

C. (?) 1. C is the third letter of the English alphabet. It is from the Latin letter C, which in old Laton represend the sounds of k, and g (in go); its original value being the latter. In AngloÐSaxon words, or Old English before the Norman Conques, it always has the sound of k. The Latin C was the same letter as the Greek ?, ?, and came from the Greek alphabet. The Greek got it from the Phoenicians. The English name of C is from the Latin name ce, and was derived, probably, through the French Etymalogically C is related to g, h, k, q, s (and other sibilant sounds). Examples of these relations are in L. acutus, E. acute, aque; E. acrid, eagar; L. cornu, E. horn; E. cat, kitten; E. coy, quiet; L. circare, OF. cerchier, E. search.

See Guide to Pronunciation, ?? 221Ð228.

(Mus.) (a) The keynote of the normal or ½natural, scale, which has neither flats nor sharps in its signature; also, the third note of the relative minor scale of the same (b) C after the clef is the mark of common time, in which each measure is a semibreve (four fourths or crotchets); for alla breve time it is written ? (c) The ½C clef,, a modification of the letter C, placed on any line of the staff, abows that line to be middle C.

As a numeral, C stands for Latin centum or 100, CC for 200, etc.

C spring, a spring in the from of the letter C.

ØCaïaba (?), n. [Ar. ka'ban, let, a square building, fr. ka'b cude] The small and nearly cubical stone building, toward which all Mohammedans must pray. [Written also kaaba.]

µThe Caaba is situated in Messa, a city of Arabia, and contains a famous black stone said to have been brought from heaven. Before the time of Mohammed, the Caaba was an idolatrouse temple, but it has since been the chief sanctuary and object of pilgrimage of the Mohammedan world.

Caas (?), n, sing. ? pl. Case [Obs.] Chaucer.

Cab (?), n [Abrev. fr. cabriolet.] 1. A kind of close carriage with two or four wheesl, usually a public vehicle. ½A cab came clattering up., Thackeray.

µ A cab may have two seats at right to the driver's seat, and a door behind; or one seat parallel to the driver's, with the entrance from the side or front.

Hansom cab. See Hansom.

The covered part of a locomotive, in which the engineer has his station.

Knight.

Cab (?), n. [Heb. gab, fr. q¾bab to hollow.] A Hebrew dry measure, containing a little over two (2,37) pints.

W.H.Ward. 2 Kings vi. 25.

Caïbal (?), n. [F. cabale cabal, cabala LL. cabala cabala, fr. Heb. qabb¾l?h reception, tradition, mysterious doctrine, fr. q¾bal to take or receive, in Pi‰l qibbel to abopt (a doctrine).] 1. Tradition; occult doctrine. See Cabala [Obs.]
Hakewill.

A secret. [Obs.] ½The measuring of the temple, a cabal found out but lately.„

B.Jonson.

A number of persons united in some close design, usually to pronote their private views and interests in church or state by intrigue; a secret association composed of a few designing persons; a junto.

It so happend, by a whimsical coincidence, thet in 1671 the cabinet consisted of five persons, the initial letters of whose names made up the word cabal; Clifford, Arlington, Buckingham, Ashley, and Lauderdale.
Macaulay.

The secret artifices or machinations of a few persons united in a close desing; in intrigue.

By cursed cabals of women.
Dryden.
Syn. Ð Junto; intrigue; plot; combination; conspiracy. Ð Cabal, Combination, Faction. An association for some purpose considered to be bad is the idea common to these terms. A combination is an organized union of individuals for mutual support, in urging their demands or resisting the clams of others, and may be good or bad according to circumstances; as, a combiviation of workmen or of employers to effect or to prevent a chang in prices. A cabal is a secret association of a few individuals who seek by cunning practices to abtain affice and power. A faction is a larger body that a cabal, employed for selfish purpoeses in agitating the community and working up an excitement with a view to chenge the existing order of things. ½Selfishness, insubordination, and laxity of morals give rise to combinations, which belong particularly to the lower orders of society. Restlase, jealous, ambitious, and little minds are ever forming cabals. Factions belong especially to free governments, and are raised by busy and turbulent spirits for selfish parposes„.
Crabb.

Caïbal, v. i. [int. & p.p. Caballed (?); p. pr. & vb. n. Caballing]. [Cf. F. cabaler.] To unite in a small party to promote private views and interests by intrigue; to intrigue; to plot.

Caballing still against it with the great.
Dryden.

CabaÐla (?), n. [LL. See Cabal, n.] 1. A kind of occult theosophy or traditional interpretation of the Scriptures among Jewish rabbis and certain mediaeval Christians, which treats of the nature of god and the mystery of humsn existence. It assumed that every letter, word, number, and accent of Scripture contains a hidden sense; and it teaches the methods of interpretation for ascertaining these occult meanings. The cabalists pretend even to foretell events by this means.

Secret science in general; mystic art; mystery.

Caballism (?), n. [Cf. F. cabalisme.]

The secret science of the cabalists.

A superstitious devotion to the mysteries of the religion which one professes. [R]

Emerson.

Caballist (?), n. [Cf.F. cabaliste.] One versed in the cabala, or the mysteries of Jewish traditions. ½Studions cabalists.

Swift.

Cab·allistic (?), Cab·aÐlisticÐal (?)} a. Of or pertaining to the cabala; containing or conveying an occult meaning; mysic.

The Heptarchus is a cabalistic of the first chapter of Genesia.

Hallam.

Caba·allisticIalIly, adv. In a cabalistic manner.

Caballize (?), v.i. [Cf.F. cabaliser.] To use cabalistic language. [R]
Dr.H.More.

Calballer (?), n. One who cabals.

A close caballer and togueÐvaliant lord.

Dryden.

Caballliney(?), a. [L.caballinus, fr. caballus a nag. Cf. Cavalier.] Of or pertaining to a horse. Ðn. Caballine aloes.

Caballine aloes, an inferior and impure kind of aloes formerly used in veterinary practice; Ð called also horse aloes. Ð Caballine spring, the fountsain of Hippocrene, on Mount Helicon; Ð fabled to have been formed by a stoke from the foot of the winged horse Pegasus.

Cabalret (?), n. [F.] A tavern; a house where liquors are retailed. [Obs. as an English word.]

ØCalbas (?), n. [F.] A flat basket or for figs, etc.; Hence, a lady's flat workbasket, reticule, or hand bag; Ð often written caba.

C.Bront,.

ØCalbassony(?), n. (Zo"l.) A speciec of armadillo of the genus Xenurus (X. unicinctusand X. hispidus); the tatouay. [Written also Kabassou.]

Cabbage (?), n. [OE. cabage, fr. F. cabus headed (of cabbages), chou cobus headed cabbage, cabbage head; cf. It. capuccio a little head, cappuccio cowl, hood, cabbage, fr. capo head, L. caput, or fr. It. cappa cape. See Chiff, Cape.] (Bot.) 1. An esculent vegetable of many varieties, derived from the wild Brassica oleracea of Europe. The common cabbage has a compact head of leaves. The caulifliwer, Brussels sprouts, etc., are sonaetimes classed as cabbages.

The terminal bud of certain palm trees, used, like, cabbage, for food. See Cabbage free, below.

The cabbage palmetto. See below.

Cabbage aphis (Zo"l.), a green plantÐlouse (Aphis brassic?) which lives upon the leaves of the cabbage. Ð Cabbage Beetle (Zo"l.), a small, striped fleaÐbeetle (Phyllotreta viltat) which lives, in the larval state, on the roots, and when adult, on the leaves, of cabbage and other cruciferous plants. Ð Cabbage butterfly (Zo"l.), a white butterbly (Pieris rap? of both Europe and America, and the Allied P. oleracea, a native American species) which, in the larval state, devours the leaves of the cabbage and the turnip. See Cabbage worm, below. Ð Cabbage Fly (Zo"l.), a small twoÐwinged fly (Anthomyia brassic?), which feeds, in the larval or maggot state roots of the cabbage, often doing much damage to the crop. Ð Cabbage head, the compact head formed by the leaves of a cabbage; Ð contemptuously or humorously, and colloquially, a very stupid and silly person; a numskull. Ð Cabbage palmetto, a spesies of palm tree (Cabal Palmetto) found along the coast from North Carolina to Florida. Ð Cabbage rose (Bot.), a spesies of rose (Rosa centifolia) haveng large and heavy blossoms. Ð Cabbage tree, Cabbage palm, a name given to palms having a terminal bud called a cabbag, as the Sabal Palmetto of the United States, and the Euterpe oleracea and Oreodoxa oleracea of the West Indies. Ð Cabbage worm (Zo"l.), the larva of several species of moths and butterfies, which attacks cabbages. The most common is usully the larva of a white butterfly. See Cabbage Butterfly, above. The cabbage cutworms, which eat off the stalks oryoung plants during the night, are the larv' of several species of moths, of the genus Agrotis. See Cutworm. Ð Sea cabbage.(Bot.) (a) Sea kale (b). The original Plant (Brassica oleracea), from which the cabbage, cauliflower, , broccoli, etc., have been derived by cultivation. Ð ThousandÐheadeu cabbage. See Brussels sprouts.

Cabage, v.i. To from a head like that the cabbage; as, to make lettuce cabbage.

Johnson.

Cabbage, v.i. [imp. & p.p Cabbaged (?); p. pr. & vb. n. Cabbagingÿ3.] [F.cabasser, fr. OF. cabas theft; cf. F. cabas basket, and OF. cabuser to cheat.] To purloin or embezzle, as the pieces of cloth remaining after cutting out a garment; to pilfer.

Your tailor ... cabbages whole yards of cloth.

Arbuthnot.

Cabbage, n. Cloth or clippings cabbaged or purloined by one who cuts out garments.

Cabbler (?), n. One who works at cabbling.

Cabbling (?), n. (Metal) The process of breaking up the flat measses into which wrought iron is first hammered, in order that the pieces may be reheated and wrought into bar iron.

∅**Caïbe?aÿ?, Caïbesseÿ**(?), n. [Pg. cabe?a, F. cabesse.] The finest king of silk received from India.

∅**Caber** (?), n. [Gael] A pole or beam used in Scottish games for tossing as a trial of strength.

Cab · eĺzonÿ(?), n. [Sp., properly, big head. Cf. Cavesson.] (Zo"l.) A California fist (Hemilepidotus spinosus), allied to the sculpin.

Cablíat (?), n. [Native South American name.] (Zo"l.) The capybara. See Capybara.

Cabin (?), n. [OF. caban, fr. W. caban booth, cabin, dim. of cab cot, tent; or fr. F. cabane, cabine, LL. cabanna, perh. from the Celtic.] 1. A cottage or small house; a hum.

Swift.

A hunting cabin in the west.

E.Everett.

A small room; an inclosed plase.

So long in secret cabin there he held
Her captive.
Spenser.

A room in ship for officers or passengers.

Cabin boy, a boy whose duty is wait on the officers and passengers in the cabin of a ship.

Cabin v. i. [Imp. &p. p. Cabined (Đ?nd); p. pr. & vb. n. Cabining.] To live in, or as in, a cabin; to lodge.

I'll make you ... cabin in a cave.

Shak.

Cabin, v. t. To confine in, or as in, a cabin.

I am cabined, cribbed, confined, dound in
To saucy doubts and fears.
Shak.

Cabiĺnetÿ3, n. [F., dim. of cabine or cabane. See Cabin, n.] 1. A hut; a cottage; a small house. [Obs.]

Hearken a while from thy green cabinet,
The rural song of careful Colinet.
Spenser.

A small room, or retired apartment; a closet.

A private room in which consultations are held.

Philip passed some hours every day in his father's cabinet.
Prescott.

The advisory council of the chief executive officer of a nation; a cabinet council.

μ In England, the cabinet or cabinet council consista of those privy coucilors who actually transact the immediate business of the government. Mozley & W. Ð In the United States, the cabinet is composed of the heads of the executive departments of the government, namely, the Secretary of State, of the Treasury, of War, of the Navy, of the Interior, and of Agiculture, the PostmasterÐgeneral ,and the AttorneyÐgeneral.

(a) A set of drawers or a cupboard intended to contain articles of value. Hence: (b) A decorative piece of furniture, whether open like an ,tagŠre or closed with doors. See Etagere.

Any building or room set apart for the safe keeping and exhibition of works of art, etc.; also, the colleotion itself.

Cabinet council. (a) Same as Cabinet, n., 4 (of which bode it was formerly the full title). (b) A meting of the cabinet. Ð Cabinet councilor, a member of a cabinet council. Ð Cabinet photograph, a photograph of a size smaller than an imperial, though larger than a carie de visite. Ð Cabinet picture, a small and generally highly finished picture, suitable for a small room and for close inspection.

Cabĭnet, a. Suitable for a cabinet; small.

Yt [Varnhagen von Ense] is a walking cabinet edition of Goethe.

For. Quar. Rev.

Cabĭnet, v. i. [imp. & p. p. Cabineted; p. pr. & vb. n. Cabineting.] To inclose [R.]

Hewyt.

CabĭnetĭmakˑerÿҊ(?), n. One whose occupation is to make cabinets or other choice articles of household furniture, as tables, bedsteads, bureaus, etc.

CabĭnetĭmakˑÊing, n. The art or occupation of making the finer articles of household furniture.

CabĭnetĭmorkˑÊ(?), n. The art or occupation of working upon wooden furniture requiring nice workmanship; also, such furniture.

CabˑÊiÍreanÿ3, n. One of the Cabiri.

ØCabĭbiriÿ(?), n. pl. [NL., fr. Gr. ????????.] (Myth) Certain deities originally worshiped with mystical rites by the Pelasgians in Lemnos and Samothrace and afterwards throughout Greece; Ð also called sons of eph'stus (or Vulcan), as begin masters of the art ofworking metals. [Written also Cabeiri.]

Liddell & Scott.

Caĭbiriĭanÿ(?), a. Same as Cabidic.

Caïbiricÿ3, a. [Cf. F. Cabirique] Of or pertaining to the Cabiri, or to their mystical worship. [Written also Cabiritic.]

Cableÿ3, n. [F. Cfble,m LL. capulum, caplum, a rope, fr. L. capere to take; cf. D., Dan., & G. rabel, from the French. See Capable.] 1. A large, strong rope or chain, of considerable length, used to retain a vesel at anchor, and for other purposes. It is made of hemp, of steel wire, or of iron links.

> A rope of steel wire, or copper wire, usually covered with some protecting, or insulating substance; as, the cable of a suspension bridge; a telegraphiccable.

> (Arch) A nolding, shaft of a column, or any other member of convex, rounded section, made to resemble the spiral twist of a rope; Đ called also cable molding.

Bower cable, the cable belonging to the bower anchor. Đ Cable road, a railway on which the cars are moved by a continuously running endless rope operated by a stationary motor. Đ Cables length, the length of a ship's cable. Cables in the merchant service vary in length from 100 to 140 fathoms or; but as a maritime measure, a cable's length is either 120 fathoms (720 feet), or about 100 fathoms (600 feet, an approximation to one tenth of a nautical mile). Đ Cable tier. (a) That part of a vessel where the cables are stowed. (b) A coll of a cable. Đ Street cable, the cable belonging to the sheet anchor. Đ Stream cable, a hawser or rope, smaller than the bower cables, to moor a ship in a plase sheltered from wind and heavy seas. Đ Submarina cable .See Telegraph. Đ To pay out the cable. To vear out the cable, to slacken it, that it may run out of the ship; to let more cable run out of the hawse hole. Đ To serve the cable, to bind it round with ropes, canvas, etc., to prevent its being, worn or galled in the hawse, et. Đ To slip the cable, to let go the end on board and let it all run out and go overboard, as when there is not time to weigh anchor. Hence, in sailor's use, to die.

<— p. 200 —>

End of 's Webster's Unabridged Dictionary, by Noa Webster